GETTIN

FOR THE 20

KAPLAN SCHWESER CPA REVIEW

Welcome

We're pleased to have the opportunity to help you prepare for the CPA Exam. The CPA curriculum is demanding. Getting an early start is the best way to increase your chances for success on exam day. Here's how to begin:

Step 1: Access your online assets at **www.schweser.com/cpa**.

- Under the **Online Access** heading in the left navigation bar, click the "Login" button. Enter your username and password (sent to you via email 2 business days after you placed your order).

Step 2: Create a customized study plan by clicking **Study Calendar** in the left navigation bar. Click "Create a New Calendar" to get started. Select the start date and desired length of study that fit your timeline for preparing for the CPA Exam.

Step 3: Begin your prep process by becoming familiar with your print and online study tools.

- Begin reading your **Study Manual** and developing an understanding of the material that will be covered in the course.

- View clips in the **Video Library** for introductory lessons and information not covered in the Online Review Course.

- Pinpoint problem areas by creating custom exams with **SchweserPro™ QBank**.

- Reach out to your CPA content team and instructors, using the **InstructorLink™** assets located in the left navigation bar:
  - › Instructor Email Access
  - › Searchable FAQs
  - › Instructor-led Office Hours
  - › Exam-tips Blog

Step 4: Follow the daily assignments in your **Study Calendar**. This is your step-by-step roadmap to success on the CPA Exam.

For additional information, call 800-CPA-2DAY.

ISBN: 1427790140   PPN: 45280CPA

CPA Exam Study Manual

Financial Accounting & Reporting

2009/2010

Kaplan Schweser

This publication is designed to provide accurate and authoritative information in regard to the subject matter covered. It is sold with the understanding that the publisher is not engaged in rendering legal, accounting, or other professional service. If legal advice or other expert assistance is required, the services of a competent professional should be sought.

President and CEO: Dr. Andrew Temte, CFA
Chief Learning Officer: Dr. Tim Smaby, CFA
Vice President of CPA Education: Denise Probert, CPA, MPA

CPA EXAM STUDY MANUAL – FINANCIAL ACCOUNTING & REPORTING

©2009 Kaplan, Inc. All rights reserved.

Published in April 2009 by Kaplan Schweser.

Printed in the United States of America.

ISBN: 1-42778-863-4

PPN: 45265CPA

CONTENTS

©2009 Kaplan, Inc.

INTRODUCTION

Thank you for choosing Kaplan Schweser CPA Review to guide your preparation for the CPA exam. You are about to embark on a journey that is unparalleled in your academic and professional training until now. Success on the CPA exam requires your total commitment of focus, discipline, time, and energy. We are here to guide you to those all-important words: "I passed!"

Kaplan, the leader in standardized test preparation for nearly 70 years, is dedicated to helping you pass the CPA exam the first time. Inside this book, you will find study notes and outlines as well as comprehensive questions and answers for the Regulation section of the CPA exam. Other volumes published by Kaplan Schweser CPA Review cover the remaining three sections of the exam. We realize you have a very busy life, and we have structured this volume to include only the topics you need to know for the exam. We do not include a lot of extra material that is unlikely to be tested. You do not have time for that!

We realize that everyone's needs are different when it comes to preparing for an important exam. Some people require only a brief refresher of well-known concepts; others look for a more in-depth review. Our Kaplan Schweser CPA Review Learning System is designed to provide you with the level of preparation *you* need. In addition to this Kaplan Schweser CPA Review Study Manual, the following companion products in our Learning System include study tools that are geared to all learning styles and that provide the flexibility today's busy professionals require:

- Kaplan Interactive Study Calendars to provide day-by-day guidance.
- Online Review Course providing more than 90 hours of instruction across all four sections.
- Online CPA QBank containing 3,000 T/F and 2,200 M/C questions, Testlets, and Simulations.
- Audio MP3s presented as a series of Q&As providing more than 22 hours of strategic retention exercises across all four sections.
- 2,100 Flashcards for hours of critical topic review.
- E-mail an Instructor and Instructor-led Office Hours provide additional assistance.
- Video library provides additional instruction to supplement the Online Review Courses.

We appreciate the opportunity to guide your study for the CPA exam. We wish you the best of success. Check our Web site at *www.kaplanCPAreview.com* for free resources to help you get ready for the exam, and practice with sample exam-like questions. Call us today at 800-CPA-2DAY (800-272-2329) or e-mail us at *cpainfo@kaplan.com* to take the first step toward passing the exam and getting on with the beginning of the rest of your life.

FREQUENTLY ASKED QUESTIONS

Q: How do I know the requirements to take the CPA exam?

A: Read an overview of your state's requirements by going to *www.kaplancpareview.com*, and click on "Exam Information." Information for all the available jurisdictions can be found here, along with special information for international candidates.

Q: When should I start the application process to take the CPA exam?

A: First, you should make sure that you have all education and other requirements fulfilled for the state where you want to have your scores reported. Go to *www.cpa-exam.org* and click on "Apply Now" and then follow the links to find your state. Make certain that you have (or will have) the hours and the courses that are required. Laws vary considerably by state and tend to change over time. Do not take the requirements for granted; check on the rules of your state. Second, keep in mind that the approval process can take up to six or seven weeks. You probably need to send in your application at least two months prior to when you want to sit for one or more parts of the exam.

Q: Can I begin the application process prior to completing all requirements so that I can sit for the exam as soon as I am qualified?

A: Check your state requirements. However, most states specify that the requirements have to be completed prior to beginning the application process.

Q: What is an NTS?

A: The NTS is your "notice to schedule," which indicates that your application has been approved. At that point, you can contact Prometric at *www.prometric.com/CPA* to find a test center and schedule an exam. Prometric is the company that administers the CPA exam. Make sure that you carefully read the NTS; it contains a lot of helpful information.

Q: Do I have to take the CPA exam in a particular state?

A: No, as long as you are properly scheduled, you can take the CPA exam in any Prometric Center regardless of its location. For example, you can take the exam as an Iowa candidate but sit in a center in Hawaii.

Q: How long do I have to pass all four parts of the CPA exam?

A: That depends entirely on the law of the state where you are having your scores reported. Be certain to check by reading the rules of your state when you go to *www.cpa-exam.org*. The time can vary considerably by state (normally 18 months).

Q: When is the CPA exam offered?

A: The CPA exam is given in four windows during the year: January-February, April-May, July-August, and October-November. Each section of the exam can be taken once in each window. Thus, you could sit for Financial Accounting & Reporting (as well as all other sections) a maximum of four times in any calendar year.

Q: Should I take all four parts of the CPA exam in one window?

A: That depends almost entirely on your ability to prepare for the exam. Most experts feel that a total of 250-400 hours is needed to prepare properly for all four sections of the exam. Many individuals take one or two parts per window unless they have a sufficient amount of time available to prepare for more than two parts. It is not unusual, though, for a candidate to take one part at the beginning of a window and a second part toward the end of that same window.

Q: Which part of the CPA exam should I take first?

A: There are a lot of different theories about which part should be taken first. One theory holds that you should take the part that you feel most positive about first so that you increase the chances of getting off to a good start. Other theories, though, do exist.

Q: Is the CPA exam only given by computer?

A: Correct. Starting back in 2004, the CPA exam was switched from a paper and pencil exam to a computerized exam. A multitude of changes in the exam took place at that time.

Q: What does the Financial Accounting and Reporting (FAR) exam look like?

A: FAR opens with 30 multiple-choice questions. When those 30 are submitted by the candidate, then a second testlet of 30 more questions are given, and then a final 30 appear. For FAR, there are a total of 90 multiple-choice questions that make up the first portion of the exam, followed by simulations, which we will discuss in another question.

Q: Should I guess if I do not know an answer?

A: The grade is computed based on the questions that you get correct. Therefore, you should answer all questions even if you have to guess.

Q: After I answer a question can I go back and change my answer?

A: Each of the three testlets in FAR has 30 multiple-choice questions. Until you finish a testlet, you can always change answers. Once a testlet has been submitted, you cannot go back and change those answers.

Q: Are all of those multiple-choice questions in FAR actually graded?

A: Of the 90 multiple-choice questions, 75 are graded while the other 15 are being tested for future use and do not affect the candidate's grade. However, you cannot tell which ones are graded. For example, it is possible to spend a long time attempting to answer a question that is not even graded.

Q: Do all of those multiple-choice questions have the same value?

A: No. Each question is individually weighted through a complicated mathematical process. In simple terms, answering a complex question correctly is worth more than answering an easy question correctly.

Q: After finishing the 90 multiple-choice questions, what happens next in FAR?

A: In all parts of the CPA exam other than Business Environment and Concepts (BEC), there are also two simulation questions. Each is like a small case study. A piece of information is provided and then a wide variety of questions are asked that can include matching, fill-in-the-blank, and spreadsheet work. In addition, the simulation contains a written communications question where the candidate has to write a memo, audit documentation, a letter, or the like. Finally, there is a research question. In that question, you are given access to a database of official pronouncements and you enter search terms to find a passage that answers a query that has been given. This research is very much like an Internet search.

Q: So, FAR is made up of 90 multiple-choice questions and two simulations. How is a grade determined?

A: Three grades are determined: one for multiple-choice, one for the written communications question, and one for the remainder of the simulation. Those grades are then weighted by factors of 70, 10, and 20 to arrive at a final grade. For example, a grade is determined for the multiple-choice questions and then that grade is multiplied by 70% to arrive at that portion of a candidate's total grade.

Q: What is a passing score?

A: A candidate must make a score of 75 to pass. However, because of the complex weighting system, that does not equal getting 75% of the questions correct.

Q: I understand what multiple-choice questions look like. How can I see an example of a simulation?

A: The AICPA provides candidates with access to one practice simulation for AUD, FAR, and REG. These simulations are available at *www.cpa-exam.org* under the "Tutorial and Sample exams" link. Kaplan Schweser's Learning Systems provide candidates with more than 30 practice simulations as part of your "Online Tools." Or if you purchase our Study Manual as an individual text, you receive online access to four practice simulations per section.

Q: How long are the exams?

A: FAR is 4 hours, Auditing and Attestation is 4.5 hours, Regulation is 3 hours, and BEC is 2.5 hours.

Q: How much of that time should be used for the two simulations?

A: The AICPA recommends 45 minutes for each simulation in FAR and also in Auditing and Attestation with 35 minutes for each simulation in Regulation. That is probably a good allocation of time. Therefore, in FAR, the candidate should spend about 2.5 hours on the 90 multiple-choice questions and 1.5 hours on the two simulations. Note that this means that you would need to average answering each multiple-choice question in FAR in 100 seconds. You can certainly make that pace, but you have to stay focused to do so.

Q: How difficult are the questions on the CPA exam?

A: Not surprisingly, the complexity of the questions tends to vary significantly. However, almost anyone who has been around the CPA exam will tell you that the breadth of the questions is more challenging than the depth. In other words, most questions are not too difficult, but the exam tends to cover every possible topic. You have to move your thinking from one topic to another very quickly. The first question might be on earnings per share and the second on leases and the third on pensions. Each question may not be too difficult but that constant movement of topics poses a challenge.

Q: What is the pass rate on FAR?

A: The pass rate on each of the four parts is roughly in the 40% to 45% range. It is a difficult exam, but it is certainly not impossible. People who put in enough hours tend to pass.

Q: Where can I get more information on Kaplan Schweser?

A: Go to *www.kaplanCPAreview.com* or send an e-mail to CPAinfo@kaplan.com.

EXAM STRATEGIES

Kaplan Schweser CPA Review applauds your desire to earn the CPA designation, one of the most prestigious and respected professional credentials in the world. Employing Kaplan's proven system for CPA examination preparation, you will be giving yourself a tremendous advantage in your efforts to join the more than 350,000 fellow CPAs and members of the American Institute of Certified Public Accountants (AICPA).

We have assembled some of the best minds in academia, along with a highly skilled professional staff, to develop a comprehensive review course for enhancing your chances of passing the CPA exam. We recommend that you follow the guidelines in this book and use the supporting course materials to ensure your success.

You should also be commended for working hard to complete your accounting degree. It is one of the most rigorous programs in business. With Kaplan Schweser's proven tools and CPA exam preparation formula, we can assist you with taking the knowledge you have acquired through the years and applying it to the CPA exam. Rigorous study alone will not ensure success. Your approach must focus your energy in a logical and organized manner, combining hard work with more effective and successful techniques. **Once you see that the "how" of studying is as crucial as the "what" to study, the effort and results will become readily apparent.**

This Strategies chapter will serve as a valuable tool to help you navigate the Kaplan Schweser course material, organize your study approach, and gain an understanding of the big picture regarding the CPA exam. We know that your chances for success will increase if you begin with this chapter and follow its recommendations, instructions, and advice.

The chapter will cover the following topics:

- Planning to Take the Exam
- Developing a Study Plan
- Preparation for the Exam
- Guidance on Exam Day
- Post-Exam Analysis

PLANNING TO TAKE THE EXAM

AICPA TESTING GOALS

In 2004, the CPA exam entered a new era, one that recognizes the context of your current educational environment and work experience. The old, paper-based exam sought to test problem-solving skills and knowledge of financial literature. It required more memorization than demonstration of critical thinking and analytical and communication skills. Today's computerized exam focus requires more than a general familiarity with the material. It requires a complete grasp of the concepts and the ability to clearly communicate your knowledge to the graders. This reflects today's business environment, which requires more advanced skills in researching technical information; applying informed, sound judgment in decision making; and communicating more effectively with many different stakeholder groups.

What is the driving force behind all this change? Corporations and other organizations are demanding accounting professionals who possess skills in communication, critical thinking, and problem and opportunity definition and analysis to guide their institutions in the 21st century's global economy. Accountants have become business partners and not just "bean counters." In response to the growing need for CPAs to possess broader skills, curricula are changing at colleges and universities to promote more experiential and cooperative learning (e.g., internships, group projects and class presentations). Likewise, the AICPA has incorporated the demands of the marketplace into the new CPA exam by transforming it from a paper-based to a computer-based test leveraging the benefits of a technology-based environment. Specifically, the computerized exam expands the learning goals and expectations beyond simply content and problem-solving skills. On the CBT (computerized-based testing) exam, the candidate is expected to demonstrate mastery of the competencies listed below.

- *Research relevant financial literature.* The candidate should possess the ability to review current rules, regulations, and interpretations in a particular context, such as revenue recognition or impairment of goodwill. The CBT exam requires the candidate to demonstrate the ability to research an issue, identify the appropriate authoritative literature, understand its application to the issue, and offer an opinion or structure a transaction in compliance with the proper rules. This is now tested under the simulation dimension of the exam. The questions will require you to access, during the exam, an online database of literature from which you will determine your answer.

- *Communicate business information.* Through analysis, evaluation, and conclusion, a candidate should demonstrate the ability to conduct the appropriate research of financial literature. Findings must then be communicated in an effective, clear, and relevant manner. This part of the exam, requiring written communications, will be graded manually by the AICPA. Scoring will focus on your ability to write well (including developing, organizing, and expressing your ideas) as well as the technical content of your answer.

- *Analyze and interpret business information.* The candidate will review and evaluate information in context (e.g., business combinations), in order to offer opinions, conclusions, further discussions, or actions related to the analysis.

- *Render judgment based on available business information.* Traditional quantitative problems focus on generating an exact answer [e.g., net present value (NPV) of a proposed capital investment]. The computerized exam will test the candidate's ability to review the business context and relevant information, and offer an opinion beyond the formula. For example, while the NPV of a project may be positive, other risk factors, such as declining revenue and increasing expenses, may render the validity of the underlying assumptions (e.g., cash flow predictions) less reliable. Perhaps management should consider these issues prior to authorizing the investment.

- *Gain an understanding of key business terms, facts, and processes.* One major complaint by accounting firms and corporations has been that accounting graduates are not familiar with business in general, but know only how to record accounting entries. The pencil and paper CPA exam did not historically test for a breadth of understanding behind these entries. The paper-based exam assessed the candidate's proficiency in answering quantitative problems and memorizing rules. The essence of accounting is the interpretation of economic events and the translation of events into financial information. Therefore, it is critical for the candidate to understand the business environment and operations to ensure the proper evaluation of economic events along with their related recording and disclosure.

We feel confident that the knowledge gained from your college curriculum and current professional work experience, along with our guidance, will help you successfully demonstrate your mastery of these competencies.

So, yes, the CPA exam has entered the 21st century. It is more relevant than before. It is testing different skills, and testing the same skills in different ways. Does this make it more difficult to pass? Not really. Read on. There are actually some new features that will make you happy. This is not your grandfather's CPA exam!

ADVANTAGES OF THE COMPUTERIZED CPA EXAM

Probably the biggest advantage of the computerized exam is that you no longer have to prepare for all four parts of the exam at once. This is the best thing that has ever happened to a CPA exam candidate!

The CPA exam was changed from a paper-based test to a computer-based test (CBT) in April 2004. The CBT exam allows candidates to plan and schedule the time that they wish to take the exam, based on the following requirements:

- The exam is offered in more than 300 Prometric centers across the United States and its jurisdictions.
- Candidates can take the exam two months out of each quarter of each year (January–February, April–May, July–August, and October–November).
- Candidates can take just one or as many as all four sections at a time and in any order desired.
- Each section is graded independently, and the outcome does not impact the other section results or qualification.
- Once you pass a section and earn credit, you have 18 months to pass the other three sections of the exam.
- There is no minimum score requirement for failed sections. That is, you don't have to obtain a certain minimum score to continue sitting for sections in the future.

The new exam mirrors the flexibility that technology has brought to the workplace, most notably through telecommuting and flexible work arrangements. Candidates can now schedule sections within a testing window (i.e., 2-month period) and take the sections of the exam at a pace that meets their work schedule, study/readiness plan, and general preference.

Candidates should be careful to understand the rules imposed by the CBT exam. Under the paper-based method, there was a lack of uniformity among the jurisdictions in qualifying for sections as they were passed. For example, in some jurisdictions, you had to have a minimum score on all parts taken, or your passing grade on another part was not accepted. All jurisdictions now follow the same guidelines for granting credit. Each section is graded independently, without regard to your score on another section of the exam.

However, once you pass any section, your time clock begins, and you have 18 months from that passing notification to complete the remaining sections. It is imperative that you fully understand the time constraint that is imposed once a section is passed. Your professional career or personal demands could easily consume months, and before you know it, time has expired and you could be working under pressure to pass or face forfeiture of the sections for which you previously earned credit.

We will assist you in passing the exam as soon as possible to avoid this potential planning and scheduling challenge. We want you to be aware of the potential risk and avoid it with effective planning.

Do not procrastinate. Once you pass the first part of the exam, maintain your study schedule, with appropriate rest breaks, and keep going. Prepare for and pass sections on a time schedule that works for you, but just ensure that you pass all four sections before that 18-month period slips by!

CBT VS. PAPER-BASED EXAM

A CBT exam presents some unique advantages, which were noted above, along with some limitations listed in the following:

- The examination is linear; you must take each portion of an exam section (called a "testlet") in a series. You cannot start in the middle of the exam as you could do in the paper-based mode.
- Once you complete a portion (testlet) and exit from it, you cannot go back to review and/or change answers.
- The time limits are even more critical as the system will close the exam once the time expires. You must manage your time on each testlet to ensure that you complete the entire exam on time. The exam software includes a clock which counts backwards to "zero time left." Be sure you do not spend too much time on one testlet, or you may run out of time on the other testlets.

The candidate should visit the AICPA's Web site, *www.cpa-exam.org,* to become familiar with the CBT exam. The AICPA has developed and made available a free comprehensive tutorial, use of which is highly recommended. The tutorial provides examples of test questions and, more importantly, the technical mode of presentation and delivery. Utilizing these resources will ensure that you will be confident, prepared, and efficient when the time comes. **We cannot overemphasize the importance of this step in your preparation.** The actual exam administration location (i.e., the Prometric Center) is not the place to learn what the exam looks like!

Remember the last time you drove a car that you had never seen before? You had to get in, locate all the buttons and dials, adjust the seat, set the air conditioner and radio, etc. This is similar to how you will become familiar with the exam experience. Do this on your own time with the tutorial, and our online materials, not at the exam, where your time is precious!

We recognize that you began your career in the information age, and you are probably quite adept at using technology. However, one aspect of technology is navigation, and it is essential that you gain an understanding of the software and mode of operation used for the CPA exam prior to exam day. Coaches and their players often visit a football field in advance of the game to ensure they know the stadium and the unique dimensions of the field, and to remove the fear of the unknown. Likewise, we want you to invest the necessary effort with the AICPA's tutorial and the Kaplan Schweser online materials. Take the opportunity to practice in a CBT environment similar to that where the test will be given. We want you to be free of exam-day jitters and be ready to pass.

EXAMINATION OVERVIEW

The CPA exam is prepared and administered by the AICPA for the 55 jurisdictions, including the District of Columbia, Virgin Islands, Puerto Rico, Guam, and the Commonwealth of the Northern Mariana Islands (CNMI). The AICPA is responsible for exam development, administration, and scoring. The AICPA has partnered with Prometrics Testing Services to administer the computerized examination at Prometric centers within the 55 jurisdictions.

Each state and jurisdiction has its own board of accountancy that administers the licensing function. For example, if you live, sit for, and pass the exam in Houston, Texas, the Texas State Board of Accountancy will issue your license to practice and your CPA certificate. The requirements for licensure vary from state to state. Be sure to check with your own state's board of accountancy for the requirements, both to sit for the exam and to become licensed after you pass.

The CPA exam is given in four sections as follows:

Section	Test Format	Allowed Time
Auditing and Attestation	• Multiple choice given in three separate testlets of 24 or 30 questions each • 2 Simulation questions	4.5 hours
Financial Accounting and Reporting	• Multiple choice given in three separate testlets of 24 or 30 questions each • 2 Simulation questions	4.0 hours
Regulation	• Multiple choice given in three separate testlets of 24 or 30 questions each • 2 Simulation questions	3.0 hours
Business Environment and Concepts	• Multiple choice given in three separate testlets of 24 or 30 questions each • There are no simulations on BEC.	2.5 hours
Total		14 hours

Topic coverage of CPA exam:

Section	Content Coverage Percent (approximate)	Relevant Supporting Literature
Auditing and Attestation	• 100%	• Generally Accepted Auditing Standards • Standards for Attestation Engagements and for Accounting and Review Services • Government Auditing Standards • Audit Risk Alerts • PCAOB Standards • For simulations, a research database such as the AICPA Standards database

Financial Accounting and Reporting	• Business Enterprises—80%
	• Government Entities—10%
	• Not-for-Profits—10%
		• Generally Accepted Accounting Principles for:
		  ♦ Business enterprises
		  ♦ Not-for-profit organizations
		  ♦ Government entities
		• For simulations, a research database such as FARS

Regulation	• Federal Taxation—60% • Law and Professional Responsibilities—40%	• Internal Revenue Code • Ethics pronouncements of AICPA • Sarbanes-Oxley Act of 2002 • PCAOB Pronouncements • Business Law textbook • For simulations, a tax research database tool
Business Environment and Concepts	• Business Structures—20% • Economics—15% • Finance—20% • IT—25% • Planning & Measurement—25%	• Current textbooks and business periodicals provide good coverage for BEC • There are currently no plans to include simulations on BEC

Note: Because the ability to research technical questions is tested in the simulations, the AICPA makes a sample research database available to candidates for a period of time while they are preparing for the CPA exam. See www.cpa-exam.org for more details. Kaplan Schweser's simulations also provide a sample research tool for your use in practicing with simulations.

Your initial response could be "Wow! That is a lot of material to cover in such a short period of time," or "I have never had an exam that lasted more than three hours, even when I had back-to-back exams in college." Please relax. We will teach you how to navigate through the material, develop an effective study plan, and efficiently use your time to focus on the relevant topics required to successfully pass the exam.

Remember: You are *not* learning all these topics for the first time; you are learning how to pass the exam. There's a big difference. You are not trying to become an expert in all of these topical areas. What you need is a structured and focused review and a proper strategic approach. We will provide that, along with flexibility and content to support any areas where you have had little or no prior exposure.

Hopefully, after looking at this schedule, you can begin to see how this guide, along with other Kaplan Schweser materials, will assist you in using your time wisely. This allows you to more effectively plan your time to properly manage the volume of material and breadth of topic coverage. With Kaplan Schweser materials, your focus can easily be tailored to reflect your particular background and you can efficiently and effectively prepare for the CPA exam.

BENEFITS OF THE KAPLAN SCHWESER CPA REVIEW MATERIALS

Kaplan Schweser has developed a comprehensive set of materials that will greatly assist candidates in their preparation to pass the CPA exam. The following is a guideline for each study aid and its recommended use and value:

Study Tool	Recommended Use	Benefit
Lectures (offered via live, interactive Web-based class or Web-based Self-Study of those classes.)	• Focus only on topics that are tested, as well as how they are tested (e.g., basic auditing standards). • Demonstration of how to effectively solve problems in a specific content area (e.g., lease accounting)	• Provides audio/visual lecture in a dynamic, interesting, and comprehensive manner. • Archives are available for viewing if you miss the live class, or if you just want to view the class again. • Archives are useful for those who cannot make a scheduled class.
Study Manuals	• Reference guides to support the review and study process for each topic. • Also includes multiple choice questions, essential outlines, exam strategy and technique, and a writing styles guide.	• Provides a comprehensive resource for each topic area for ongoing reference and review. • Provides summary outlines for quick review. • Provides multiple-choice questions for more practice. • Helps you understand the exam and the entire exam process. • Helps you structure your writing assignment in the simulations to gain maximum points.
Interactive Study Calendars	• Schedule the practice and review time in order to prepare for the CPA exam. • Impose discipline on your study schedule.	• Provides a terrific planning tool that integrates all of the Kaplan Schweser CPA Review materials by topic with a suggested study approach.
Audio MP3s	• A question/answer format to reinforce the content.	• Allows you to listen while you commute, go for a run or walk, or any other time it is appropriate for you to multi-task!
Flashcards	• More than 2,000 cards organized by exam topic, in question-and- answer format.	• Provides additional reinforcement of the topics, in a format that is convenient to use and carry with you.
Online Exam Testlets	• Evaluation and practice mechanism to determine progress and areas where more work is required.	• Provides an opportunity for candidates to evaluate progress in an environment that simulates the actual CPA exam CBT format. This is an invaluable opportunity for candidates, not only to demonstrate their readiness in terms of the topic coverage, but also to increase their level of comfort with navigating the computerized exam environment.

Study Tool	Recommended Use	Benefit
Online Exam Simulations	• Simulations provide the opportunity to practice with exam-like case problems and with an online research database tool. • While simulations definitely give you the opportunity to reinforce content, the major benefit of using simulations is to practice with the functionality of the software and the use of the research tool.	• Provides an opportunity for candidates to evaluate progress in an environment that simulates the actual CPA exam CBT format. Since the simulations are the newest component of the CPA exam, it is critical that the candidate understand the process and functionality of the software in this testing context. The simulations consist of multiple points-and-clicks, screen accesses, and other navigational requirements (e.g., professional literature review prior to responding to the specific questions). You should feel very comfortable with this process prior to exam day to ensure that you can maximize your available time to answer the questions, as opposed to being confused by the functions of the software. We want to minimize your stress on exam day by preparing you to anticipate every dimension of the exam, including content and operation.
Online Question Bank	• True/False questions sequenced to develop your learning of the topics; • Multiple-choice questions that are similar to exam questions.	• The T/F questions are similar to a "Socratic method" for learning the CPA Exam content. They are designed for Learning and not for Testing. • The M/C questions provide candidates with additional testing opportunities to identify strengths and weaknesses and to reinforce the learning.
E-mail-an-Instructor	• Resource for timely response to your questions.	• Provides candidates with a feedback mechanism to address issues and concerns as they arise. This is where our course becomes a personal tool, as this will complement any of our materials with the ability for you to ask specific questions. We want you to view this function as having access to a personal coach who will ensure that, as you practice, any issues or concerns you have will be addressed in a timely manner. We will be there for you and with you throughout this whole preparation period. You are not alone!
Blog	• Help CPA Certification candidates to understand and communicate about the CPA Exam throughout the year.	• Candidates use this Blog to gather information from Kaplan Schweser staff members as well as from each other. Sometimes it's nice to hear about the experiences of other candidates like you.
Instructor-led Office Hours	• "Live Chat" with an instructor who can answer your questions on the spot.	• Similar to "live" office hours with your college professors, this feature allows you to communicate directly with the content experts and discuss any issues you have with the material or your study plan.

KEY STEPS FOR PASSING THE EXAM

We recommend that you follow these guidelines to ensure that you maximize your time and appropriately utilize the resources made available through the Kaplan Schweser course.

1. **Visit the AICPA dedicated Web site for the CPA exam to gain a thorough understanding of the exam.** Use the tutorial, which gives you a sample of the test questions and mode of examination: *www.cpa-exam.org*. The AICPA has created for eligible candidates a wealth of free instructional information, such as tutorials, guides, and resources. This will allow you to be clear on the nature of the exam in terms of content and operation. It will also give you guidance on preparation and other critical information, such as scheduling the exam. **Be sure to obtain and read the <u>Candidate Bulletin</u> from that Web site.**

2. **Enroll in the following:** The AICPA is offering eligible candidates (refer to preceding Web site for more information) a 6-month free subscription to the AICPA Professional Standards, FASB Current Text, and FASB Original Pronouncements, which will provide students with a rich resource base to prepare for the research element of the simulation questions. Since the simulation questions will require research of the professional literature, the AICPA is providing this for free so you can practice conducting research prior to the exam. This will allow you to become familiar with both the content and the operation. This will greatly benefit you on exam day because you will have already mastered the research and the navigation effort. And it's free. What a great bargain!

3. **Determine when you plan to take the exam and contact your state board of accountancy and Prometric Center to apply and schedule a time.** As working professionals or students nearing graduation, your time is both limited and precious. Make sure you fully understand the "testing windows" concept and your availability prior to scheduling the exam. Keep in mind that you have new flexibility that was not previously available. But also note that you have an 18-month limitation once you pass a section to complete the remaining parts of the exam. We want you to avoid the last-minute or "cram" approach to the exam. Your success depends on having sufficient time to study for and pass the exam.

4. **Use the Kaplan Schweser materials in conjunction with your study plan to ensure your readiness on exam day.** The Kaplan Schweser materials have been developed to support each section of the exam. The Kaplan Schweser materials also help prepare the candidate to perform effectively within the new computerized exam environment by providing CBT examples relevant to each topic and testing format (i.e., multiple-choice or simulations). We strongly urge you to use these materials to prepare for the exam.

5. **Follow the suggestions in our CPA Survival Guide (see *www.schweser.com/cpa*, under Free Resources).** This guide is a personal reminder to make sure you plan, prepare, relax, and succeed. Kaplan Schweser understands that you will work very hard to prepare for the exam. **We will assist you in planning your time effectively so your preparation activities are efficient and effective.** This should ensure that you can physically and mentally relax, both during your preparation and on exam day. We do encourage dedicated days off to refresh and rejuvenate during the practice period. Finally, we feel that if you are properly prepared, you can relax and minimize or even eliminate stress before and on exam day. We want you to just go out and do your very best. Remember: you practiced, practiced, and practiced; all you have to do now is demonstrate what you know. And, while there is no such thing as being overly prepared, you do want to reach your exam day in an optimistic frame of mind.

DEVELOPING A STUDY PLAN

Once you have determined that you are fully committed to taking the exam, we recommend you develop a careful, sensible, and comprehensive study plan. This will ensure that you use your time and Kaplan Schweser materials effectively and efficiently. This will help you manage the process of preparation and control the degree of stress that is often related to such endeavors. As you progress with your studies, you will also begin to see that, while this is a big effort, it is absolutely not an impossible effort. You will begin to develop the confidence needed to believe in yourself and to keep heading toward your goal.

The CBT exam is more focused on assessing the competencies previously noted than on the memorization of certain rules and techniques. A quote from a recent presentation by an AICPA representative, "More thought than rote," indicates a focus toward more critical thinking. It is essential that you invest the proper time to plan, because the process of demonstrating mastery of the five competencies is different from a cursory memorization process.

The paper-based exam emphasized the ability to recall facts and rules. Preparing for the new exam requires effective application of the accounting foundation you acquired in college and/or work to the various contextual situations found throughout the exam.

Our review process focuses on providing you with adequate time to practice applying your knowledge, enhancing your knowledge in areas where you need support, and learning the testing environment. Therefore, you can relax and not be overwhelmed with the amount of material covered, or be concerned about your ability to memorize the complete set of GAAP and GAAS. We will help you prepare for this exam with proven methods that are relevant to the current expectations. **We cannot emphasize enough that *how* you study is as important as *what* you study.**

PREPARATION FRAMEWORK

When coaches prepare their teams for the forthcoming season, they develop a comprehensive plan that seeks to address every dimension of the competitive environment: game plan, winning strategy, physical component, and their team's mental readiness. Likewise, serving as your coach, Kaplan Schweser fully recognizes your world-class talent and capabilities and seeks to ensure that you walk away from the exam having given a winning effort.

We also want to address every key aspect of the CPA exam, relative to your strengths, talents, and professional, personal, and physical dimensions, so you are adequately prepared. Specifically, we will focus on strengthening and conditioning the following dimensions of your life related to preparing for the exam:

- Knowing the rules.
- Knowing how to implement the rules.
- Managing your emotional and mental energy while preparing.
- Maintaining your health and energy during the preparation period.

This chapter will provide you with a comprehensive and current review of the rules of the CPA exam. These Kaplan Schweser references provide a complete description of the exam and its objectives, explanation of its administration, registration information, and recommendations on how to leverage knowledge of the rules to your advantage. It is critical that you understand how the exam works. We go beyond the basics, giving you a background of the exam so you can fully appreciate why the current exam has been transformed from a paper-based, memorization-oriented test into a computerized exam that emphasizes critical thinking and analytical skills. We also feel it is important for you to know the registration process so you can make sure you are enrolled and eligible to sit for the exam when the time comes.

Kaplan Schweser will provide you with a rich set of tools that will assist in your preparation for the CPA exam. These tools were outlined in a table on page 10 of this study manual. Kaplan Schweser's tools are your manual for success, ensuring that your talents and mental attitude are ready to be put to the test.

We make an all-out effort to support your mental attitude by acting as your coach and cheerleader. We do this with our Blog, E-mail-an-instructor, and Instructor office hours. We know you have already worked hard to become eligible for the exam. We feel that our proven techniques will not only provide adequate preparation, but will instill the confidence needed to face the challenges of the CPA exam. In addition, if you ever feel an anxiety attack approaching, you can e-mail us and we will provide helpful feedback to resolve whatever issues are causing you stress. We will be there for you throughout the preparation period. Your coach will be on the sideline cheering, encouraging, and providing guidance right up to exam day.

The Interactive Study Calendar and the CPA Survival Guide encourage you to rest, relax, and refresh your energy throughout the preparation period. We recognize the fatigue that will arise from executing the recommended preparation schedule. We strongly encourage you to take periodic breaks at least once a week and also right before the exam. We want you to have the energy to rally all of your talents and knowledge to achieve peak performance. We want you to be as stress-free as possible during the preparation period. In fact, we want you to enjoy this process and anticipate and visualize your success. Most of all, we want you to enjoy the relief, satisfaction, and professional recognition that will come your way when you pass. So keeping healthy, alert, and confident is a very important part of this process.

DEVELOPING A STUDY PLAN AND SCHEDULE

Now that you fully understand the rules of the game, we need to focus on learning to play the game by practice, practice, and more practice. However, we want you to practice in an efficient, effective, and organized manner, and not just plunge into a set of materials. Besides not being very efficient, a haphazard approach may even lead to burnout.

We have developed a process for you to design a comprehensive study plan. This will prepare you for the planned "testing window" when you take the exam. You must consider your level of knowledge section by section, your schedule, and the rules of your jurisdiction to outline a plan that will lead to successfully passing the exam.

Please review the following steps and begin to design your study plan.

Determine when you are going to take the exam and calculate how many weeks of study you have available. We recommend seven weeks for AUD, BEC and REG, plus an additional two weeks for final review. For FAR, the schedule is nine weeks plus two for final review. The Kaplan Schweser materials are built around this schedule, and it is designed to work for you even if you are working full-time. If you are not working and have more time to study, you can shorten the schedule somewhat by using the self-study product based around archives of the live Web-based classes (Online Review Course—ORC). Your schedule should include planned days of NO study to provide balance and an opportunity to refresh and relax; this will help you avoid burnout and a negative attitude. We want you to be extremely realistic when considering your current responsibilities, and professional and personal commitments, and then, with our Kaplan Schweser Interactive Study Calendar, outline a study plan that you can fulfill. It is essential that you commit to the study days as well as to the days off. We want you to develop a balanced preparation approach that considers your intellectual efforts, as well as the need to maintain your mental and physical health. Another reason to be realistic in planning your study schedule is to ensure that you do not "over-schedule" yourself and then feel negative about yourself when you cannot meet that schedule. Set yourself up for success by being realistic from the beginning. Remember: this is really not a difficult exam, but it is a very long exam! Have someone who knows you well review your planned schedule and offer their opinion on whether you have a great chance of sticking with it.

Access the online Kaplan Schweser CPA Review Interactive Study Planner that is available for each topic. The Planner outlines exactly what you need to do each week. The foundation of the week's study is the class, which is available as a live, interactive class via the Web. You can take the live class anywhere you have a computer and Web access! You can ask questions and receive answers during class. You can e-mail your instructor between classes for additional questions. You can watch the archives of the class as many times as you like, either for catching up on a missed class or for further reinforcement of a topic. The nature of the Planner makes it easy for the candidate to identify the course material required and the recommended use of that material for each topical area.

UNDERSTAND THE "TESTING WINDOWS" FOR TAKING THE CPA EXAM AT THE PROMETRIC CENTERS

Testing Windows*	Closed Periods per Quarter
January and February	March
April and May	June
July and August	September
October and November	December

*A window is a consecutive 2-month period within a quarter that the exam is available via Prometric. Candidates can take one, two, three or all four parts during a "window." Candidates cannot repeat a part during a window.

As noted earlier in this chapter, the CBT exam gives the candidate considerable flexibility. For example, during the January and February window, a candidate could elect to take Auditing and Attestation during the first week of January. This could be followed by Regulation during the third week of January. They could then take Financial Accounting and Reporting during the second week of February and complete the exam with the Business Environment and Concepts section during the last week of February. Now, this would be a very aggressive schedule, perhaps more suitable to a candidate who is not working full-time!

Another candidate might elect to take two of the sections during this period and defer the other two to the April and May window. Or another candidate might elect to take one section per window to complete the whole exam in a year. The number of sections you elect to take during a window is your choice. Just remember, you cannot repeat a section within a window. In other words, you cannot take Regulation twice in the January and February window.

Whatever your schedule, take full advantage of the ability to take one part at a time. The improved flexibility in the exam scheduling is a great benefit to candidates. Not only does it allow you to create your own schedule, but it also enables you to prepare for and take only one section at a time. Compared to the old exam requirement of sitting for all four sections at once, this is a huge stress reliever for you. If you have not experienced preparing for and sitting for all four sections over two days, just ask some of your colleagues at work how much fun that was!

Along with this great benefit from flexibility comes a huge responsibility. (There is no free lunch, right?) You have the responsibility to discipline yourself to begin the process. It is far too easy for some people to say, "Oh, well, I'll just take it next month." While it is much better for you to have this flexible scheduling, it is also easier for you to let yourself procrastinate. Think about this. Do not put it off. Get the process out of the way, and move on to other learning opportunities in your life and career. The hardest part of a difficult undertaking is just taking the first step.

Another scheduling consideration is when to schedule a re-take in the event something unexpected arises that prevents you from preparing sufficiently. You always want to get your scores on a section of the exam before you schedule a re-take. Realistically, you will probably not receive your grades in time to retake a section within the same window. Thus, the AICPA has a rule allowing you to take a section only once per window. In addition, we would want you to spend sufficient time addressing the weaknesses noted on any failed section so that we can assist you in avoiding the same mistakes. With adequate preparation, you can expect to pass. If something prevents you from preparing completely, we will help you assess what your next steps should be.

Here's another point to consider. Experience shows that few people leave the exam site saying, "Oh, great, I passed that with no problem." It just doesn't happen. Most candidates leave the exam with at least some doubt as to whether they passed. This is perfectly normal. Many of them find out their immediate assessment was wrong, and they did pass. So *always* know your score before scheduling another sitting of any part of the exam. In fact, the best thing to do after a part is over is to make note of any areas you felt very weak in while taking the exam, and then put away that note until you get your score. Next, go have some fun! You earned it. After a few days off, you can start preparing for the next section of the exam you plan to take.

Before going any further, take the time to review your plan. Consider whether the schedule you selected is realistic. For example, if you have just been promoted and your new position will require extensive travel, will you have online access to the Kaplan Schweser materials while you are on the road? Will you have the time to study adequately? We do not want you to design a plan that is not attainable. It is essential that you develop a program that makes sense for your professional and personal schedule, commitments, and responsibilities.

We want you to be committed to your schedule. Our tools, such as the Interactive Study Calendar by section, are very useful. But these tools are only as good as how you use them to support your practice and preparation period. We recommend you document this plan in your PDA, online, or in the tool that best keeps you organized. This will provide an additional mechanism and the ability to track your progress, modify plans as your schedule changes, and ensure that you have considered all aspects of your professional and personal activities.

REGISTER TO TAKE THE EXAM

We want you to be mentally, physically, and emotionally ready for the exam. However, it will all be moot if you do not follow the process of enrollment and eligibility. We urge you to take sufficient time to understand the specific rules for registering to take the exam in your jurisdiction.

We have provided a list of steps for you to follow, which are relevant in each of the 55 jurisdictions.

Please note, these steps are general and you need to augment them after researching your respective jurisdiction.

Apply to your state board of accountancy. Your jurisdiction should have a Web site containing the registration information online. We recommend you pay particular attention to the eligibility rules (e.g., number of college credits and the lead time for filing). For example, if you want to sit for the exam in the April through May "testing window," identify the deadline for registering for that time. This is critical, since missing the deadline to register for a desired testing window will impact your study plan.

Be sure to notice your jurisdictions's requirements for number of credits in accounting courses, number of credits in other business courses, rules for accepting online courses, and any requirement for courses specifically dedicated to Accounting Ethics (not general ethics). Some states are adopting new rules in these areas. Be sure you know exactly what is required to be eligible to sit for the exam. Don't make the assumption that because you hold an accounting degree, you have met all requirements. Do your research to be sure. We will assist you in this area if you have questions.

Obtain your Notice to Schedule (NTS). This is your confirmation of eligibility to sit for the exam. You will need to keep this in a safe place since it will be required for admission [along with the approved form(s) of identification] to the Prometric Center where you take the exam. The NTS also qualifies you for enrollment in the AICPA Professional Literature subscription, as noted previously.

DETERMINE YOUR TESTING WINDOW SCHEDULE BASED ON THE STUDY PLAN YOU HAVE DEVELOPED

Again, you need to consider your professional and personal commitments. The rules for changing your testing window and any related refund for registration will vary by jurisdiction. We feel it is better to be certain and retain your scheduled testing window unless there is an emergency.

Schedule your examination appointment with Prometric. You can use the online or telephone contact information below. We recommend that you make your appointment as soon as you receive your NTS from your jurisdiction. This will ensure that your planned time and location are available.

- *www.prometric.com/cpa* (there is some very useful information on this site; visit it early in your planning).
- 800-580-9648.

We recommend you take the time to visit the Web site for the state board of accountancy in your jurisdiction to learn the process specific to your state. Some states process applications directly, and some have delegated this function to the National Association of State Boards of Accountancy (NASBA). NASBA is the central organization that the AICPA works with to facilitate the grade distribution process. Some states have authorized NASBA to serve as the registration unit for their candidates. It is imperative that you know what organization is responsible for registration. This will allow you to determine their procedures, gather the appropriate information, and complete the application in a timely manner. Completion will include verification of your eligibility (i.e., sufficient hours in accounting and undergraduate coursework in compliance with your jurisdiction's requirements, which may be 150 hours).

AICPA GRADING PROCESS

We have given you information regarding the rules of the exam, which have included a comprehensive description of the how, what, when, and why of the exam's administration and delivery processes. It is important that you also know how your performance will be evaluated by the AICPA. Remember, we are concerned about you in every aspect and want to eliminate any ambiguity regarding the grading process. This will help eliminate any stress you may have over this particular issue.

The following table provides an outline of the process that occurs once you complete the exam, whether you take one section or all four sections. The table makes a distinction between the multiple-choice testlets and the simulation testlets, since the latter possess a written portion, which is manually, rather than electronically, graded.

Function	Performer	Action
CPA exam	Candidate	**Complete scheduled section(s) of exam.** Once you finish a section (i.e., FAR, AUD, BEC, REG), it is independently graded and processed. Each section is graded separately, based on its own merit. Multiple-choice testlets are graded electronically; simulations are graded both electronically (the objective questions) and manually (the writing assignment).
Exam distribution	Prometric Testing Services	**Distribute candidate's electronic files to AICPA.** The AICPA has the sole responsibility for grading, assembling the grades, and distributing the grades to NASBA and/or the candidate's jurisdiction.
Grading—multiple-choice testlets and objective portions of simulation testlets	AICPA	**Conduct a sampling of answers to determine grading scales and any adjustments for defective questions with multiple answers.** This allows the AICPA to calibrate the grading scales to reflect desired passing ranges and to consider overall candidate responses for each question. For example, if there is a noted trend on a multiple-choice question, it may indicate that the question is defective or that the intended clarity was not achieved, and consideration for an alternative answer may be valid. Review answers electronically and assign scores to candidates. Once the grading scales have been calibrated, the scoring process is electronically completed, summarized, and prepared for distribution.

Function	Performer	Action
Grading—written communication portion of simulation testlets	AICPA	**Conduct a sampling of written questions to develop a grading guide for point assignment.** This process mirrors the paper-based examination in regard to its manual nature. However, they must read your response for both content and writing proficiency. The clarity, organization, accuracy, relevance, and content of your responses are critical because these characteristics will impact the graders' ability to determine your grade. If your response is not clear, then the grader will make a quick determination that you are not worthy of passing the written portion of this simulation question. Graders have a large workload and have less than three minutes to look at your particular response. If in the first minute they feel you do not communicate effectively, they will suspend their effort and make a general assessment of failure. **Execute manual review, evaluation, and grading of written communications.** It is important for you to realize that, while you will have two written communication questions on AUD, FAR and REG (i.e. two simulations, each with a writing component), only one of these will be graded. The AICPA selects which one to score, and then a maximum of ten points is allocated to that question. Therefore, you must do well on the writing portion of each sim. Do not omit either one. You will not know which one is scored.
Grade distribution	NASBA/State Board of Accountancy	Distribute grades to candidate. You will receive a notice of your performance via the United States Post Office. You will not receive an e-mail or voice mail.

Now you have a customized study plan that reflects your practice and preparation needs and considers your professional and personal commitments. This plan will be your critical guide over the coming weeks to help you navigate the process of being prepared for exam day. You should congratulate yourself for reaching this stage, because it reflects your commitment to investing the appropriate resources to pass the CPA exam.

PREPARATION FOR THE EXAM

Now it's time to practice, and, as they say, practice makes perfect. You are now aware of how the exam is scheduled throughout the year, as well as what is required in terms of your eligibility to sit for the exam. Let's now concentrate on how to practice, so you will be prepared on exam day.

APPROACH

All work and no play will burn you out and result in fatigue, impairing your ability to be successful on exam day. To avoid this problem, we have developed a holistic approach to studying for the exam. Our Interactive Study Calendar balances your preparation period by considering what it will take to pass the exam, while also recognizing that you have a full personal and professional life. We do not recommend that you put your personal life, including social and health management–related activities, completely on hold until you take the exam. In fact, we strongly encourage you to take time out, enjoy yourself, and relax periodically. This will allow you to return to your preparation activities with energy, enthusiasm, and clarity.

Now that you have elected to take the exam, you must look ahead at your schedule and consider your forthcoming personal and professional commitments. You may then make a realistic decision on how many sections of the exam you will take and when. You have 18 months to complete the entire exam once you have passed any one of the four sections. For example, if you pass Auditing and Attestation in the January/February testing window, you have 18 months from that time forward to pass the other three sections. We feel confident that our process for exam preparation will enable you to complete the exam successfully within this time period.

PROGRESS EVALUATION

Kaplan Schweser has assembled an array of online materials to assist you with monitoring your preparation, as well as its quality and effectiveness. By using Kaplan Schweser's tools, you will always know how your study is progressing. The tools will indicate whether or not you have mastered a given subject matter and focus your attention on areas where you are not performing as well.

So how can you measure your progress? Each time you take one of our online sample tests in a specific subject area, you receive a comprehensive view of where you stand. Testing also gives you the chance to see the actual testing experience. Once you complete the testlet, you can review your scores as well as an explanation for each answer to determine why you missed any particular question.

We hope this method of evaluation will serve as a source of encouragement. As you progress, we expect that your scores will improve. Use your improvement to boost your self esteem and confidence, and know that your hard work will pay off on exam day. Are you still visualizing that CPA certificate on your wall?

FINAL STRETCH

It's the fourth quarter and you have a comfortable lead. You have scheduled to take the exam on July 10, and it is now July 1. You may have told all of your friends and relatives that you cannot attend any of the Fourth of July festivities. Wrong! Now is just the time to take a break, and we will show you how to take a break and still be prepared. Having some fun in the final stretch is okay. After working so hard, you deserve a break!

We have outlined some key steps to follow during that final stretch period. Following, you will find a reference tool that you can use during the final few days before the exam to guide your activities effectively. Keep in mind, if you have consistently tested at a level of 80% or more, you are already testing at a level above the minimum passing rate of 75%. This fact should help keep your anxiety level down and enhance your confidence.

Also, understand there are certain things you should not do during the following few days. Do not try to learn new material. Doing so will cause unnecessary stress. Do not focus on areas of material that you don't know well or have consistently failed during the review period. Instead, focus on those areas where you have performed well and feel confident. Remember, you do not need to score 100%. Relax and look back at how well you have done during the practice period. You should review with a smile on your face, knowing that your hard work will allow you to take the exam with confidence.

FINAL STRETCH REFERENCE GUIDE

Use the following guide on July 1 (from our hypothetical example above, about 10 days before the Exam) to review your work during the practice season. The guide serves as a checklist and, hopefully, confirmation of your efforts to pass the CPA exam. We have listed seven questions, which we want you to answer.

Tip: Print this guide and place it on top of each of the planners that you have in use (e.g., Financial Accounting and Reporting).

Once you have completed your comments next to each question, step back and see where you stand. Answering yes to questions 1, 2, and 3 indicates that you have followed our recommendations for executing a structured process of exam preparation. It also shows that your hard work has consistently scored at 75% or better, which is what you need to pass the exam. Answering "no" to any of the seven questions is your indication of where to review during the coming days.

The remaining four questions will determine how you feel about navigating the exam (e.g., MCQ or simulation questions, or the specific CBT technology). If you have issues or concerns in this area, please feel free to e-mail us, or review the AICPA tutorial again to make sure you are comfortable with the technology.

Assuming you launch the Final Stretch period on July 1, you have nine days to answer questions 1 through 7 in the Final Stretch Reference Guide. This will allow you time to review what you have covered, evaluate how well you performed, review the technology, and determine your proficiency in answering questions in a variety of formats. Hopefully, you will complete the guide and get the big picture! That is: you have read, reviewed, and completed a vast amount of material over the past weeks; you were committed, faithful, and diligent; and you are ready to give your best on exam day.

It is critical that you do not allow the rigors of the preparation process to overwhelm, discourage, or distract you from the overall goal of becoming a CPA. Yes, it is a lot of work, but the rewards are outstanding, and you deserve to experience all of them. Therefore, we have developed a "CPA Survival Guide," which is a digital pocket guide of recommendations that we hope you will use to succeed in your goal of becoming a CPA.

Final Stretch Reference Guide

Action Steps	Candidates Review Comments
1. Have you completed all key steps outlined in the Interactive Study Calendar?	
2. Did you score at least 75% on all of the key topic areas?	
3. Did you review any area where you did not score 75%? If so, how did you do on the next test?	
4. Are there any areas where you still have trouble? What are they? What is the expected coverage on the exam?	
5. Overall, how do you feel about the multiple-choice questions?	
6. Overall, how do you feel about the simulation questions?	
7. Do you feel comfortable with the exam technology? Did you use the tutorial on the AICPA Web site? Have you used our testlets, which look just like the CBT CPA exam technology? Did you have any trouble navigating through the technology?	

In the next section, we will continue with our review of preparation for the exam, but our focus will be on exam day. We will use the same example (i.e., sitting for the exam on July 10) to help illustrate our key points.

REST, REST, AND REST

It is the night before the exam, and all through the house not a soul is stirring, not even your computer mouse. That is exactly the atmosphere we want for you: peaceful and quiet the evening before the exam. The Final Stretch Reference Guide provided above will direct you to conduct a high-level review, but we don't want you to do anything on the day before the exam other than the following:

1. **Take the day of July 9 off from work; schedule a vacation or personal day, whatever is available.** If your family environment mandates, check into a hotel the night before the exam. Yes, that means in addition to the day(s) required to sit for two sections, you will also need a day of rest prior to the exam. Therefore, assuming you take one section per day, you will need a minimum of three days.

2. **Locate your Notice to Schedule (NTS).** Make sure you place the NTS next to your two forms of identification to ensure you will have it with you when you proceed to the exam on July 10. Without this ID, you will not be admitted to the exam.

3. **Go to the Internet and print out the directions to the testing site.** We actually recommend you do this when you first receive your NTS. Hopefully, you have physically visited the location and know all of the alternative routes in case of heavy traffic.

4. **Review the rules for Prometric Testing Centers.** The AICPA and NASBA, along with Prometric's standard policies, prohibit candidates from wearing certain articles of clothing without significant security reviews. This is intended to prevent the use of electronic devices such as hidden cameras or unauthorized transmitters.

5. **Look in your closet and locate comfortable clothes.** Remember to follow the instructions from the Prometric Web site, and adhere to the limitations of what you can wear and take to the exam.

6. **Go to your kitchen and identify what you will eat for breakfast.** Make sure the breakfast you select is something that will promote energy, such as low-fat protein and complex carbohydrates. Select high-fiber cereal and fruit rather than sugary donuts.

7. **Get a good night's sleep.** Now it is time to go to bed. If you have cable or satellite service, find a comedian, listen to a joke, and go to bed prepared to sleep and dream about the sweet success to come.

GUIDANCE ON EXAM DAY

Finally, it's July 10 and it's a beautiful morning. It is time to go outside and conquer the world of passing the CPA exam. This is the day we have been waiting for. Just like the Olympians who practice very hard in hopes of earning a gold medal, you have also worked very hard. Just remember, a bronze is good enough to pass the exam, but keep your eye on the gold medal.

So here we are. We have done what we promised. If you followed our steps, you should be prepared and ready to demonstrate just how well you know the underlying material. Before you leave for the Prometric Testing Center, please remember the following:

1. Be confident—you worked really hard to be prepared.

2. Do not forget your NTS and two forms of identification (e.g., driver's license and passport).

3. You will be provided with scratch paper and pencils, along with lockers for small bags or wallets. These are the only items you should bring to the exam. The only other thing to bring is the knowledge that you have acquired over the past few weeks and the confidence that you are prepared!

4. Do not bring large bags, briefcases, or laptops, because they will not be allowed and they do not fit in the lockers. If you bring such items, you will have to go back to your car or even back home (if you did not drive), which could adversely impact your time.

One last thing before you leave home: look in the mirror and what do you see? We see a CPA in the making, and the next step is successfully passing the sections you are taking today.

POST-EXAM ANALYSIS

You have just completed one of the most significant testing marathons of your life. How do you feel? You may be exhausted, but, hopefully, you feel relieved and confident. If you followed our program, you should have had some time to relax as you studied for the exam. Now you have to wait for the results. Even though the exam is computer-based, there are still portions that are manually graded the old-fashioned way. What should you do in the mean time? Do you wonder what you missed and think back about each question to see if you made a mistake? Certainly not! We want you to enjoy the break and think ahead to the remaining sections with optimism. Do not spend time reliving the exam you just completed. Most people who spend time trying to analyze their own results will underestimate how well they did. Move on. Have some fun. Don't try to mentally grade your own exam. Wait for the results before you even think about that section again.

The pass rates in the CBT are in the range of 45-50%, plus or minus a few points. This rate is higher than the pass rate of the paper-based test. We sincerely hope that you are in that passing group, and feel that we can make the difference when it comes to your success. We now recommend that you resume your regular schedule and not dwell on or worry about the results.

IT'S IN THE MAIL

The scores have finally arrived. You open the envelope and find that you passed Financial Accounting and Reporting with a score of 76%, but failed to pass Auditing and Attestation, receiving a score of 70%. Congratulations, you deserve to celebrate! You have just passed part of the CPA exam, and you are on your way to earning one of the toughest professional certifications in the world.

What we need to do now is find out what happened with Auditing and Attestation. You did so well on the practice questions, testlets, and simulations that we were sure you would pass. Let's go back to the score reporting envelope and look at the diagnostic analysis of your score. This analysis should tell you how you performed on the MCQs and two simulation testlets by topic area. For example, you will know if you did well on the MCQs but performed poorly on the simulation tests. Use this information to direct your review for the next exam.

You should also review your score for the section that you passed to identify any trends (e.g., you performed marginally on the simulation questions in that section as well). Any such trends would suggest the need to work harder at becoming more proficient and comfortable with the simulation format questions.

So now you know your score. You passed one of the two sections and came very close to passing the other section. We still want you to celebrate and have some fun. When you return, we have more work to do; you now have 18 months remaining to become a CPA.

We hope you have found this chapter to be a beneficial preparation tool. As you continue preparing for the remainder of the CPA exam, be sure to use this chapter as one of your central resources for navigation and support.

Types of Questions on the CPA Exam

In order to prepare efficiently, you need to understand how the CPA exam questions are designed, the types of answers that are expected, and the recommended solution approach that will best help you achieve your goal of passing the CPA exam.

This chapter provides a guide based on the current approach the AICPA has developed for the CBT exam. We will discuss the multiple-choice question testlets for each section and address the different types of multiple-choice questions and recommended approaches to providing an answer. We will also do the same for the simulation questions that will be used on all of the sections except the Business Environment and Concepts.

MULTIPLE-CHOICE QUESTIONS (MCQs)

In the rest of this chapter, you will see representative samples of every type of multiple-choice question from each of the four sections of the exam. It is key to your success that you become familiar with all the various types of questions, and that you practice with them in our materials and on *www.cpa-exam.org*. Strategy is undeniably important to your success on the exam. Take a look at the kinds of questions, and you will feel less like you are going into a mysterious event called the CPA exam. You will know what to expect, and that in itself is worth some points in your score!

We have selected multiple-choice questions (MCQs) and simulation questions from our online materials to help reinforce your study approach.

SCREEN OUTLINE FOR MULTIPLE-CHOICE QUESTIONS (ILLUSTRATION 1)

The screen for MCQs is outlined as follows for the CBT CPA exam. We feel it is important that through the AICPA tutorial and our online testlets and question bank, you become familiar and proficient with using this format and the related available tools, such as a calculator or review selection feature. Illustration 1 shows a screen-shot of a multiple choice question from AUD.

Illustration 1

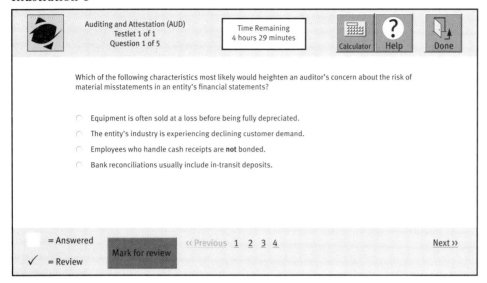

Top of Screen from Left to Right

- *AICPA logo.*
- *Testlet number* (e.g., Testlet 1 of 5). (This sample is from the AICPA's tutorial, where there is only one testlet. On the actual exam, there will be five testlets.)
- *Question number* (e.g., 1 of 30). (This sample is from the AICPA's tutorial, where there are only five questions on the testlet. On the actual exam, there will be 30 questions on the AUD testlets.)
- *Time clock.* Shows remaining time for the total section, so it is counting down to zero.
- *Calculator.* You should practice using this online calculator for various exercises to ensure that you are comfortable with its operations. Yes, it looks and operates like the handheld calculators, as well as the one on your PC or laptop. However, we want you to feel confident with its operation so that on exam day you will not waste any unnecessary energy learning to use it. (You can practice with the calculator in the AICPA Tutorial and in our online questions.)
- *Help.* Provides guidance on the CBT technical dimension, the MCQ aspect of the exam, and what to do if you need to ask a Prometric representative a question (does not provide help with correct answers! Sorry!).
- *Done.* Indicates that you have completed the section. Just as with most Windows-based operations, it will ask you to confirm (yes or no) your decision to leave the section through the appearance of a dialogue box.

Bottom of the Screen from Left to Right

- *Answer status box.*
  - A check in one box indicates that you answered the question and are finished with that one.
  - A check in the other box indicates that you marked the question for another review. This is an important feature, whereby the question will be highlighted in a sequential list, allowing you to quickly determine which questions you need to complete prior to clicking the *Done* button.
- *Mark for review button.* Allows you to mark an individual question for review, enabling a check mark to appear in the Status box.
- *Previous.* Click here to return to the previous question.
- *Question sequence.* This is a horizontal list of question numbers, e.g., 1 2 3. Indicates the answer status as follows:
  - Answered questions appear in a white box.

- ◆ The current question appears in a black box.
- ◆ Questions marked for review have a check that appears below the number. This allows you to identify the unanswered questions quickly so that they may be completed. In Illustration 1, question 1 is the current question. Questions 4-5 have not been attempted. (There are only 5 questions, because this is a screen shot of the AICPA tutorial.)
- • *Next.* Click here to move to the next question.

The actual question appears in the middle of the screen in a format that you will see illustrated in the following sections. You answer the MCQs by clicking in the box next to the answer choice. The answer status boxes will indicate your completion and selection to mark for review.

It is critically important to become familiar with the screen design and the online practice tests (on Kaplan Schweser's Web site and on the Exam Web site—*www.cpa-exam.org*) so that you can position yourself to be successful on exam day and not be overwhelmed by the exam's method of delivery. We cannot overemphasize how important it is to be prepared for the "look and feel" of the screens.

TYPES OF MULTIPLE-CHOICE QUESTIONS

Let's first discuss the types of MCQs that exist. The two primary categories are *quantitative* and *qualitative*. *Quantitative* questions require that you make a calculation based on a set of facts. *Qualitative* MCQs seek to determine your understanding of a principle and/or rule or its application, in view of a set of presented facts or procedures. In addition, some qualitative questions ask you to evaluate the four answer choices by selecting the "best," "least," or "most likely" answer. At times, you will see more than one correct answer, but one is better than the other. This is why practice-practice-practice with MCQs is so important. You can master this technique.

We have provided examples of both qualitative and quantitative MCQs with solutions to get you familiar with both types. In addition, we have provided commentary regarding the type of information that was required to answer the question correctly, such as knowledge of a specific rule.

You have probably heard this advice before, but it bears repeating: Most MCQs will have a best answer, an almost correct answer, and two other answers that are much less correct. **Be sure to read all the answers before making your choice. In fact, you should read the question and try to think of the correct answer before you even look at the answer choices.** At least two of the distractors (wrong answers) are usually close to being correct. And, if you read the question too fast, or do not give adequate consideration to each answer, it will be easy for you to select the "almost" right answer. And never leave an answer blank. If you should run out of time, or have no idea, try to make an educated guess and record something. Even if you do not know the answer, you have a 25% chance of getting it correct by guessing. There are no penalties for guessing.

AUDITING & ATTESTATION QUESTIONS

The examination of Auditing and Attestation focuses on your ability to interpret a set of facts and select the answer based on the generally accepted auditing standards (GAAS). The nature of this topic lends itself to qualitative versus quantitative MCQs since GAAS and the related pronouncements are policies-, principles-and procedures-based.

This also makes the choices tougher to select unless you are properly prepared. As you will see during our discussion, various types of qualitative MCQs can be used. By using our online material and this information, you should feel comfortable and confident when seeing questions similar to these on exam day.

MCQ TESTING A SPECIFIC RULE OR PRINCIPLE

When a company issues an income statement but no statement of cash flows, what is the only opinion that can be rendered?
A. Adverse.
B. Qualified.
C. Unqualified with an explanatory paragraph.
D. Unqualified.

The correct answer is "B." The auditor must issue a *qualified* report. This question is designed to test a specific auditing rule, which states that when an income statement is provided, but no statement of cash flows is included, the CPA must give a qualified opinion. Neither an adverse opinion nor an unqualified opinion can be given in this particular case. In this example you needed to know the specific rule regarding issuing an audit report.

MCQ TESTING AN APPLICATION BASED ON A SET OF FACTS

A client has $1 million in assets and $600,000 in income. Which of the following is *most likely* to be material?
A. Accidentally expensing a $20,000 asset.
B. An extraordinary item of $30,000 was reported.
C. The treasurer making an illegal bribe in a foreign country of $15,000.
D. Accidentally capitalizing an expense of $12,000.

The correct answer is "C." An illegal act is always material due to the fact that a violation of a law exists. In deciding about materiality, the CPA faces both a quantitative issue as well as a qualitative issue. The *quantitative* issue is purely a question of size and all of the misstatements here are relatively the same size. The *qualitative* issue rests on the seriousness and/or the nature of the problem. In other words, the cause would concern the auditor even if the discovered result were comparatively small. Here, the bribe will cause the most worry because it is both an intentional and illegal act. Moreover, it can be representative of a wider problem that needs to be further examined.

This question required you to identify which item was material. You had to compare the amount noted in each choice to the asset and income size of the company to determine if it was material. Initially, you may have thought "none of these are material." So, your next step would be to determine "what is there about these answers that makes one of them stand out from the others?" Answer "C" involved an illegal act, whereas "A" and "D" are both accidents, and "B" is a legitimate transaction. The existence of fraud or illegal activity renders any transaction as material because of its nature. Thus, you could have selected "C" without any further analysis.

Tip: Finding the correct answer efficiently and effectively allows you to save time for a subsequent review prior to exiting and closing the testlet.

MCQ REQUIRING THE EVALUATION OF THE FOUR ANSWER CHOICES

The following question is one where you need to know the rule and apply it by evaluating the four choices to select "the least." In this question, you should know the reasons why auditors must hire a specialist and then select which reason is the *least likely*.

> The CPA firm of Acme and Ball has hired an outside specialist to help with the audit of
> Keystone Corporation. Which of the following is the *least likely* reason for hiring the specialist?
> A. Keystone is an art gallery and the firm wants to determine the value of the inventory of paintings.
> B. Keystone is a jewelry store and the firm wants to determine the value of the diamonds held in inventory.
> C. Keystone is a construction company and the firm wants to determine the degree of completion of several big projects.
> D. Keystone owns an office supply company and the firm wants to determine the assessed value of its warehouse.

First, in reading this question, note the italicized words (least likely); these are the keys to getting this question correct.

The correct answer is "D." The nature of office supply inventory does not merit the hiring of a specialist. A specialist is most often hired when the CPA needs certain information that is not readily available in any other way, or the nature of the information needed is highly technical and outside the breadth of the CPA's knowledge. For example, the **value** of assets in "A" and "B" and the **status of completion** for construction projects would be essential information in an audit and very few auditors possess the expertise to make that determination without the use of a specialist. However, an **assessed value** is done for tax purposes and really provides little value to the auditor. In addition, the client should have physical proof from the government of the assessment so the auditor would not need a specialist. In this case, the question asked for the "least likely." Therefore, answer "D" is the least likely in view of the other three answer choices.

It is essential that you become familiar with these very common forms of questions. Often, all of the answers will be correct to some degree, but only one is the right selection—or more correct than the others—in the context of the question.

QUANTITATIVE MULTIPLE-CHOICE QUESTIONS

Quantitative MCQs require you to review a set of data and then perform a calculation. The CBT exam has a built-in calculator, which appears as an icon on the top right of the screen. You can use this calculator at any time. Quantitative questions require you to know the underlying accounting or regulatory principle, as well as the procedure for executing the calculation. Therefore, we recommend plenty of practice so you can become very familiar with how concepts can be presented and tested. This will allow you to effectively and efficiently respond to each quantitative MCQ.

QUANTITATIVE AUDITING AND ATTESTATION QUESTION

The next question requires you to understand the concept of audit sampling and related procedures for establishing an error rate or tolerance level. You must then apply the formulas for calculating a sample size.

> A client has processed 200,000 sales invoices, and the CPA must consider the error rate associated with these invoices. The auditor expects 2% to have mistakes but could tolerate having mistakes up to 6%. A sample of 200 invoices was selected and three were found to have errors. Using a statistical sampling chart, an upper deviation rate of 5% was determined. What was the allowance for sampling risk?
> A. 1.5%.
> B. 2.0%.
> C. 3.5%.
> D. 4.0%.

The correct answer is "C," which is the difference between the upper deviation rate of 5%, less the actual upper level rate of occurrence, which is 1.5%. In a sampling for attributes plan such as this, the difference between the sample rate (1.5% or 3 out of 200) and the upper deviation rate determined statistically (5%) is known as the allowance for sampling risk.

This question required you to understand sampling procedures, the auditor's role in establishing a tolerance rate, and how to apply the two concepts to select the best answer. The goal is to have practiced enough of these questions from our question material that you can effectively identify the appropriate approach and calculate the answer efficiently.

COMBINATION MULTIPLE-CHOICE QUESTIONS

We have illustrated both quantitative and qualitative questions in terms of the types and approach within Auditing and Attestation. There is also a presentation approach for the *answer choices*, which applies to both qualitative and quantitative MCQs. Both types of MCQs can use the following type of answer choices:

- *Combination Choices.* You are given a set of facts about a situation, where a *selection* of the facts make up the answer. For example, you are given a list of various cash flows, and asked which one(s) are Investing Cash Flows. Or, you must choose answers with multiple variable choices for each lettered answer (e.g., balances for both current assets and retained earnings). These are like two questions in one.

COMBINATION AUDITING AND ATTESTATION QUESTION—EXAMPLE

In the following question, you must answer two questions, "yes" or "no" for each column heading:

An auditor would express an unqualified opinion with an explanatory paragraph added to the auditor's report for:

	An unjustified accounting change	A material weakness in the internal control structure
A.	Yes	Yes
B.	Yes	No
C.	No	Yes
D.	No	No

The correct answer is "D." Both of these conditions mandate a qualified opinion. If the auditors are not satisfied that management's justification for a change in accounting principle is appropriate, their opinion should be qualified for a departure from GAAP. Material weaknesses in internal control must be reported to the audit committee. Such weaknesses affect the design of substantive tests, but are not noted in the auditor's opinion. Answers "A," "B," and "C" are incorrect because an unqualified opinion would not be issued when there is a departure from GAAP, and an explanatory paragraph would not be added for internal control weaknesses.

There are numerous examples of all these question types in our Kaplan Schweser materials, whether you are using the online multiple-choice questions or the books. Practice, practice, practice is the key to getting used to these styles of questions. And, if in doubt, you can usually eliminate two of the answers with your base of knowledge. (That's just how multiple-choice questions are designed.) So, even if there is a question where you are unsure, you will usually have a 50/50 chance of getting it right on that basis alone.

FINANCIAL ACCOUNTING AND REPORTING QUESTIONS

The Financial Accounting and Reporting (FAR) section tests the various sources of generally accepted accounting principles, including the application of these standards. Therefore, expect a lot of the MCQs in the FAR section to be quantitative. Even the ones that have a qualitative set of answer choices often require you to perform some degree of calculation.

In working MCQs in FAR, always read the actual question before you begin reading the facts. In other words, you may have a paragraph of facts, with the last sentence reading "What is the amount of the lease payment?" If you read the "question" part of the MCQ first, you will be better prepared to note useful information as you read the facts, or *fact pattern*, as we call it. Plus, knowing what your goal is (determine the lease payment) may allow you to ignore unrelated data that might appear in the question.

In this section, we have identified examples of both qualitative and quantitative MCQs for FAR.

QUALITATIVE MULTIPLE-CHOICE QUESTIONS IN FAR

The most common type of qualitative FAR MCQ is one that tests a specific rule, such as revenue recognition, and provides four answer choices based on a set of facts. Often, two of the answer choices are in obvious contradiction to the specific rule (i.e., obviously wrong), which should allow you to narrow the choice down to the other two and, ideally, quickly identify which of the remaining two is the correct one.

TESTING A SPECIFIC RULE OR PRINCIPLE IN FAR

The following question tests your knowledge of the statement of cash flows.

> Which of the following cash flows per share should be reported in a statement of cash flows?
> A. Primary cash flows per share only.
> B. Fully diluted cash flows per share only.
> C. Both primary and fully diluted cash flows per share.
> D. Cash flows per share should not be reported.

The correct answer is D. Cash flow is *never* expressed on a per share basis. Cash flow per share should *not* be reported in financial statements. Cash flow per share is not an acceptable alternative to net income or earnings per share as a measure of performance. This is an example of testing the specific rules regarding cash flow.

COMBINATION QUALITATIVE MULTIPLE-CHOICE QUESTIONS IN FAR

This question requires you to know the concepts regarding the nature of trademarks, along with the implications of their amortization, deferred taxes, and proper presentation on the financial statements. The combination dimension of the question requires you to provide two answers, one for each of two years. In this case, you must determine the current and deferred income tax impact of the amortization of the trademark.

> Cahn Co. applies straight-line amortization to its trademark costs for both income taxes and financial statement reporting. However, for tax purposes a 5-year period is used, and for financial statement purposes a 10-year period is used. Cahn has no other temporary differences, has an operating cycle of less than one year, and has taxable income in all years. Cahn should report both current and non-current deferred income tax liabilities at the end of:
>
> | | Year 1 | Year 2 |
> |----|--------|--------|
> | A. | No | Yes |
> | B. | No | No |
> | C. | Yes | Yes |
> | D. | Yes | No |

The correct answer is B. Since the related asset is *not* a current asset, the deferred tax liability will be classified as non-current at the end of Year 1 and Year 2. This question requires you to understand the classification of a trademark on the balance sheet, its amortization, and the related tax implications and presentation on the balance sheet. However, since the trademark is not a current asset, its related impact on deferred taxes will also be non-current. Understanding this rule will allow you to eliminate answers A, C, and D.

TESTING AN APPLICATION BASED ON A SET OF FACTS IN FAR

The following question provides a set of facts where you must apply your knowledge of the underlying concept (valuation and financial reporting of inventory) to select the correct qualitative answer.

> An inventory loss from a market price decline occurred in the first quarter, and the decline was not expected to reverse during the fiscal year. However, in the third quarter, the inventory's market price recovery exceeded the market decline that had occurred in the first quarter. For interim financial reporting, the dollar amount of net inventory should:
> A. decrease in the first quarter by the amount of the market price decline and increase in the third quarter by the amount of the decrease in the first quarter.
> B. decrease in the first quarter by the amount of the market price decline and increase in the third quarter by the amount of the market price recovery.
> C. decrease in the first quarter by the amount of the market price decline and **not** be affected in the third quarter.
> D. not be affected in either the first quarter or the third quarter.

The correct answer is A. Applying the matching and conservatism principles to inventory (lower-of-cost-or-market), you reduce the value of the inventory in the first quarter. Specifically, the inventory decline in the first quarter should be recognized in that quarter because at that point it was the company's judgment that the decline was not expected to reverse during the fiscal year. However, the decline was recovered in the third quarter. In that case, the recovery recognized is limited to the amount of the decrease in the first quarter. To do otherwise would violate the cost and conservatism principles for inventory. Inventory should not be written up above its original historical cost.

The first thing that happens when you read this question is you get lost in all the words—this went up and this went down and increase and decrease, and so on. If you are not totally relaxed, you probably forget the question by the time you read the answer choices. So, stop! Use your scratch paper at the exam site to doodle a picture of this, or make up some numbers that fit the description of the events in the MCQ, and make sure you are totally grasping the facts and the question. Then, try to answer it BEFORE you look at choices A through D. Also, you will note that choice C contained the word "not" in bold letters, which would naturally attract your attention during the exam. *Do not focus on fonts and other format issues versus content.* In this case, the bold emphasis was not relevant.

QUANTITATIVE MULTIPLE-CHOICE QUESTIONS IN FAR

As noted above, the nature of the FAR section lends itself to quantitative MCQs. Below, we have outlined the various types that will commonly appear on the exam. It is important that you practice with the quantitative MCQs and with the supporting tools like the calculator. Unlike with qualitative MCQs, calculations will be required. The calculator is available on the screen in the upper right-hand area. Naturally, use of these "practice calculators" is easy, but remember you will be under exam conditions at the Prometric center, and you want to be so accustomed to this type of device that it is second nature. Practice with our Kaplan Schweser materials and with the AICPA tutorial to be sure you that the use of this calculator is very comfortable to you.

MIXED QUALITATIVE AND QUANTITATIVE MULTIPLE-CHOICE QUESTION IN FAR

The following question is an example of the blend of qualitative and quantitative dimensions of an MCQ. The question requires you to understand the concepts of current assets and liabilities and their related transactions. In addition, you must be able to select the answer choice that properly expresses the transaction qualitatively as well as quantitatively. In this example, you have to express the impact of a transaction on the current ratio, which means you have to qualitatively be correct on the impact of the transaction as well as be quantitatively correct regarding the amount.

> Gil Corp. has current assets of $90,000 and current liabilities of $180,000. Which of the following transactions would improve Gil's current ratio?
> A. Refinancing a $30,000 long-term mortgage with a short-term note.
> B. Purchasing $50,000 of merchandise inventory with a short-term account payable.
> C. Paying $20,000 of short-term accounts payable.
> D. Collecting $10,000 of short-term accounts receivable.

The correct answer is B. This question requires you to conceptually understand the components of the current ratio. The current ratio is the result of dividing current assets by current liabilities. Any transaction that will either increase current assets proportionately more than current liabilities, or decrease current liabilities proportionately more than current assets, will increase the current ratio.

When solving this type of MCQ, you may be able to just think through this in your head without using your scratch paper. But, it's always safer to jot down the numbers on your scratch paper or type them into your spreadsheet and actually make the calculations. Do this quickly; don't waste a lot of time. Seeing the actual numbers will give you a better chance of getting it right.

On your scratch paper, jot down 90 / 180 = 0.5. That represents the "given information." Then, for Answer A, you are moving a long-term item to short-term. So, now jot down 90 / (180 + 30) = 90 / 210, which is 0.4. Answer A represents a decrease in the current ratio, so this answer is wrong. Answer A is incorrect, since it will increase only current liabilities, decreasing the current ratio. Follow this pattern with all the answer choices. It is much easier to determine the correct answer this way than spending a lot of time thinking about it.

Answer B says you are purchasing $50,000 of inventory with a short-term account payable will increase both current assets and current liabilities by $50,000. However, because the current ratio is less than 1-to-1, the purchase will increase current assets proportionately more than current liabilities and, therefore, increase the current ratio.

Answer C is incorrect, because it will decrease current assets proportionately more than current liabilities, decreasing the current ratio. Answer D is incorrect, as it will not affect either current assets or current liabilities. Therefore, the current ratio will be unchanged.

This is a challenging question. A lot of people see this question and then close their eyes or stare up at the ceiling and run through the steps of the MCQ in their mind. It is much better if you will make up a numerical example on that scratch paper, then manipulate it by using the information in the answer choices, and SEE what happens to the current ratio. A picture (of the hypothetical numbers) is really worth a thousand words here.

In all of the examples provided, it is critical that you are comfortable with the underlying concepts. Furthermore, you must be able to quickly identify the appropriate rule or principle, apply it to the question, and select the correct answer. Like appearing at Carnegie Hall, this can only be achieved through practice, practice, and practice. We feel confident that if you use our MCQ materials, you will be adequately prepared to successfully solve the real exam questions.

VARIABLE DEGREE OF CALCULATION COMPLEXITY IN MULTIPLE-CHOICE QUESTIONS IN FAR

We have noted that there is a range of complexity in the calculations required to solve a quantitative MCQ. We have listed a few examples ranging from basic to complex, to illustrate a recommended solution approach. The examples also show how you can reduce each MCQ into basic calculations once you fully understand the underlying concepts.

The following question is an example of a basic calculation requirement for a quantitative MCQ. Based on the set of facts, a basic calculation of the operating cycle is required.

The following computations were made from Clay Co.'s Year 1 books:

Number of days' sales in inventory   61
Number of days' sales in trade account receivables   33

What was the number of days in Clay's Year 1 operating cycle?
A. 33.
B. 47.
C. 61.
D. 94.

The correct answer is D, based on the definition of the operating cycle. The operating cycle is the average time for a company to outlay cash for inventory, to process and sell the inventory, and collect the resulting receivables, converting them back into cash. The number of days in the operating cycle (94) is equal to the number of days' sales in inventory (61), plus the number of days' sales in accounts receivable (33). This question required you to know the definition of the operating cycle and then perform an easy calculation in accordance with the concept. By knowing the concept and then applying the formula, you should be able to solve this question in less than a minute. Since the exam allows you approximately two minutes on average (and sometimes more), this allows you to bank some extra time for those harder questions or for review at the end of the testlet.

The next question requires the candidate to have a general knowledge of depreciation and the related presentation of book value on the balance sheet, and to perform two sets of calculations. In terms of the level of effort required, this MCQ is classified as intermediate in complexity.

First, go to the end of the question and read the actual question: what is the carrying amount (another name for book value). Now you know what you are doing and you will pay closer attention to the facts as you read the question.

On January 1, Year 3, Lane, Inc., acquired equipment for $100,000 with an estimated 10-year useful life. Lane estimated a $10,000 salvage value and used the straight-line method of depreciation. During Year 7, after its Year 6 financial statements had been issued, Lane determined that, due to obsolescence, this equipment's remaining useful life was only four more years and its salvage value would be $4,000. In Lane's December 31, Year 7, balance sheet, what was the carrying amount of this asset?
A. $51,500.
B. $49,000.
C. $41,500.
D. $39,000.

The correct answer is B, which is based on the following calculation:

Cost of the asset on 1/1/Year 3 = $100,000

Straight-line depreciation of ($100,000 – $10,000 salvage value) / 10 years = $9,000 per year

Book value as of 12/31/Year 6 ($100,000 – 4 years depreciation of $36,000) = $64,000

Recognition of new book value:

Straight-line depreciation of ($64,000 – $4,000 salvage value) / 4 years = $15,000 per year

Book value as of 12/31/Year 7 ($64,000 – one year of depreciation of $15,000) = $49,000

This required a more complex set of calculations based on the concepts of depreciation.

The following question requires a multiple series of calculations and is probably one of the most complex examples of a quantitative MCQ. This example could easily be separated into more than one MCQ using a common set of facts. Be sure to read the question part first—how many shares of common stock outstanding?

Rudd Corp. had 700,000 shares of common stock authorized and 300,000 shares outstanding at December 31, Year 9. The following events occurred during Year 10:

January 31	Declared 10% stock dividend
June 30	100,000 shares acquired as treasury stock
August 11	Reissued 50,000 shares
November 30	Declared 2-for-1 stock split

At December 31, Year 10, how many shares of common stock did Rudd have outstanding?
A. 560,000.
B. 600,000.
C. 630,000.
D. 660,000.

The correct answer is A, based on the following series of calculations:

Balance of stock on January 1		300,000sh
Declaration of stock dividend	30,000	
New balance		330,000sh
Treasury stock acquired	−100,000	
New balance		230,000sh
Reissue of stock	50,000	
New balance		280,000sh
Stock split	2 × 280,000	
Balance of stock on December 31		560,000sh

This question was not difficult and only required a fundamental understanding of basic equity transactions related to common stock. However, it did require you to go through translating a sequence of events in order to arrive at the answer. Each of the steps (treatment of the stock dividend or treasury stock) could have been a separate MCQ. In this case, the complexity is based on the fact that you had multiple calculations to execute before selecting the correct answer. This approach will be common on the CPA exam, making it essential that you are able to solve the basic or qualitative MCQs as efficiently as possible, saving you time for other similar types of MCQs.

A good tidbit of advice on this type of question is to read very carefully, and be as relaxed as possible, because you do not want to make a tiny error half-way through the solution. The CPAs who write the exam questions know from experience what the most common errors are; if you make that common error, you will derive an answer that will show up among the answer choices. So, when there are multiple steps to a question, be very careful and jot down the intermediate steps on your scratch paper.

COMBINATION QUANTITATIVE MULTIPLE-CHOICE QUESTIONS IN FAR

There are combination questions in FAR that require you to select at least two variables per set of information, and to also select combinations of information. Below, we have identified some examples of both to illustrate the common forms.

The following question requires you to select a combination of four variables in each answer choice. While it may appear to be complicated, once you review the material and follow our recommended solution approach, you will see how to simplify this MCQ.

Read the question first (What accounts and amounts should Newt credit in Year 10 to record the issuance of the 3,000 shares?) so you know what your goal is as you read the facts.

In Year 9, Newt Corp. acquired 6,000 shares of its own $1 par value common stock at $18 per share. In Year 10, Newt issued 3,000 of these shares at $25 per share. Newt uses the cost method to account for its treasury stock transactions. What accounts and amounts should Newt credit in Year 10 to record the issuance of the 3,000 shares?

	Treasury stock	Additional paid-in capital	Retained earnings	Common stock
A.	$54,000		$21,000	
B.	$54,000	$21,000		
C.	$72,000			$3,000
D.	$51,000		$21,000	$3,000

The correct answer is B. The best way to determine the solution is to create the related journal entry to record this transaction, while jotting it down on your scratch paper. The journal entry would be as follows:

Debit cash for $75,000; this reflects the 3,000 shares at $25 per share.

Credit treasury stock for $54,000; which is 3,000 shares at the cost per share of $18.

Also credit additional paid-in capital (APIC) for $21,000; this is the excess of reissue price above cost ($75,000 minus $54,000).

Under the cost method, when treasury stock is sold at a price in excess of its cost, the difference is credited to APIC-treasury stock. Answers A and D are incorrect because retained earnings cannot be increased by treasury stock transactions. Answers C and D are incorrect because treasury stock transactions do not affect the capital stock (common or preferred) accounts.

This is one of the most complicated and comprehensive examples of a combination quantitative MCQ. It required you to generate two answers, and the four options (A through D) each had four variables (treasury stock, APIC, retained earnings, and common stock). This is why practicing using our MCQs is critical. It is essential that you are able to confidently and efficiently take something that appears complex and break it into small pieces to solve.

EXTENSIVE SET OF FACTS TYPE OF MULTIPLE-CHOICE QUESTIONS FAR

Another type of quantitative MCQ presents an extensive amount of information, which can be overwhelming. It is easy to get lost among all the facts. But, with practice, you can solve these types of questions just as easily as the ones that present only a sentence or two of information. These questions, an example of which follows, still seek to test your understanding of the underlying concepts. Once you grasp the issues, you can simplify the information and quickly identify what is relevant, determining the correct answer among the four choices. (As you read the following MCQ, you may think this is a problem, but it is just a long MCQ!) Be sure to read the question part first, so you know how to organize the information (in your mind and on your scratch paper or "scratch" spreadsheet.) And, be sure to notice which year is involved ... year 1.

The Ajax Company has several investments:
- It owns 38% of Turtle Company and has the ability to apply significant influence.
- It owns 18% of Snail Company and has the ability to apply significant influence.
- It owns 19% of Elephant Company but does not have the ability to apply significant influence.
- It owns 7% of Cat Company but does not have the ability to apply significant influence.

Ajax received the following cash dividends:
- $40,000 from Turtle on November 1, Year 1.
- $30,000 from Snail on November 20, Year 1.
- $20,000 from Elephant that was declared on December 1, Year 1, and collected on December 20, Year 1.
- $15,000 from Cat that was declared on December 15, Year 1, with a date of record of January 5, Year 2, and was collected on January 20, Year 2.

Ajax also received 1,000 shares of Cat as a 12% stock dividend on July 5, Year 1. The shares have a par value of $10 per share but a fair value of $18 per share. How much dividend revenue should Ajax recognize for Year 1?
A. $20,000.
B. $35,000.
C. $50,000.
D. $68,000.

Wow! At first glance, before we even solve this question, it appears that it should be worth more than one MCQ. However, after you read the information you will note that this involves the equity method of accounting for investments. If you know the rules, you can quickly determine that this will be an easy question to solve. (Don't let those scary-looking questions slow you down; take a deep breath, relax, get out that scratch paper, and proceed to the correct solution.)

It is quite useful in a question like this one to first read the actual requirement of the problem (i.e., the actual question you are trying to answer): "How much dividend revenue..." in this case. Reading the requirement first will enable you to sort through the facts as you read them, because you will be better prepared to ignore facts that are not pertinent to the calculation of your answer.

Dividends from equity method investments are not reported as dividend revenue. Likewise, the receipt of a stock dividend is not reported as dividend revenue. That leaves only the cash dividends from Elephant and Cat. However, dividends to be received are not reported by the owner until the date of record. Thus, the dividend from Cat will not be reported until Year 2. Only the $20,000 in cash dividends from Elephant should be reported in Year 1, so the answer is A.

The answer was quite simple once you applied the basic concepts of investments based on the equity method of accounting. All of the information presented did not require an extensive series of calculations, merely the understanding of the basic concepts. Do not let a lengthy question like this one intimidate you. Sometimes, many of the facts are really irrelevant to your calculations anyway.

So, now you should feel better about those FAR questions. You have a strategy for solving them. You have lots of MCQs in our materials to give you the needed practice. Practice is the key here. And, any time you solve a MCQ and initially get the wrong answer, be sure to analyze WHY you missed it. Do not let this get you down, either. You are in a learning mode as you work through these study materials. The testing mode is at the Prometric center. Each time you miss a question you have yet another opportunity to learn from your mistake.

Next, we take a look at the REG questions.

REGULATION QUESTIONS

The Regulation, or REG, section will test your understanding of prevailing federal taxation, business law, ethics for CPAs, SEC rules, and other significant and relevant regulatory matters. Given these topics, you can expect a mix of quantitative and qualitative MCQs. Regulation is very similar to auditing in that you are expected to interpret various policies, rules, and procedures. Federal taxation lends itself to the testing of the application of rules, which is the primary source of quantitative questions in this section.

MCQs TESTING A SPECIFIC RULE OR PRINCIPLE IN REG

The following question tests your knowledge of a specific law. You must understand contract law as it applies to minors, and no interpretation or calculation is required. The solution is strictly based on understanding the law, using it to evaluate each response, and finding the correct answer.

> Fritz, a minor who appeared to be in his early 20s, purchased a used Jet Ski from Mill's for $2,750 in cash. Fritz ran the Jet Ski aground the first week he used it, causing it considerable damage. Fritz can:
> A. return the Jet Ski to Mills for a partial refund only.
> B. return the Jet Ski to Mills for a full refund if he first has it repaired.
> C. not cancel his contract with Mills.
> D. return the Jet Ski to Mills, without repairs, for a full refund.

The correct answer is D. A minor cannot enter into a legally binding contract without parental consent. Specifically, a minor can void a contract by returning the item, regardless of its condition. If the item has been lost or stolen, the minor can disaffirm, even though he or she returns nothing. This is a business law question based on contract law, which is very clear about the eligibility of a minor to engage in an agreement. Consequently, you did not need to calculate or debate the issue; it is very clear. You could have eliminated any choice that did not relieve the minor of all responsibility, which quickly eliminates the other three choices. It is critical, though, that you first realize that the question states Fritz is a minor. "Appearing to be in his early 20s" does not matter in this case.

Now let's look at a question involving federal taxation and see how important it is to know the Internal Revenue Code and be able to apply it to a given situation as well. We have selected a question involving rules for dependency, a topic that is heavily tested.

Peter and Susan Dillon are married and have two children: Paul, aged 22, who was a full time student during the year, and Mary, aged 18. Paul has $6,000 in taxable income and Mary has $5,000 in taxable income. Peter and Susan provide over half of the support for both children, although neither lives at home. Neither child is married. Which of the following statements is true?

A. Mary qualifies as a dependent of the Dillons if she is a full-time student for at least five months.
B. Paul must file a tax return and gets one personal exemption.
C. Paul qualifies as a dependent of the Dillons.
D. Because of her age, Mary need not file a tax return.

The correct answer is C. The gross income test for dependency does not apply to Paul because he is under 24 and a full-time student. Mary need not be a full-time student to qualify as a dependent because she is under the age of 19. Because of Mary's age and Paul's status as a student, either can earn any amount of income and still qualify for dependency. Furthermore, as long as the Dillons are providing greater than 50% of their children's support, they also meet the support test. Both Paul and Mary will have to file their own tax returns, while neither will be entitled to claim their own exemption. Understanding the rules for dependency is key to answering the question. We strongly recommend that you understand the Internal Revenue Code as it applies to an Individual Form 1040, and our materials will assist you in that mastery.

TESTING AN APPLICATION BASED ON A SET OF FACTS IN REG

The next type of qualitative MCQ involves making a decision based on a set of facts, which is very common in either the federal taxation or business law sections. We have identified an example of each for your review.

Due to favorable prices, Hunt, a purchasing agent for Petri, ordered 15,000 gallons of #2 heating oil from Grace for $0.99 per gallon. Hunt was not authorized to make purchases for Petri that exceeded $1,000. Even though the purchase was not authorized, Petri wishes to hold Grace to the contract. To do this, Petri must:

A. receive and accept the benefits of the contract.
B. pay for the heating oil prior to delivery.
C. grant Hunt the requisite purchasing authority.
D. ratify the contract before withdrawal by Grace.

The correct answer is D. Even though the agent was not authorized to make the purchase, the principal can still ratify the agreement. A principal can ratify an unauthorized contract that was entered into by an agent as long as ratification takes place prior to withdrawal by the other party to the contract. This is a basic element of contract law, where you have to apply the rule to the set of facts as presented.

We can now review a similar question from Corporate Federal Taxation. Specifically, the following question involves tax treatment of corporate capital gains and losses and how that treatment differs between corporations and individuals.

> The Ace Corporation has sales revenues of $300,000, normal and necessary operating expenses of $200,000, a short-term capital gain of $3,000, and a long-term capital loss of $10,000. What is the amount of capital loss that can be deducted for this year?
> A. $3,000.
> B. $7,000.
> C. $10,000.
> D. $0.

The correct answer is D. Corporations are not allowed to deduct net capital losses to receive a current year benefit. Instead, capital gains and losses are netted to determine a single net gain or loss position. Where net capital gains are fully taxable, net capital losses must be carried either back three years or forward five years and netted with capital gains in those years. The result is a refund of prior years' taxes or reduction in future years' taxes. Individuals, on the other hand, can deduct net capital losses of up to $3,000 per year, carrying excess net losses into the future to net with other capital gains.

We have just covered two major types of qualitative MCQs we expect to appear on the exam, which test a specific rule or the application of a rule to a set of facts. The next common type of qualitative MCQ is a combination question, which involves both qualitative and quantitative answer choices.

EXAMPLES OF COMBINATION MULTIPLE-CHOICE QUESTIONS IN REG

The next question requires you to know the concepts (e.g., the rules regarding corporate capital gain and loss treatment as discussed earlier) as well as to calculate the correct amount for the right year or entity. You will be required to provide two answers for one question.

> A corporation has capital gains of $8,000 in Year 1 and $4,000 in Year 2. The same corporation has capital losses of $9,000 in Year 1 and $1,000 in Year 2. There have been no other transactions resulting in capital gains and losses. How do these gains and losses impact taxable income?
> A. No tax effect in Year 1 and a $2,000 gain in Year 2.
> B. An $8,000 gain in Year 1 and a $3,000 gain in Year 2.
> C. A loss of $1,000 in Year 1 and a $3,000 gain in Year 2.
> D. No tax effect in Year 1 and $3,000 gain in Year 2.

The correct answer is A. In Year 1, the gains and losses are netted to arrive at a $1,000 loss. As a corporation, that loss is not deductible, but can be carried back for three years and forward for five years. Because there are no past capital gains, this loss can only be carried forward. In Year 2, the gains and losses are netted to a $3,000 capital gain. However, the $1,000 loss carryforward reduces that taxable amount to a $2,000 capital gain. Again, there are two issues to consider. The first addresses the qualitative dimension of whether the corporation is eligible for any capital gain or loss and in which years. The other relies on the specific calculation of capital gains and losses for both years.

The next question also involves two issues. The first requires understanding the difference between cash and accrual basis accounting for tax purposes. The second requires an actual calculation of taxable income for each category.

> Dr. Jekyl starts the current year with accounts receivable of $50,000. During the year, he provides services to patients and charges them $210,000. He actually collects cash of $180,000 and has ending accounts receivable of $80,000. Which of the following is true about his taxable income?
> A.   Cash based—$130,000; accrual based—$210,000.
> B.   Cash based—$180,000; accrual based—$210,000.
> C.   Cash based—$180,000; accrual based—$240,000.
> D.   Cash based—$130,000; accrual based—$240,000.

The correct answer is B. A cash basis taxpayer recognizes income when cash is actually collected. Here, the doctor received $180,000 in cash. An accrual basis taxpayer recognizes income when the work is done. In this case, the doctor provided $210,000 in services. To correctly answer this question you had to first categorize the information: cash basis versus accrual basis. Then you had to perform the actual calculation for each accounting method. Again, it was critical that you first understood the qualitative dimension of accounting basis, before performing the quantitative requirement.

Also helpful in answering the previous question would be the use of a T-account for accounts receivable. You should recognize that an increase in the receivables account represents current-year credit sales, while a decrease in the account represents cash collections from customers. Not all sales are made on credit, however, so you should watch for cash sales, since they will not affect the receivables account but will increase income under either cash or accrual basis accounting methods.

By now you should see the patterns of MCQs that appear consistently in each of the sections. There will always be the testing of a rule, the application of a rule, and some combination of testing and application MCQs in each of the four sections on the exam. Let's now proceed to the quantitative type of REG questions. These will primarily be based on federal taxation since the law and ethics questions in REG will tend to be rule-based.

QUANTITATIVE MULTIPLE-CHOICE QUESTIONS IN REG

As noted previously, the nature of federal taxation lends itself to quantitative MCQs. We have outlined the various types that will commonly appear on the exam. It is important that you know the types of MCQs and be familiar with using the supporting tools like the calculator. The calculator is available on the screen in the upper right hand area. We recommend that you use the one available in testlets and test modes of our online question bank, along with the examples available in the AICPA tutorial, so that you become proficient with using the software-based calculator.

Our first question requires a very brief calculation of taxable income for a corporation. Shortly, we will cover the calculation of taxable income for an individual. It is essential that you review the federal taxation portions of our materials to ensure that you are very familiar with the two income tax reporting forms for the individual and corporation. We also recommend that you know the key supporting schedules such as the Schedule A for Itemized Deductions, since there will likely be several questions taken from these forms and schedules.

During the current year, the Daily Corp. had revenues of $300,000, ordinary and necessary expenses of $180,000, and dividend revenue of $5,000. (Daily owned 30% of the company that paid the dividend, and it was a domestic company.) What was Daily's taxable income?

A. $120,000.
B. $121,000.
C. $125,000.
D. $121,500.

The correct answer is B. The income prior to the dividends-received deduction is $125,000 ($300,000 + $5,000 – $180,000). Based on 30% ownership, the dividends-received deduction is 80% of $5,000, or $4,000. This reduces the taxable income to $121,000. We recommend that you know both the IRS Form 1040 for individuals and IRS Form 1120 for corporations. This question is based on the form 1120C for corporations, and follows the guidelines noted on the form for determination of taxable income.

Barbara and Kevin get a divorce on January 1 of the current year. Barbara gets $200,000 in cash at that time and a house worth $240,000. Six months later she receives a car worth $30,000 from Kevin as part of the settlement. Kevin also makes monthly payments of $6,000 to Barbara during the year: $2,000 in child support and $4,000 in alimony. What is Barbara's income for the year?

A. $72,000.
B. $78,000.
C. $248,000.
D. $48,000.

The correct answer is D. Periodic cash payments after a legal separation are viewed as alimony, as long as they contain no child-related contingencies. These amounts are taxable to the recipient and deductible by the person making the payment. Any payment or part of a payment that is viewed as child support is not included as alimony, nor is it taxable to the recipient, nor deductible by the payer.

Twelve alimony payments of $4,000 per month were made in this case. Property settlements pursuant to a divorce are also not taxable as income, regardless of whether cash or property changes hands. Determining the correct answer to this question was contingent upon your understanding what constitutes gross income versus exclusions from gross income for an individual.

Our last question in this section involves the calculation of a capital gain for an individual. Capital gains are a common source of quantitative MCQs. You can expect several quantitative questions to focus on the calculation of adjusted gross income, taxable income, or some dimension of a capital gain for an individual, partnership, or corporation.

William and Sandra file a joint return each year. They bought a house as their principal residence in Year 1 for $190,000. In Year 9, when they are both 67 years old, they sell this house for $700,000 and buy a new principal residence for $300,000. What is their taxable capital gain?

A. $0.
B. $10,000.
C. $400,000.
D. $500,000.

The correct answer is B. The taxpayers have a gain of $510,000 ($700,000 less $190,000). However, because it is their principal residence and they file a joint return, the first $500,000 of that gain is excluded from gross income and not taxable. The calculation for this problem was not difficult, assuming you are aware that each taxpayer is allowed to exclude up to $250,000 of gain on the sale of their principal residence as often as every two years, and they need not reinvest the proceeds of the sale into a new residence to receive the exclusion. Furthermore, because they file a joint tax return, they can exclude twice the amount, or $500,000.

BUSINESS ENVIRONMENT AND CONCEPTS QUESTIONS

The Business Environment and Concepts (BEC) section will test your understanding of key general business concepts, processes, practices, and emerging issues. The AICPA added the BEC section to further enhance its ability to test your proficiency in the real world of business. As we discussed earlier, the CPA exam was changed to ensure that CPAs were better educated, more well-rounded, and proficient in skills beyond the technical dimension of debits and credits. The AICPA also wanted to ensure that CPAs could effectively communicate, understand the impact of the business environment on their clients' organizations, and keep up to date with contemporary practices and emerging issues. This is reflective of a life-long learning environment, and the broadening of the role of the accounting profession and accounting professionals in business.

The specific areas of coverage consist of:

- Business Structures (corporations, partnerships, sole proprietorships).
- Economic Concepts (from your basic economics classes).
- Financial Management (from your basic finance course).
- Information Technology (basic concepts from Accounting Information Systems and Management Information Systems).
- Planning and Measurement (we used to call this Cost and Managerial accounting).

The five concepts noted above represent general knowledge categories that are not heavily rule-driven, but more factual (e.g., the types of legal entities, such as sole proprietorships, partnerships and corporations; or the key essence of the balanced scorecard). Of all parts of the CPA Exam, this is the one where frequent reading of the general business press will help you.

Remember, Finance, Economics and IT are fairly new topics for the CPA exam, and the AICPA has not yet developed simulation questions. Therefore, the BEC section consists of MCQs.

BUSINESS STRUCTURES

Business Structures is really a law topic. Most formation, operation and termination issues related to business forms derive from a law. You will see similarities between the MCQs in BEC and in REG. This area will primarily test your understanding of current business structures and how they operate.

Let's review a few questions in this section so you can fully understand what to expect and will feel comfortable with your ability to successfully answer each MCQ.

Grant and Ames are partners in a car repair business trading as G & A Services. Without authorization from Ames, Grant signed a contract for G & A Services to purchase an expensive automotive diagnostic machine from Harper Equipment, Inc., Harper Equipment, Inc., may pursue a claim for payment:

A. against Grant and Ames.
B. against Grant only.
C. only against the partnership, G & A Services.
D. against Grant, Ames or G & A Services, but only for what the cost of the equipment was to Harper Equipment, Inc.

The correct answer is A. Since G & A is a partnership, both Grant and Ames are liable, and G & A Services is liable as well, since every partner has the implied power to bind the partnership (and all partners) to contracts in the ordinary course of business. Once you understand partnerships, you will know that unless it is a limited partnership every partner is exposed to joint and several liability for activities of the entity.

Let's continue our review of business structures with a question that involves the sharing of profits.

Lucy, Duff, and Gordon are general partners in a dress-making business. Lucy works full time in the business, while Duff and Gordon work only part-time. As a consequence of this, the partners have agreed that Lucy should receive one-half of the partnership profits. As a result:

A. Lucy must be paid a salary.
B. Lucy has greater voting rights than her partners.
C. Lucy will be liable for half the losses, unless otherwise agreed.
D. Duff and Gordon will have limited liability for partnership debts.

The correct answer is C. Unless specifically stated otherwise, profits and losses are shared equally by default. If a partnership has an agreement regarding the sharing of profits, but the agreement is silent with respect to losses, losses will be shared the same as profits. This is a fundamental concept of partnerships and is expected knowledge of anyone with a business degree, whether or not they are an accounting major. These concepts are not hard to grasp, rather they are simply general business knowledge. Much of the new material on BEC falls into the category of general business knowledge.

We should look at one more question just to make sure you see the nature and scope of the coverage in this area.

Bernard, Chang, and Dorset are partners in a limited partnership, in which Bernard and Dorset are limited partners and Chang is the sole general partner. Chang withdraws from the partnership, but the business continues to operate. Which of the following statements is true?

A. Withdrawal of one partner has no effect on the partnership's continued existence.
B. The partnership can avoid dissolution by replacing Chang within 90 days.
C. The limited partnership immediately dissolves.
D. The limited partnership immediately becomes a general partnership.

The correct answer is B. Under the latest version of the Uniform Limited Partnership Act, withdrawal of the sole general partner from a limited partnership no longer results in the automatic dissolution of the limited partnership. Partners have 90 days to find and replace a general partner. This question validates the importance of reviewing our online material for BEC since it represents the most current information for those sections. In this case, your old business law book or advanced accounting book may not contain the latest version of the Uniform Limited Partnership Act, and you should be careful when choosing additional materials for review.

We have covered three aspects of business structures: binding a partnership; sharing profits and losses; and what occurs when a partners leaves. We feel this is very representative of the MCQs that will be covered in the BEC section under the business structures area.

Now on to economics—the topic you enjoyed with a passion in college and hear about each day in the news. This area is tested to determine your ability to understand the macro and micro events surrounding your client.

ECONOMIC CONCEPTS

We believe that using the newspaper to stay current on the economy and reviewing our online material will provide sufficient preparation for this portion of BEC. We will provide some MCQs to demonstrate the nature of the coverage.

> Economic activity does not occur at an even pace over time. An economic cycle occurs where the economy goes from a valley to a peak in activity and then repeats the cycle. Which of the following *best* describes the normal sequence of a business cycle?
> A. Expansion, contraction, recession, boom.
> B. Recession, contraction, boom, expansion.
> C. Expansion, boom, contraction, recession.
> D. Boom, contraction, expansion, recession.

The correct answer is C. This is general knowledge you would have obtained in your Economics 101 course. Now, just in case you have forgotten, here is a more detailed explanation. A series of short-term ups and downs in economic performance is a business cycle. Rather than moving along at a steady rate of growth, an economy goes through different stages of growth in production. The expansion phase is an early growth period, where: levels of income rise, unemployment remains flat or slowly begins to fall; interest rates are low and begin to rise; and inflation is low, but price pressure begins to build. From the expansion base the economy eventually reaches a boom phase, where: rates of production reach a peak; income growth is high; unemployment begins to reach a low; interest rates rise to high levels; and inflation becomes a problem due to excess demand as the economy reaches peak production. When the boom peaks, interest rates, inflation, and inventory levels are high. Businesses carry high inventories to accommodate strong sales. But when sales and expected sales slow due to higher interest rates, inflation, or any other factor, businesses cut investment and aggregate demand stalls or weakens. This is the start of a contraction phase. Economic performance levels are good, but the direction of growth begins to slow and ultimately reverse. Following a contraction, the economy enters a recession (defined as two successive quarters of negative growth in gross domestic product), where: unemployment rises; incomes fall; personal consumption begins to fall; business investment continues to fall; inflation rates fall; and interest rates fall. As the recession reaches its deepest point, we are in the valley of the cycle. The valley of the recession is the beginning of the next expansion phase and the cycle repeats.

Hopefully you get the point that this area is not hard; you just have to refresh your review of economic basics. Okay, let's cover one you hear in the news all the time: What makes our economy grow? You may have thought listening to the news would be of no value, but remember, the AICPA wants future CPAs to be well-informed about how the world businesses operate, which includes knowing about the economy.

Which of the following should help promote expansion in the economy?
A. Higher taxes.
B. Increased imports.
C. Falling inventory-to-sales ratio.
D. Lower levels of government spending.

The correct answer is C. Falling inventories are an indication that consumers are buying and businesses will have to stock. The increase in production in turn means more jobs. The following answer is a bit more detailed and refers to the economic cycle discussed previously. Falling inventory-to-sales ratio will help promote an expansion. When the level of inventory is low relative to sales, businesses must increase production, bringing inventory levels back up to prevent stock-outs and lost sales. The increase in production stimulates job growth, income growth, and output growth which helps fuel an expansion. On the other hand, higher taxes take disposable income away from consumers. Lower consumer spending reduces aggregate demand and lowers economic growth. Imports are a "leakage" in that they are produced in other countries but take part of consumer disposable income. Net exports (exports – imports) contribute to higher gross domestic product (GDP), so higher imports will lower GDP. Government spending contributes to GDP, so lower spending slows down GDP growth.

Now let's look at a question with a quantitative requirement before we move on to the financial management area.

If the nominal interest rate is 6% and the market expects inflation to be 2%, then the expected real interest rate must be:
A. 8%.
B. 6%.
C. 2%.
D. 4%.

The correct answer is D. You may remember this point from Economics 101. While this subject is discussed in the news, most of us have forgotten the detailed calculation. A nominal interest rate includes both the real rate and an inflation premium. It follows then that with a nominal rate of 6% and expected inflation of 2%, the difference—or real rate—must be 4%. This assumes a risk-free rate with no risk premium.

We can now proceed to the Planning and Measurement section where we expect to find a wide variety and greater number of quantitative questions.

PLANNING AND MEASUREMENT

In recent years, business leaders complained that our profession was weak in the area of planning and measurement during the 1980s and early 1990s. As a result, it is now tested on the CPA exam. Performance measurement is a major activity within management, and accounting is the key source of underlying information.

The area of Planning and Measurement covers an array of topics including cost-volume-profit analysis, planning and budgeting, cost measurement and performance measurement. We have selected both quantitative and qualitative questions so you can see the scope of coverage that we believe will be tested.

A company had sales of $2 million last year with variable costs of $1.2 million and fixed costs of $500,000. What was breakeven point?
A. $1.7 million.
B. $1.25 million.
C. $1.5 million.
D. $1.45 million.

The correct answer is B. This is a basic cost behavior analysis and cost-volume-profit question, where you must understand the cost relationships before you can calculate the breakeven point. Breakeven point (BEP) is the point where a company will make neither a profit nor a loss. So, the results of operations are set up as a formula, where:

net income = sales – variable cost – fixed costs

Or: NI = S – VC – FC

And sales (S) is the unknown.

Variable costs "vary" with sales and can be expressed as a constant percentage of sales: VC / S = 1.2 / 2 = 0.6

If variable costs are 60% of sales, then VC = 0.6S

Fixed costs (FC) = $500,000

Net Income (NI) = $0

Therefore: S – (0.6)S – 500,000 = 0

Solving the equation for S, we find sales at the break-even point = $1,250,000.

This is not a difficult question, and if you know the formula for calculating a BEP, you can easily answer a variety of BEP type questions.

The following question is a manipulation of the BEP equation since one of the variables, fixed costs, is missing. Once you know the formula for BEP, you will be prepared to respond to any version of MCQ.

Last year, a company had sales of $500,000, variable costs of $300,000, and a net loss of $40,000. How much must sales *increase* this year in order for the company to make a net income equal to 10% of sales?
A. $90,000.
B. $200,000.
C. $300,000.
D. $210,000.

The correct answer is C. Here fixed costs are not known, and the figure must be determined before the equation can be established to solve for sales (and the needed increase in sales). From last year we know:

$$S - VC - FC = NI, \text{ so: } 500,000 - 300,000 - FC = (40,000)$$

So fixed costs must have been $240,000. That figure can then be used in making the computation for the current year, recognizing that "fixed" implies no change relative to changes in sales. Also notice in this problem that variable costs are again 60% of sales since 300,000 / 500,000 = 0.6. Finally, we would like to generate an income that is 10% of the current year's sales. So: $S - 0.6S - 240,000 = 0.1S$

Solving for S, we determine that sales must be $800,000 in order to meet the target net income.

Since the question asks about the increase in sales, the final answer is $300,000 or the difference between this year's and last year's sales. Once again this MCQ was not difficult and is similar to the last question, where it relies on the formula for BEP.

The following is a good example of a qualitative or conceptual MCQ.

> A balanced scorecard is a methodology for assessing an organization's business performance via four major components of the organization. Which of the following *most accurately* outlines those four major components?
> A. Financial areas, internal business processes, employee characteristics and satisfaction, and innovation and improvement activities.
> B. Marketing areas, internal business processes, customer characteristics and satisfaction, and innovation and improvement activities.
> C. Financial areas, external business processes, customer characteristics and satisfaction, and innovation and improvement activities.
> D. Financial areas, internal business processes, customer characteristics and satisfaction, and innovation and improvement activities.

The correct answer is D. The key here is to determine what has a direct impact on an organization's overall business performance. Management would certainly be concerned with employee concerns, characteristics, and job satisfaction, as well as external business processes. However, these are indirect business performance metrics on a balanced scorecard. Customer attributes and satisfaction are directly related to business performance. Marketing areas are also very important but would fall within the innovation and improvement activities.

These three MCQ examples demonstrate the level of coverage in the Planning and Measurement area. Let's now review the coverage under the Information Technology section.

INFORMATION TECHNOLOGY

This is a broad area within BEC. It's a lot of vocabulary and very basic concepts that you probably already know. The AICPA does not expect you to be a systems analyst, but you are expected to possess a general understanding of information technology, since it is a critical dimension of business and is especially relevant to the accounting profession.

Our first question is not difficult, and anyone who was in school or graduated around the era of Y2K should know about ERPs.

Enterprise Resource Planning (ERP) systems are integrated software applications designed to provide complete integration of an organization's business information processing systems. Certain activities within an ERP system, such as entering client data, managing different levels of inventory, and any specialized subsystem of the MIS related to accounting are all considered integral parts of the enterprise system. Which of the following specific systems is not considered part of the accounting information system of the ERP application?

A. Taxation.
B. Land, building, and equipment recordation.
C. Cash management.
D. Payroll.

The correct answer is C. This question required you to understand the components of an ERP system related to a particular function. Tax accounting, capital asset accounting, and payroll accounting are all integral parts of the accounting and reporting function, and would be included in the accounting information system. Cash management, along with financial forecasting, portfolio management, and credit analysis, are all functions of the separate financial information systems. These are not difficult concepts, but they do require you to be current on the subject matter.

Let's look at one more question so we can see the diversity of coverage in this area.

Which of the following types of reports are not considered a particular category of accounting information systems reports?

A. Summary reports.
B. Detail reports.
C. Exception reports.
D. Incremental reports.

The correct answer is D. The incremental report is not one of the normal outcomes of an accounting system. Accounting information systems must be able to generate summary reports, which include the balance sheet, income statement, statement of cash flows, and statement of equity changes. These reports should depict accurate information and conform to GAAP—at any level of detail. Three types of reporting are defined by accounting information systems: detail reports, which list detailed information, perhaps account balances; summary reports, which outline summarized information, such as balances summarized by geographic divisions; and exception reports, which list exceptions to normal reporting, such as a report on sales that do not meet a plan. This is why it is critical to practice taking MCQs in each of the areas within all of the sections to gain an understanding of the terminology used—so if there is something you are not familiar with, you can overcome this limitation prior to the exam.

The final area we will cover here, Financial Management, is one of the newest additions to the exam.

FINANCIAL MANAGEMENT

Financial Management topics include many from your basic finance course in college. There is some overlap between finance and accounting, so this is helpful here. Topics tested include financial models such as cash flow, net present value, internal rate of return, and payback, along with the tax considerations of these methods. Financing options, cost of capital, derivatives, and cash management are included. Financial statement analysis (ratios) is included here as well. (Note that ratio analysis may be tested in both FAR and BEC, according to the AICPA Content Specification Outlines.)

Let's review an example of what we might expect to find for MCQs in this area.

> A BBB-rated Simpson Company bond pays a coupon rate of 6.5% (paid semiannually) and has a maturity of 10 years. The market rate of interest on bonds of similar risk (BBB) and maturity (10 years) is currently 7.5%. The price of this bond will be:
> A. greater than face value.
> B. equal to face value.
> C. cannot be determined from the information given.
> D. less than face value.

The correct answer is D. The Simpson bond pays $65 a year (6.5% of face value, which is by definition $1,000), while other bonds of the same maturity and risk are paying $75 in interest. Bonds of the same maturity and risk must provide the same total yield to maturity (YTM). Therefore, investors will bid down the price of this bond until its YTM is 7.5%. Rules of thumb: if the coupon rate is less than the market rate of interest (MRI) it will sell at a discount; if the coupon rate is greater than the MRI, it will sell at a premium; if the coupon equals the MRI, the bond will sell at face or par value. Here's a good example of a question that could easily be in BEC finance or FAR bonds.

Again, though not difficult, this section of the exam requires you to be current on a lot of material. We will help you review these concepts so that you are prepared for exam day.

FINAL COMMENTS ABOUT MCQS

The CBT CPA exam offers a valuable tool to assist you with the MCQs on the exam—*mark for review*. As described previously, this feature allows you to visually see all of the questions you have not completed. Once you have sequentially gone through a testlet and answered as many questions as possible, you should go back through and complete those that remain unanswered.

We want you to use your time wisely. When you approach a question, review the context of the question or its actual "question" prior to looking at the answer choices. Then apply the recommended approach to selecting an answer. If a question appears to be too difficult to resolve, continue on to the next question. Do not let a question frustrate you or cause any stress. Do not waste a lot of time on a question for which you do not know the answer. The key is to remain positive and confident, so do what is necessary to maintain your composure and progress through the exam, knowing that you are managing your time toward a successful completion.

Once you have answered all of the questions you feel comfortable with, return to those you skipped. Perhaps by answering the other questions, your memory was jolted and/or your confidence has been boosted so that you can tackle these remaining questions effectively. Amazingly, sometimes you may "learn" an idea in a subsequent question that reminds you of the answer to a previous one.

It is critical that you complete every question. The CPA exam does not penalize guessing like some other exams you may have taken. While we want you to be prepared and minimize guessing, please do not leave any question blank. Your attempt will at least increase the possibility of receiving some points— and we hope we have prepared you to take an educated guess on those questions where you are unclear of the approach. Never, never, never leave blanks.

Finally, time management is a required skill of CPAs; it was expected on the paper-based exam, and it is just as essential on the CBT exam. Always be aware of your time and keep an eye on the "remaining time" feature on your screens. You will actually have plenty of time, and many candidates will leave early. You will probably be surprised to learn that you do have sufficient time. But use that time wisely and maximize the amount of benefit in terms of points scored! Practice working with time constraints when you are preparing for the exam.

SIMULATION QUESTIONS

Now that you understand MCQs, we will continue with the other type of question on the CPA exam—the simulations.

The simulation questions are structured to reflect real-world scenarios by going beyond the static nature of a long problem or essay that offers only historical information. Simulation questions require the candidate to respond to a multiple set of objective questions, which could include true/false, multiple choice, matching, or journal entries. In addition, simulation questions include a subjective component. This component will require a written response based on the candidate's interpretation of a given situation and research of the appropriate auditing, tax, or financial accounting literature.

The simulation format attempts to place the candidate in a "real world" environment. In the real world, you will be faced with a situation, such as a potential merger or acquisition, or the spin-off of a line of business, that demands an informal decision be made concerning accounting or auditing issues. To effectively develop a response, you would consult the current financial accounting literature (GAAP) or generally accepted auditing standards (GAAS) for guidance.

The REG, FAR, and AUD sections of the exam contain three testlets of MCQs and two testlets of simulation questions. There are no plans at the current time to include sims on BEC. In this section, we will discuss both the nature and operation of the simulation questions to assist you in becoming proficient at solving them on the exam. It is particularly important that you become familiar and comfortable with how simulation questions operate, since you must be able to navigate the software and access multiple tabs in order to answer the question. For example, you will be required to access related authoritative literature on some questions, requiring use of the appropriate tab to execute your research effort.

Tip: We highly recommend that you take the time to practice using both the AICPA tutorial and our replication of the CPA exam simulations. Both will provide valuable experience with respect to content and functional format. However, the most beneficial aspect of the practice simulations is your practice with the functionality of the software. The content is also presented elsewhere in our program. Your major goal in working sims should be to learn the software and practice timing yourself.

DIAGRAM OF A SIMULATION QUESTION

You should understand why the CBT exam contains simulation questions. Let's go back to our earlier discussion where we noted that the profession was asked by key stakeholders, such as employers, to test the following competencies:

- Research, interpretation, and application of current financial literature.
- Communication of business information.

- Analysis and interpretation of business information.
- Render judgment based on available business information.
- Gain an understanding of key business terms, facts, and processes.

Simulations create the opportunity to meet these testing goals in a way that multiple-choice questions cannot.

SCREEN OUTLINE FOR SIMULATION QUESTIONS

You are able to access simulations on our Web site, *www.schweser.com/cpa*. If you purchased our entire program, you have access to all our online sims. If you purchased only the Study Manual, you can practice with a limited number of sims by accessing the Web site mentioned on the back of the Study Manual. As you read the following paragraphs about sims, it will be helpful to have the online sims available to you for examination of their features.

The screen for simulation questions is outlined as follows for the CBT CPA exam. We strongly believe it is important that, through the AICPA tutorial and our online simulations, you become familiar and proficient with using this format and related available tools (e.g., calculator or professional literature feature).

Illustration 2

This sample AUD sim is from the AICPA Sample Test found at *www.cpa-exam.org*. This is one tab (Audit Risk) showing an objective question. Once you double-click in the answer area (under "Impact on component of audit risk") the box headed "Select Item" pops up, allowing you to select your answer from the choices.

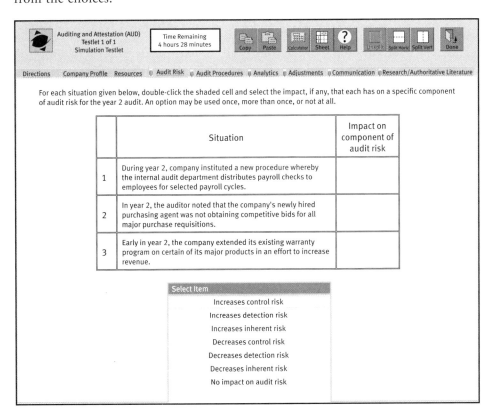

Top of Screen

Top Bar

The top bar on the top of the screen contains a series of buttons and windows, providing an array of tools and resources to assist you in completing the simulation questions. As you read through the descriptions below, try clicking on the various buttons of a real sim (either a Kaplan Schweser sim or an AICPA Tutorial sim) to experience the functionality.

Top of Screen From Left to Right

- *AICPA logo.*
- *Name and Testlet number of the sim.*
- *Time clock.* Shows remaining time for the total section (e.g., 3 hours and 5 minutes). This is a critical and valuable tool that will assist with time management as you complete the exam. Please use the clock as a tool and do not let it alarm you as you proceed. With practice, you will learn how to use your time wisely during the exam, and we will provide you with the necessary guidance to do so.
- *Copy/Paste.* There are copy/paste functions on the work tabs other than Research/Authoritative Literature as well as on the calculator and the electronic spreadsheet. (No copying/pasting is allowed on the Research/Authoritative Literature tab because of the nature of the answer. On this tab, you do not write or calculate an answer, but instead, you perform a search function, then click on a button to identify the answer. Copy/paste is not needed here.) You can copy answers you calculate in the spreadsheet and the calculator into answer boxes. You can copy/paste between tabs. You can make calculations in the spreadsheet and copy/paste them into the data entry area of the calculator. We strongly recommend that you practice with these functions, beginning with the Tutorial on the Web site www.cpa-exam.org.
- *Calculator.* You should practice with this online calculator to ensure that you are comfortable with its operations.
- *Spreadsheet.* A worksheet similar to commercially provided ones, used to facilitate calculations or arrange data. Practice with this one, because it is similar, but NOT identical to, those you may have used in the past.
- *Help.* Provides you with guidance on the CBT technical dimension, on the simulation questions part of the exam, and what to do if you need to ask a Prometric representative a question. (Does not "help" you with answers to the exam!)
- *Split.* This feature allows you to split the screen; this split displays various screens, depending on which tab you are viewing at the time you "split." For example, if you are viewing the Audit Risk tab in this example, splitting the screen will give you the Company Profile next to the Audit Risk question. Practice using the Split Screen buttons from each of the question tabs to see how this works for you.
- *Done.* Indicates that you have completed the section. Just as with most Windows-based operations, it will ask you to confirm (yes or no) your decision to leave the section through the appearance of a dialogue box.

We have just outlined how the simulation questions look in terms of their online design, features, and functionality. Next we will discuss the contents of the questions in a manner similar to our earlier coverage of the MCQs. This is where you can begin to experience these questions in their actual environment.

Lower Top Bar

This bar consists of "tabs" that you can click to obtain information, resources, or an objective or subjective question. The tabs are noted as "work" tabs by the AICPA.

Tabs

- *Directions*. Provides general instructions and a description of the various types of tabs.
- *Situation* or *Company Profile*. Provides a set of conditions and facts that will be used to answer the questions.
- *Series of multipart objective and subjective questions*. Each of these work tabs will ask a series of objective questions, including formats such as true/false, MCQ, short calculations, matching, etc
- *Written Communication*. Used when you need to write a memorandum to someone regarding an issue. Depending on the particular simulation, you may be addressing the accountant, the CFO, or the partner of the CPA firm. In any case, pay attention to the addressee of your communication and consider that when developing your answer. You may write differently to the CFO versus the entry-level staff accountant because of their differing levels of experience with the topic.
- *Research/Authoritative Literature*. Provides the access to the database of authoritative literature used in constructing your answer to a Research question. Here, you simply find the passage in the database, and click on it to identify it. There is no writing involved here.
- *Resources*. Resources will vary from question to question depending on the tools required for answering that question. You might find a Time Value of Money Table or a MACRS Depreciation Schedule, or various other items.

Note: The objective question work tabs will be graded electronically by the AICPA. The written communication will be graded manually.

TYPES OF SIMULATION QUESTIONS

Simulation questions represent a combination of objective and subjective questions. Objective questions can include multiple-choice, completion, matching, true/false and other formats. They can also include questions that require completion of a spreadsheet, calculation of amounts, and preparation of journal entries.

Each simulation question contains two subjective questions, written communications (Communication tab) and research (Research/Authoritative Literature tab). Your written responses to the Communications question must be "on topic" (quoting the AICPA), meaning that you answer the question that is asked and do not include information that is unrelated to the question. The AICPA expects that you will be specific, clear, and concise, using language that indicates your understanding of the situation. The graders will be looking for sentences and paragraphs that are well written, and you should avoid simply making lists with bullet points. (For more on writing on the CPA exam, see the Simulation Writing Guide.)

TIME OUT! LET'S SEE WHERE WE ARE

Let's take a break to review what we have covered. The following points summarize what you need to know about simulations.

1. Simulation questions are divided into objective and subjective parts, which appear in separate work tabs.

2. The objective and subjective questions are based on a situation that presents a set of facts.

3. Each of the objective work tabs will contain a series of questions, which could be in MCQ, completion, true/false, matching, etc.

4. The work tabs and the series of questions contained therein are independent, but they share the common situation.

5. You should answer the work tabs in order. Select the questions within each work tab that you understand and can definitively answer. This will allow you to reduce the number of questions on which you have to guess.

6. Answering the questions in order will help you on each subsequent question, since all the questions are based on the same situation and require an understanding of the same authoritative literature.

7. If you practice using our online material, the objective questions should not be difficult for you to answer and should help prepare you to respond to the subjective questions.

Hopefully you feel more comfortable regarding the objective questions and understand how they are presented so that you can effectively practice and prepare for the exam.

SIMULATION WRITING GUIDE

HOW TO USE THIS COURSE

The Kaplan Schweser CPA Review course is designed to get you started on the road to CPA success. Since the writing portion of the exam makes up a significant portion of your score, we created this special writing course to help you prepare for the writing portion of the CPA Exam.

This chapter accompanies a series of videos that are available on our Web site, *www.schweser.com/cpa*. The best way to use these materials is to watch the video, then review that section in the chapter before moving on. We'll tackle various steps in the writing process, and we recommend that you review each section carefully. You will review key concepts in grammar, punctuation, and spelling. Finally, you will have the chance to practice what you've learned by writing answers to the practice questions available in the last section of the chapter. You can then review sample answers to these questions.

WRITING QUESTIONS ON THE CPA EXAM

WHERE THEY APPEAR

As you know, the computer-based CPA exam is divided into multiple-choice questions and case-based simulations. The writing or communication portion of the exam appears as part of the simulations. Three content areas—Financial Accounting and Reporting, Auditing and Attestation, and Regulation— will have two simulations, and each will include one Communication tab. Note that no simulations currently appear on the Business Environment and Concepts section of the exam. You can review the contents of the exam and find sample tutorials by visiting *www.cpa-exam.org*.

HOW THEY APPEAR

Let's take a quick look at a real simulation so you know what the writing component looks like. If you are a student in our program, you have access to all the online sims. If you purchased only the Study Manual, look on the back cover for information about accessing sample Kaplan Schweser sims. Just select one now, and look at it as you read along. The purpose of practice sims is to learn their functionality. Fingers-on-keyboard is the only way to do that!

The first tab will give you the situation, which is the basic knowledge you will need to answer the questions. In order to answer the various questions, you will use the tabs to navigate (click on the Situation Tab to view the information).

The simulation tab that contains the writing question will be labeled Communication. On this tab, you will get some information about the question you are expected to answer. In some cases, the answer will be started for you, with a salutation or greeting at the top. You will type your answer into the field at the bottom of the screen. You will also notice that the Communication screen has a toolbar. These are tools that you are probably accustomed to using in word processing programs, including cut, copy, paste, undo/redo, and spell check.

Take a look at this by clicking on the Communication Tab now.

How Much They Count

The Communication part of your score will be a relatively large portion of your total score. The writing portion will count for about 10% of your score. If you are feeling good about the Communication portion, this is good news. If you are feeling nervous about the Communication portion, you are doing the right thing by committing to a serious schedule of practice for this part of the exam. *Note: The AICPA graders will select only one of your two Communication answers to score; you must do a good job on both of them because you do not know which one will be selected for grading.*

When to do Them

Students sometimes ask whether they should do the simulation tabs in the order presented, or whether they should skip around. Usually we tell students that completing the tabs in order is the best way to stay focused. However, if you are particularly anxious about the Communication tab, you may want to try doing it first, so you can be sure that you can give it your best attention. You should make your own decision, based on your experience as you practice.

How to Practice for the Communication Portion

As you work through your Kaplan Schweser CPA Review materials, you will be learning lots of ways to cope with the Communication tab portion of the exam. You will want to practice these techniques so that they become second nature. Once you have assimilated our methods, you will find that you can use them on the exam and in all your future business writing.

Learn From the AICPA

The best way to familiarize yourself with the appearance and behavior of the simulations is to view the official simulation tutorials, which are available at *www.cpa-exam.org*. This will be an essential part of your preparation for the exam. Keep an eye on this Web site, because the AICPA makes frequent updates to the materials.

Use Your Kaplan Schweser Materials

Make the most of these materials. If you need to watch a video more than once to be sure you are getting the point, go ahead! Write out all the practice Communication questions in the back of this chapter. Take our suggestions, and you are sure to improve your writing and your score!

PRACTICE WRITING

As you prepare to take the exam, you will run across topics and questions that you know need extra review. Those might be topics studied in your earlier years of college or areas in which you always struggled. Try writing short answers on these topics. It will give you excellent practice at writing, and it will also help those tough concepts sink in. Making up your own questions will also help you get inside the mind of the test authors, and better understand how CPA Communication questions work.

READ CRITICALLY

As you read the newspaper, magazines, or any other non-fiction, take a critical look at the author's writing. Is it solid? Does she make a strong argument? How does he back up his assertions? Think about how you would improve the article, or how you might take the opposite side of an argument. Reading critically will help you to write critically, which is a key component of success on the Communication portion.

WHAT GRADERS ARE LOOKING FOR

Kaplan Schweser CPA Review has done a careful review of the Communication question grading system. Unlike the multiple-choice part of the exam, your Communication tabs will be read by real human graders. They will have very specific criteria to look for, and they will grade you on how closely your response meets those criteria. So what do the Communication tab graders look for?

- *They want your written communication to be on-topic.* If you stray from the topic at hand or lose focus, you will lose points. In fact, the AICPA says that once the grader starts reading your answer, if your answer is not on-topic, they will discontinue the grading process and give you no points.
- *Your answer must address the concept of the question.* Your response should answer the question that is being asked! (It is more common than you might imagine for candidates to give a good answer, but to a question other than the one asked on the exam.) When certain accounting concepts come up, the graders want to be sure that you can understand those concepts and write about them.
- *Your answer should have solid structure.* This means that you should be able to construct a strong, well-supported argument, a topic we'll cover later in this chapter.
- *Finally, graders are looking for clear, coherent writing.* This is where concepts like grammar, spelling, sentence structure, and punctuation come into play. We will spend time looking at all of these issues later in this chapter.

To write an answer that graders will love, keep these points in mind, and use the Kaplan Schweser CPA Review system!

HOW TO ANSWER THE QUESTION

In this section, we will review the same question that we cover in the video course. That way, you can follow along in your book or you can review what you learned in the video tutorials. If you have already reviewed this question and answer thoroughly, turn to the last section of this book and practice the writing steps with one of the other sample questions that are available for you.

THE IMPORTANCE OF PREWRITING

Prewriting is everything you do before you actually start writing your answer. It includes thinking through the question, planning the structure of your answer, and constructing the basis and support of your argument. Prewriting is an essential part of all writing, but it is particularly important when you have limited time. The prewriting process will help you organize your thoughts and will improve your final product. Prewriting will actually save time in the long run. You will see what we mean as you work through the rest of this chapter.

REPHRASING THE QUESTION

Most Communication questions will be very wordy and will include a lot of detail. When you read the question, ask yourself the following:

- What do the graders want to know?
- How can I cut through the detail and get to the gist?

Following are some examples of rephrasing questions.

1. Easy Question Example

Don Marcus, the partner in charge of the Franken engagement, is considering whether confirmation of accounts receivable is necessary in this engagement. Write a memo to Mr. Marcus describing situations, if any exist, when confirmation of accounts receivable can be omitted.

So what is the question? Translated into plain English, the exam wants to know: Is it always necessary to confirm accounts receivable? If not, describe when it is not necessary.

2. Harder Question Example

Here is another question for you to rephrase.

TFC has hired your firm to audit its financial statements. The president of TFC has heard the term "control risk," but is not sure of its impact on the audit process. Write a memo to the president to explain the nature of control risk, and also describe the work of the external auditor in connection with control risk and the impact of that work on the overall audit.

Translated into English, the exam wants to know: What is control risk? What does the auditor do with control risk? How does control risk relate to the overall audit?

That is a little more complex than the last Communication question, but still, you can rely on your knowledge of auditing to come up with the answer.

3. Question Requiring More Information

Take a look at another question.

Garden, Inc. is negotiating the lease of property to FarmCom. Identify the type of lease from the accounting perspective of the lessee, FarmCom, and provide reasons for this classification. Then identify the type of lease from the accounting perspective of the lessor, Garden, Inc., and provide reasons for this classification.

Translated, this question is asking: Based on the information you know about this negotiation, what type of lease is it for the lessee? Why? What type is it for the lessor? Why? (To answer this question, you would obtain facts from the Situation tab of the simulation.)

4. Question Requiring Calculations

Take a look at one more question.

Mr. Roseman is scheduled to receive $200,000 as a result of his wife's life insurance policy. The life insurance company will give him the money immediately or allow him to take ten annual payments of $26,000 each. Write a memo to Mr. Roseman explaining the tax ramifications of this decision.

Translated, the question is: Should the client take the money now, or take annual payments? What are the pros and cons?

To answer this question in detail, you will need background knowledge about the nature of taxation and annual payments. You will also need to apply your knowledge to this specific situation, and perform some basic calculations.

POINTERS ON REPHRASING

If you have trouble translating a question, look for words like "how" and "why." Look for words that point to specific accounting principles. Remember to ask yourself, "What do the graders want to know?"

NOTE TAKING

Note taking is a key part of the prewriting process. You will be given scrap paper when you take the exam, and you will want to make good use of it. No one will be grading your notes, so as long as you can read and understand them, they are O.K.

Start your notes by writing down your rephrasing of the question. As you progress through the prewriting process, you will want to make notes to track your thoughts. You will use these notes as a basis for writing your answer.

Some things you may want to convey in your notes are lists, like pros and cons. You can write down important numbers and calculations, so you will not have to manipulate numbers when you are trying to write your answer. You can use arrows and symbols to point out specific pieces of information. When your question has multiple parts, you will want to label the questions and notes as A, B, and C. If you do not know every aspect of the answer, write down what you do know.

QUESTION #1: NOTE TAKING

Here is the first question we will focus on as we work through the prewriting process.

> Beverage, Inc., (BI) operates beverage machines that do not maintain a record of sales, and accept only cash. BI is a privately held company owned by three investment groups. One of the investor groups serves as the operator. The former auditor for BI went bankrupt due to malpractice claims. The CPA firm Trust LLP is now planning a year-end audit.

> Provide an overall assessment of BI's risk, and note the impact to the audit process that Trust must execute. In addition, describe specifically how control risk relates to this assessment.

REPHRASING THE QUESTIONS

Here is how we would translate the questions:

A. How much risk is there and why?
B. What should Trust do about it?
C. What is the control risk implication?

SITUATION NOTES

Now we can start to formulate answers for these questions. Begin by taking notes on the situation.

1. The first sentence tells us: Beverage, Inc., (BI) operates beverage machines that do not maintain a record of sales, and accept only cash. Our notes say: Cash-only bev. corp.

2. The next two sentences say: BI is a privately held corporation owned by three investment groups. One of the investor groups serves as the operator. Our notes say: One op owner.

3. Finally, the last sentences say: The former auditor for BI went bankrupt due to malpractice claims. The CPA firm Trust LLP is now planning a year-end audit. Our notes say: Old auditor no good.

Your notes might look different, but make sure that you have at least covered all the key points of the situation.

KEY CONCEPTS NOTES

Next, you will want to reread the question and think about the key accounting concepts and principles you will use. Take some notes on these key concepts. Provide an overall assessment of BI's risk, and note the impact to the audit process that Trust must execute. In addition, describe specifically how control risk relates to this assessment.

What key concepts do we need to take into account? Make some notes that make sense to you.

Our notes say:

Internal Controls—Risk Assessment—Substantive Testing—Analytical Procedures—Control risk

QUESTION NOTES

Next you will want to take some notes on the questions so that you have an instant reference when you are ready to write your answer. This is where you will begin to formulate your answers. Our first question, Question A, is: *How much risk is there and why?* Here is our answer: *It is a cash-only industry, there are no good past records, and the past auditor is no help, since he went bankrupt (and is thus unreliable and probably unavailable for comment.)* Make some quick notes about these risk factors under the letter A.

Now let us move on to Question B, which is: *What should Trust do about it?* Here, your notes can come directly from your Key Concepts notes. *The auditing firm needs to think about analytical procedures and substantive tests.* You can abbreviate these however you like.

Question C asks for some detail. *What's the control risk implication?* What are the specific issues surrounding control risk that we need to cover? *We need to think about material misstatements. We need to consider how trustworthy the operating owner might be. And we need to take into account the issue of opening balances, due to the problem with the previous auditor.* Make some notes on the control risk implications. Make sure they are legible and clear.

HOW TO STRUCTURE YOUR THOUGHTS

STRUCTURE OF AN ARGUMENT

Many of the writing questions on the exam will have relatively simple answers. If they were multiple-choice questions, you would click a choice and that would be all. However, on the Communication part of the exam, you cannot just answer the question and move on. If the exam just wanted a quick answer, the test would be all multiple-choice. **The graders want to see how well you can construct an argument and back up your theories.** As you well know, accounting is not just playing with a calculator all day. There is a great deal of analytical thought and communication required in this profession, and the exam wants to be sure that you are ready!

To construct a strong argument, you need to begin with a main point, or thesis. On the CPA exam, your main point is the answer to the question. You also need support for your thesis. This support can consist of facts, key concepts, examples, calculations and other relevant information. As we continue to answer our sample question, we will review how you can construct support for your argument.

HOW TO STRUCTURE YOUR ARGUMENT

Here is our question again:

> Beverage, Inc., (BI) operates beverage machines that do not maintain a record of sales, and accept only cash. BI is a privately held corporation owned by three investment groups. One of the investor groups serves as the operator. The former auditor for BI went bankrupt due to malpractice claims. The CPA firm Trust LLP is now planning a year-end audit. Provide an overall assessment of BI's risk, and note the impact to the audit process that Trust must execute. In addition, describe specifically how control risk relates to this assessment.

Begin by reviewing your notes:

> *Situation Notes:* Cash-only bev. corp./One op owner/Old auditor no good

> *Key Concepts Notes:* Internal Controls, Risk Assess, Sub testing/An. Proc., Control risk specific

QUESTION A

We will begin our focus with Question A: *How much risk is there and why? Do you think that BI represents a high or low audit risk?* Take a look at all the notes you made about risks, and you can conclude that *BI represents a high audit risk*. That is the main point of your argument.

That is not the end of your answer, though. You also need to explain why the risk is high. That is where the rest of your notes will come into play, so let us take a look.

According to the notes for Question A, BI is cash only, there are no good records, and the previous auditor is no help. These details will form the support for your main point. For Question A, you now have the basic underlying structure of your argument.

QUESTION B

Take a look at Question B: *What should Trust do about the high audit risk of BI?* Analytical procedures and substantive testing comprise the basic answer to this question. But again, this is not multiple-choice, and we need more information. Where is the support for our main idea? If you get stuck, try asking yourself some questions.

> *Ask the question: why?* Or, in other words: What would be the reason for performing analytical procedures and substantive testing? Well, these are done to gain assurance about the validity of reported revenue.

Now ask the question: How? Or, how could Trust gain the necessary assurance? To answer this question, provide examples. Examples are a great way to provide supporting data for your main point. For example, Trust could look at vendor payments and observe a sales sample to develop estimates. So now Question B has a main idea and adequate support for that main idea.

QUESTION C

Finally, look at Question C: *What is the control risk implication?* Looking back at our notes, we see that based on the risk of material misstatements, our doubt about the trustworthiness of the operating owner, and our concern about the reliability of the opening balances, we would have to say that internal controls will have a high risk of failure. So that becomes our main point, and the reasons for concern form the support for that main point.

STRUCTURE: QUICK REVIEW

We've organized our notes into an outline, or skeleton, that we can use to write our answer. *Each question has a clear response, with a main point and supporting details. Remember that a well-structured argument is crucial. It is one of the key things for which the graders look.* Be sure that all your main ideas are supported with details, evidence, and key concepts.

HOW TO WRITE YOUR ANSWER

ANSWER STRUCTURE

One of the key things that the graders are looking for is an answer with a solid structure. On the CPA exam, structure is your friend. Having a good sense of structure at your fingertips will make it easier to put your answer together quickly and clearly, and that will help you earn points on the exam.

THE THREE- OR FIVE-PARAGRAPH ANSWER

In high school, you probably learned how to write the five-paragraph answer, a classic essay structure. The same type of structure also works well in a three-paragraph answer, especially where you have a limited topic and a limited amount of time, as on the CPA exam.

The three- or five-paragraph answer begins with an *introductory paragraph*. This is where the topic is outlined, and the goal of the question is stated. If your answer is in response to one question and has one main idea, this is where you state that main idea. If your answer responds to more than one question, you may or may not want to use this paragraph to express the main ideas, or answers, to all the questions.

The next one to three paragraphs are the *development*. In this section, information is presented, and data and support are supplied. Other opinions and contrary facts can be presented here, if they are relevant.

In the final paragraph, a *conclusion* is drawn, and the author makes a summary of the facts and theories stated in the answer.

Understanding the three- or five-paragraph answer format will help you structure any answer you write. However, you probably will not need to write a full five paragraphs, and you may not even need to write three paragraphs. There are some questions that can be answered without an elaborate introduction or conclusion. There are other questions that may require a different type of structure. With this in mind, let us consider some alternatives.

THE INVERTED PYRAMID STRUCTURE

A structure commonly used in business writing and in journalism is the inverted pyramid structure. In this structure, you begin with the most important point. On the CPA exam, that would be the main point, or the answer to the question. You then follow up with supporting information, like examples and other supporting details. Finally, you close with any other information, such as less-important details.

This structure is called an inverted pyramid because it is large at the top, in terms of importance, and small at the bottom. When no formal introduction or conclusion is called for, the pyramid structure will serve you well.

OTHER STRUCTURES

Now let us talk about a few other types of structure that may come in handy. You may be asked to describe a problem and solution.

> **Example:** *Describe the issues inherent in dischargeability of debts in bankruptcy and propose a solution.* You might need to describe cause and effect.

> **Example:** *What would cause a legal repossession to occur, and what would be the consequences of this result?* You may need to compare and contrast two things.

> **Example:** *What are the similarities and differences between the security interests described here?* You may need to describe a chronology or timeline.

In each of these cases, you want to follow the pattern of the question, answering in the order suggested by the question.

You do not need to memorize all of these structures. What you need to know is that sometimes the structure will be spelled out for you in the question. In these cases, it is better to stick with the structure presented than to try to shoehorn your response into the three or five paragraph structure or the pyramid structure.

STRUCTURING OUR SAMPLE ANSWER

Now that we have described some structures, let us go back to the sample question and decide on a structure for our answer.

> *Question: Provide an overall assessment of BI's risk, and note the impact to the audit process that Trust must execute. In addition, describe specifically how control risk relates to this assessment.*

Here is the translation for the questions that we prepared earlier:

- *How much risk is there and why?*
- *What should Trust do about it?*
- *What is the control risk implication?*

Given these questions, how would you structure this answer? Well, we have three questions, making this one suitable for three paragraphs. The questions go from general to specific, so we can begin with Question A, and move down the line, with one paragraph per question. Let us use the three-paragraph answer format.

If we felt a need for an introduction and conclusion, we could expand into the five-paragraph format. However, we already have enough to tackle here, and we can omit the added formality of the introduction and conclusion, as long as our argument has a clear structure. We will be sure of that by reinforcing our main points with strong details.

PARAGRAPHS

Paragraphs can have all kinds of structures in articles, essays, stories, and other kinds of writing. The main thing you need to know to do well on the CPA exam is *keep it simple*. There is no need for complex paragraph structure to make your point.

The other thing to keep in mind is that a paragraph is much like a mini-essay. Your main idea is your topic sentence, and your supporting details make up the rest of the paragraph. If your paragraphs have strong structure, your answer will have strong structure.

SENTENCES

Before we begin to write, let us talk very briefly about sentence structure. Once again, keep it simple. You are not going to impress the graders with long, convoluted sentences. You are going to impress them with clear, logical sentences. Keep your sentences logical and well-organized, and you will maximize your points.

TURNING NOTES INTO SENTENCES

The process you will follow here is the same process you will use whenever you translate notes into sentences and paragraphs. Start with your topic sentence, and continue with your support. This is the most basic structure you can use, and it is the best for the CPA exam.

CHOOSING A VOICE

First, we choose a voice. Sometimes you will be asked to write as a certain party, with a certain audience. For example, the question may state that you are an audit senior preparing a memo to the audit partner. In other cases, you will need to make a decision on your own. In still other cases, a salutation will already be included in the answer window, which should make clear which voice you should use.

In this case, we have a choice, since the voice is not specified. Let us write from the perspective of Trust LLP, using the voice "*we.*" This is a pretty safe decision, since there is no specified voice.

Here is one more thing to think about before you begin. You need to keep in mind your purpose as you write. For whom are you writing and why?

- Is the answer intended to be a memo to a client? If so, do not assume that the client will understand abbreviations or accounting jargon. Spell everything out clearly, as you would for an actual client.
- If the answer is intended for a colleague or superior, it is acceptable to assume that she will have knowledge of typical accounting language. However, be careful to answer all parts of the question. You cannot assume that the reader will be able to make inferences from a sketchy answer.

PARAGRAPH 1

Let us take our notes for Question 1, and turn them into the sentences that make up Paragraph 1.

First, there is our main point: *The audit is high risk.* We then need support for the main point. *Our support is that the business is cash only, there are no good records, and the old auditor is no help.*

Let us write some sentences! We begin with a topic sentence for Paragraph 1. The topic is that the audit is high risk. Here is a sentence that expresses that:

> *Overall, we have determined that there are several serious issues surrounding the upcoming audit of Beverage, Inc., by Trust LLP.*

Your sentence might be slightly different, but in general, this is a good way to start. Now we need support sentences for Paragraph 1. Try translating your notes into sentences.

Note: *Cash only.*

Sentence: *Beverage, Inc., operates in an industry with no debit or credit card technology, so cash reflects 100% of sales activity.*

Note: *No good records.*

©2009 Kaplan, Inc.

Sentence: *This presents an internal control challenge to BI's management and an audit risk to Trust since there is no written or electronic documentation of each sales transaction.*

Note: *Old auditor no help.*

Sentence: *Furthermore, the lack of supporting audit documents from previous audits, due to the unreliability of the previous auditor, presents a serious risk of failure.*

Here is our Paragraph 1.

Overall, we have determined that there are several serious issues surrounding the upcoming audit of Beverage, Inc., by Trust LLP. Beverage, Inc., operates in an industry with no debit or credit card technology, so cash reflects 100% of sales activity. This presents an internal control challenge to BI's management and an audit risk to Trust since there is no written or electronic documentation of each sales transaction. Furthermore, the lack of supporting audit documents from previous audits, due to the unreliability of the previous auditor, presents a serious risk of failure.

Before we move on, let us look at how we used some linking words to contribute to the logic of the paragraph.

- We began with the word "*overall,*" which signals that a general point is about to be made. In this case, it is the main point.
- The last sentence in the paragraph begins with the word "*furthermore,*" which indicates that additional information that is parallel with the previous information is about to follow.

Using linking words will help to reinforce the logic and structure of your answer.

PARAGRAPH 2

The question we will address in this paragraph is: *What should Trust do about the high audit risk of BI?* Our main idea is that Trust should do analytical procedures and substantive tests. Supporting this main idea is the answer to the question "why?" It is to gain assurance about validity of reported revenue. Let us see if we can turn that into one concise sentence.

Due to the overall risk presented by BI's situation, Trust must execute analytical procedures and related substantive tests to gain assurance regarding the validity of reported revenue.

Now incorporate the examples that will form your support. The examples are: *looking at vendor payments and observing a sales sample to develop estimates.*

Sentences:

Trust could use an analytical procedure where they use vendor payment records. Trust could also observe a sample of vending machine sales to develop an estimate for inventory balances and activity for the fiscal period.

Here is Paragraph 2.

Due to the overall risk presented by BI's situation, Trust must execute analytical procedures and related substantive tests to gain assurance regarding the validity of reported revenue. Trust could use an analytical procedure where they use vendor payment records. Trust could also observe a sample of vending machine sales to develop an estimate for inventory balances and activity for the fiscal period.

PARAGRAPH 3

Paragraph 3 must answer the question: *What is the control risk implication?*

Note: *Internal controls have high risk of failure.*

Sentence: *The audit presents certain issues which have specific relevance to high control risk.*

Now, let us write the sentences that provide support for the main idea.

Note: *Failure to detect material misstatements.*

Sentence: *Without an audit trail of sales transactions, there is a high risk of failure of the internal control system to detect material misstatements in the reporting of revenue for BI for a stated fiscal period.*

Note: *No process to be sure operating owner is accounting for all transactions.*

Sentence: *As far as we can determine, there is no internal control process in place to ensure that the operating owner is accounting for all sales transactions during a fiscal period or detecting if any material misstatements have occurred.*

Note: *No way to verify opening balances, due to old auditor.*

Sentence: *Since BI's prior auditor is bankrupt, and Trust does not have access to the prior year's auditing audit documents, Trust cannot verify the opening balances for the current fiscal period.*

Here is the third paragraph.

The audit presents certain issues which have specific relevance to high control risk. Without an audit trail of sales transactions, there is a high risk of failure of the internal control system to detect material misstatements in the reporting of revenue for BI for a stated fiscal period. As far as we can determine, there is no internal control process in place to ensure that the operating owner is accounting for all sales transactions during a fiscal period or detecting if any material misstatements have occurred. Since BI's prior auditor is bankrupt, and Trust does not have access to the prior year's audit documents, Trust cannot verify the opening balances for the current fiscal period.

This answer takes on a basic three-paragraph structure, and there is no need for a formal concluding paragraph.

WRITING THE ANSWER: QUICK REVIEW

When you write your answer, stay focused. Do not go off on tangents or include extra information. Just answer the question as simply as you can. Lay out the simplest possible structure. Use one of the structures we talked about, or follow the structure suggested by the question. Your paragraphs should have one main idea, plus the support for that main idea. Finally, keep your sentences clear and simple. One sentence per idea is usually just right.

EDITING

READING OUT LOUD

One of the most important things you can do when you have finished writing your answer is to read it out loud. During the exam, you will not be able to read it out loud, but you can read silently to yourself. Hearing the voice of your answer in your head will help you to "hear" any mistakes that are there.

DOUBLE-CHECK YOUR PUNCTUATION

- On the CPA exam, you will probably end all of your sentences with *periods. The lessor has met the criteria.* Question marks occasionally come up in business writing when the writer is using a rhetorical style. *Has the lessor met the criteria? Yes, she is qualified.* It is hard to imagine a use for an exclamation point in business communication. (The following is unlikely to gain points on the exam: *The lessor has met the criteria! Hooray!*) Ensure that all your sentences have ending punctuation.
- Use a *comma* to separate parts of dates and places. *January 12, 2007,* and *Cleveland, Ohio.* Use a comma to separate items in a series. Examples: *I eat apples, oranges, and bananas. The Sarbanes-Oxley Act of 2002 seeks to institutionalize objectivity, independence, and reliability in corporate governance, audit committee performance, and external auditor activities.*
- *Commas* are used before certain linking words (e.g., *and, but, for, nor,* and *yet*). Examples: *Detection is reduced by carrying out additional substantive testing, or by performing substantive testing that renders a higher quality of audit evidence. The accountant is prepared for a more senior role, yet he lacks experience in certain areas.*
- Use a *comma* to separate an introductory part, or clause, of the sentence from the rest of the sentence. Examples: *If control risk is assessed as high, the auditor will need to gather more evidence. In*

some cases, the reliability is not strong enough. For example, government confirmations normally require no corroboration.

- Use a *comma* to set off descriptive information. Examples: *XMG, a technology firm, has retained our services. Ms. Templeton, an auditor, will be visiting the office today.* Keep in mind that a comma indicates a pause. As you read your answer silently, listen for spots where there should be a pause. Consider adding a comma. If a comma appears where a pause is not called for, consider omitting the comma.

- Use a *colon* after the salutation in a business letter. Examples: *Dear Investor: Dear Ms. Abernathy:*

- Use a *colon* to introduce a list of items after a complete sentence. Example: *There are three different classifications of payments by the securitization mechanism: pay-through, pass-through, or revolving-period.* A colon is not required if the list is not preceded by a complete sentence. Example: *The firms retained by the client are Smith, Harvey, and Brustein.* Edit check: Does your salutation end with a colon? Look for lists in your answer. If they are preceded by a complete sentence, there should be a colon before the list.

- Use a *semicolon* when you are connecting two closely related sentences. Example: *The fair value is known; our information is complete.* Use a semicolon before certain linking words that demonstrate consequence. These are words such as: *therefore, thus,* and *consequently.* The linking word however also requires a semicolon. Example: *The fair value of the first bond is known; however, the value of the second is unknown.* Edit check: If you have connected related sentences, consider using a semicolon as the connector. Watch for adverbs such as *thus* and *therefore*, and be sure that you have added a semicolon where necessary.

SPELLING: FREQUENTLY CONFUSED WORDS

Spell check on the exam cannot catch everything! Watch out for homonyms, which are words that sound alike. Learn the ones that usually trip you up, and be sure to review and memorize them. Following is a list of words that are commonly confused.

Accept/except
Accept means "to receive." *Except* means "not including."
We will accept all of the provisions, except the third one.

Access/excess
Access is a noun meaning "the ability to enter." *Excess* is a noun or adjective meaning "extra."
If you gain access to the storage room, you will find the excess files.

Affect/effect
Affect is a verb that means "to produce an influence or effect on something." *Effect* is a noun that means "a result" or "a fulfillment." Effect is the word used in the phrase "in effect."
This move will affect our profit margins. The effect will be shrinkage.

Among/between
Use *among* when you are writing about more than two people or things. Use *between* when you are writing about two people or things.
The client needs to decide among the many accounting firms that are available. The two partners have an agreement between them.

Less/fewer
Less means "not as much," and *fewer* means "not as many."
Fewer jobs means less income for the city.

Personal/personnel
Personal means "relating to a particular person." *Personnel* means "staff."
The personal records of our personnel are kept confidential.

Precede/proceed
Precede is a verb meaning "to go before." *Proceed* is a verb meaning
"to go forward, or continue."
The audit will precede the final work paper review. We will proceed with the review after the audit.

Principal/principle
Principal as a noun means the leader of a school. As an adjective, it means "main" or "primary."
Principle means a fact or law, like the principles of accounting.
The principal topics on the exam are the principles of accounting.

Edit check: After you have run the spell check, look for frequently confused words. Know which ones give you trouble, and keep a special eye out for those.

APOSTROPHES

Use an apostrophe to substitute for missing letters when you make a contraction. *We will merge = we'll merge. It is prudent = it's prudent. Do not assume = don't assume. The company will not retain = the company won't retain.* Use an apostrophe to indicate possession—the idea that something belongs to someone. *The firm's assets = the assets belonging to the firm. The partner's workload = the workload belonging to the partner. The accountants' case = the case belonging to the accountants.* Note here that there are multiple accountants, so the apostrophe goes after the "s," not before it.

These frequently confused words with apostrophes may come up in your writing: *Its and it's. Your and you're. Whose and who's. Their and they're.*

Its is a possessive word, indicating that something belongs to "it." It's is a contraction meaning "it is." *See the dog? It's wagging its tail. Have you heard about the loss taken by the firm? It's a reflection of its poor management practices.*

Your is a possessive word, indicating that something belongs to "you." You're is a contraction meaning "you are." *You're planning to file your return by April 15, aren't you?*

Whose is a possessive word, indicating that something belongs to "who." Who's is a contraction meaning "who is." *Whose files are these on my desk? Who's going to come to the audit meeting?*

Their is a possessive word, indicating that something belongs to "them." They're is a contraction meaning "they are." *They're on the way to their meeting with the attorneys.*

Edit check: If you are prone to sprinkling extra apostrophes through your writing, do this test as you read through your draft.

- Can the word be expanded? (Does the apostrophe indicate a contraction?)
- Does something belong to someone?

If the answer to both of these questions is no, then the apostrophe is not necessary.

CAPITALIZATION

Each sentence should begin with a capital. Titles such as President or Chairman of the Board begin with capitals. Some abbreviations, such as LLP or FASB, are made up of capitals. Edit check: Do you see capital letters in your draft? Are they necessary according to the conditions above? If not, make them lowercase.

SENTENCE FRAGMENTS

A fragment is an incomplete sentence. Examples: *The goal of this requirement. Providing protection. Consummation of an agreement.* All of these are fragments. A complete sentence requires a subject and a verb. Examples: *The goal of this requirement is to ensure an effective system. Providing protection is the responsibility of the firm. Consummation of an agreement is to be expected within the week.* Edit check: Does your sentence have a subject and a verb?

RUN-ON SENTENCES

A run-on occurs when you have two or more complete sentences without adequate separation. *Management is responsible for maintaining internal controls they must also present an assessment of the effectiveness of the controls.* Fix this run-on this way: *Management is responsible for maintaining internal controls. They must also present an assessment of the effectiveness of the controls.* Or: *Management is responsible for maintaining internal controls, and must also present an assessment of the effectiveness of the controls.* Edit check: If you suspect a run-on, read the sentence again. Does it contain two or more complete sentences without separation? If so, provide separation, either by breaking it into two sentences, or by adding connecting words and/or punctuation.

SUBJECT-VERB AGREEMENT

In a sentence, your subject and verb must agree. If your subject is singular, your verb must be singular. Example: *John Smith, CPA, undertakes audits.* If your subject is plural, your verb must be plural. Example: *Many CPA firms undertake audits.* The concept of agreement can be tricky with collective nouns like "staff" or "faculty." If a group is working together to perform the same action, you need a singular verb. Example: *The staff prepares for the overhaul. The faculty strives toward excellence.* Be especially careful when the subject and verb are not right next to each other. Example: *The importance of the reports is high.* The importance is high, not the reports. Therefore, we use a singular verb.

Edit check: As you read, be sure that each subject and verb agree. Especially watch for collective nouns. If the subject and verb are not next to each other, tune out the words that get in the way, and listen for the right subject-verb agreement.

PARALLEL STRUCTURE

Words that are linked by "and" need to be in the same form, as do words in a list. You can usually diagnose parallelism problems by listening. Listen for the mistake: *The plan will be formulated and I will undertake it in the near future.* Since the verbs are joined by "and," they should be in the same form and tense. Here is the right way to structure this sentence: *The plan will be formulated and undertaken in the near future.* Here, formulated and undertaken are in the same, parallel form. Parallel structure is also necessary among ideas in a list. Look for the mistakes in this sentence: *An understanding of internal control is needed to determine the nature, degree to which testing should be performed and when is best to do the substantive testing.* Here is the way to structure this sentence correctly: *An understanding of internal control is needed to determine the nature, extent, and timing of the substantive testing.* Edit check: Listen to your sentence. Any words, phrases, or verbs that are set in parallel structure need to have the same form, tense, and structure.

PRONOUN ANTECEDENTS

A pronoun is a word that substitutes for another word. Example: *John is an accountant. He works very long hours.* "He" stands in for "John." It is clear who we are talking about, so we can say that the pronoun "he" has a clear antecedent. Now read these sentences: *Under some circumstances, the reliability of confirmation of accounts receivable is not strong enough to merit the effort, and the firm may omit the confirmation. They are in a position to gain very little.* To what or to whom does the word "they" refer? The firm? The accounts receivable? Also, what will "they" gain very little of? Reliability? Information? Here is a better follow-up sentence: *In this case, the firm will gain very little information.* Edit check: As you read through your answer, look for pronouns like "he," "she," "it," and "they." Make sure that it will be clear to the reader to whom or to what these pronouns refer.

CLARITY AND CONCISENESS

CPA Communication graders will pay special attention to the clarity and conciseness of your writing. There are no hard and fast rules here, but here is our key recommendation: think simple. This is not the time to impress anyone with mile-long sentences or ten-dollar vocabulary words. You want to get your answer across as clearly and concisely as possible. The clearest way to say something is usually the simplest way. Minimize the number of phrases and clauses in each sentence, and you are well on your way.

Here is an example of how to avoid wordiness. Instead of: *We intend to take this opportunity to fulfill your request by providing you with the information which it has been our pleasure to enclose.* Try: *Enclosed is the information you requested.* Or: *We are pleased to provide you the enclosed information.* Edit check: Read through your answer. Does any of the language seem excessively wordy? See if you can state your case in a simpler manner.

CHECKLIST FOR EDITING

Use it to check all your practice writing, and the items on the list will become second nature. When you take the exam, you will do this check automatically:

- Is the purpose of the answer clear?
- Is the answer appropriate for the reader?
- Is the answer complete and accurate?
- Is there extra information that should be removed?
- Is any necessary information missing?

- Is the information well-organized?
- Does the flow of the answer make sense?
- Are the paragraphs of reasonable length?
- Does each paragraph have one main idea?
- Should shorter paragraphs be combined, or longer paragraphs be split or trimmed?
- Is the language clear and direct? Is it easy to read?
- Are the grammar, punctuation, and spelling correct?

FINAL REVIEW AND QUESTION #2

So let us take it from the top once again. You are at the exam center, working your way through your exam. You are in one of the simulations, cranking through the drag-and-drop questions, the matching questions, the true/false questions … and then, there is the Communication tab!

The Ulysses Corporation began operations early in Year 1 and, by the end of that year, the company had generated $400,000 in credit sales. During that year, many of the company's customers made payments on their accounts so that on the last day of Year 1, Ulysses was reporting Accounts Receivable of $160,000. Leo Brown is president of the Ulysses Corporation and has hired the CPA firm of Stern and Ross to prepare financial statements for the first year of operations according to U.S. generally accepted accounting principles. These statements are scheduled to be released on February 16, Year 2. Brown is concerned about the reporting of bad debt expense. Brown believes that approximately 3% of the Year 1 credit sales will prove to be uncollectible. However, the company will not be able to identify the specific accounts to be written off until June or July of Year 2. Although Brown believes the 3% figure is a reasonable estimation, he realizes that the actual amount of bad accounts could be either higher or lower. Brown has asked the CPA firm as to whether these bad debts should be recognized immediately in Year 1 or not until Year 2 when the actual bad accounts will be determined. You are employed as a staff auditor for Stern and Ross, CPAs. Your supervisor has asked you to write a memo to Leo Brown to explain the proper accounting for bad debts according to U.S. generally accepted accounting principles.

This question looks like one that might appear on the Financial Accounting and Reporting section of the exam.

PREWRITING REVIEW: REPHRASING

What do you do first? You read the question and start your prewriting. Remember, prewriting gives you the freedom to construct the best possible sentences without having to think too much about your topic. If it is all there in your notes, you can focus on writing clearly. Begin to prewrite by putting the question into your own words, or rephrasing it. How would you rephrase this question?

Your supervisor has asked you to write a memo to Leo Brown to explain the proper accounting for bad debts according to U.S. generally accepted accounting principles. It should sound something like … Given the situation provided about the Ulysses Corporation, explain how bad debts are accounted for.

©2009 Kaplan, Inc.

PREWRITING REVIEW: NOTE TAKING

First, take notes on the situation. Your notes might look something like this:

- *400,000 in credit sales.*
- *160,000 A/R.*
- *About 3% uncollectible.*
- *Recognize in Year 1 or Year 2?*

Then, take notes on the key concepts, the principles you will want to take into account. Here is what we wrote as notes.

- *Accrual accounting.*
- *The matching principle: recognize expenses in same period as revenues.*
- *Reasonable estimation.*
- *Report A/R at net realizable value.*

PREWRITING REVIEW: STRUCTURING YOUR ARGUMENT

Now find your main point and your support: the structure of your argument. Your main point will be your answer to the question, "How should Ulysses account for bad debt?" and your support will be your review of the key concepts, particularly the matching principle. We are not going to answer the question for you here. Take what we have done so far and work on this one on your own. You will find our sample answer in the last section of this chapter. Keep reading, though, and we'll give you some more pointers.

PREWRITING REVIEW: STRUCTURING YOUR ANSWER

It is time to decide on a structure for your answer. Remember the different types of structure we talked about: the three- or five-paragraph answer, the pyramid structure, and structure based on the question. What's the best way to structure this answer? *How should Ulysses account for bad debt?* This is a straightforward question. You can begin with your main point—the answer to the question. You can then support that main point with your theoretical key concepts.

Try covering this in three paragraphs, with a basic pyramid structure. Start with the most important information, then fill in the key details you need. Use this structure and attempt to write your own answer. A model solution is provided later in this chapter.

EDITING REVIEW

Before we move on, let us review the key concepts of editing. One of the most important things you can do when you have finished writing your answer is to read it out loud. Hearing the voice of your answer in your head will help you to "hear" any mistakes that exist. Remember that spell check only goes so far. You need to be sure to read and evaluate every word of your writing.

Finally, be sure to use your editing checklist as you practice, and it will become second nature. Know your weaknesses and pay special attention to them as you practice editing.

PREPARING FOR THE EXAM

Let us go over what you can do to prepare for the test. First, remember to *practice writing*. As you prepare to take the exam, write short answers on topics that you need to review. Make up your own questions. This will give you great writing practice, and it will also help you with the multiple-choice part of the exam.

The next thing you can do is to *read critically*. Remember to look at the author's argument when you read the newspaper or magazines. Look at the structure of the piece, and search for the support for the main point. Think about how you would improve the article, or how you might take the opposite side of an argument. You will probably find that plenty of professional writers make some of the structure mistakes that we talked about.

Finally, *edit everything* you write, even your e-mails to colleagues or friends. Make every word perfect. If you write a note to your roommate on the fridge, make sure your punctuation and spelling check out. It sounds silly, but proper grammar, punctuation, and spelling are habits. Once you get in the habit, it will help you for the rest of your life. In the next section, you will find several sample questions, complete with notes and sample answers. Use the prewriting and writing process techniques you have learned as you practice writing these answers. The more you practice, the easier it will be to write your answers on the exam. Good luck on exam day!

COMMUNICATION QUESTIONS, OUTLINES, AND ANSWERS

QUESTION #2: SAMPLE QUESTION

The Ulysses Corporation began operations early in Year 1 and, by the end of that year, the company had generated $400,000 in credit sales. During that year, many of the company's customers made payments on their accounts so that on the last day of Year 1, Ulysses was reporting accounts receivable of $160,000.

Leo Brown is president of the Ulysses Corporation and has hired the CPA firm of Stern and Ross to prepare financial statements for the first year of operations, according to U.S. generally accepted accounting principles. These statements are scheduled to be released on February 16, Year 2.

Brown is concerned about the reporting of bad debt expense. Brown believes that approximately 3% of the Year 1 credit sales will prove to be uncollectible. However, the company will not be able to identify the specific accounts to be written off until June or July of Year 2. Although Brown believes the 3% figure is a reasonable estimation, he realizes that the actual amount of bad accounts could be either higher or lower. Brown has asked the CPA firm as to whether these bad debts should be recognized immediately in Year 1 or not until Year 2 when the actual bad accounts will be determined.

You are employed as a staff auditor for Stern and Ross, CPAs. Your supervisor has asked you to write a memo to Leo Brown to explain the proper accounting for bad debts according to U.S. generally accepted accounting principles.

QUESTION #2: SAMPLE NOTES

Question: Given the situation provided about the Ulysses Corporation, explain how bad debts are accounted for.

Situation: 400,000 in credit sales—160,000 A/R—About 3% uncollectible—Recognize in Year 1 or Year 2?

Key Concepts: Accrual accounting—The matching principle: recognize expenses in same period as revenues—reasonable estimation—report A/R at net realizable value

Structure: Three-paragraph pyramid

QUESTION #2: SAMPLE RESPONSE

To: Leo Brown, President of Ulysses Corporation
From: Staff Auditor, Stern and Ross, CPAs
Subject: Recognition of Bad Debt Expense

Bad debt expense of $12,000 (3% of sales) should be recognized in Year 1. Under U.S. generally accepted accounting principles, the timing of revenue and expense recognition is governed by accrual accounting. Here, the issue in question specifically concerns the recording of an expense. According to accrual accounting, the matching principle is used to guide the recognition of an expense. The matching principle states that expenses should be recognized in the same time period as the revenues that they help to generate.

With regard to the Ulysses Corporation, the company incurred uncollectible accounts as a result of the sales process in Year 1. These revenues were appropriately recognized in Year 1. Thus, the matching principle requires the related bad debt expense to be recognized in the same period. This reporting is used even though the actual amount and identity of the uncollectible accounts will not be known until Year 2. The company, though, must be able to make a reasonable estimation of the amount of expense to be reported.

Recognition of the uncollectible accounts in Year 1 also reduces the reported year-end balance of accounts receivable to its net realizable value, which is the amount that the company expects to collect. Reporting this asset at the lower net realizable value figure is conservative, and this approach is favored by U.S. generally accepted accounting principles.

QUESTION #3: SAMPLE QUESTION

To: Information Technology Partner
From: Engagement Partner
Re: ConnMart's supply-chain management process
Date: May 17, Year 6

ConnMart, a publicly held entity, operates in a paperless environment. The complete supply-chain management process, including the purchase order, delivery, and vendor payment, is electronic.

The recent issuance of the Public Company Accounting Oversight Board Auditing Standard No. 2 requires our firm to issue a separate report regarding the system of internal controls developed, documented, maintained, and evaluated by management. We want to verify the reliability and effectiveness of ConnMart's system of internal controls over their supply-chain management process.

Please direct your information systems audit team to assist in the development of substantive testing procedures to verify the accuracy, reliability, and completeness of the financial information reported by the supply-chain management system.

QUESTION #3: SAMPLE NOTES

Question: Describe the necessary substantive testing procedures.

Situation: Supply-chain management system: paperless.

Legal entity: Publicly held, subject to Sarbanes-Oxley Act of 2002.

Auditor: Must be registered with PCAOB.

Key Concepts: Internal controls, substantive testing to confirm inventory balances, expenses and related liabilities along with revenue, analytical procedures, expenses, liabilities.

Computer-based auditing procedures—Revenue

- Program analysis.
- Program testing.
- Continuous auditing.

Structure: Two paragraphs, each describing a key aspect of the question to be answered.

QUESTION #3: SAMPLE RESPONSE

To: Engagement Partner, Little Rock, Arkansas
From: Information Technology Partner, Little Rock, Arkansas
Reference: ConnMart's supply-chain management process
Date: May 17, Year 6

The information audit team has considered the outcome of the risk assessment process, and the team will develop the following substantive testing procedures. The audit team can use analytical procedures to gain insight into the reliability and reasonableness of the financial information reported by ConnMart's supply-chain management system. For example, the team can develop contribution margin ratios for each inventory category and compare these to sales activity, vendor payment activity, and inventory activity to determine reasonableness. The auditors can project the level of sales, costs, and remaining inventory using this technique. In addition, the team can review management's forecast, annual budget, and monthly operational reports to detect trends, and can compare these to the current results. This should identify any major variances and areas where additional investigation is required.

As for computer-based auditing procedures, the audit team can use program software to analyze various aspects of the supply-chain system, and can implement controls to ensure the accuracy of data output. They can review the existing system to ensure there are no coding problems that would lead to errors. The team can also run audit software to trace actual transactions from purchase order to vendor payment to the reorder process when a sale occurs. The team can input dummy transactions to ensure accurate processing throughout the system, and they can install a continuous auditing feature to monitor transactions as they occur. Finally, the team can run audit software that will allow for parallel simulation of actual data to be compared to output from the supply-chain management system.

QUESTION #4: SAMPLE QUESTION

Netco, Inc., filed for an Initial Public Offering in Year 6. Also in Year 6, Netco experienced significant sales growth and generated a profit of approximately $85 million on sales of almost $1 billion.

Netco launched the IPO to generate additional capital to finance growth and expansion as well as provide additional incentives for employees. Specifically, Netco used the funds to acquire new buildings and equipment to expand their technology infrastructure, and to establish a stock option plan. When the CFO directs the generation of the statement of cash flows for the year ending December 31, Year 6, describe the impact of the following in terms of the three sections of the statement of cash flows:

- Generation of equity and related proceeds from the sale of stock via the IPO.
- Treatment of costs for going public.
- Acquisition of buildings.
- Purchase of equipment.
- Creation of stock option plan.
- Generation of net income.

QUESTION #4: SAMPLE NOTES

Question: Describe the impact of the listed items on the statement of cash flows.

Situation: Company industry: Internet; Legal entity: issued an IPO; Acquisitions: purchased new buildings and equipment; Revenue: generated $1 billion with net income of $85 million.

Key Concepts: Statement of cash flows, investing activities, financing activities, operating activities, accruals, direct and indirect approach.

Structure: Introduction, plus three paragraphs, each focused on an aspect of the statement of cash flows.

QUESTION #4: SAMPLE RESPONSE

The CFO of Netco, Inc., will translate the key events for the current fiscal period into the three areas of the statement of cash flows as follows:

With regard to operating activities, the revenue generated from routine sales activities, adjusted for accruals and other non-cash transactions such as depreciation, will result in cash flow from operations.

Specifically, the $85 million in net income will be adjusted for the net impact of current accounts and non-cash activities, such as amortization, to establish the cash flow from operations.

As for financing activities, the proceeds from the IPO represent an equity-based transaction that generated cash flow. The use of the funds is not relevant, but the net effect from the equity-based activity represents cash flows from financing. The costs for an IPO are expensed as part of the issuance and are included in the net proceeds amount and, accordingly, there is no amortization. The creation of a stock option plan does not constitute an investing or financing activity until the stock is exercised.

As for investing activities, the acquisition of a long-term asset, such as a building or equipment, represents an investing activity. In this case, cash flows were used to invest in the expansion of assets.

QUESTION #5: SAMPLE QUESTION

To: General Counsel, Construction Firm, Inc.
From: CFO, Construction Firm, Inc.
Reference: Plaintiffs and Municipal Airport Project Subcontractors
Date: May 11, Year 6

Construction Firm, Inc., (CFI) has received a letter of intent to litigate from counsel representing a contractor who responded to our Request for Quotation (RFQ) to provide electrical and mechanical services for the Municipal Airport Project. The letter claims that counsel's client has incurred proposal costs, as well as injury to his business, because CFI elected to perform the work internally instead of using an external contractor.

CFI's RFQ is the industry standard solicitation that requests that potential and eligible suppliers provide their estimated price schedule for a specified set of goods and services. We clearly indicate that this RFQ is not a binding agreement that constitutes a contract between CFI and the offeror. Furthermore, we indicate that CFI reserves the right to secure the specified goods and services. Finally, the RFQ also states that all information submitted by the offeror becomes the property of CFI.

The overall claim of the plaintiff is that CFI improperly used the RFQ process to obtain prices and to use that information as a resource base to direct internal resources to secure the goods and services to support the Municipal Airport Project.

As the CFI general counsel, we need your opinion on this potential lawsuit. Specifically, does the RFQ process commit CFI to an obligation to select a potential supplier and execute a procurement contract?

QUESTION #5: SAMPLE NOTES

Question: Is CFI committed to this selection and contract execution?

Situation: Company industry: construction; contract issue: municipal airport project; legal entity: corporation; sourcing: decision to in-source or out-source a project.

Key Concepts: Outline the appropriate key contract law terms related to the memorandum:

Contract law; Existence of an offer; Evidence of consideration; Acceptance of an offer; Invitation to make an offer versus an offer; Definiteness of terms; Type of agreement (written, oral, unilateral or bilateral); Uniform Commercial Code

Structure: Introduction stating the answer, plus two paragraphs of support describing reasons for the answer.

QUESTION #5: SAMPLE RESPONSE

The plaintiff does not have legal recourse against CFI for our decision to use internal resources to provide electrical and mechanical services for the Municipal Airport Project for the following reasons.

An offer is a definite proposal or undertaking made by one party to another that, by its terms, is conditional upon an act or return promise given in exchange. An RFQ is not an offer, but an invitation to bid in the same manner as an advertisement. As such, an RFQ does not constitute an offer or any legally binding event.

The RFQ does possess the three essential components of an offer: intent, communication, and definite and certain terms. However, the CFI RFQ clearly indicates the intent to solicit non-binding prices, and not bids. Further, there was no commitment to select a respondent for procurement. Consequently, the criteria for an offer were not met, and there is no binding element.

QUESTION #6: SAMPLE QUESTION

The passage of Sarbanes-Oxley Act of 2002 represents the most significant changes to the regulation of capital markets, corporate governance, and the auditing profession since the Securities Acts of 1933 and 1934. Congress passed the Act in response to an unprecedented wave of fraudulent financial reporting that ultimately led to the erosion of investor confidence in capital markets.

The Act targets management, auditors, and audit committees, among other stakeholders, and charges them with responsibilities. Outline the major requirements of the Act as it relates to one of the three stakeholders. Also discuss the purpose and implications of the Act for restoring investor confidence in each of the three respective responses for the stakeholders.

QUESTION #6: SAMPLE NOTES

Question: Identify the major points of Sarbanes-Oxley for one of the three stakeholders. Note that you only need to choose one stakeholder to write about. Discuss purpose of the act as it relates to investor confidence.

Situation: Outline the appropriate key aspects of Sarbanes-Oxley related to the question; major rules as they relate to management, audit committee, or external auditor, PCAOB.

Key Concepts: Fraudulent financial reporting; Corporate governance; Investor confidence; Role of audit committee; Role of external auditor.

Structure: Two paragraphs, each addressing one of the two aspects of the question.

QUESTION #6: SAMPLE RESPONSE—THREE OPTIONS FOR YOUR RESPONSE

1. Management

The Sarbanes-Oxley Act mandates that management is responsible for creating and maintaining adequate internal controls and presenting its assessment of the effectiveness of those controls. The goal of this requirement is to ensure that there is an effective system to prevent material misstatements in the financial statements generated by management.

The wave of fraudulent financial reporting cases caused significant erosion to investor confidence in the reliability, accuracy, objectivity, and validity of financial information disclosed by corporate America. The Act requires that the CEO and CFO must sign a separate statement to accompany the financial statements certifying the propriety, reliability, fairness, and completeness of the financial reports. It also requires that the financial reports and disclosures fairly present the company's operations and the financial condition. This sends a signal to investors that management is ultimately responsible for the financial information released and will be held accountable, including being held liable and subject to criminal prosecution for any known false statements.

2. Audit Committee

The Sarbanes-Oxley Act outlines a comprehensive role for the audit committee that did not exist in the past. The audit committee is responsible for ensuring that management adheres to the rules of the Act, including the establishment of a system of internal controls. The act requires that the audit committee oversee the relationship with the registered external audit firm, including hiring, compensation, and verification of their continued independence. The Act also specifies that the audit committee should consist of independent directors and a financial expert.

The increased role of the audit committee ensures that there is an independent and strong monitoring function on the board of directors that will review both management and external auditor activities. This will help to ensure that external auditor performance is optimal. The Act further requires that audit committees have procedures in place to receive and address complaints regarding accounting, internal control, or auditing issues. Further, it provides protection for corporate whistle blowers by specifying that audit committees establish procedures for handling employees' anonymous submission of concerns regarding accounting or auditing matters.

3. External Auditor

The Sarbanes-Oxley Act prescribes the nature of the relationship of the external auditor with the company, and identifies the services that an auditor can provide to a company for which it performs an audit. The Act also details services that are prohibited, such as executing accounting services or performing the functions of management. The audit committee must approve all services that are allowed per the Act, such as tax services, prior to consummating an agreement.

In addition, the Act created the Public Company Accounting Oversight Board. The PCAOB is granted the authority by the Act to publicize auditing rules, regulate registered accounting firms, and invoke sanctions for any violations. Accounting firms must register with the PCAOB, and must adhere to its standards for independence and its auditing standards. The creation of the PCAOB seeks to enhance the regulation and performance monitoring of the external auditor, who plays a key role in ensuring the reliability of financial reports.

BE CONFIDENT!

You are ready to begin your studies for the CPA exam. You can be confident that the content found in the study manuals is adequate for your studies. You should, however, supplement your studies by watching the Online Review Courses, reviewing the flashcards, listening to the audio files, and practicing with the Qbank questions found online at www.schweser.com/cpa.

We are confident in your abilities to pass the CPA Exam. It does require diligent studies and our Kaplan Interactive Study Calendar will provide a study strategy that will ensure your successful completion of all material.

CHAPTER 1 – RECEIVABLES AND BAD DEBT EXPENSE

STUDY TIP

Almost every person has some habit or fondness that eats up a lot of their time. For some, it is television, while for others it is card playing, going to the movies, or the like. When you first begin to study for the CPA exam, determine what activity you use to waste time. Do not avoid this activity completely, but work to reduce that time to a specific but reasonable amount each week. That helps you take control over your time and find the time needed to prepare properly.

CHAPTER 1 – RECEIVABLES AND BAD DEBT EXPENSE

BASIC DESCRIPTION

DEFINITION OF ACCOUNTS RECEIVABLE

A. Also known as **trade accounts receivable**, it is a current asset listed on the balance sheet (normally with a debit balance) that arose from past transactions typically involving sales of goods and/or rendering of services where cash was not yet exchanged.

B. Accounts receivable are reasonably expected to be converted to cash at some time during the company's next year or operating cycle, whichever is longer.

C. For companies with accounts receivable balances, the opportunity cost incurred by the delayed cash receipts may be viewed as a necessary cost of financing.

D. A typical journal entry to record a transaction involving accounts receivable would be as follows:

Dr   Accounts receivable

    Cr   Revenue

COMPONENTS OF THE ACCOUNTS RECEIVABLE BALANCE

A. The accounts receivable balance is composed of four parts:

1. Beginning balance for the period.

2. Add: Credit sales for the period.

3. Deduct: Cash receipts (collections) from credit sales.

4. Deduct: Balances written off because of returns, discounts, or doubtful accounts.

    a. *Allowance for sales returns and allowances* represents an estimated amount of sales included in receivables that are expected to be returned.

    b. *Allowance for sales discounts* represents an estimate of the sales discounts to be utilized by customers who pay within a certain time period.

    c. *Allowance for doubtful accounts* represents an estimate of uncollectible receivables due to customer nonpayment.

5. This calculation yields the net realizable value of the accounts receivable; NRV is the proper carrying amount for the balance sheet.

SALES DISCOUNTS

There are two ways to account for sales discounts:

A. The net method:

1. The net method records the initial credit sale as a debit to accounts receivable and a credit to sales at the net amount (sales amount minus the discount).

2. If the cash payment is received within the discount period, then an entry crediting accounts receivable and debiting cash is recorded, all at the net amount.

3. If the full cash payment is received, but received *after* the discount period, then the cash received is recorded at the gross sales amount. This is balanced by an entry crediting accounts receivable for the recorded sales amount along with a credit (or a "gain") to an account "discounts not taken."

4. This method, then, records sales at the "net of discount" amount, and if the discount is not taken, an income statement account shows a credit balance for the "discounts not taken."

B. The gross method:

1. Recording the sale is similar to the net method, except the accounts receivable and revenue/sales are recorded at the gross amounts.

2. If the cash payment is received within the discount period, then the amount of cash received will be less than the gross amount of sales recorded initially. An entry crediting accounts receivable for the gross sales amount is required along with a debit to cash for the net amount received. Because less cash will be received when the discount is taken, the difference becomes an income statement expense called "sales discounts taken."

3. If the cash payment is received *after* the discount period, then there is simply an entry debiting cash and crediting accounts receivable.

4. This method, then, records sales at the "gross" amount, and if the discount is not taken, no other entries are made. If the discount is taken, there is an income statement account with a debit balance for the "discounts taken."

Example: Sales Discounts, Net and Gross Method

Facts: Sales, $100   Sales Discounts Offered, $5

Journal Entries for Gross and Net Method of Handling Sales Discounts

Net Method

	Sales Discount Taken		Sales Discount Not Taken	
Sale	A/R 95		A/R 95	
	Sales	95	Sales	95
Cash Collection	Cash 95		Cash 100	
	A/R	95	A/R	95
			Discounts Not Taken* 5	

Gross Method

	Sales Discount Taken		Sales Discount Not Taken	
Sale	A/R 100		A/R 100	
	Sales	100	Sales	100
Cash Collection	Cash 95		Cash 100	
	Discount Taken* 5		A/R	100
	A/R	100		

* *Discounts not taken* appears on the income statement as a credit balance (net method).
  Discounts taken appears on the income statement as a debit balance (gross method).

If discounts are *taken* under the Net Method, no income statement account is necessary for discounts.

If discounts are *not taken* under the Gross Method, no income statement account is necessary for discounts.

VALUING ACCOUNTS RECEIVABLE

A. Whereas the allowances for sales returns and sales discounts may be incorporated in calculating the "gross" accounts receivable figure, the allowance for doubtful accounts (AFDA) is disclosed separately.

B. The AFDA is a contra-account (i.e., negative account) to accounts receivable. The two amounts combined will result in the proper reporting of the accounts receivables at net realizable value.

BAD DEBT EXPENSE

COMPONENTS OF THE ALLOWANCE FOR DOUBTFUL ACCOUNTS (AFDA)

A. Beginning balance for the period (should usually start with a credit balance). *[Note: Candidates frequently ask, "What if the ending balance in the Allowance was a 'debit' at the end of last year because more accounts were written off than were 'allowed for' in the allowance account? Wouldn't it begin the year with that same debit balance?" The answer (at least on the CPA exam) is that even if Year 1 ends with a debit in the AFDA, proper accounting would require an adjustment to the expense at year-end, bringing the allowance to a credit balance.]*

B. Deduct: Write-offs of any uncollectible accounts receivables.

This practice makes sense because the allowance was made in anticipation of the write-off. Once the write-off is made, it would be reasonable to reduce the allowance.

C. Add: Subsequent collection of an account previously written off as bad.

1. The journal entry would be to debit cash (increase) and credit allowance for doubtful accounts (increase). This practice makes sense because the receivable has previously been written off. The receivable needs to be re-established before a collection can be recorded.

2. If the allowance is determined to be excessive because of a high percentage of such subsequent collections, then an adjustment could be made to debit the allowance (decrease) and credit bad debt expense (decrease). This would have a positive effect on net income.

D. Add: Recognition of bad debt expense for the current period (debit bad debts expense and credit allowance for bad debts).

E. Remember: The AFDA is an estimate because we record the expense and the allowance when the revenues are earned, in order to "match" revenues and expenses. Thus, the allowance account represents an estimate of future bad debts. Once the bad accounts are "known" and written off, then they are no longer needed in the allowance, so the allowance account is reduced by the amount of the bad debt.

F. Another good point to remember: When uncollectible accounts are written off (debit allowance, credit A/R), there is no overall effect on the balance sheet. You are reducing assets (A/R) and reducing a contra-asset (allowance) by the same amount, so the overall effect on current assets is zero.

DIRECT WRITE-OFF METHOD

A. The direct write-off method is sometimes used by smaller businesses to report bad debts. This is the method used for tax purposes but it is not acceptable for financial statement reporting purposes. An exam question might test your understanding that this is *not* acceptable in financial accounting.

B. No allowance account is established, and the bad debt expense is only recognized once the account is actually written off.

C. This practice violates the matching principle because the bad debt expense is recognized in the period in which the specific receivable becomes uncollectible, rather than in the period in which the related sales are recognized.

D. Illustrative journal entry:

Dr   Bad debt expense
    Cr   Accounts receivable

E. Net income is reduced by the amount of the bad debt expense recognized, and current assets are reduced by the amount of the A/R written off.

PERCENTAGE OF SALES METHOD (A.K.A. INCOME STATEMENT APPROACH)

A. In this approach, the company uses its past experience and knowledge of the industry and current economic conditions to determine a percentage of its credit (not cash, because there are no bad debts on cash sales!) sales that will typically not be collectible.

B. Once the proper percentage is taken of credit sales, the resulting figure is the bad debt expense for the period as well as the increase in the allowance for doubtful accounts.

C. The resulting amount is recorded as bad debt expense for the period using the following journal entry:

Dr Bad debt expense

Cr AFDA

D. This approach follows the matching principle on the income statement because bad debt expense is computed on the basis of credit sales so that the expense is matched with the related revenue. Notice that any previous balance in the AFDA account is ignored in calculating the current year bad debt expense.

PERCENTAGE OF RECEIVABLES METHOD (A.K.A. AGING METHOD OR BALANCE SHEET METHOD)

A. Here the company prepares an aging schedule of accounts receivables— current, 30 days past due, 60 days past due, 90 days past due, etc.

B. A percentage is taken of each category based on the company's knowledge of the likelihood that an account will be uncollectible once it exceeds a certain time period of collection.

C. The total of all the amounts computed for each aging category will be the amount that will be expected to be uncollectible and should be the ending balance in the AFDA account. Any previous balance in the AFDA account is taken into consideration when determining the current year bad debt expense.

D. An entry will be prepared for an amount equal to the difference between the existing balance in the AFDA account and the ending balance calculated above. It is the same journal entry as under the percentage of sales method (debit bad debt expense and credit AFDA), but with different amounts. The bad debt expense is equal to the increase in the AFDA.

E. This approach is justified under the concept of asset measurement (NRV on the balance sheet).

Note: Sometimes on the CPA exam you will be given one percentage and asked to apply it to the ending balance in A/R. This procedure substitutes for having a unique percentage for each age category of A/R. So, the exam may say "uncollectible accounts are expected to be 10% of accounts receivable." You would multiply 10% times the ending A/R balance, and that would be the ending balance in AFDA. The journal entry would be the amount required to bring the AFDA to the number you just calculated. (You calculated the desired ending balance in AFDA, not the expense amount.)

WRITING OFF AN UNCOLLECTIBLE ACCOUNT

A. The actual write-off of an uncollectible account may occur at any time but usually occurs when there is an indication that the receivable has become uncollectible (e.g., notification of bankruptcy filing).

B. The write-off of an uncollectible account has no net financial statement effect (i.e., no effect on bad debt expense nor the *net* amount of the receivables balance).

C. The journal entry is simply a reclassification between the two components of the accounts receivable balance:

Dr   AFDA

    Cr   Accounts receivable

SUMMARY OF BAD DEBT

A.

Accounts receivable	
(Debit)	**(Credit)**
Beginning balance	– Collections
+ Credit sales	– Write-offs
+ Reinstatements	
= Ending balance	

B.

AFDA	
(Debit)	**(Credit)**
– Write-offs	Beginning balance
	+ Bad debt expense
	+ Reinstatements
	= Ending balance

USING ACCOUNTS RECEIVABLE TO OBTAIN CASH PRIOR TO COLLECTIONS FROM CUSTOMERS

PLEDGING ACCOUNTS RECEIVABLES

A. Accounts receivables may be used as collateral for loans. This practice is known as *pledging*.

B. If the loan is not paid as it comes due, then the lender may force the liquidation of the pledged asset to pay the account receivable balance.

C. Proper disclosure is required, and it is usually provided in the financial statement footnote disclosures. Pledging accounts receivables does not require a journal entry.

FACTORING ACCOUNTS RECEIVABLES

A. Factoring of receivables is a sale of the receivables to another party. The buyer usually bears the collection risk of the receivables (see "factor holdback" below, however).

B. The difference between the factoring sale price and the carrying value of the receivables is most likely recorded as a loss (see below). The "loss" may also be seen in the form of interest expense and/or factoring fees.

C. Two benefits of factoring are as follows:

    1. Cash flow: Seller obtains the cash immediately.

    2. Risk management: Seller transfers away the collection risk.

"Factor Holdback"

A. The buyer of the receivables can reduce the cash payment to the seller by a specific percentage intended to cover anticipated merchandise returns and some portion of bad accounts. This reduction is called a "factor holdback" and can still be paid to the seller if returns and bad debts are less than a stipulated amount.

B. A factor holdback is a receivable for the seller of the accounts and a payable for the buyer. The final amount is not known until the accounts have all been settled.

Control and the Financial Component Approach as Applied to the Accounting Treatment of Receivables

A. It is sometimes difficult to determine whether a sale has been made or if the receivables are being used as security for a loan.

B. Financial accounting dictates that both buyer and seller must recognize the respective assets and liabilities that they control.

C. Under SFAS 140, the financial component approach is used to determine control. It specifies that any element of the receivable is considered to be sold if three criteria have been met indicating a change in control:

1. The asset is isolated from the seller.

2. The buyer now has the right to sell or pledge the asset.

3. The seller has not retained control through agreements to repurchase or redeem the asset.

D. Do not treat a problem as a factoring problem unless these three criteria have been met.

JOURNAL ENTRY FOR THE SALE OF ACCOUNTS RECEIVABLE WITHOUT RECOURSE

(*Without recourse* means that if the receivable is not paid by the customer when due, then the buyer *cannot* then demand payment from the seller. The buyer bears the risk of uncollectibility.)

A. To record the sale, debit cash received and credit receivables sold.

B. Seller has no further obligation; therefore, no additional liability needs to be recorded.

C. A loss will be recorded because the sale must almost always occur at a discount to the face amount of the A/R.

1. Clearly accounts receivables are not as liquid as cash.

2. Buyer bears some risk in that the full amounts of the receivables may not be ultimately realized.

D. Illustrative journal entry: Seller

Dr   Cash
Dr   Loss on sale
Dr   Factor holdback receivable
    Cr   Accounts receivable

Illustrative journal entry: Buyer

Dr   Accounts receivable

    Cr   Cash

    Cr   Factor Holdback Payable

JOURNAL ENTRY FOR THE SALE OF ACCOUNTS RECEIVABLE WITH RECOURSE

A. *With recourse* means that if the receivable is not paid by the customer when due, the buyer can then demand payment from the seller.

B. To record the sale, debit cash received and credit receivables sold. Seller must also record a potential liability equal to the fair value of any "recourse obligation" that is expected to arise because of the failure of some customers to pay.

C. The difference between the cash received and the summation of the asset lost and the recourse obligation incurred is recognized as a loss.

D. Illustrative journal entry: Seller

Dr   Cash

Dr   Loss on sale

Dr   Factor holdback receivable

    Cr   Accounts receivable

    Cr   Recourse obligation (liability)

E. Illustrative journal entry: Buyer

Dr   Accounts receivable

    Cr   Cash

    Cr   Factor holdback payable

SALE OF NOTES RECEIVABLE (DISCOUNTING)

A. Discounting refers to the sale of a note receivable and so the amount to be conveyed to the seller must be computed.

B. Interest to be paid on the note is computed (face value × annual rate × period of the year from date of issuance until maturity). This interest is added to the face value to get the maturity value of the note.

C. The maturity value is then multiplied by the buyer's discount (profit) rate for the period of time that is remaining until maturity. The resulting figure is the profit that the buyer wants to make.

D. The buyer's profit is subtracted from the maturity value to get the price paid for the note receivable.

E. Example: Smith owns an N/R with a face of $1,000, an interest rate of 10%, and a maturity date six months from issuance. The maturity value is $1,000 + [$1,000 × 10% × 6/12], or $1,050. If the note is discounted at 12% after two months (i.e., four more months to maturity), the cash received by the seller is $1,050 – [$1,050 × 12% × 4/12] or $1,008. The seller earns $8 interest by holding the note for two months; the buyer pays $1,008 but eventually collects $1,050, for a profit to the buyer of $42.

QUESTIONS: RECEIVABLES AND BAD DEBT EXPENSE

1. On January 1, 2006, Markham, Inc.'s allowance for doubtful accounts had a credit balance of $30,000. During 2006, Markham charged $64,000 to bad debt expense, wrote off $46,000 of uncollectible accounts receivable, and unexpectedly recovered $12,000 of bad debts written off in the prior year. The allowance for doubtful accounts balance at December 31, 2006, would be:
    A. $48,000.
    B. $60,000.
    C. $64,000.
    D. $94,000.

2. Clarkson, Inc.'s allowance for doubtful accounts had a credit balance of $12,000 at December 31, 2005. Clarkson accrues bad debt expense at the rate of 4% of credit sales. During 2006, Clarkson's credit sales amount to $1,500,000 and uncollectible accounts totaling $48,000 were written off. The aging of accounts receivable indicated that a $50,000 allowance for doubtful accounts was required at December 31, 2006. Clarkson's bad debt expense for the year would be:
    A. $48,000.
    B. $50,000.
    C. $60,000.
    D. $86,000.

3. The following accounts were abstracted from Chloe, Inc.'s unadjusted trial balance at December 31, 2005:

	Debit	Credit
Accounts receivable	$1,000,000	
Allowance for doubtful accounts	$8,000	
Net credit sales		$4,000,000

    Chloe estimates that 3% of the gross accounts receivable balance will become uncollectible. After adjustment on December 31, 2005, the allowance for doubtful accounts should have a credit balance of:
    A. $22,000.
    B. $30,000.
    C. $38,000.
    D. $120,000.

4.   Rondo Co. has the following information relating to its accounts receivables:

Accounts receivable at 12/31/2005	$1,300,000
Credit sales for 2006	$5,400,000
Collections from customers for 2006	$4,750,000
Accounts written off 9/30/2006	$125,000
Collection of accounts written off in prior years (customer credit was not reestablished)	$25,000
Estimated uncollectible receivables per aging of receivables at 12/31/2006	$165,000

At December 31, 2006, Rondo's accounts receivable balance (before allowance for doubtful accounts) should be:
A. $1,825,000.
B. $1,850,000.
C. $1,950,000.
D. $1,990,000.

5.   The following information pertains to Oren Corp.:

Credit sales for the year ended December 31, 2006	$450,000
Allowance for doubtful accounts balance at January 1, 2006	$10,800 (credit)
Bad debts written off during 2006	$18,000

According to past experience, 3% of Oren's credit sales have been uncollectible.

After a provision is made for bad debt expense for the year ended December 31, 2006, the allowance for doubtful accounts balance would be:
A. $6,300.
B. $13,500.
C. $24,300.
D. $31,500.

6.   Adam Co. reported sales revenue of $2,300,000 in its income statement for the year ended December 31, 2006. Additional information is as follows:

	12/31/05	12/31/06
Accounts receivable	$500,000	$650,000
Allowance for doubtful accounts	($30,000)	($55,000)

Doubtful accounts totaling $10,000 were written off during 2006.

Under the cash basis of accounting, Adam would have reported 2006 sales of:
A. $2,140,000.
B. $2,150,000.
C. $2,175,000.
D. $2,450,000.

7. For the year ended December 31, 2006, Bower Co. estimated its allowance for doubtful accounts using the year-end aging of accounts receivable. The following data is available:

Allowance for doubtful accounts at 1/1/06	$42,000 (credit)
Bad debt expense during 2006	$40,000
Doubtful accounts written off (11/30/06)	$46,000
Estimated doubtful accounts per aging schedule (12/31/06)	$52,000

After the year-end adjustment, the bad debt expense for the year should be:
A. $46,000.
B. $48,000.
C. $52,000.
D. $56,000.

8. Moutouzkine Co. prepared an aging of its accounts receivables at December 31, 2006 and determined that the net realizable value of the receivables was $250,000. Additional information is available as follows:

Allowance for doubtful accounts at 1/1/06	$28,000 (credit)
Accounts written off as uncollectible in 2006	$23,000
Accounts receivable at 12/31/06	$270,000
Uncollectible accounts recovery during 2006	$5,000

For the year ended December 31, 2006, Moutouzkine's bad debt expense would be:
A. $10,000.
B. $15,000.
C. $20,000.
D. $23,000.

9. Milne Co.'s allowance for doubtful accounts was $100,000 at the end of 2006 and $90,000 at the end of 2005. For the year ended December 31, 2006, Milne reported bad debt expense of $16,000 on its income statement.

What amount did Milne debit to the appropriate account in 2006 to write off actual bad debts?
A. $6,000.
B. $10,000.
C. $16,000.
D. $26,000.

10. Under the allowance method of recognizing doubtful accounts, the entry to write off an uncollectible account:
A. decreases net income.
B. has no effect on net income.
C. increases the allowance for doubtful accounts.
D. has no effect on the allowance for doubtful accounts.

11. Revard Co. uses the direct write-off method to account for doubtful accounts receivables. During an accounting period, Revard's cash collections from customers equal sales adjusted for the addition or deduction of the following amounts:

| | Increase in accounts |
Accounts written off	receivable balance
A. Addition	Addition
B. Addition	Deduction
C. Deduction	Addition
D. Deduction	Deduction

12. When the allowance method of recognizing doubtful accounts is used, the entries at the time of the collection of an account previously written off would:
   A. increase net income.
   B. decrease the allowance for doubtful accounts.
   C. increase the allowance for doubtful accounts.
   D. have no effect on the allowance for doubtful accounts.

13. When the allowance method of recognizing bad debt expense is used, the allowance would decrease when a(n):
   A. account previously written off is collected.
   B. account previously written off becomes collectible.
   C. specific uncollectible account is written off.
   D. provision for uncollectible accounts is recorded.

14. The following information relates to the Jesper Co.'s accounts receivable for 2006:

Accounts receivable, 1/1/06	$650,000
Credit sales for 2006	$2,700,000
Sales returns for 2006	$75,000
Accounts written off during 2006	$40,000
Collections from customers during 2006	$2,150,000
Estimated future sales returns at 12/31/06	$50,000
Estimated uncollectible accounts at 12/31/06	$110,000

On December 31, 2006, what amount should Jesper record for accounts receivable, before allowance for sales returns and uncollectible accounts?
   A. $925,000.
   B. $1,085,000.
   C. $1,125,000.
   D. $1,200,000.

15. The following information pertains to Tara Co.'s accounts receivable at December 31, 2006:

Days outstanding	Amount	Estimated % uncollectible
0–60	$120,000	1%
61–120	$ 90,000	2%
Over 120	$100,000	6%

During 2006, Tara wrote off $7,000 in receivables and recovered $4,000 that had been written off in prior years. Tara's December 31, 2005 allowance for doubtful accounts balance was $22,000 (credit).

Under the aging method, what amount of allowance for doubtful accounts should Tara record at December 31, 2006?
A. $9,000.
B. $10,000.
C. $13,000.
D. $19,000.

16. Rosario Co.'s allowance for doubtful accounts had a credit balance of $24,000 at December 31, 2005. During 2006, Rosario wrote off doubtful accounts of $96,000. The aging of accounts receivables indicated that a $100,000 allowance was required at December 31, 2006.

What amount of bad debt expense should Rosario report for 2006?
A. $96,000.
B. $100,000.
C. $120,000.
D. $172,000.

17. Western Co. estimates its bad debt expense to be 2% of credit sales. Western's credit sales for 2006 were $1,000,000. During 2006, Western wrote off $18,000 of doubtful accounts. Western's allowance for doubtful accounts has a $15,000 credit balance on January 1, 2006.

In its December 31, 2006 income statement, what amount should Western record as bad debt expense?
A. $17,000.
B. $18,000.
C. $20,000.
D. $23,000.

18. On March 31, 2006, Viduiera Co. had an unadjusted credit balance of $1,000 in its allowance for doubtful accounts. An analysis of Viduiera's trade accounts receivables on that date revealed the following:

Days outstanding	Amount estimated	% uncollectible
0–30	$60,000	5%
31–60	$4,000	10%
Over 60	$2,000	$1,400

Under the aging method, what amount should Viduiera record as additional bad debt expense?
A. $3,000.
B. $3,800.
C. $4,000.
D. $4,800.

19. Delta, Inc. sells to wholesalers on terms of 2/15, net 30. Delta has no cash sales but 50% of Delta's customers take advantage of the discount. Delta uses the gross method of recording sales and trade receivables. An analysis of Delta's trade receivables balances at December 31, 2006 revealed the following:

Age	Amount	Estimated % collectible
0–15 days	$100,000	100%
16–30 days	$60,000	95%
31–60 days	$5,000	90%
Over 60 days	$2,500	20%

On its December 31, 2006 balance sheet, what amount should Delta report for allowance for discounts?
A. $1,000.
B. $1,620.
C. $1,675.
D. $2,000.

20. After being held for 40 days, a 120-day 12% interest-bearing note receivable was discounted at a bank at 15%. The proceeds received from the bank equal:
A. face value less the discount at 12%.
B. face value less the discount at 15%.
C. maturity value less the discount at 15%.
D. maturity value less the discount at 12%.

21. Apex Company accepted from a customer a $100,000 face amount, six month, 8% note dated April 15, 2006. On the same day, Apex discounted the note at Union Bank at a 10% discount rate.

How much cash should Apex receive from the bank?
A. $97,200.
B. $98,800.
C. $99,000.
D. $104,000.

22.   Garr Company received a $60,000, six month, 10% note from a customer. After holding the note for two months, Garr was in need of cash and discounted the note at the United Local Bank at a 12% discount rate. How much cash should Garr receive from the bank?
        A. $60,480.
        B. $60,630.
        C. $61,740.
        D. $62,520.

23.   Randall, Inc. accepted from a customer a $40,000, 90-day, 12% interest-bearing note dated August 31, 2006. On September 30, 2006, Randall discounted the note at Apex State Bank at 15%. However, the proceeds were not received until October 1, 2006.

        On Randall's September 30, 2006 balance sheet, the amount receivable from the bank, based on a 360-day year, includes accrued interest revenue of:
        A. $170.
        B. $200.
        C. $300.
        D. $400.

24.   On July 1, 2006, Lee Co. sold goods in exchange for a $200,000, eight-month, non-interest bearing note receivable. At the time of the sale, the note's market rate of interest was 12%. What amount did Lee receive when it discounted the note at 10% on September 1, 2006?
        A. $188,000.
        B. $190,000.
        C. $193,800.
        D. $194,000.

25.   Zane Co. factored its receivables. Control was surrendered in the transaction that was on a without recourse basis with Ross Bank. Zane received cash as a result of this transaction that is best described as a:
        A. loan from Ross collateralized by Zane's accounts receivable.
        B. loan from Ross to be repaid by the proceeds from Zane's accounts receivable.
        C. sale of Zane's accounts receivable to Ross, with the risk of uncollectible accounts retained by Zane.
        D. sale of Zane's accounts receivable to Ross, with the risk of uncollectible accounts transferred to Ross.

Use the following information to answer Questions 26 through 28.

Taylor Corp. factored $400,000 of accounts receivables to Rich Corp. on July 1, 2006. Control was surrendered by Taylor. Rich accepted the receivables subject to recourse for nonpayment. Rich assessed a fee of 2% and retains a holdback equal to 5% of accounts receivable. In addition, Rich charged 15% interest computed on a weighted-average time to maturity of the receivables of 41 days. The fair value of the recourse obligation is $12,000.

26.   Taylor will receive and record cash in the amount of:
        A. $357,260.
        B. $365,260.
        C. $377,260.
        D. $385,260.

27. Which of the following statements is correct?
     A. Rich should record an asset of $8,000 for the recourse obligation.
     B. Taylor should record a liability and corresponding loss of $12,000 related to the recourse obligation.
     C. Taylor should record a liability of $12,000, but no loss related to the recourse obligation.
     D. No entry for the recourse obligation should be made by Taylor or Rich until the debtor fails to pay.

28. Assuming all receivables are collected, Taylor's cost of factoring the receivables would be:
     A. $8,000.
     B. $14,740.
     C. $34,740.
     D. $42,740.

29. Beulah Corp. transferred financial assets to Coyle, Inc. The transfer meets the conditions to be accounted for as a sale. As the transferrer, Beulah should do each of the following except:
     A. remove all assets sold from the balance sheet.
     B. record all assets received and liabilities incurred as proceeds from the sale.
     C. measure the assets received and liabilities incurred at cost.
     D. recognize any gain or loss on the sale.

30. Cynthia Corp. factored $750,000 of accounts receivable to Victor Corp. on October 20, 2006. Control was surrendered to Cynthia. Victor accepted the receivables subject to recourse for nonpayment. Victor assessed a fee of 2% and retains a holdback equal to 4% of the accounts receivable. In addition, Victor charged 12% interest computed on a weighted-average time to maturity of the receivables of 51 days. The fair value of the recourse obligation is $15,000.

     Assuming all receivables are collected, Cynthia's cost of factoring the receivables would be:
     A. $12,575.
     B. $15,000.
     C. $27,575.
     D. $42,575.

31. The Matheson Corporation begins Year 1 with accounts receivables of $340,000 and an allowance for doubtful accounts of $20,000. During Year 1, credit sales of $800,000 were made by Matheson. Cash collections for the year were $600,000 and accounts with a balance of $15,000 were written off as uncollectible. Miwa has estimated that 5% of its credit sales this year will prove to be uncollectible. However, if, instead, Miwa had estimated that 6% of its ending accounts receivable would eventually become uncollectible, how much higher would the company's reported net income have been? (Ignore income taxes effects.)
     A. $3,500.
     B. $7,500.
     C. $9,500.
     D. $13,500.

32.   The Anderson Company holds $400,000 in accounts receivable which it sells to the First American Bank. The sale is for $340,000. However, Anderson only collects $310,000 at the present time. The remainder will be paid based on the specific amount collected by the bank. If the bank collects $360,000 or more, Anderson receives the entire holdback amount. If the bank collects less then $360,000, an amount of this holdback will be retained to compensate the bank up to a maximum of the entire $30,000 figure. Anderson believes that the bank will be able to collect $342,000. What is the amount of loss that Anderson should recognize on this sale?
   A. $18,000.
   B. $60,000.
   C. $78,000.
   D. $90,000.

33.   Wren Company had the following account balances at December 31, Year 1:

Accounts receivable	$900,000
Allowance for doubtful accounts (before recognition of the current expense)	$16,000 (credit)
Credit sales for the year	$1,750,000

Wren is considering the following two methods of estimating doubtful accounts expense for the current year:
   •   Based on credit sales at a 2% rate.
   •   Based on accounts receivable at a 5% rate.

What amount should Wren charge to doubtful accounts expense under each method?

	Percentage of credit sales	Percentage of gross receivables
A.	$35,000	$29,000
B.	$35,000	$45,000
C.	$51,000	$29,000
D.	$51,000	$45,000

34.   At the end of the current year, a company collects a trade receivable from a major customer. Which of the following ratios will be increased by this transaction?
   A. Receivable turnover ratio.
   B. Inventory turnover ratio.
   C. Current ratio.
   D. Quick ratio.

35.   Harkness Corporation starts the current year with accounts receivable of $400,000 and ends the year with accounts that total $600,000 despite having to write off $20,000 as uncollectible. Cash collections for the year were $900,000. The company also started the year with an allowance for doubtful accounts of $17,000 but ended with a balance of $19,000. What was bad debt expense for the current year?
   A. $19,000.
   B. $20,000.
   C. $21,000.
   D. $22,000.

36.   The Armstrong Corporation has receivables of $700,000. Armstrong goes to ten different banks and other finance institutions and sells each one 10% of the future cash to be collected from these receivables for $62,000 each. This process is known as:
        A.   factoring.
        B.   securitization.
        C.   discounting.
        D.   leveraging.

37.   A company transfers $300,000 in receivables to a bank for cash of $270,000. This transaction is not viewed as a sale if which of the following takes place?
        A.   The company has an agreement to repurchase the receivables from the bank.
        B.   The company physically transfers all rights to the receivables to the bank.
        C.   The bank has the right to sell the receivables to another outside party.
        D.   The bank has the right to pledge the receivables to another outside party.

ANSWERS: RECEIVABLES AND BAD DEBT EXPENSE

1. **B**   The $30,000 credit balance in the allowance for doubtful accounts at 1/1/06 would be increased by the current year bad debt expense of $64,000 and reduced by write-offs of $46,000. The recovery of the accounts that have previously been written off are recorded with an increase in the allowance for the amount recovered, $12,000.

   In summary, the balance in allowance for doubtful accounts at 12/31/06 will be $30,000 + $64,000 – $46,000 + $12,000 = $60,000.

2. **D**   Clarkson's allowance for doubtful accounts had a beginning credit balance of $12,000. During the year, bad debt expense of 4% of credit sales (4% × $1,500,000 = $60,000) was accrued, increasing the credit balance to $72,000. Accounts totaling $48,000 were written off, leaving a credit balance of $24,000. Because the aged analysis indicated that a $50,000 credit balance was required, an additional $26,000 of bad debt expense would need to be accrued.

   Total bad debt expense for the period is $60,000 + $26,000 = $86,000.

   This question demonstrates the importance of carefully reading the question. The question asks for bad debt expense, and there are two steps to getting the answer: (1) the normal periodic adjusting entry recorded for bad debts based on the income statement method (% × credit sales) and (2) the year-end adjusting entry, where they adjust the Allowance account to a percent of A/R based on the balance sheet aging method. Because the question did not ask about the allowance balance, the $48,000 of write-offs is irrelevant.

3. **B**   Because Chloe estimates that 3% of gross accounts receivable will become uncollectible, this percentage is applied to gross accounts receivable to determine the desired balance in the allowance for doubtful accounts. The amount would be 3% × $1,000,000 = $30,000.

   It would be recorded with a debit to bad debt expense and a credit to the allowance of $38,000. This would offset the existing $8,000 debit balance in the allowance and result in a $30,000 credit balance.

4. **A**   Accounts receivable has a beginning balance of $1,300,000 that will be increased by credit sales of $5,400,000 and decreased by collections of $4,750,000, resulting in a balance before adjustment of $1,950,000. Accounts written off would decrease accounts receivable by $125,000 to $1,825,000.

   When an account that was previously written off is collected, it is first reinstated with an increase to the receivables balance and a corresponding reduction (debit) to the allowance for doubtful accounts. Then the collection is recorded as a decrease to accounts receivable, resulting in no overall net change to the receivables balance.

5. **A**   The allowance for doubtful accounts balance at January 1, 2006 of $10,800 would increase by $13,500 ($450,000 × 3% = $13,500) as a result of credit sales. It would decrease by $18,000 as a result of write-offs. The resulting balance is $10,800 + $13,500 – $18,000 = $6,300.

6. **A**   Accounts receivable had a beginning debit balance of $500,000. Sales of $2,300,000 would increase the balance to $2,800,000. The write-off of $10,000 reduces the balance to $2,790,000. Because the ending balance was given was $650,000, collections must have been $2,790,000 – $650,000 = $2,140,000. This is the amount that would have been reported as sales under the cash basis.

7. **D**   Bower uses a year-end aging of accounts receivables to determine uncollectible amounts. As a result, Bower will want to adjust the allowance at year-end such that the ending balance will be $52,000. There was a beginning balance in the allowance for doubtful accounts of $42,000. During the year, estimated bad debt expense of $40,000 was recognized, increasing the balance to $82,000. Accounts totaling $46,000 were written off, giving a balance of $36,000.

In order to increase the balance to $52,000, an additional $16,000 in bad debt expense is required, giving a total of $40,000 + $16,000 = $56,000 for the year.

8.   A   The allowance for doubtful account balances at 1/1/06 was $28,000. Accounts written off as uncollectible of $23,000 reduce the allowance to $5,000, while recoveries of $5,000 increase the allowance to $10,000.

         Because the accounts receivable at 12/31/06 were $270,000 and the net realizable value of those accounts was $250,000, then the allowance must have been $20,000 at 12/31/06. As adjustment of the allowance to that amount, with an offsetting entry to bad debt expense, is made for $20,000 – $10,000 = $10,000.

9.   A   The allowance at the beginning of 2006 was $90,000, and $16,000 was added to the allowance when bad debt expense was recorded, increasing the allowance to $106,000. If it ended the year at $100,000, then $6,000 must have been subtracted from the allowance as a result of bad debt write-offs (net of recoveries).

10.   B   Under the allowance method, the entry to write off an uncollectible account includes a debit to the allowance for uncollectible accounts and a credit to accounts receivable. Because the allowance account is a contra-asset with a credit balance, a debit to that account decreases its value. Because no entries are made to income accounts as a result of the write-off, the entry has no effect on net income.

11.   D   Accounts written off represent reductions in accounts receivable that did not result in a collection of cash. To convert accrual sales to cash collections, accounts written off would be deducted. In addition, an increase in accounts receivable indicates that sales were made that have not yet been collected and these too must be deducted from sales to determine collections.

12.   C   When an account that has been previously written off is collected, it is reinstated by increasing the receivable and allowance accounts. Collection is then recorded in the same manner as for an account that had not been written off.

13.   C   The allowance for doubtful accounts is increased by the recognition of bad debt expense. It decreased when a specific account is written off and increased if an account previously written off either becomes collectible or is collected.

14.   B   The beginning balance in accounts receivable of $650,000 would be increased by credit sales of $2,700,000, decreased by sales returns of $75,000, decreased by accounts written off of $40,000, and decreased by collections of $2,150,000. The resulting balance would be $1,085,000.

15.   A   Under the aged analysis approach, the allowance for doubtful accounts will consist of 1% of the $120,000 ($1,200) that are 0 to 60 days old, plus 2% of the $90,000 ($1,800) that are 61 to 120 days old, and 6% of the $100,000 ($6,000) that are over 120 days old, for a total of $9,000.

         The previous balance in the allowance is only considered in determining the adjustment needed to bring the balance to the desired $9,000 amount.

16.   D   With a credit balance of $24,000 and write-offs of $96,000, the allowance would have a debit balance of $72,000 before recognition of any bad debt expense. In order to establish the desired credit balance of $100,000, a credit to the allowance and a debit to bad debt expense in the amount of $172,000 would be required.

17.   C   Because Western estimates bad debt expense at 2% of credit sales, the balance in the allowance for doubtful accounts will be ignored. Bad debt expense will be 2% of credit sales of $1,000,000 = $20,000.

18.   B   Using the aged analysis, the allowance for doubtful accounts will consist of 5% of $60,000 = $3,000 + 10% of $4,000 = 400 + $1,400 for a total of $4,800. Because there is already a credit balance of $1,000 in the allowance, an adjustment of $3,800 (credit allowance, debit bad debt expense) will be required to give the desired $4,800 balance.

19. **A**   Only those accounts aged 0–15 days ($100,000) would still qualify for the discount. Of those, 50% ($50,000) are expected to take advantage of the 2% discount, resulting in a discount amount of $50,000 × 2% = $1,000.

20. **C**   When a note is discounted, the proceeds will be equal to the maturity value of the note less the discount. The discount is calculated by multiplying the discount rate by the maturity value and multiplying the result by the portion of a year from the date of the discounting to the maturity date.

21. **B**   The $100,000 note will bear interest at 8% for six months, thereby indicating a maturity value of $104,000. This will be the amount at which the bank discount will be computed. The bank discount will be $104,000 × 10% × 6/12 = $5,200. So the proceeds from discounting the note will be $104,000 – $5,200 = $98,800.

22. **A**   The maturity value of the note will be $60,000 plus interest of $3,000 ($60,000 × 10% × 6/12) for a total of $63,000. This amount will be discounted at 12% for the remaining four months, resulting in a discount of $2,520 ($63,000 × 12% × 4/12). The proceeds will be $63,000 – $2,520 = $60,480.

23. **A**   The receivable will have a maturity value of $40,000 plus interest equal to $1,200 ($40,000 × 12% × 90/360) for a total of $41,200. This amount will be the basis for the discount which will be equal to $1,030 ($41,200 × 15% × 60/360). As of 9/30/06, the receivable from the bank would include accrued interest revenue of $170 ($1,200 – $1,030).

24. **B**   As of September 1, 2006, two months after receiving the eight-month note, the note had a remaining term of six months. The discount on the note would be calculated by multiplying the maturity value of $200,000 by the discount rate of 10% by the portion of the year remaining (6/12). This results in a discount of $10,000 ($200,000 × 10% × 6/12). The proceeds from discounting will be $200,000 – $10,000 = $190,000.

25. **D**   When receivables are factored and control is surrendered, the transaction is treated as a sale. Under SFAS 140, a transfer in which control is surrendered will not be treated as borrowing. The risk of uncollectible accounts is not retained by the seller in a sale without recourse.

26. **B**   Taylor will receive the value of the receivables ($400,000), reduced by $20,000 for the amount of the holdback ($400,000 × 0.05), $8,000 withheld as fee income ($400,000 × 0.02), and $6,740 withheld as interest expense ($400,000 × 0.15 × 41/365).

Total proceeds equals $400,000 – $8,000 – $6,740 – $20,000 = $365,260.

27. **B**   Under SFAS 140, a sale of receivables with recourse is recorded using a financial components approach because the seller has a continuing involvement. Under this approach, the seller would reduce receivables, recognize assets obtained and liabilities incurred, and record gain or loss.

The entry would be as follows:

Cash	$365,260	
Factor holdback	$20,000	
Loss	$26,740	
Accounts receivable		$400,000
Recourse liability		$12,000

28. **B**   If all receivables are collected, Taylor would eliminate its recourse liability and the corresponding loss. The costs incurred by Taylor would include a fee of $8,000 ($400,000 × 0.02) and interest expense of $6,740 ($400,000 × 0.15 × 41/365) for a total of $14,740.

29. **C**   According to SFAS 140, the transferrer, Beulah, should measure the assets received and liabilities incurred at fair value, not at cost. The transferee, Coyle, should record assets obtained and liabilities incurred at fair value.

30. **C** If all receivables are collected, Cynthia would eliminate its recourse liability and the corresponding loss. The costs incurred by Cynthia would include a fee of $15,000 ($750,000 × 0.02) and interest expense of $12,575 ($750,000 × 0.12 × 51/365) for a total of $27,575.

31. **D** Miwa's bad debt expense for Year 1 is reported as $40,000 or 5% of $800,000 in credit sales. However, had the company estimated that 6% of its ending accounts receivable would prove uncollectible, only a bad debt expense of $26,500 is recognized in Year 1. The expense is $13,500 lower, so reported net income is that much higher.

    The $26,500 is found by determining (1) that the unadjusted balance in the allowance for doubtful accounts is a $5,000 credit (beginning balance of $20,000 less the $15,000 in accounts written off) and (2) that the ending balance in accounts receivable is $525,000 ($340,000 beginning balance plus $800,000 in credit sales less $600,000 in collections and less $15,000 in accounts written off). If 6% of ending receivables are expected to be bad, then the allowance for doubtful accounts should be reported as $31,500 ($525,000 times 6%). Raising the $5,000 credit balance to a $31,500 credit requires the recognition of $26,500 in bad debt expense.

32. **C** Anderson has already received $310,000. Because collections are expected to come up $18,000 short of $360,000 ($360,000 – $342,000), Anderson will not receive the entire $30,000 remaining amount but only $12,000 ($30,000 – $18,000). Thus, Anderson expects to collect $322,000 for its $400,000 in accounts receivable leaving it with a $78,000 loss.

33. **A** For the percent of credit sales method, the expense is the current credit sales of $1,750,000 × 2% or $35,000.

    For the percentage of gross receivables, the expense is the adjustment necessary to establish the proper balance in the allowance for doubtful accounts.

    The allowance account should be adjusted to $45,000 ($900,000 receivable balance × 5%). With a current, unadjusted balance of $16,000 (as a credit), an adjustment of $29,000 is needed which serves as the expense balance.

34. **A** Accounts receivable goes down whereas cash goes up. So neither the total of the current assets or the quick assets is changed. In addition, neither inventory nor cost of goods sold is affected so inventory turnover does not change. However, the receivable turnover is credit sales divided by the average receivables for the period. The collection decreases receivables so that the resulting ratio is higher.

35. **D** The company wrote off $20,000 in accounts receivable during the year as uncollectible. However, instead of going down by $20,000, the allowance balance went up by $2,000. That would only happen if bad debt expense of $22,000 is recognized for the year.

36. **B** Factoring usually refers to selling of accounts receivable, and discounting is a technique for determining the price when a note receivable is sold. Leveraging is a measure of the amount of debts a company. Securitization is a term referring to the sale of a right to future cash flows from an asset.

37. **A** The question of whether the receivables have been sold to the bank or are just serving as security for a loan is based on which party really has control over the receivables. If the receivables are isolated from the company, the bank can sell or pledge the receivables, and the seller has no repurchase agreement, then control over the receivables is clearly in the hands of the buyer. However, if the "selling" company has the right to repurchase the receivables, then that party really has control over these assets and no sale has taken place.

Chapter 2 – Present Value Computations

Study Tip

Decide how many days you will be able to use to prepare for each section of the CPA exam. Divide that number of days into three equal periods of time. During the first third, focus 100% of your time on learning new material. In the second third, allocate 60–70% of your time to new subjects with the remainder for reviewing previously covered topics. For the final days, 30–40% of the coverage should be new areas with the rest for review. When taking the exam, all topics need to be kept fresh in your memory until you walk in to take and pass the CPA exam.

Chapter 2 – Present Value Computations

Overview of Time Value of Money Coverage on the CPA Exam

Time value of money (TVM) is a basic concept that is necessary to understand before moving on to four major topics in which TVM applications are used extensively: (1) bonds payable and bond investments, (2) debt restructure, (3) pensions, and (4) leases. TVM will likely be tested in the context of those topics as opposed to being tested on a stand-alone basis. We will look at the concept of present value of an amount and present value of an annuity, where we discount future amounts back to today's value. We will also examine the concept of future value of an amount and of an annuity in order to calculate the amount to which a sum or series of sums will grow with compound interest.

Tables for present value and future value factors for amounts and ordinary annuities are located in the Appendix of this study manual.

Overview of Present Value (PV)

A. In order for money to have time value, it must be possible to invest it at a positive rate of return.

B. GAAP states that all future contractual cash flows must have an interest factor attached.

1. Interest must be recognized virtually any time that money is paid or received over time.

2. If cash is to be paid over time (a liability exists), interest expense is recognized.

3. If cash is to be received over time (a receivable exists), interest revenue is recognized.

C. The interest factor can be explicitly stated and paid, thus causing no valuation problems, as seen in the following example:

1. A $1,000 note payable pays 9% annual cash interest.

2. $1,000 is the principal and $90 per year is the interest.

3. A present value calculation is not needed, as a reasonable interest rate is stated and paid. The amount of principal and interest are easily distinguishable. The combination of the present value of principal and interest equals the amount to be paid in the future.

D. If a reasonable rate of interest is not stated and paid, the future cash is assumed to be part interest and part principal, as seen in the following example:

1. Land is acquired for a single payment of $2,000 to be made in two years.

2. Part of the $2,000 is viewed as principal (cost of land).

3. Remainder is recorded as interest to be recognized over the 2-year period. Present value is required to separate this interest component.

E. Present value computations are designed to compute the portion of any future cash flows that represent the principal.

 1. If a purchase is made that requires future cash payments, but a reasonable interest rate is not stated and paid, the present value is the cost assigned to the purchase.

 2. For a sale with future payments that do not include a reasonable interest rate, the present value is the amount of the sales revenue to be recorded immediately.

F. One major exception exists in connection with the use of present value.

 1. When all cash flows arising from normal business operations are to be made within one year, present value computations are not used, even if no reasonable interest rate is stated and paid. An example of this is Accounts Receivable.

CALCULATION OF PRESENT VALUE (PV)

A. The present value of a future amount is the amount you would pay now for an amount to be received n periods in the future, given an interest rate of i.

B. PV is based on the following formula:

Present Value = Future Cash Flows × Conversion Rate (or Factor)

C. Future cash flows are usually specified in an agreement or contract.

D. Factor comes from a table provided to you on the CPA exam. More than one factor may be given to you to test your understanding of how to use the following three variables:

 1. Number of time periods.

 2. A reasonable interest rate (sometimes called the yield rate, effective rate, or market rate).

 3. Whether the cash flow is a single amount or an annuity. An annuity is a series of payments, where the payments are always the same amount, they are made on the same day of the period (i.e., always on the same day of the year or month), and the interest rate is the same over the entire series of payments. All these conditions must be met to have an annuity.

E. If future cash flow is a single amount, the factor comes from the "Present Value of $1" table.

F. If future cash flow is an annuity, the "Present Value of Annuity" table is used (more on annuities below).

G. If future cash flow is several unequal payments, "Present Value of $1" table is used:

 1. A separate factor is used for each payment to get individual present values.

 2. These values are added to get total present value.

H. If future cash flow is both a single payment and an annuity, as it would be in many debt notes, the following applies:

 1. The factor for the annuity comes from the annuity table.

2. The factor for the single amount comes from the single amount table.

3. Then, the present values for the annuity and the single amount are added together to arrive at a total present value.

OVERVIEW OF ANNUITIES

A. Ordinary annuity.

1. An ordinary annuity exists when the payments are made at the end of each period. The "start" or "beginning" of the annuity is today, and the first annuity payment is made one period FROM today.

2. Interest on a payable or receivable is paid at the end of the period.

3. Examples: An annual annuity begins January 13, and the first payment is made one year from that date. Subsequent payments are made on January 13. A monthly annuity begins on March 20, and the first payment is on April 20, and on the 20th of each consecutive month. Ordinary annuities can begin on days other than the first day of the year or the first day of the month. They can *start* on any of 365 days. As long as the remaining payments are made on the same day of the month or year, and the first payment is made a month or year from the start date, you have an ordinary annuity.

    Note: When solving a CPA exam question, write down the first day of the period and the last day of the period. Then note when the payment is made. This will help you determine the proper treatment of the annuity.

B. Annuity due.

1. An annuity due exists when the payments are made at the beginning of each period. The "start" or "beginning" of the annuity and the first annuity payment are the same day. As with ordinary annuities, the annuity due can *start* on any day of the period (month, year, quarter, etc.) as long as the first payment is made on the same day.

2. Most rents and leases require payments at the beginning of the period.

C. If necessary, ordinary annuity table factors can be used to solve an annuity due question.

1. Solve the annuity problem as if it were an ordinary annuity.

2. Multiply your answer by 1 plus the interest rate $(1 + i)$.

3. The result is the annuity due value. This technique can be used for solving both future and present value problems.

NET PRESENT VALUE AND FUTURE VALUES

NET PRESENT VALUE (NPV)

A. NPV is used in a capital budgeting context, which is generally tested on BEC, but understanding the concepts of NPV might also earn you some points on the FAR exam.

B. NPV represents the difference between the present value of an asset's future cash flows and its cost.

C. The PV Factor is determined based on a minimum interest rate (a.k.a. required rate of return) that the company wants to earn on the investment.

D. If the present value is higher than the cost of the asset, the NPV will be positive and the asset is considered to be a good acquisition. It will add value to the firm.

CALCULATION OF FUTURE VALUES (FV)

A. You may be asked to calculate the future value or the amount that a set of cash flows will be worth at a specified point in the future, as seen in the following example:

1. $1,000 is deposited in a savings account that adds 5% interest per year (compounded—more on compounding follows).

2. A future value computation can be used to determine the amount in the account at any future point in time.

B. Formula:

Future Value = Cash Flows (Payment Amount) × Factor

1. Factor is based on the number of time periods, a reasonable interest rate, and whether a single amount or an annuity is involved.

2. Factor comes from a future value table on the CPA exam. If the cash flows are in the form of an annuity, you can use the FV of an annuity table factor. If the future cash flows are not in the form of an annuity, then you must do a separate FV of an amount calculation for each one, then sum those to get the FV of the entire series.

C. The future value of $1 is the inverse of the present value of $1.

CALCULATING OTHER VARIABLES USING THE SIMPLE FORMULAS

Sometimes, the hardest part of a time value of money question is to know which factors to use to solve the problem. You will ask yourself (as will the exam) is this PV or FV? Is this a lump sum or annuity? Is this an ordinary annuity or an annuity due? What, exactly, am I solving for: the present or future value, the payment amount of an annuity, the interest rate, or the number of time periods? Remember all of these are variables in any TVM question, and you could be asked to determine any of them. Yes, most of the time, the question asks you to calculate either the present value or the future value, but not always. So, just remember that if you are given a factor or a table of factors on the exam, you will be given some of the variables and asked to solve for an unknown variable. Knowing the present and future value equations will help you organize the known variables and identify the unknown variable for which you will solve.

A. Formula for present value of a lump sum:

Present Value = Future Value in $ × Present Value of $1 Factor

The factor is selected by knowing the interest rate and the associated time period. If the interest rate is given as 3% annually, the time periods are years. If the interest rate is expressed as 3% per quarter, then the time periods are quarters or three months long.

Example:

The question just above was "what is the present value of a future lump sum?" What if the question was "what is the annual interest rate associated with a present value of $100 and a future value of $110 in one year?"

Solution:

Using the formula above, you could calculate the FACTOR.

PV of a lump sum = $FV × FACTOR for PV of lump sum

$100 = $110 × FACTOR

Solving for FACTOR, $100/$110 yields a factor of 0.90909 (a PV factor).

By looking at a PV table for lump sum, under the row for one year, you find the factor 0.90909 under the column for 10%. So, you have used the PV of a lump sum formula to determine the interest rate. Likewise, if you knew the interest rate was 10%, but wanted to know the time period, you could look at the same table under 10% and you would find 0.90909 under the line for one year. Using that one simple formula, you can calculate any of its components if you know the others.

B. Formula for future value of a lump sum.

Future Value = Present Value in $ × Future Value of $1 Factor

The factor is selected by knowing the interest rate and the associated time period. If the interest rate is given as 3% annually, the time periods are years. If the interest rate is expressed as 3% per quarter, then the time periods are quarters or three months long.

Example:

The previous question was "what is the future value of a present lump sum?" What if the question was "what is the annual interest rate associated with a present value of $100 and a future value of $110 in one year?"

Solution:

Using the formula above, you could calculate the FACTOR.

FV of a lump sum = $PV × FACTOR for FV of lump sum or $110 = $100 × FACTOR

Solving for FACTOR, $110/$100 yields a factor of 1.1 (a FV factor).

By looking at a FV table for lump sum, under the row for one year, you find the factor 1.1 under the column for 10%. So, you have used the FV of a lump sum formula to determine the interest rate. Likewise, if you knew the interest rate was 10%, but wanted to know the time period, you could look at the same table under 10% and you would find 1.1 under the line for one year. Using that one simple formula, you can calculate any of its components if you know the others.

Did you also notice that the present value factor is less than 1 and the future value factor is more than 1? PV is a process of removing interest, making an amount smaller. FV is a process of adding interest, making an amount larger. Remembering this fact will help you check yourself on the exam.

C. Formula for present value of an annuity:

Present Value = Payment Amount in $ × Present Value of Annuity Factor

The factor is selected by knowing the interest rate and the associated time period. If the interest rate is given as 3% annually, the time periods are years. If the interest rate is expressed as 3% per quarter, then the time periods are quarters or three months long.

Example:

The question might be: "what is the payment amount associated with a given present value of an annuity?" Here, you would know the amount of money you have available (PV) and you want to know, for example, "how much can I pay myself as a retirement benefit if I know the interest rate and the number of payments I want to pay?"

Solution:

Use the same formula as above, but the "present value of an annuity" and the "present value of an annuity factor" will be the known information, and you will solve the formula for the unknown, or the payment amount. Remember, in this case, you must realize which formula to use. This is the key to solving the problem. This is still a present value of an annuity problem, but the unknown is the payment.

D. Formula for future value of an annuity:

Future Value = Payment Amount in $ × Future Value of Annuity Factor

The factor is selected by knowing the interest rate and the associated time period. If the interest rate is given as 3% annually, the time periods are years. If the interest rate is expressed as 3% per quarter, then the time periods are quarters or three months long.

Example:

Assume the question is: "what is the payment amount associated with a given future value of an annuity?" Here, you would know the amount of money you expect to have available at a future date, so you want to calculate the payment amount you need to deposit into the bank if you know the interest rate and the number of payments you want to deposit. This is a future value of an annuity problem, where you want to calculate the payment.

Solution:

Use the same formula as above, but the "future value of an annuity" and the "future value of an annuity factor" will be the known information, and you will solve the formula for the unknown, or the payment amount. Remember, in this case, you must realize which formula to use. This is the key to solving the problem. This is still a future value of an annuity problem, but the unknown is the payment.

CALCULATIONS USING ANNUITY FACTORS

A. If the total amount comes at the end of a series of payments, it is a future value of annuity situation. The process of computing future values involves projecting the cash flows forward, on the basis of a reasonable compound interest rate, to the end of the investment's life (i.e., this adds the applicable interest to the principal that will be repaid).

B. If the total amount comes at the beginning of the series of payments, it is a present value of annuity situation. The computation of present value works in the opposite direction of future value—it brings the cash flows from an investment back to the beginning of the investment's life on the basis of a reasonable compound rate of return (i.e., subtracts interest).

C. Drawing a time line for the cash flows in each question is often a good idea as it will help you determine if you need to solve for a present value or a future value.

1. A cash flow that occurs in the present (today) is put at time 0.

2. Cash outflows (payments) are given a negative sign.

3. Cash inflows (receipts) are given a positive sign.

4. Once the cash flows are assigned to a timeline, they may be "moved" to the beginning of the investment period to calculate the present value through a process called discounting.

5. Or they may be "moved" to the end of the period to calculate the future value using the compounding process.

Figure 1: Sample Timeline for Future Value

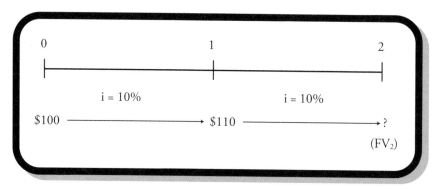

(2 Periods, 10% Interest, Lump Sum, Calculate the Future Value of $100)

COMPOUND INTEREST

A. When interest is compounded more than once a year, the following two extra steps are needed:

1. Multiply n by the number of times interest is compounded annually. This will give you the total number of interest periods ("n" refers to number of years).

2. Divide the annual interest rate, i, by the number of times interest is compounded annually. This will give you the appropriate interest rate for each interest period.

When an investment is subjected to compound interest, the growth in the value of the investment from period to period not only reflects the interest earned on the original principal amount but also interest earned on the previous period's interest earnings—**the interest on interest**.

B. Example:

If the 10% was compounded semiannually, the amount of $100 at the end of one year would be $110.25 instead of $110. The extra $0.25 is 5% of $5 interest earned in the first half of the year.

$100 × 1.10 = $110, if interest of 10% is compounded annually.

$100 × 1.05 × 1.05 = $110.25, if interest of 10% is compounded semiannually.

QUESTIONS: PRESENT VALUE COMPUTATIONS

1. On March 15, 2006, Dominique Corp. (Dominique) adopted a plan to accumulate $1,000,000 by September 1, 2010. Dominique plans to make four equal annual deposits to a fund that will earn interest at 10% compounded annually. Dominique made the first deposit on September 1, 2006.

    Future value and future amount factors are as follows:

Future value of $1 at 10% for four periods	1.46
Future amount of ordinary annuity of $1 at 10% for four periods	4.64
Future amount of annuity in advance (annuity due) of $1 at 10% for four periods	5.11

    Dominique should make four annual deposits (rounded) of:
    A. $146,000.
    B. $195,700.
    C. $215,500.
    D. $250,000.

2. On July 1, 2006, Marcy Darcy (Darcy) signed an agreement to operate as a franchisee of Qwicky Mart, Inc. for an initial franchise fee of $60,000. Of this amount, $20,000 was paid when the agreement was signed and the balance is payable in four equal annual payments of $10,000 beginning July 1, 2007.

    The agreement provides that the down payment is not refundable and no future services are required of the franchisor. Darcy's credit rating indicates that she can borrow money at 14% for a loan of this type. Information on present and future value factors is as follows:

Present value of $1 at 14% for four periods	0.59
Future amount of $1 at 14% for four periods	1.69
Present value of an ordinary annuity of $1 at 14% for four periods	2.91

    Darcy should record the acquisition cost of the franchise on July 1, 2006 at:
    A. $43,600.
    B. $49,100.
    C. $60,000.
    D. $67,600.

3. On November 1, 2006, a company purchased a new machine that it does not have to pay for until November 1, 2008. The total payment on November 1, 2008, will include both principal and interest. Assuming interest at a 10% rate, the cost of the machine would be the total payment multiplied by what time value of money concept?
    A. Present value of $1.
    B. Present value of annuity of $1.
    C. Future value of $1.
    D. Future value of annuity of $.

4. On December 31, 2005, Roberge Co. (Roberge) issued a $10,000 face value note payable to Wilma Co. (Wilma) in exchange for services rendered to Roberge. The note, made at usual trade terms, is due in nine months and bears interest, payable at maturity, at the annual rate of 3%. The market interest rate is 8%. The compound interest factor of $1 due in nine months at 8% is 0.944. At what amount should the note payable be reported in Roberge's December 31, 2005 balance sheet?
   A. $9,440.
   B. $9,652.
   C. $10,000.
   D. $10,300.

5. Leif Co. (Leif) purchased from Ove Co. (Ove) a $20,000, 8%, 5-year note that required five equal annual year-end payments of $5,009. The note was discounted to yield a 9% return to Leif. At the date of purchase, Leif recorded the note at its present value of $19,485. What should be the total interest revenue earned by Leif over the life of this note?
   A. $5,045.
   B. $5,560.
   C. $8,000.
   D. $9,000.

6. A company recently took out a $25,000 loan with interest payable at the rate of 9%, compounded annually. The loan is to be paid off in one lump sum, at the end of three years. Time value of money factors are listed below. Given that it is to include both principal and interest, the amount of the loan payment will be *closest* to which of the following?

   FV of $1 @ 9% for 3 years = 1.295
   PV of $1 @ 9% for 3 years = 0.7722

   A. $32,375.
   B. $27,250.
   C. $31,750.
   D. $34,000.

7. On January 1, 2005, Ott Company sold goods to Fox Company. Fox signed a non-interest-bearing note requiring payment of $60,000 annually for seven years. The first payment was made on January 1, 2005. The prevailing rate of interest for this type of note at date of issuance was 10%. Information on present value factors is as follows:

Periods	Present value of $1 at 10%	Present value of ordinary annuity of $1 at 10%
6	0.56	4.36
7	0.51	4.87

   Ott should record the sales revenue in January 2005 of:
   A. $321,600.
   B. $292,200.
   C. $261,600.
   D. $214,200.

8. What's the maximum an investor should be willing to pay for an annuity that will pay out $10,000 at the beginning of each of the next 10 years, given the investor wants to earn 12.5%, compounded annually?

	9 Years	10 Years
PV ordinary annuity of $1@12.5%	5.2285	5.5364
PV annuity due of $1@12.5%	5.8820	6.2285

    A. $62,285.
    B. $55,364.
    C. $52,285.
    D. $69,620.

9. What is the value in five years of $100 invested today at an interest rate of 10% compounded quarterly?

n	i	FV of $1
5	10.0%	1.6105
10	5.0%	1.6289
20	2.5%	1.6386

    A. $163.86.
    B. $150.00.
    C. $159.33.
    D. $161.05.

10. An annuity will pay four annual payments of $100, with the first payment to be received three years from now. If the interest rate is 12% per year, what is the present value of this annuity?

n	PV of $1 @ 12%	PV of an ordinary annuity of $1 @ 12%
2	0.7972	1.6901
3	0.7118	2.4018
4	0.6355	3.0373
5	0.5674	3.6048
6	0.5066	4.1114
7	0.4523	4.5638

    A. $242.13.
    B. $303.73.
    C. $180.93.
    D. $400.00.

11. On January 1, Year 1, the Stafford Company sells a piece of land with a cost of $600,000 to a buyer for $900,000. However, the $900,000 amount will not be collected until December 31, Year 2. No other payment will be made although a reasonable annual interest rate for this type of transaction is normally 10%. The present value of $1 in two years at an annual interest rate of 10% is assumed to be 0.83. The present value of an ordinary annuity of $1 over two years at an annual interest rate of 10% is assumed to be 1.74. What total income effect should Stafford recognize in Year 1?
    A. $147,000.
    B. $221,700.
    C. $300,000.
    D. $390,000.

12. Equipment is bought by a company for $100,000 on January 1, Year 1. It is to be used for ten years. A $60,000 payment is made in exactly one year and the remaining $40,000 payment is to be made in two years. A reasonable annual interest rate is 10%. The present value of an ordinary annuity for one year at a 10% annual rate is 0.909 whereas the present value of an ordinary annuity for two years at a 10% annual rate is 1.735. The present value of a single dollar in one year at a 10% annual rate is 0.909, whereas the present value of a single dollar in two years at a 10% annual rate is 0.826. If the straight-line method is being used and the asset has no residual value, what is the amount of depreciation expense for Year 2?
   A. $8,675.
   B. $8,692.
   C. $8,758.
   D. $10,000.

13. A company sells a 2-year bond with a face value of $100,000 and a cash stated annual interest rate of 10%. The interest is paid at the end of each year. Initially, no one will buy the bond so it has to be sold at an amount that will yield an annual interest rate of 12%. The present value of an ordinary annuity for one year at a 10% annual rate is 0.909 and at 12% is 0.893, whereas the present value of an ordinary annuity for two years at a 10% annual rate is 1.735 and at 12% is 1.690. The present value of a single dollar in one year at a 10% annual rate is 0.909 and at 12% is 0.893 whereas the present value of a single dollar in two years at a 10% annual rate is 0.826 and at 12% is 0.797. For how much will the bond be sold?
   A. $95,340.
   B. $96,600.
   C. $97,070.
   D. $97,800.

Use the following information to answer Questions 14 and 15.

A company owns land with a cost of $65,000. It is sold to another company for $100,000 to be paid in exactly two years. The buyer believes that an annual interest rate of 10% is reasonable for this type of transaction. The seller believes that an annual interest rate of 12% is reasonable for this type of transaction. The present value of an ordinary annuity for one year at a 10% annual rate is 0.909 and at 12% is 0.893, whereas the present value of an ordinary annuity for two years at a 10% annual rate is 1.735 and at 12% is 1.690. The present value of a single dollar in one year at a 10% annual rate is 0.909 and at 12% is 0.893 whereas the present value of a single dollar in two years at a 10% annual rate is 0.826 and at 12% is 0.797.

14. What amount of gain does the seller recognize on this transaction?
   A. $14,700.
   B. $15,800.
   C. $16,100.
   D. $17,600.

15. What is the cost of this land to the buyer?
   A. $65.000.
   B. $79,700.
   C. $82,600.
   D. $89,300.

ANSWERS: PRESENT VALUE COMPUTATIONS

1. **B**   The desired fund balance on September 1, 2010 ($1,000,000) is a future amount. The series of four equal annual deposits is an annuity in advance, rather than an ordinary annuity, because the last deposit (9/1/09) is made one year prior to the date the future amount is needed.

   Draw a picture for clarification:

9/1/06	9/1/07	9/1/08	9/1/09	9/1/10
$Pmnt	$Pmnt	$Pmnt	$Pmnt	Total $1 million End of Period

   Therefore, these are beginning-of-year payments. The following simple formula for this is the future value of an annuity due:

   FV = Payment Amount × Factor

   To solve for the payment amount, you can use the following:

   $1,000,000 = ?Pmnt Amt? × 5.11 (annuity due, four periods)

   Therefore, the deposit (or payment) amount is computed by dividing the *future amount* by the *factor for the future amount of an annuity in advance.*

   $1,000,000 / 5.11 = $195,700

2. **B**   The requirement is to determine the acquisition cost of a franchise. The cost of this franchise is the down payment of $20,000 plus the present value of the four equal annual payments of $10,000. The annual payments represent an ordinary annuity since the first payment is made one year after the agreement is signed. The $10,000 annual payment is multiplied by the present value factor of 2.91. Therefore, the franchise cost is $49,100 ($20,000 + $29,100).

3. **A**   The requirement is to determine what time value of money concept would be used to determine the cost of a machine when a payment (principal plus interest) is to be made in two years.

   Answer A is correct because the cost of the machine is to be recorded immediately; therefore, the cost of the present value of a lump-sum payment would be used.

   Answer B is incorrect because a lump-sum payment is involved, not an annuity. Answer C is incorrect because a future amount would be used in computing the payment and not the cost of the machine. Also, a lump-sum payment is involved and not an annuity. Answer D is incorrect because a future amount would be used in computing the payment and not the cost.

4. **C**   According to GAAP, receivables and payables are subject to present value measurement techniques and interest imputation, if necessary, with certain exceptions. One exception is "normal course of business" receivables and payables maturing in less than one year. Therefore, this note payable, due in nine months at usual trade terms, would be reported at face value ($10,000) rather than at present value ($10,225 × 0.944 = $9,652).

5. **B**   The total interest revenue earned over the life of the note equals the excess of the cash received over the cash paid to acquire the note. The cash received over the five years is $25,045 (five receipts of $5,009 each). The cash paid to acquire the $20,000 note was $19,485. Therefore, the total interest revenue is $5,560 ($25,045 – $19,485).

6. **A** $32,375

This can be solved with either the PV or FV of $1 equation, using the correct factor:

PV = FV × PV Factor

So: $25,000 = FV × 0.7722 = $32,375

Or, $25,000/0.7722 = $32,375

(Start with the PV equation, use the PV factor, but solve for the FV.)

OR, alternatively, use the following formula:

FV = PV × FV Factor

Therefore, FV = $25,000 × 1.295 = $32,375

(You start with the FV equation, use the FV factor, and solve for the FV.)

7. **A** The sales price is equivalent to the present value of the note payments:

Present value of first payment	$60,000
Present value of last six payments:	
$60,000 × 4.36	<u>$261,600</u>
Sales price	$321,600

Note that the present value of annuity factors which are given are "ordinary" annuity factors. Therefore, the present value of the first payment must be considered separately.

If you were given the present value of an annuity due (or annuity in advance) factors, this would be a 7-period annuity due and you could simply multiply $60,000 by the factor for the 7-period annuity due.

8. **A** You can solve this in two ways: (1) an ordinary annuity that started a year ago, so that today's payment is the first "end-of-year" payment, or (2) an annuity due that started today.

Remember: The annuity due corresponds to payments made at the first of the period. An ordinary annuity corresponds to payments made at the end of the period. The "beginning" or "start" date of an annuity due is the same as the date of the first payment. The "beginning" or "start" date of an ordinary annuity is one year before the first payment.

You can solve by using the ordinary annuity factor for nine periods and adding the first payment as follows:

PV Ordinary Annuity = (10,000 × 5.2285) + 10,000 = $62,285

Or, you can solve by using the annuity due factor for ten periods:

PV Annuity Due = 10,000 × 6.2285 = $62,285

9. **A** This is a future value of a single sum problem, where the challenge is to select the proper interest rate and periods to use in the table of factors. Because the interest is compounded quarterly, you must divide the 10% by four to obtain 2.5%. Then, you take the five years and multiply by four (four quarters in a year) to obtain the number of periods of 20. This is a 2.5%, 20-period problem, so the factor is 1.6386.

FV = 100 × 1.6386 = $163.86

10. **A**   This is a good place to analyze your timeline very carefully:

Today is Point 0. In three years, the payments will begin. There are four payments.

Today	1 year later	2 years later	3 years later	4 years later	5 years later	6 years later
What is PV?		beginning of 4-pmnt annuity	1st pmnt	2nd pmnt	3rd pmnt	4th pmnt

Viewing this as an ordinary annuity, taking the present value of that ordinary annuity would place you at the point "two years from today." (Remember, the first payment is "three years from today," so "three years from today" is the end of the year that begins "two years from today.") Then, you still need to discount that PV of an ordinary annuity back two more years in order to obtain the present value of today. So, this is a 2-part problem: (1) take the PV of the 4-period annuity, yielding a lump sum, then (2) discount back that lump sum two more years to get the PV as of today.

First, solve for present value of the 4-period ordinary annuity (as of "two years later"): N = 4, PMT = 100, interest rate = 12%, PVA factor is 3.0373. So, PV of the annuity = $100 × 3.0373 = $303.33.

Now discount back two years: N = 2, interest rate = 12%, FV = $303.73, PV = 303.73 × 0.7972 = $242.13.

Note: While the first payment occurs in three years, that payment is actually at the end of the first year of the annuity. So, the beginning of the annuity is two years from today; the payment is three years from today. Thus, by taking the present value of the annuity, you are at the beginning of the 4-year-period of the annuity, which is two years from today. (The third year from today corresponds with the first year of the annuity.)

11. **B**   Because the cash flows are not being collected within one year and because no reasonable cash interest rate is being included in the payments, the receivable must be recorded at its present value of $747,000 ($900,000 future cash collection × 0.83). The land had a cost of $600,000; therefore, Stafford recognizes an immediate gain of $147,000.

At the end of Year 1, interest revenue of $74,700 ($747,000 × 10%) must also be recognized on the amount of the receivable for the period. The gain of $147,000 plus the interest of $74,700 gives a total increase in income of $221,700.

12. **C**   Because a reasonable interest rate is not being paid, the equipment and the liability must be recorded at the present value of the cash flows with is $87,580.

$60,000 × 0.909 = $54,540

$40,000 × 0.826 = $33,040 for a total of $87,580

Using the straight-line method of depreciation over a 10-year life with no residual value gives annual depreciation of $8,758.

13. **B**   The contractual cash flows are $10,000 per year for two years based on the 10% stated rate and the $100,000 face value. In addition, the company has to make a single payment of $100,000 at the end of two years.

The bond will be sold at a present value amount that equals 12% annual interest.

$10,000 × 1.690 = $16,900 and $100,000 × 0.797 = $79,700 for a total of $96,600

14. **A**   The seller believes a reasonable interest rate is 12% per year. Thus, the present value of the future cash flows in this contract is $100,000 × 0.797, or $79,700. Because the cost of the land had only been $65,000, the seller has a gain of $14,700.

15. **C**   The buyer believes a reasonable interest rate is 10% per year. Thus, the present value of the $100,000 payment in two years is $100,000 × 0.826, or $82,600.

CHAPTER 3 – LAND, BUILDINGS, AND EQUIPMENT

STUDY TIP

No matter how busy you get preparing for the CPA exam, make time to exercise several times each week. Even 15 minutes of walking around your neighborhood every other day will help you release tension and keep your mind clear. Continue to take good care of yourself during this review process. Your ability to concentrate will improve and careless mistakes will disappear. Get enough exercise so you can maximize the efficiency of your study time.

CHAPTER 3 – LAND, BUILDINGS, AND EQUIPMENT

OVERVIEW OF THE LAND, BUILDINGS, AND EQUIPMENT COVERAGE ON THE CPA EXAM

In thinking about land, buildings, and equipment, it is useful to think of the following 3-step timeline as your framework:

1. Acquire land, buildings, and equipment (issues relate to acquisition cost determination).

2. Use of land, buildings, and equipment (issues are recording depreciation; recording additional expenditures associated with use, either as revenue or capital expenses; impairment in value).

3. Disposal of land, buildings, and equipment (by sale, trade, or otherwise).

ACQUIRING LAND, BUILDINGS, AND EQUIPMENT

ACQUISITION COST

A. Capitalized expenditures are classified on the balance sheet as tangible and long-lived assets that are being used to generate revenues.

B. Period of use will exceed one year.

C. Tangible property includes the following:

    1. Land.

    2. Buildings.

    3. Equipment.

    4. Any other property that physically exists.

D. Tangible property is also referred to as *operational assets* and *property, plant, and equipment.*

EXPENDITURES: CAPITAL VS. REVENUE EXPENDITURES

A. For new acquisitions, all normal and necessary costs to acquire the asset and get it into the condition and location to be used will be capitalized.

B. *Capitalization* means the costs are added to an asset account (balance sheet) rather than an expense account (income statement). Capitalized amounts are subsequently allocated to expense (depreciated) over time (more on this later).

C. For an asset already in use, any new expenditure on that asset is capitalized only if it provides additional future benefits. Those expenditures that benefit only the current year are expensed. Items that are immediately expensed are called *revenue expenditures.*

D. To be capitalized and then depreciated, an expenditure must make the asset "bigger, better, or longer." In other words, the asset must have increased or improved functionality, make better products, or have a longer life. Following are three examples of this concept.

1. The estimated useful life of the asset is extended beyond the original estimation (i.e., expenditures for a major overhaul of a bread oven in a commercial bread bakery might extend the life of the oven beyond the original estimate).

2. The asset becomes more efficient or productive, meaning it can produce higher quantities or operate at a lower cost (i.e., a new laser product sorter might be added to a machine, replacing human efforts to sort out defective products. This would speed up the process).

3. Quality of the asset's output is improved (i.e., upgrades to equipment for a textile company, which enable it to produce a higher thread count sheet).

E. If an expenditure merely maintains the asset at its anticipated level of productivity and length of life, the following occurs:

1. The cost is not capitalized on the balance sheet.

2. Instead, it is recorded as a maintenance expense on the income statement.

   Be familiar with the following terms for capitalizable expenditures:

   a. An *addition* is a new major component of the asset, such as an additional room on a building, that did not exist before.

   b. An *improvement* is the replacement of a major component of the asset, such as a replacement of the air conditioning system for a building. Improvements are recorded by using one of the following methods:
      - *Substitution*—remove the old air conditioner and record the new one.
      - *Reduction of accumulated depreciation* on the old air conditioner.
      - In either case, the cost of the new item will be depreciated over time.

   c. A *rearrangement* is a restructuring of an asset that does not extend its life, but creates a new type of benefit. Relocation of a company to another city is an example.

   d. *Materiality.* In all these cases, immaterial amounts will most likely be expensed as incurred.

Items Typically Capitalized for Land, Buildings, and Equipment

A. Invoice price (less any discounts).

B. Sales taxes.

C. Cost of delivery.

D. Cost of installation.

E. Any costs incurred in razing an old building are added to the acquisition cost of the land on which the old building formerly stood. The cost of razing the old building is accounted for as a cost of getting the land ready to be used. (On the CPA exam, candidates often miss this. They mistakenly put the cost of razing the land into the building account. This is incorrect.)

Self-Constructed Fixed Assets: Capitalized Costs

A. Direct materials.

B. Direct construction labor.

C. Variable overhead.

D. A fair share of fixed overhead.

E. Capitalized interest (will be discussed later).

F. On the exam, items A–D above would most likely be tested conceptually. Item E, capitalized interest, would be tested conceptually and computationally.

Accounting for the Cost of Land to be Used as an Office or Plant Site

A. Classified as a long-term asset under land, buildings, and equipment.

B. Cost of land will include the following:

　1. Basic land cost.

　2. Costs of acquisition of the land, such as broker's commissions, title insurance.

　3. Costs of improvements that will have *unlimited* useful life, such as clearing and grading of land.

C. It is extremely important to remember that land costs are *not* depreciated over time! However, land improvements that have *limited* useful lives, such as sidewalks and fences, are depreciated over their useful lives. These amounts are not technically included in the cost of land. They would appear in a separate account called *Land Improvements.*

Interest Capitalization for Self-Constructed Assets

A. In what cases are interest costs capitalized?

　1. Interest costs incurred in the construction of land, buildings, and equipment categorized as "operational assets" (i.e., assets to be used by the company that is self-constructing them).

　2. Interest costs incurred in the construction of inventory specifically being built for a customer (e.g., a major project requiring a long period for completion, such as a road).

　Note: Interest is not capitalized on the production of regularly manufactured inventory items that are produced repetitively and in large quantities. (No interest is capitalized on the production of food products or diapers.)

B. Again, the interest cost is added to the asset account rather than being recorded as interest expense.

C. The amount of interest to be capitalized each year is calculated by multiplying the weighted average accumulated expenditures (WAAE) to date times an interest rate.

　1. If specific debt is incurred to finance the construction, the interest rate on that debt is used in this computation.

　2. Otherwise, the weighted average interest rate for all of the company's outstanding debt is used.

3. If the calculation of capitalized interest gives a figure that is more than the actual interest incurred during the period, only the actual interest incurred is capitalized.

4. WAAE is an amount calculated by *weighting* the expenditures on the project by a fraction representing the portion of the year remaining when those expenditures are made. For example, an amount spent on July 1 would be weighted by a fraction of 6/12 (months remaining divided by total months of the year). In other words, the expenditures are "outstanding for half of the year."

5. If the project is completed before the end of the year, the fraction is different. The numerator will be months remaining until the end of the project divided by number of months in the project. Example: if the project is January 1 through August 31, and an expenditure is made on March 1, the fraction would be 6/8, because the project is 8 months long, and the expenditure was made when 6 months were remaining.

D. The amount of interest to be capitalized cannot exceed total actual interest costs incurred during the entire reporting period.

E. Interest earned on temporarily invested borrowings may not be offset against interest to be capitalized.

F. Interest capitalization begins when the first expenditure is made and ceases when the asset is substantially complete and ready for use, or when interest is no longer being incurred on either the project or other debt.

G. Numerical example:

Example:

During the current year, a company has been constructing a building to be used for its production facility. The *average cost* of the building in process is $1,000,000. Two other ways you may see this on the exam are as follows:

1. Weighted average accumulated expenditures (WAAE) are $1,000,000.

2. Spending on the building was a total of $2,000,000, incurred evenly throughout the year, meaning an *average* of [$0 at the beginning of the year + $2,000,000 by the end of the year]/2 = $1,000,000.

The company has borrowed $500,000 at 5% interest to finance this construction. For several years now, the company has had $3,000,000 of 10% debentures and $600,000 of 8% debentures outstanding.

Calculate the amount of interest to be capitalized (added to the cost of the building) and the total interest expense to be reported on the income statement.

Solution:

Capitalized interest is calculated using the interest rate on funds borrowed to finance the actual construction, as long as the WAAE is equal to or less than the actual amount of construction borrowing. In this case, the WAAE is $1,000,000, and the construction debt is only half that. Therefore, we must calculate the weighted average interest rate on all other debt, as follows:

$3,000,000 × 10% = $300,000 interest payable for one year

$600,000 × 8% = $48,000 interest payable for one year

[$300,000 + $48,000]/[$3,000,000 + $600,000] = $348,000/$3,600,000

Equals 9.7% weighted average rate

What interest rates are used in this case?

Interest on construction debt: ($500,000 × 0.05) = $25,000

Interest on debentures: ($500,000 × 0.097) = $48,500

Total capitalized interest on WAAE of $1 million = $73,500

Note: The $500,000 of the actual construction loan plus an additional $500,000 from the debentures makes up the total WAAE of $1,000,000. So, given WAAE of $1 million, half is multiplied by the interest rate on the construction loan and the remainder is multiplied by the weighted average rate.

total interest expense = total interest paid – capitalized interest

$25,000 + $300,000 + $48,000 – $73,500 = $299,500

The total interest expense is what is reported on the income statement. Note the difference between the actual interest paid and the calculation of the capitalized interest. Actual interest is based on the actual loan amounts and the actual rates, not the weighted average rate. It's only the capitalized interest that uses a weighted average rate, and that only happens when the specific construction loans are less than WAAE AND there are multiple loans in addition to the construction loan.

If the company's only debt was the $500,000, 5% construction loan, then only the interest paid on that debt ($25,000) would be capitalized.

If the project goes into a *second year*, interest capitalization is calculated much the same as in the first year. The major difference to remember for the second year is that [Year 1's WAAE + Year 1's capitalized interest] will become an "expenditure" for Year 2, assumed to have been made on the first day of the year for the purposes of calculating Year 2's WAAE. Otherwise, calculations are the same as for the first year. Also, remember that if the project is under construction for less than 12 months, the fraction to determine WAAE will have a denominator of less than 12. We discussed this earlier in item C-5.

Theoretical Reasons for Interest Capitalization

A. To reflect the true or full acquisition cost of the asset.

B. To match the asset's cost with revenue of future periods that benefit from its use, because the capitalized interest will become a part of depreciation expense.

Accounting for Assets Received as Gifts

A. SFAS 116 requires that donated assets received from an unrelated party be initially recorded on the balance sheet at their fair value (FV). FV can be obtained from a ready market price or from an appraisal.

B. There is a corresponding increase to a donated revenue account on the income statement. (The journal entry, therefore, is debit Asset Account and credit Donated Revenue, for the fair value of the asset. Assets increase and net income increases.)

C. Donated assets are considered to be the equivalent of a donation of cash, where the corporation uses the cash to buy an asset.

D. Once received and put into use, donated assets are depreciated the same as assets purchased or developed.

Asset Retirement Obligation Provisions of SFAS 143

A. The ownership of some tangible, long-lived assets creates a liability that must be paid at the eventual point of retirement. These are called *asset retirement obligations.*

B. For example, the acquisition of an off-shore oil or gas drilling facility may necessitate its eventual removal because of legal requirements.

C. As soon as this retirement obligation becomes *probable*, its current fair value must be determined and recognized as a liability, offset by a debit to the asset itself. (The obligation must be a legal requirement, and may become probable at acquisition or at some point during its useful life.)

D. If a current fair value cannot be ascertained, the present value of the future obligation is recognized as the debt.

   1. A credit-adjusted risk-free interest rate is used to determine the present value, as well as the computation of the interest expense, that should be recognized each period.

   2. The credit-adjusted risk-free interest rate is calculated as the current interest rate for a U.S. government obligation for the time period, adjusted upward based on the credit rating of the company.

   3. If present value is used, the future cash flows are determined based on a weighted average. For example, if there is a 40% chance the obligation will cost $1 million and a 60% chance it will cost $2 million, then the company would use $1.6 million (40% of $1 million plus 60% of $2 million).

E. The liability that is recognized also serves to increase the capitalized cost of the asset. This increases the annual recognition of depreciation expense.

F. Example of asset retirement liability:

   Jones Mining recently purchased a silver mine. Acquisition, exploration and development costs totaled $5.6 million, and were paid in cash. Once the silver is all extracted (in about five years), Jones is obligated to restore the land to its original condition. The company's accountant has developed three different possibilities for the cash flows expected to be required for the restoration costs, shown in the following table. The company's credit-adjusted, risk-free rate of interest is 6%. Prepare the journal entry to record this acquisition.

   Possible Restoration Costs

Alternative 1	$500,000	20% probability
Alternative 2	$550,000	45% probability
Alternative 3	$650,000	35% probability

   First, we must calculate the cost of the asset.

   Cost of silver mine:

Acquisition, exploration, and development	$5,600,000
Restoration costs	429,675 †
	$6,029,675

   † $500,000 × 20% = $100,000
           550,000 × 45% = $247,500
           650,000 × 35% = $227,500
                     $575,000 × 0.74726* = $429,675   *Present value of $1, n = 5, i = 6%

Journal Entry:

Intangible Asset—Silver Mine	$6,029,675	
Asset Retirement Liability		$429,675
Cash		$5,600,000

Each year, interest is accrued on the Retirement Liability at the rate of 6% (debit interest expense, credit asset retirement liability).

When the mine reaches the end of its useful life, a journal entry will be made to reduce the liability and credit various accounts required to complete the restoration process. If the actual costs to restore the land exceed the originally-recorded liability, the journal entry will reflect a retirement loss to balance the entry. If the actual costs are less than the originally-recorded liability, the journal entry will reflect a retirement gain.

Acquisition and Sale of Assets with Payments Made or Received Over Time

A. Assets may be acquired (or sold) for *future* cash payments (receipts).

   1. A payable is created by a purchase.

   2. A receivable is created by a sale.

B. If a reasonable interest rate is not stated and paid, the cost of the asset, or revenue if it is a sale, will be the present value of the cash flows based on a reasonable interest rate.

"Basket Purchases" or Lump-Sum Purchases

A. Assets can be acquired in a "basket purchase" or lump-sum purchase. When several assets are acquired for one lump-sum amount, and the purchase price of each one is not separately stated, the lump-sum purchase price should be allocated to the assets according to each asset's fair value as a percentage of the total fair value of the "basket." For example, Johnson Publishers acquires two printing presses for $100,000. The fair value of one is $50,000, and the fair value of the other is $60,000. The first press is recorded at ($50,000/$110,000) × $100,000. The second is recorded at ($60,000/$110,000) × $100,000.

Discounts Arising on the Purchase or Sale of Assets with Future Cash Payments

A. The asset (or sales revenue) is recorded at the present value of the future cash flows.

B. The payable (or receivable) is recorded in the amount of the total undiscounted cash flow.

C. A discount is set up for the difference.

   1. This is a contra-account to the payable (or receivable).

   2. The discount represents the portion of the total cash flows that is viewed as interest rather than principal. (Remember, interest is not a part of the cost of the asset purchased, nor a part of the revenue from the asset sold. It is either an expense or an income item reported separately as interest.)

   3. As an alternative, the payable (or receivable) could be reported as a single number net of the discount.

D. Over the life of the payable/receivable, the discount will gradually be reclassified (amortized) as interest.

   1. Reducing the discount causes an increase in the net balance of the payable/receivable.

2. If the payable/receivable is shown as a single net figure, recognition of interest within the cash flows increases the payable/receivable balance being reported.

E. Interest to be recognized each period is computed by multiplying the payable/receivable net of the discount times a reasonable interest rate. This is referred to as the effective rate method.

F. As an alternative, if the results are not materially different, the *straight-line method* can be used to compute interest expense. Here, the discount is divided evenly over the time period that payment will be made.

G. Example:

On January 2, Year 1, Marshall Co. acquires an asset for three annual payments of $100,000, payable on January 2 of Year 1, Year 2, and Year 3. Interest is stated in the contract at 10%, payable on the same dates as the principal payments. The cost of the asset to Marshall is $300,000, because the interest is stated separately and recorded as interest expense each year. However, if Marshall acquired the same asset with three $100,000 payments on the first day of years 1, 2, and 3, and *no interest* was mentioned in the contract, Marshall would need to take the present value of the three payments at a *reasonable interest rate* to determine the purchase price, as follows:

Cost of Asset = $100,000 paid immediately, thus no discounting

Plus, Present Value of $100,000 to be paid in one year at x% interest,

Plus, Present Value of $100,000 to be paid in two years at x% interest, where x% is the "reasonable interest rate"

H. More details about present value calculations can be found in Chapter 2, which discusses the time value of money.

USE OF LAND, BUILDINGS, AND EQUIPMENT

DEPRECIATION

A. *Depreciation* is the process of assigning or allocating the cost of a fixed asset to expense for the years in which it is used to generate revenues. It must be done in some systematic and rational way that will be determined by applying the matching concept.

B. It should also be noted that although depreciation expense appears on the income statement, it has no impact on the direct method statement of cash flows, because depreciation is a non-cash expense. However, on the indirect method statement of cash flows, depreciation expense is added back to net income in adjusting net income to cash flows for operating activities.

C. The depreciation amount is computed and recorded at the end of each year in which the asset is in use. Depreciation expense is also recorded at the date an asset is sold, traded, or otherwise disposed of, in order to allocate the cost of the asset to the partial year it was used.

1. The journal entry is a debit to *depreciation expense* and a credit to *accumulated depreciation*.

2. Depreciation expense is shown on the income statement and is closed out each year.

3. Accumulated depreciation is a contra-account to the asset and is reported on the balance sheet so that it is not closed out at the end of every period.

D. The asset's book value (or carrying value) is its cost less total accumulated depreciation recognized to date.

E. For convenience, a half-year convention (or some variation) is sometimes used.

1. Only one half-year of depreciation is recorded in the year of acquisition and again in the year of disposal.

2. This practice is used regardless of the exact dates of purchase or disposition.

F. If an asset is not being used to generate revenues, it is reported as an *other asset,* and depreciation is not recorded.

DEPRECIATION METHODS

There are multiple acceptable methods of calculating depreciation. Companies select a method based on their own economic circumstances.

Straight-Line Method of Depreciation

A. The straight-line method records the same depreciation expense for each full year.

B. The annual figure is computed using this formula: (cost – salvage value)/estimated useful life

C. Alternatively, the "straight-line rate" (1/number of years of useful life) can be multiplied by the (cost – salvage value) to get the annual expense.

Accelerated Methods of Depreciation

A. Accelerated methods of depreciation record a higher percentage of depreciation expense in the early years of asset use (when the asset is most productive and subject to quick losses of value). These methods also result in lower amounts being recorded later, when repair and maintenance expense is most likely to be higher.

B. *Double-declining balance method* (also called 200%-declining balance method) computes the current expense as follows:

1. [(Cost – accumulated depreciation)] × [2 × the straight-line rate] (Note that in the first year, accumulated depreciation will be zero. In subsequent years, it will be a positive number, so that the *rate* is applied to the book value of the asset.)

2. Because accumulated depreciation gets larger each year, the resulting book value figure (and hence, depreciation expense) will get smaller each year.

3. An alternative method is 150%-declining balance, where the rate is 1.5 times the straight-line rate.

4. Because the salvage value is not deducted from the asset cost, once the book value (cost – accumulated depreciation) is equal to the salvage value, no further depreciation expense is taken.

C. *Sum-of-the-years'-digits method* computes the current expense as follows:

1. (Cost – salvage value) × fraction.

2. The fraction is determined as follows:

   a. Denominator: the sum of the years of the asset's life. An asset with a 5-year life would have a denominator of 15 (5 + 4 + 3 + 2 + 1).

   b. Numerator: the number in the asset's life that corresponds to the current year (in descending order). For an asset with a 5-year life, 5 would be used for the first year, 4 for the second, and so on. This clearly reflects the accelerated nature of depreciation; 5/15 in Year 1, 4/15 in Year 2, etc.).

Group Depreciation

Group depreciation is used when a company has a group of similar assets that all need to be depreciated. Rather than depreciating each asset separately, the group method can be used. If the group of assets is dissimilar, the composite method should be used.

A. The group method applies one straight-line rate to an entire group of assets that are all acquired in the same year but have different estimated useful lives.

B. For example, 20 different small machines might be depreciated as a group.

C. In the year of acquisition, the following applies:

   1. Annual depreciation is computed for each asset.

   2. The total annual depreciation is divided by the total cost of these assets to get a depreciation rate (a weighted average).

   3. Each year, this same rate is multiplied by the remaining cost of the group.

   4. Depreciation stops with the disposal of the last item in the group or when any remaining cost has been fully depreciated.

D. For the disposal of an item within the group, the following applies:

   1. Cash received is recorded, the original cost of that particular asset is removed, and the difference is a reduction in accumulated depreciation. (debit cash, credit asset cost, "plug" to accumulated depreciation, i.e., accumulated depreciation is a balancing amount)

   2. No gain or loss is recognized.

   3. The assumption is that all gains and losses within the group will eventually offset.

   4. Any residual gain or loss is recorded at the retirement of the last asset.

Cost Allocation (i.e., Depletion) of Wasting Assets

A. Examples include oil wells and gold mines.

B. Computed on the straight-line method but based on units, not years. The method is very similar to the units of production method explained in the next section.

C. The per unit rate is calculated by dividing the cost less any anticipated residual value by the number of expected units of output of the asset.

D. When units are removed, the cost (the number of units times the rate) is first recorded in an inventory account. At the eventual time of sale, the cost is reclassified from inventory to cost of goods sold.

E. Because the number of units is an estimate, a new depletion rate may have to be computed each year.

    1. Estimated residual value is subtracted from the remaining book value.

    2. The resulting figure is divided by the estimated number of units remaining.

Units of Production Method of Depreciation

A. Similar to the depletion calculation (based on units).

B. Annual depreciation = (units of current activity or output/total expected activity or output) × depreciation base.

C. For example, depreciation of a taxicab could be based on miles driven in the given year as a percentage of the total mileage of expected use.

Changes in Estimates Used in Depreciation

A. An exam question may test your ability to calculate changes in depreciation due to changes in expected useful life, expected salvage value, and/or depreciation method.

B. Be sure to make the change *prospectively* from the beginning of the year in which the change in estimate is made.

C. Calculation:

    1. Divide the new estimate of number of periods remaining (from the beginning of the year of the change) into the remaining depreciation base (i.e., the undepreciated cost to date less revised estimate of salvage value).

D. This is considered a *change in estimate*.

Reported Earnings and Estimates for Useful Life and Salvage Value: Opportunities for Manipulation of Income

A. The utilization of a longer useful life will result in higher net asset values, lower depreciation expense, and increased net income over the years of useful life. Management can then write down the overstated assets in a restructuring later on.

B. Management might also write down assets (taking an immediate charge against income) and then record less future depreciation expense based on the written-down assets. This results in higher future net income in exchange for a one-time charge to current net income.

C. A company estimates the salvage value of an asset when the asset is placed into service.

    1. For the straight-line and sum-of-years-digits methods, salvage value is deducted from the purchase price to calculate the amount that is depreciated each year.

    2. The higher the salvage value, the lower the amount of depreciation expense applied each year.

3. Consequently, management can increase reported income by estimating higher salvage values for its assets.

4. This will also result in an overstatement of loss when the asset is retired.

DISPOSAL OF LAND, BUILDINGS, AND EQUIPMENT

DISPOSALS OF ASSETS

A. A disposal occurs when an asset is sold, destroyed, or otherwise disposed.

B. Depreciation must be recorded through the date of disposal.

C. Both the cost of the asset and the related accumulated depreciation are removed from the balance sheet.

D. If the amount received is different from the book value being removed, a gain is recorded if more is collected or a loss is recorded if less is collected.

IMPAIRMENT OF ASSETS

Impairment of Operational Assets

A. *Impairment* of operational assets (assets currently in use).

1. Occurs when the total of expected net future cash inflows (undiscounted, meaning no present value calculation required) is less than the current book value. This is called the *recoverability* test. ("Net" future cash inflows means cash outflows net of cash inflows related to a particular asset.)

2. If impaired (i.e., sum of net cash flows is less than the book value), the book value of the asset is written down to fair value and a corresponding impairment loss is recorded on the income statement in the Loss on Asset Impairment account (normal balance is a debit). Lower the book value to fair value by crediting Accumulated Depreciation. The new smaller book value becomes the basis for future depreciation calculations. No future recovery of an impairment loss is permitted.

   Record a loss on impairment for the difference between book value and fair value with this entry:

   Loss on Impairment
       Accumulated Depreciation

   a. If the fair value of the assets is not readily available, it may need to be determined.

   b. One method for estimating fair value is to calculate the discounted present value of the future cash flows expected from the asset. *(Note: The recoverability test above uses non-discounted cash flows; when present value is used as a proxy for fair value, discounted cash flows are used.)*

3. Summary:

   1. Impairment means the sum of the future cash flows (netting cash inflows with cash outflows) expected for a given asset *is less than* the book value of that asset. So, we will not *recover the book value* in the future.

   2. If impairment occurs, then we have to record it, but need to calculate the amounts for the journal entry. The impairment loss is the Book Value minus the Fair Value.

3. If we don't have a good way to find the Fair Value, then we must calculate it using the Present Value of the future net cash flows.

B. There is a rule for *when* we must test for impairment. Test for impairment should be made when any of the following six conditions apply:

1. There is a significant decline in the market price of an asset.

2. There is a significant change in the usage rate, market value, or condition of the asset.

3. There are significantly higher than expected costs involved in the acquisition or construction of an asset.

4. The company decides to sell the asset significantly before the end of its expected life.

5. There are significant and unfavorable changes in the business environment or laws and regulations.

6. There is a forecast for a significant decline in profitability related to the asset.

Note: You are not likely to be required to recite this list on the exam. However, you should be familiar with these in such a way that you would recognize them. All six are situations causing the asset to be worth less to the company than they originally expected.

Points to Consider in Testing for Impairment

Assets should be grouped at the lowest possible level for which cash flows can be identified and distinguished from the cash flows of other assets.

A. Building and equipment might be tested separately or together.

B. Future cash flows should be determined for the period equal to the expected life of the asset.

1. If various assets are grouped, the expected life should be the one for the primary asset in the group.

2. The primary asset is the one that is most significant for generating cash flows.

3. Any asset in the group with a longer expected life is assumed to be sold at the end of the primary asset's expected life.

C. If a loss is determined for a group of assets, the following applies:

1. The loss is allocated to the various assets proportionally based on individual book values.

2. Through this allocation process, however, no asset should be reported below its current market value.

Impairment of Assets to be Sold or Abandoned

A. Assets to be sold must be *reclassified* on the balance sheet under certain conditions:

1. The asset should be reclassified into a "held for sale" category when several requirements have been met, including the following:

a. The company is actively looking for a buyer.

      b.   A sale is probable within one year.

      c.   The asset is available for immediate sale.

  2. Any asset that qualifies as "held for sale" should be reported at the lower of its book value or net realizable value (fair value or expected sales price less anticipated selling expenses). An impairment loss is recorded for any write down necessary.

      a.   If the asset remains unsold at the end of subsequent reporting periods, gains in net realizable value can be recognized, but only to the extent of previously recorded losses.

B. If an asset is simply to be abandoned, the asset remains on the books, and depreciation is continued as long as the asset is still in use. At the time of abandonment, the book value is removed, and a loss is recognized.

C. Sometimes assets are disposed of by "involuntary conversion," such as a natural disaster. There may or may not be insurance proceeds. This disposition is treated the same as any other disposition. The book value is removed from the books, any cash received is recorded, and the journal entry is "balanced" with a gain or loss.

Disclosures Related to Land, Buildings, and Equipment

A. The amount of depreciation expense for the period (income statement).

B. Balances of major classes of depreciable assets classified by their nature or function at the balance sheet date (balance sheet and footnotes).

C. Balances of accumulated depreciation either by class of asset or in total, at the balance sheet date (balance sheet and footnotes).

D. A general description of the method(s) used in computing depreciation with respect to major classes of depreciable assets (footnotes).

ASSET EXCHANGES

Accounting Issues Related to Asset Exchanges

A. The following two questions must be addressed when accounting for asset exchanges:

  1. What value is recorded as the "acquisition cost" of the item received?

  2. Is a gain or a loss to be recognized?

B. The general rule is to record the asset received at the fair value of the asset(s) given up. This is similar to the concept of acquiring an asset for cash, and then recording the new asset at the fair value of the cash given up. (The fair value of cash is easily determinable; the fair value of assets given up may not be.)

C. If the fair value of the asset exchanged can not be readily determined, the fair value of the asset received can be used as the acquisition cost of the asset received.

D. A minor amount of cash given or received to balance the transaction does not change the basic nature of an asset exchange. If given, cash is added to the fair value of the non-cash asset given up to determine the recorded cost of the asset received. If cash is received, then the fair value of the asset given up will be spread over the non-cash asset(s) received and the cash to determine their recorded costs.

E. In extremely rare occasions, a company may not be able to determine the fair value of either the asset given up or the asset received. In these unusual cases, the transaction is recorded at the book value of the asset given up, and no gain or loss is recorded.

F. Recording an asset exchange at fair value may result in a gain or loss equal to the difference between the fair value and the book value of the asset(s) given up. In order to prevent companies from trading appreciated assets solely to recognize gains, the FASB requires that asset transactions recorded at fair value must have commercial substance. *Commercial substance* is defined as "causing a significant change in the future cash flows of the company." If there is no commercial substance to the transaction, the asset exchange must be recorded at book value.

G. On the CPA exam, you may be asked to calculate gain or loss when there is no commercial substance. They may just tell you "there is no commercial substance" or they may tell you "this exchange does not cause a significant change..." Either way, the determination of whether or not there is "commercial substance" will be fairly straightforward. Just be sure to know that there will be no gain or loss because the asset will be recorded at "book value." The journal entry would remove the book value of the old asset, and record the cost of the new asset equal to the same amount. Therefore, given the laws of debit and credit, there is no gain or loss on such a journal entry!

H. A related issue occurs when a company issues its own stock for an asset. No gains or losses will be recorded. The new asset is recorded at the fair value of the stock issued, with the appropriate amounts recorded in the stock and paid-in-capital-in-excess-of-par accounts.

QUESTIONS: LAND, BUILDINGS, AND EQUIPMENT

1. On June 18, Year 6, Lee Printing Co. (Lee) incurred the following costs for one of its printing presses:

• Purchase of collating and stapling attachment	$84,000
• Installation of attachment	$36,000
• Replacement parts for overhaul of press	$26,000
• Labor and overhead in connection with overhaul	$14,000

    The overhaul resulted in a significant increase in production. Neither the attachment nor the overhaul increased the estimated useful life of the process.

    Based on the above, what amount of costs should Lee capitalize?
    A. $0.
    B. $84,000.
    C. $120,000.
    D. $160,000.

2. On April 1, Year 4, Dogg Co. (Dogg) purchased new machinery for $300,000. The machinery has zero salvage value. The machinery has an estimated useful life of five years and depreciation is computed by the sum-of-the-years'-digits method. The accumulated depreciation on this machinery at March 31, Year 6 would be:
    A. $100,000.
    B. $120,000.
    C. $180,000.
    D. $192,000.

3. A fixed asset with a 5-year estimated useful life and no residual value is sold at the end of the second year. How would using the sum-of-the-years'-digits method instead of the double-declining balance method affect a gain or loss on the sale of the fixed asset?

	Gain	Loss
A.	Decrease	Decrease
B.	Decrease	Increase
C.	Increase	Decrease
D.	Increase	Increase

4. On July 1, Year 3, Irina Corp. (Irina) purchased computer equipment at a cost of $360,000. This equipment was estimated to have a 6-year useful life with no residual value and was depreciated by the straight-line method.

    On January 3, Year 6, Irina determined that this equipment could no longer process data efficiently, its value had been permanently impaired, and $70,000 could be recovered over the remaining useful life of the equipment.

    What carrying amount should Irina report on its December 31, Year 6 balance sheet for this equipment?
    A. $0.
    B. $50,000.
    C. $70,000.
    D. $150,000.

©2009 Kaplan, Inc.

5. Zulu Corp.'s (Zulu) comparative balance sheet at December 31, Year 6 and Year 5 reported accumulated depreciation balances of $800,000 and $600,000, respectively. Property with a cost of $50,000 and a carrying amount of $40,000 was the only property sold in Year 6. How much depreciation was charged to Zulu's operations in Year 6?
    A. $190,000.
    B. $200,000.
    C. $210,000.
    D. $220,000.

6. Vos Corp. (Vos) bought equipment on January 2, Year 5 for $200,000. This equipment had an estimated useful life of five years and a salvage value of $20,000. Depreciation was computed by the 150%-declining balance method. The accumulated depreciation balance at December 31, Year 6 should be:
    A. $72,000.
    B. $91,800.
    C. $98,000.
    D. $102,000.

7. On October 1, Year 6, Stumpy Corp. (Stumpy) purchased a machine for $126,000 that was placed in service on November 30, Year 6. Stumpy incurred additional costs for this machine as follows:

Shipping	$3,000
Installation	$4,000
Testing	$5,000

    In Stumpy's December 31, Year 6 balance sheet, the machine's cost should be reported as:
    A. $126,000.
    B. $129,000.
    C. $133,000.
    D. $138,000.

8. During Year 6, Bay Co. (Bay) constructed machinery for its own use and for sale to customers. Bank loans financed these assets both during construction and after construction was complete. How much of the interest incurred should be reported as interest expense on Bay's Year 6 income statement?

	Machinery for own use	Machinery constructed for sale to customers
A.	All interest incurred	All interest incurred
B.	All interest incurred	Interest incurred after completion
C.	Interest incurred after completion	Interest incurred after completion
D.	Interest incurred after completion	All interest incurred

9. Southwick, Inc. (Southwick) purchased a machine that was installed and placed in service on January 1, Year 5 at a cost of $240,000. Salvage value was estimated at $40,000. The machine is being depreciated over ten years by the double-declining balance method. For the year ended December 31, Year 6, what amount should Southwick report as depreciation expense?
    A. $21,600.
    B. $32,000.
    C. $38,400.
    D. $48,000.

10. Derbyshire, Inc. (Derbyshire) incurred costs to modify its building and to rearrange its production line. As a result, an overall reduction in production costs is expected. However, the modifications did not increase the building's market value, and the rearrangement did not extend the production line's expected life. Should the building modification costs and the production line rearrangement costs be capitalized, respectively?

	Building modification costs	Production line rearrangement
A.	Yes	No
B.	Yes	Yes
C.	No	No
D.	No	Yes

11. On January 2, Year 3, Renard Co. (Renard) purchased a machine for $800,000 and established an annual depreciation charge of $100,000 over an 8-year life. During Year 6, after issuing its Year 5 financial statements, Renard concluded:

1. The machine suffered permanent impairment of its operational value.

2. $200,000 is a reasonable estimate of the amount expected to be recovered through the use of the machine for the period January 1, Year 6 through December 31, Year 10.

In Renard's December 31, Year 6 balance sheet, the machine should be reported at a carrying amount of:
A. $0.
B. $100,000.
C. $160,000.
D. $400,000.

12. On January 1, Year 2, Kramer, Inc. (Kramer) purchased equipment having an estimated salvage value equal to 20% of its original cost at the end of a 10-year life. The equipment was sold December 31, Year 6, for 50% of its original cost. If the equipment's disposition resulted in a reported loss, which of the following depreciation methods did Kramer use?
A. Double-declining balance.
B. Sum-of-the-years'-digits.
C. Straight-line.
D. Composite.

13. Weir Co. (Weir) uses straight-line depreciation for its PP&E, which is stated as follows:

	Dec 31/Year 6	Dec 31/Year 5
Land	$25,000	$25,000
Buildings	195,000	195,000
Machinery & equipment	695,000	650,000
Less: accumulated depreciation	(400,000)	(370,000)
	$515,000	$500,000

Weir's depreciation expense for Year 6 and Year 5 was $55,000 and $50,000, respectively.

What amount was debited to accumulated depreciation during Year 6 because of land, buildings, and equipment retirements?
A. $10,000.
B. $20,000.
C. $25,000.
D. $40,000.

14. Geo, Inc. (Geo) determined that, due to obsolescence, equipment with an original cost of $900,000 and accumulated depreciation at January 1, Year 6 of $420,000, had suffered permanent impairment, and as a result, should have a carrying value of only $300,000 as of the beginning of the year.

    In addition, the remaining useful life of the equipment was reduced from eight years to three years.

    In its December 31, Year 6 balance sheet, what amount should Geo report as accumulated depreciation?
    A. $100,000.
    B. $520,000.
    C. $600,000.
    D. $700,000.

15. Cole Co. (Cole) began constructing a house for its own use in January, Year 6. During Year 6, Cole incurred interest costs of $50,000 on specific construction debt and $20,000 on other borrowings. Interest computed on the weighted-average amount of accumulated expenditures for the building during Year 6 was $40,000. What amount of interest should Cole capitalize in Year 6?
    A. $20,000.
    B. $40,000.
    C. $50,000.
    D. $70,000.

16. Which of the following uses the straight-line depreciation method?

	Group depreciation	Composite depreciation
A.	No	No
B.	Yes	Yes
C.	No	Yes
D.	Yes	No

17. Turtle Co. (Turtle) purchased equipment on January 2, Year 4 for $50,000. The equipment had an estimated 5-year service life. Turtle's policy for 5-year assets is to use the double-declining method for the first two years of the asset's life and then switch to straight-line method for the remainder. The equipment has no salvage value. On its December 31, Year 6 balance sheet, what amount should Turtle report as accumulated depreciation for the equipment?
    A. $30,000.
    B. $38,000.
    C. $39,200.
    D. $42,000.

18. On January 2, Year 6, Leonore Corp. (Leonore) bought machinery under a contract that required a down payment of $10,000 plus 24 monthly payments of $5,000 each, for total cash payments of $130,000. The cash equivalent price of the machinery was $110,000. The machinery has an estimated useful life of ten years and estimated salvage value of $5,000. Leonore uses straight-line depreciation. In its Year 6 income statement, what amount should Leonore report as depreciation for this machinery?
    A. $10,500.
    B. $11,000.
    C. $12,500.
    D. $13,000.

19.   In January Year 6, Mosario Co. (Mosario) purchased a mineral mine for $2,640,000 with removable ore estimated at 1,200,000 tons. After it has extracted all the ore, Mosario will be required by law to restore the land to its original condition at an estimated cost of $220,000. The present value of the estimated restoration costs is $180,000. Mosario believes it will be able to sell the property afterwards for $300,000. During Year 6, Mosario incurred $360,000 of development costs preparing the mine for production and removed and sold 60,000 tons or ore. In its Year 6 income statement, what amount should Mosario report as depletion?
A. $135,000.
B. $144,000.
C. $150,000.
D. $159,000.

20.   Only July 1, Year 6, Bali Co. (Bali) exchanged a truck for 25 shares of Adam, Inc. (Adam) common shares. On that date, the truck's carrying amount was $2,500, and its fair value was $3,000. Also, the book value of Adam's stock was $60 per share on that date. On December 31, Year 6, Adam had 250 shares of common stock outstanding and its book value per share was $50. What amount should Bali report in its December 31, Year 6 balance as an investment in Adam?
A. $1,250.
B. $1,500.
C. $2,500.
D. $3,000.

21.   On March 31, Year 6, Franck, Inc. (Franck) traded in an old machine having a carrying amount of $16,800 and paid a cash difference of $6,000 for a new machine having a total cash price of $20,500. On this date, what amount of loss should Franck recognize on the exchange?
A. $0.
B. $2,300.
C. $3,700.
D. $6,000.

22.   Which of the following conditions must exist in order for an impairment loss to be recognized on a long-lived asset, such as a building?

I.   The carrying amount of the long-lived asset is less than its fair value.
II. The carrying amount of the long-lived asset is not recoverable.

A. I only.
B. II only.
C. Both I and II.
D. Neither I nor II.

23.   Mellow Co. depreciated a $12,000 asset over five years, using the straight-line method with no salvage value. At the beginning of the fifth year, it was determined that the asset will last another four years. What amount should Mellow report as depreciation expense for Year 5?
A. $600.
B. $900.
C. $1,500.
D. $2,400.

24. Cantor Co. purchased a coal mine for $2,000,000. It cost $500,000 to prepare the coal mine for extraction of the coal. It was estimated that 750,000 tons of coal would be extracted from the mind during its useful life. Cantor planned to sell the property for $100,000 at the end of its useful life. During the current year, 15,000 tons of coal were extracted and sold. What would be Cantor's depletion amount per ton for the current year?
    A. $2.50.
    B. $2.60.
    C. $3.20.
    D. $3.30.

25. Miller Co. discovered that in the prior year, it failed to report $40,000 of depreciation related to a newly constructed building. The depreciation was computed correctly for tax purposes. The tax rate for the current year was 40%. What was the impact of the error on Miller's financial statement for the prior year?
    A. Understatement of accumulated depreciation of $24,000.
    B. Understatement of accumulated depreciation of $40,000.
    C. Understatement of depreciation expense of $24,000.
    D. Understatement of net income of $24,000.

26. A company buys a computer on March 1, Year 1, for $30,000 with a 5-year life and no salvage value. Straight-line depreciation is used along with the half-year convention. On August 1, Year 3, when this computer is now worth $14,000, it is traded along with cash of $6,000 for a new computer valued at $20,000. The new computer is similar to the old computer. What gain or loss is recognized on the trade?
    A. $0.
    B. $2,000 loss.
    C. $4,000 loss.
    D. $6,000 loss.

27. A trade is made that is said to have "no commercial substance." What does that mean?
    A. The assets are similar.
    B. The assets are dissimilar.
    C. The trade creates no significant change in future cash flows.
    D. The assets are tangible in nature.

28. On January 1, Year 1, a company agrees to pay $80,000 in exactly three years for a machine. The asset has a 10-year life and a salvage value of $10,000. The double-declining balance method is being applied based on the number of months held during the year. No interest is to be paid, although a reasonable rate is 8%. The present value of $1 in three years at an 8% annual rate is assumed to be 0.735. The present value of a $1 ordinary annuity over three years at an 8% annual rate is assumed to be 2.577. The present value of a $1 annuity due over three years at an 8% annual rate is assumed to be 2.783. How much depreciation expense should be recognized on this machine for Year 2?
    A. $7,808.
    B. $8,232.
    C. $8,878.
    D. $9,408.

29. On January 1, Year 1, the Moses Corporation buys 100 small production machines that should each last for five years. Of the total, 70 cost $4,000 each and the remaining 30 cost $3,000 each for a total cost of $370,000 (70 × $4,000 + 30 × $3,000). At the end of Year 1, three of the $4,000 models are sold for $3,100 each. If group depreciation is being applied, what gain or loss should be recorded on these initial sales?
    A. $0.
    B. $300 loss.
    C. $300 gain.
    D. $600 loss.

30. On January 1, Year 1, the Moses Corporation buys 100 small production machines that should each last for five years. Of the total, 70 cost $4,000 each and the remaining 30 cost $3,000 each for a total cost of $370,000 (70 × $4,000 + 30 × $3,000). At the end of Year 1, three of the $4,000 models are sold for $3,100 each. If group depreciation is being applied, what amount of depreciation expense should be recognized in Year 2?
    A. $74,000.
    B. $73,200.
    C. $72,400.
    D. $71,600.

31. Ames, Inc. buys an electric power plant for $400 million. The plant will last for 20 years, and then Ames will be legally obligated to clean up the environment around the plant. A current fair value for this requirement cannot be determined, but the anticipated future cash flows are $80 million. A risk-free interest rate at this time is 5% but a credit-adjusted risk-free interest rate for Ames is 8%. The present value of $1 at 5% annual interest in 20 years is assumed to be 0.375. The present value of $1 at 8% annual interest in 20 years is assumed to be 0.215. On the date of the acquisition, what is the capitalized cost of the power plant?
    A. $400 million.
    B. $417.2 million.
    C. $430 million.
    D. $480 million.

32. A company owns a large manufacturing plant with a book value of $13 million. The plant has a current fair value of $11.7 million. The company expects this plant to generate a positive cash flow of $1 million each year for its remaining life of 15 years. The present value of these cash flows is assumed to be $9.6 million. What amount of impairment loss should the company recognize in connection with this plant?
    A. $0.
    B. $1.3 million.
    C. $2 million.
    D. $3.4 million.

33. A company has a small retail outlet that it wants to sell. The company is trying to determine whether this asset should be reclassified on its balance sheet to a "held for resale" category. Which of the following is not required for this reclassification to be necessary?
    A. The company is actively seeking a buyer.
    B. Sale is probable within one year.
    C. The asset is available for immediate sale.
    D. A probable buyer has been located although a contract has not been signed.

34. A company holds an asset that qualifies as being held for sale. The asset has a cost of $12 million and accumulated depreciation of $3 million. The company expects to sell this asset for $10 million after spending $2 million for costs necessary to create the sale. At what amount should this asset be reported on the company's balance sheet?
    A. $12 million.
    B. $10 million.
    C. $9 million.
    D. $8 million.

35. On January 1, Year 1, Naughton Corporation borrowed $1 million at an annual interest rate of 8%. The company immediately began to use a large portion of this money to build a new warehouse. The construction was done evenly throughout the year and completed on the last day of Year 1 at a total cost of $800,000. What amount of interest expense should Naughton recognize on its income statement for Year 1?
    A. $0.
    B. $16,000.
    C. $48,000.
    D. $80,000.

36. A company buys an oil platform in the Gulf of Mexico to use to pump oil. The platform was bought on January 1, Year 1, at a cost of $60 million and should last for ten years. However, at the end of that time, the company is legally required to dismantle the platform. That cost is estimated to be $15 million, which, at a reasonable annual of 10%, has a present value of $5.8 million. If the straight-line method is used for depreciation and the effective rate method is used for interest, what amount of expense will this company recognize for Year 1?
    A. $6,580,000.
    B. $6,820,000.
    C. $7,050,000.
    D. $7,160,000.

37. A company buys an oil platform in the Gulf of Mexico to use to pump oil. The platform was bought on January 1, Year 1, at a cost of $80 million and should last for 10 years. However, at the end of that time, the company is legally required to dismantle the platform. The company is not certain as to how much this retirement obligation will cost in ten years but has made the following projections: 30% chance that it will cost cash flows of $20 million, 60% chance that it will cost $15 million, and 10% chance that it will cost $10 million. A 10% annual interest rate is being used, and the present value of $1 in ten years at an annual interest rate of 10% is 0.39. What amount of liability should be reported by the company on January 1, Year 1?
    A. $3,900,000.
    B. $5,850,000.
    C. $6,240,000.
    D. $7,800,000.

38. A company buys an oil platform in the Gulf of Mexico to use to pump oil. The platform was bought on January 1, Year 1, at a cost of $80 million and should last for ten years. However, at the end of that time, the company is legally required to dismantle the platform. The company believes this retirement obligation will cost $22 million in cash. The company recently issued a 3-year bond, paying 7% annual interest, when the U.S. government was issuing 3-year bonds paying 5% annual interest. Currently, the U.S. government is issuing 10-year bonds that are paying 6% annual interest. When computing the present value of the asset retirement obligation, what annual interest rate should be used?
    A. 8%.
    B. 7%.
    C. 6%.
    D. 5%.

39. The Alexander Company holds asset A with a cost of $90,000 and accumulated depreciation of $30,000. However, the asset is currently worth $69,000. That asset is traded for another asset that is dissimilar in nature and has a fair value of approximately $60,000. To even up the trade, the parties negotiate and finally, Alexander is given cash of $10,000. At what figure does Alexander recognize the new asset received?
    A. $50,000.
    B. $59,000.
    C. $60,000.
    D. $69,000.

40. A company applies double-declining balance depreciation and uses the half-year convention. Equipment was bought on May 1, Year 1, for $12,000 with an estimated 10-year life and residual value of $2,000. The equipment is sold on November 1, Year 3, for its fair value of $7,100. What gain or loss is reported on the sale?
    A. $676 loss.
    B. $288 loss.
    C. $305 gain.
    D. $620 gain.

41. On December 31, Year 1, the Barker Corporation decides to sell a large manufacturing plant that it operates in Montana. The company begins to actively seek a buyer and believes it is probable that the sale can be completed within eight months. Which of the following is true?
    A. Because the sale is expected to take eight months to complete, the asset should not be reported as the Asset Held for Sale.
    B. If the company continues to operate the plant in Year 2, it must continue to record depreciation even though it is in the process of being sold.
    C. A loss should be recognized on the plant on December 31, Year 1.
    D. Because the sale will not occur in Year 1, the possibility of the sale should be disclosed but should have no impact on the company's balance sheet.

42. The Jackson Corporation owns a large building that is located near Roanoke, Virginia. When producing its Year 1 balance sheet, company officials decide to test this asset to see if its value had been impaired. Which of the following is not a reason that might have led these officials to conclude that such testing was necessary?
   A. The building had been used as a warehouse but has recently been converted to office space.
   B. The building has a remaining life of 20 years, but company officials now believe it will be sold within the next four years.
   C. Construction of the building was recently completed by the company at a cost 5% below the amount expected.
   D. Real estate market values in this area of Virginia have experienced a significant decrease over the past 12 months.

43. Equipment is bought on January 1, Year 1 for $190,000 with an expected life of ten years and a salvage value of $10,000. Straight-line depreciation is used. During Year 3, it became apparent that the total life of the equipment would be only seven years (to December 31, Year 7) and that no salvage value would remain at that time. What depreciation expense should be recognized for Year 3?
   A. $27,800.
   B. $28,800.
   C. $29,800.
   D. $30,800.

44. On June 27, 20X6, Brite Co. distributed to its common stockholders 100,000 outstanding common shares of its investment in Quik, Inc., an unrelated party. The carrying amount on Brite's books of Quik's $1 par common stock was $2 per share. Immediately before the distribution, the market price of Quik's stock was $2.50 per share. In its income statement for the year ended June 30, 20X6, what amount should Brite report as gain before income taxes on disposal of the stock?
   A. $250,000.
   B. $200,000.
   C. $50,000.
   D. $0.

45. In October 20X6 Allen Company exchanged a used packaging machine, having a book value of $120,000, for a dissimilar new machine and paid a cash difference of $15,000. The market value of the used packaging machine was determined to be $140,000. Assume that the transaction has commercial substance. In its income statement for the year ended December 31, 20X6, how much gain should Allen recognize on this exchange?
   A. $0.
   B. $5,000.
   C. $15,000.
   D. $20,000.

46.   Caine Motor Sales Exchanged a car from its inventory for a computer to be used as a long-term
        asset. The following information relates to this exchange that took place on July 31, 20X5:
        Carrying amount of the car $30,000
        Listed selling price of the car $45,000
        Fair value of the computer $43,000
        Cash difference paid by Caine $5,000

        Caine states that there will be a significant change in cash flows as a result of this transaction.
        Therefore, the transaction has commercial substance.

        On July 31, 20X5, what amount of profit should Caine recognize on this exchange?
        A. $0.
        B. $8,000.
        C. $10,000.
        D. $13,000.

47.   On March 31, 20X5, Winn Company traded in an old machine having a carrying amount of
        $16,800, and paid a cash difference of $6,000 for a new machine having a total cash price of
        $20,500. Winn states that because of the difference in age of the assets, there should be a
        significant difference in cash flow. Therefore, the transaction has commercial substance.

        On March 31, 20X5, what amount of loss should Winn recognize on this exchange?
        A. $0.
        B. $2,300.
        C. $3,700.
        D. $6,000.

48.   On December 30, 20X5, Diamond Company traded in an old machine with a book value of
        $10,000 for a similar new machine having a list price of $32,000, and paid a cash difference of
        $19,000.

        Diamond does not think there will be a significant change in cash flows as a result of this
        transaction. Therefore, the transaction lacks commercial substance.

        Diamond should record the new machine at:
        A. $32,000.
        B. $29,000.
        C. $22,000.
        D. $19,000.

49.   Pine Football Company had a player contract with Duff that is recorded in its books at $500,000
        on July 1, 20X5. Ace Football Company had a player contract with Terry that is recorded in its
        books at $600,000 on July 1, 20X5. On this date, Pine traded Duff to Ace for Terry and paid a
        cash difference of $50,000. The fair value of the Terry contract was $700,000 on the exchange
        date. Pine stated that this transaction lacked commercial substance. The Terry contract should be
        recorded in Pine's books at:
        A. $550,000.
        B. $600,000.
        C. $650,000.
        D. $700,000.

50. Good Deal Company received $20,000 in cash and a used computer with a fair value of $180,000 from Harvest Corporation for Good Deal's existing computer having a fair value of $200,000 and an undepreciated cost of $160,000 recorded on its books.

   Good Deal does not think that there will be significant change in cash flows. Therefore, the transaction lacks commercial substance.

   How much gain should Good Deal recognize on this exchange, and at what amount should the acquired computer be recorded, respectively?
   A. $0 and $140,000.
   B. $4,000 and $144,000.
   C. $20,000 and $160,000.
   D. $40,000 and $180,000.

51. SFAS 153 – Accounting for Nonmonetary Transactions states that if the transaction causes a significant change in cash flows, the transaction has commercial substance. In transactions of this type, at what amount should the entity record the asset received?
   A. Book Value.
   B. Intrinsic Value.
   C. Book Value plus Boot.
   D. Fair Value.

52. May Co. and Sty Co. exchanged nonmonetary assets and May paid cash to Sty in the transaction. May stated that the exchange had commercial substance. However, the assets exchanged were so specialized that there was not an objective basis to determine a fair value. In cases like this, the FASB suggest that May record the asset at:
   A. Estimated Fair Value.
   B. Book Value.
   C. Book Value of asset traded plus cash paid.
   D. Intrinsic Value.

ANSWERS: LAND, BUILDINGS, AND EQUIPMENT

1. **D** The collating and stapling attachment, including the cost of installation, is an addition to existing land, buildings, and equipment. As such, the entire $120,000 would be capitalized. Because the overhaul of the press resulted in a significant increase in production, it would be considered a betterment and the parts, labor, and overhead would all be capitalized in the amount of $40,000. As a result, the entire $160,000 in costs would be capitalized.

2. **C** As of 3/31/06, the machine would have been held for two full years. Depreciation under the sum-of-the-years'-digits method, with a 5-year life and apparently no salvage value, would involve multiplying the cost of $300,000 by 5/15 for Year 1 and 4/15 for Year 2. Accumulated depreciation would then be 9/15 × $300,000 or $180,000 after two years.

3. **B** Under the double-declining balance method of depreciation, using a 5-year estimated life, depreciation in the first year would be 40% of the cost of the asset. In the second year, depreciation would be 40% of the remaining book value or an additional (40% × 60%) 24% for a total of 64%. The remaining book value would be 36% of the cost.

   Under the sum-of-the-years'-digits method, depreciation in the first year would be 5/15 of the cost and in the second year it would be 4/15 of the cost for a total of 9/15 and a remaining book value of 6/15 or 40%.

   As a result, the carrying value would be higher after the second year under sum-of-the-years'-digits method. This would cause a gain to be lower and a loss to be higher than that computed under the double-declining balance method.

4. **B** At January 3, Year 6, the carrying value of the asset will be reduced to $70,000. As of that date, 2.5 years had passed since the acquisition of the equipment on July 1, Year 3. As a result, 3.5 years of the original 6-year life remains. The $70,000 impaired value will be depreciated over the 3.5 years at the rate of $20,000 per year. December 31, Year 6, after one year, depreciation of $20,000 will reduce the carrying value to $50,000.

5. **C** Accumulated depreciation began the year at $600,000. The property with a $50,000 cost and $40,000 carrying amount must have had accumulated depreciation of $10,000. When the property was sold, the accumulated depreciation would have been reduced from $600,000 to $590,000. Because accumulated depreciation ended the year at $800,000, depreciation must have been recorded in the amount of $800,000 – $590,000 = $210,000.

6. **D** Over a 5-year life, straight-line depreciation comes to 20% per year. The 150%-declining applies a rate of 150% × 20% = 30% on the book value each year. The initial book value in Year 5 is the cost of $200,000, so depreciation in Year 5 is $200,000 × 30% = $60,000. The book value to begin Year 6 is the cost of $200,000 minus the accumulated depreciation of $60,000, or $140,000. Depreciation in Year 6 is $140,000 × 30% = $42,000. Accumulated depreciation at December 31, Year 6 is $60,000 + $42,000 = $102,000.

7. **D** All costs incurred to acquire the machine and prepare it for use are capitalized. This includes the invoice price of $126,000, shipping of $3,000, installation of $4,000, and testing of $5,000, for a total of $138,000.

8. **D** Interest on construction loans for machinery the company will be using itself should be capitalized during the construction period. Interest is not capitalized when it relates to construction loans for the manufacture of inventory held for sale.

9. **C** Under the double-declining-balance method, salvage value is ignored and the book value is multiplied by a rate equal to two times the straight-line rate. With a 10-year life, the straight-line rate is 10% and the double-declining-balance rate is 20%. Depreciation in Year 5 would be 20% of $240,000 or $48,000, reducing the book value to $192,000 in Year 6. Depreciation in Year 6 would be 20% of $192,000 or $38,400.

10. **B** Because the building modification and the production line rearrangement result in an increase in production efficiency, evidenced by a decrease in production costs, both costs would be capitalized.

11. **C** As a result of the permanent impairment to the operational value of the machine, the carrying value would be written down to $200,000 as of 1/1/06. That amount would then be depreciated over the remaining 5-year useful life from 1/1/06 through 12/31/10 at the rate of $40,000 per year. The carrying value at 12/31/06 would be $200,000 – $40,000 or $160,000.

12. **C** If equipment was sold at a loss for 50% of its original cost, the book value is apparently more than 50%. Because the equipment was acquired on 1/1/02 and sold on 12/31/06, five years of its 10-year life had expired. With a salvage value of 20%, the depreciable basis is 80% and, under straight-line, accumulated depreciation would be 40% of the cost. The book value would be 60%, indicating a loss.

    Under sum-of-the-years'-digits, accumulated depreciation would be (10/55 + 9/55 + 8/55 + 7/55 + 6/55) × 80% of the cost or 40/55 × 80%, which is about 58% of cost.

    Under double-declining balance, depreciation in Year 2 would be 20% of the cost. In each subsequent year, depreciation would be 20% of the remaining book value, which works out to 16% in Year 3, 12.8% in Year 4, 10.24% in Year 5, and 8.192% in Year 6 for a total of 67.232%. Both are clearly more than 50% and the sale would result in a gain.

    Under composite depreciation, it is assumed that any sales result in no gain or loss.

13. **C** With accumulated depreciation of $370,000 at 12/31/05 and depreciation expense of $55,000 in Year 6, the balance in accumulated depreciation would be $425,000 before recording any retirements. Because the correct balance at 12/31/06 was $400,000, accumulated depreciation must have been decreased by $25,000 due to retirements.

14. **D** It was determined that the equipment had been permanently impaired and should have a carrying value of $300,000 at 1/1/06 with a remaining useful life of three years. As a result, additional depreciation in Year 6 would be $100,000, reducing the carrying value to $200,000. With an original cost of $900,000, accumulated depreciation would be the difference of $700,000 at 12/31/06.

15. **B** Capitalized interest will be based on the weighted average of accumulated expenditures. When that amount exceeds the funds borrowed, interest on unrelated liabilities will be capitalized. When that amount is lower than the funds borrowed, as is the case here, the amount to be capitalized will be the lower amount of $40,000.

16. **B** Under both the group and composite depreciation approaches, assets are depreciated in groups, rather than individually. Both calculate depreciation under the straight-line method.

17. **B** Under double-declining balance depreciation over a 5-year life, depreciation on the $50,000 machine would have been 40% or $20,000 in the first year, and 40% of the remaining $30,000 or $12,000 in the second year, for a total of $32,000. The remaining $18,000 would be depreciated straight-line over the remaining three years at the rate of $6,000 per year. As a result, after the first three years, accumulated depreciation would have been $32,000 + $6,000 or $38,000.

18. **A** The machine would be recorded at its cash equivalent price of $110,000. With a salvage value of $5,000 and a useful life of ten years, annual depreciation would be 10% of the depreciable basis of $105,000 or $10,500.

19. **B**   The depletion charge per unit is depletion base (net cost of the resource) divided by the estimated units of the resource. Mosario's depletion base is $2,880,000, as computed below:

Cost of mine	$2,640,000
Development cost	$360,000
Restoration cost	$180,000
Residual value	($300,000)
	$2,880,000

Note that the present value of the restoration costs is recorded as required by SFAS 143. The depletion charge is $2.40 per ton ($2,880,000/1,200,000 tons). Because 60,000 tons were removed and sold, depletion of $144,000 (60,000 × $2.40) is included in Mosario's Year 6 income statement.

20. **D**   When the investment in Adam, Inc. stock was acquired, it was recorded at its cost. In this case, the cost was measured at the fair value of that which was given up to acquire the stock. The truck given up had a fair value of $3,000. As a result the investment in Adam would be reported at $3,000 in its December 31, Year 6 balance sheet.

21. **B**   The cash price of the new machine represents its fair value (FV). The FV of the old machine can be determined by subtracting the cash portion of the purchase price ($6,000) from the total cost of the new machine: $20,500 – $6,000 = $14,500. Because the book value of the machine ($16,800) exceeds its FV on the date of the trade in ($14,500), the difference of $2,300 must be recognized as a loss.

22. **B**   An impairment loss on long-lived asset is only possible if the future cash flows to be generated are anticipated to be less than the current carrying value of the asset. In other words, the company cannot recover the carrying value of the asset being reported. Thus, II is required. At that point, a loss is actually recognized if the fair value is below the carrying value. Therefore, I is backwards for a loss to be recognized.

23. **A**   After four years, the asset will be 4/5 depreciated down to a book value of $2,400 (20% of $12,000). The asset, though, now has four remaining years so that depreciation should be adjusted to $600 per year ($2,400 over four years).

24. **C**   The total cost of the coal mine is $2.5 million. However, there is a residual value of $100,000. That leaves $2.4 million in cost to be written off over 750,000 tons, which equates to $3.20 per ton.

25. **B**   The tax effect was correct so the company simply had depreciation expense and accumulated depreciation too low by $40,000. That would cause net income and retained earnings to be too high by $40,000.

26. **C**   The old computer depreciates at a rate of $6,000 per year ($30,000/five years). At the time of the trade, accumulated depreciation is $12,000 ($3,000 for Years 1 and 3 and $6,000 for Year 2). The book value is $18,000 ($30,000 – $12,000), but the value is only $14,000, creating a loss of $4,000 to be recognized.

27. **C**   If a trade takes place and the cash flows before and after the trade are basically the same (in terms of amounts, timing, and risk), there is no rationale for making the trade. In that case, the asset being received is valued at the book value of the asset being surrendered rather than its fair value.

28. **D**   Because a reasonable interest rate is not being paid, the asset is recorded at the present value of the future cash flows or $58,800 ($80,000 × 0.735). Depreciation in Year 1 is $11,760 ($58,800 × 2/10). This reduces the book value from $58,800 to $47,040. Depreciation for Year 2 is $9,408 ($47,040 × 2/10).

29. **A**   In applying the group (or composite) depreciation method, the assumption is that some of these assets will be sold at a gain and some will be sold at a loss. Likely, those gains and losses will come close to offsetting. Therefore, to simplify the process, no gain or loss is recorded on any sales until the very last item in the group is sold. In that way, only the amount that did not offset exactly is recognized. Here, the first three assets are sold; thus, no gain or loss is recognized.

30. **D** Because all the assets will last for five years, depreciation each year is 20% (1/5) multiplied times the cost. The original cost was $370,000, but three assets costing $4,000 each were sold so that the cost of this group has been reduced to $358,000. Depreciation for Year 2 is 20% of $358,000 or $71,600.

31. **B** A current fair value for this legal obligation cannot be determined so the present value of the future cash flows is used for reporting purposes. For this computation, a credit-adjusted risk-free interest rate is applied. Here, that rate is 8%. Thus, the present value of this obligation is $17.2 million or $80 million times 0.215. This amount increases the company's cost for this power plant to $417.2 million.

32. **A** An asset is not viewed as being impaired if the company anticipates it will be able to generate sufficient cash flows to recover the present book value of the item. Here, the company expects positive cash flows of $15 million ($1 million per year for 15 years), which is larger than the book value of $13 million. Thus, no loss is recognized.

33. **D** A company is required to reclassify an asset as held for resale if a buyer is being actively sought, the sale will probably occur within one year, and the asset is immediately available as soon as a buyer is found. However, a probable buyer does not have to be located before the reclassification is necessary.

34. **D** When an asset is to be reported on a company's balance sheet as being held for resale, it should be shown at the lower of its book value ($12 million – $3 million or $9 million) and its net realizable value ($10 million – $2 million or $8 million).

35. **C** When a company chooses to build a fixed asset, such as this warehouse or a specially ordered piece of inventory, interest during the construction is capitalized rather than being recognized as interest expense. The average accumulated expenditure for the year was $400,000: the $800,000 cost was incurred evenly during the year. At an 8% rate, $32,000 of the interest should be capitalized rather than expensed. On the debt, the interest incurred was $80,000 ($1 million – 8%). Because $32,000 is capitalized along with the cost of the warehouse, only $48,000 remains to be recognized at interest expense.

36. **D** The oil platform has a capitalized cost of $65,800,000, the cost of the acquisition plus the present value of the retirement obligations (which is included because it is legally required). Over ten years, using the straight-line method, annual depreciation expense is $6,580,000. The obligation for the required retirement begins as a liability of $5,800,000. As a present value figure, interest expense (often called an accretion expense because there is no actual debt instrument) is computed at the 10% annual rate as $580,000. Hence, total expense is $7,160,000 ($6,580,000 depreciation + $580,000 interest).

37. **C** The FASB requires a weighted average cash flow figure to be used when determining the liability to be recognized.

> 30% × $20 million = $6 million
> 60% × $15 million = $9 million
> 10% × $10 million = $1 million
> Weighted average $16 million

Because the cash payments are in the future, the liability is recognized today at its present value or $16 million times 0.39 to arrive at $6,240,000.

38. **A** The FASB held that a company in this type of situation should determine its credit-adjusted risk-free rate. Recently, the company issued a 3-year bond at a rate that was 2% higher than the rate for similar U.S. government bonds. Apparently, the credit risk associated with this company required the company to pay an interest rate that was 2% higher than the U.S. government (a risk-free rate). Because the U.S. government is currently issuing 10-year bonds at a 6% rate, this company could probably issue similar debt at a rate 2% higher or 8%. The risk-free rate has been adjusted based on the credit rating of the company.

39. **B**   Alexander Company is sacrificing an asset with a value of $69,000. Therefore, the two assets being received must be recorded at this same $69,000 figure; that is really their cost to the company. Because the cash has to be recorded at $10,000, the remaining $59,000 is assigned to the other asset being received.

40. **A**   Year 1: $12,000 cost minus zero accumulated depreciation equals a book value of $12,000 multiplied by 2/10 and 1/2 year to get depreciation expense of $1,200.

     Year 2: $12,000 cost minus $1,200 accumulated depreciation equals a book value of $10,800 multiplied by 2/10 to get depreciation expense of $2,160.

     Year 3: $12,000 cost minus $3,360 accumulated depreciation equals a book value of $8,640 multiplied by 2/10 and 1/2 year to get depreciation expense of $864.

     The $864 expense reduces the book value from $8,640 to $7,776. Since the sale was only for $7,100, the company reports a loss of $676 on the sale.

41. **B**   Depreciation continues to be carried out in order to match the cost of an asset with the periods in which it generates revenue. Thus, if the plant will operate in Year 2, depreciation should also be recognized. Answer A is incorrect because an asset can qualify as being held for sale as long as the owner believes it is probable that a sale will occur within 12 months. Answer C is incorrect because once the asset is labeled as "held for sale" it should be reported at the lower of book value of fair value less any costs to sale. If the book value is reduced, a loss is recognized. If the book value is not reduced, no loss is recognized. Answer D is incorrect because the asset is separated on the balance sheet and labeled as "held for sale" as soon as it qualifies.

42. **C**   The FASB has provided a rather lengthy list of events or changes in circumstances that would require a company to test an asset for impairment. Most of these fall into examples similar to Answers A, B, and D, where uncertainty is introduced that might indicate a value problem: a new use, the decision to see more quickly than expected, a general change in values, and the like. In addition, if an asset is being built and turns out to cost more than expected, then a question arises as to whether that added cost can be recovered. In Answer C, though, the asset cost less than expected to construct so that recovering the investment is even more likely.

43. **D**   Depreciation for each of the first two years was $190,000 minus $10,000 (or $180,000), allocated over ten years at a rate of $18,000 per year. After two years, the book value of this equipment has been reduced to $154,000 ($190,000 less $36,000). Because of the change in estimated life, there are only five years of useful life left for this equipment. With no salvage value, that remaining book value will be expensed at the rate of $30,800 per year ($154,000 / 5 years).

44. **C**   This is a non-reciprocal transfer. Non-reciprocal transfers are recorded at FV (100,000 shares × $2.50 per share = $250,000). The difference between the FV ($250,000) and the carrying value ($200,000) is recorded as a $50,000 gain.

45. **D**   Since the transaction has commercial substance, the asset received should be recorded at fair value and a gain on the trade recorded immediately.

     The gain is measured by the difference between the market value and the book value of the machine exchanged or $140,000 − $120,000 = $20,000. The new machine will be recorded at $140,000 + $15,000 or $155,000.

46. **B**   Since the transaction has commercial substance, the asset received should be recorded at fair value and a gain on the trade recorded immediately.

Fair value of computer		$43,000
Book value of auto given up	$30,000	
Cash paid	5,000	35,000
Gain on the exchange		$ 8,000

47. **B** Since the transaction has commercial substance, the asset received should be recorded at fair value and a loss on the trade should be recorded immediately.

    In order to determine the loss, the trade-in value must be compared to the book value:

Cash price of new machine	$20,500
Less: Cash payment	6,000
Trade-in value of old machine	$14,500
Book value of old machine	16,800
Loss to be recognized	$ 2,300

48. **B** Since the transaction lacks commercial substance, the asset received should be recorded at the book value of the asset(s) given up and the theoretical gain deferred. The theoretical gain is the fair value of the machine of $32,000 versus the book value given up of $29,000 (cash of $19,000 + book value of old asset $10,000), for a theoretical gain of $3,000.

Book value of old asset	$10,000
Cash Paid	19,000
Recorded cost of new asset	$29,000

49. **A** Since the transaction lacks commercial substance, the asset received should be recorded at the book value of the asset(s) given up and the theoretical gain deferred. The theoretical gain is the $700,000 fair value of Terry versus the book value of $550,000 given up (cash of $50,000 plus the book value of Duff of $500,000) for a theoretical gain of $150,000. The journal entry would be as follows:

Terry, Player (cost)	$550,000	
Duff, Player		$500,000
Cash		$50,000

50. **B** Since the transaction lacks commercial substance and Good Deal received cash, a gain should be recognized on the portion of the asset sold and the "cost" of the new asset should be recorded at book value of the portion of asset traded.

    $$\text{ratio: } \frac{\text{monetary consideration}}{\text{total consideration}} = \frac{\$20,000}{\$20,000 + \$180,000} = 10\%$$

    Portion of book value applicable to monetary consideration = 10% × $160,000 = $16,000

Monetary consideration	$20,000
Less: Applicable book value	16,000
Gain realized	$ 4,000

Book value of asset given up	$160,000
Less: Book value applicable to monetary consideration	16,000
Recorded amount of acquired asset	$144,000

51. **D** The asset received should be recorded at the fair value of the asset given up or the asset received, whichever is more evident, and a gain or loss recognized immediately.

52. **C** The general rule is that the asset should be recorded at fair value. However, in this situation in which the fair value cannot be determined, the FASB makes an exception and allows the recording of the asset at the book value of the asset(s) given up. May gave up two assets, the book value of the asset traded and cash, so the answer would be C.

CHAPTER 4 – BONDS PAYABLE, NOTES PAYABLE, AND INVESTMENTS IN BONDS OR NOTES HELD TO MATURITY

STUDY TIP

Before you get too involved in studying for the CPA exam, make sure you know exactly why you want to pass this exam. It is much easier to do the necessary work if you have a clear understanding of why you want to pass.

CHAPTER 4 – BONDS PAYABLE, NOTES PAYABLE, AND INVESTMENTS IN BONDS OR NOTES HELD TO MATURITY

BONDS AND NOTES

A. **Bonds** and **notes** are formal promises to pay a certain amount of money (principal) along with a specified amount of interest at a certain time in the future.

B. Bonds and notes can be negotiated with a single party or they can be structured as a negotiable instrument to be bought and sold at whatever price can be achieved.

C. **Serial bonds** are those that make periodic payments of interest and principal; they mature in installments, such as on the same date each year over a period of years.

D. **Term bonds** are those that make interest payments each period, but the principal is paid as a lump sum on a single maturity date.

E. **Debenture bonds** are not secured by collateral but rather by the general assets of the company. Mortgage bonds are secured by collateral.

COMMON FEATURES FOUND IN BONDS

A. **Bond indenture** is a document that describes the legal terms of the bond. The indenture is the bond contract.

B. **Bond issuance costs** paid by the debtor are reported as an asset (deferred charge) and amortized as an expense through the straight-line method over the life of the bond. If the bond is paid off early, any remaining cost must be removed. Examples of bond issuance costs include printing and engraving costs, legal and accounting fees, promotion costs, commissions.

Selling Price of a Bond on the Market

A. Price is usually stated as a percentage of face value (e.g., a price of 98 would mean 98% of face value).

B. If investors want an interest rate that is the same rate as the cash rate stated on the indenture, they will pay an amount equal to the face value of the bond. Note the following formula:

   stated interest rate × face value = annual amount of interest to be paid

C. If the investor and debtor negotiate an effective yield rate that is different than the stated cash interest rate, the price of the bond must be calculated.

D. The present value of the cash flows set by the indenture is determined using the effective yield rate negotiated by the parties.

Using the effective interest method:

carrying amount of the bonds × effective rate = interest expense

The resulting price will be:

1. Below face value if the negotiated yield rate is higher than the stated interest rate (discount); carrying amount increases each year, so interest expense increases each year.

2. Above face value if the negotiated yield rate is below the stated interest rate (premium); carrying amount decreases each year, so interest expense decreases each year.

E. A present value computation is also necessary if the stated interest rate is unreasonable (such as a zero rate). Interest is assumed to be hidden inside of the note or bond.

Example: A bond is issued with a face value (or, maturity value) of $1,000 and a stated interest rate of 1%. It matures in 10 years. The current market rate for similar bonds is 5%. The stated interest rate is unreasonable, and the selling price must be calculated. The calculation would be the present value of the future cash flows, a lump sum of $1,000 for the maturity value, and an ordinary annuity for interest ($10.00 each year for 10 years). The appropriate interest rate for the present value calculation would be market rate, or 5%. The sum of the PV of the principal and the PV of the interest payments would be the selling price of this bond. Because the current market rate is greater than the stated interest rate, the bond will sell at a discount (i.e., selling price will be less than $1,000).

F. Summary:

If the bond's market rate of interest on the date of acquisition is *different* than the stated rate, the bonds will have a premium or discount.

1. If the market rate of interest is higher than the bond's stated rate, the price will be lower than the face value (i.e., discounted). The discount will be recognized over the life of the investment as an addition to interest expense. Annual interest expense will equal the cash interest paid plus the discount amortization for the year.

2. If bonds are purchased at par (face value), the interest expense will equal the cash interest received. There will be no discount or premium. Interest expense will stay constant throughout the life of the bond.

3. If the market rate of interest is lower than the bond's stated rate, the price will be higher than the face value (i.e., premium). The premium will be recognized over the life of the investment as a reduction in interest expense. The interest expense for a bond purchased at a premium would equal the cash interest paid less the premium amortization for the year.

FEATURES OF PREMIUMS AND DISCOUNTS

A. If a premium or discount is recorded on a bond, that amount must be amortized to interest over the life of the bond.

B. Amortization entries are made at the date of each interest payment, as well as at the end of each fiscal year.

METHODS OF AMORTIZING PREMIUMS AND DISCOUNTS

A. Effective rate method.

1. The effective rate method calculates the true interest by multiplying current book value of the debt (face value plus premium or minus discount) by the effective interest rate.

2. The difference between this interest figure and the cash interest payment reduces the discount or premium.

3. Because of the change in the discount or premium, the book value of the bond or note changes each time amortization is recorded.

    For example, assume a bond with a $100,000 face value and an annual 6% stated cash interest rate is sold for $90,000 to yield an annual rate of 9%. Then, after one year, $6,000 interest is actually paid ($100,000 × 6%) but interest is recognized on the income statement as $8,100 ($90,000 × 9%). The $2,100 difference ($8,100 less $6,000) is added to the book value of the bond to raise it to $92,100.

4. The effective interest rate is the market rate at the time the bond is originally issued.

5. The effective interest rate can be calculated as follows:

    [current year discount or premium amortization + (coupon rate × face value)]/ beginning net debt (beginning book value of bond)

    Using the information in the previous example, the effective interest rate can be proven using this formula. This formula verifies that the effective interest rate equals the market rate at the time the bond was originally sold.

    [$2,100 + (0.06 × $100,000)] / $90,000 = 9%

B. Straight-line method.

1. The straight-line method is sometimes used to amortize the discount or premium, although the effective rate method is preferred.

2. The straight-line method divides premium or discount evenly over the life of the bond; the same amount is amortized each period.

3. Straight-line method can be used when recognized amounts are not materially different than figures that would have been reported by the effective rate method.

C. Under either method, interest expense to be recognized is the cash interest plus the amortization of any discount or less the amortization of any premium.

D. Bond issuance costs must be amortized as well as any discount or premium.

E. For a long-term bond, the portion that should be reported as a current liability is equal to any principal payment in the upcoming year less amortization of any discount or plus amortization of any premium.

ACCOUNTING ENTRIES WHEN BONDS ARE CALLED BY THE ISSUER

A. If a bond is called by the issuer before its maturity date, the debtor must repay the outstanding amounts immediately or within a reasonable amount of time.

B. A final amortization entry must be recorded to bring the bond's book value to its current amount.

C. Face value along with any remaining bond issuance costs and any unamortized discount or premium gives the book value of the bond.

   1. The difference between this book value and the cash payment to the issuer is recognized as a gain or loss.

   2. For the debtor, the gain or loss is classified as an ordinary part of net income. It is no longer viewed as an extraordinary item.

ACCOUNTING ENTRIES FOR DETACHABLE STOCK WARRANTS

A. A bond is sometimes sold along with detachable stock warrants, all for one price.

B. Warrants are long-term equity call options (i.e., the right to purchase the bond-issuing company's stock) and are typically issued with bonds as a sweetener to make the company's bonds appear more attractive to potential investors.

C. To record both the bond and the warrant, the price must be allocated between debt and equity.

   1. If market value of only one item is known, that amount is assigned to that item. The remainder is "plugged" to the other item.

   2. If both items have a known fair value, the price is allocated between debt and equity based on their relative market values. If the fair value of the warrant is $100, and the fair value of the bond is $200, then 1/3 of the total price of the bond + warrant issue is assigned to the warrants and 2/3 is assigned to the bonds.

D. If bonds with warrants are issued at a discount or premium, then the discount or premium must be amortized in the same way other bond discounts and premiums are amortized.

COMMON CLASSIFICATION ISSUES ARISING WITH DEBT

A. Some financial instruments have characteristics of both liabilities and equities, so classification on the balance sheet can be a problem.

B. The following are considered to be liabilities rather than equities:

   1. Any financial instrument (even a share of the company's own stock) is reported as a liability if assets will have to be used to satisfy a mandatory redemption.

      The best example is preferred stock that must eventually be redeemed with cash. It is listed as a liability on the balance sheet. This is called "mandatorily redeemable preferred stock."

   2. A financial instrument that must or may be settled by a variable number of the company's own equity shares is reported as a liability:

a. The monetary amount may be fixed (so that the number of shares required will vary based on market price).

b. The number of shares to be issued may be based on some other value (such as the current price of gold).

C. If a company has a debt coming due within 12 months of the balance sheet date, the debt is classified as long term if either one of two conditions is met before the financial statements are issued:

1. The debt is refinanced on a long-term basis.

2. A noncancellable agreement to refinance on a long-term basis is signed with a financially sound lending institution.

FEATURES OF CONVERTIBLE BONDS

A. Bonds are frequently issued with the right to convert the bonds into common stock by the investor.

1. Upon conversion, the investor exchanges the bond for a prespecified number of common shares (the conversion rate).

2. For example, a bond issued with a 10-to-1 conversion factor may be exchanged for 10 shares of common equity.

B. The equity option or conversion feature embedded in convertible bonds is *not* detachable—you cannot trade or act on this option separately. You either hold a bond or you convert that bond into common stock by exercising the conversion feature.

C. The convertability feature of a bond is ignored when the bond is issued; no value is apportioned to the conversion feature.

1. The entire proceeds of the bond are recorded as a liability.

2. When a convertible bond is converted into equity, the entire proceeds will be reclassified from debt to equity.

ACCOUNTING FOR CONVERSION OF BONDS

There are two methods presented below. Use whichever method is more reliable in the circumstances.

A. Book Value Method. This method values the transaction at the book value of the bonds. (This is absolutely the most commonly used method.)

1. The book value of the bond payable is removed from books, the common stock is recorded at par, and the difference between the book value of the bonds and the par value of the common stock is recorded as Additional Paid in Capital (APIC)—Common Stock. Therefore, common equity is increased and long-term debt is reduced by the same amount. No gain or loss is recorded and none should result from an equity transaction.

2. Journal entry:

Bonds payable   (book value)
    Common stock   (par)
    APIC—common stock   (book value of bonds – par value of stock)

B. Market Value Method. This method records the shares issued at the market value of the shares at the time of conversion. The difference between this market value of the shares and the book value of the bonds is recorded as a loss on conversion of the bonds.

For the purposes of the illustration, we will assume market value exceeds book value.

1. This method assumes a culmination of earnings process which justifies recording a loss on the conversion. The market value of the bonds or the market value of the stock can be used, depending on which is more readily determinable.

2. On the issuing company's books, the loss would be the difference between the market value of the stock and the book value of the bonds.

3. Journal entry:

Loss on redemption	(plug)
Bonds payable	(book value)
Common stock	(par)
APIC—common stock	(market value – par value)

4. Additional paid-in capital (APIC) is credited for the excess of market value over the par value.

EXTINGUISHMENT OF DEBT

A. Debt is considered extinguished whenever the debtor pays the creditor and is relieved of all obligations relating to the debt.

B. Examples:

1. The calling of a bond by the debtor, requiring the bondholder to sell the bond to the issuing company at a certain date and stated price.

2. Open market repurchase of a debt issue by the debtor.

3. Refunding of debt (replacement of debt with other debt).

   Note: Troubled debt restructures and debt conversions are not considered extinguishment of debt.

C. All gains or losses resulting from the extinguishment of debt should be recognized in the period of extinguishment.

1. The gain or loss is the difference between the bond's reacquisition price and its net book value (face value +/– any unamortized premium or discount and issue costs).

2. The gain or loss is considered an ordinary one and is a separate item in net income from continuing operations. *Note: Gains and losses on extinguishment of debt are no longer considered to be extraordinary; they are ordinary.*

TROUBLED DEBT RESTRUCTURING

A. A troubled debt restructuring occurs when a debtor faces default and the creditor gives more lenient terms in hopes of improving future collection.

B. If payment is made immediately with a noncash asset (such as land), the asset is first adjusted to market value so that the debtor has an ordinary gain or loss.

    1. The difference between the market value of the asset and the book value of the debt is an ordinary gain or loss for the debtor.

    2. The creditor accounts for any loss as an ordinary loss.

C. If debt is restructured so that the debtor has better terms, the debtor and creditor record the restructuring differently.

    1. Debtor.

        a. Records a gain if the new agreement calls for less to be paid (over the entire life of revised note) than is currently due (principal plus unpaid interest to date). No present value calculations are required here.

        b. If less is to be paid, the debt is reduced to that amount and a gain is recognized.

        c. If gain is recognized by debtor, no future interest amounts are recorded even if a payment is called "interest."

        d. If more will be paid than is currently owed, no gain is recorded. That excess is recognized as interest over the remaining life of the payments.

    2. Creditor.

        a. Computes the present value of future cash flows (specified by the restructuring) based on the original interest rate. The future cash flows are those determined by the restructuring agreement.

        b. If present value is less than the current debt (principal plus interest), a loss is recorded for the difference.

        c. Future interest revenue to be recognized is the original interest rate times book value, which is the present value of future cash flows.

QUESTIONS: BONDS PAYABLE, NOTES PAYABLE, AND INVESTMENTS IN BONDS OR NOTES HELD TO MATURITY

1. On July 1, Year 6, Novotny Corp. (Novotny) issued 600 of its 10%, $1,000 bonds at 99 plus accrued interest. The bonds are dated April 1, Year 6 and mature on April 1, 2016. Interest is payable semiannually on April 1 and October 1.

   What amount did Novotny receive from the bond issuance?
   A. $579,000.
   B. $594,000.
   C. $600,000.
   D. $609,000.

2. During Year 6, Kinney, Inc. (Kinney) issued 3,000 of its 9%, $1,000 face value bonds at 101.5. In connection with the sale of these bonds, Kinney paid the following expenses:

Promotion costs	$20,000
Engraving and printing	$25,000
Underwriters' commission	$200,000

   What amount should Kinney record as bond issue costs to be amortized over the term of the bonds?
   A. $0.
   B. $220,000.
   C. $225,000.
   D. $245,000.

3. Samilski Corp. (Samilski) incurred costs of $3,300 when it issued, on August 31, Year 6, 5-year debenture bonds dated April 1, Year 6. What amount of bond issue expense should Samilski report in its income statement for the year ended December 31, Year 6?
   A. $220.
   B. $240.
   C. $495.
   D. $3,300.

Use the following information to answer Questions 4 and 5.

Schmidt, Inc. (Schmidt) issues a $10 million bond with a 6% coupon rate, 4-year maturity, and annual interest payments when market interest rates are 7%.

4. What is the initial book value of the bonds?
   A. $9,400,000.
   B. $9,661,279.
   C. $10,000,000.
   D. $10,338,721.

5.   For the first period, the interest expense is:
     A. $600,000.
     B. $676,290.
     C. $700,000.
     D. $723,710.

6.   On January 2, Year 6, Cabassi Co. (Cabassi) issued 9% bonds in the amount of $500,000, which
     mature on January 2, 2016. The bonds were issued for $469,500 to yield 10%. Interest is payable
     annually on December 31. Cabassi uses the effective interest method of amortization.

     In its June 30, Year 6 balance sheet, what amount should Cabassi report as bonds payable?
     A. $469,500.
     B. $470,475.
     C. $471,025.
     D. $500,000.

7.   Luna Co. (Luna) has outstanding a 7%, 10-year $100,000 face value bond. The bond was
     originally sold to yield 6% annual interest. Luna uses the effective interest rate method of
     amortization. On June 30, Year 5, the carrying amount of the outstanding bond was $105,000.

     What amount of unamortized bond premium or discount should Luna report on its June 30, Year
     6 balance sheet?
     A. $1,050.
     B. $3,950.
     C. $4,300.
     D. $4,500.

8.   On January 2, Year 6, Nash Co. (Nash) issued 8% bonds with a face amount of $1,000,000 that
     mature on January 2, 2012. The bonds were issued to yield 12%, resulting in a discount of
     $150,000. Nash incorrectly used the straight-line method instead of the effective interest method
     to amortize the discount. How is the carrying amount of the bonds affected by the error?

	At December 31, Year 6	At January 2, 2012
A.	Overstated	Understated
B.	Overstated	No effect
C.	Understated	Overstated
D.	Understated	No effect

9.   On July 1, Year 6, Kyle Co. (Kyle) purchased as a long-term investment $500,000 face amount,
     8% bonds of Rubba Co. (Rubba) for $461,500 to yield 10% per year. The bonds pay interest
     semiannually on January 1 and July 1. In its December 31, Year 6 balance sheet, Kyle should
     report interest receivable of:
     A. $18,460.
     B. $20,000.
     C. $23,075.
     D. $25,000.

10. An investor purchased a bond as a long-term investment on January 1. Annual interest was received on December 31. The investor's interest income for the year would be highest if the bond was purchased at:
    A. par.
    B. face value.
    C. a discount.
    D. a premium.

11. Jenn Corp. (Jenn) purchased bonds at a discount of $10,000. Subsequently, Jenn sold these bonds at a premium of $14,000. During the period that Jenn held this investment, amortization of the discount amounted to $2,000. What amount should Jenn report as a gain on the sale of the bonds?
    A. $12,000.
    B. $22,000.
    C. $24,000.
    D. $26,000.

12. On July 1, Year 6, after recording interest and amortization, Yorkville Co. (Yorkville) converted $1,000,000 of its 12% convertible bonds into 50,000 shares of $1 par value common stock. On the conversion date, the carrying amount of the bonds was $1,300,000, the market value of the bonds was $1,400,000, and Yorkville's common stock was publicly trading at $30 per share.

    Using the book value method, what amount of additional paid-in capital should Yorkville record as a result of the conversion?
    A. $950,000.
    B. $1,250,000.
    C. $1,350,000.
    D. $1,500,000.

13. On December 30, Year 6, Fortin, Inc. (Fortin) issued 1,000 of its 8%, 10-year, $1,000 face value bonds with detachable stock warrants at par. Each bond carried a detachable warrant for one share of Fortin's common stock at a specific option price of $25 per share. Immediately after issuance, the market value of the bonds without warrants was $1,080,000 and the market value of the warrants was $120,000.

    In its December 31, Year 6 balance sheet, what amount should Fortin report as bonds payable?
    A. $880,000.
    B. $900,000.
    C. $975,000.
    D. $1,000,000.

14. Maren Co. (Maren) issued bonds with detachable common stock warrants. Only the warrants had a known market value. The sum of the fair value of the warrants and the face amount of the bonds exceeds the cash proceeds. The excess is reported as:
    A. discount on bonds payable.
    B. premium on bonds payable.
    C. common stock subscribed.
    D. contributed capital in excess of par—stock warrants.

15. On June 30, Year 6, King Co. (King) had outstanding 9%, $5,000,000 face value bonds maturing on June 30, 2011. Interest was payable semiannually every June 30 and December 31. On June 30, Year 6, after amortization was recorded for the period, the unamortized bond premium and bond issue costs were $30,000 and $50,000, respectively. On that date, King acquired all its outstanding bonds on the open market at 98 and retired them. On June 30, Year 6, what amount should King recognize as a gain (before income taxes) on the redemption of the bonds?
    A. $20,000.
    B. $80,000.
    C. $120,000.
    D. $180,000.

16. Casper Corp. (Casper) entered into a troubled debt restructuring agreement with the First State Bank (First State). First State agreed to accept land with a carrying amount of $85,000 and a fair value of $120,000 in exchange for a note with a carrying amount of $185,000. What amount should Casper report as a gain from extinguishment of debt in its income statement?
    A. $0.
    B. $35,000.
    C. $65,000.
    D. $100,000.

17. On October 15, Year 6, Rica Corp. (Rica) informed Flor Co. (Flor) that Rica would be unable to repay its $100,000 note due on October 31 to Flor. Flor agreed to accept title to Rica's computer equipment in full settlement of the note. The equipment's carrying value was $80,000 and its fair value was $75,000. What amounts should Rica report as the gain (loss) on the transfer of assets and the gain on restructuring of debt?

	Transfer gain/(loss)	Restructuring gain
A.	($5,000)	$25,000
B.	$0	$30,000
C.	$0	$20,000
D.	$20,000	$0

18. Pastorale, Inc. (Pastorale) is indebted to Tempest, Inc. (Tempest) under an $800,000, 10%, 4-year note dated December 31, 2003. Annual interest of $80,000 was paid on December 31, Year 4 and Year 5. During Year 6, Pastorale experienced financial difficulties and is likely to default unless concessions are made. On December 31, Year 6, Tempest agreed to restructure the debt as follows:
    • Interest of $80,000 for Year 6, due on December 31, Year 6, was made payable December 31, Year 7.
    • Interest for Year 7 was waived.
    • The principal amount was reduced to $700,000.

    How much should Pastorale report as a gain in its income statement for the year ended December 31, Year 6?
    A. $0.
    B. $60,000.
    C. $100,000.
    D. $120,000.

19. Maui, Inc. (Maui) had a $4,000,000 note payable due on March 15, Year 6. On January 28, Year 6, before the issuance of its Year 5 financial statements, Maui issued long-term bonds in the amount of $4,500,000. Proceeds from the bonds were used to repay the note when it came due. How should Maui classify the note in its December 31, Year 5 financial statements?
    A. As a current liability, with separate disclosure of the note refinancing.
    B. As a current liability with no separate disclosure required.
    C. As a noncurrent liability, with separate disclosure of the note refinancing.
    D. As a noncurrent liability, with no separate disclosure required.

20. On January 1, Year 1, a company agrees to pay $80,000 in exactly three years for a machine. No interest is to be paid although a reasonable rate is 8%. The present value of $1 in three years at an 8% annual rate is assumed to be 0.735. The present value of a $1 ordinary annuity over three years at an 8% annual rate is assumed to be 2.577. The present value of a $1 annuity due over three years at an 8% annual rate is assumed to be 2.783. Approximately how much interest expense should be recognized on this liability for Year 2?
    A. $0.
    B. $4,704.
    C. $5,080.
    D. $5,346.

21. A company issues a $5 million bond on January 1, Year 1 paying 6% annual interest. A buyer for the bond cannot be found initially. Eventually, the company locates a buyer by issuing the bond to generate an effective annual interest rate of 8%. The bond is sold at 84% of its face value. What is the book value of this bond on December 31, Year 2?
    A. $4,274,880.
    B. $4,258,620.
    C. $4,252,190.
    D. $4,248,770.

22. On August 18, Year 3, the Chelsea Corporation owes the bank $500,000 on an 8% note and $60,000 in accrued interest. The note itself comes due in four years. Because Chelsea is undergoing financial difficulties, the two parties restructure the note. The accrued interest is eliminated and the principal of the note is reduced to $300,000 which is due in 10 years. The annual interest rate drops from 8% to 5%. The present value of these future cash flows at an 8% annual rate is assumed to be $240,000. What gain should Chelsea recognize on this troubled debt restructuring?
    A. $0.
    B. $110,000.
    C. $260,000.
    D. $320,000.

23. On January 1, Year 1, the Alexandria Company issues bonds with a face value of $100,000 and a stated annual cash interest rate of 7% for $91,000 to yield an assumed effective interest rate of 8%. Interest is paid every December 31 and the effective rate method is being applied. This issuance was done on a date when the market rate of interest for companies like Alexandria was 9%. Which of the following is false?
    A. To the buyers of the bonds, this company looks particularly risky.
    B. The 9% figure will have no impact on the financial statements of Alexandria.
    C. Interest expense to be recognized on the income statement for Year 1 will be $7,280.
    D. On Alexandria's financial statements, a $7,000 figure will only appear as a reduction in the Cash account.

24. On January 1, Year 1, the Charleston Company issues bonds with a face value of $100,000 and a stated annual cash interest rate of 6% for $80,000 to yield an assumed effective interest rate of 8%. Interest is paid every December 31 and the effective rate method is being applied. What amount of interest expense should Charleston report for the year ending December 31, Year 2?
    A. $6,000.
    B. $6,400.
    C. $6,432.
    D. $7,040.

25. On January 1, Year 1, Barcelona Corporation buys a 10-year $300,000 bond paying an annual cash interest of 5% every December 31. Assume that Barcelona pays $240,000 in order to create a mathematical yield rate of 7%. Barcelona plans to hold the bond until its maturity date. What would be the impact on net income reported for Year 1 if Barcelona uses the straight-line method rather than the effective-rate method? (Ignore income taxes.)
    A. The net income would be the same as under the effective rate method.
    B. Net income would be $4,200 higher than if the effective-rate method had been used.
    C. Net income would be $5,400 higher than if the effective-rate method had been used.
    D. Net income would be $6,000 higher than if the effective-rate method had been used.

26. On July 1, Year 1, the Albemarle Corporation buys a 10-year $400,000 bond paying an annual cash interest of 9% every June 30. Assume that Albemarle pays $420,000 in order to create a mathematical yield rate of 7.5%. Albemarle plans to hold the bond until its maturity date. If the straight-line method of amortization is applied, what amount of interest revenue should Albemarle recognize for Year 1?
    A. $15,750.
    B. $17,000.
    C. $18,900.
    D. $19,000.

27. On December 31, Year 1, a company borrows $1 million from a bank on a six-month note paying an annual stated interest rate of 6% (the prime interest rate on that date). When the note comes due on June 30, Year 2, the bank pays the interest and refinances the $1 million with a new six-month note at the current prime rate. The company and the bank continue to follow this pattern for years: The interest is paid every six months and a new note is signed for $1 million to refinance the principal. On December 31, Year 6, the latest interest payment and note signing takes place. Once again, this note is for six months. The company will issue its Year 6 financial statements on March 4, Year 7. Which of the following is true?
    A. The note should be reported as a current liability in all cases because it is due in six months.
    B. The note should be reported as a long-term liability in all cases because there is sufficient evidence that the note will not be paid with cash.
    C. The company has the option of reporting the note as a long-term liability or as a current liability.
    D. If the company and the bank sign a non-cancelable agreement on February 26, Year 7 that states that the note will continue to be refinanced through the end of Year 7, the note must be reported as a long-term liability.

28. A company has a bond outstanding with a book value of $367,000. The bond is paid off before its maturity. Which of the following is true about the gain or loss resulting from the early extinguishment?
    A. The gain or loss must be reported as an extraordinary item.
    B. The gain or loss must not be reported as an extraordinary item.
    C. The gain or loss must be reported as an extraordinary item if it is viewed as both unusual in nature and infrequent in occurrence.
    D. To avoid income manipulation, gains must be reported as extraordinary whereas losses cannot be recorded as extraordinary.

29. On January 1, Year 1, the Depth Corporation (Depth) borrows $1 million from a bank on a 10-year note paying cash interest at the end of each year of 10%. Interest is properly paid for the first three years but the interest payment is missed on December 31, Year 4. On January 1, Year 5, the company and the bank restructure the loan. The principal is dropped from $1 million to $600,000 and the interest rate is dropped from 10% to 8%. The maturity date is moved from December 31, Year 10 to December 31, Year 15 (11 years from the date of refinancing). The present value of these new future cash flows discounted at a 10% annual interest rate is assumed to be $522,000. What amount of gain should Depth recognize on this restructuring?
    A. $0.
    B. $400,000.
    C. $500,000.
    D. $578,000.

30. On January 1, Year 1, the Cincinnati Corporation borrows $1 million from the First National Bank of Ohio on a 10-year note paying cash interest at the end of each year of 10%. Interest is properly paid for the first three years but the interest payment is missed on December 31, Year 4. On January 1, Year 5, the company and the bank restructure the loan. The principal is dropped from $1 million to $600,000 and the interest rate is dropped from 10% to 8%. The maturity date is moved from December 31, Year 10 to December 31, Year 15 (11 years from the date of refinancing). The present value of these future cash flows discounted at a 10% annual interest rate is assumed to be $522,000. What amount of loss should the bank recognize on this restructuring?
    A. $0.
    B. $400,000.
    C. $500,000.
    D. $578,000.

31. On December 31, Year 1, Arnold, Inc., issued $200,000 in annual 8% serial bonds, to be repaid in the amount of $40,000 each year plus interest on December 31. The bonds were issued for $190,280 to yield 10% interest each year. Arnold uses the effective rate method to determine the interest to be recognized. In its December 31, Year 2, balance sheet, at what amount should Arnold report the carrying value of the bonds?
    A. $139,380.
    B. $149,100.
    C. $150,280.
    D. $153,308.

32.   On January 1, Year 1, Grey Company owes the local bank $800,000 on a payable that will come
       due in exactly seven years (January 1, Year 8). The company also owes accrued interest of $64,000
       based on an annual interest rate of 8%. Grey and the bank have now agreed to the following
       restructuring arrangement:
       • Reduced the principal obligation from $800,000 to $600,000.
       • Forgave the $64,000 accrued interest.
       • Set the maturity date at January 1, Year 3.
       • Set the annual interest at 6% per year to be paid to Grey on December 31, Year 1 and Year 2.

       Based on an annual interest rate of 8%, the present value of the cash flows after the restructuring
       was $578,000.

       At the date of the restructuring, what gain, if any, should Grey (the debtor) recognize?
       A. $0.
       B. $192,000.
       C. $200,000.
       D. $264,000.

ANSWERS: BONDS PAYABLE, NOTES PAYABLE, AND INVESTMENTS IN BONDS OR NOTES HELD TO MATURITY

1. **D** To determine the net cash received from the bond issuance, we should look at the journal entries.

Cash	$609,000	
Discount on bonds payable	$6,000	
Bonds payable		$600,000
Interest expense		$15,000

    The bonds were issued at 99 ($600,000 × 99% = $594,000), so the discount is $6,000. The accrued interest covers the three months from April 1, Year 6 to July 1, Year 6 ($600,000 × 10% × 3/12 = $15,000). The cash received includes the $594,000 for the bonds and the $15,000 for the accrued interest, for a total of $609,000.

2. **D** SFAS 91 states that engraving and printing costs, legal and accounting fees, commissions, promotion costs, and other similar costs should be recorded as bond issue costs and amortized over the term of the bonds. All the costs given are bond issue costs, so the amount reported is $245,000 ($20,000 + $25,000 + $200,000).

3. **B** Bond issue costs are treated as deferred charges and amortized on a straight-line basis over the life of the bond. These five-year bonds were issued five months late (4/1/04 to 8/31/04), so they will be outstanding only 55 months (60 – 5). During Year 6, the bonds were outstanding for four months (8/31/04 to 12/31/04). Therefore, the bond issue costs must be amortized for four months out of 55 months total, resulting in bond issue expense of $250 ($3,300 × 4/55).

4. **B** The present value of a four-year annuity of $600,000 plus a four-year lump sum of $10 million, all valued at a discount rate of 7%, which equals $9,661,279. Note that the process of elimination takes out Choices C and D because the bond is selling at a discount.

5. **B** The market interest rate multiplied by the book value = 7% × $9,661,279 = $676,290.

6. **B** Under the effective interest method, interest expense is computed as follows:

    book value of bonds × yield rate × time period = interest expense

    $469,500 × 10% × 6/12 = $23,475

    The cash interest payable is computed as follows:

    face value of bonds × stated rate × time period = interest payable

    $500,000 × 9% × 6/12 = $22,500

    The bond discount amortization is the difference between these two amounts computed above ($23,475 – $22,500 = $975). The amortization would increase the carrying amount of the bonds to $470,475 ($469,500 original carrying amount + $975 amortization).

7. **C** Under the effective interest method, interest expense is computed as follows:

    book value of bonds × yield rate × time period = interest expense

    $105,000 × 6% ×12/12 = $6,300

    The cash interest payable is computed as follows:

    face value of bonds × stated rate × time period = interest payable

    $100,000 × 7% × 12/12 = $7,000

The bond premium amortization is the difference between these two amounts computed above ($7,000 – $6,300 = $700). Therefore, the unamortized premium at June 30, Year 6 would be $4,300 ($5,000 – $700).

8. **B**   Under the effective interest method, the discount amortization amount increases yearly. Under the straight-line method, discount amortization is constant each period. After one year, the incorrect use of the straight-line method would overstate the carrying amount of the bonds because more discount would have been amortized than under the effective interest method. By the time the bonds mature on January 2, 2012, the entire discount would have been amortized under both methods, so the carrying amount would be the same for both methods.

9. **B**   Interest receivable on an investment in bonds is computed using the basic interest formula:

face value × stated rate × time period = interest receivable

$500,000 × 8% × 6/12 = $20,000

Note that interest revenue is $23,075 ($461,500 × 10% × 6/12) using the effective interest method.

10. **C**   Bonds purchased at a discount—the discount will increase the amount of interest income even though the cash amount of interest received is the same.

11. **B**   The gain on the sale of the bond investment is the excess of the selling price over the carrying amount. The selling price was $14,000 above face value. The bonds were purchased at a discount of $10,000 but after amortization of $2,000, the carrying amount at the time of the sale was $8,000 below face value. Therefore, the selling price exceeded the carrying amount by $22,000 ($14,000 premium + $8,000 remaining discount).

12. **B**   Using the book value method, the common stock is recorded at the carrying amount of the converted bonds, less any conversion expenses. Because there are no conversion expenses in this case, the common stock is recorded at the $1,300,000 carrying amount of the converted bonds. The par value of the stock issued is $50,000 (50,000 × $1), so additional paid-in capital (APIC) of $1,250,000 ($1,300,000 – $50,000) is recorded. Note that when the book value is used, fair values are not considered and no gain or loss is recognized.

13. **B**   APB 14 states that the proceeds of bonds issued with detachable warrants are allocated between the bonds and the warrants based on their relative fair values at the time of issuance. In this case, the portion allocated to the bonds is $900,000, calculated as follows:

$1,080,000 / ($1,080,000 + $120,000) × $1,000,000 = $900,000

Therefore, the bonds payable are reported at $900,000 (face value $1,000,000 less $100,000 discount).

14. **A**   The approach is to set up the original journal entry on the books of the issuer.

Cash	(proceeds)	
Discount on bonds payable	(plug)	
Bonds payable		(face value)
APIC–stock warrants		(fair value)

Because the APIC–stock warrants account is already stated at market value, any remaining difference must be allocated to the bonds. Bonds payable would be credited only at their face (par) value. Therefore, discount on bonds payable is debited for the excess of fair value of the warrants and the face amount of the bonds over cash proceeds.

15. **B**   A gain or loss on redemption of bonds is the difference between the cash paid ($5,000,000 × 98% = $4,900,000) and the net book value of the bonds. To compute the net book value, premium or discount and bond issue costs must be considered. Book value is $4,980,000 ($5,000,000 face value, less $50,000 bond issue costs, plus $30,000 premium). Therefore, the gain or redemption is $80,000 ($4,980,000 book value less $4,900,000 cash paid).

16. **C**   If a debt is settled by the exchange of assets, a restructuring gain is recognized for the difference between the carrying amount of the debt and the fair value of the consideration given up to extinguish the debt. If a noncash asset is given, a separate gain or loss is recorded to revalue the noncash asset to fair value as the basis of the noncash asset given.

Therefore, a gain of $35,000 ($120,000 – $85,000) will be recorded to revalue the land to fair value, and a gain of $65,000 ($185,000 – $120,000) will be recorded for the extinguishment of the debt in Casper's income statement.

17. **A**   In this restructure, the debt is retired by the transfer of equipment to the creditor. Per SFAS 15, a gain or loss is recognized on the transfer of the equipment and a gain or loss is recognized on the retirement of the debt. The loss on the transfer of equipment is the excess of the equipment's carrying amount over its fair value ($80,000 – $75,000 = $5,000). The gain on retirement of debt is the excess of the carrying amount of the debt over the fair value of the equipment transferred ($100,000 – $75,000 = $25,000).

18. **C**   According to SFAS 15, if the debt is continued with a modification of terms, a gain is recognized by the debtor if the future cash payments on the debt are less than the carrying value of the debt. For troubled debt restructures, carrying value is defined as the principal amount ($800,000) plus accrued interest ($80,000) for a total of $880,000. The future payments total $780,000 ($700,000 reduced principal and $80,000 interest). The $100,000 difference ($880,000 – $780,000) is recognized as a restructuring gain.

19. **C**   The $4,000,000 note is due March 15, Year 6, and normally would be classified as a current liability in the December 31, Year 5 financial statements. However, SFAS 6 states that a short-term obligation can be reclassified as long-term if the company intends to refinance the obligation on a long-term basis and the intent is supported by the ability to refinance.

Maui demonstrated its ability to refinance by actually issuing bonds and refinancing the note prior to the issuance of the December 31, Year 5 financial statements. Since the proceeds from the bonds exceeded the amount needed to retire the note, the entire $4,000,000 notes payable would be classified as a noncurrent liability, with separate disclosure of the note refinancing required by SFAS 6.

20. **C**   The liability is recorded initially at its present value of $58,800 ($80,000 × 0.735). Interest for the first year is 8% of that balance or $4,704. Because no cash interest is being paid, this amount is compounded to bring the liability balance up to $63,504. At 8% interest, this new balance leads to interest expense for the second year of $5,080.

21. **A**   The bond was issued for $4.2 million (84% of $5 million). Interest recognized the first year was $336,000 (8% of $4.2 million) but the interest paid at the time was only $300,000 (6% of $5 million). The $36,000 difference was not paid so it had to be compounded, bringing the bond up to $4,236,000. Interest recognized the second year was $338,880 (8% of $4,236,000) but the interest paid at the time was again $300,000. The $38,880 difference was compounded to bring the bond up to $4,274,880.

22. **B**   In a troubled debt restructuring, for the debtor, the amount currently owed is compared to the future cash flows to be paid. Thus, the debt today of $560,000 is compared to the $450,000 that will be paid in total ($300,000 plus $15,000 in interest annually for ten years). The reduction creates the gain to be reported.

23. **A**   The bond was sold at a yield rate (8%) that was below the current market rate (9%). Buyers would only acquire an investment at this lower interest rate if they felt that the company or the structure of the bond was particularly strong. Interest expense for the first year is computed as the $91,000 book value times the 8% yield rate (or $7,280) while the amount of cash paid is the $100,000 face value times the 7% stated cash rate (or $7,000).

24. **C**   In Year 1, interest expense recognized is $6,400 ($80,000 book value times 8% yield rate). However, the cash interest paid is only $6,000 ($100,000 face value times 6% stated rate). The $400 interest amount that is recognized but not paid during the period is compounded or added to the book value. Hence, the book value for Year 2 is now $80,400 and interest expense is calculated by taking 8% of that new balance.

25. **B**   Under the effective rate method, Barcelona will recognize interest revenue in Year 1 of $16,800 ($240,000 book value times the yield rate of 7%). Under the straight-line method, the interest revenue is the $15,000 cash payment ($300,000 face value times the 5% stated rate) plus the amortization of the discount. The $60,000 discount is amortized over ten years at a rate of $6,000 per year. Thus, the straight-line method gives interest revenue of $21,000 ($15,000 plus $6,000), which is $4,200 higher than the $16,800 figure for the effective-rate method.

26. **B**   The cash interest for these six months is the $400,000 face value times the 9% stated rate times 1/2 year or $18,000. Using the straight-line method over ten years, the amortization of the $20,000 premium is $2,000 per year or $1,000 for six months. Because the bond was sold for a rate lower than the stated rate, the amortization reduces the interest being recognized. Consequently, interest expense for this period is $18,000 less $1,000 amortization or $17,000.

27. **D**   Because the due date is within six months, the note has to be reported as a current liability unless it is assured that no cash will be paid during Year 7. That proof has to be derived prior to issuance of the statements on March 7 and can either come from a non-cancelable agreement to refinance or from an actual refinancing arrangement. Here, the first of these criteria is met.

28. **C**   For several decades, gains and losses on the early extinguishment of debt had to be reported as extraordinary. That rule has been abandoned by the FASB and now these gains and losses are viewed exactly like any other gains and losses: if they are unusual in nature and infrequent in occurrence, they must be reported as extraordinary.

29. **A**   The debtor only recognizes a gain on a restructuring if the total amount of cash flows to be paid after the restructuring is less than the liability at the current time. The annual interest in the future will now be $48,000 ($600,000 × 8%) so that, over an eleven-year period, the total interest payments will amount to $528,000. The final principal payment of $600,000 brings the total cash payments up to $1,128,000 which is larger than the debt at present ($1.1 million–the $1 million principal plus one year of accrued interest at 10%). No income effect is recognized for the debtor at the time of the restructuring by the debtor.

30. **D**   The creditor recognizes a loss on a restructuring based on the difference between the amount owed at present ($1.1 million) and the present value of the future cash flows discounted at the rate of interest on the loan before it was restructured (10% in this case). Dropping the balance from $1.1 million to a present value of $522,000 creates a loss for the bank of $578,000.

31. **D**   The cash interest payment at the end of Year 2 should be the $200,000 face value times 8% interest or $16,000. The interest expense to be recognized is the $190,280 book value multiplied by the 10% yield rate or $19,028. The $3,028 difference that is recognized as interest expense but is not paid at this time must be capitalized or added to the principal. Consequently, at the end of Year 2, the original balance of $190,280 is increased by this $3,028 in interest that has not yet been paid. In addition, though, a $40,000 payment is made on the debt on that date so that the balance to be reported is now $153,308.

32. **B**   After a debt restructuring, the debtor only recognizes a gain if the amount to be paid in the future is less than the current amount of the reported liability. That is the case here as the total amount to be paid of $672,000 ($600,000 plus two payments of $36,000 each) is less than the $864,000 debt previously reported ($800,000 + $64,000). In that case, the carrying amount is simply reduced down to the total amount to be paid and this drop in the liability is the recorded gain. A reduction from $864,000 to $672,000 leads to a recognized gain of $192,000.

CHAPTER 5 – MISCELLANEOUS FINANCIAL STATEMENTS

STUDY TIP

Know as much as you can about the CPA exam before you sit. In addition to the content tested on the exam, you should be familiar with the testing and grading processes. This will improve your confidence and will prepare you for what is to come on the exam. The beginning of this study manual contains very useful information that you should review carefully as part of your preparation for exam day. The more you know about the CPA exam, the more chance you have for success. Before you get too far into your preparation, go to www.cpa-exam.org and read the official "Candidate Bulletin."

Chapter 5 – Miscellaneous Financial Statements

INTERIM REPORTING

A. Interim financial statements are produced for any period less than one year; most frequently every three months (e.g., quarterly statements for public companies).

   1. The purpose of interim statements is to provide more timely information than annual reports and to illustrate potential business turning points that may occur during the year.

B. U.S. GAAP takes an "integral view" approach to interim reporting, where each interim period is considered an integral part of an annual period.

   1. Expectations for the annual period must be reflected in interim reports.

   2. Special accruals, deferrals, and allocations are utilized.

C. Revenue recognition is the same as in regular accounting.

   1. Revenues are recognized when earned and the transaction is substantially complete.

   2. Certain income items such as extraordinary items are recorded when incurred and not allocated over the entire year.

D. Expenses are accrued in order to match them against the revenues they have helped generate. Expenses, such as property taxes and rents, that are for longer than a single quarter must be allocated to the periods benefited.

E. Income taxes must be anticipated and recognized each quarter.

   1. Each quarter, the effective tax rate for the entire year is estimated.

   2. This rate is multiplied by the total income to date to derive total income tax expense to date.

   3. Any tax expense previously recognized is subtracted to determine the appropriate expense for the current period.

F. If inventory declines in value during a quarter, a loss is not recognized if the drop in value is considered temporary.

   1. However, if the value decline is viewed as permanent, the loss is recognized immediately.

   2. A subsequent recovery of market value should be recognized as a cost recovery in the period of increase, but never above original cost.

PERSONAL FINANCIAL STATEMENTS AND DEVELOPMENT STAGE ENTERPRISES

A. **Personal financial statements** are prepared for individuals.

1. **Statement of financial condition** presents assets and liabilities at current values rather than historical cost. The difference is referred to as net worth.

   a. Because assets and liabilities are reported at fair value, the potential tax effects of realizing gains and losses in value must also be reported.

   b. Estimated tax effect on potential gains/losses is reported between the liabilities and net worth section of the balance sheet.

2. **A statement of changes in net worth** is also reported.

B. A **development stage enterprise** is a company that is working to establish its business and has not yet generated significant revenues. The reporting process is normal except that the income statement and cash flow figures are reported twice: for the current period and as cumulative amounts since the inception of the business.

QUESTIONS: MISCELLANEOUS FINANCIAL STATEMENTS

1. Wilson Corp. (Wilson) experienced a $50,000 decline in the market value of its inventory in the first quarter of its fiscal year. Wilson expected this decline to reverse in the third quarter, and in fact, the third quarter recovery exceeded the previous decline by $10,000. Wilson's inventory did not experience any other declines in market value during the fiscal year.

    What amounts of loss and/or gain should Wilson report in its interim financial statements for the first and third quarters?

	First quarter	Third quarter
A.	$0	$0
B.	$0	$10,000 gain
C.	$50,000 loss	$50,000 gain
D.	$50,000 loss	$60,000 gain

2. For interim financial reporting, a company's income tax provision for the second quarter of Year 6 should be determined by using which of the following?
    A. Effective tax rate expected to be applicable for the full year of Year 6 as estimated at the end of the first quarter of Year 6.
    B. Effective tax rate expected to be applicable for the full year of Year 6 as estimated at the end of the second quarter of Year 6.
    C. Effective tax rate expected to be applicable for the second quarter of Year 6.
    D. Statutory tax rate for Year 6.

3. Advertising costs may be accrued or deferred to provide an appropriate expense in each period under which of the following?

	Interim financial reporting	Year-end financial reporting
A.	Yes	No
B.	Yes	Yes
C.	No	No
D.	No	Yes

4. In general, an enterprise preparing interim financial statements should:
    A. defer recognition of seasonal revenue.
    B. disregard permanent decreases in the market value of its inventory.
    C. allocate revenues and expenses evenly over the quarters, regardless of when they actually occurred.
    D. use the same accounting principles followed in preparing its latest annual financial statements.

5. Which of the following is true for personal financial statements?
    A. Assets and liabilities are both reported at fair value.
    B. Assets are reported at fair value, but liabilities are not.
    C. Liabilities are reported at fair value, but assets are not.
    D. Neither assets nor liabilities are reported at fair value.

6.   Personal financial statements are being prepared for Dr. Abraham Jones. Dr. Jones holds land with a cost of $100,000 but a fair value of $500,000. The doctor has an effective tax rate of 40%. Which of the following statements is true?
      A.   A future tax obligation of $160,000 should be recognized by Dr. Jones as a liability.
      B.   A future tax obligation of $160,000 should be recognized by Dr. Jones as part of the net worth.
      C.   A future tax obligation of $160,000 should be recognized by Dr. Jones between the liabilities being reported and net worth.
      D.   No future tax obligation should be recognized by Dr. Jones.

7.   A company produces quarterly financial statements. At the end of the second quarter, the company's inventory account is valued at $60,000 below cost, but this drop in value is viewed as temporary. However, at the end of the third quarter, the inventory is $50,000 below cost, and this reduction is now viewed as a permanent decline. What gain or loss should the company recognize in its third quarter?
      A. $0.
      B. $10,000 gain.
      C. $12,500 loss.
      D. $50,000 loss.

8.   A CPA has been asked to produce personal financial statements for Dr. Tran. Dr. Tran owns a rental house that costs $280,000 but is now worth $480,000. The tax rate on gains of this type is assumed to be 20%. Which of the following is false?
      A.   There has been an increase in Dr. Tran's net worth of $160,000.
      B.   A potential tax obligation should be recognized of $40,000.
      C.   The rental house should be reported at $480,000.
      D.   The rental house should be reported at $480,000, but if this had been Dr. Tran's personal residence, it would have been reported at $280,000.

9.   A company is viewed as a development stage enterprise, because it has not begun to generate revenues. In Year 1, the company incurred $60,000 in expenses and in Year 2, the company incurred another $70,000 in expenses. Which of the following statements is true?
      A.   As a development stage enterprise, the entire $130,000 should be capitalized.
      B.   As a development stage enterprise, the entire $130,000 should be recorded directly within other comprehensive income in stockholders' equity.
      C.   As a development stage enterprise, at the end of Year 2, the $70,000 is shown as an expense for that period and the $130,000 as the cumulative total of expenses.
      D.   As a development stage enterprise, the only information that is shown is the income statement for the current period, which reports an expense of $70,000.

ANSWERS: MISCELLANEOUS FINANCIAL STATEMENTS

1. **A** Temporary declines in inventory market values are not recognized. Only declines that are apparently permanent or other than temporary need to be recognized. In this case, Wilson expected the decline to reverse in the third quarter; therefore, the decline is temporary, and no loss would be recorded in the first quarter. Because no loss was recorded for the decline, no gain will be recognized in the third quarter for the recovery of the $50,000 decline.

    Also, assuming the inventory was valued at cost at the beginning of the fiscal year, no gain will be recorded for the recovery excess of $10,000, because inventory may not be valued at an amount in excess of cost.

2. **B** Each interim period is considered to be an integral part of the annual period. Therefore, expectations for the annual period must be reflected in the interim period. The income tax expense should be calculated using the estimated annual effective tax rate. The estimated tax rate should be updated as of the end of each interim period (here, as of the second quarter). The statutory tax rate is only a part of the effective tax. The effective tax rate includes the statutory tax rate and a variety of other items.

3. **B** Advertising costs may be deferred within a fiscal year, if the benefits clearly extend beyond the interim that the expense was paid. Also, advertising costs may be accrued and assigned to interim periods in relation to sales. Year-end accruals and deferrals of costs are also considered appropriate accounting treatment. Note, however, that deferral in year-end reporting is permitted only if the advertising has not be run in the media.

4. **D** In general, interim financial statements are prepared as if each separate period is the same as a separate year, and thus, the handling of any recognition follows that used by the company for its annual financial statements.

5. **A** On personal financial statements, all assets and liabilities are reported at fair value.

6. **C** On personal financial statements, the land should be reported at $500,000. That amount contains a $400,000 gain ($500,000 – $100,000) that can only be realized by selling the property. Thus, in recognizing this gain in value, the resulting tax effect must also be reported. Because no liability will exist until the land is sold, the tax amount is shown between Dr. Jones' liabilities and net worth.

7. **D** For interim reporting purposes, declines in inventory value are only recognized when they become viewed as permanent, Thus, the $50,000 permanent loss is recognized in the third quarter of the year.

8. **D** On personal financial statements, all assets and liabilities are reported at their fair values. However, to realize these changes in value, a sale would occur, which, in most cases, would lead to a tax effect. Because the change in value is being reported, the potential tax obligation must also be shown.

9. **C** A development state enterprise must show its current income statement based on normal accounting principles. However, to better reflect the impact of operating without significant revenues, cumulative figures should be shown on the income statement and statement of cash flows.

CHAPTER 6 – STOCKHOLDERS' EQUITY

STUDY TIP

It is critical that you structure your study time. Those items that you structure into your day get accomplished. And those structured items drive out those that are unstructured. If you don't structure study time into your day, the study time is less likely to get done. Be deliberate.

CHAPTER 6 – STOCKHOLDERS' EQUITY

STOCKHOLDERS' EQUITY

A. Contributed capital (or paid-in capital).

   1. Contributed capital results when any class of stock is issued. It can also occur when owners make contributions for reasons other than the issuance of stock.

   2. Includes:

      a. Legal capital—the par or stated value of stock issued.

      b. Paid-in capital in excess of par or stated value.

      c. Paid-in capital from other transactions.

B. Retained earnings.

C. Accumulated other comprehensive income.

D. Contra stockholders' equity items (i.e., treasury stock-cost method).

When major changes occur in stockholders' equity accounts, companies are required to disclose them in the notes to the financial statements.

CAPITAL STOCK

A. Shares authorized is the total number of shares that can be legally issued by a corporation according to its charter or certificate of incorporation.

B. Shares issued is the number of shares that have been sold for cash or other consideration.

C. Shares outstanding is the number of shares that are presently being held by the public. It is equal to shares issued less treasury shares. (More on treasury shares below.)

D. Par value.

   1. Par value is a relatively arbitrary value attached to a share by the company in order to comply with state law.

   2. Anyone buying a share for less than par value risks having to make up the difference if the company ever goes bankrupt.

   3. When stock is sold, its par value is recorded in the stock account (legal capital) with any excess received recorded as additional paid-in capital (APIC).

   4. Stock issued in exchange for noncash assets or services is recorded at fair value of those assets or services.

E. Subscribed stock is a term that describes the shares that have been ordered by a potential investor but not yet fully paid (i.e., paid in installments). Usually, shares cannot be issued until the full subscription price is paid.

COMMON STOCK

Corporations issue capital stock. Depending on specific state law, ownership of common stock usually provides the following:

A. The right to vote for members of Boards of Directors (to ensure investors' interests are considered).

B. The right to share in any dividends that are declared (to provide an income source).

C. The right to share in any assets remaining after liquidation (to ensure some recoverability of initial investment).

ACCOUNTING ENTRIES FOR THE ISSUANCE OF COMMON STOCK

A. Cash   (amount received)
  Common stock   (par or stated value)
  Paid-in capital in excess of par (plug to balance)

B. Costs of registering and issuing common stock are usually netted against the proceeds (i.e., reduce "paid-in capital in excess of par"). This makes sense because these costs are unrelated to corporate operations and should not be expensed.

PREFERRED STOCK

A. Common stockholders can give up one or more of their basic rights to the owners for a second type of stock called *preferred stock*.

B. The right given up is often connected with dividend payments.

Preferred stock is given preference over common stock when dividends are declared. Preferred stockholders are given their dividend first. Preferred stock dividends are usually set at a percentage of par and can be cumulative. Cumulative dividends require that all past dividends be paid before common stockholders can receive any dividends. The preferred stock dividend is usually calculated based on both the par value and the dividend rate. For example, 5% preferred stock, $100 par value means that the annual dividend will be $5.

1. If a *cumulative* dividend is not paid, it is referred to as *dividends in arrears* and must be disclosed in the financial statements. The unpaid dividend is accumulated and will be paid in a subsequent period when dividends are declared and before any current dividends are paid to preferred or common stockholders.

2. In the case of *noncumulative* preferred stock, if a preferred dividend is not paid in a particular year, it is not required to be paid in the future (i.e., it is "lost").

3. Although dividends may be cumulative, it is extremely important to note that no dividend is viewed as a liability until it is declared by the company's Board of Directors.

4. Furthermore, there must be a distinction between participating and nonparticipating preferred stock.

   a. *Participating* preferred stock refers to the sharing with common stockholders in dividend distributions after both preferred and common stockholders receive a specified level of dividend payment.

      • They may be fully participating with common stockholders. For example, 7% preferred shares receive 7% of their par value in dividends before common stockholders receive dividends. Fully participating preferred shares would receive the same percentage dividend as common stockholders if the common stockholders received over a 7% (of par value) dividend.

      • They may also be participating to a certain limit. Therefore, the total of the current dividends and the additional dividends cannot exceed this limit. (Dividends in arrears do not apply to this limit.)

   b. *Nonparticipating* preferred stock means that the preferred stockholders will receive their normal dividends (and dividends in arrears, if applicable) but will not receive any additional dividends, regardless of the amount paid to common shareholders.

CONVERTIBLE AND CALLABLE PREFERRED STOCK

A. The *convertible* feature allows preferred stockholders the option of exchanging their stock for common stock at a predetermined ratio.

   1. Conversions are usually accounted for at book value.

Preferred stock	(par converted)
Preferred paid-in accounts	(related balances)
Common stock	(par)
Paid-in capital in excess of par	(plug)

   2. If market value is used, common stock and paid-in excess are credited for the market value, usually resulting in a debit to retained earnings. The retained earnings figure becomes the plug.

B. The *callable* feature allows the issuing company the option to repurchase the preferred stock at a predetermined price.

   1. If called, no gain or loss is recognized on the income statement.

   2. The gains are taken to a paid-in capital account.

   3. The losses are charged to retained earnings.

   4. Note that, per SFAS 150, mandatorily redeemable preferred stock must be classified as a liability on the balance sheet.

TREASURY STOCK (COMPANY BUYS ITS OWN STOCK)

Accounting for the Acquisition and Reselling of Treasury Stock

Treasury stock is the stock of a company that was issued and later repurchased by the company. Such stock is not formally retired, however. Companies can never record a gain or loss on buying or selling their own stock. Treasury stock is a negative balance in stockholders' equity, and is *not* reported as an asset.

Treasury stock can be accounted for by using one of three methods.

A. Method 1: Cost method.

   1. Treasury stock is recorded at cost.

   2. If shares are later resold above cost, APIC is increased.

   3. If shares are later resold below cost, APIC is reduced. If APIC is not sufficient to cover the difference, then the remainder is a reduction in retained earnings.

B. Method 2: Par value method.

   1. Treasury stock is recorded at its par value with any APIC that was originally recorded being removed.

   2. Any difference in original issuance price and the reacquisition price increases or decreases APIC—Treasury Stock. Once again, if need be, retained earnings can be reduced.

C. Under either of the above methods, treasury stock is shown as a reduction figure within the Stockholders' Equity section of the balance sheet. The resale of shares is handled just like an original issuance.

D. Method 3: Retirement method.

   1. Stock can be bought back and then retired so that it is removed entirely from the records.

   2. The entry is the same as a repurchase entry under the par value method, except that common stock is reduced rather than treasury stock.

E. Example of cost method:

Example:

In Year 5, Waldstein, Inc. (Waldstein) acquired 6,000 shares of its own $1 par value common stock at $18 per share. In Year 6, Waldstein issued 3,000 of these shares at $25 per share. Waldstein uses the cost method to account for its treasury stock transactions. What accounts and amounts should Waldstein credit in Year 6 to record the issuance of the 3,000 shares?

Solution:

Upon issuance of the treasury shares, Waldstein would record a debit to cash of 3,000 × $25 = $75,000. The treasury stock account would be credited for the original cost of the shares (3,000 × $18 = $54,000). The difference of $21,000 would be recorded with a credit to APIC.

F. Example of par value method:

Example:

Klavier, Inc. (Klavier) was organized on January 10, Year 6 with 100,000 authorized shares of $20 par value common stock. During Year 6, Klavier had the following capital transaction:

January 31 – issued 48,000 shares at $27 per share
December 8 – purchased 6,000 shares at $22 per share

Klavier used the par value method to record the purchase of the treasury shares.

What would be the balance in Klavier's paid-in capital from treasury stock account at December 31, Year 6?

Solution:

Using the par value method, treasury stock is debited for par value (6,000 × $20, or $120,000) when purchased. Any excess over par from the original issuance (6,000 × $7, or $42,000) is removed from the appropriate paid-in capital account.

In effect, the total original issuance price (6,000 × $27, or $162,000) is charged to two accounts. Any difference between the original issue price ($162,000) and the cost of the treasury stock (6,000 × $22, or $132,000) is credited to paid-in capital from treasury stock, as illustrated below.

Treasury stock (6,000 × $20)	$120,000	
APIC (6,000 × $7)	$42,000	
Cash (6,000 × $22)		$132,000
APIC—treasury stock ($162,000 – $132,000)		$30,000

RETAINED EARNINGS

A. The retained earnings account is a measure of net assets held by the company that were generated originally by the operations.

   1. It begins with the accumulated net earnings of the company minus the accumulated losses of the company.

   2. Retained earnings may have a debit balance (deficit) in cases where losses exceed profits.

B. It is further decreased by dividends (on the date of declaration). Dividends may be paid if there is a credit balance in retained earnings, even if there was no income in the current year.

C. If a company has decided to limit the amount of dividends, retained earnings is shown as two figures:

   1. Unappropriated—the maximum amount of dividends that would be paid.

   2. Appropriated—the remainder.

      a. Appropriations of retained earnings are a means of communicating a future need to users of financial statements.

      b. They may be set up for plant expansion, contingent liabilities, or repayment of debt.

      c. The appearance of an appropriation informs users that dividends may not be paid so that funds are available for this special need.

MISCELLANEOUS ISSUES RELATING TO CORPORATE ENTITIES

INCORPORATION OF A SOLE PROPRIETORSHIP OR A PARTNERSHIP

A. All assets and liabilities are adjusted to fair value.

B. Stock is issued to owners based on this total fair value.

C. Retained earnings is set at zero since this is the beginning of a new corporation.

QUASI-REORGANIZATION

A. Quasi-reorganization is a technique used by the company (with the approval of the creditors and stockholders where required) in hopes of avoiding bankruptcy.

B. It is an informal proceeding that is applicable during a period of declining price levels and for a situation where a going concern exists except for overvalued assets and a possible deficit.

   1. The overvalued assets result in high depreciation charges and losses and therefore, lower net income.

   2. The deficit precludes payment of dividends.

C. Assets and liabilities are revalued to current fair value.

   1. Liabilities are also usually reduced by creditors.

   2. All gains and losses directly impact retained earnings.

D. Par value of common stock account is reduced with an offsetting increase in APIC.

E. Negative balance in retained earnings is offset against APIC. Retained earnings is now reported as a zero balance.

DIVIDENDS

A. Dividends are distributions (cash or noncash) made to stockholders as a reward of ownership.

B. Three dates are important:

   1. Date of declaration—Board of Directors declares dividend so that it becomes a legal liability (it is accrued), and retained earnings is reduced.

   2. Date of record—Ownership of stock is established; company makes no entry, but stockholder records a receivable.

   3. Date of payment—Journal entry is recorded to reduce cash paid and liability accrued on the date of declaration.

PROPERTY AND LIQUIDATING DIVIDENDS

A. A *property dividend* is an example of a noncash distribution.

   1. Property is adjusted by the company to fair value on the date of declaration with a gain or loss being recognized.

2. Dividend is then recorded—decrease retained earnings and the property being distributed.

B. When dividends are declared for an amount that exceeds the retained earnings balance, the excess is treated as a return of capital, referred to as a *liquidating dividend*.

STOCK DIVIDENDS AND STOCK SPLITS

A. Stock dividends are distributions made in the stock of the company.

B. Stockholders do not make a journal entry and do not record income but must reallocate book value over a greater number of shares.

C. Company records the dividends as a decrease in retained earnings for the fair value of the shares, an increase in the common stock for the par value, and the difference between the fair value and par value as an adjustment to the APIC account.

   1. If the stock dividend is less than 20% (owner gets less than two shares for every ten being held), the dividend is recorded at the fair value of the newly issued shares.

   2. If the stock dividend is between 20% and 25%, the company may choose to record the dividend at fair value or at par value of the shares.

   3. If the stock dividend is over 25%, the dividend is recorded at the par value of the newly issued shares. No adjustment to APIC is required since the transaction is being recorded at par.

STOCK SPLITS

A. A stock split occurs where the old shares are cancelled and all new shares (with new par value) are issued.

B. It is not a distribution of income but simply a means of increasing the number of shares outstanding.

C. No journal entry is necessary and the stock split does not affect stock accounts or retained earnings.

D. When a stock split occurs, the company will usually reduce the par value per share so that the total par value of the shares outstanding after the split will be equal to the par value of the shares outstanding before the split.

E. Example:

   Assume that 1,000 shares outstanding with a $100 par value are split 2 for 1. The company will now have 2,000 shares outstanding with a $50 par value. Total par value does not change—it was $100,000 both before and after the split.

STOCK DIVIDEND VS. STOCK SPLIT

A. The key difference between a stock dividend and a stock split lies with the intent of management.

B. A stock dividend is a means by which management can provide evidence of the stockholders' interest in earnings without distributing assets.

C. A stock split is management's method for increasing the number of shares outstanding, decreasing the market price, and causing wider distribution and greater marketability of the shares.

STOCK WARRANTS AND STOCK OPTIONS

A. A *stock warrant* is the right to acquire shares of stock at a set price known as an *option price*. Consequently, these are also referred to as *stock options*.

B. If a stock warrant is sold by a company to raise capital, then:

    1. The inflow of assets is reflected through an increase in paid-in capital.

    2. The company, if subsequently converted, records any additional cash received and removes the amount of the stock warrant.

C. The new stock is then recorded at the total of these two amounts using both the Common Stock and APIC if the total is more or less than par.

NONCOMPENSATORY STOCK OPTION PLAN

A. No value is assigned by the company at the time of grant.

B. If later these stock options are converted into shares, the company makes the normal entry for the issuance of stock.

C. Stock options given to employees are deemed noncompensatory if both:

    1. Substantially, all employees share in the distribution on an equitable basis.

    2. The discount in price below market value is relatively small (under 5%).

D. If there is a set purchase price, the employee must convert within 31 days to eliminate the chance for significant gains. If a percentage of market value is used to set the option price, then the 31-day limitation is not necessary.

COMPENSATORY PLAN

A. A compensatory plan is anything that does not qualify as noncompensatory.

B. An expense must be determined and recognized over the period that the employee is required to provide services.

    1. The fair value of the warrants on the grant date is used to determine the amount of the expense.

    2. In some cases, fair value is obvious by looking at market prices for the same type or similar options.

    3. If market price is not available, an option pricing model such as Black-Scholes-Merton or a binomial model must be used. No single model is required, but the model must take the following factors into account:

        a. Exercise price.

        b. Expected term of option.

        c. Current price of stock.

        d. Expected volatility of stock price.

  e. Expected amount of dividends.

  f. Risk-free interest rate.

ACCOUNTING FOR STOCK OPTIONS

When accounting for stock option plans, the key accounting issue is how to calculate the compensation expense.

A. GAAP Requirements—Fair Value Method:

  1. The fair value method bases the compensation expense on external factors such as stock volatility or expected length of option life. Fair value of the stock options issued is calculated using an option pricing model to determine the compensation expense on the grant date.

  2. Compensation expense is allocated equally over the employee's service period which is the time from the grant date to the vesting date.

B. Example:

On January 1, Year 6, Tiberghien, Inc. granted options to purchase 20,000 shares of the company's stock at $20 per share to several of its key employees. The options will expire on January 1, Year 10. At the grant date, the market price was $25. Using the Black-Scholes option pricing method, the compensation expense based on the fair value of the stock options granted is $6.75 per share. The service period is four years.

Calculate the annual compensation expense.

Fair value method: ($6.75 × 20,000)/4 years = $33,750

DISCLOSURES RELATING TO STOCK OPTIONS

The following financial statement disclosures are required for stock options:

A. Effect on income and earnings per share (EPS).

B. The number of options outstanding and their related characteristics (expiration dates, exercise prices, whether they are currently exercisable).

C. The fair value of the options issued during the year, valued at the grant date, and whether or not these options are in-the-money, out-of-the-money, or at-the-money.

D. A description of the method and specific assumptions used to value the options, including the risk-free interest rate, the option's maturity, the stock's volatility, and any expected dividends.

E. Any compensation cost recognized during the period.

F. Data related to option repricing during the period.

G. Data related to other compensation using equity instruments, such as restricted stock or phantom stock.

STOCK APPRECIATION RIGHTS

A. These rights can be awarded by a company to give potential cash bonuses to employees based on changes in the stock price over a specified period of time.

B. The company recognizes expense and creates a liability over the period that the services must be rendered.

   1. At the end of each period, the value of these rights is determined using an option pricing model.

   2. At the end of each period, the total benefit estimated at that time is multiplied by the percentage of the total time that has passed to get the benefits.

   3. Any previous expense that has been recognized is subtracted from the benefits earned to date to arrive at the expense to be recognized for the current period.

   4. In some cases, the liability may have to be reduced so that a decrease in the expense is necessary.

QUESTIONS: STOCKHOLDERS' EQUITY

1. Beckham Corp. (Beckham) issued 200,000 shares of common stock when it began operations in 2004 and issued an additional 100,000 shares in Year 5. Beckham also issued preferred stock convertible to 100,000 shares of common stock. In Year 6, Beckham purchased 75,000 shares of its common stock and held it in treasury stock.

    At December 31, Year 6, how many shares of Beckham's common stock were outstanding?
    A. 225,000.
    B. 300,000.
    C. 325,000.
    D. 400,000.

2. A company was organized in January Year 6 with authorized capital of $10 par value common stock. On February 1, Year 6, shares were issued at par for cash. On March 1, Year 6, the company's attorney accepted 5,000 shares of the common stock in settlement for legal services with a fair value of $60,000. Additional paid-in capital would increase on:

	February 1, Year 6	March 1, Year 6
A.	Yes	No
B.	Yes	Yes
C.	No	No
D.	No	Yes

3. During Year 4, Brad Co. (Brad) issued 5,000 shares of $100 par convertible preferred stock for $110 per share. One share of preferred stock can be converted into three shares of Brad's $25 par common stock at the option of the preferred shareholder. On December 31, Year 6, when the market value of the common stock was $40 per share, all of the preferred stock was converted.

    What amount should Brad credit to common stock and APIC—common stock as a result of the conversion?

	Common stock	APIC
A.	$375,000	$175,000
B.	$375,000	$225,000
C.	$500,000	$50,000
D.	$600,000	$0

4. Hill, Inc. (Hill) issued preferred stock with detachable common stock warrants. The issue price exceeded the sum of the warrants' fair value and the preferred stock's par value. The preferred stock's fair value was not determinable.

    What amount should be assigned to the warrants outstanding?
    A. Total proceeds.
    B. Excess of proceeds over the par value of the preferred stock.
    C. The proportion of the proceeds that the warrants' fair value bears to the preferred stock's par value.
    D. The fair value of the warrants.

5.   On December 1, Year 6, shares of authorized common stock were issued on a subscription basis at a price in excess of par value. A total of 20% of the subscription price of each share was collected as a down payment on December 1, Year 6, with the remaining 80% of the subscription price of each share due in Year 7. Collectibility was reasonably assured.

   At December 31, Year 6, the stockholders' equity section of the balance sheet would report APIC for the excess of the subscription price over the par value of the shares of common stock subscribed and common stock:
   A.   issued for 20% of the par value of the shares of common stock subscribed.
   B.   issued for the par value of the shares of common stock subscribed.
   C.   subscribed for 80% of the par value of the shares of common stock subscribed.
   D.   subscribed for the par value of the shares of common stock subscribed.

6.   At December 31, Year 5, Roanna Co. (Roanna) had 20,000 shares of $1 par value treasury stock that had been acquired in Year 5 at $12 per share. In May Year 6, Roanna issued 15,000 of these treasury shares at $10 per share. The cost method is used to record treasury stock transactions. Roanna is located in a state where laws relating to acquisition of treasury stock restrict the availability of retained earnings for declaration of dividends.

   At December 31, Year 6, what amount should Roanna show in notes to financial statements as a restriction of retained earnings as a result of its treasury stock transactions?
   A. $5,000.
   B. $10,000.
   C. $60,000.
   D. $90,000.

7.   Vivian Corporation (Vivian) was organized on January 2, Year 6, with 100,000 authorized shares of $10 par value common stock. During Year 6, Vivian had the following capital transaction:

   January 5—issued 75,000 shares at $14 per share
   December 27—purchased 5,000 shares at $11 per share

   Vivian used the par value method to record the purchase of the treasury shares.

   What would be the balance in Vivian's paid-in capital from treasury stock account at December 31, Year 6?
   A. $0.
   B. $5,000.
   C. $15,000.
   D. $20,000.

8.   Pirelli Corp. (Pirelli) acquired treasury shares at an amount greater than par value but less than the original issue price. Compared to the cost method of accounting for treasury stock, does the par value method report a greater amount for APIC and a greater amount for retained earnings?

	APIC	Retained earnings
A.	Yes	Yes
B.	Yes	No
C.	No	No
D.	No	Yes

9.   In 2004, Martha Corp. (Martha) issued 5,000 shares of $10 par value common stock for $100 per share. In Year 6, Martha reacquired 2,000 of its shares at $150 per share from the estate of one of its deceased officers and immediately cancelled these 2,000 shares. Martha uses the cost method in accounting for its treasury stock transactions.

   In connection with the retirement of these 2,000 shares, Martha should debit which of the following?

	APIC	Retained earnings
A.	$20,000	$280,000
B.	$100,000	$180,000
C.	$180,000	$100,000
D.	$280,000	$0

10. On December 31, Year 6, Packard Corp.'s (Packard) board of directors canceled 50,000 shares of $2.50 par value common stock held in treasury at an average cost of $13 per share. Before the cancellation of treasury stock, Packard had the following balances in its stockholders' equity accounts:

Common stock	$540,000
Additional paid-in capital	$750,000
Retained earnings	$900,000
Treasury stock, at cost	$650,000

   In its balance sheet at December 31, Year 6, Packard should report a common stock balance of:
   A. $0.
   B. $250,000.
   C. $415,000.
   D. $540,000.

11. At December 31, Year 5 and Year 6, Apex Co. (Apex) had 3,000 shares of $100 par, 5% cumulative preferred stock outstanding. No dividends were in arrears as of December 31, 2004. Apex did not declare a dividend during Year 5. During Year 6, Apex paid a cash dividend of $10,000 on its preferred stock.

   Apex should report dividends in arrears in its Year 6 financial statements as a(n):
   A. accrued liability of $15,000.
   B. disclosure of $15,000.
   C. accrued liability of $20,000.
   D. disclosure of $20,000.

12. On January 2, Year 6, Andreas Co.'s (Andreas) board of directors declared a cash dividend of $400,000 to stockholders of record on January 18, Year 6, payable on February 10, Year 6. The dividend is permissible under law in Andreas' state of incorporation. Selected data from Andreas' December 31, Year 5 balance sheet are as follows:

Accumulated depletion	$100,000
Capital stock	$500,000
APIC	$150,000
Retained earnings	$300,000

    The $400,000 dividend includes a liquidating dividend of:
    A. $0.
    B. $100,000.
    C. $150,000.
    D. $300,000.

13. On December 1, Year 6, Nazareth Corp. (Nazareth) declared a property dividend of marketable securities to be distributed on December 31, Year 6, to stockholders of record on December 15, Year 6. On December 1, Year 6, the trading securities had a carrying amount of $60,000 and a fair value of $78,000.

    What is the effect of this property dividend on Nazareth's Year 6 retained earnings, after all nominal accounts are closed?
    A. $0.
    B. $18,000 increase.
    C. $60,000 decrease.
    D. $78,000 decrease.

14. Liszt Co. (Liszt) had 100,000 shares of common stock issued and outstanding at January 1, Year 6. During Year 6, Liszt took the following actions:

    March 15—declared a 2-for-1 stock split, when the fair value of the stock was $80 per share.
    December 15—declared a $0.50 per share cash dividend.

    In Liszt's statement of stockholders' equity for Year 6, what amount should Liszt report as dividends?
    A. $50,000.
    B. $100,000.
    C. $850,000.
    D. $950,000.

15. The following stock dividends were declared and distributed by Schachter Corp. (Schachter):

Percent of Common Shares Outstanding at Declaration Date	Fair Value	Par Value
10	$15,000	$10,000
28	$40,000	$30,800

What aggregate amount should be debited to retained earnings for these stock dividends?
A. $40,800.
B. $45,800.
C. $50,000.
D. $55,000.

16. On July 1, Year 6, Campbell Co. (Campbell) has 200,000 of $10 par common stock outstanding, and the market price is $12 per share. On the same date, Campbell declared a 1-for-2 reverse stock split. The par of the stock was increased from $10 to $20 and one new $20 par share was issued for each two $10 par shares outstanding. Immediately before the 1-for-2 reverse stock split. Campbell's APIC was $450,000.

What should be the balance in Campbell's APIC account immediately after the reverse stock split is affected?
A. $0.
B. $450,000.
C. $650,000.
D. $850,000.

17. How would a stock split in which the par value per share decreases in proportion to the number of additional shares issued affect each of the following?

	APIC	Retained earnings
A.	Increase	No effect
B.	No effect	No effect
C.	No effect	Decrease
D.	Increase	Decrease

18. At December 31, Year 5, Eagle Corp. (Eagle) reported $1,750,000 of appropriated retained earnings for the construction of a new office building that was completed in Year 6 at a total cost of $1,500,000. In Year 6, Eagle appropriated $1,200,000 of retained earnings for the construction of a new plant. Also, $2,000,000 of cash was restricted for the retirement of bonds due in Year 7.

In its Year 6 balance sheet, Eagle should report what amount of appropriated retained earnings?
A. $1,200,000.
B. $1,450,000.
C. $2,950,000.
D. $3,200,000.

19. Porter Co. began its business last year and issued 10,000 shares of common stock at $3 per share. The par value of the stock is $1 per share. During January of the current year, Porter bought back 500 shares at $6 per share, which were reported by Porter as treasury stock. The treasury stock shares were reissued later in the current year at $10 per share. Porter used the cost method to account for its equity transactions. What amount should Porter report as paid-in capital related to its treasury stock transactions on its balance sheet for the current year?
    A. $1,500.
    B. $2,000.
    C. $4,500.
    D. $20,000.

20. A company has issued stock options to all of its employees. There are 10,000 options, and an option pricing model values these options at $4 each. The employees have 28 days to convert the options, and the option price is set at an amount which is $5 below the fair value of the stock. That is a discount of exactly 5%. The options are distributed to substantially all employees in an equitable manner. The options are all, eventually, converted when the option price is $4.78 below the fair value of the stock. What is the total amount of expense to be recognized by the company?
    A. $0.
    B. $40,000.
    C. $47,800.
    D. $50,000.

21. Jackson, Inc. is a publicly-held corporation. At the beginning of Year 1, the company issues 10,000 stock options to its president. They can be exercised if the president works for four additional years. An option pricing model is used to determine the value of the options on January 1, Year 1 ($8), December 31, Year 1 ($10), and December 31, Year 2 ($14). How much expense should the company recognize for Year 2?
    A. $20,000.
    B. $35,000.
    C. $45,000.
    D. $50,000.

22. The Truman Corporation is a publicly-held corporation. At the beginning of Year 1, the company issues 10,000 stock appreciation rights to its president. They can be exercised if the president works for four additional years. The president will receive cash equal to the value of the company's stock after the four years have passed. An option pricing model is used to determine the value of the rights on January 1, Year 1 ($8), December 31, Year 1 ($10), and December 31, Year 2 ($14). How much expense should the company recognize for Year 2?
    A. $20,000.
    B. $35,000.
    C. $45,000.
    D. $50,000.

23. A company issues 1,000 shares of its $10 par value common stock for $12 per share. Later, the company buys back 100 of these shares for $13 each. Still later, the company resells one of these shares for $16. Which of the following statements is true? If the:
    A. cost method is used to record treasury stock, a $3 gain is reported on the company's income statement.
    B. par value method is used to record treasury stock, additional paid-in capital of $3 is reported when the stock is resold.
    C. cost method is used to record treasury stock, the remaining shares are reported in stockholders' equity at $1,287.
    D. par value method is used to record treasury stock, the remaining shares are reported as assets at $990.

24. A company starts the current year with 50,000 shares of common stock outstanding. The stock has a par value of $10 per share but the shares were sold at $16 each. Then, the company issues 5,000 new shares because of a 10% stock dividend. At that date, the price of the stock was $25 per share. Still later during the year, another 22,000 shares are issued as a 40% stock dividend. At that date, the price of the stock was $30 per share. What is the total amount reported as additional paid-in capital?
    A. $300,000.
    B. $375,000.
    C. $740,000.
    D. $815,000.

25. The Arizona Corporation has 100,000 authorized shares of $10 par value common stock. The company issues 10,000 shares for $18 per share. Later, 1,000 of these shares were repurchased for $21 per share as treasury stock. After a few weeks, 100 shares of the treasury stock were resold for $25 per share. If the par value method is utilized to record treasury stock transactions, what should the company report as its total additional paid-in capital?
    A. $69,400.
    B. $70,500.
    C. $72,400.
    D. $73,500.

26. A partnership has assets of $200,000, liabilities of $40,000, and partners' capital of $160,000. The assets are actually worth $240,000, and the liabilities are worth $50,000. The partnership is incorporated by issuing 15,000 shares of $10 par value common stock to each of the three partners. In creating the opening records of the new corporation, what should be reported as additional paid-in capital?
    A. $20,000.
    B. $30,000.
    C. $40,000.
    D. $50,000.

27. The Alatar Corporation issues 20,000 shares of $10 par value common stock for $19 per share. A few years later, the company issues 10,000 additional shares for $22 per share. The following year, the company issues 9,000 more shares as a stock dividend when shares are selling for $25 each on the open market. For the 39,000 shares, what amount of additional paid-in capital should be reported?
    A. $300,000.
    B. $327,000.
    C. $435,000.
    D. $468,000.

28. On January 1, Year 1, the president of the Atkins Company received 1,000 stock options. It is a compensatory plan. However, he had to work for the company for four additional years in order to be able to convert these options. A computer pricing model was used to determine the value of one option on January 1, Year 1, as $20. The computer pricing model was used again on December 31, Year 1, to arrive at a value for one option of $30. How much expense should the company recognize for Year 1?
    A. $5,000.
    B. $7,500.
    C. $20,000.
    D. $30,000.

29. In valuing a compensatory stock option using a computer pricing model, several variables must be included in arriving at the value. Which of the following is not one of those variables? The:
    A. length of time that the employee has to convert.
    B. historical volatility of the stock price.
    C. current difference between the stock price and the option price.
    D. salary level of the employee.

30. Copper, Inc. initially issued 100,000 shares of $1 par value stock for $500,000 in Year 1. In Year 3, the company repurchased 10,000 of these shares for $100,000. In Year 5, 5,000 of the repurchased shares were resold for $80,000. If the cost method is being applied, what is now the balance to be reported as additional paid-in capital?
    A. $340,000.
    B. $390,000.
    C. $430,000.
    D. $445,000.

31. Assuming that a company's stock has a fair value in excess of its par value, how would the declaration of a 15% stock dividend by a corporation affect each of the following?

	Additional paid-in capital	Total stockholders' equity
A.	Increase	No effect
B.	No effect	No effect
C.	No effect	Decrease
D.	Decrease	Decrease

32. Which of the following disclosures regarding employee stock options is not required under SFAS 123?
    A. The number of options authorized to be issued.
    B. The effects of option repricing during the period.
    C. The cumulative fair value of the options issued to date.
    D. The fair value of the options at the end of the reporting period.

ANSWERS: STOCKHOLDERS' EQUITY

1. **A**   The number of common shares outstanding is equal to the issued shares less treasury shares. Beckham had 300,000 shares outstanding at 1/1/04. The purchase of treasury shares in Year 6 reduced the number of shares outstanding to 225,000 (300,000 – 75,000). The preferred stock convertible into 100,000 shares of common stock is recorded as preferred stock until it is converted by the stockholder.

2. **D**   On February 1, Year 6, when shares were issued at par for cash, the following journal entry would have been made:

Cash	(cash received)	
Common stock	(par)	

    On March 1, Year 6, however, the issuance of 5,000 shares in settlement for legal services rendered would have been recorded as follows:

Legal fees	$60,000	
Common stock ($10 × 5,000 shares)		$50,000
APIC		$10,000

    Per APB 29, stock issued for services (i.e., in a nonmonetary transaction) should be recorded at the fair value of those services (in this case, $60,000).

3. **A**   All 5,000 shares of convertible preferred stock were converted to common stock at a rate of three shares of common for every share of preferred. Therefore, 15,000 shares of common stock were issued (5,000 × 3). The common stock account is credited for the par value of these shares (15,000 × $25 = $375,000). APIC – common stock is credited for $175,000, the difference between the carrying amount of the preferred stock (5,000 × $110 = $550,000) and the par value of the common stock.

    The journal entry is as follows:

Preferred stock	$500,000	
APIC—preferred stock	$50,000	
Common stock		$375,000
APIC—common stock		$175,000

    Note that the $40 market value of the common stock is ignored. The book value method must be used for conversion of preferred stock, so no gains or losses can be recognized.

4. **D**   Note that this question is mainly a review of material in the previous chapter.

    Per APB 14, when an issuance of debt, or in this case preferred stock, contains detachable common stock warrants, the total proceeds from the sale should be allocated to both the preferred stock and the detachable stock warrants. This treatment arises due to the separability of the stock and the detachable warrants.

    The allocation of the proceeds is based on the relative fair values of both the stock and the warrants at the time of the issuance. However, in instances where only one of the fair values is known, the known fair value will be used to allocate proceeds to the security in which the fair value is determinable. The remainder is then allocated to the security for which the fair value is unknown. Therefore, because only the fair value of the warrants is known, answer D is correct.

    Answers A and B are incorrect because fair value is used to allocate proceeds to the warrants, not the total proceeds or excess proceeds over par value. Answer C is incorrect because proceeds are allocated in proportion to both fair values, if determinable, not the fair value and par value.

5. **D** When stock is sold on a subscription basis, the full price of the stock is not received initially, and the stock is not issued until the full subscription price is received. On the subscription contract date of December 1, Year 6, the journal entry would be:

Cash	(amount received)
Subscriptions receivable	(balance due)
Common stock subscribed	(par)
APIC	(plug)

6. **C** The entry that Roanna made on acquisition of treasury stock was as follows using the cost method:

Treasury stock (20,000 × $12)	$240,000	
Cash		$240,000

When some of the shares are later reissued, the entry is as follows:

Cash (15,000 × $10)	$150,000	
Retained earnings	$30,000	
Treasury stock (15,000 × $12)		$180,000

It is assumed there was no balance in APIC—treasury stock prior to this entry. If the problem had stated that there was a credit balance, APIC—treasury stock would be debited before retained earnings to the extent a credit balance existed in APIC—treasury stock. SFAS 5 requires disclosure when retained earnings are legally restricted. In this case, the net treasury stock account balance is $60,000 ($240,000 – $180,000), and this is the amount of retained earnings that must be disclosed as legally restricted.

7. **C** The requirement is to determine the balance in the paid-in capital from treasury stock account at 12/31/06. Using the par value method, treasury stock is debited for par value (5,000 × $10, or $50,000) when purchased. Any excess over par from the original issuance (5,000 × $4, or $20,000) is removed from the appropriate paid-in capital account.

In effect, the total original issuance price (5,000 × $14, or $70,000) is charged to two accounts. Any difference between the original issue price ($70,000) and the cost of the treasury stock (5,000 × $11, or $55,000) is credited to paid-in capital from treasury stock, as illustrated below.

Treasury stock (5,000 × $10)	$50,000	
APIC (5,000 × $4)	$20,000	
Cash (5,000 × $11)		$55,000
APIC—treasury stock ($70,000 – $55,000)		$15,000

8. **C** In this case, the par value method does not report a greater amount for APIC or retained earnings than the cost method. The entries for an acquisition of treasury shares at greater than par but less than the original issue price are as follows:

Cost method	Par value method
Treasury stock	Treasury stock (par value)
Cash	PIC in excess of par (from original issue)
	Cash
	PIC from treasury stock

Because under the par value method the original PIC in excess of par must be removed from the accounts upon reacquisition, the par value method actually reports a decrease in APIC. On the other hand, under the cost method no change in APIC is recorded. There is no change in retained earnings under either method.

9. **C** When accounting for the retirement of stock, common stock and APIC are removed from the books based on the original issuance of the stock. Cash is credited for the cost of the shares. Any difference is debited to retained earnings or credited to paid-in capital from retirement. The entry in this case is as follows:

Common stock (2,000 × $10) $20,000
APIC (2,000 × $90) $180,000
Retained earnings (2,000 × $50) $100,000
  Cash $300,000

Therefore, APIC should be debited for $180,000 and retained earnings should be debited for $100,000.

10. **C** When accounting for the retirement of treasury stock that was initially recorded using the cost method, common stock and APIC are removed from the books based on the original issuance of the stock. Treasury stock is credited for the cost of the shares acquired. Any difference is debited to retained earnings or credited to paid-in capital from retirement. In this problem, common stock should be debited for $125,000 (50,000 shares × $2.50), and the common stock balance at December 31, Year 6, is $415,000 ($540,000 – $125,000).

11. **D** For cumulative preferred stock, dividends not paid in any year will accumulate and must be paid in a later year before any dividends can be paid to common stockholders. The unpaid prior year dividends are called "dividends in arrears." The balance of dividends in arrears should be disclosed in the financial statements rather than accrued, as they are not considered a liability until they are declared. Dividends in arrears at 12/31/06 total $20,000, as computed below:

Year 5: $300,000 × 5% $15,000
Year 6: $300,000 × 5%   15,000
Total cumulative preferred dividends $30,000
Less Year 6 dividend payment   (10,000)
Balance of dividends in arrears $20,000

Answer C is incorrect because dividends in arrears are not considered to be liability until they are declared. They should be disclosed parenthetically or in the notes to the financial statements. Answer B is incorrect because the total dividends amount needs to reflect both the Year 5 and Year 6 unpaid dividends since it is cumulative preferred stock. Answer A is incorrect because the dividends in arrears would not be considered a liability until they are declared and the $15,000 amount is the incorrect balance as discussed above.

12. **B** Dividends that are based on funds other than retained earnings are considered to be liquidating dividends. The cash dividend declared of $400,000 is first assumed to be a return on capital for the distribution of the retained earnings balance of $300,000. The excess of $400,000 dividend – $300,000 retained earnings = $100,000 is considered to be a return of capital or a liquidating dividend rather than a return on capital. Note that the amount of liquidating dividend also equals the balance in accumulated depletion. Companies in the extractive industries may pay dividends equal to the accumulated income and depletion.

13. **C** Per APB 29, a transfer of a nonmonetary asset to a stockholder or to another entity in a nonreciprocal transfer should be recorded at the fair value of the asset transferred, and a gain or loss should be recognized on the disposition of the asset. At the date of declaration, Nazareth records the following:

Trading securities $18,000
  Gain on disposition of securities $18,000
Retained earnings (dividends) $78,000
  Property dividends payable $78,000

At the date of distribution, Nazareth records the following:

Property dividends payable $78,000
  Trading securities $78,000

After all nominal accounts are closed, the effect on retained earnings from the above entries would be $60,000 ($78,000 debit to retained earnings less $18,000 credit to retained earnings when the "gain on disposition" account is closed out).

14. **B** A stock split is not a dividend. Stock splits change the number of shares outstanding and the par value per share. Par value per share is reduced in proportion to the increase in the number of shares. Therefore, the total par value outstanding does not change, and no journal entry is required. The only dividend to be reported on Liszt's Year 6 statement of stockholders' equity is the Dec 15 cash dividend. The stock split increased the number of shares outstanding to 200,000 (100,000 × 2), so the amount of the cash dividend is $100,000 (200,000 × $0.50).

15. **B** The requirement is to determine the amount to be debited to retained earnings for these stock dividends. Per ARB 43, chapter 7B, the issuance of a stock dividend less than 20% to 25% (a "small" stock dividend) requires that the market value of the stock be transferred from retained earnings, and a dividend greater than 20% to 25% (a "large" stock dividend) requires the par value of the stock to be transferred from retained earnings.

    Thus, a 10% stock dividend is considered to be "small" and should be transferred from retained earnings at the FV of $15,000. At 28%, stock dividend is considered to be "large" and should be transferred at the par value of $30,800. The aggregate amount to be transferred from retained earnings is $45,800.

16. **B** The requirement is to determine the balance of APIC immediately after a reverse stock split. Stock splits change the number of shares outstanding and the par value per share, but the total par value outstanding does not change. Stock splits do not affect any account balances, including APIC. Therefore, the balance of APIC remains at $450,000.

17. **B** A stock split does not affect either the balance of the APIC or retained earnings accounts. The number of shares outstanding and the par value per share merely change in proportion to each other. When this occurs, only a memorandum entry is made.

18. **A** The requirement is to determine the amount of appropriated retained earnings Eagle should report in its Year 6 balance sheet. The entry to record the appropriated of retained earnings in Year 6 for the construction of a new plant is as follows:

RE (or unappropriated RE)	$1,200,000
RE appropriated for plant expansion	$1,200,000

    The cash restricted for the retirement of bonds due in Year 7 should not be reported as an appropriation of retained earnings because the facts in the question do not indicate that appropriation was made by management. SFAS 5 requires that when an appropriation is no longer needed, it must be returned directly to unappropriated retained earnings by reversing the entry that created it. Therefore, when the office building was completed in Year 6, the following entry was made:

RE appropriated for plant expansion	$1,750,000
RE (or unappropriated RE)	$1,750,000

    The total cost to complete the building has no effect on appropriated retained earnings.

19. **B** The company bought 500 shares of its own stock which was recorded at cost. When it was later resold, a gain of $4 per share was made. However, no income statement effect can result from a company's dealings in its own stock. Thus, this $2,000 gain (500 shares times $4) is reported as an increase in paid-in capital.

20. **A** This is a noncompensatory stock option plan so that no expense is recognized. Noncompensatory plans have a discount from the fair value of the stock of 5% or less; they are given to substantially all employees on an equitable basis, and the employee has 31 days or less to convert once the price is set. These options are viewed as an enticement to get the employees to invest in the company rather than a reward for work done. Thus, no expense is recorded.

21. **A** This is a compensatory stock option because only the president is being rewarded. For a compensatory stock option, the recorded value is determined on the grant date and is not remeasured over time. On the grant date, the 10,000 options are valued at $8 each or $80,000. Because the president has to work for four years to earn these options, an expense of $20,000 is recognized each year.

22. **C** Because a specific cash figure will have to be paid, the liability is recomputed at the end of each year. At the end of Year 1, the 10,000 rights are worth $10 each or $100,000. Because one year out of four has been worked, an expense and a liability of $25,000 are recognized at that time. At the end of Year 2, these rights are now worth $14 each or $140,000. Two years out of four have been worked so the liability should be remeasured to $70,000. Increasing the liability from $25,000 to $70,000 necessitates an expense for Year 2 of $45,000.

23. **C** There is no income statement effect created by the buying and selling of treasury stock. All balances and transactions impact paid-in capital and stockholders' equity. In the cost method, the shares are recorded at their $13 cost, and that figure is then reduced for each subsequent resell. In the par value method, the shares are recorded at their $10 par value, and that figure is then reduced for each subsequent resell. The initial cost was $13 each or $1,300. Because one share has been reissued, that balance has been reduced by $13.

24. **B** When the first 50,000 shares were issued, the company received $6 per share over par value or additional paid-in capital of $300,000. The 10% stock dividend was below the 20–25% level and is, therefore, reported at the fair value of $25 per share. That is $15 over par value so there is a $75,000 increase in additional paid-in capital ($15 × 5,000 shares). The 40% stock dividend is above the 20% to 25% level so these shares are recorded at par value with no further increase in additional paid-in capital.

25. **B** When the 10,000 shares are sold originally, the additional paid-in capital balance was increased by $8 per share, or $80,000. That amount received is over and above the par value of the stock. When 1,000 shares are later bought back, under the par value method of accounting for treasury stock, $8 per share ($8,000 in total) is removed from the APIC account to eliminate the original APIC received on this stock. An additional $3 per share ($3,000 in total) must also be charged to the APIC account to reflect the additional amount that was paid to reacquire the stock. Later, the sale of 100 shares is made at $15 per share above par value ($25 – $10 par), or $1,500 in total. Thus, the Arizona Corporation's total additional paid-in capital after these transactions are recorded would amount to $80,000 less $8,000 less $3,000 plus $1,500, or $70,500.

26. **C** The corporation is looked on as a new entity so that all of the assets and liabilities held by the old partnership should initially be recorded at their fair values. Also, because it is a new entity, retained earnings starts with a zero balance. If assets minus liabilities is $190,000 ($240,000 – $50,000) and if retained earnings is now zero, then contributed capital must be $190,000 for the balance sheet to balance. A total of 15,000 shares were issued with a par value of $10 each or $150,000 in total. The remaining $40,000 of the contributed capital has to be reported as additional paid-in capital.

27. **A** The 20,000 shares are issued at $9 above par so that additional paid-in capital is $180,000. The 10,000 shares are issued at $12 above par so that additional paid-in capital goes up by another $120,000 to $300,000. The stock dividend is a 30% stock dividend (9,000 shares / 30,000 shares) which is a large stock dividend (one that is over 20% to 25% of the outstanding shares). As a large stock dividend, it is recorded at par value; additional paid-in capital is not increased.

28. **A** For a compensatory stock option plan, the value is determined only on the grant date and only using a computer pricing model (unless fair value can be determined by a current market value for such instruments). That amount of $20,000 has to be allocated to expense over the four years that the president has to work or $5,000 per year.

29. **D** The variables to be considered include anything that will influence the eventual value of the option. For example, the length of time is included because the longer the available time, the more chance the employee has of waiting for a particular high price. In addition, the price volatility is also a factor because if the price goes up and down a lot, it is more likely that the employee will be able to wait for a higher stock price before converting. Finally, the bigger the difference there is between stock price and option price, the more likely that difference will expand and get larger. The salary level has nothing to do with the value of a stock option.

30. **C**   When the first 100,000 shares are sold, the company receives $400,000 more than the $1 per share par value. That is the initial balance in additional paid-in capital. When the cost method is applied, the purchase of treasury stock has no impact on additional paid-in capital. The subsequent sale, though, treats the gain as an increase in additional paid-in capital. Those 5,000 shares had cost $10 each ($100,000/10,000 shares) or $50,000. The sale for $80,000 creates an increase of $30,000 in additional paid-in capital to raise the balance to $430,000.

31. **A**   Issuing stock dividends does not impact stockholders' equity because there is neither an increase nor a decrease in the net assets of the company. Because the dividend was less than 20% to 25%, it is viewed as small stock dividend, and, hence, it is recorded at fair value. Because fair value is greater here than par value, the extra amount will go to increase additional paid-in capital.

32. **B**   The number of options outstanding is required. The fair value of options issued during the year is required. The fair value of the options issued at the grant date is required.

CHAPTER 7 – ACCOUNTING FOR LEASES

STUDY TIP

Before you go to bed each night, write down what exam preparation you plan to accomplish the following day and when you will do it. In that way, you begin each day with an organized plan and do not have to waste time determining what to do as the day progresses.

CHAPTER 7 – ACCOUNTING FOR LEASES

BASIC LEASE CONCEPTS

A. A **lease** is a contract between two parties.

B. One party (the lessor) owns the leased property.

C. Through the contract, a different party (the lessee) rents and is given the right to use the lessor's property for a specified period of time in return for periodic cash payments (rent) to the lessor.

CRITERIA FOR A CAPITAL LEASE

A. A major goal in accounting for leases is to recognize the economic substance of the lease agreement over its mere legal form.

B. A lease may be recorded by the lessee as a capitalized lease if the rights and obligations of ownership are conveyed to the lessee.

   1. A capitalized lease is viewed as a transfer of ownership rights—the effective transfer of all the risks and benefits of the property to the lessee.

   2. Capital leases are economically equivalent to sales and, for accounting purposes, are treated as sales.

C. A lease is viewed as a capitalized lease if it meets *any one* (or more) of the following four criteria:

   1. Title of the property (the leased asset) transfers to the lessee at the end of the lease term.

   2. There is a bargain purchase option. In other words, the lessee has the option to buy property at the end of the lease for a price that is significantly below market value (on the option exercise date) so that there is a reasonable expectation that the price will be paid.

   3. The term of the lease is 75% or more of the estimated economic life of the leased asset.

   4. The present value of the minimum lease payments is 90% or more of the fair value of the leased asset.

D. If none of the criteria are met, it is a rental of property and must be recorded as an operating lease.

   1. When the lease is signed, the lessee does not record an asset or a liability.

      a. The avoidance of a liability on the lessee's balance sheet is one of the "shortcomings" in the accounting for operating leases. This is called "off-balance sheet financing."

      b. Managers have every incentive to classify a lease as an operating lease to improve or minimize a company's debt-to-equity ratio.

2. Rent expense is recognized by the lessee as incurred.

   a. If a prepayment of rent is required, and it is not refundable, then the prepayment is amortized over the lease term.

   b. If a refundable deposit is paid, it is recorded as a long-term receivable by the lessee and a long-term liability by the lessor, unless it is not expected to be refunded. (Assuming the lease is for more than one year, these amounts are recorded as long-term.)

   c. If the lease calls for a rent abatement, or a period of "free rent," then the payments for the lease term are allocated evenly to all the periods of the lease term. ("A year's free rent" in a 5-year lease would result in the payments for the four years being amortized evenly over the five years, and would result in a credit to a "rent payable" account for the lessee in the first year.)

3. The lessor retains the asset on its books and records rent revenue as it is earned. The lessor recognizes rent revenue on the same basis as the lessee recognizes rent expense, as explained above.

INTEREST (OR DISCOUNT) RATE FOR NONOPERATING CAPITALIZED LEASES

A. An appropriate interest rate has to be used for the calculation of the present value of minimum lease payments (criterion C. 4. above).

   1. The lessor uses the imputed interest rate built into the cash flows of the lease contract.

   2. The lessee uses its incremental borrowing rate unless the lessor's imputed interest rate on the lease is known, and it is lower.

      a. In other words, the lessee must use the lower of the two rates.

      b. Using the lower of the two rates increases the present value of the lease payments and increases the likelihood that the lease will satisfy the 90% criterion and therefore be classified as a capital lease (general objective of GAAP is to encourage capitalization of leases).

BARGAIN PURCHASE OPTION AND RESIDUAL VALUE

A. As shown above, both parties to a capitalized lease base the computation on the minimum lease payments.

B. For the lessor, the minimum lease payments includes the total annual payment *plus* any amount to be received as a bargain purchase option.

   However, if the lessor anticipates getting the asset back because the title does not transfer and there is not a bargain purchase option, the expected residual value of the asset when returned is also viewed as a future collection.

C. For the lessee, any amount to be paid as a bargain purchase option is included as part of the minimum lease payments.

   If, instead, the asset is to be returned to the lessor, then only a value that has been guaranteed is included by the lessee.

D. Residual value can be unguaranteed or guaranteed.

   1. Some lease contracts require lessees to guarantee residual value to lessors.

2. The lessee can either buy the leased asset at the end of the lease term for the guaranteed residual value (GRV) or allow the lessor to sell the leased asset (with the lessee paying any deficiency or receiving any excess over the GRV).

3. In the case of GRV, at the end of the lease term, the receivable and payable on the respective lessor's and lessee's books should be equal to the GRV.

   a. Both lessor and lessee consider the GRV to be final lease payment.

   b. The lessee should depreciate the asset down to the GRV only.

LESSEE ACCOUNTING FOR A CAPITALIZED LEASE

A. The lessee accounts for a capitalized lease as if the property were being purchased over a period of time.

   1. On the balance sheet, part of the lease liability is shown as current with the remaining amount being long-term.

   2. The current portion consists of the payments to be made in the next 12 months less the amount of interest to be recognized during the period. Thus, only the principal portion is shown as a liability, and interest becomes a liability as it is incurred.

B. Both asset and liability are recorded at an amount equal to the present value of the minimum lease payments.

   1. The liability can be shown as a single figure (net of interest), or as a payable for total payments less a separate discount account to reduce the value to present value.

   2. The difference between total payments and present value is the interest to be recognized over the life of the lease.

   3. Interest is recognized each period, based on the effective rate method.

C. Although the asset is not legally owned by the lessee, the lessee depreciates the asset as if it were owned because the leased asset was set up as an asset on the balance sheet.

   1. The straight-line method is normally applied over the expected useful life of the asset.

   2. Specifically, if there is a transfer of title or there is a bargain purchase option, the depreciation period is over the life of the asset. Otherwise, it is for the term of the lease.

D. Maintenance, property taxes, and the like are executory costs.

   1. Such payments are not part of the minimum lease payments and are not included as part of the lease liability or the leased asset.

   2. Executory costs are expensed as incurred.

EXAMPLE

A. Situation:

   1. Dodevski, Inc. leases a machine for four years with annual payments of $10,000.

   2. At the end of the lease, the lessor regains possession of the asset that will be sold for scrap.

3. The implicit rate on the lease (known to Dodevski) is 6% and Dodevski's incremental borrowing rate is 7%.

4. Depreciation of all assets is on the straight-line basis, and the lease payments are made at the end of the year.

B. Analysis:

1. The lease is classified as a capital lease because the asset is being leased for at least 75% of its useful life (at the end of the lease term the asset will be sold for scrap).

2. The discount rate that should be used to value the lease is 6%, which is the lower of the discount rate on the lease and Dodevski's incremental borrowing rate. Using the ordinary annuity present value tables, the present value of the lease payments at 6% for 4 years is $34,651.

3. This amount is immediately recorded as both an asset and a liability.

4. Over the next four years, depreciation will be $34,651 / 4 = $8,663 per year.

5. The asset carrying value will decline each year by the depreciation amount and will be $25,988, $17,326, $8,663, and $0 at the end of each of the next four years, respectively.

C. Summary amortization schedule for the lease:

Year	Beginning Value	Interest Expense	Lease Payment	Liability
0				$34,651
1	$34,651	$2,079	$10,000	$26,730
2	$26,730	$1,604	$10,000	$18,334
3	$18,334	$1,100	$10,000	$9,434
4	$9,434	$566	$10,000	$0

1. Interest expense is calculated by multiplying the beginning value by the interest rate of 6%.

2. The lease liability is the beginning value plus the interest expense minus the lease payment (e.g., $34,651 + $2,079 – $10,000 = $26,730).

OPERATING LEASES

LEASE TERMINATION COSTS PAID BY A LESSEE

A. Occasionally, a lessee will decide to terminate an operating lease and incur costs to do so.

B. The fair value of the termination costs paid must be recognized as an expense or loss in calculating income from continuing operations in the year the lease was terminated.

ACCOUNTING FOR LEASEHOLD IMPROVEMENTS

A. Frequently, the lessee will make improvements to leased property by constructing new buildings or improving existing structures.

1. The lessee has the right to use these leasehold improvements over the term of the lease. Once attached, the lessor owns the leasehold improvements.

2. These improvements will revert to the lessor at the expiration of the lease.

B. Leasehold improvements are capitalized to an intangible asset account by the lessee and are amortized over the shorter of either the remaining lease term or useful life of the improvement.

C. Improvements made in lieu of rent should be expensed in the period incurred.

D. If the lease contains an option to renew and the likelihood of renewal is uncertain, the leasehold improvement should be written off over the life of the initial lease term or the useful life of the improvement, whichever is shorter.

E. Moveable equipment or office furniture that is not attached to the leased property is not considered a leasehold improvement.

ACCOUNTING FOR INITIAL DIRECT COSTS

A. The lessor may incur costs associated with setting up the lease agreement.

B. Such costs might include finder's fees, appraisal fees, and other costs in closing the transaction.

C. These costs are carried as an asset (deferred charge) on the lessor's balance sheet and amortized to expense by the lessor on a straight-line basis over the term of the lease.

ACCOUNTING FOR UNEVEN PAYMENTS OR FREE RENT

A. Some operating lease agreements might call for uneven payments or scheduled rent increases over the lease term. Other agreements might include, as an incentive to the lessee, several months of "free rent."

B. In these cases, rental revenue (expense) is still recognized by the lessor (lessee) in a straight-line basis and prorated over the full term of the lease during which the lessee has possession of the asset.

C. This is logical given the matching principle—if physical usage is relatively the same over the lease term, then an equal amount of benefit is being obtained by both parties to the lease.

LESSOR

CRITERIA TO DETERMINE WHEN A LESSOR MUST CLASSIFY ITS LEASES AS NONOPERATING

A. As with the lessee, the lessor must fulfill at least one of the four criteria discussed previously to qualify for capital lease treatment. The lessor refers to a capital lease as either a direct financing lease or a sales type lease.

B. Additionally, the collectibility of lease payments must be predictable *and* there should be no significant uncertainties about the amount of unreimbursable costs yet to be incurred by the lessor.

LESSOR ACCOUNTING FOR NONOPERATING CAPITALIZED LEASES

A. To account for a nonoperating lease, the lessor removes the leased asset from its balance sheet and recognizes revenue from the lease on its income statement.

B. Two different methods can be used to determine the pattern of revenue recognition:

1. It is a *direct financing lease* if the lessor is not a dealer or manufacturer of the product (i.e., it is a finance company instead). The lessor merely leases the item to other parties and does not sell the item in the normal course of business. Because of this, the present value of the lease payments equals the cost of the asset and the only revenue is interest on the receivable.

   a. A receivable and any cash immediately received are both recorded. The receivable amount is recorded for the gross amount of the payments to be received.

   b. The cost of the leased asset is removed from the books but no immediate gain is recorded. The difference is recorded as unearned interest revenue to be allocated to revenue over the period of payments. Under a direct financing-type lease, there is no sales or manufacturing profit. Only interest income will be recognized.

   c. Interest revenue equals the implicit interest rate times net lease receivable at the beginning of the period. The net receivable equals the lease receivable balance less the unearned interest revenue balance.

   d. The interest is initially recorded as unearned interest and then amortized to interest revenue based on the implicit rate and the net receivable balance.

   Entry at inception:

Lease receivable	(gross)	
Asset		(cost)
Unearned interest revenue		(plug)

2. It is a *sales-type lease* if the lessor is a dealer or manufacturer of the leased asset who may also sell the item in the normal course of business.

   a. A lease receivable for all the required payments and any cash immediately received are recorded at the gross amounts. This is called the gross investment. The present value of the gross investment is the net investment.

   b. The cost of the asset, inventory, is removed from the books.

   c. Sales revenue is recorded at the present value of the minimum lease payments.

   d. Cost of goods sold (COGS) is recorded as the cost of the asset plus initial direct costs less the present value of any unguaranteed residual value.

   e. Unearned interest revenue is the amount of the gross investment over the the net investment. This unearned interest will be recognized as interest revenue over the term of the lease using the effective rate method using the implicit rate and the net receivable balance.

EXAMPLE OF A SALES-TYPE LEASE

A. Situation (same information as in the example above plus some additional details):

1. Maciej, Inc. leases a machine to Dodevski, Inc. for four years with annual payments of $10,000.

2. It cost Maciej $30,000 to produce the machine.

3. At the end of the lease, Maciej (the lessor) regains possession of the asset and estimates that it will be able to sell the machine for $6,000.

B. Analysis:

1. The gross investment is $46,000 ($40,000 + $6,000).

2. Sales revenue is recorded as the present value of the four $10,000 lease payments at 6%, or $34,651. The present value of the unguaranteed residual value is $4,753 (using PV of a lump sum table).

3. The COGS is the cost of the inventory less the present value of any unguaranteed residual value, or $30,000 – $4,753 = $25,247.

4. The net investment is the present value of the gross investment, or $34,651 + $4,753 = $39,404.

5. The unearned revenue is the difference between the gross investment of $46,000 and the net investment of $39,404.

    The journal entry at inception is:

Lease receivable	$46,000	
COGS	$25,247	
Sales revenue		$34,651
Inventory		$30,000
Unearned interest revenue		$6,596

C. Summary

Year	Beginning Net Investment in Lease	Interest Revenue	Lease Payment	Ending Net Investment in Lease
0				$39,404
1	$39,404	$2,364	$10,000	$31,768
2	$31,768	$1,906	$10,000	$23,674
3	$23,674	$1,420	$10,000	$15,094
4	$15,094	$906	$10,000	$6,000

1. Interest revenue is calculated by multiplying the beginning investment in the lease by the interest rate of 6%.

2. Ending value of the investment in the lease is the beginning value plus the interest revenue minus the lease payment.

3. The ending value at the end of Year 4 should be equal to the expected salvage value.

    At the end of the first year, the first annual payment will be received and unearned interest revenue will be amortized to interest revenue.

Cash	$10,000	
Interest		$10,000

Unearned interest revenue	$2,364	
Interest revenue		$2,364

    These entries will be replicated at the end of each year for the appropriate interest revenue amount.

D. Practice problem for sales-type lease:

Wilson is a dealer in widgets, normally buying them for $30,000 and selling them for $39,000. On December 31, Year 0, Wilson buys a widget for $30,000 and immediately leases it to Thomas for five years at $11,000 per year, with the first payment being made immediately. Assume, for convenience, that the implicit interest rate built into the contract was 10% per year.

Determine what journal entry should be recorded by Wilson at the start of this lease. Then, determine the amount of income to be recognized in Year 0, Year 1, and Year 2.

E. Analysis and solution:

In this lease, the lessor (Wilson) will receive a total of $55,000 ($11,000 per year for five years). The cost of the widget is only $30,000. Wilson is a dealer in widgets so that the transaction is recorded as a sales-type lease. For that reason, the profit from a sale must be recognized immediately and the interest revenue is reported as time passes.

The first payment is made immediately so the initial entry on December 31, Year 1 is:

Cash	$11,000	
Lease receivable	$44,000	
Sales revenue		$45,869
Unearned interest revenue		$9,131
Cost of goods sold	$30,000	
Inventory—Widget		$30,000

Year	Beginning Net Investment in Lease	Earned Interest Revenue	Lease Payment	Ending Net Investment in Lease
12/31/Year 1	$45,869		$11,000	$34,869
12/31/Year 2	$34,869	$3,487	$11,000	$27,356
12/31/Year 3	$27,356	$2,736	$11,000	$19,091
12/31/Year 4	$19,091	$1,909	$11,000	$10,001
12/31/Year 5	$10,001	$1,000	$11,000	$1*

*Rounding error.

Year 1: The only income is the $45,869 revenue from the sales-type lease less cost of goods sold of $30,000, or $15,869.

Year 2: The net receivable balance for this year is the $44,000 receivable less the $9,131 unearned interest revenue, or $34,869. Based on a 10% rate, interest revenue of $3,487 should be recognized on December 31, Year 2 bringing unearned interest revenue down to $5,644.

Year 3: A second payment is made at the end of Year 2 so that the receivable is reduced from $44,000 to $33,000. On that same day, interest revenue of $2,736 is recorded, which decreases the unearned interest revenue to $2,908. The net receivable for Year 3 is $19,091.

ACCOUNTING OF DIRECT COSTS INCURRED BY THE LESSOR

A. The lessor may have to pay direct costs such as legal fees and commissions associated with creating the lease agreement.

B. If it is an operating lease, these costs are recorded as an asset and amortized as an expense over the term of the lease.

C. If it is a sales type lease, the cost is expensed immediately.

D. If it is a direct financing lease, the cost is a reduction in the unearned interest account so that less interest is recognized over the term of the lease.

SALE-LEASEBACK ARRANGEMENTS

A. A sale-leaseback arrangement occurs when an asset is sold and then leased back to the original owner.

B. If book value exceeds fair value at the inception of the lease, the seller/lessee recognizes the loss immediately. (This is viewed the same as selling an asset for a loss: The book value is greater than the selling/market price.)

C. If there is a gain, the principle of conservatism states that the seller/lessee may have to defer recognition of part of the gain, given that the seller/lessee has not truly given up control of the asset.

1. If only a minor portion of the property is leased back, any gain is recognized by the seller/lessee immediately. A minor portion exists when the present value of payments is 10% or less of the fair value.

2. If substantially all of the property (90%) is leased back, the entire gain is initially deferred.

    a. If it is a capital lease, the deferred gain is gradually amortized to reduce depreciation expense over the term of the lease.

    b. If it is an operating lease, the deferred gain is amortized in proportion to rent expense over the term of the lease.

3. If the leaseback is more than a minor portion but less than substantially all, the seller/lessee recognizes part of the gain and defers the rest.

    a. The deferred gain is written off to reduce the depreciation expense over the term of the lease.

    b. The deferred gain is the amount up to the present value of the lease payments.

    c. Any additional amount is recognized immediately as a gain.

D. Also, when the leaseback is more than minor but does not meet the criteria of a capital lease, the gain is recognized immediately.

E. Note that a modification to a capital lease that changes the classification of the lease to an operating lease requires the transaction be accounted for as a sale-leaseback transaction.

DISCLOSURES

A. A general description of the leasing arrangement is required.

B. The disclosure of future minimum lease payments is required for each of the next five years.

QUESTIONS: ACCOUNTING FOR LEASES

1. A company leases an asset for eight years. At the end of that time, the company can buy the asset for $16,000. Which of the following statements is true?
    A. The availability of this option makes the lease a capital lease.
    B. If this option price is below the expected fair value of the asset at that time, the lease must be a capital lease.
    C. If the asset has an expected life of ten years, the lease is a capital lease.
    D. To be a capital lease, both the option rule and the life rule must be met.

2. The Ace Rental Company leases an apartment to Smith for $1,000 per month for 24 months on July 1, Year 1. However, to encourage Smith to take the apartment, Ace agreed to skip the first three months of rental fees. This is an operating lease. What amount of rental revenue should Ace recognize for Year 1?
    A. $3,000.
    B. $5,250.
    C. $5,400.
    D. $6,000.

3. The Higgens Corporation is neither a dealer nor a manufacturer of widgets. On January 1, Year 1, Higgens buys a widget for $20,286 and leases it to Testani Corporation for its entire life of ten years for $2,900 per year. Assume that this payment was determined based on a 9% annual interest rate. Testani has an incremental borrowing rate of 12%. Both parties are aware of these rates. The first payment is made immediately. How much income should Higgens recognize in Year 1?
    A. $1,565.
    B. $1,800.
    C. $2,052.
    D. $2,400.

4. The Higgins Corporation is neither a dealer nor a manufacturer of widgets. On January 1, Year 1, Higgins buys a widget for $20,000 and leases it to Testane Corporation for its entire life of ten years for $2,900 per year. This is a capital lease. Assume that this payment was determined based on a 9% annual interest rate. Testane has an incremental borrowing rate of 12%. Both parties are aware of these rates. The first payment is made immediately. Assume, for convenience, that interest revenue of $2,000 is recognized at the end of Year 1. How much income should Higgins recognize in Year 2?
    A. $1,484.
    B. $1,719.
    C. $1,944.
    D. $2,292.

5. The Huggens Corporation is a dealer in widgets. Huggens normally sells widgets for $4,000 above their cost. On January 1, Year 1, Huggens buys a widget for $20,000 and leases it to Tostani Corporation for its entire life of ten years for $3,500 per year. This is a capital lease. Assume that this payment was determined based on a 9% annual interest rate. Tostani has an incremental borrowing rate of 12%. Both parties are aware of these rates. The first payment is made immediately. How much income should Huggens recognize in Year 1?
    A. $6,371.
    B. $6,160.
    C. $6,460.
    D. $6,880.

6. The Histron Corp. holds a building with a book value of $2.4 million. The building has a 20-year remaining life. The building is sold for $3.0 million. Histron immediately leases the building back from the buyer for one year for a single payment of $310,000. What amount of the gain on the sale of the building should Histron recognize this year?
    A. $0.
    B. $290,000.
    C. $310,000.
    D. $600,000.

7. A company (the lessor) buys a car and then leases it to one of its customers (lessee). Which of the following is correct?
    A. Unless the title eventually transfers to the lessee, the lease should be reported as an operating lease.
    B. If the car has a life of ten years and the lease is for eight years, the lease must be reported as a capital lease.
    C. If the lease is a capital lease, then the lessee must account for the contract as either a direct financing lease or a sales type lease.
    D. If the lessee is given the option to purchase the car at the end of the lease, both parties will account for the contract as a capital lease.

8. On January 1, Year 1, the Lexington Corporation leases a machine to use for eight years, its entire life. Payments will be $10,000 per year beginning immediately. Lexington has an incremental borrowing rate of 6%. The present value of an ordinary annuity for eight years at an annual interest rate of 6% is assumed to be 6.21. The present value of an annuity due for eight years at an annual interest rate of 6% is assumed to be 6.58. Assume the straight-line method is used for depreciation but the effective-rate method is used in recognizing interest. What amount of interest expense should be recognized for Year 2? (Round to the nearest dollar.)
    A. $2,547.
    B. $2,714.
    C. $2,949.
    D. $3,585.

9. The Joshua Corporation is a dealer in automobiles. One particular line of cars is bought by Joshua for $39,000 each and then sold for $50,000. On January 1, Year 1, one of these cars is leased to a customer for five years (its entire useful life). The annual payments are $12,000 based on an assumed implicit interest rate of 10%. The first payment is made immediately and every January 1 thereafter. What increase in net income should Joshua recognize for Year 1?
    A. $3,842.
    B. $11,138.
    C. $14,842.
    D. $16,989.

10. Acme Leasing keeps no inventory. However, when a customer wants virtually any item, Acme will buy the item and then lease it to the customer. In that way, the customer gets financing and Acme makes a predetermined and acceptable rate of return. On January 1, Year 1, a customer wants a computer. Acme buys the proper model for $24,000 and leases it immediately to the customer for the expected seven year life of the asset. Payments are made annually on January 1 with the first one made immediately. Acme always uses an implicit interest rate of 8% and the annual payments charged for this computer are assumed to be $4,300. What net receivable figure should Acme report on its December 31, Year 1, balance sheet?
   A. $21,276.
   B. $21,620.
   C. $25,920.
   D. $27,864.

11. On January 1, Year 1, the Trimble Corporation leases a piece of equipment to use for eight years. The equipment has an expected life of ten years and no anticipated salvage value. Trimble has an incremental borrowing rate of 5%. Annual payments for this asset are $9,000 with the first payment to be made immediately. At the end of the eight years, Trimble has the right to buy the asset for $10,000 in cash. This amount is expected to be significantly below the expected fair value of the equipment on that date so it is reasonable to expect Trimble to pay this amount. Trimble records depreciation based on the straight-line method and interest based on the effective rate method. The present value of an annuity due of $1 at 5% for eight years is assumed to be 6.80. The present value of an ordinary annuity of $1 at 5% for eight years is assumed to be 6.50. The present value of a single amount of $1 at 5% in eight years is assumed to be 0.66. What amount of depreciation expense should Trimble record for Year 1?
   A. $6,120.
   B. $6,510.
   C. $6,780.
   D. $7,650.

12. On January 1, Year 1, the Hawthorne Corporation buys a building with 20 floors for $8 million. The building is immediately sold to Rosebud Corporation for $9.2 million. Hawthorne then leases back one floor of the building for 20 years (the expected life of the building). The lease payments are $200,000 per year with the payments being made annually beginning on January 1, Year 1. The present value of the $200,000 payments for 20 years using an incremental borrowing rate of 10% is assumed to be $1.8 million. Depreciation is recorded by applying the straight-line method and interest is determined using the effective-rate method. What is the overall impact on the reported net income for Hawthorne for Year 1?
   A. Increase of $1,200,000.
   B. Increase of $950,000.
   C. Decrease of $190,000.
   D. Decrease of $250,000.

ANSWERS: ACCOUNTING FOR LEASES

1. **C** There are four criteria for determining a capital lease. Only one of the four must be met. One of these states that a lease is a capital lease if there is a bargain purchase option. A bargain purchase option is one where the lessee can buy the leased asset for significantly below the expected fair value of the property at that time so that it is reasonable to believe that the lessee will take advantage of the opportunity. A second criterion states that a lease is a capital lease if the life of the lease is 75% or more of the life of the asset. Here, that criterion is being met (8/10 = 80% of the asset's life).

2. **B** Ace has signed a contract that will generate $21,000 in revenues (after skipping the first three months) over 24 months. That is rental revenue of $875 per month. For the last six months of Year 1, that is a total of $5,250.

3. **A** This is a capital lease because the life of the lease is 75% or more of the life of the asset. Because the lessor is not a dealer or manufacturer, this is a direct financing lease. As a direct financing lease, no profit is recognized at the time of the lease and all profit is recognized as interest over the life of the lease. The lease receivable here is initially $29,000, but the asset has a cost of $20,286 so that the unearned interest revenue is $8,714. The first immediate payment reduces the receivable from $29,000 to $26,100. That drops the net receivable balance to $17,386 ($26,100 minus $8,714). At 9% interest, the interest revenue for the first year is $1,565.

   The journal entry at inception is:

Lease Receivable	29,000	
Asset		20,286
Unearned Interest Revenue		8,714
Cash	2,900	
Lease Receivable		2,900

4. **A** Because the lessor is not a dealer or manufacturer, this is a direct financing lease. As a direct financing lease, no profit is recognized at the time of the lease and all profit is recognized as interest over the life of the lease. The lease receivable here is initially $29,000 but the asset has a cost of $20,286 so that the unearned interest revenue is $8,714. The first payment reduces the receivable from $29,000 to $26,100. That drops the net receivable balance to $17,386 ($26,100 minus $8,714). At the end of Year 1, interest of $2,000 is recognized and compounded to bring the net receivable up to $19,386. Then, the next payment of $2,900 reduces that figure to $16,486, which is the balance throughout the second year. At an interest rate of 9%, that gives interest revenue of $1,484.

5. **A** Because the lessor is a dealer (or a manufacturer), this is a sales type lease. As a sales type lease, the sales revenue and COGS are recognized at the beginning of the lease and all remaining profit is recognized as interest over the life of the lease. The gross investment (lease receivable) is initially $35,000, the present value of lease payments (net investment) is $24,483 using the implicit rate of 9%, so the unearned interest revenue is $10,517 (the extra amount being received over time). Sales revenue less COGS is $4,483. The first payment reduces the receivable from $35,000 to $31,500. That drops the net receivable balance for Year 1 to $20,983 ($31,500 minus $10,517). At a 9% annual interest rate, the interest revenue for the first year is $1,888. The total income for the year is $4,483 plus $1,888, or $6,371.

6. **D** Because the leaseback is for less than 10% of the life of the asset that was sold, it is viewed as a minor portion and the entire gain is recognized immediately.

7. **B** The FASB has established four criteria for a capital lease. If any one of these is met, then the lease has to be recorded as a capital lease:

   - The title transfers to the lessee.
   - There is a bargain purchase option (a bargain is viewed as an option price that is significantly below expected fair value so that it is reasonable to expect the lessee to acquire the asset).

- The life of the lease is 75% or more of the life of the asset.
- The present value of the minimum lease payments is 90% or more of the fair value of the asset.

For a capital lease, the lessee only has one method of reporting (basically, the asset is being recorded as an acquisition using long-term financing). However, the lessor must classify the lease as a sales type lease or an operating lease based on certain factors.

8. **C**   This is an annuity due since the first payment is made immediately. Thus, the liability (and the asset) are initially recorded at $65,800 ($10,000 times 6.58). The first payment then reduces the liability to $55,800. At the end of the first year, interest expense of $3,348 ($55,800 times 6%) is recognized and compounded to increase the liability. Interest is not specifically paid in a lease and, so it is compounded. The second payment is made at the beginning of Year 2. For Year 2, the liability balance is now $49,148 ($55,800 plus $3,348 minus $10,000). Interest expense for Year 2 is $2,949 (or $49,148 times 6%).

9. **C**   This is a sales type lease because the lessor is either a dealer or manufacturer of the item being leased. As such, sales revenue equal to the present value of lease payments and COGS are recognized immediately on January 1, Year 1. This leads to an increase in net income of $11,038.

In addition, interest revenue must be recognized over the five years of the lease. The receivable is $60,000, but the unearned interest revenue within the receivable is $9,962 for a beginning net receivable value of $50,038. The first payment of $12,000 immediately reduces that net receivable balance to $38,038 for the duration of Year 1. At a 10% interest rate, the interest revenue for Year 1 is $3,804 ($38,038 times 10%). The gain of $11,038 plus the first year interest of $3,804 gives an increase in income for Year 1 of $14,842.

10. **A**   For the lessor, this is viewed as a direct financing lease because Acme does not appear to be either a dealer or a manufacturer of computers. Thus, no immediate profit is recognized; all of the profit is interest revenue to be reported over this seven-year period. The initial receivable is $30,100 ($4,300 times seven payments). Because the asset only cost the lessor $24,000, the additional amount to be received of $6,100 ($30,100 less $24,000) is unearned interest buried inside of the payments. After the first payment is made, the gross receivable is reduced to $25,800 ($30,100 less $4,300) so that the net receivable balance for the first year is $19,700 ($25,800 receivable after removing the $6,100 in unearned interest revenue). Based on an 8% interest rate, interest revenue of $1,576 is recognized for Year 1. Interest is not directly paid in lease arrangements so the amount being recognized must be capitalized (added to the net receivable balance). Hence, the net receivable at the end of that year is raised from $19,700 to $21,276.

11. **C**   Because the purchase option is expected to be paid, it is viewed as a bargain and is included as a cash flow. Trimble expects to pay the $10,000 and use the asset for its entire 10-year life and that is how the transaction should be recorded. Because the first payment is made immediately, the annual payments represent an annuity due. The present value of the cash flows is $9,000 times 6.80 ($61,200) plus $10,000 times 0.66 ($6,600) for a total of $67,800. The company plans to use the asset for all ten years so the depreciation expense each year is $6,780.

12. **B**   Because the leaseback is for a minor portion of the building (less than 10% of the asset or less than 10% of its life), the $1.2 million gain on the sale is recognized immediately by Hawthorne. In addition, because the floor of the building is being leased for 75% or more of the asset's life, this qualifies as a capital lease. The leased asset (the rental space) is capitalized at $1.8 million and depreciated over 20 years or at the rate of $90,000 per year. The liability is also recorded at $1.8 million but the first payment of $200,000 immediately drops that amount to $1.6 million. Based on an interest rate of 10%, interest expense of $160,000 is recorded for Year 1. Thus, the gain of $1.2 million less depreciation of $90,000 and less interest of $160,000 gives an increase in profit for the year of $950,000.

CHAPTER 8 – MISCELLANEOUS ACCOUNTING CONCEPTS

STUDY TIP

Keep a diary of your study time. Each day, write down the amount of time you spend and what you get accomplished. People often tend to overestimate their study hours and, thus, quit too soon. A diary will help you monitor whether you are investing an adequate amount of time so that you can take corrective action if necessary.

Chapter 8 – Miscellaneous Accounting Concepts

Overview of the Concepts and Standards for Financial Statements Coverage on the CPA Exam

According to the AICPA Content Specification Outline, the candidates should be aware of the following four aspects of Concepts and Standards for financial statements:

1. Financial accounting concepts.

2. Financial accounting standards for presentation and disclosure in general-purpose financial statements.

3. Other presentations of financial data—financial statements prepared in conformity with comprehensive bases of accounting other than generally accepted accounting principles (GAAP).

4. Financial statement analysis.

This chapter will cover *financial accounting concepts* only (with the remaining three topics to be covered in subsequent chapters).

In this chapter, we examine the process by which standards are set and the roles of standard-setting bodies. This will be followed with a discussion of the conceptual basis for accounting standards.

The material contained in this chapter provides the student with a general introduction to financial statements. It is crucial to note that subsequent chapters will build on and refer back to these fundamental concepts.

Financial Accounting Standards Board

Basic Description

Please note that all of the material in the following outlines has been taken exclusively from publicly available information contained on the Financial Accounting Standards Board (FASB) website, *www.fasb.org*, and from *Facts about FASB*, published by FASB. We have summarized what we believe are the most relevant sections for the CPA Exam.

The FASB has the following three responsibilities:

1. Since 1973, it is the designated private sector organization in the United States that establishes financial accounting and reporting standards.

2. The FASB's standards govern the preparation of financial reports.

3. The mission of the FASB is to establish and improve standards of financial accounting and reporting for the guidance and education of the public including issuers, auditors, and users of financial information.

HOW FASB ACCOMPLISHES ITS MISSION

To accomplish its mission, FASB does the following five things:

1. Improves on the usefulness of financial reporting by focusing on the primary characteristics of *relevance* and *reliability* and on the qualities of *comparability* and *consistency* (four concepts to be discussed in much more detail in the next section).

2. Keeps standards current to reflect changes in methods of doing business and changes in the economic environment.

3. Considers promptly any significant areas of deficiency in financial reporting that might be improved through the standard-setting process.

4. Promotes the international convergence of accounting standards concurrent with improving the quality of financial reporting.

5. Improves the common understanding of the nature and purposes of information contained in financial reports.

STANDARD-SETTING PROCESS

Accounting standards are essential to the efficient functioning of the economy because decisions about the allocation of resources rely heavily on credible, concise, transparent, and understandable financial information. Financial information about the operations and financial position of individual entities also is used by the public in making various other kinds of decisions.

A. An Open Decision-Making Process.

1. Actions of the FASB have an impact on many organizations within its large and diverse constituency.

2. It is essential that the decision making process be evenhanded.

3. Accordingly, the FASB follows an extensive "due process" that is open to public observation and participation.

B. FASB Due Process Steps.

The FASB has established the following procedures for developing accounting standards. These procedures are used for major agenda projects. Not all of the steps may be necessary for application and implementation projects. Often, many other steps are followed during the course of the project that are not mentioned below.

1. FASB receives requests and recommendations for possible projects and reconsideration of existing standards from various sources.

2. The FASB staff summarizes the information it receives and discusses its findings at a public FASB meeting as part of the agenda decision making process.

3. FASB votes on whether to add the project to its agenda. A simple majority vote is needed.

4. FASB deliberates the various issues identified and analyzed by the staff at a series of public meetings.

5.   FASB issues the Exposure Draft. (In some projects, the staff may prepare and issue an Invitation to Comment or Preliminary Views prior to FASB issuing an Exposure Draft.)

6.   FASB holds a public roundtable meeting on the Exposure Draft, if necessary.

7.   The FASB staff analyzes comment letters, public roundtable discussion, and any other information, and the FASB re-deliberates the proposed provisions at public meetings.

8.   FASB issues a Statement or Interpretation by simple majority vote.

ROLE OF FASB

A.   General.

   1.   FASB develops broad accounting *concepts* as well as *standards* for financial reporting.

   2.   The FASB also provides guidance on implementation of standards.

   3.   Concepts are useful in guiding FASB in establishing standards and in providing a frame of reference, or conceptual framework, for resolving accounting issues.

   4.   FASB's framework will help to establish reasonable bounds for judgment in preparing financial information and to increase understanding of, and confidence in, financial information on the part of users of financial reports.

   5.   The FASB framework also will help the public to understand the nature and limitations of information supplied by financial reporting.

B.   Concepts and Standards.

   1.   FASB's work on both concepts and standards is based on research aimed at gaining new insights and ideas.

   2.   Research is conducted by the FASB staff and others, including foreign national and international accounting standard-setting bodies.

   3.   As mentioned above, FASB's activities are open to public participation and observation under a mandated "due process" system.

   4.   The FASB actively solicits the views of its various constituencies on accounting issues.

GENERALLY ACCEPTED ACCOUNTING PRINCIPLES (GAAP)

FUNDAMENTALS

A.   The generally accepted accounting principles (GAAP) are the backbone of financial accounting and include the conventions, rules, and procedures that make up what is acceptable practice.

B.   However, GAAP is always adapting and evolving with the new developments in business and industry.

C.   The key point to remember is that GAAP is flexible and that the technical guidance is only that, guidance.

D. There may be several alternative (and valid) ways to interpret a particular accounting rule and as a result, several potentially different treatments on the financial statements.

HIERARCHY

A. GAAP has been set up in a hierarchical structure.

B. When more than one pronouncement relates to a given issue or type of transaction, an individual can determine which pronouncement is the most authoritative based upon this hierarchy.

C. The structure divides sources of accounting principles into the following four categories:

1. Category A.

    a. FASB Statements of Financial Accounting Standards (SFAS).

        FASB Statement 133 Implementation Issues

        FASB Staff Positions

    b. FASB Interpretations.

    c. Accounting Principles Board (APB) Opinions that are not superseded by actions of the FASB.

    d. AICPA Accounting Research Bulletins (ARB).

2. Category B.

    a. FASB Technical Bulletins.

    b. AICPA Industry Audit and Accounting Guides cleared by the FASB.

    c. AICPA Statements of Position cleared by the FASB.

3. Category C.

    a. AICPA Accounting Standards Executive Committee (AcSEC) Practice Bulletins cleared by the FASB.

    b. Consensus positions of the FASB Emerging Issues Task Force the Topics discussed in Appendix D of EITF Abstracts (EITF D-Topics).

4. Category D.

    a. AICPA accounting interpretations.

    b. Implementation guides (Q&As) published by the FASB staff.

    c. AICPA Industry Audit and Accounting Guides and Statements of Positions not cleared by the FASB.

    d. Practices that are widely recognized and prevalent either generally or in a specific industry.

5. The higher category is usually predominant over the lower category in case of any conflict in the interpretation for the treatment of a particular transaction.

CONCEPTUAL FRAMEWORK OF ACCOUNTING

A. FASB undertook a project to establish a conceptual framework for accounting. The project was intended to more clearly define the objectives and concepts underlying financial accounting and reporting.

B. As a result of the work performed, the FASB has created a series of pronouncements entitled Statements of Financial Accounting Concepts (SFAC).

C. In relation to financial accounting by the business enterprise, the following five major issues have been addressed:

1. Objectives of Financial Reporting.

2. Qualitative Characteristics of Accounting Information.

3. Elements of Financial Statements.

4. Recognition and Measurement in Financial Statements.

5. Using Cash Flow Information and Present Value in Accounting Measurements.

IMPLICATIONS OF THE CONCEPTUAL FRAMEWORK FOR ACCOUNTING

A. The conceptual framework will have many short-range and long-range effects on the way financial information and reporting are viewed both within the profession and by users of the information.

B. Eventually, it is anticipated that all financial accounting standards will be directly traceable to the underlying objectives and concepts established in the conceptual framework.

C. It will also result in the eventual restructuring of what is viewed as a complete set of financial statements and what is included under the "umbrella" of financial reporting.

D. Although much of what makes up generally accepted accounting principles was derived prior to the development of the conceptual framework, previous studies of a similar nature had been performed by the appropriate authoritative bodies.

E. The conceptual framework will be referred to as a basis for the development of all future financial accounting standards promulgated by the FASB.

INTRODUCTION TO FINANCIAL REPORTING

BASIC DESCRIPTION

A. Before addressing the objectives of financial reporting, it must be understood that financial reporting includes, but is not limited to, the financial statements issued by an entity.

B. Financial reporting also refers to any means of communication that is directly provided by the entity's accounting system.

C. Financial reporting refers to the general purpose external financial reporting by business enterprises. Although internal users, such as the enterprise's management, will need and use the same information as external users, they will generally need additional information.

D. The conceptual framework is intended to relate to external users for their investment and credit decisions.

USES AND USERS OF FINANCIAL REPORTING

A. The objectives of financial reporting must also contemplate certain basic aspects of the environment in which financial reports will be used.

B. Financial reports are used largely for the purpose of making business and economic decisions about the best allocation of resources.

C. The reporting is used by: investors, creditors, and business managers.

D. The government is also a user of financial reporting for: regulatory purposes, tax purposes, and purposes of accumulating information in fulfilling its role as provider of economic statistics and other information pertaining to the economy as a whole or to large segments of the economy.

HOW FINANCIAL REPORTING MUST BE EVALUATED IN TERMS OF ITS CHARACTERISTICS AND LIMITATIONS

A. There is a cost associated with providing and using the information.

B. Financial information is generally quantitative in nature and must be measured on the basis of some common denominator, money.

C. Presentation of financial information involves measurement by means of: estimation, classification, summarization, judgment, and allocation.

D. Although financial information is often used to make decisions about the future, the information is historical in nature. It is difficult to assess the future based entirely upon information from the past. In many cases, the economic impact of events and transactions cannot be precisely measured until some point in the future.

E. Users must look to other sources for information about the economy, politics, and industry to better be able to use financial information provided by an enterprise.

OBJECTIVES OF FINANCIAL REPORTING BY BUSINESS ENTERPRISES

ROLE OF FINANCIAL REPORTING

The role of financial reporting is to assist in the making of decisions and to establish a favorable environment for decision making. It is not intended to determine or to influence the outcome of the decision-making process. As a result, financial reporting must provide *evenhanded*, *neutral*, or *unbiased* information.

A. To provide information for present and potential investors and creditors (users) in making rational investment, credit, and similar decisions.

The information should be understandable to users having *reasonable* knowledge of business and economic matters and who are willing to study the information.

B. To provide information for users in assessing the amounts, timing, and uncertainty of prospective cash receipts from dividends or interest and proceeds from sale, redemption, or maturity of securities or loans.

The availability of these cash receipts is largely dependent on the enterprise's ability to generate and manage cash, resulting in the need for information enabling users to assess the amounts, timing, and uncertainty of prospective cash inflows to the enterprise.

C. To provide information about an enterprise's economic resources, claims against those resources, and the effects of transactions, events, and circumstances that change resources and claims against them. Information can be placed in five categories:

1. Economic resources, obligations and owners' equity.

2. Enterprise performance and earnings.

3. Liquidity, solvency, and fund flows.

4. Management stewardship and performance.

5. Management explanations and interpretations.

INFORMATION CONTAINED IN AN ENTERPRISE'S FINANCIAL STATEMENTS

A. Information about an enterprise's *resources, obligations,* and *owners' equity* helps users identify financial strengths and weaknesses and to assess liquidity and solvency. Such information also provides indications of cash flow potentials.

B. Information about an enterprise's *performance* and *earnings* provides a basis for assessing potential future performance. Although the users' primary emphasis is to assess future cash flows, the enterprise's ability to generate future positive cash flows will be based on the enterprise's ability to generate earnings. As a result, information about an enterprise's performance and earnings is best provided by applying accrual basis accounting.

C. Information about an enterprise's *liquidity, solvency,* and *fund flows* provides users with a means of assessing how the enterprise obtains and spends cash, how it borrows and repays borrowed funds, how it handles its capital transactions, and how it evaluates other factors affecting the enterprise's liquidity or solvency.

D. Management of an enterprise has a fiduciary duty to the owners for the custody of its resources and for the efficient and profitable use of them. Information about *management's stewardship* and *performance,* often best provided through reports on earnings, allows users to assess management's attendance to this fiduciary duty.

E. Information provided in the form of management *explanations* and *interpretations* assist users in understanding financial information. This is especially true when the financial information is largely based on management's estimates and judgment.

QUALITATIVE CHARACTERISTICS OF ACCOUNTING INFORMATION

USEFULNESS

A. The qualitative characteristics of accounting information are those characteristics that make the information useful to users in the decision-making process.

B. These qualitative characteristics are the basis for evaluating the information against the cost of providing and using it and help distinguish more useful from less useful information.

C. The qualitative characteristics of accounting information should be used when making choices among different alternatives by both the FASB and others who set down reporting requirements as well as those within the enterprise who make decisions as to what shall be included in financial reports and in what manner it shall be presented. (*Note: Constraints to usefulness will be discussed later in this chapter.*)

PRIMARY QUALITATIVE CHARACTERISTICS OF ACCOUNTING INFORMATION

The primary qualitative characteristics are *relevance* and *reliability*. If the accounting information lacks either relevance or reliability the information would automatically not be useful.

RELEVANCE

A. *Relevance* indicates that the information will make a difference in the decision-making process.

B. Three ingredients contribute to the relevance of accounting information:

1. It must be timely.

2. It must have predictive value.

3. It must have feedback value.

Timeliness indicates that the information is available while it can still influence decisions.

Predictive value indicates that the information is helpful in forecasting the outcome of past or present events.

Feedback value indicates that the information is helpful in confirming or correcting prior expectations.

RELIABILITY

A. *Reliability* indicates that the information is adequately free from error and bias and faithfully represents what it purports to represent. In context, accounting information is reasonably free from bias if it is not consistently overstated or consistently understated.

B. The ingredients that make accounting information reliable include: representational faithfulness, verifiability, and neutrality.

Representational faithfulness, sometimes referred to as validity, indicates that the information corresponds to what it purports to represent or that the information says what it appears to say.

Verifiability indicates that the method of measurement in use has been applied without error or bias and is usually determined through consensus among those making similar measurement.

Neutrality indicates that the information is reported without bias and is not presented to create a particular result.

SECONDARY QUALITATIVE CHARACTERISTICS OF ACCOUNTING INFORMATION

A. Accounting information should also have the secondary qualitative characteristics of *comparability* and *consistency*.

1. *Comparability* indicates that the information can be compared to other data for the purpose of identifying similarities and differences.

2. *Consistency* indicates that accounting policies and procedures remain unchanged from period to period.

CONSTRAINTS TO USEFULNESS

A. The most pervasive constraint is that the usefulness and benefit to be derived from having certain information *must exceed the cost* of providing it.

B. A secondary constraint is materiality. *Materiality* is a threshold for recognition in that information can still be reliable if it contains immaterial errors.

1. Materiality is a consideration if it is probable that a person relying on certain information will be influenced in making investment or credit decisions by an error or omission.

2. The materiality of an item must be considered simultaneously with the importance of the item. A small amount, considered immaterial in normal transactions, might influence users of the information when it pertains to an unusual item.

UNDERSTANDABILITY

A. To be useful to a particular individual, the information must be understandable.

1. *Understandability* indicates that a user is able to perceive the significance of the information. If a user is not qualified to comprehend the information, it does not make the information irrelevant but creates a necessity for the user to broaden his knowledge or seek assistance in interpreting the information.

2. Information is considered understandable if it is comprehensible to those with a *reasonable* (not necessarily expert) understanding of business and economics and who are willing to study the information.

PRECISION, BIAS, COMPLETENESS, VERIFIABILITY, AND CONSERVATISM AFFECT RELIABILITY

A. To be reliable, information does not necessarily have to have absolute *precision* or exactness. In some circumstances, a range or an approximate amount may be adequately precise to enable the user of the information to make the appropriate decisions.

B. *Bias* may affect the reliability of accounting information in two different respects. On one hand, the means of measurement may be biased causing the resulting information to be unreliable. On the other hand, a lack of skill or integrity by the measurer may cause the information to be biased.

C. To be reliable, accounting information must be complete. *Completeness* indicates that everything that is material and that is necessary for faithful representation is included in the information.

D. Bias resulting from a measurer's lack of skill or integrity can be minimized through *verifiability* of the information. *Verifiability* implies that more than one measurer would have the same results using the same measurement methods. It does not provide assurance that the most appropriate method of measurement was selected.

CONSERVATISM

A. There is a relationship between the relevance and reliability of accounting information with the convention of conservatism.

B. *Conservatism*, meaning prudence, ensures that the uncertainty and risks inherent in business situations are adequately considered.

C. Conservatism should not imply the deliberate understatement of assets and profits and should lead toward fairness of presentation. An attempt to understate results on a consistent basis will lead accounting information to be unreliable.

ELEMENTS OF FINANCIAL STATEMENTS OF BUSINESS ENTERPRISES

The elements of financial statements include:

A. Assets.

B. Liabilities.

C. Equity.

D. Investments by owners.

E. Distributions to owners.

F. Comprehensive income.

G. Revenues.

H. Expenses.

I. Gains.

J. Losses.

TWO CLASSES OF ELEMENTS

A. One class of elements is used to describe the status of the enterprise as of a particular date (balance sheet). Elements that describe the status of the enterprise include **assets**, **liabilities**, and **equity**.

B. The other class describes the **effects of events and transactions** on the enterprise for a particular period of time (income statement). Elements that describe the effects of events and transactions include revenues and expenses.

C. The two classes of elements are related in that the elements of the first class are changed by the elements of the latter class.

D. The elements in that first class—assets, liabilities, and equity—represent the cumulative result of the elements of the latter class.

E. In addition, an increase or decrease in an asset cannot occur unless there is a corresponding decrease or increase in another asset or a corresponding increase or decrease in a liability or equity.

F. These relationships, referred to as *articulation*, result in a cohesive set of interrelated financial statements.

G. Notes to financial statements are an integral part of the financial statements but are not considered elements. They serve the functions of amplifying and complementing information about items in the financial statements.

ASSETS, LIABILITIES, AND EQUITY

CHARACTERISTICS OF AN ASSET

A. An asset involves a probable future benefit that can contribute to future net cash inflows.

B. The enterprise can obtain the benefit and control the access of others to it.

C. The event creating the benefit has already occurred.

D. Once an asset is acquired, it remains an asset of the enterprise until it is collected, transferred, or used, or until some event makes the future benefit unobtainable to the enterprise.

CHARACTERISTICS OF A LIABILITY

A. Liability involves the responsibility to use or transfer assets to others on a specific date, upon occurrence of a specific event, or on demand.

B. The responsibility leaves little or no opportunity for avoiding the future sacrifice.

C. The transaction creating the obligation has already occurred.

D. Once a liability is incurred, it remains a liability of the enterprise until it is settled or another event or transaction eliminates the enterprise's responsibility to settle it.

THE CONCEPT OF EQUITY IN A FINANCIAL STATEMENT CONTEXT

A. *Equity* is the ownership interest in an enterprise's assets after deducting its liabilities.

B. Equity is the same as *net assets* (assets minus liabilities) and is enhanced or burdened by increases and decreases in net assets resulting from nonowner sources.

TRANSACTIONS AND EVENTS THAT AFFECT A BUSINESS ENTERPRISE

A. Changes in assets and liabilities that are not associated with changes in equity include:

1. Exchanges of assets for assets.

2. Exchanges of liabilities for liabilities.

3. Acquisition of assets by incurring liabilities.

4. Settling liabilities by transferring assets.

B. Changes in assets and liabilities that are accompanied by changes in equity include:

1. Comprehensive income incorporating revenues and expenses and gains and losses.

2. Investments by owners and distributions to owners.

C. Changes in equity that do not affect assets or liabilities include:

1. Stock dividends.

2. Conversions of preferred shares into common stock.

3. Some recapitalizations.

FINANCIAL STATEMENT EFFECTS OF TRANSACTIONS INVOLVING OWNERS

A. *Investments by owners* are transfers to the enterprise of assets or services or the satisfaction of the enterprise's liabilities in exchange for obtaining or increasing ownership interest in the enterprise.

B. *Distributions to owners* decrease ownership interest in the enterprise by transferring assets, rendering services, or incurring liabilities by the enterprise to the owners.

COMPREHENSIVE INCOME

A. *Comprehensive income* includes all changes in net assets (equity) except those resulting from investments by owners or distributions to owners. Comprehensive income can be divided into components using two distinct approaches.

1. The basic components of comprehensive income are the revenues, expenses, gains, and losses of the enterprise. These are individually listed as elements of financial statements.

2. Comprehensive income is segregated into intermediate components that result from combining various basic components.

B. Over the life of an enterprise, comprehensive income will equal the net cash inflow or outflow of the business excluding cash investments by owners and cash distributions to owners.

C. A significant aspect of measuring comprehensive income becomes the timing of the recognition of the components.

D. In summary, comprehensive income includes the effects of:

1. Exchange transactions and other transfers between the enterprise and nonowners.

2. Productive efforts by the enterprise.

3. Price changes, casualties, and other effects of interactions between the enterprise and its environment.

E.   Comprehensive income is closely related to the concept of capital maintenance, described in the following section.

Capital Maintenance

A.   *Capital maintenance* can be viewed from two separate viewpoints: a *financial capital* approach and a *physical capital* approach.

   1.   The financial capital approach relates to the value of the resources available to an enterprise.

      a.   If, for example, a piece of equipment were to increase in value, the value of the company would also increase.

      b.   Under the financial capital approach, this holding gain would be included in comprehensive income.

   2.   The physical capital approach relates to the actual resources available to an enterprise, disregarding changes in value.

      a.   If, for example, a piece of equipment were to increase in value, the company would still own the same amount of equipment as it did prior to the increase in value.

      b.   Under the physical capital approach, this holding gain would not be included in comprehensive income.

B.   The concept of capital maintenance applied to a particular enterprise will have a direct effect on what is included in comprehensive income.

C.   Under the financial capital approach the effects of changing prices, to the extent recognized, will be included in comprehensive income. For example, gains and losses on marketable securities are recognized, some in net income and some in other comprehensive income.

D.   Under the physical capital approach the effects of changing prices will *not* be included in comprehensive income.

E.   Comprehensive income can be divided into components using two distinct approaches:

   1.   The basic components of comprehensive income are the revenues, expenses, gains, and losses of the enterprise. These are individually listed as elements of financial statements.

   2.   Comprehensive income is segregated into intermediate components that result from combining various basic components.

Revenues, Expenses, Gains, and Losses

A.   *Revenues* are *inflows and other increases* in assets, reductions of liabilities, or some combination resulting from ongoing operations.

B.   *Expenses* are *outflows and other decreases* in assets, increases in liabilities, or some combination resulting from ongoing operations.

C.   The activities that produce revenues and expenses may include delivering or producing goods and providing services, for example.

D. *Gains* are *increases* in net assets (equity) that result from transactions other than those related to the normal ongoing operations of the enterprise as well as from events and circumstances that affect the enterprise other than revenues or owner investments.

E. *Losses* are *decreases* in net assets (equity) that result from transactions other than those related to the normal ongoing operations of the enterprise as well as from events and circumstances that affect the enterprise other than revenues or owner investments.

CLASSIFICATION OF GAINS AND LOSSES

A. Gains and losses can be classified according to their sources. Examples of categories by sources may include:

1. Incidental transactions such as sales of investments and dispositions of used equipment.

2. Nonreciprocal transfers such as gifts or donations, effects of lawsuits, or thefts.

3. Holding of assets or liabilities such as write-downs of inventories and changes in foreign currency exchange rates.

4. Environmental factors such as damage due to earthquake or flood.

B. Although gains and losses result from transactions other than those related to the normal ongoing operations of the entity, they may still be categorized as *operating* or *nonoperating*.

1. Operating gains and losses.

a. Write-downs of inventory to the lower of cost or market.

b. Gains and losses on disposals of property, plant, and equipment.

2. Nonoperating gains and losses.

a. Losses incurred by a creditor as a result of a troubled debt restructuring.

b. Casualty losses.

ACCRUAL ACCOUNTING

A. Elements of financial statements that meet the criteria for recognition and measurement are accounted for according to the accrual basis of accounting.

B. Items to be reported result from (1) *Transactions*, (2) *Events*, and (3) *Circumstances*

1. *Transactions* are particular types of external events involving transfers between two or more entities.

2. *Events* are happenings of significance to the enterprise and may include internal events such as production and external events such as transactions with other entities, changes in prices, and casualties.

3. *Circumstances* are sets of conditions that result from an event. For example, if a debtor were to declare bankruptcy (an event), the creditor would have to deal with a potentially uncollectible receivable (a circumstance).

IMPLICATIONS OF NONCASH EVENTS AND CIRCUMSTANCES ON THE FINANCIAL STATEMENTS

A. Under the accrual basis of accounting, the effects of transactions, events, and circumstances are recognized in the period when they take place (earlier), *not* when the effects occur (later).

B. Recognizing noncash events and circumstances when they take place will result in accruals and deferrals as well as allocations and amortizations.

   1. Accruals relate to expected future cash receipts or payments.

   2. Deferrals relate to past cash receipts or payments.

   3. *Allocation* (includes amortization) is the distribution of an amount according to a plan or formula.

   4. Amortization (includes depreciation) specifically relates to the recognition of:

      a. Income to reduce a liability from a cash receipt.

      b. Expenses or costs of production to reduce an asset resulting from a cash payment.

CONCEPTS THAT HELP TO DISTINGUISH ACCRUAL ACCOUNTING FROM CASH ACCOUNTING

A. Realization actually occurs when noncash resources and rights are converted into cash or receivables.

   1. *Realized* refers to revenues, gains, or losses on assets sold.

   2. *Unrealized* refers to revenues, gains, or losses on assets *not* sold.

B. Recognition relates to the actual reporting of an item in the financial statements of an enterprise.

C. *Matching* is the process whereby costs that are associated with particular revenues are recognized as reductions of those revenues or as expenses in the same period in which the corresponding revenues are recognized.

THE APPROACHES USED IN ACCRUAL ACCOUNTING TO RECOGNIZE COSTS INCURRED AS REDUCTIONS IN INCOME

A. Some transactions or events will result in both revenues and one or more expenses in which case the matching concept is applied. A sale of inventory, for example, will result in cost of sales along with other expenses such as transportation to the customer, sales commissions, and other selling costs.

B. Costs are recognized in the period incurred in all of the following situations:

   1. Costs not attributable to particular revenues but can be related to a particular period based on the transactions or events occurring in that period.

   2. Costs incurred in order to obtain benefits that will be used up in that same period.

   3. Costs incurred, but the period when the benefits will be derived is indeterminate.

C. Some costs are expected to yield benefits over several periods, such as prepaid insurance and the cost of fixed assets.

  1. These costs are allocated over their estimated useful lives, including the periods over which benefits are expected to be derived.

  2. A systematic and rational allocation procedure such as depreciation is used.

RECOGNITION AND MEASUREMENT IN FINANCIAL STATEMENTS OF BUSINESS ENTERPRISES

FINANCIAL STATEMENTS

A. A full set of financial statements, prepared in conformity with generally accepted accounting principles, should be adequate to meet the objectives of financial reporting of a business enterprise.

B. Preparation of a full set of financial statements involves the proper recognition of those items that fall within the definitions of assets, liabilities, revenues, expenses, etc., where appropriate recognition and measurement criteria apply.

C. Recognition involves the presentation of the item on the financial statements with words of identification as well as numbers, and with the quantities included in the totals of the financial statements.

D. A full set of financial statements for a period should show the following:

  1. Financial position as of the end of the period.

  2. Earnings or net income for the period.

  3. Comprehensive income for the period.

  4. Investments by and distributions to owners during the period.

E. The financial information may be provided in a series of separate statements or may be combined in various ways to result in a set of financial statements with each depicting one or more of the above types of information.

F. The common goal of the financial statements is to report the financial position of the enterprise as of the end of a period and all factors that caused changes in that financial position during that period.

G. As a general rule, the information will be provided in four separate financial statements:

  1. Statement of Financial Position (Balance Sheet).

  2. Statement of Earnings and Comprehensive Income.

  3. Statement of Cash Flows.

  4. Statement of Investments by and Distributions to Owners.

H. In preparing financial statements, items with essentially similar characteristics should be grouped while items with essentially different characteristics should be separated.

I. In addition, due to the vast amount of data that is compiled in making up financial statements, a means of combining and aggregating data is necessary to condense and simplify the financial statements.

STATEMENT OF FINANCIAL POSITION (BALANCE SHEET)

A. It provides information about an enterprise's assets, liabilities, and equity, as well as their relationships to one another as of a particular point in time.

B. It reports the structure of the enterprise's resources and financing by presenting the information in a classified manner.

C. The statement of financial position is not intended to report the current value of the business enterprise because amounts are reported at historical cost. But it may assist users in making their own estimates as to the enterprise's value.

D. This statement may be used in conjunction with others to assist investors, creditors, and others in performing financial analysis.

STATEMENT OF EARNINGS AND COMPREHENSIVE INCOME (INCOME STATEMENT)

A. In order to be most effective to users, the statement of earnings and comprehensive income must clearly separate earnings from comprehensive income.

B. Earnings, often referred to as net income, will include the effects of *all* revenues, expenses, gains, and losses occurring during the period.

C. Although earnings will be similar to net income as it is currently presented, it will be different in that it will not include the cumulative effects of changes in accounting principles. This will be included in comprehensive income, as will certain other items.

D. As discussed previously, comprehensive income more broadly measures all recognized changes in equity during the period other than those resulting from investments by owners and distributions to owners.

E. Comprehensive income incorporates earnings as well as items that are excluded from earnings. These items include:

1. Effects of accounting adjustments of earlier periods recognized in the current period such as the cumulative effect of a change in accounting principles.

2. Other changes in net assets recognized during the period are often classified as holding gains or losses. These changes may include changes in the market value of investments in marketable securities available for sale and foreign currency translation adjustments.

F. As previously discussed, the concept of comprehensive income is based upon the financial capital maintenance approach rather than the physical capital maintenance approach.

1. Under the financial capital maintenance approach, the effects of changing prices result in holding gains and losses that are included in comprehensive income.

2. If the physical capital maintenance approach were applied, the effects of changing prices would be incorporated in the maintenance of the same physical capabilities and would be direct adjustments to equity, excluded from comprehensive income.

STATEMENT OF CASH FLOWS

A. It simply reflects the enterprise's cash receipts, classified by major sources, and the enterprise's cash payments, also classified by major uses, for the period.

B. Those sources and outflows include:

   1. Operating activities.

   2. Investing activities.

   3. Financing activities.

STATEMENT OF INVESTMENTS BY AND DISTRIBUTIONS TO OWNERS (OWNERS' EQUITY)

A. It reflects the increases or decreases in equity resulting from transactions with the owners acting in the capacity as owners.

B. It excludes transactions with the owners as suppliers, employees, customers, or lenders. These transactions would be reflected in the statement of earnings and comprehensive income or the statement of cash flows, as appropriate.

C. A combination of the statement of earnings and comprehensive income and the statement of investments by and distributions to owners will provide information about all changes in equity for the period.

RECOGNITION IN FINANCIAL STATEMENTS

A. Subject to the constraint that the cost of reporting an item should not exceed its benefit, and subject to the threshold of materiality, an item should be recognized when four criteria have been met.

B. These criteria relate to definitions, measurability, relevance, and reliability.

RECOGNITION CRITERIA: DEFINITIONS, MEASURABILITY, RELEVANCE, AND RELIABILITY

A. In order for an item to be recognized in the financial statements, it must conform to the appropriate *definitions* as set out in the pronouncement related to the elements of financial statements of business enterprises. A resource must conform to the definition of an asset, an obligation to the definition of a liability, and so on, in order to be recognized on the financial statements.

B. *Measurability* must be considered along with relevance and reliability. In order to be recognized on the financial statements, an asset, liability, or change in equity must be measurable in monetary terms and have the following five attributes:

   1. **Historical cost** equals what was paid for the item adjusted for amortization or other allocation.

   2. **Current cost** equals what would have to be paid if the item were to be acquired currently.

   3. **Current market value** equals the amount that could be obtained by selling the item.

   4. **Net realizable (settlement) value** equals the nondiscounted amount that the item will be converted into, net of costs of making that conversion, in the ordinary course of business.

5. **Present (or discounted) value of future cash flows** equals the present value of future cash inflows expected to be derived from converting the item in the ordinary course of business less the present value of future cash outflows that will be incurred in making the conversion.

C. *Relevance* indicates that the information has predictive value or feedback value, or both, and is timely.

D. *Reliability* indicates that the information has representational faithfulness and is verifiable and neutral.

E. In applying these fundamental four criteria to items that affect changes in equity, certain guidelines must be followed in determining if the items will be included in earnings.

F. Certain changes in equity that meet the four criteria above may not be included in earnings but would be reported as a part of comprehensive income.

FACTORS TO CONSIDER IN INCLUDING REVENUES AND GAINS IN EARNINGS

A. *Item must be realized or realizable*—Realization takes place when goods, services, or other assets are exchanged for cash or claims to cash. Revenues and gains are realizable when related assets received or held are readily convertible to known amounts of cash or claims to cash.

B. *Item must be earned*—Revenues are earned when goods have been delivered or produced, services have been rendered, or other activities that are part of ongoing operations have been performed. Gains do not generally result from an earnings process and their realization or *realizability* is the key factor for recognition.

C. Following are seven examples:

1. Revenues are generally recognized when goods or services are delivered to customers, and gains are generally recognized at the point of sale.

2. If a sale occurs prior to production or delivery, revenue is recognized as production and delivery occurs.

3. If a product is contracted for prior to production, revenue may be recognized as production takes place such as under the percentage-of-completion method.

4. When services are rendered over time or the rights to use assets are granted over time, revenues may be recognized as time passes, as in the case of rents or interest.

5. If products are easily absorbed in the marketplace at determinable prices, such as often is the case with scarce resources including precious metals, revenues may be recognized at the completion of production.

6. When items are exchanged for nonmonetary assets, revenues or gains may be recognized on the basis that they have been earned and the transaction is complete. This would also be the case if nonmonetary assets are received or distributed in nonreciprocal transactions.

7. When collectibility of assets received is doubtful, revenues and gains may be recognized as cash is received (e.g., cost recovery method or installment sales).

RECOGNITION CRITERIA FOR EXPENSES AND LOSSES

Expenses or losses are generally recognized when the enterprise's economic benefits are used up or when previously recognized assets are expected to provide reduced future benefits or no future benefits.

QUESTIONS: MISCELLANEOUS ACCOUNTING CONCEPTS

1.   Under Statements of Financial Accounting Concepts, which of the following relates to both *relevance* and *reliability*?
   A.   Consistency.
   B.   Feedback value.
   C.   Neutrality.
   D.   Timeliness.

2.   According to Statements of Financial Accounting Concepts, *neutrality* is an ingredient of

	Relevance	Reliability
A.	Yes	Yes
B.	Yes	No
C.	No	No
D.	No	Yes

3.   According to the FASB Conceptual Framework, which of the following relates to both *relevance* and *reliability*?

	Consistency	Verifiability
A.	Yes	Yes
B.	No	No
C.	Yes	No
D.	No	Yes

4.   According to the FASB Conceptual Framework, earnings:
   A.   are the same as comprehensive income.
   B.   exclude certain gains and losses that are included in comprehensive income.
   C.   include certain gains and losses that are excluded from comprehensive income.
   D.   include certain losses that are excluded from comprehensive income.

5.   According to the FASB's conceptual framework, comprehensive income includes which of the following?

	Operating income	Investment by owners
A.	Yes	No
B.	Yes	Yes
C.	No	Yes
D.	No	No

6.   The FASB's conceptual framework classifies gains and losses based on whether they are related to an entity's major ongoing or central operations. These gains or losses may be classified as which of the following?

	Nonoperating	Operating
A.	Yes	No
B.	Yes	Yes
C.	No	Yes
D.	No	No

7. According to FASB's conceptual framework, the process of reporting an item in the financial statements of an entity is known as:
    A. allocation.
    B. matching.
    C. realization.
    D. recognition.

8. Under FASB Statement of Financial Accounting Concepts No. 5, which of the following items would cause earnings to differ from comprehensive income for an enterprise in an industry not having specialized accounting principles?
    A. Unrealized loss on investments in securities available for sale.
    B. Unrealized loss on investments in trading securities.
    C. Loss on exchange of similar assets.
    D. Loss on exchange of dissimilar assets.

9. FASB's conceptual framework explains both financial and physical capital maintenance concepts. Which capital maintenance concept is correctly applied to currently reported net income, and which is applied to comprehensive income?

	Currently reported net income	Comprehensive income
A.	Financial capital	Physical capital
B.	Physical capital	Physical capital
C.	Financial capital	Financial capital
D.	Physical capital	Financial capital

10. FASB Interpretations of Statements of Financial Accounting Standards have the same authority as FASB's:
    A. Technical Bulletins.
    B. Emerging Issues Task Force Consensus.
    C. Statements of Financial Accounting Concepts.
    D. Statements of Financial Accounting Standards.

11. According to the FASB conceptual framework, which of the following is an essential characteristic of an asset?
    A. An asset has value.
    B. An asset is tangible.
    C. An asset is obtained at a cost.
    D. An asset provides future benefits.

12. According to the FASB conceptual framework, predictive value is an ingredient of:

	Reliability	Relevance
A.	Yes	Yes
B.	No	Yes
C.	No	No
D.	Yes	No

13. Which of the following accounting pronouncements is the *most* authoritative?
    A. FASB Statement of Financial Accounting Concepts.
    B. FASB Technical Bulletin.
    C. AICPA Accounting Principles Board Opinion.
    D. AICPA Statement of Position.

14. According to the FASB conceptual framework, which of the following relates to both relevance and reliability?
   A. Comparability.
   B. Feedback value.
   C. Timeliness.
   D. Verifiability.

15. According to the FASB conceptual framework, an entity's revenue may result from a(n):
   A. decrease in an asset from primary operations.
   B. increase in an asset from incidental transactions.
   C. increase in a liability from incidental transactions.
   D. decrease in a liability from primary operations.

16. According to the FASB conceptual framework, which of the following situations violates the concept of reliability?
   A. Financial statements were issued nine months late.
   B. Report data on segments having the same expected risks and growth rates to analysts estimating future profits.
   C. Financial statement data included in property, plant and equipment with a carrying value increased to management's estimate of market value.
   D. Management reports to stockholders regularly refer to new projects undertaken, but the financial statements never report project results.

17. According to the FASB conceptual framework, the objectives of financial reporting for business enterprises are based on:
   A. the need for conservatism.
   B. reporting on management's stewardship.
   C. generally accepted accounting principles.
   D. the needs of the users of the information.

18. According to the FASB conceptual framework, which of the following practices conforms to the realization concept?
   A. Equipment depreciation was assigned to a production department and then to product unit costs.
   B. Depreciated equipment was sold in exchange for a note receivable.
   C. Cash was collected on accounts receivable.
   D. Product unit costs were assigned to cost of goods sold when the units were sold.

19. What are the Statements of Financial Accounting Concepts intended to establish?
   A. The hierarchy of sources of generally accepted accounting principles.
   B. Generally accepted accounting principles in financial reporting by business enterprises.
   C. The meaning of "present fairly in accordance with generally accepted accounting principles."
   D. The objectives and concepts for use in developing standards of financial accounting and reporting.

20. Reporting inventory at the lower of cost or market is a departure from the accounting principle of:
   A. conservatism.
   B. consistency.
   C. full disclosure.
   D. historical cost.

21. During a period when an enterprise is under the direction of a particular management group, its financial statements will directly provide information about:
     A. both enterprise performance and management performance.
     B. management performance but not directly provide information about enterprise performance.
     C. enterprise performance but not directly provide information about management performance.
     D. neither enterprise performance nor management performance.

22. What is the purpose of information presented in the notes to the financial statements?
     A. To present management's responses to auditor comments.
     B. To correct improper presentation in the financial statements.
     C. To provide disclosures required by generally accepted accounting principles.
     D. To provide recognition of amounts not included in the totals of the financial statements.

23. According to the FASB conceptual framework, the quality of information that helps users increase the likelihood of correctly forecasting the outcome of past or present events is called:
     A. feedback value.
     B. predictive value.
     C. representational faithfulness.
     D. reliability.

ANSWERS: MISCELLANEOUS ACCOUNTING CONCEPTS

1. **A** Both timeliness and feedback value, along with predictive value, are ingredients relating to the qualitative characteristic of relevance. Neutrality (free from bias), along with representational faithfulness and freedom from error, are ingredients of reliability. Comparability, which includes consistency, are secondary qualitative characteristics that relate to *both* reliability and relevance.

2. **D** The ingredients of the qualitative characteristic of relevance are that the information must provide feedback value or predictive value and must be timely. To be reliable, the information should be free from error, representationally faithful, and free from bias (or neutral).

3. **C** Consistency in financial presentation means the use of the same accounting procedures for presenting information in different periods. Because trend analysis is a strong element in projecting the future, investors and creditors find consistency important in making data useful, or relevant in making decisions. Consistent presentation also removes potential bias from presentation that might be caused by selecting the procedure each year that makes the company look best. A consistent presentation enhances the neutrality of the information, which is an element of reliability. Thus, consistency relates to both relevance and reliability.

    Verifiability means the development of information by an approach that would cause different people to arrive at the same figures. Verifiability makes information more reliable but does not tell us whether the information being developed happens to be relevant to the user.

4. **B** Comprehensive income includes all changes in net assets from nonowner sources. It would include items—such as unrealized losses on decline in marketable securities available for sale and foreign currency translation adjustments—that are excluded from the calculation of earnings.

5. **A** Comprehensive income represents all changes to equities other than those that result from investments by owners or distributions to owners. As a result, comprehensive income would include operating income but exclude investments by owners.

6. **B** Gains or losses that are related to an entity's major ongoing or central operations are operating items, while gains or losses that do not result from the entity's primary activities would be considered nonoperating in nature. Either may appear in the financial statements.

7. **D** Recognition relates to the actual reporting of an item in the financial statements of the enterprise. Realization occurs when noncash resources and rights are converted into money. Allocation is the distribution of an amount according to a plan or formula. Matching is the process that attempts to recognize costs along with the related revenue.

8. **A** An unrealized loss on investments in securities available for sale reduces net assets, making it a part of the determination of comprehensive income, but such a loss is reported as a contra-equity account and not included in earnings. An unrealized loss on investments in trading securities is included in both comprehensive income and earnings. A loss on exchange of similar assets is also reported in both. Both gains and losses on exchanges of dissimilar assets are fully included in earnings as well as comprehensive income.

9. **C** Capital maintenance is an approach to measuring income that compares the company's capital, or equity, at the end of the period to that at the beginning. The financial capital concept takes into account changes in prices, while the physical capital concept takes into account changes in physical capacity. Thus, the financial capital concept is applied to currently reported net income and to comprehensive income.

10. **D** Current standards have established a hierarchy of accounting principles in which Accounting Research Bulletins, Accounting Principles Board Opinions, FASB Statements of Financial Accounting Standards, and FASB Interpretations are at the highest level. Technical Bulletins are at the second level, Emerging Issues Task Force Consensus Positions are at the third level, and Statements of Financial Accounting Concepts are at an even lower level.

11. **D** According to the FASB conceptual framework, an asset is an economic resource that will provide a probable future benefit, is within the control of the entity, and results from an event or transaction that has already occurred.

12. **B** Predictive value, along with feedback value and timeliness, are ingredients of relevance. Faithful representation, verifiability, and neutrality are the ingredients associated with reliability.

13. **C** Pronouncements with the highest level of authoritative support include FASB Statements of Financial Accounting Standards, FASB Interpretations, AICPA Accounting Principle Board Opinions, and AICPA Accounting Research Bulletins.

14. **A** Feedback value and timeliness relate to relevance, while verifiability relates to reliability. Comparability is a secondary qualitative characteristic that relates to both relevance and reliability.

15. **D** A decrease in an asset from primary operations might result in an expense, rather than revenue. An increase in an asset or an increase in a liability from incidental transactions might result in a gain or a loss. A decrease in a liability from primary operations might result in revenue.

16. **C** Issuance of financial statements nine months late would be a violation of the concept of timeliness. Reporting data on segments having the same expected risks and growth rates to analysts estimating future profits would relate to predictive value. Reporting on new projects without reporting on project results would be a violation of the concept of feedback value. Each of these relate to ingredients of relevance, but not reliability. Using management estimates violates the concept of verifiability, which is an ingredient of reliability.

17. **D** Because financial statements are used by investors, creditors, and managers for the purpose of making business and economic decisions, the needs of the users must be taken into account when evaluating the objectives of financial reporting.

18. **B** Realization occurs when noncash resources and rights are converted into money or claims to money. This would be the case when equipment is sold for a note receivable. Assigning of costs is a form of allocation. Realization occurs at the time that sales of merchandise are made in exchange for accounts receivable, not when the receivables are collected.

19. **D** Statements of Financial Accounting Concepts (SFAC) establish a conceptual framework for accounting that includes the objectives and concepts used in developing standards of financial accounting and reporting. Generally accepted accounting principles (GAAP) are based upon the conceptual framework and must be followed in order for the financial statements to be presented fairly in accordance with GAAP. When there are two or more principles that may apply to a given situation, the hierarchy of sources of GAAP provides guidance as to which principle or principles should be given priority.

20. **D** Reporting inventory at the lower of cost or market is an application of the concept of conservatism. It would be a departure from the historical cost concept that requires assets to be recorded at historical cost and continue to be reported on that basis.

21. **C** Financial statements, primarily in the form of the income statement, provide direct information about enterprise performance. Information about management performance can only be derived indirectly from the financial statements under the assumption that enterprise performance is closely related to management performance. There are many factors that may contribute to enterprise performance, however, that do not relate to management performance.

22. **C** The purpose of information presented in notes to the financial statements is to enhance the information included in the statements. This may include providing further detail of amounts that are included in totals on the statements. There should not be information that is improperly presented in the financial statements, and management's responses to auditor comments would not be presented in the statements or the notes to them.

23. **B** The users of financial statements want to be able to predict a company's earnings and cash flows. The financial statements are constructed to enhance such predictions. This quality is referred to as having "predictive value."

CHAPTER 9 – OVERVIEW OF FINANCIAL STATEMENT ANALYSIS ON THE CPA EXAM

STUDY TIP

People get tired of studying, especially when studying seems to get into a rut. As long as you are preparing efficiently, do not make any changes. However, if putting in the hours of study has become a real trial, try changing your location. For example, if you normally study in your den, begin working at the kitchen table for a few days. Creating any type of change can be refreshing, and it can keep the preparation process from becoming drudgery.

CHAPTER 9 – OVERVIEW OF FINANCIAL STATEMENT ANALYSIS ON THE CPA EXAM

Financial statement analysis is tested in FAR, BEC, and AUD.

Financial ratios were briefly discussed previously in the sections on receivables, inventories, and current liabilities. The emphasis now will be on a more in-depth coverage of financial ratios that should solidify your appreciation of the interrelationships between the various financial statements—balance sheet, income statement, and statement of cash flows. Comparison techniques and trend analysis are introduced to demonstrate how to use the financial ratios to help you evaluate financial statements.

FEATURES OF FINANCIAL RATIOS

A. A ratio is one figure or balance divided by another. By dividing (and obtaining the resulting percentage), we remove the issue of size and can compare companies of different sizes based on ratios.

B. Ratios have certain "acceptable ranges."

C. The key is to be able to measure whether a company's figures and balances fall within these acceptable ranges.

PERFORMING ANALYSIS WITH FINANCIAL RATIOS

A. A single value of a financial ratio is not meaningful by itself but must be examined in context of the company's history (past performance), the industry, the major competitors, and the economy.

B. One reviews a company's financial statements to gain insight into the company's financial decision making and operating performance.

C. Financial data is converted into ratios to facilitate the analysis. Although literally dozens of ratios can be computed, there is a relatively small subset of ratios that provides most of the relevant information about a company.

COMMON-SIZE BALANCE SHEETS AND INCOME STATEMENTS

A. Common-size balance sheets and income statements allow one to more easily compare companies of different sizes.

   1. A common-size balance sheet expresses all balance sheet accounts as a percentage of total assets.

   2. A common-size income statement expresses all income statement items as a percentage of sales.

B. In addition to the comparison of financial data across firms and time, common-size analysis is appropriate for quickly viewing certain financial ratios.

   1. For example, the gross profit margin, operating profit margin, and net profit margin are all clearly indicated within a common-size income statement.

2. Common-size income statement ratios are especially useful in studying trends in costs and profit margins:

> common-size income statement ratios = income statement account/sales

3. Balance sheet accounts can also be converted to common-size ratios by dividing each balance sheet by total assets:

> common-size balance sheet ratios = balance sheet account/total assets

COMMON BENCHMARKS FOR RATIO ANALYSIS

A. In order for a ratio to provide information, it must be compared to a standard or benchmark. The value of a single financial ratio is not meaningful by itself but must be interpreted relative to trend analysis and cross-sectional analysis.

B. Trend analysis (time series).

1. Comparing a company with its history is very common. Indeed, it is problematic to simply consider long-term average of ratios without taking their trend into account.

2. Five years of data is desirable.

C. Cross-section analysis.

1. Cross-section analysis considers only a subset of firms with similar characteristics, including size.

2. In any given time period, such analysis tells how the company is doing compared to:

a. Industry average.

- The most common method of comparison. Industry comparisons are particularly valid when the products generated by the industry are similar.

b. Specific competitors.

c. The overall economy.

- Important to do so when overall business conditions are changing.
- For example, a stable profit margin might be considered good if the economy is in recession and the economy-wide average profit margin is declining. On the other hand, it might be considered problematic if a stable profit margin occurs during an economic expansion when average overall profit margins are increasing.

USERS OF RATIOS

A. Creditors—Want to know if the company can repay its debts. Liquidity, debt, and coverage ratios are of most interest.

B. Investors—Want to know how much money the company is making. Profitability ratios are key!

C. Management—Sets standards for each ratio and compares actual results to those standards. Variances need to be investigated.

FIVE MAJOR TYPES OF FINANCIAL RATIOS

A. **Liquidity ratios.** These ratios help show the ability of the company to pay short-term obligations based on balance sheet strength.

B. **Debt ratios.** These ratios help show the ability of the company to pay long-term obligations based on balance sheet strength.

C. **Coverage ratios.** These ratios help show the ability of the company to pay short-term obligations based on income statement strength.

D. **Activity or efficiency ratios.** These are output-to-input ratios. In other words, how effectively does the company manage its assets and use its resources to generate revenue?

E. **Profitability ratios.** These ratios help to measure the success of the company in generating net income.

MEASURES OF A COMPANY'S INTERNAL LIQUIDITY

A. Current ratio.

   1. **Current assets (CA) / current liabilities (CL)**

   2. Higher is generally better as it is more likely that the company will be able to pay its short-term bills.

   3. Historically, the benchmark for a manufacturing company is 2.0.

       a. A current ratio of less than 1.0 means that the company has negative working capital (CL > CA) and is probably facing a liquidity crisis.

       b. However, if the current ratio gets too high, the company may be sacrificing profitability for liquidity.

B. Quick (acid test) ratio.

   1. **(Cash + short-term investments + net receivables)/CL**

       A much more stringent measure of liquidity. Clearly, inventories might not be very liquid so they are excluded from this calculation.

   2. Again, higher is normally better and the benchmark for a manufacturing company is about 1.0.

C. Net working capital.

   1. **CA – CL**

       This is a dollar measure and not technically a ratio.

   2. But it is a common loan covenant that a borrowing company must maintain a minimum level of net working capital.

MEASURES OF A COMPANY'S LEVERAGE

A. Total debt to total asset ratio.

   1. **Total debt (both current and long-term) / total assets**

2. This is a measure of leverage and risk—the additional volatility of equity returns caused by the company's use of debt. Increases and decreases in this ratio suggest a greater or lesser reliance on debt as a source of financing.

B. Debt to equity ratio.

1. Generally, **long-term debt / total stockholders' equity**

2. One issue here is how to treat preferred stock—is it debt or equity? Opinions differ on the inclusion or exclusion of preferred stock, which may have a material impact on the ratio calculations. Read your exam question carefully. If there is no indication that preferred stock should be treated as debt, include it in Stockholder's Equity.

3. Again, increases and decreases in this ratio suggest a greater or lesser reliance on debt as a source of financing.

MEASURES OF A COMPANY'S DEBT-SERVICING CAPABILITY

A. Times interest earned ratio.

1. **Earnings before interest and taxes (EBIT) / required interest payments**

2. Obviously, the higher the ratio, the better. The lower the ratio, the more likely it is that the company will have difficulty meeting its debt payments.

MEASURES OF A COMPANY'S ACTIVITY AND EFFICIENCY

A. Receivables turnover ratio.

1. **Net annual sales / average receivables**

2. A measure of accounts receivable liquidity. It is considered desirable to have a receivables turnover figure close to the industry norm.

Note: For exam purposes, average receivables will either be given or you will have to compute it by adding the beginning-of-year account value and the end-of-year account value and then dividing the sum by two.

B. Average receivables collection period ratio.

1. **365 / receivables turnover**

2. This is the average number of days it takes for the company's customers to pay their bills. It is considered desirable to have the collection period be close to the industry norm.

3. The company's credit terms are another important benchmark used to interpret this ratio.

   a. A collection period that is too high might mean that customers are too slow in paying their bills, which means too much capital is tied up in assets. In other words, the company's credit policy might be too loose.

   b. A collection period that is too low might indicate that the company's credit policy is too strict, which might be hampering sales.

C. Inventory turnover ratio.

   1. **Cost of goods sold / average inventory**

   2. Measures a company's efficiency with respect to its production and inventory management.

   3. Generally, the higher the figure, the better, in order to avoid the problem of inventory obsolescence.

D. Average inventory processing period ratio.

   1. **365 / inventory turnover**

   2. As is the case with accounts receivable, it is considered desirable to have a figure close to industry norm.

      a. A processing period that is too high might mean that too much capital is tied up in inventory and could mean that inventory is obsolete.

      b. A processing period that is too low might mean that the company has inadequate stock on hand, which could adversely impact sales.

E. Payables turnover ratio.

   1. **Cost of goods sold / average trade payables**

   2. A measure of the use of trade credit by the company.

F. Average payables payment period ratio.

   1. **365 / payables turnover ratio**

   2. The average amount of time it takes the company to pay its bills.

G. Cash conversion cycle.

   1. **Average receivables collection period + average inventory processing period – average payables payment period**

   2. Measures the length of time it takes to outlay cash for inventory, make the product, sell the product, and collect the cash back from customers.

   3. Sometimes called *cash to cash,* the cash conversion cycle is the length of time it takes to turn the firm's investment into cash. It is the number of days a firm's cash is tied up in the business in accounts such as inventory and accounts receivable.

   4. High cash conversion cycles are considered undesirable.

      A figure that is too high implies that the company has an excessive amount of capital investment in the sales process.

   5. Although not technically a ratio, the cash conversion cycle calculation is useful to study as it clearly integrates the previous six ratio calculations nicely (see the following figure).

Cash Conversion Cycle Example

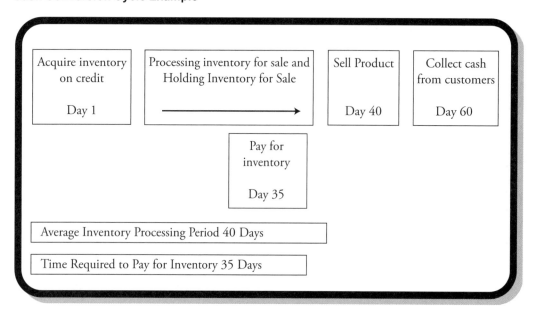

Period from Acquiring Inventory to Collecting Cash minus	+ 60 days
Period before Inventory is Paid for	−35 days
Cash Conversion Cycle	= 25 days

or

Average Receivables Collection Period plus	+20 days
Average Inventory Processing Period minus	+40 days
Average Payables Payment Period	−35 days
= Cash Conversion Cycle	= 25 days

H. Total asset turnover ratio.

1. **Net sales / average total net assets**

2. Different types of industries might have considerably different turnover ratios.

    a. Manufacturing businesses that are capital-intensive might have asset turnover ratios near 1.

    b. Retail businesses might have turnover ratios near 10.

3. Once again, it is desirable for an asset turnover ratio to be close to the industry norm.

    a. Low asset turnover ratios might mean that the company has too much capital tied up in its asset base.

    b. A turnover ratio that is too high might imply that the company has too few assets for potential sales or that the asset base is outdated.

I. Net fixed asset turnover ratio.

1. **Net sales / average net fixed assets**

2. Close to industry norm is desirable.

    a. A high turnover ratio might imply that the company has obsolete equipment, or at a minimum, the company will probably have to incur (significant) capital expenditures in the near future to increase capacity to support growing revenues.

MEASURES OF A COMPANY'S PROFITABILITY

A. Profit margin ratio.

1. Gross margin ratio.

    a. **(Sales – COGS) / sales**

    b. Examining the changes in gross margin over time and in comparison to competitors helps to evaluate the company.

    c. Should be concerned if this ratio is too low or if there are sudden and large swings from year to year.

2. Operating margin ratio.

    a. **EBIT / sales**; EBIT = gross profit less operating expenses but excluding interest and taxes. (Earnings Before Interest and Taxes)

    b. Again, should be concerned if this ratio is too low.

3. Net margin ratio.

    a. **Net income (NI) / sales**; used often in making future projections about the company

    b. Only considers "NI from continuing operations." "Below the line" (i.e., below net income from continuing operations) items such as discontinued operations or extraordinary items are ignored as they have no impact on the company in the future.

    c. This is a common measure of the strength of the income statement.

B. Return on assets (ROA) ratio.

1. **(NI + gross interest expense) / average total assets**

2. The higher the ROA, the better.

3. DuPont ratio decomposition breaks down ROA into two components: net margin × total asset turnover.

Example:

Sales are $1,000,000, total assets are $500,000, and net income is $50,000.

ROA = $50,000 / $500,000 = 10%

DuPont = ($50,000 / $1,000,000) × ($1,000,000 / $500,000) = 5% × 2 = 10%

Therefore, DuPont shows the income statement impact times the balance sheet impact.

C. Return on equity (ROE) ratio.

   1. **(NI – preferred dividends) / average stockholders' equity**

   2. This is the return on the owners' capital.

   3. The greater the spread between ROA and ROE, the more leverage the company has. In other words, the better use the company is making of the money that it receives from its debts.

LIMITATIONS OF FINANCIAL RATIOS

A. Financial ratios are not useful when viewed in isolation. They are valid only when compared to those of other (similar) companies or to the company's historical performance.

B. Conclusions cannot be made from viewing one set of ratios. All ratios must be viewed relative to one another.

C. Determining the target or comparison value for a ratio is difficult—requires some range of acceptable values.

BALANCE SHEET

A. The balance sheet is also known as a *statement of financial position*.

   1. It presents assets, liabilities, stockholders' equity, and the cumulative effects of all past transactions at one point in time.

   2. It is divided into two main columns—left side is assets and right side is liabilities plus stockholders' equity.

   3. Amounts are presented in order of descending liquidity. For example, current assets and current liabilities are listed first within the assets and liabilities sections.

B. An important feature is the distinction between current and noncurrent items.

   1. Current assets are "cash and other assets or resources commonly identified as those that are reasonably expected to be *realized in cash* or *sold* or *consumed* during the normal operating cycle of the business."

      Examples include cash available for current operations, short-term (marketable) securities, trade receivables, other receivables collectible within one year, inventories, and prepaid expenses (all in roughly descending order by liquidity).

   2. Current liabilities are "obligations whose liquidation is reasonably expected to require the *use* of existing resources properly classifiable as *current assets* or the creation of *other current liabilities*" (during the normal operating cycle of the business).

      Examples include trade payables, deferred/unearned revenues, accruals of expenses, other liabilities coming due within one year, including the current portions of long-term liabilities (again, all in roughly descending order by liquidity).

   3. In practice, current assets and liabilities have a maximum "life" of the greater of one operating cycle or one year.

C. Noncurrent assets have lives of more than one year and include (in roughly descending liquidity order):

1. Long-term investments (e.g., securities, cash surrender value of life insurance policies).

2. Property, plant, and equipment (e.g., land, buildings, machinery, furniture).

3. Intangible assets (e.g., patents, trademarks).

4. Other assets (e.g., unamortized bond issue costs).

D. Noncurrent liabilities are expected to be fully paid in more than one year into the future and include notes payable, long-term bonds, accrued pension liabilities, deferred tax liabilities, and capital lease liabilities.

E. Stockholders' equity includes:

1. Capital stock (i.e., common stock, preferred stock).

2. Additional paid-in capital (APIC)—based on capital stock transactions, for example.

3. Retained earnings (i.e., appropriated and unappropriated, if applicable).

4. Accumulated other comprehensive income (i.e., some transactions with marketable securities and pensions are recorded here).

F. Keep in mind that much of the purely numerical information on the balance sheet may be amplified by discussion in the notes to the financial statements (more on that later).

ACCOUNTING POLICIES AND OTHER NOTES TO FINANCIAL STATEMENTS

The purpose of disclosure is to avoid misleading financial statement users.

A. Accounting policies can affect reported results significantly. The usefulness of the financial statements depends on the user's understanding of the accounting policies adopted by the company.

B. Disclosure of accounting policies is:

1. Essential to users.

2. An integral part of the financial statements.

3. Not required for unaudited interim statements if no change in accounting policy has occurred.

C. Accounting policies must be set forth as the first footnote to the financial statements (Summary of Significant Accounting Policies). Must disclose at least the following:

1. Accounting principles followed and the methods of applying those principles.

2. Accounting principles involving a selection from acceptable alternatives.

3. Principles peculiar to a particular industry.

4. Unusual or innovative applications of accounting principles.

5. Examples:

    a. Revenue recognition method.

    b. Inventory pricing (FIFO versus LIFO).

    c. Translation of foreign currencies.

    d. Depreciation method.

D. Other disclosures commonly required in the notes to financial statements (not part of the summary of significant accounting policies) to comply with GAAP are the following:

1. Related-party disclosures (more on this later).

2. Subsequent events (more on this later).

3. Leases (especially off-balance sheet operating leases).

4. Pensions.

5. Stock options.

6. Accounting changes and error corrections.

7. Contingencies (i.e., lawsuits).

8. Commitments (i.e., unconditional purchase obligations—disclosure of aggregate amount of payments for each of the five years following the date of the balance sheet—similar requirement for leases).

IMPORTANT TERMS FOR RELATED-PARTY DISCLOSURES

A. *Affiliates*—Party is controlled by another company that controls, or is under the common control with another company, directly or indirectly.

B. *Control*—Power to direct or cause direction of management through ownership contract or other means.

C. *Immediate family*—Family members whom principal owners or management might control/influence or be controlled/influenced by.

D. *Management*—Persons responsible for company objectives who have policy-making and decision-making authority. Examples include: board of directors, CEO, CFO, and vice presidents.

E. *Principal owners* (includes *beneficial owners*)—Owners of more than 10% of a company's voting interests.

F. *Related parties*—Affiliates, equity method investees, employee benefit trusts, principal owners, management, or any party that can significantly influence a transaction.

DISCLOSURES REQUIRED FOR RELATED-PARTY TRANSACTIONS

A. Material related party transactions must generally be disclosed.

    1. Two exceptions:

        a. Compensation agreements, expense allowances, and other similar items in the ordinary course of business.

        b. Transactions that are eliminated in the preparation of consolidated/combined financial statements.

B. For material related party transactions, the following is disclosed:

    1. The nature of the relationship(s).

    2. A description and terms of the transaction, including those assigned zero or nominal amounts.

    3. Dollar amounts of transactions for each income statement period.

    4. Amounts due to and from related parties, including terms and manner of settlement.

C. Representations concerning related-party transactions shall not imply that terms were equivalent to those resulting in arm's length bargaining unless such a statement can be substantiated.

D. When a control relationship exists, disclose such a relationship even though no transactions have occurred.

SUBSEQUENT EVENTS AND SUBSEQUENT PERIOD

A. *Subsequent events* are events or transactions having a material effect on the financial statements that occur subsequent to the balance sheet date but prior to issuance of the financial statements.

    1. Type 1 subsequent events are such events that provide additional evidence about conditions that existed at the date of the balance sheet and affect the estimates used in preparing financial statements.

    2. Type 2 subsequent events are such events that provide evidence with respect to conditions that did *not* exist at the balance sheet date being reported on, but arose after that date.

B. *Subsequent period* is the period after the balance sheet date, extending to the reporting date.

ACCOUNTING FOR SUBSEQUENT EVENTS

A. Type 1 subsequent events require making an adjusting entry to the financial statements.

    1. Example #1: Settlement of litigation for an amount different from the liability recorded in the accounts, assuming the event causing the litigation occurred before year-end.

    2. Example #2: Loss on an uncollectible account receivable as a result of a customer's deteriorating financial condition *on* the balance sheet date but that further led to bankruptcy *subsequent* to the balance sheet date.

B. Type 2 subsequent events have no impact on year-end balances but are so significant that they should be disclosed in the footnotes.

Examples include:

1. Sale of bonds (incurrence of a large debt) or issuance of capital stock.

2. Purchase of a business.

3. A large casualty loss (e.g., fire, flood).

4. Loss on receivables, but only when the loss occurred due to a post-balance sheet event such as a customer's deteriorating financial condition subsequent to the balance sheet date that also led to bankruptcy subsequent to the balance sheet date. *(Note: It is important to clearly distinguish between the example here and in A2 above.)*

The disclosures related to a subsequent event might include pro forma statements to be included in the notes.

QUESTIONS: OVERVIEW OF FINANCIAL STATEMENT ANALYSIS ON THE CPA EXAM

1. To study trends in a company's COGS, one should standardize the COGS numbers to a common-sized basis by dividing COGS by:
    A. assets.
    B. sales.
    C. net income.
    D. the prior years' COGS.

2. Dragi, Inc.'s (Dragi) current ratio is 1.9. If some of Dragi's accounts payable are paid off from the cash account, the:
    A. numerator and the current ratio would remain unchanged.
    B. numerator would decrease more than the denominator, resulting in a lower current ratio.
    C. denominator would decrease more than the numerator, resulting in a higher current ratio.
    D. numerator and denominator would decrease proportionally, leaving the current ratio unchanged.

3. Dreamspace, Inc.'s (Dreamspace) quick ratio is 1.2. If Dreamspace purchased inventory for cash, the:
    A. numerator and the quick ratio would remain unchanged.
    B. numerator would decrease more than the denominator, resulting in a lower quick ratio.
    C. denominator would decrease more than the numerator, resulting in a higher current ratio.
    D. numerator and denominator would decrease proportionally, leaving the current ratio unchanged.

4. Bouwens Co.'s (Bouwens) income statement indicates COGS of $100,000. The balance sheet shows an average accounts payable balance of $12,000. What is Bouwens' average payables payment period?
    A. 28 days.
    B. 37 days.
    C. 44 days.
    D. 52 days.

5. Marcel, Inc. (Marcel) has a gross profit margin of $45,000 on sales of $150,000. The balance sheet shows average total assets of $75,000 with an average inventory balance of $15,000. What are Marcel's total asset turnover and inventory turnover amounts, respectively?

	Total asset turnover	Inventory turnover
A.	7.00 times	2.00 times
B.	2.00 times	7.00 times
C.	0.50 times	0.33 times
D.	10.00 times	0.60 times

6. Raphal, Inc.'s (Raphal) receivable turnover is 10 times, its inventory turnover is 5 times, and its payables turnover is 9 times. What is Raphal's cash conversion cycle?
    A. 69 days.
    B. 104 days.
    C. 150 days.
    D. 170 days.

7. Vassily Co's (Vassily) income statement shows sales of $1,000, COGS of $500, pre-interest operating expense of $200, and interest expense of $100. What is Vassily's interest coverage ratio?
    A. 1 times.
    B. 2 times.
    C. 3 times.
    D. 4 times.

Use the following information to answer Questions 8 and 9 (answers will need to be rounded).

Monique Co. (Monique)	
Sales	$5,000
Cost of goods sold	$2,500
Average account balances:	
Inventories	$600
Accounts receivable	450
Working capital	750
Cash	200
Accounts payable	500
Fixed assets	4,750
Total	$6,000
Annual purchases	$2,400

8. Monique's average inventory processing period is:
    A. 37 days.
    B. 44 days.
    C. 65 days.
    D. 88 days.

9. Monique's cash conversion cycle is:
    A. 19 days.
    B. 33 days.
    C. 48 days.
    D. 127 days.

Use the following information to answer Questions 10 through 13.

Beta Co. (Beta) has a loan covenant requiring it to maintain a current ratio of 1.5 or better. As Beta approaches year-end, current assets are $20 million ($1 million in cash, $9 million in accounts receivable and $10 million in inventory) and current liabilities are $13.5 million.

10. Beta's current ratio is closest to:
    A. 0.675 times.
    B. 0.74 times.
    C. 1.48 times.
    D. 1.5 times.

11. Beta's quick ratio is closest to:
   A. 0.675 times.
   B. 0.74 times.
   C. 0.81 times.
   D. 1.48 times.

12. What can Beta do to meet its loan covenant?
   A. Sell $1 million in inventory and deposit the proceeds in the company's checking account.
   B. Borrow $1 million short term and deposit the funds in the company's checking account.
   C. Sell $1 million in inventory and pay off some of its short-term creditors.
   D. Do nothing at all.

13. If Beta sells $2 million in inventory on credit, the current ratio will:
   A. increase, and if Beta sells $1 million in inventory and pays off accounts payable, the quick ratio will remain the same.
   B. remain the same, and if Beta sells $1 million in inventory and pays off accounts payable, the quick ratio will decrease.
   C. remain the same, and if Beta sells $1 million in inventory and pays off accounts payable, the quick ratio will increase.
   D. increase, and if Beta sells $1 million in inventory and pays off accounts payable, the quick ratio will increase.

14. Which of the following pieces of information should be included in Melay, Inc.'s (Melay) Year 6 summary of significant accounting policies?
   A. Property, plant, and equipment is recorded at cost with depreciation computed principally by the straight-line method.
   B. During Year 6, the Delay business component was sold.
   C. Business component revenues in Year 6 are Alay $1 million, Delay $2 million, and Celay $3 million.
   D. Future common share dividends are expected to approximate 60% of earnings.

15. Miri, Inc. (Miri) was incorporated on January 1, Year 6, with proceeds from the issuance of $750,000 in stock and borrowed funds of $110,000. During the first year of operations, revenues from sales and consulting amounted to $82,000, and operating costs and expenses totaled $64,000. On December 15, Miri declared a $3,000 cash dividend, payable to stockholders on January 15, Year 7. No additional activities affected owner's equity in Year 6. Miri's liabilities increased to $120,000 by December 31, Year 6.

   On Miri's December 31, Year 6 balance sheet, total assets should be reported at:
   A. $875,000.
   B. $878,000.
   C. $882,000.
   D. $885,000.

16. Financial statements shall include disclosures of material transactions between related parties except:
   A. nonmonetary exchanges by affiliates.
   B. sales of inventory by a subsidiary to its parent.
   C. expense allowances for executives that exceed normal business practice.
   D. a company's agreement to act as surety for a loan to its chief executive officer.

17. Zero Corp. (Zero) suffered a loss that would have a material effect on its financial statements on an uncollectible trade account receivable due to a customer's bankruptcy. This occurred suddenly due to a natural disaster ten days after Zero's balance sheet date, but one month before the issuance of the financial statements. Under these circumstances:

	Adjust statements	Disclose in statements but do not adjust
A.	Yes	No
B.	Yes	Yes
C.	No	No
D.	No	Yes

18. Holmquist, Inc. (Holmquist) acquired 25% of its capital stock after year-end and prior to the issuance of the financial statements. Which of the following is required?
    A. An adjustment to the balance sheet to reflect the acquisition.
    B. Issuance of pro forma financial statements giving effect to the acquisition as if it had occurred at year-end.
    C. Disclosure of the acquisition in the notes to the financial statements.
    D. No disclosure nor adjustment is needed.

19. Which of the following should be disclosed in a summary of significant accounting policies?
    A. Basis of profit recognition on long-term construction contracts.
    B. Future minimum lease payments in the aggregate and for each of the five succeeding fiscal years.
    C. Depreciation expense.
    D. Composition of sales by segment.

ANSWERS: OVERVIEW OF FINANCIAL STATEMENT ANALYSIS ON THE CPA EXAM

1. **B** With a common-size income statement, all income statement accounts are divided by sales.

2. **C** Current ratio = (cash + A/R + inventory)/A/P. If cash and A/P decrease by the same amount and the current ratio > 1, then the denominator falls faster than the numerator and the current ratio increases. (Because the denominator is smaller than the numerator, removing the same amount from each results in a smaller percentage drop in the numerator than in the denominator, so the whole fraction gets larger.)
   Example: Because the ratio starts at 1.9, assume it is 1.9/1, and assume you remove 0.2 from both numerator and denominator. The new fraction is now 1.7/0.8, or 2.13.

3. **B** Quick ratio = (cash + A/R)/A/P. If cash decreases, the quick ratio will also decrease. The denominator is unchanged.

4. **C** payables turnover = COGS/average A/P = 100/12 = 8.33. Average payables payment period = 365/8.33 = 43.8 days

5. **B** total asset turnover = sales/total assets = 150/75 = 2 times

   inventory turnover = COGS/average inventory = (150 – 45)/15 = 7 times

6. **A** (365/10) + (365/5) – (365/9) = 69 days

7. **C** interest coverage ratio = EBIT/interest expense = (1,000 – 500 – 200)/100 = 3 times

8. **D** inventory turnover = COGS/average inventory = 2,500/600 = 4.166 times

   average inventory processing period = 365 inventory turnover = 365/4.166 = 87.6 days

9. **C** receivables turnover = 5,000/450 = 11.11

   average receivables collection period = 365/11.11 = 32.85 days

   payables turnover = 2,500/500 = 5

   average payables payment period = 365/5 = 73 days

   cash conversion cycle = 33 + 88 – 73 = 48 days

10. **C** current ratio = current assets/current liabilities = [{1 + 9 + 10)/13.5] = 20/13.5 = 1.48 times

11. **B** quick ratio = (cash + marketable securities + receivables)/current liabilities = (1 + 9)/13.5 = 10/13.5 = 0.74 times

12. **C** This transaction would increase the current ratio: (20 – 1)/(13.5 – 1) = 19/12.5 = 1.52. Selling $1 million in inventory and depositing the proceeds in the company's checking account would leave the ratio unchanged: (20 + 1 – 1)/13.5 = 1.48. Borrowing $1 million short term and depositing the funds in their checking account would decrease the current ratio: (20 + 1)/(13.5 + 1) = 21/14.5 = 1.45

13. **C** If inventory goes down and receivables rise by the same amount, the numerator would be unchanged.

   Quick ratio = (cash + A/R)/A/P. A/P would decrease without any change to the numerator, thus increasing the overall quick ratio.

14. **A**   Per APB 22, disclosure of accounting policies should identify and describe the accounting principles followed by the reporting company and methods applying those principles.

Answer A is correct because the method of recording and depreciating assets is an example of such a required disclosure. Answers B and C are incorrect because both represent detail presented elsewhere in the financial statements. Answer D is incorrect because it is an estimate of earnings rather than an accounting policy.

15. **D**   Miri began operations on 1/1/Year 6 with the following balance sheet elements:

assets ($860,000) = liabilities ($110,000) + owners' equity ($750,000)

During Year 6, liabilities increased to $120,000 and owners' equity increased to $765,000 [$750,000 beginning balance + $18,000 net income ($82,000 revenues – $64,000 expenses) – $3,000 dividends declared].

Therefore, 12/31/Year 6 assets must be $885,000.

liabilities ($120,000) + owners' equity ($765,000) = assets ($885,000)

16. **B**   Because sales of inventory between subsidiary and parent are eliminated in preparing consolidated financial statements, such sales need not be disclosed as a related-party transaction.

Nonmonetary exchanges by affiliates are not specifically exempted from disclosure by SFAS 57, and therefore must be disclosed as related-party transactions.

In this case, the expense allowances are in excess of normal business practice and therefore must be disclosed.

Surety and guarantee agreements between related parties are not specifically exempted from disclosure by SFAS 57, and therefore must be disclosed as related-party transactions.

17. **D**   Answer D is correct because a customer's major casualty loss after year-end will result in a financial statement note disclosure with no adjustment to the financial statements.

18. **C**   Answer C is correct because the transaction described is a Type 2 subsequent event (because the acquisition provided evidence of a condition that came into existence after year-end) and therefore the accounting approach would be note disclosure rather than adjustment.

Answer A is incorrect because adjustments are only appropriate for Type 1 subsequent events (events that provide evidence the condition was in existence at year-end). Answer B is incorrect because the pro forma statements are optional and not mandatory. Based on the above, answer D is clearly incorrect because at a minimum, disclosure in the footnotes is required.

19. **A**   The summary of significant accounting policies is normally the first note to the financial statements or is included just in front of the notes. As the name implies, it allows readers to know which accounting policies were utilized by the management of the reporting company in creating the financial statements. The basis of profit recognition on long-term contracts (between the percentage of completion method and the completed contract method) is a policy decision that impacts the determination of net income and must be disclosed.

CHAPTER 10 – MARKETABLE SECURITIES (INCLUDING CASH AND CASH EQUIVALENTS)

STUDY TIP

Do not dwell on whether you are going to pass or fail the CPA exam. That is pure speculation and can harm your chances. Your only goal is to add a point or two to your score every day. That is a reasonable goal and one that will bring you success faster than you might think possible.

Chapter 10 – Marketable Securities (Including Cash and Cash Equivalents)

Cash and Cash Equivalents

Examples

A. Cash on hand.

B. Demand deposits.

Cash Equivalents

A. The characteristics of short-term and liquid investments are as follows:

1. Readily convertible into known amounts of cash.

2. Near maturity (original maturity of three months or less from the original *date of purchase*) and present virtually no risk of changes in value due to changes in interest rates.

B. Examples:

1. Treasury bills.

2. Commercial paper.

3. Money market funds.

Financial Statement Disclosures for Cash

A. Unrestricted cash available for general use.

1. Listed as a current asset on the balance sheet.

2. Simply reported as cash as a separate line item.

B. Restricted cash set aside for special use.

1. Separately disclosed.

2. If not available for use within the next year, then cannot be classified as a current asset.

Bank Reconciliations for Cash

A. Purpose is to move from the bank's *cash balance stated on a "pure cash" basis* to an accrual basis.

B. The starting point is the actual bank statement.

C. Then, identify reconciling items not on the bank statement (Type A).

1. Outstanding checks (decreases cash balance).

2. Deposits in transit (increases cash balance).

3. Bank errors (decrease or increase cash balance).

D. Next, find reconciling items not in the company's cash records (Type B).

   1. Unrecorded returned nonsufficient funds (NSF) checks (decreases cash balance).

   2. Unrecorded bank charges (decreases cash balance).

   3. Errors in the cash account (decrease or increase cash balance).

E. Note that Type A adjustments do not require a journal entry, but Type B adjustments do.

MARKETABLE SECURITIES AS INVESTMENTS

PURPOSE FOR INVESTING IN MARKETABLE SECURITIES

A. To generate a favorable return on excess cash until it is needed for operating purposes (generate interest income).

B. To accumulate funds for a long-term cash requirement.

   1. Repayment of debt.

   2. Acquisition of property, plant, and equipment.

   3. Part of a long-term investment policy developed as part of the overall business plan.

   4. To enhance a relationship with a supplier, customer, or other company.

   5. To attempt to gain actual or effective control of another company.

ACCOUNTING FOR INVESTMENTS IN MARKETABLE SECURITIES

A. The accounting treatment of securities that have a public market or a readily estimated fair value is determined based upon *management's designation of the purpose of the security holdings.*

B. In the United States, the *cost method* must be used for securities that have no public market or readily determined fair value.

C. GAAP requires a company to *classify* its marketable securities into categories based upon the *company's intent* relative to the eventual disposition of the securities.

D. This classification will determine the accounting method used.

CATEGORIES OF INVESTMENTS

A. Held-to-maturity (debt securities only).

B. Available-for-sale (debt or equity securities).

C. Trading (debt or equity securities).

GAAP TREATMENT OF BOND TRANSACTIONS IN WHICH THE UNDERLYING SECURITIES ARE CLASSIFIED AS "HELD-TO-MATURITY"

A. There must be the *intention* to hold until maturity (very subjective). In other words, there is no expectation to dispose of or reclassify the securities despite changes in the following:

    1. Market interest rates or the bonds' risk of being called by the issuer.

    2. The investor's liquidity needs.

    3. The availability of alternative investments.

B. Bonds are recorded at cost either as a current or long-term investment, depending on the maturity date.

C. Any discount or premium is amortized (assume effective-interest method) to the income statement.

D. Interest income is reported on the income statement as part of income from continuing operations. Interest income cash flows are reported as operating cash flows on the Statement of Cash Flows.

E. Cash flows from purchases and sales would be recorded in the *investing* activities section of the Statement of Cash Flows.

GAAP TREATMENT OF STOCK AND BOND TRANSACTIONS IN WHICH THE UNDERLYING SECURITIES ARE CLASSIFIED AS "AVAILABLE-FOR-SALE"

A. Not actively traded but yet not held with the intention of reaching maturity. Purpose could be to maximize the company's return on excess working capital or to accomplish some long-term goal.

B. Could be sold at any time if cash is needed. Differentiated from trading securities as these Available-for-Sale (AFS) securities are *not* actively being bought or traded.

C. Depending on circumstances, securities are classified as current or long-term assets on the balance sheet but are always recorded at market value.

D. "Unrealized" change in value is recorded directly to stockholders' equity (bypasses the income statement). It is included in Other Comprehensive Income.

E. Interest income and dividend income are reported on the income statement as earned and as part of income from continuing operations.

F. If sold, the gain or loss is "realized" and is the difference between original cost and sales price. The amount is recorded on the income statement.

G. Cash flows for purchases and sales would be recorded in the *investing* activities section.

H. Changes in value of available-for-sale securities are used to convert a company's net income figure to comprehensive income.

GAAP TREATMENT OF STOCK AND BOND TRANSACTIONS THAT ARE CLASSIFIED AS "TRADING"

A. Held for current resale.

1. Intended to be held for a short period only (current asset) and acquired principally for the purpose of selling in the near future.

2. Associated with active and frequent purchases and sales.

3. Purchased with the objective of generating profits due to short term fluctuations in price.

B. Securities are initially recorded on the balance sheet at cost and adjusted to market value for each reporting period. Bond investments discounts/premiums are amortized over the life of the bond.

C. "Unrealized" holding gain or loss is recorded directly on the income statement as part of income from continuing operations.

D. If sold, the gain or loss is "realized" and is the difference between the fair value at the beginning of the year and the sales price. It is also recorded on the income statement as part of income from continuing operations.

E. Interest income and dividend income reported on the income statement as earned and as part of income from continuing operations.

F. Cash flows would be recorded in the *operating* activities section.

	Held-to-Maturity	*Available-for-Sale*	*Trading*
Balance sheet carrying value	amortized cost	fair value (unrealized amounts in other comprehensive income)	fair value (unrealized amounts in income)
Income statement recognition	interest realized amounts	interest/dividends realized amounts	interest/dividends realized amounts unrealized amounts

Because securities listed in the available-for-sale and trading categories are measured at fair value, a portfolio of investment securities can have a value *above* or *below* original cost at any balance sheet date.

IMPAIRMENT ISSUES WITH MARKETABLE SECURITIES

A. For securities classified as held-to-maturity or available-for-sale, permanent impairment may occur, in which case the investment will be handled as follows:

1. The investment will be written *down* to market value.

2. The decrease will be reported on the income statement as if it were a realized loss.

3. The reduced amount will be considered the **new cost basis** of the security and the **cost** will *not* be adjusted upwards for subsequent recoveries of fair value. (The A-for-S securities will continue to be carried at fair value, but the *cost* will not be written up.)

ACCOUNTING IMPLICATIONS OF TRANSFERRING SECURITIES FROM ONE PORTFOLIO TO ANOTHER IF THE INTENTIONS OF THE OWNER CHANGE

A. Changes in circumstances will periodically cause companies to reclassify investments in debt and equity securities from one of the categories to another.

B. Management determines the appropriate classification at the time of purchase, reevaluates such determinations at each balance sheet date, and transfers securities from one category to another if appropriate.

C. *Remember the general rule:* When securities are transferred between reporting categories, the security is transferred at its fair value on the date of the transfer. Any unrealized holding gain or loss at reclassification should be accounted for consistent with the reporting category *into which* the security is transferred. (For example, transfers to trading securities would result in the unrealized gains/losses being reported in income on the income statement.)

D. The nature of *held-to-maturity* securities should make transfers *from* that category rare.

E. Only an investment in a debt security may be changed *to* the "held to maturity" classification.

1. Carrying value of the old classification is removed, and its face value is recorded in the new classification along with the related discount or premium. So, the old and new book value will be the same.

2. If transferred from trading securities, the reclassification is complete.

3. If transferred from available-for-sale, any unrealized gain or loss in stockholder's equity remains and the balance is amortized as an adjustment to interest income over the remaining life of the security.

F. The nature of *trading* securities should make transfers *to* or *from* that category rare.

G. If a security is changed to either trading securities or available-for-sale, the following applies:

1. The previous carrying value (along with any unrealized gain or loss in the stockholders' equity account) is removed.

2. The market value on the date of the transfer is recorded in the new classification.

3. If a difference exists between (1) and (2), an unrealized gain or loss is recorded as follows:

a. In the income statement if changed to a trading security.

b. In stockholders' equity if changed to an available-for-sale security.

EXTENDED EXAMPLE

The following example illustrates the application of the accounting for held-to-maturity, available-for-sale, and trading securities, and their respective impacts on the financial statements. Focus your attention on both the calculations and how the financial statements are affected by the classification of the securities.

Figure 1 contains transactions for investments made by Jagger, Inc., together with associated market data and year-end values. Figure 2 displays the income statement effects of Jagger's securities transactions, categorized as returns on investments and realized and unrealized gains and losses due to price changes. Figure 3 provides an analysis of the income statement effects based on varying assumptions regarding the nature of the portfolio holdings. Finally, Figure 4 shows the balance sheet carrying amounts for the securities.

Figure 1: Market and Trading Data for Jagger

	Year 4	Year 5	Year 6
Shares bought (sold)	1,000	(300)	500
Total shares: year-end	1,000	700	1,200
Purchase price	$50		$50
Sale price		$30	
Year-end market price	$60	$40	$60
Year-end holdings at cost	$50,000	$35,000 (Note 1)	$60,000 (Note 2)
Year-end holdings at market	$60,000	$28,000	$72,000

Figure 2: Jagger Portfolio Income Data

	Year 4	Year 5	Year 6
Total return (i.e., interest for debt securities, dividends for equity securities)	$1,000	$700	$1,200
Realized gains/(losses)	$0	($6,000) (Note 3)	$0
Unrealized gains/(losses)	$10,000	($17,000) (Note 4)	$19,000 (Note 5)

Notes Relating to Figure 1 and Figure 2:

1. 700 shares × $50/share = $35,000

2. (700 shares × $50/share) + (500 shares × $50/shares) = $60,000

3. 300 shares × ($30/share – $50/share) = ($6,000)

4. [700 shares × ($40/share – $60/share)] + [300 shares × ($50/share – $60/share)] = ($17,000). The second part of the calculation ($3,000 unrealized loss) represents the reversal of the unrealized gain (of the write-up from $50/share to $60/share) previously recorded in Year 4 on the 300 shares sold in Year 5.

   An alternative way to look at this is: The change in market value was a debit of $10,000 at the end of Year 4 (market above cost). This resulted from the increase in the market value of the stock from $50 to $60 per share × 1,000 shares during Year 4.

   In Year 5, the change in market value was a credit of $7,000 because the year-end holdings have a cost of $35,000 and a fair value of $28,000, for a difference of $7,000.

   To go from an increase of $10,000 to a decrease of $7,000 requires a change of $17,000.

5. [700 shares × ($60/share – $40/share)] + [500 shares × ($60/share – $50/share)] = $19,000

Or, because the decrease in the market value at the end of Year 5 was $7,000 (credit to the investment), there is an increase of $12,000 (debit to the investment) ($72,000 – $60,000) and a total unrealized gain of $19,000.

Figure 3: Reported Income for Jagger Portfolio

Based on three different assumptions regarding the category of the securities. (Assume total portfolio represents one category.)				
		Income Statement		
Assumptions	*Year 4*	*Year 5*	*Year 6*	
Held-to-maturity	$1,000	($5,300)	$1,200	dividends and realized losses
Available-for-sale	$1,000	($5,300)	$1,200	
Trading	$11,000	($22,300)	$20,200	

The previous figure represents the pretax income statement effects of the three reporting methods. Recall that the three methods are virtually identical except that unrealized gains and losses related to trading securities are included in current period income from continuing operations.

Unrealized gains and losses are *not included* for the other two categories, resulting in the same income for those two methods.

In general, the resulting reported income for trading securities is more volatile than it is for income associated with available-for-sale and held-to-maturity securities.

Figure 4: Balance Sheet Carrying Values for Jagger Portfolio

Assumptions	*Year 4*	*Year 5*	*Year 6*
Held-to-maturity	$50,000	$35,000	$60,000
Available-for-sale	$60,000	$28,000	$72,000
Trading	$60,000	$28,000	$72,000

For the trading and the available-for-sale securities, the carrying value on the balance sheet is adjusted to reflect changes in the market value of the securities. Unrealized gains and losses are reported as a separate component of other comprehensive income.

For held-to-maturity securities, there are no adjustments to the carrying value on the balance sheet or to comprehensive income.

OTHER ACCOUNTING ISSUES RELATED TO MARKETABLE SECURITIES

A. Cash dividends are recorded as revenue on the date of record.

B. Stock dividends and stock splits are not recorded by the owner. The book value of the investment is simply allocated over more shares.

C. Receipt of stock rights is not recorded as revenue. However, if rights have a value, the book value of the investment should be divided between the stock and the rights based on their relative fair values.

D. A liquidating dividend is a payment by a company that does not have income.

1. The owner reduces the investment account.

2. No income is recorded.

OTHER INVESTMENTS

A. A life insurance policy can have a cash surrender value (CSV), which is reported as an asset. Annual payment on the policy less the increase in the CSV is recorded as an expense for the period.

B. When a company insures the lives of employees and names itself as the beneficiary, the cash surrender value (CSV) of the policies is considered an asset. During the first few years of a policy, no CSV may accrue, and in that case, the journal entry to record a premium paid would be to debit insurance expense and credit cash.

C. A bond sinking fund is money set aside to pay off a bond.

1. If debt will be paid this year, the sinking fund is classified as a current asset.

2. Otherwise, the amount is classified as a long-term investment.

QUESTIONS: MARKETABLE SECURITIES (INCLUDING CASH AND CASH EQUIVALENTS)

1. Data regarding Dzegniuk Co.'s (Dzegniuk) available-for-sale securities is as follows:

	Cost	Market value
December 31, Year 5	$150,000	$130,000
December 31, Year 6	$150,000	$160,000

    Differences between cost and market values are considered to be temporary. Dzegniuk's Year 6 other comprehensive income would be:
    A. $0.
    B. $10,000.
    C. $20,000.
    D. $30,000.

2. On January 2, Year 3, Beus, Inc. (Beus) acquired a $70,000 whole-life insurance policy on its president. The annual premium is $2,000. The company is the owner and beneficiary. Beus charged officer's life insurance expense as follows:

2003	$2,000
2004	$1,800
2005	$1,500
2006	$1,100

    On Beus's December 31, Year 6 balance sheet, the investment in cash surrender value should be:
    A. $0.
    B. $1,600.
    C. $6,400.
    D. $8,000.

3. Day Corp. (Day) began operations in Year 6. An analysis of Day's marketable equity securities portfolio acquired in Year 6 shows the following totals at December 31, Year 6:

	Trading	Available-for-sale
Aggregate cost	$45,000	$65,000
Aggregate market value	$39,000	$57,000
Aggregate lower of cost or market value applied to each security in the portfolio	$38,000	$56,000

    The market declines are determined to be temporary.

    What amount should Day report in its Year 6 income statement for the unrealized losses?
    A. $6,000.
    B. $7,000.
    C. $9,000.
    D. $14,000.

4.   Buechner Co. (Buechner) had the following balances at December 31, Year 5:

Cash in checking account	$35,000
Cash in money market account	$75,000
U.S. Treasury bill, purchased Nov. 1, Year 5, maturing Jan. 31, Year 6	$350,000
U.S. Treasury bill, purchased Dec. 1, Year 5, maturing Mar. 31, Year 6	$400,000

According to SFAS 95, what amount should Buechner report as cash and cash equivalents on its December 31, Year 5 balance sheet?
A. $110,000.
B. $385,000.
C. $460,000.
D. $860,000.

5.   In preparing its August 31, Year 6, bank reconciliation, Malexa Corp. (Malexa) has the following information:

Balance per bank statement, 8/31/Year 6	$18,050
Deposit in transit, 8/31/Year 6	$3,250
Return of customer's check for insufficient funds, 8/31/Year 6	$600
Outstanding checks, 8/31/Year 6	$2,750
Bank service charges for August Year 6	$100

At August 31, Year 6, Malexa's correct cash balance is:
A. $17,550.
B. $17,850.
C. $17,950.
D. $18,550.

6.   Information regarding Drupinski Co.'s (Drupinski) portfolio of available-for-sale securities is as follows:

Aggregate cost as at 12/31/Year 6	$170,000
Unrealized gains as at 12/31/Year 6	$4,000
Unrealized losses as at 12/31/Year 6	$26,000
Net realized gains during Year 6	$30,000

At December 31, Year 5, Drupinski reported an unrealized loss of $1,500 in other comprehensive income to reduce these securities to market.

Under the accumulated other comprehensive income in stockholders' equity section of its December 31, Year 6 balance sheet, what amount should Drupinski report?
A. $0.
B. $20,500.
C. $22,000.
D. $26,000.

7. For a marketable equity securities portfolio classified as held-to-maturity, which of the following amounts should be included in the period's net income?

   1. Unrealized temporary losses during the period.
   2. Realized gains during the period.
   3. Changes in the valuation allowance during the period.

   A. 2 only.
   B. 3 only.
   C. 1 and 2.
   D. 1, 2, and 3.

8. A marketable equity security is transferred from the trading portfolio to the available-for-sale portfolio. At the transfer date, the security's cost exceeds its market value. What amount is used at the transfer date to record the security in the available-for-sale portfolio?
   A. Market value, regardless of whether the decline in market value below cost is considered permanent or temporary.
   B. Market value, only if the decline in market value below cost is considered permanent.
   C. Cost, if the decline in market value below cost is considered temporary.
   D. Cost, regardless of whether the decline in market value below cost is considered permanent or temporary.

9. In Year 1, Ota, Inc. (Ota) purchased a $1,000,000 life insurance policy on its president, of which Ota is the beneficiary. Information regarding the policy for the year ended December 31, Year 6, follows:

Cash surrender value, 1/1/Year 6	$87,000
Cash surrender value, 12/31/Year 6	$108,000
Annual advance premium paid 1/1/Year 6	$40,000

   What amount should Ota report as life insurance expense for Year 6?
   A. $13,000.
   B. $19,000.
   C. $25,000.
   D. $40,000.

10. When the market value of an investment in debt securities *exceeds* its carrying amount, how should each of the following assets be reported at the end of the year?

	Held-to-maturity	Trading
A.	Market value	Amortized cost
B.	Amortized cost	Market value
C.	Amortized cost	Amortized cost
D.	Market value	Market value

11.	Hally Corp. (Hally) has a checkbook balance of $5,000 on December 31, Year 5. In addition, Hally held the following items in its safe on that date:

$2,000	Check payable to Hally, dated December 31, Year 5, in payment of a sale made in December Year 5, not included in December 31, Year 5 checkbook balance.

$500	Check payable to Hally, deposited December 15 and included in December 31 checkbook balance, but returned by the bank on December 30 stamped NSF. The check was redeposited on January 2, Year 6, and cleared on January 9.

$300	Check drawn on Hally's account, payable to a vendor, dated and recorded in Hally's books on December 31 but not mailed until January 10, Year 6.

What is the proper amount to be shown as cash on Hally's balance sheet on December 31, Year 5?
A.	$4,800.
B.	$5,300.
C.	$6,500.
D.	$6,800.

Use the following information to answer Questions 12 and 13.

The following data pertains to Tyne Co.'s (Tyne) investments in marketable equity securities:

	Cost	Market value 12/31/Year 6	Market value 12/31/Year 5
Trading	$150,000	$155,000	$100,000
Available-for-sale	$150,000	$130,000	$120,000

12.	What amount should Tyne report as an unrealized holding gain in its Year 6 income statement?
A.	$50,000.
B.	$55,000.
C.	$60,000.
D.	$65,000.

13.	What amount should Tyne report as a net unrealized loss on marketable equity securities at December 31, Year 6, in accumulated other comprehensive income in stockholders' equity?
A.	$0.
B.	$10,000.
C.	$15,000.
D.	$20,000.

14.   Norina Co. (Norina) has a portfolio of marketable equity securities that it does not intend to sell in the near term.

How should Norina classify these securities *and* how should it report unrealized gains and losses from these securities?

	Classify as	Report as a
A.	Trading securities	Component of income from continuing operations
B.	Available-for-sale securities	Separate component of other comprehensive income
C.	Trading securities	Separate component of other comprehensive income
D.	Available-for-sale	Component of income from continuing operations securities

15.   An increase in the cash surrender value of a life insurance policy owned by a company would be recorded by:
A. decreasing annual insurance expense.
B. increasing investment income.
C. recording a memorandum entry only.
D. decreasing a deferred charge.

16.   Schulte, Inc. (Schulte) had the following bank reconciliation at March 31, Year 6:

Balance per bank statement, 3/31/Year 6	$46,500
Add: deposit in transit	10,300
Less: outstanding checks	(12,600)
Balance per books, 3/31/Year 6	$44,200

Data per bank for the month of April Year 6 follow:

Deposits	$58,400
Disbursements	$49,700

All reconciling items at March 31, Year 6 cleared the bank in April. Outstanding checks at April 30, Year 6 totaled $7,000. There were no deposits in transit at April 30, Year 6.

What is Schulte's cash balance per books at April 30, Year 6?
A. $48,200.
B. $52,900.
C. $55,200.
D. $58,500.

17.   On January 10, Year 6, Brixton, Inc. (Brixton) purchased marketable securities of Knightsbridge, Inc. (Knightsbridge) and Scott, Inc. (Scott), neither of which Brixton could significantly influence. Brixton classified both securities as available-for-sale.

At December 31, Year 6, the cost of each investment was greater than its fair value. The loss on the Knightsbridge investment was considered other-than-temporary and that on Scott was considered temporary.

How should Brixton report the effects of these investments in its Year 6 income statement?

I.   Excess of cost of Knightsbridge stock over its market value.
II. Excess of cost of Scott stock over its market value.

A.   An unrealized loss equal to I plus II.
B.   An unrealized loss equal to I only.
C.   A realized loss equal to I only.
D.   No income statement effect.

18.   A marketable security is transferred from available-for-sale to held-to-maturity. At the transfer date, the security's carrying amount exceeds its market value. What amount is used at the transfer date to record the security in the held-to-maturity portfolio?
A.   Market value, regardless of whether the decline in market value below cost is considered permanent or temporary.
B.   Market value, only if the decline in market value below cost is considered permanent.
C.   Cost, if the decline in market value below cost is considered temporary.
D.   Cost, regardless of whether the decline in market value below cost is considered permanent or temporary.

19.   Upon the death of an officer, Jacob Co. (Jacob) received the proceeds of a life insurance policy held by Jacob on the officer. The proceeds were not taxable. The policy's cash surrender value had been recorded on Jacob's books at the time that the proceeds were received. What amount of revenue should Jacob report in its income statement?
A.   Proceeds received.
B.   Proceeds received less cash surrender value.
C.   Proceeds received plus cash surrender value.
D.   None.

Use the following information to answer Questions 20 and 21.

Sun Corp. (Sun) had investments in marketable debt securities costing $650,000 that were classified as available-for-sale. On June 30, Year 6, Sun decided to hold the investments to maturity and accordingly reclassified them. The investments' market value was $575,000 at December 31, Year 5; $530,000 at June 30, Year 6; and $490,000 at December 31, Year 6.

20.   What amount of loss from investments should Sun report in its Year 6 income statement?
A. $0.
B. $45,000.
C. $85,000.
D. $120,000.

21. What amount should Sun report as net unrealized loss on marketable debt securities in its Year 6 statement of stockholders' equity?
    A. $40,000.
    B. $45,000.
    C. $120,000.
    D. $160,000.

22. At year-end, Rim Co. held several investments with the intent of selling them in the near term. The investments consisted of $100,000, 8%, 5-year bonds, purchased for $92,000, and equity securities purchased for $35,000. At year-end, the bonds were selling on the open market for $105,000 and the equity securities had a market value of $50,000. What amount should Rim report as trading securities in its year-end balance sheet?
    A. $50,000.
    B. $127,000.
    C. $142,000.
    D. $155,000.

23. A company buys a portfolio of equity investments in Year 1 for a cost of $19,000. By the end of this first year, these stocks were worth $21,000. However, at the end of the subsequent year, the value of the stocks had dropped to $18,000. Which of the following statements is not true?
    A. If the stocks are viewed as trading securities, there is a $3,000 decrease to net income in the second year.
    B. If the stocks are viewed as available for sale, there is a $3,000 decrease in switching from net income to comprehensive income in the second year.
    C. If the stocks are viewed as trading securities and are sold on the first day of Year 3 for $18,000, there is a $1,000 drop in net income.
    D. If the stocks are viewed as available for sale and are sold on the first day of Year 3 for $18,000, there is a $1,000 drop in net income.

24. The Oregon Company bought 100 shares of XYZ Company on January 1, Year 1 for $40 per share. On the same day, the company bought 100 shares of ABC Company for $20 per share. At the end of Year 1, XYZ stock was selling for $39 per share and ABC was selling for $25 per share. The Oregon Company sold the shares of ABC on March 3, Year 2 for $18 per share. What was the impact of ownership of these marketable securities on Oregon's reported net income for Year 1 and what was the gain or loss reported in the Year 2 net income on the sale of ABC? Assume these investments were probably classified as being trading securities.
    A. Zero and $200 loss.
    B. $100 loss and $200 loss.
    C. $100 loss and $700 loss.
    D. $400 gain and $700 loss.

25. The Mississippi Company bought 100 shares of XYZ Company on January 1, Year 1 for $60 per share. On the same day, the company bought 100 shares of ABC Company for $30 per share. At the end of Year 1, XYZ stock was selling for $64 per share and ABC was selling for $29 per share. The Mississippi Company sold the shares of ABC on March 3, Year 2 for $33 per share. What was the impact of ownership of these marketable securities on Mississippi's reported net income for Year 1 and what was the gain or loss reported in the Year 2 net income on the sale of ABC? Assume these investments were probably classified as being available for sale.
   A. Zero and $300 gain.
   B. Zero and $400 gain.
   C. $300 gain and $300 gain.
   D. $300 gain and $300 gain.

26. In the current year, a company only had one item of income reported in other comprehensive income. That amount came from the change in value of an investment that was being reported as available for sale. For the current year, the company reported net income of $30,000 and comprehensive income of $32,000. If the company had viewed this investment as a trading security rather than available for sale, how would that have changed the reported income figures for the year?
   A. Net income would be $30,000 and comprehensive income would be $30,000.
   B. Net income would be $30,000 and comprehensive income would be $32,000.
   C. Net income would be $32,000 and comprehensive income would be $32,000.
   D. Net income would be $32,000 and comprehensive income would be $34,000.

ANSWERS: MARKETABLE SECURITIES (INCLUDING CASH AND CASH EQUIVALENTS)

1. **D** SFAS 115, as amended by SFAS 130, dictates that unrealized holding gains and losses on available-for-sale securities be reported as other comprehensive income. At 12/31/Year 5, available-for-sale securities would have been reported on the balance sheet at their fair value of $130,000, with a corresponding loss of $20,000.

   At 12/31/Year 6, the fair value of these securities is $160,000. Therefore, an unrealized gain of $30,000 ($160,000 – $130,000) would be reported in other comprehensive income.

2. **B** From Year 3 to Year 6, a total of four premium payments of $2,000 each, or $8,000, have occurred. If the company has reported $6,400 of expense over that period, the remaining $1,600 must have been capitalized on the balance sheet as the cash surrender value of the policy.

3. **A** The unrealized loss on current marketable trading securities is the difference between the aggregate cost of $45,000 and the aggregate market value of $39,000, or $6,000. This is reported on the income statement.

   The unrealized loss on the marketable securities available for sale is reported as an adjustment to comprehensive income on the balance sheet, and is not reported on the income statement.

4. **C** Per SFAS 95, *Statement of Cash Flows*, the definition of cash includes both cash (cash on hand and demand deposits) and cash equivalents (short-term, highly liquid investments). Cash equivalents have to be readily convertible into cash and so near maturity that they carry little risk of changing in value due to interest rate changes. This will include only those investments with original maturities of three months or less from the date of purchase by the company.

   Common examples of cash equivalents include treasury bills, commercial paper, and money market funds. Buechner should report a total of $460,000 ($35,000 + $75,000 + $350,000) on its December 31, Year 5, balance sheet.

   The U.S. treasury bill purchased on December 1, Year 5 is not included in the calculation because its original maturity is not within three months or less from the date of purchase.

5. **D** To determine the correct balance at August 31, Year 6, a partial bank reconciliation should be prepared. The balance per bank statement ($18,050) must be adjusted for any items that the bank has not yet recorded and also for any bank errors (none in this question).

Balance per bank statement	$18,050
Deposits in transit	3,250
Outstanding check	(2,750)
Correct balance	$18,550

   The deposits in transit and the outstanding checks represent transactions that the company has recorded but the bank has not yet recorded. The insufficient funds check ($600) and bank service charge ($100) are both items that the bank has recorded but the company has not. They would be adjustments to the book balance, not the bank balance.

6. **C** Available-for-sale securities are reported at market value on the balance sheet. At 12/31/Year 6, Drupinski has incurred gross unrealized gains of $4,000 and gross unrealized losses of $26,000 on its available-for-sale securities. Therefore, at 12/31/Year 6, the net unrealized loss is $22,000 ($26,000 – $4,000). Drupinski would have to increase the balance in accumulated other comprehensive income from $1,500 to $22,000 at 12/31/Year 6.

7. **A** Per SFAS 115, held-to-maturity securities are carried at cost, so unrealized holding gains and losses are not reported. However, realized gains and losses on held-to-maturity securities should always be included in the income statement of the appropriate period. No valuation allowance exists for any marketable debt or equity securities. Realized gains for the period are the only item listed that is included in that period's net income.

---

8. **A**   When a marketable security is reclassified from a trading security to an available-for-sale security, the transfer is at the market value as of the date of the transfer.

9. **B**   Ota paid a premium on the life insurance in the amount of $40,000, but the cash surrender value of the insurance increased by $21,000 from $87,000 to $108,000. As a result, $21,000 would be applied to the asset account and the remaining $19,000 of the premium would be recognized as an expense.

10. **B**   When market value exceeds amortized cost, debt securities classified as trading securities are reported at market value. When investments in debt securities are expected to be held to maturity, they are reported at the amortized cost.

11. **D**   To be classified as cash, the item must be readily available for current needs with no legal restrictions limiting its use. Thus, the $2,000 check was incorrectly excluded from the 12/31 checkbook balance and an adjustment is necessary.

An NSF check should not be included in cash until it has been redeposited and has cleared the bank. At 12/31, the NSF check ($500) had not yet been redeposited, so it was incorrectly included in the 12/31 checkbook balance, and an adjustment must be made.

The check that was not mailed until 1/10/Year 6 ($300) should not be subtracted from cash until the company gives up physical control of that amount. Therefore, $300 must be added back to the checkbook balance.

As a result of these adjustments, the correct cash balance is $5,000 + $2,000 – $500 + $300 = $6,800.

12. **B**   Debt and equity securities that are classified as trading securities are reported at fair value with unrealized gains and losses included in earnings. During Year 6, Tyne had an unrealized holding gain of $55,000 ($155,000 – $100,000) on its trading securities.

The unrealized holding gain on available-for-sale securities of $10,000 ($130,000 – $120,000) is excluded from earnings and reported as other comprehensive income.

13. **D**   The requirement is to determine the accumulated other comprehensive income to be reported in the December 31, Year 6 statement of stockholders' equity. Unrealized gains and losses on trading securities are included in earnings. Unrealized gains and losses on available-for-sale securities are excluded from earnings and reported as accumulated other comprehensive income in a separate component of shareholders' equity. This amount is the net unrealized loss on available-for-sale securities at 12/31/Year 6 of $20,000 ($150,000 – $130,000).

14. **B**   In accordance with SFAS 115, marketable equity securities (MES) are classified as either trading (held for current resale) or available-for-sale (if not categorized as trading). Because Norina does not intend to sell these securities in the near term, they should be classified as available-for-sale.

SFAS 115 requires MES to be carried at market value. The unrealized gains or losses of available-for-sale MES are reported as a separate component of other comprehensive income. It is important to note that unrealized gains or losses on trading securities would be reported as a component of continuing operations on the income statement.

Thus, Answer B is correct because the securities would be classified as available-for-sale and unrealized gains or losses from these securities would be reported as other comprehensive income.

15. **A**   When a company insures the lives of employees and names itself as the beneficiary, the cash surrender value (CSV) of the policies is considered an asset. During the first few years of a policy, no CSV may accrue and in that case, the journal entry to record a premium paid would be to debit insurance expense and credit cash.

However, if CSV increases, part of the cash paid is received as an increase in the CSV. The entry becomes debit insurance expense, debit CSV (asset) and credit cash. So the increase in CSV actually decreases insurance expense because the same amount of cash paid must be allocated between the two accounts.

The increase in CSV does not affect investment income or deferred charges.

16. **A**   The balance per books at 3/31/Year 6 is $44,200. The amount would be increased by cash receipts per books and decreased by cash disbursements per books. Cash receipts per the bank in April were $58,400, but this amount includes the $10,300 in transit at 3/31/Year 6. Therefore, cash receipts per books in April are $48,100 ($58,400 – $10,300).

Cash disbursements per the bank in April were $49,700. This amount includes the 3/31/Year 6 outstanding checks ($12,600) but does not include the 4/30/Year 6 outstanding checks ($7,000). Therefore, April cash disbursements per books is $44,100 ($49,700 – $12,600 + $7,000).

The cash balance per books at 4/30/Year 6 is $48,200 ($44,200 at 3/31/Year 6 plus $48,100 receipts and less $44,100 disbursements).

An alternative solution approach is to first compute the 4/30/Year 6 bank balance ($46,500 + $58,400 – $49,700 = $55,200), and then adjust for outstanding checks ($55,200 – $7,000 = $48,200).

17. **C**   The requirement is to determine how the losses on the securities classified as available-for-sale should be reported. In accordance with SFAS 115, a decline in market value of a security, which is considered to be other-than-temporary, should be reported in the income statement in the current period.

A decline in market value, which is considered to be temporary, would be recorded as an unrealized loss, and recognized as other comprehensive income.

Therefore, Answer C is correct, as the loss on the Knightsbridge stock is considered to be other-than-temporary and it would be reported on the income statement.

Answer A is incorrect because the unrealized loss on the Scott stock would be reported as other comprehensive income.

Answer B is incorrect because the loss on the Knightsbridge stock is considered to be a realized loss as it is other-than-temporary.

Answer D is incorrect because the other-than-temporary decline in Knightsbridge stock results in a realized loss that is reported on the income statement.

18. **A**   SFAS 115 states that "the transfer of a security between categories of investments shall be accounted for at fair value." If fair value is less than the security's carrying amount at the date of transfer, it is irrelevant whether the decline is temporary or permanent.

19. **B**   When a company insures the lives of employees and names itself as the beneficiary, the cash surrender value (CSV) of the policy is considered an asset. Premiums paid are debited to CSV for the increase in CSV that year and to insurance expense for the excess of cash paid over the increase in CSV. Upon the death of an insured employee, the company recognizes a gain for the excess of proceeds received over CSV.

20. **A**   The requirement is to determine the amount of loss on investments to be reported on Sun's Year 6 income statement. SFAS 115 requires this transfer to be accounted for at fair value and any holding gains or losses on securities that are transferred to held-to-maturity from available-for-sale be reported as accumulated other comprehensive income.

This amount is then amortized over the remaining life of the security as an adjustment to yield. Because cost is greater than market value by $75,000 at 12/31/Year 5 ($650,000 cost – $575,000 fair value), there would be a debit to unrealized loss and a credit to marketable debt securities, both for $75,000.

Then on June 30, Year 6, when Sun decides to hold the investments to maturity, an additional $45,000 will be recorded in the valuation account ($575,000 value on books – $530,000 FV) to reflect the change in the FV. There would be a debit to unrealized loss and a credit to marketable debt securities, both for $45,000.

Each year the unrealized loss would be reported as other comprehensive income that would be closed to "accumulated other comprehensive income."

21. C   Per SFAS 115, when a security is transferred to held-to-maturity from available-for-sale, the unrealized holding gain or loss continues to be reported as a separate component of stockholders' equity.

Held-to-maturity securities are carried at amortized cost and any unrealized holding gains or losses are not reported. Thus, the balance in the "accumulated other comprehensive income" in stockholders' equity on the Year 6 statement of stockholders' equity would be $120,000 ($75,000 amount reported at 12/31/Year 5 plus the $45,000 reported at June 30, Year 6).

The $120,000 will be amortized over the remaining life of the security as an adjustment to yield. The additional decline in value from 6/30/Year 6 to 12/31/Year 6 would not be reported, as held-to-maturity securities do not report unrealized losses.

22. D   Because both groups of securities were acquired with the "intent of selling them in the near future," they are classified as Trading Securities and reported on the balance sheet at the year-end fair value.

23. C   For trading securities, changes in value are reported in net income and gains and losses on sales are only measured based on a change in value during the current fiscal period. There was no noted change in value during Year 3, so no income effect will be recognized at the time of sale if this is a trading security portfolio. For available for sale securities, changes in value are reported in other comprehensive income within stockholders' equity and as an adjustment figure in converting net income to comprehensive income. The only income statement effect occurs at sale and is based on the difference between the original cost and the amount received.

24. D   As trading securities, the entire portfolio is updated each year to fair value and changes in this value are reported within net income. The initial cost of $6,000 ($4,000 plus $2,000) is adjusted to $6,400 ($3,900 plus $2,500) at the end of Year 1 and a $400 gain is recognized. Because the investments have been adjusted to fair value, the gain or loss to be recognized on the sale is measured against that balance. The company received $1,800 for the shares of ABC but its adjusted book value would have been $2,500. That creates a loss of $700.

25. A   As available for sale securities, the entire portfolio is updated each year to fair value but the changes in value are only reported within other comprehensive income in the stockholders' equity section of the balance sheet. There is no impact on net income caused by any changes in value. When the stock is eventually sold, the entire income effect is then reported in net income. The company received $3,300 for the shares of ABC but the original cost was $3,000. That creates a gain of $300.

26. C   At the current time, the company is reporting $30,000 as net income and has a $2,000 adjustment for the value of the securities which brings comprehensive income up to $32,000. Changing the classification from available for sale to a trading security only moves the $2,000 adjustment directly into net income. Net income is then reported at $32,000 and there are no longer any other comprehensive income adjustments. Thus, comprehensive income is the same $32,000 figure as net income.

CHAPTER 11 – REVENUE RECOGNITION (INCLUDING LONG-TERM CONTRACTS) AND INSTALLMENT SALES METHOD

STUDY TIP

Don't make any sudden changes in your sleeping or eating habits right before you take the CPA exam. Keep life as normal as possible so there is not any unnecessary stress on you. The CPA exam is a challenge; don't make your body and mind adapt to new circumstances at this critical juncture.

CHAPTER 11 – REVENUE RECOGNITION (INCLUDING LONG-TERM CONTRACTS) AND INSTALLMENT SALES METHOD

CRITERIA FOR REVENUE RECOGNITION

A. The following conditions must be met in order to recognize revenues on the income statement:

1. The earnings process must have been substantially complete (a key criterion).

    a. The risk of ownership must have been transferred from the seller to the purchaser, or the company must have provided virtually all of the goods or services for which it is to be paid.

    b. The expected cost of providing the goods or services must be measurable.

2. The company must have reasonable assurance of payment (a key criterion).

    a. In other words, has the seller received or will the seller receive cash or some other asset whose value can be precisely measured?

3. The transaction cannot be cancelled or revoked (more or less implied from the first two criteria).

B. If any of the conditions have not been met, then the company should not recognize the revenue on their income statement; revenue will have to be deferred (recorded as a liability on the balance) until an appropriate time in the future.

1. However, the generality of these conditions provides companies with flexibility in selecting how they recognize revenues.

2. This introduces the potential for unscrupulous managers to manipulate reported income for their personal benefit or for the benefit of the company.

BASIC ISSUES INVOLVED IN THE ANALYSIS OF REVENUE RECOGNITION METHODS

A. Most companies recognize revenue at the time they sell goods or render services. However, some companies may opt to prematurely recognize revenues (aggressive revenue recognition).

1. As a result, there could be significant distortion in its financial results and ratios.

2. One should carefully review the revenue recognition method chosen by a company to determine if the method is appropriate and meaningful.

B. Companies can recognize revenue at the following times:

1. At the time of production/construction.

2. At the time of sale.

3. At the time of cash collection.

C. The revenue recognition method the company selects will not affect the total amount of revenue recognized over the life of the business. However, the method selected will affect the timing of revenue recognition.

SALES BASIS METHOD OF REVENUE RECOGNITION

A. The sales basis method is the most common method, and most businesses generate revenue under these assumptions, which are discussed at the very beginning in the Criteria for Revenue Recognition" section of this chapter.

B. This method is the standard to which one should compare alternative methods.

C. Goods and services are provided when the sale is made, and the sale is for cash or credit to a customer with a high probability of payment.

D. As mentioned earlier, if cash is received before goods or services are provided, the revenue is not recognized until it is earned.

E. Examples:

1. Revenue from the sale of magazines is not recognized until delivery.

2. Credit card fees received in advance are not revenue until the passage of time.

   a. In each of these cases, revenue is not recognized until it is earned and cash collection is assured. The cost of the goods or services will be recognized as an expense only when the corresponding revenue is recorded (the matching principle).

REVENUE RECOGNITION METHODS FOR LONG-TERM CONSTRUCTION CONTRACTS

A. Percentage-of-completion method.

1. This is the method normally used for financial reporting purposes for a construction job that will take over a year to complete.

2. A contract must exist and there must be reliable estimates of the revenues, costs, and completion time. In addition, no significant uncertainties can exist.

3. It recognizes a percentage of total profit (revenues net of expenses) each year as the job progresses and in proportion to the amount of work completed, as follows:

   a. A construction-in-progress account is maintained at cost plus the gain recognized to date.

   b. Percentage of work done is usually determined as the cost to date divided by the total of the estimated cost of the project.

   c. This percentage is multiplied by the total estimated profit to get the profit earned to date.

   d. Any previously recognized revenue is subtracted from revenue earned to date to get revenue to be recognized in the current year.

   e. If a loss is anticipated, the entire amount of the loss must be immediately recognized.

4. It approximates the sales basis method and is a logical extension of the sales basis method for long-term contracts. It is designed to measure current operating performance.

5. Example:

Example:

Canucks, Inc. is building a hockey arena for $100 million, to be received in equal installments over four years. At its inception, a reliable estimate of the total cost of this contract is $80 million.

During the first year of construction, the total cost incurred was $16 million. How much revenue and profit/loss are recognized in the first year?

During the second year, the total cost incurred was $20 million. Additionally, Canucks has revised its estimate of the total cost to $90 million. How much revenue and profit (loss) is recognized in the second year?

Solution:

First year:

1. Calculate expected total revenue: $100 million – 80 million = $20 million
2. Calculate percent complete based on costs-to-date and expected total costs: $16 million / $80 million = 20% complete
3. Calculate profit to be recognized to date: $20 million × 20% = $4 million
4. Calculate current period profit taking into consideration any previous profit recognized: $4 million – 0 = $4 million

Second year:

1. Calculate expected total revenue: $100 million – 90 million = $10 million
2. Calculate percent complete based on costs-to-date and expected total costs: $36 million / $90 million = 40% complete
3. Calculate profit to be recognized to date: $10 million × 40% = $4 million
4. Calculate current period profit taking into consideration any previous profit recognized: $4 million – 4 million = $0 current period profit recognized

Extension of Example: Expected Loss

Assume that at the beginning of Year 3, the company realized the costs were going to total $105 million, but revenue was still $100 million. The expected loss on the entire project would be $5 million. Because $4 million in profit had been recorded in Year 1 (and $0 in Year 2), a loss of $9 million would be recorded in Year 3 to bring the cumulative loss to $5 million. Even if the loss was not expected to occur until Year 4, it would still be recorded in Year 3, based on the principle of conservatism.

B. Completed contract method.

1. An alternate method of revenue recognition; it is not considered appropriate unless reasonable estimates cannot be made about a job. Often some significant uncertainty exists about the estimates of revenues or costs, which makes the percentage-of-completion method unavailable.

   a. Cost is recorded in the construction-in-progress account with no income effect recognized until the project is completed.

   b. Any anticipated losses must be recognized immediately.

2. It is more suitable for shorter-term contracts.

3. It is more conservative than the percentage-of-completion method, so revenues will lag those of the percentage-of-completion method.

4. Also, income will be less stable under the completed contract method.

5. Example:

    a. Using the same example as before, if no reliable estimate can be made of its total cost, then no revenue or expenses will be recognized until the fourth year under the completed contract method.

C. Other reporting issues related to both methods.

1. Under either method, invoices are periodically sent to the buyer. The invoices do not affect recognition of revenue.

    a. Accounts receivable and a billings account are both recorded with a debit to Accounts Receivable and a credit to Progress Billings. Progress Billings is a credit-balance balance sheet account.

    b. For balance sheet reporting, the construction-in-progress and the billings accounts are netted.
- If the billings account is higher, the net amount is reported as a liability.
- If the construction-in-progress account is higher, the net amount is reported as an asset.

2. Summary of journal entries:

| Incur costs: | Debit Construction in Progress (CIP) |
| | Credit Cash or Payables |

| Record invoices sent to customer: | Debit Accounts Receivable |
| | Credit Progress Billings |

| Customer remits cash: | Debit Cash |
| | Credit Accounts Receivable |

Record revenue:	Debit CIP (the gross profit amount)
	Debit Cost of Goods Sold (COGS)
	Credit Revenue

    a. *Note:*
- CIP is now equal to the "selling price" of the item because we debited it for both costs incurred and gross profit (revenue – COGS).
- Progress Billings is the amount billed to the customer; it is not reduced when cash is collected. Over the life of the project, it grows to become equal to total amount billed, or total revenue.
- CIP will eventually equal Progress Billings because of the costs plus gross profit recorded in CIP.
- At the end of the project, CIP and Progress Billings will be netted against each other.
- At any balance sheet date, we net the CIP and Progress Billings for each project. All with a net CIP balance are shown on the balance sheet under inventory. All with a net Progress Billings balance are shown on the balance sheet under liabilities.

SUMMARY

Completion of Earnings Process	Assurance of Revenue	Revenue Recognition Method
Complete	Assured	Sales basis
Complete	Not assured	Installment basis
Complete with contingencies	Assured	Cost recovery
Complete with contingencies	Not assured	Cost recovery
Incomplete & costs can be estimated	Assured	Percentage-of-completion
Incomplete & costs can be estimated	Not assured	Completed contract
Incomplete & costs cannot be estimated	Assured	Completed contract
Incomplete & costs cannot be estimated	Not assured	Completed contract

INSTALLMENT SALES METHODS OF REVENUE RECOGNITION

A. Installment sales method.

1. Appropriately used to recognize profits for any sale when collection will take over a year AND a significant uncertainty exists. In other words, there is no way to estimate the likelihood of collecting the sales proceeds, but the costs of the goods and services are known.

   a. No profit is recognized at the time of sale, but rather when the cash is collected.

   b. Until cash is collected, all profit is recorded in a deferred revenue account.

2. Profit to be recognized equals gross profit percentage times the cash collected.

   gross profit percentage = gross profit / sales price

   The gross profit percentage multiplied by the remaining receivable balance represents the gross profit still deferred.

3. Example:

Example:

Maguire, Inc. (Maguire) uses the installment sales method to account for its sales. In Year 3, Maguire sold goods costing $14 million for $20 million, representing a gross profit of $6 million and a gross profit margin of 30% ($6 million divided by $20 million). Maguire collected $10 million of this sale in Year 4, $5 million in Year 5 and $5 million in Year 6. How much did Maguire recognize as gross profit in Year 4, Year 5, and Year 6?

The gross profit margin is 30%, so the cost of goods sold is 70% of sales.

Solution:

Year 4:

Cash Collections of $10 million × Gross Profit Margin of 30% = $3 million of recognized gross profit. The Accounts Receivable balance is now $10 million.

Year 5 and Year 6:

Cash Collections in each year = $5 million

30% × $5 million equals $1.5 million in each year

Total gross profit recognized: $3 million + $1.5 million + $1.5 million = $6 million (Sales were $20 million; COGS was $14 million.)

Sometimes the CPA exam might ask for the gross profit *deferred* rather than the amount recognized in a year. The deferred portion is always the gross profit percentage multiplied by the Accounts Receivable balance. For the previous example:

Deferred Gross Profit

Year 4   30% × $10 million = $3 million

Year 5   30% × $5 million = $1.5 million

Year 6   no more is deferred

B. Cost recovery method.

1. Appropriately used for any sale where collection is highly doubtful.

    a.   For example, a sale could be made to a company on the verge of bankruptcy.

    b.   No profit is recorded until cash equal to the cost of the asset is collected. For all further collections of cash, an equal amount of profit is recognized.

2. Could also be used when the costs to provide goods or services is not known at the outset.

3. Example:

    a.   Using the same example as for the installment sales method, we can also calculate the amount of gross profit to recognize under the cost recovery method.

    Year 4:

    A gross profit of $0 because the $10 million of cash collected for the year is less than the cost of the goods ($14 million).

    Year 5:

    A gross profit of $1 million because total cash collections to date, $15 million ($10 million in Year 4 and $5 million in Year 5), are $1 million greater than the cost of goods sold.

    Year 6:

    A gross profit of $5 million. The final payment for the sale is received in this year. Total cash collections to date, $20 million, are $6 million more than the cost of goods sold. Because $1 million of the total gross profit of the sale was recognized in Year 5, the remainder of the gross profit is recognized in Year 6.

QUESTIONS: REVENUE RECOGNITION (INCLUDING LONG-TERM CONTRACTS) AND INSTALLMENT SALES METHOD

Use the following information to answer Questions 1 and 2.

Windsor Co. (Windsor) has a contract to build a building for $100,000, with an estimated completion time of three years. A reliable cost estimate for the project would be $60,000. In the first year of the project, Windsor incurred costs totaling $24,000.

1. Under the percentage-of-completion method, in the first year Windsor will report a profit of:
    A. $16,000.
    B. $36,000.
    C. $40,000.
    D. $76,000.

2. Under the completed contract method, in the first year Windsor will report a profit of:
    A. $0.
    B. $16,000.
    C. $36,000.
    D. $40,000.

3. When accounting for long-term projects, which revenue recognition method should be used when the revenues are paid up front, but the costs, which can be estimated, will be incurred over the next three years?
    A. Sales basis method.
    B. Percentage-of-completion method.
    C. Completed contract method.
    D. Installment sales method.

4. Construction Project R has both a reliable price contract and an unknown cost estimate. Construction Project S has an unreliable cost estimate. Based on the information provided, which revenue recognition methods should be used?

	Project R	Project S
A.	Completed contract	Percentage-of-completion
B.	Completed contract	Completed contract
C.	Percentage-of-completion	Completed contract
D.	Percentage-of-completion	Percentage-of-completion

5. When accounting for long-term projects, which revenue recognition method should be used when the revenues are paid up front, but the costs are highly uncertain and will be incurred over the next three years?
    A. Sales basis method.
    B. Percentage-of-completion method.
    C. Completed contract method.
    D. Installment sales method.

6. Which of the following statements about the percentage-of-completion and completed contract methods during the life of a project is true?
   A. Reported earnings are higher under the completed contract method.
   B. The percentage-of-completion method can be used with unreliable cost estimates.
   C. The completed contract method must be used if reliable cost estimates can be obtained.
   D. Periodic profit is not recognized under the completed contract method prior to the completion of the project.

7. Rachel, Inc. (Rachel) has a $500,000 airport construction project contract. The estimated total costs are $400,000. In the first year, incurred costs are $200,000.

   What is Rachel's change in retained earnings at the end of the first fiscal year, if it uses the following revenue recognition methods?

	Percentage-of-completion	Completed contact
A.	$0	$0
B.	$50,000	$50,000
C.	$50,000	$0
D.	$100,000	$50,000

8. The following information is available for the current fiscal year of the Ashley Construction Company (Ashley):

   Ashley has a 10-year project to build a canal for $5,000,000.
   Cash received on the contract during the year was $500,000.
   Ashley incurred costs of $400,000 during the year.
   An unreliable estimate of the total project cost is $4,000,000.

   In the current fiscal year, Ashley would report gross profit for the project of:
   A. $0.
   B. $100,000.
   C. $600,000.
   D. $1,000,000.

9. Diamond, Inc. (Diamond) has a 5-year construction contract to build a canal for $600,000. The estimate of total costs is $400,000. Year 1 and Year 2 incurred costs are, respectively, $100,000 and $20,000.

   If the ultimate payment is assured and the cost estimate is reliable, which of the following realized profits would Diamond report?

	Year 1	Year 2
A.	$0	$0
B.	$10,000	$50,000
C.	$40,000	$40,000
D.	$50,000	$10,000

10.   The Linton Corporation signs a contract with the state of Missouri to build a bridge across a river. The contract price is $24 million. The company expects the job to cost $19 million. The work should occur relatively evenly over four years. In Year 1, $4 million is expended, and the estimation is then made that another $16 million will be necessary to complete the project. In Year 2, another $5 million is expended, and the estimate is that another $9 million will be needed to finish the work. If the percentage-of-completion method is to be used, what amount of profit will Linton recognize in Year 2?
A. $1,500,000.
B. $1,666,667.
C. $2,000,000.
D. $2,200,000.

11.   The Allen Construction Company is building a bridge across the Elizabeth River for the state of Virginia. The profit to be earned on the construction project is $800,000. The first year of work has been relatively uncomplicated, and the project is one-fourth completed. However, at the end of that first year, the company encounters some particularly treacherous sand deposits that have created a significant amount of uncertainty for the remainder of the work to be done. Which of the following is true?
A. Allen has the option of choosing between the percentage-of-completion method and the completed contract method.
B. No profits should be recognized at the end of the first year of the project.
C. Profits are recognized in this type of project based on the amount that has been billed by the construction company to the government.
D. A profit of $200,000 should be recognized for this first year.

12.   The Major Construction Company is building a large apartment building for $15 million. The work should take several years, so the percentage-of-completion method is being applied. The company spends $3 million in Year 1 and, at that time, expects to spend another $7 million to complete the job. In Year 2, the company spends another $2.5 million, but now believes that an additional $5.5 million will have to be spent to finish the work. What amount of profit should the company recognize in Year 2?
A. $0.
B. $500,000.
C. $909,090.
D. $2,000,000.

13.   Trojan Corporation is currently working on the first year of two long-term construction projects. Because of several uncertainty issues, the company is properly applying the completed-contract method. What amount of profit should be recognized at the end of this initial year?

	Job A-98	Job B-17
Contact price	$890,000	$790,000
Costs incurred this year	$400,000	$500,000
Estimated cost necessary to complete	$400,000	$300,000
Amounts billed to customers to date	$330,000	$470,000
Cash collections	$280,000	$450,000

   A. $10,000 loss.
   B. $6,250 loss.
   C. $0.
   D. $35,000 gain.

14.   In Year 1, James, Inc. sells a motorcycle to Wilson for $10,000. The money is to be collected over three years. Of this amount, 20% was collected in the first year and 50% in the second year. The installment sales method is being applied by James for financial reporting purposes. If the motorcycle had a book value of $4,000 to James, what is the deferred gross profit to be reported at the end of Year 2?
   A. $1,800.
   B. $2,000.
   C. $2,200.
   D. $2,400.

15.   A company holds land with a cost of $300,000 that is sold for $500,000 on January 1, Year 1. The buyer will make five annual payments of $100,000 each plus interest on the unpaid balance for the period at a 9% annual rate that is viewed as reasonable. The first payment will be made on December 31, Year 1 and each year thereafter. If the installment sales method is used for financial reporting purposes, what is the company's increase in income in Year 2 relating to this transaction?
   A. $36,000.
   B. $40,000.
   C. $76,000.
   D. $136,000.

16.   A company holds land with a cost of $300,000 that is sold for $500,000 on January 1, Year 1. The buyer will make five annual payments of $100,000 each plus interest on the unpaid balance for the period at a 9% annual rate that is viewed as reasonable. The first payment will be made on December 31, Year 1 and each year thereafter. If the cost recovery method is used for financial reporting purposes, what is the company's increase in income in Year 2?
   A. $36,000.
   B. $0.
   C. $76,000.
   D. $136,000.

17. Karr Co. began operations on January 1, Year 1 and appropriately uses the installment method of accounting for financial reporting purposes. The following information pertains to Karr's operations for Year 1:

Installment sales	$1,200,000
Collections on installment sales	$500,000
General and administrative expenses	$180,000
Cost of goods sold – installment sales	$720,000

The balance in Karr's deferred gross profit account at December 31, Year 1, should be:
A. $160,000.
B. $175,000.
C. $200,000.
D. $280,000.

18. Gant Co. (Gant), which began operations on January 1, Year 6, appropriately uses the installment method of accounting. The following information pertains to Gant's operations for Year 6:

Installment sales	$500,000
Regular sales	$300,000
Cost of installment sales	$250,000
Cost of regular sales	$150,000
General and administrative expenses	$50,000
Collections on installments sales	$100,000

On its December 31, Year 6 balance sheet, what amount should Gant report as deferred gross profit?
A. $75,000.
B. $160,000.
C. $200,000.
D. $250,000.

19. Wren Co. (Wren) sells equipment on installment contracts. Which of the following statements best justifies Wren's use of the cost recovery method of revenue recognition to account for these installment sales?
A. Sales are subject to a high rate of return.
B. There is no reasonable basis for estimating collectibility.
C. No cash payments are due until one year from the date of sale.
D. The sales contract provides that title to the equipment only passes to the purchaser when all payments have been made.

20. For financial statement purposes, the installment sales method may be used if the:
A. collection period extends over more than 12 months.
B. installments are due in different years.
C. ultimate amount collectible is indeterminate.
D. percentage-of-completion method is inappropriate.

Use the following information to answer Questions 21 and 22.

In Year 1, Markus, Inc. (Markus) sells $5,000 of goods with a total cost of $2,500 on installment. During Year 1, Markus collects $2,000 and then collects $3,000 in Year 2.

21.   Using the *cost recovery method*, how much will Markus report as gross profit in Year 1 and Year 2, respectively?

	Year 1	Year 2
A.	$1,000	$1,500
B.	$1,500	$1,000
C.	$0	$2,500
D.	$1,250	$1,250

22.   Using the *installment sales method*, how much will Markus report as gross profit in Year 1 and in Year 2, respectively?

	Year 1	Year 2
A.	$1,000	$1,500
B.	$1,500	$1,000
C.	$0	$2,500
D.	$1,250	$1,250

23.   On December 31, Year 5, L'Abbe Co. (L'Abbe) sold construction equipment to Devon Co. (Devon) for $1,800,000. The equipment had a carrying amount of $1,200,000. Devon paid $300,000 cash on December 31, Year 5 and signed a $1,500,000 note bearing interest at 10%, payable in five annual installments of $300,000.

L'Abbe appropriately accounts for the sale under the installment method. On December 31, Year 6, Devon paid $300,000 principal and $150,000 interest.

For the year ended December 31, Year 6, what total amount of revenue should L'Abbe recognize from the construction equipment sale and financing?
A. $100,000.
B. $120,000.
C. $150,000.
D. $250,000.

24.   The following information pertains to a sale of real estate for $3 million by Ryan Co. (Ryan) to Katie Co. (Katie) on December 31, Year 5:

Carrying amount on Ryan's books		$2,000,000
Sales price:		
Cash received	$300,000	
Mortgage given by Ryan	$2,700,000	$3,000,000

The mortgage is payable in nine annual installments of $300,000, beginning December 31, Year 6, plus interest of 10%. The December 31, Year 6 installment was paid as scheduled, together with interest of $270,000. Ryan uses the cost recovery method to account for this sale.

What amount of income should Ryan recognize in Year 6 from the real estate sale and its financing?
A. $0.
B. $270,000.
C. $370,000.
D. $570,000.

25.   Luge Co. (Luge), which began operations on January 2, Year 6, appropriately uses the installment sales method of accounting. The following information is available for Year 6:

Installment accounts receivable, December 31, Year 6	$800,000
Deferred gross profit, December 31, Year 6 (before recognition of realized gross profit for Year 6)	$560,000
Gross profit on sales	40%

For the year ended December 31, Year 6, what should be the cash collections and realized gross profit on sale?

	Cash collections	Realized gross profit
A.	$400,000	$320,000
B.	$400,000	$240,000
C.	$600,000	$320,000
D.	$600,000	$240,000

ANSWERS: REVENUE RECOGNITION (INCLUDING LONG-TERM CONTRACTS) AND INSTALLMENT SALES METHOD

1. **A** $24,000 costs incurred / $60,000 total expected costs = 40% of the project completed. For the first year, 40% × $100,000 = $40,000 revenue. For the period, $40,000 revenue × 40% = $16,000 profit.

2. **A** The completed contract method does not recognize any revenue until the entire project is complete.

3. **B** The percentage-of-completion method is used when there are reliable estimates of revenues and expenses.

4. **B** The completed contract method should be used when the selling price or cost estimates are unreliable, while the percentage-of-completion method can be used when collection of the contract price is assured and cost estimates are reliable. Neither Project R nor Project S meet the requirements for using percentage-of-completion.

5. **C** The completed contract method is used when estimates of costs are unreliable.

6. **D** Generally, companies with a continuing flow of profitable projects will have higher earnings (because of earlier recognition of profit) by using the percentage-of-completion method as compared to the completed contract method. The completed contract method should be used when the selling price or cost estimates are unreliable, while the percentage-of-completion method can be used when ultimate payment of the contract is assured and cost estimates are reliable. The completed contract method does not report periodic profit.

7. **C** The completed contract method does not report periodic profit. Hence, if the company uses the completed contract method, retained earnings will be $0 in Year 1. If the percentage-of-completion method is used, retained earnings will increase by $50,000 [(200,000 / 400,000) × (500,000 – 400,000)].

8. **A** Because the cost estimate is unreliable, the completed contract method for the revenue recognition should be used. This method does not recognize periodic profit prior to the completion of the contract period.

9. **D** Because ultimate payment is assured and the cost estimate is reliable, Diamond may use the percentage-of-completion method. Total expected profit is $200,000 ($600,000) – $400,000). In Year 1, 25% of the total costs of the project ($100,000 / $400,000) are incurred, hence, reported Year 1 profit is 25% × $200,000 = $50,000. In Year 2, 30% of the total costs of the project ($120,000 / $400,000) are incurred. Total profit to be recognized after two years should be $60,000 ($200,000 × 30%). In Year 1, $50,000 was recognized. Therefore, only $10,000 should be recognized in Year 2 ($60,000 – $10,000).

10. **D** At the end of the first year, the company expects the total cost to be $20 million ($4 million + $16 million). That leaves an estimated profit of $4 million ($24 million – $20 million). Because $4 million has been spent to date, the job is 20% complete ($4 million / $20 million), and $800,000 in profit should be recognized (20% × $4 million). In the second year, the company expects the total cost to be $18 million ($4 million + $5 million + $9 million). That changes the expected profit to $6 million ($24 million – $18 million). Because $9 million has been spent to date, the job is 50% complete ($9 million / $18 million), and a total profit of $3 million should be recognized (50% × $6 million). Since a profit of $800,000 was recognized in Year 1, only $2,200,000 should be recognized in Year 2.

11. **B** A company can only use the percentage-of-construction method for long-term construction projects where a reasonable estimation of the degree of completion can be made, and there are no significant uncertainties. Because of the problems with the sand deposits that were experienced at the end of the first year, there are significant uncertainties, so the completed contract method must be used. Under that method, no profits are recognized until the job is completed.

12. **B**   At the end of the first year of this job, the company will recognize a profit of $1.5 million. The company has spent $3 million out of a total expected cost of $10 million ($3 million to date + the expected additional amount of $7 million). The job is 30% completed ($3 million / $10 million) and the total expected profit is $5 million ($15 million – $10 million). Thus, for the first year, the profit to be recognized would be $1.5 million ($5 million × 30%). By the end of the second year, the company has spent a total of $5.5 million ($3 million + $2.5 million). Because another $5.5 million is expected to be spent, the total cost has escalated to $11 million, reducing the expected profit to $4 million. The job is 50% complete ($5.5 million out of a total cost of $11 million) so the profit to be recognized to date is $2 million (50% of $4 million). The company recognized $1.5 million in profit in the first year so another $500,000 should be recognized in the second year ($2 million – $1.5 million).

13. **A**   Under the completed-contract method, profits are recognized when a job is completed or when a loss can be anticipated. Job A-98 is not finished and, while a profit of $90,000 is expected, no profit at all is recognized in this initial year. However, for Job B-17, the company believes it will spend a total of $800,000 ($500,000 + $300,000) in order to get a contract price of only $790,000. The $10,000 difference is a loss and must be recognized immediately because of conservatism.

14. **A**   Initially, the deferred gross profit was $6,000 ($10,000 – $4,000) or 60%. After two years, 70% of the cash has been collected, leaving a remaining receivable balance equal to 30% of the sales price or $3,000. The portion of this balance that represents deferred gross profit is $1,800 ($3,000 × 60%) at the end of the second year.

15. **C**   In applying the installment sales method, the gross profit percentage must be determined which is the $200,000 gross profit divided by the $500,000 sales price, or 40%. A payment of $100,000 was made on the sale in Year 2 so the profit on the sale to be recognized in that year is $40,000 ($100,000 × 40%). Interest revenue must also be recognized. In the first year, $500,000 was owed but a principal payment of $100,000 was made on the last day of Year 1. The remaining $400,000 (principal for Year 2) times the 9% interest rate means that interest revenue in year two will be $36,000. Profit on the sale of $40,000 plus interest revenue of $36,000 leads to a $76,000 increase in income.

16. **B**   In the cost recovery method, no profit is recognized until cash equal to the cost of the item sold has been collected on the sales transaction. The cost of the land was $300,000, but as of the end of Year 2, only $200,000 has been collected in connection with the sale. Therefore, no profit on the sale is yet recognized. Interest on the receivable is not reported at this point in time. The deferred interest income for Year 2 is the receivable balance of $400,000 times 9% rate or $36,000. If interest has been received for Year 2, it would be considered as a reduction of the principal balance owing. If interest has not been received, it will not be accrued on the company's books. *Only* when cash receipts (interest or principal) exceed the cost of the item is profit or interest income recognized.

17. **D**   The gross profit is $480,000 ($1,200,000 in sales – $720,000 in cost of goods sold). Thus, the gross profit percentage is 40%: $480,000 / $1,200,000. The company still has $700,000 in receivables from the installment sales ($1,200,000 – collections of $500,000). Of that amount, 40% represents the gross profit that will not be recognized until the cash is collected. Deferred gross profit is $280,000, or $700,000 × 40%.

18. **C**   *Note: This question is asking for the deferred gross profit. There is a lot of information here that you will not need. Read the question carefully.*

       Under the installment sales method, gross profit is deferred at the time of sale and is recognized by applying the gross profit rate to subsequent cash collections. At the time of sale, gross profit of $250,000 is deferred ($500,000 installment sales – $250,000 cost of installment sales). The gross profit rate is 50% ($250,000 / $500,000).

       Because Year 6 collections on installment sales were $100,000, gross profit of $50,000 (50% × $100,000) is recognized in Year 6. This would decrease the deferred gross profit account to a 12/31/Year 6 balance of $200,000 ($250,000 – $50,000).

Or, you could begin with Accounts Receivable for Installment Sales of $500,000 minus collections of $100,000, leaving $400,000 not collected. Multiply the AR times the gross profit percentage of 50% to yield the answer of $200,000.

Note that regular sales, cost of regular sales, and general and administrative expenses do not affect the deferred gross profit account.

19. **B**   The installment method is used when collection of the selling price is not reasonably assured. However, when the uncertainty of collection is so great that even the use of the installment method is precluded, then the cost recovery method may be used. Having no reasonable basis for estimating collectibility would provide a great enough uncertainty to use the cost recovery method. It is important to note that any time the installment method is used, some risk of less than 100% collection exists, but the risk must be extreme before the cost recovery method is used.

20. **C**   The profit on a sale in the ordinary course of business is considered to be realized at the time of the sale unless it is uncertain whether the sale price will be collected. The use of the installment method of accounting is not acceptable unless this uncertainty exists.

21. **C**   The cost recovery method does not recognize a profit until all COGS are collected. In Year 1, $500 of COGS have yet to be collected, so no profit is recognized until Year 2.

22. **A**   Cost is 50% of sales (2,500 / 5,000 = 50%). For both years, 50% of the amount collected will be recognized as COGS with the other 50% recognized as profit.

23. **D**   The equipment sale is accounted for using the installment sales method. The gross percentage profit on the sale is 33 1/3% ($600,000 profit / $1,800,000 selling price). Because $300,000 of the sales price is collected in Year 6, gross profit of $100,000 is recognized (33 1/3% × $300,000). The total revenue recognized is $250,000 ($100,000 gross profit + $150,000 interest revenue).

24. **A**   Under the cost recovery method, no profit of any type is recognized until the cumulative receipts (principal and interest) exceeds the COGS. This means that the entire gross profit ($3,000,000 – $2,000,000 = $1,000,000) and the Year 6 interest received ($270,000) will be deferred until cash collections exceed $2,000,000. Therefore, no income is recognized in Year 6.

25. **D**   Under the installment sales method, gross profit is deferred to future periods and is recognized proportionately as cash is collected. To determine cash collections in this case, first compute the Year 6 installment sales by dividing deferred gross profit by the gross profit percentage ($560,000 / 40% = $1,400,000).

Then, the 12/31/Year 6 installment accounts receivable is subtracted to determine cash collections ($1,400,000 – $800,000 = $600,000). Realized gross profit is then computed by multiplying cash collections by the gross profit percentage ($600,000 × 40% = $240,000).

CHAPTER 12 – STRUCTURE OF AN INCOME STATEMENT

STUDY TIP

Always focus on learning the essentials of each topic. The CPA exam rarely gets into much depth on any topic, but instead prefers to focus on testing a very broad range of questions. It is better to know the essentials about every topic than to know any topic in serious depth and detail.

Chapter 12 – Structure of an Income Statement

STATEMENT OF INCOME

A. An income statement can be reported by the single-step format where all revenues and gains are listed first, followed by all expenses and losses.

B. An income statement can also be constructed using a multiple-step format.

1. Revenue from major operations are listed first, followed by cost of goods sold to arrive at gross profit.

2. Operating expenses are subtracted next. These expenses are usually presented as two categories:

    a. Selling expenses such as commissions, advertising, and bad debt expense.

    b. General and administrative expenses such as insurance, repairs, and accounting.

3. Other revenues and expenses are reported next. This category typically reports most gains and losses as well as interest revenues and interest expense.

4. Gains and losses that are unusual in nature or infrequent in occurrence are reported next.

5. For most income statements, the final reduction is for income tax expense, split into two components: current and deferred.

6. If a company is publicly held, EPS information must also be reported along with each income statement.

7. Items that are unusual or infrequent but not both should not be presented as extraordinary items. They are placed as part of income from continuing operations after normal recurring revenues and expenses. An example would be a corporate "restructuring charge" that is planned and controlled by the company's management.

8. Regardless of format, two figures are always reported at the bottom of the income statement, net of the applicable tax effect. They will all be discussed in more detail in subsequent chapters. They are:

    a. The income effect of a discontinued operation.

    b. Extraordinary gains and losses.

STATEMENT OF COMPREHENSIVE INCOME

A. A company must now produce a statement of comprehensive income in order to report all changes in the net assets of a company other than investments by owners and distributions to owners.

    1. Three alternative display options:

        a. At the bottom of the income statement by continuing from net income to arrive at a comprehensive income figure.

        b. In a separate statement that starts with net income.

        c. In the statement of changes in stockholders' equity.

    (Note that FASB prefers a or b.)

B. At present, several changes in net assets are reflected in stockholders' equity instead of within net income.

    1. Translation of the financial statements of a foreign subsidiary creates a translation adjustment.

    2. Changes in the value of marketable securities classified as available-for-sale creates an unrealized gain or unrealized loss.

    3. Recognition of prior service cost and net gains/losses related to pension plans.

C. The statement of comprehensive income starts with net income and adjusts that figure for changes during the period in each of the preceding equity figures.

    1. For example, if marketable securities that are available for sale go up in value, the change is not reported in net income but would be reported in comprehensive income.

D. The net income figure may contain items that have been previously recognized in computing comprehensive income.

    1. For example, if available-for-sale securities go up one year but are sold for a gain at the start of the following year, comprehensive income increases in the first year but net income increases in the second.

EXTRAORDINARY ITEMS

A. Extraordinary items are reported at the bottom of the income statement net of any tax effect and in a separate category after discontinued operations.

B. To be classified as extraordinary, gains and losses must have the following three characteristics:

    1. Must be material in size. That means being of a size and/or nature that will affect the decision making of an outside party.

    2. Unusual in nature.

    3. Infrequent in occurrence.

C. Certain gains and losses, such as the following, cannot be considered extraordinary:

   1. Write-offs of assets not caused by a specific external event, such as the write-off of obsolete inventory or equipment.

   2. Gains or losses created by changes in the value of a foreign currency.

   3. Gains or losses resulting from a strike.

   4. Gains or losses on extinguishment of debt, since the release of SFAS 145 in 2002, are now treated as a part of income from continuing operations.

D. Items that are unusual or frequent, but not both, do not qualify as extraordinary. An example is a restructuring charge. It should be placed as part of income from continuing operations after normal recurring revenues and expenses.

STATEMENT OF CHANGES IN EQUITY ACCOUNTS

A. As mentioned previously, there are four major categories of stockholders' equity accounts: capital stock, additional paid-in capital (APIC), retained earnings, and accumulated other comprehensive income.

B. When significant changes occur in such accounts, companies are required to disclose the changes. Most companies satisfy this requirement by issuing a statement of changes in stockholders' equity.

   1. Must show changes (in between balance sheet dates) in the number of shares and the dollar amounts.

C. As mentioned previously, the statement of changes in stockholders' equity may also be used to report comprehensive income, but this is FASB's least preferred method.

D. The change in retained earnings is shown by taking the beginning balance for the period and adding net income (or subtracting a net loss) and then subtracting any cash or stock dividends that were declared.

CORRECTION OF ERRORS

A. Errors that are made and discovered in the same year are corrected by the following:

   1. Determining the entry that was made.

   2. Determining the correct entry.

   3. Analyzing increases or decreases needed in the affected accounts.

   4. Making the correcting entry.

B. Nonsystematic errors in adjusting entries (e.g., an error in ending inventory in one period) affect two periods and are known as self-correcting (counterbalancing) errors.

   1. Example: Overstating ending inventory of Year 5 will overstate the income of Year 5 and understate the income of Year 6 (income statement errors have opposite effects in both years). At the end of Year 6, the balance sheet accounts will be correct.

C. Other errors will affect the income of several periods, such as the incorrect recording of the cost of a long-lived asset (i.e., depreciation will be misstated for all periods).

D. When an error is discovered in a period subsequent to the period in which the error occurred, an entry must be made to correct the amounts as if the error had not been made.

1. Example: An entry to accrue wages expense of $10,000 is omitted on December 31, Year 4. The effects that would be caused by such an omission are as follows:

	Year 4	Year 5	Year 6
Expense	Understated	Overstated	Correct
Net income	Overstated	Understated	Correct
Wages payable	Understated	Correct	Correct
Retained earnings	Overstated	Correct	Correct

If the company follows the policy of reversing adjusting entries for accruals, then the correction of the error any time during Year 5 will be to debit adjustment to correct error and credit wages expense. The adjustment account, when closed to retained earnings, will correct for the January 1, Year 5 overstatement in retained earnings due to the overstatement of Year 4 net income. The credit to wages expense will reduce the expense account balance for Year 5 to an amount equal to Year 5 wages payable.

If the error was discovered in Year 6, no entry would be required because the error self-corrects during Year 5. The Year 6 balances would be the same with or without the error.

E. Correction of errors meets the criteria for prior period adjustments.

1. Must adjust beginning retained earnings of single-year statements and adjust retained earnings of each year presented in comparative statements for the error effects prior to each of the years presented.

2. Note that reporting of prior years' errors is required even if a journal entry is not required because the errors have self-corrected.

3. Adjustments to the comparative years should be made to reflect retroactive application of the prior period adjustments to specific accounts affected.

F. When solving error analysis questions, note the following:

1. Be sure to distinguish between the effect of the error and the correction of the error; they are opposite. For example, a revenue overstatement means the error is a "plus" and to correct the error, one must "subtract" the amount.

2. Be sure to distinguish between an adjusting entry (a necessary part of accrual accounting) and a correcting entry (to correct errors).

QUESTIONS: STRUCTURE OF AN INCOME STATEMENT

1. Brocket Corp. (Brocket) reports operating expenses in two categories: (1) selling, and (2) general and administrative. The adjusted trial balance on December 31, Year 6, included the following expense and loss accounts:

Accounting and legal fees	$120,000
Advertising	$150,000
Freight-out	$80,000
Interest	$70,000
Loss on sale of long-term investment	$30,000
Officers' salary	$225,000
Rent for office space	$220,000
Sales salaries and commissions	$140,000

    One-half of the rented premises is occupied by the sales department.

    Brocket's total selling expenses for Year 6 are:
    A. $360,000.
    B. $370,000.
    C. $400,000.
    D. $480,000.

2. On January 1, Year 6, Bretagne, Inc. (Bretagne) installed cabinets to display its merchandise in the customers' store. Bretagne expects to use these cabinets for five years. Bretagne's Year 6 multi-step income statement should include:
    A. one-fifth of the cabinet costs in COGS.
    B. one-fifth of the cabinet costs in selling, general, and administrative expenses.
    C. all of the cabinet costs in COGS.
    D. all of the cabinet costs in selling, general, and administrative expenses.

3. The following costs were incurred by Griffin, Inc. (Griffin), a manufacturer, during Year 6:

Accounting and legal fees	$25,000
Freight-in	$175,000
Freight-out	$160,000
Officers' salaries	$150,000
Insurance	$85,000
Sales representatives' salaries	$215,000

    What amount of these costs should Griffin report as general and administrative expenses for Year 6?
    A. $260,000.
    B. $550,000.
    C. $635,000.
    D. $810,000.

4.   Craig Co.'s (Craig) income statement for the year ended December 31, Year 6, reported net income of $74,100. The auditor raised questions about the following amounts that had been included in net income:

Unrealized loss on decline in market value of noncurrent investments in stock classified as available-for-sale (net of tax)	($5,400)
Gain on early retirement of bonds payable (net of $11,000 tax effect)	$22,000
Adjustment to profits of prior years for errors in depreciation (net of $3,750 tax effect)	($7,500)
Loss from fire (net of $7,000 tax effect)	($14,000)

The loss from the fire was an infrequent but not unusual occurrence in Craig's line of business.

Craig's December 31, Year 6 income statement should report net income of:
A. $65,000.
B. $66,100.
C. $81,600.
D. $87,000.

Use the following information for Question 5 and 6.

Vine Co's trial balance of income statement accounts for the year ended December 31, year 6, included the following:

	Debit	Credit
Sales		$575,000
Cost of sales	$240,000	
Administrative expenses	70,000	
Loss on sale of equipment	10,000	
Sales commissions	50,000	
Interest revenue		25,000
Freight out	15,000	
Loss from earthquake damage	20,000	
Uncollectible accounts expense	15,000	
Totals	$420,000	$600,000

Finished goods inventory:

January 1, year 6	$400,000
December 31, year 6	360,000

- Earthquakes are rare in the area in which the company is located.
- Vine's income tax rate is 30%.

5.   In Vine's Year 6 multiple-step income statement, what amount should Vine report as the cost of goods manufactured?
      A. $200,000.
      B. $215,000.
      C. $280,000.
      D. $295,000.

6.   In Vine's Year 6 multiple-step income statement, what amount should Vine report as income after income taxes from continuing operations?
      A. $126,000.
      B. $129,500.
      C. $140,000.
      D. $147,000.

7.   Dino Co. (Dino) acquired 100% of Fred Co. (Fred) prior to Year 6. During Year 6, the individual companies included the following in their financial statements:

	Dino	Fred
Officers' salaries	$75,000	$50,000
Officers' expenses	$20,000	$10,000
Loans to officers	$125,000	$50,000
Intercompany sales	$150,000	$0

      What amount should be reported as related-party disclosures in the notes to Dino's Year 6 consolidated financial statements?
      A. $150,000.
      B. $155,000.
      C. $175,000.
      D. $330,000.

8.   At the end of Year 5, Tsui Co. (Tsui) failed to accrue sales commission earned during Year 5 but paid in Year 6. The error was not repeated in Year 6. What was the effect of this error on the following?

	Year 5 Ending Working Capital	Year 6 Ending Retained Earnings
A.	Overstated	Overstated
B.	No effect	Overstated
C.	No effect	No effect
D.	Overstated	No effect

9.   Conner, Inc. (Conner) reported a retained earnings balance of $400,000 at December 31, Year 5. In August Year 6, Conner determined that insurance premiums of $60,000 for the 3-year period beginning January 1, Year 5, had been paid and fully expensed in Year 5. Conner has a 30% income tax rate.

      What amount should Conner report as adjusted beginning retained earnings in its Year 6 statement of retained earnings?
      A. $420,000.
      B. $428,000.
      C. $440,000.
      D. $442,000.

10. During Year 6, Chapman Co. (Chapman) discovered that the ending inventories reported on its financial statements were incorrect by the following amounts:

Year 4 $60,000 understated
Year 5 $75,000 overstated

Chapman uses the periodic inventory system to ascertain year-end quantities that are converted to dollar amounts using the FIFO cost method.

Prior to any adjustments for these errors and ignoring income taxes, Chapman's retained earnings balance at January 1, Year 6 would be:
A. correctly stated.
B. $15,000 overstated.
C. $75,000 overstated.
D. $135,000 overstated.

11. Which of the following errors could result in an overstatement of both current assets and stockholders' equity?
A. An understatement of accrued sales expenses.
B. Noncurrent note receivable principal is misclassified as a current asset.
C. Understatement of annual depreciation on manufacturing machinery.
D. Holiday pay expense for administrative employees misclassified as manufacturing overhead.

12. In Year 6, hail damaged several of Sancan Co.'s (Sancan) vans. Hailstorms had frequently inflicted similar damage to Sancan's vans in the past. Over the years, Sancan had saved money by not buying hail insurance and either paying for repairs, or selling damaged vans and then replacing them. In Year 6, the damaged vans were sold for less than their carrying amounts.

How should the hail damage cost be reported in Sancan's Year 6 financial statements?
A. The actual Year 6 hail damage loss as an extraordinary loss, net of income taxes.
B. The actual Year 6 hail damage loss in continuing operations, with no separate disclosure.
C. The expected average hail damage loss in continuing operations, with no separate disclosure.
D. The expected average hail damage loss in continuing operations, with separate disclosure.

13. Kent Co. (Kent) had the following transactions during Year 6:
• $1,200,000 pretax loss on foreign currency exchange due to a major unexpected devaluation by the foreign government.
• $500,000 pretax loss from discontinued operations of a division.
• $800,000 pretax loss on equipment damaged by a hurricane. This was the first hurricane ever to strike in Kent's area. Kent also received $1,000,000 from its insurance company to replace a building, with a carrying value of $300,000, that had been destroyed by the hurricane.

What amount should Kent report in its Year 6 income statement as an extraordinary loss before income taxes?
A. $100,000.
B. $1,300,000.
C. $1,800,000.
D. $2,500,000.

14.   In Year 6, Telnor Co. (Telnor) incurred losses arising from its guilty plea in its first ever antitrust action. It also incurred losses from a substantial increase in production costs, caused when a major supplier's workers went on strike.

Which of these losses should be reported as an extraordinary item?

	Antitrust Action	Production Costs
A.	No	No
B.	No	Yes
C.	Yes	No
D.	Yes	Yes

15.   In Year 4, a company discovers that a $5,000 expense was omitted from its Year 1 income statement. In the current year, financial statements are being presented but only for Years 2, 3, and 4. How is this $5,000 reported?
A. As an adjustment to the current year income.
B. As an adjustment to Year 2 income.
C. As an adjustment to beginning retained earnings for Year 4.
D. As an adjustment to beginning retained earnings for Year 2.

16.   Which of the following should not be reported within other comprehensive income shown in stockholders' equity within a corporation's balance sheet?
A. Translation adjustment.
B. Gain or loss on sale of treasury stock.
C. Gain or loss in value of available-for-sale marketable securities.
D. Minimum pension liability adjustments in excess of any unamortized prior service cost.

17.   A company incurs a loss of $100,000 in the current year (before taxes) that was viewed as being unusual in nature but not infrequent in occurrence. The loss was reported by the company as an extraordinary item. The effective tax rate is 30%. The company reported its earnings before income taxes of $500,000. The company had no temporary or permanent tax differences. On its income statement, what amount of income tax expense should the company have reported?
A. $30,000.
B. $120,000.
C. $150,000.
D. $180,000.

18.   A company owns a building that is located near what was believed to be a dead volcano. Unfortunately, the volcano erupts and destroys the buildings, causing an uninsured loss of $3.2 million. This amount is considered material. What is the most likely method for reporting this loss?
A. On the income statement as an extraordinary loss, net of any related tax effect.
B. On the balance sheet as an item within "Accumulated Other Comprehensive Income" shown in stockholders' equity.
C. On the income statement net of any tax effect as an unusual or infrequent event.
D. On the income statement as an unusual or infrequent event but with no direct tax effect taken into consideration for reporting purposes.

ANSWERS: STRUCTURE OF AN INCOME STATEMENT

1. **D**   Advertising ($150,000) and sales salaries and commissions ($140,000) are clearly selling expenses, as is the rent for the office space occupied by the sales department ($220,000 × 0.5 = $110,000). Additionally, freight-out ($80,000) is a selling expense because shipping the goods from the point of sale to the customer is the final effort in the selling process. The total selling expense is, therefore, $480,000 ($150,000 + $140,000 + $110,000 + $80,000).

    The remaining expenses given are general and administrative expenses, except for interest and the loss on sale of long-term investment that are nonoperating items (other expenses and losses).

2. **B**   In Year 6, Bretagne would report one-fifth of the cabinet costs as depreciation expense in selling, general, and administrative expenses, while four-fifths of the cabinet cost would remain capitalized as fixed assets at the end of Year 6. The cabinets are considered fixed assets and not part of COGS.

3. **A**   Operating expenses are usually divided into two categories: selling expenses and general and administrative (G&A) expenses. Selling expenses are related to the sale of a company's products, while G&A expenses are related to the company's general operations. Therefore, Griffin should include the following costs in G&A expense:

Accounting and legal fees	$35,000
Officers' salaries	150,000
Insurance	85,000
Total	$260,000

    Freight-in ($175,000) is an inventoriable cost that should be reflected in COGS and ending inventory. Freight-out, the cost of delivering goods to customers ($160,000), is included in selling expenses. Sales representatives' salaries ($215,000) is also a selling expense.

4. **D**   Net income as reported ($74,100) properly included the gain on early retirement of bonds payable ($22,000) and the loss from fire ($14,000). The fact that the gain and loss were reported net of taxes in the income statement was incorrect, but does not cause the net income amount to be in error.

    However, the other two items should not be reported in the income statement at all. An unrealized loss on noncurrent investments in stock ($5,400) is reported in other comprehensive income, not in net income. A correction of an error ($7,500) is treated as a prior period adjustment. It is reported in the financial statements as an adjustment to the beginning balance of retained earnings, rather than in the income statement. Because both of these items were subtracted in the computation of reported net income, they must be added back to compute the correct net income of $87,000 ($74,100 + $5,400 + $7,500).

5. **A**   Cost of goods manufactured has to be computed indirectly in this case, using the cost of sales formula, as follows:

Beginning finished goods	$400,000
+ Cost of goods manufactured	?
– Ending finished goods	($360,000)
Cost of sales	$240,000

    Solving for the missing amount, cost of goods manufactured is $200,000.

6. A   All of the revenues, gains, expenses, and losses given in this question are components of income from continuing operations. Income before taxes is $180,000 as computed below:

Revenues ($575,000 + $25,000)	$600,000
Expenses and losses ($240,000 + $70,000 + $10,000	
+ $50,000 + $15,000 + $15,000 + $20,000)	(420,000)
Income before income taxes	$180,000

To compute income from continuing operations (after taxes), income taxes ($180,000 × 30% = $54,000) must also be deducted ($180,000 – $54,000 = $126,000).

7. C   The officers' salaries and expenses fall into the first category of exemptions in SFAS 57 (compensation agreements and expense allowances). The intercompany sales fall into the second category (will be eliminated on consolidation). Therefore, only the loans to officers ($125,000 + $50,000 = $175,000) are reported as related-party disclosures.

8. D   The entry that Tsui should have made to accrued sales commissions earned but unpaid at the end of its Year 5 fiscal year is as follows:

Commission expense	$XXX	
Commission payable		$XXX

Because commissions payable is a current liability, the Year 5 ending working capital is overstated due to Tsui's failure to record this entry.

Because this error was not repeated the following year, the income impact of the Year 5 error "self-corrected" during Year 6, when Tsui recorded both the earned but unpaid Year 5 commissions plus the Year 6 earned commissions. Therefore, the Year 6 ending retained earnings would not be impacted by the

9. B   A correction of an error is treated as a prior period adjustment and is reported in the financial statements as an adjustment to the beginning balance of retained earnings in the year the error is discovered. The adjustment is reported net of the related tax effect. In Year 5, insurance expense of $60,000 was recorded. The correct insurance expense should have been $20,000 ($60,000 × 1/3).

Therefore, before taxes, January 1, Year 6 retained earnings is understated by $40,000. The net of tax effect is $28,000 [$40,000 – (30% × $40,000)], so the adjusted beginning retained earnings is $428,000 ($400,000 + $28,000).

10. C   The error in understating the Year 4 ending inventory would have reversed by January 1, Year 6 (Year 4 income understated by $60,000; Year 5 income overstated by $60,000). The error in overstating the Year 5 ending inventory would not have been reversed by January 1, Year 6. This error overstates both Year 5 income and the January 1, Year 6 retained earnings balance by $75,000.

11. D   The classification of holiday pay expense for administrative employees as manufacturing overhead would result in the capitalization of some or all of these costs as a component of ending inventory, while these costs should be expensed as incurred. This error could overstate ending inventory, a current asset. The overstatement of ending inventory also understates COGS and overstates net income and stockholders' equity.

The understatement of accrued sales expenses would not affect current assets.

The misclassification of the noncurrent note receivable principal as a current asset would have no impact on stockholders' equity.

The understatement of depreciation on manufacturing machinery would understate the overhead added to inventories, a current asset.

12. **B**   The hail damage losses are both common and frequent for Sancan. Thus, estimates of the losses would not be presented in the financial statements. No amount is recorded until a loss actually occurs.

13. **A**   Foreign currency losses and losses due to discontinued operations are not considered to be unusual in nature and thus are not extraordinary. Items that may qualify as extraordinary include some casualties, expropriations, and prohibitions under a new law. Kent's casualty loss appears to be extraordinary because the hurricane was the first ever to strike in Kent's area. The net pretax loss was $100,000 [$800,000 equipment loss – the $700,000 building gain ($1,000,000 – $300,000)].

14. **C**   Telnor's loss arising from its first ever antitrust action meets both the criteria of infrequency and unusual nature (particularly because they pleaded guilty) and should therefore be reported as an extraordinary item.

   The strike against Telnor's major supplier, however, should not be reported as an extraordinary item because it is unusual in nature but may be expected to recur as a consequence of customary and continuing business activities.

15. **D**   When an error has occurred, the reported figures for that specific year must be adjusted to the correct balances. However, if the income statement for that year is not being presented, the prior period adjusted should be made to the beginning retained earnings figure for the earliest year being reported.

16. **B**   Gains and losses on the sale of treasury stock are reported as increases and decreases in additional paid-in capital. They are solely events that take place with the ownership of the company. Some losses from these types of transactions can reduce retained earnings but there is no impact on the Other Comprehensive Income section.

17. **B**   The loss was not extraordinary because it was not infrequent in occurrence. Therefore, it should have been reported separately within the operating income of the company. Its inclusion causes the earnings before income taxes to be reduced to only $400,000. Based on the 30% tax rate, the Income Tax Expense figure to be reported should be $120,000.

18. **A**   When an event occurs that is unusual in nature and infrequent in occurrence, the resulting gain or loss (if material) should be reported as an extraordinary item, net of any related tax effect. Although the words "unusual" and "infrequent" do not appear here, the eruption of a seemingly dead volcano certainly seems to meet both of those standards.

CHAPTER 13 – CONTINGENCIES AND OTHER LOSSES AND LIABILITIES

STUDY TIP

Many CPA exam candidates complain that they do not have a sufficient amount of time to study. It is important to learn to study at times that would otherwise be wasted. Study at lunch or while exercising or while waiting for the bus. If candidates can make use of these wasted moments, they usually discover that they do have enough time to adequately prepare.

CHAPTER 13 – CONTINGENCIES AND OTHER LOSSES AND LIABILITIES

LIABILITIES

PAYABLES AND ACCRUALS

Given their short-term nature, payables and accruals generally fall into the classification of current liabilities on the balance sheet.

Current liabilities are obligations whose liquidation is reasonably expected to require the use of existing resources properly classified as current assets, or the creation of other current liabilities. Following are some examples:

A. Trade accounts and notes payable incurred in the ordinary course of business. These could be amounts owed to the suppliers of operating assets such as inventories.

B. Loan obligations, including the current portions of long-term debt mature or to be paid within the year.

C. Short-term obligations—if there is not intent nor ability to refinance.

D. Dividends payable—cash dividends are a liability when declared and cannot be rescinded.

E. Accrued liabilities.

F. Payroll—obligations to employees for services rendered.

G. Property taxes—generally a monthly accrual over the fiscal period.

H. Bonus arrangements.

I. Advances from customers.

ACCRUED LIABILITIES

A. Adjusting entries to reflect the use of goods or services before paying for them.

B. Will pay in future periods even though the expense is incurred in this period.

C. Examples include property taxes and payroll. They are only physically paid at certain points in time, yet they are generally incurred evenly over a given period.

D. Journal entry is to debit an expense account (income statement) and credit a liability account (balance sheet).

DEFERRED REVENUE

A. Cash receipt precedes accrual-basis recognition.

B. Postponement of recognition of revenue where cash is received but revenue not earned.

C. An example would be an advance (or deposit) from a customer where the cash is received now but the work has not yet been completed. When the work is completed, then revenue may be recognized.

D. Journal entry is in two parts:

1. Debit cash, credit deferred revenue (initial recording).

2. Debit deferred revenue, credit revenue (when earned).

OTHER LIABILITIES

A. Compensated absences.

1. Employer may have to report a liability to employees for compensated absences such as vacations, holiday pay, and sick pay.

2. Expense and liability are recognized when the following have occurred:

   a. Employee has performed services.

   b. Payment is probable.

   c. Amounts to be paid either vest (person is entitled to money without further work) or accumulate (carry over from year to year).

B. Exit activities or disposal activities.

1. If a company plans to restructure its business by selling a line of business, closing particular locations, relocating employees, et cetera.

2. Liability occurs because of the termination of employees and contracts.

3. Liabilities for such costs should be recognized when they achieve the definition of a liability (they are probable and can be reasonably estimated).

   a. They should not be anticipated.

   b. The liability should be recognized at its fair value (often its present value).

4. The cost of one-time termination of employees should be recognized when all of the following have been met and no further work is required. This information has to have been communicated to all employees.

   a. Termination plan has been approved.

   b. Number of employees to be terminated is known along with their classifications and location. The identity of the employees to be terminated does not have to be known.

   c. Benefit plans for employees have been set.

   d. It is unlikely the plan will be changed or withdrawn.

e. If the employee must still do some work, the liability is recognized over that period of work instead of immediately.

Note that items such as deferred and current income taxes, employee benefits, financial instruments, interest costs, and leases could be classified as separate liability line items on the balance sheet or somehow lumped into "other liabilities." They will all be discussed separately in subsequent chapters, with the exception of employee benefits discussed below in this chapter.

RATIOS

A. Acid-test (quick) ratio—measures ability to pay current liabilities from cash and near-cash items. Note the following formula:

(cash + net receivables + marketable securities)/current liabilities

B. Current ratio—measures ability to pay current liabilities from cash, near-cash, and cash flow items. Note the following formula:

current assets/current liabilities

CONTINGENT LIABILITIES

A. Contingent liabilities are caused by a past event but will only result in an actual loss if a future event also occurs.

B. A good example would be pending litigation where a lawsuit has been filed but no actual loss exists until the judge or jury finds the party guilty.

C. As of the balance sheet date, if chance of a loss is probable *and* the amount reasonably subject to estimation, then the loss must be immediately recognized with an accompanying liability being recorded or an asset reduced.

1. If estimation is a range, the most likely figure within the range must be recognized.

If no figure is most likely, the lowest figure in the range is recognized with the remainder of the range disclosed in the footnotes. Following is an example:

Comox, Inc. is currently involved in litigation involving patent infringement that supposedly occurred in Year 5. The financial statements for Year 5 are being prepared and Comox's legal counsel believes it is probable that Comox will lose the lawsuit and that the damages will be in the range of $500,000 to $800,000 with the most likely amount being $700,000.

Based on legal counsel's advice, Comox should have accrued the loss contingency in the following manner as at December 31, Year 5:

Loss from litigation $700,000
      Liability from litigation $700,000

The $700,000 loss from litigation is reported on the income statement and the liability on the balance sheet.

If Comox settles the litigation in Year 6 by paying damages of $600,000, the following entry should be made:

Liability from litigation	$700,000	
Cash		$600,000
Recovery of loss from litigation		$100,000

The above entry results in a loss recovery in Year 6 because the damages were settled for less than their estimated amount—not an unusual situation because the original amount was merely an estimate.

D. Other examples of loss contingencies that may be accrued:

1. Threat of expropriation of assets.

2. Actual or possible claims and assessments.

3. Guarantees of indebtedness of others.

4. Obligations of commercial banks under "standby letters of credit."

5. Agreements to purchase receivables (or the related property) that have been sold.

E. If chance of loss is only reasonably possible (not probable) or if a reasonable estimation cannot be made, the following two procedures apply:

1. The potential for loss is disclosed in the footnotes, but nothing is accrued on the financial statements.

2. If known, the range of loss would also be disclosed.

F. If chance of loss is only remote, neither disclosure nor accrual is required. Following are some examples:

1. Risk of loss or damage of company property by fire, explosion, or other hazards.

2. General or unspecified business risks.

3. Risk of loss from catastrophes assumed by property and casualty insurance companies.

    Such losses are recorded and reported only in the period in which the event occurs that causes the loss.

    As a side note, for a gain contingency, recognition is delayed until the earnings process is substantially complete. Until then, only disclosure is permitted. Based on the principle of conservatism, contingent gains are never accrued.

G. Product warranties, a specific type of contingent liability:

The concept is best explained by the following example:

Mazo Corp. has the following sales and warranty information:

Year	Sales	Actual warranty costs	Estimated warranty costs
Year 5	$500,000	$15,000	Year of sale—4% of sales
Year 6	$700,000	$47,000	Year after sale—6% of sales

Therefore, in Year 5, Mazo should accrue a loss contingency related to product warranties of $500,000 × (4% + 6%) = $50,000.

| Warranty expense | $50,000 | |
| Liability for product warranty | | $50,000 |

The actual warranty expenditures in Year 5 would be recorded as follows:

| Liability for product warranty | $15,000 | |
| Cash | | $15,000 |

The Year 5 income statement would report an expense of $50,000 related to product warranty and the December 31, Year 5 balance sheet would report a current liability for product warranty of $35,000 ($50,000 – $15,000).

In Year 6, Mazo should accrue a loss contingency related to product warranties of $700,000 × (4% + 6%) = $70,000.

The journal entries for Year 6 are similar to the ones in Year 5—$70,000 for the warranty expense and $47,000 for the warranty liability.

The current liability balance at December 31, Year 6 is $35,000 + $70,000 – $47,000 = $58,000.

OTHER CONTINGENT LIABILITIES

A. Guarantees and coupons.

   1. These are usually recorded because:

       a. The chance of loss is probable.

       b. The amount is subject to a reasonable estimation based on past history.

   2. Amount to be paid is estimated and recognized immediately as an expense.

   3. Amount that has not yet been paid is a liability to be reported.

B. Gift certificates.

   1. Company must provide the merchandise upon redemption.

   2. Initially recorded as a liability when the customer acquires it (debit cash, credit liability).

   3. Reclassified as revenue when redeemed or when time expires.

COMMITMENTS

A. A common example would be a take-or-pay contract where the purchasing company commits to a supplier to buy:

   1. A minimum quantity of an input (usually raw materials).

   2. Over a predetermined (relatively long) period of time.

B. Such arrangements are a risk management tool and are made to ensure the availability of inputs for the company's operations in the future.

C. The price may be fixed or tied to market prices.

D. From a financial reporting standpoint, if long-term financing is involved, the purchaser must disclose in the footnotes to the financial statements two items:

1. The nature of a take-or-pay contract.

2. The minimum required payments.

E. Neither the asset nor the obligation to pay is required to be recognized on the balance sheet itself.

QUESTIONS: CONTINGENCIES AND OTHER LOSSES AND LIABILITIES

1.   Spencer, Inc. (Spencer) is preparing the financial statements for the year ended December 31, Year 6. Accounts payable amounted to $360,000 before any necessary year-end adjustment related to the following:

At December 31, Year 6, Spencer has a $50,000 debit balance in its accounts payable to Wood, Inc. (Wood), a supplier, resulting from a $50,000 advance payment for goods to be manufactured to Spencer's specifications.

Checks in the amount of $100,000 were written to vendors and recorded on December 29, Year 6. The checks were mailed on January 5, Year 7.

What amount should Spencer report as accounts payable in its December 31, Year 6 balance sheet?
A. $210,000.
B. $310,000.
C. $410,000.
D. $510,000.

2.   On March 1, Year 5, Fanny Co. (Fanny) borrowed $10,000 and signed a 2-year note bearing interest at 12% per annum compounded annually. Interest is payable in full at maturity on February 28, Year 7.

What amount should Fanny report as a liability for accrued interest at December 31, Year 6?
A. $1,000.
B. $1,200.
C. $2,200.
D. $2,320.

3.   Maui, Inc. (Maui) had a $4,000,000 note payable due on March 15, Year 6. On January 28, Year 6, before the issuance of its Year 5 financial statements, Maui issued long-term bonds in the amount of $4,500,000. Proceeds from the bonds were used to repay the note when it came due.

How should Maui classify the note in its December 31, Year 5 financial statements?
A.   As a current liability, with separate disclosure of the note refinancing.
B.   As a current liability with no separate disclosure required.
C.   As a noncurrent liability, with separate disclosure of the note refinancing.
D.   As a noncurrent liability, with no separate disclosure required.

4. Rice Co. (Rice) pays its salaried employees biweekly. Advances made to employees are paid back by payroll deductions. Information relating to salaries follows:

	12/31/05	12/31/06
Employee advances	$24,000	$36,000
Accrued salaries payable	$40,000	?
Salaries expense during the year	?	$420,000
Salaries paid during the year (gross)	?	$390,000

In Rice's December 31, Year 6 balance sheet, accrued salaries payable was:
A. $30,000.
B. $58,000.
C. $70,000.
D. $82,000.

5. Kempff Co. (Kempff) must determine the December 31, Year 6 year-end accruals for advertising and rent expenses. A $500 advertising bill was received January 7, Year 7, comprising costs of $375 for advertisements in December Year 6 issues and $125 for advertisements in January Year 7 issues of the newspaper.

A store lease, effective December 16, Year 5, calls for fixed rent of $1,200 per month, payable one month from the effective date and monthly thereafter. In addition, rent equal to 5% of net sales over $300,000 per calendar year is payable on January 31 of the following year. Net sales for Year 6 were $550,000.

In its December 31, Year 6 balance sheet, Kempff should report accrued liabilities of:
A. $12,875.
B. $13,000.
C. $13,100.
D. $13,475.

6. A retail store received cash and issued gift certificates that are redeemable in merchandise. The gift certificates lapse one year after they are issued.

How would the deferred revenue account be affected by each of the following transactions?

	Redemption of Certificates	Lapse of Certificates
A.	Decrease	No effect
B.	Decrease	Decrease
C.	No effect	No effect
D.	No effect	Decrease

7. In June Year 6, Nathan Retailers (Nathan) sold refundable merchandise coupons. Nathan received $10 for each coupon redeemable from July 1 to December 31, Year 6, for merchandise with a retail price of $11.

At June 30, Year 6, how should Nathan report these coupon transactions?
A. Unearned revenues at the merchandise's retail price.
B. Unearned revenues at the cash received amount.
C. Revenues at the merchandise's retail price.
D. Revenues at the cash received amount.

8. Marek Co. (Marek) sells appliance service contracts agreeing to repair appliances for a 2-year period. Marek's past experience is that, of the total dollars spent for repairs on service contracts, 40% is incurred evenly during the first contract year and 60% evenly during the second contract year. Receipts from service contract sales for the two years ended December 31, Year 6 are as follows:

   Year 5 $500,000
   Year 6 $600,000

   Receipts from contracts are credited to unearned service contract revenue. Assume that all contract sales are made evenly during the year.

   What amount should Marek report as unearned service contract revenue at December 31, Year 6?
   A. $360,000.
   B. $470,000.
   C. $480,000.
   D. $630,000.

9. Toddler Care Co. (Toddler) offers three payment plans on its 12-month contracts. Information on the three plans and the number of children enrolled in each plan for the September 1, Year 5 through August 31, Year 6 contract year follows:

Plan	Initial Payment per Child	Monthly Fees per Child	Number of Children
1	$500	nil	15
2	$200	$30	12
3	nil	$50	9

   Toddler received $9,900 of initial payments on September 1, Year 6 and $3,240 of monthly fees during the period September 1 through December 31, Year 6.

   In its December 31, Year 6 balance sheet, what amount should Toddler report as deferred revenues?
   A. $3,300.
   B. $4,380.
   C. $6,600.
   D. $9,900.

10. On January 17, Year 6, an explosion occurred at a Sarnia Co. (Sarnia) plant causing extensive property damage to area buildings. Although no claims had yet been asserted against Sarnia by March 10, Year 6, Sarnia's management and legal counsel concluded that it is likely that claims will be asserted and that it is reasonably possible Sarnia will be responsible for damages.

   Sarnia's management believed that $1,250,000 would be a reasonable estimate of its liability. Sarnia's $5,000,000 comprehensive public policy has a $250,000 deductible clause.

   In Sarnia's December 31, Year 5 financial statements, which were issued on March 25, Year 6, how should this item be reported?
   A. As an accrued liability of $250,000.
   B. As a footnote disclosure indicating the possible loss of $250,000.
   C. As a footnote disclosure indicating the possible loss of $1,250,000.
   D. No footnote disclosure or accrual is necessary.

11.   Bryce Co. (Bryce) has the following liabilities at December 31, Year 5:

Accounts payable	$55,000
Unsecured notes, 8%, due 7/1/Year 6	$400,000
Accrued expenses	$35,000
Contingent liability	$450,000
Deferred income tax liability	$25,000
Senior bonds, 7%, due 3/31/Year 6	$1,000,000

The contingent liability is an accrual for possible losses on a $1,000,000 lawsuit filed against Bryce. Bryce's legal counsel expects the suit to be settled in Year 7, and has estimated that Bryce will be liable for damages in the range of $450,000 to $750,000.

The deferred income tax liability is not related to any particular asset for financial reporting and is expected to reverse in Year 8.

What amount should Bryce report in its December 31, Year 5 balance sheet for current liabilities?
A. $515,000.
B. $940,000.
C. $1,490,000.
D. $1,515,000.

12.   On February 5, Year 6, an employee filed a $2,000,000 lawsuit against Skywalker, Inc. (Skywalker) for damages suffered when one of Skywalker's plants exploded on December 29, Year 5. Skywalker's legal counsel expects the company will lose the lawsuit and estimates the loss to be between $500,000 and $1,000,000. The employee has offered to settle the lawsuit out of court for $900,000, but Skywalker will not agree to the settlement.

In its December 31, Year 5 balance sheet, what amount should Skywalker report as a liability from the lawsuit?
A. $500,000.
B. $900,000.
C. $1,000,000.
D. $2,000,000.

13.   On November 5, Year 6, a Dunn Corp. (Dunn) truck was in an accident with an auto driven by Kathy Wolfe (Wolfe). Dunn received notice on January 12, Year 7, of a lawsuit for $700,000 damages for personal injuries suffered by Wolfe. Dunn's legal counsel believes that Wolfe will be awarded an estimated amount in the range between $200,000 and $450,000, and that $300,000 is a better estimate of potential liability than any other amount.

Dunn's accounting year ends on December 31 and the Year 6 financial statements were issued on March 2, Year 7.

What amount of loss should Dunn accrue at December 31, Year 6?
A. $0.
B. $200,000.
C. $300,000.
D. $450,000.

14. In May 2002, Alexei Co. (Alexei) filed suit against Koltakov, Inc. (Koltakov) seeking $1,900,000 of damages for patent infringement. A court verdict in November Year 6 awarded Alexei $1,500,000 in damages but Koltakov's appeal is not expected to be decided before Year 8. Alexei's counsel believes it is probable that Alexei will be successful against Koltakov for an estimated amount in the range between $800,000 and $1,100,000, with $1,000,000 considered the most likely amount.

   What amount should Alexei record as income from the lawsuit in the year ended December 31, Year 6?
   A. $0.
   B. $800,000.
   C. $1,000,000.
   D. $1,500,000.

15. North Corp. (North) has an employee benefit plan for compensated absences that gives employees 10 paid vacation days and 10 paid sick days. Both vacation and sick days can be carried over indefinitely. Employees can elect to receive payment in lieu of vacation days; however, no payment is given for sick days not taken.

   At December 31, Year 6, North's unadjusted balance of liability for compensated absences was $21,000. North estimated that there were 150 vacation days and 75 sick days available on that date. North's employees earn an average of $100 per day.

   In its December 31, Year 6 balance sheet, what amount of liability for compensated absences is North *required* to report?
   A. $15,000.
   B. $21,000.
   C. $22,500.
   D. $36,000.

16. Gable Co. (Gable) grants all employees two weeks of paid vacation for each full year of employment. Unused vacation time can be accumulated and carried forward to succeeding years and will be paid at the salaries in effect when vacations are taken or when employment is terminated. There was no employee turnover in Year 6.

   Additional information relating to the year ended December 31, Year 6, is as follows:

Liability for accumulated vacations at 12/31/Year 5	$35,000
Pre-Year 6 accrued vacations taken from 1/1/Year 6 to 9/30/Year 6 (the authorized period for vacations)	$20,000
Vacations earned for work in Year 6 (adjusted to current rates)	$30,000

   Gable granted a 10% salary increase to all employees on October 1, Year 6, its annual salary increase date.

   For the year ended December 31, Year 6, Gable should report vacation pay expense of:
   A. $30,000.
   B. $31,500.
   C. $33,500.
   D. $45,000.

17.   Vadim Co. (Vadim) sells appliances that include a 3-year warranty. Service calls under the
        warranty are performed by an independent mechanic under a contract with Vadim. Based on
        experience, warranty costs are estimated at $30 for each machine sold.

        When should Vadim recognize these warranty costs?
        A. Evenly over the life of the warranty.
        B. When the service calls are performed.
        C. When payments are made to the mechanic.
        D. When the machines are sold.

18.   Case Cereal Co. (Case) frequently distributes coupons to promote new products. On October 1,
        Year 6, Case mailed 1,000,000 coupons for $0.45 off each box of cereal purchased. Case expects
        120,000 of these coupons to be redeemed before the December 31, Year 6 expiration date. It takes
        30 days from the redemption date for Case to receive the coupons from the retailers. Case
        reimburses the retailers an additional $0.05 for each coupon redeemed.

        As of December 31, Year 6, Case had paid retailers $25,000 related to these coupons and had
        50,000 coupons on hand that had not been processed for payment.

        What amount should Case report as a liability for coupons in its December 31, Year 6 balance
        sheet?
        A. $22,500.
        B. $25,000.
        C. $29,000.
        D. $35,000.

19.   Yang Co.'s (Yang) trial balance included the following account balances at December 31, Year 6:

Accounts payable	$15,000
Bonds payable, due Year 7	$25,000
Discount on bonds payable, due Year 7	$3,000
Dividends payable 1/31/07	$8,000
Notes payable, due Year 8	$20,000

        What amount should be included in the current liability section of Yang's December 31, Year 6
        balance sheet?
        A. $45,000.
        B. $51,000.
        C. $65,000.
        D. $78,000.

20.   A company has a contingent loss. At the end of Year 1, it is probable that the company will lose
        between $100,000 and $120,000, but it is also reasonably possible that the loss could be between
        $120,000 and $200,000. No figure within either of these ranges is more likely than any other
        figure. In Year 2, the contingency is settled for a loss of $118,000. What income statement effect
        should this company recognize in Year 2?
        A. $2,000 gain.
        B. $82,0000 gain.
        C. $18,000 loss.
        D. $8,000 loss.

21. On December 1, Year 1, a company indicates that it will fire 10% of its workforce. The terminations will initially cost the company $3 million but are expected to save $4 million annually in the future. The company is trying to decide when to recognize a liability for the costs of these terminations. Which of the following is not a requirement for recognizing this liability?
    A. Number of employees to be fired is known along with their company classifications.
    B. The identity of the employees to be fired is known.
    C. Benefit plans for employees have been set.
    D. The plan is unlikely to be changed or withdrawn.

22. A company sells toasters for $40 each. During Year 1, the company sold 10,000 toasters. Each toaster carries a warranty which requires the company to fix the toaster if it breaks within 12 months of its sales date. The company estimates that 6% of the toasters will break within that time period and cost $15 each to fix. During Year 1, 250 toasters break and are fixed for $15 each. During Year 2, another 400 toasters break; however, they cost $16 each to fix. What expense does the company recognize in Year 2?
    A. $0.
    B. $800.
    C. $1,150.
    D. $6,400.

23. The Coleman Corporation incurs a contingent liability during Year 1. At the end of Year 1, company officials believe it is probable that between $90,000 and $110,000 will be lost with no number within that range any more likely than any other number. These officials also believe it is reasonably possible that the loss could be as much as $140,000. Late in Year 2, Coleman settles the liability for $136,000. What is the change in income reported by Coleman in Year 2?
    A. $4,000 gain.
    B. $26,000 loss.
    C. $36,000 loss.
    D. $46,000 loss.

24. During Year 1, Smith Corporation filed suit against West Company because of damages that were allegedly inflicted on Smith. At the end of that year, officials of Smith believe it is reasonably possible that between $300,000 and $400,000 will be won but probable that the amount will actually be between $160,000 and $300,000. No number in either range stands out as more likely than any other number. Officials working for West have exactly the same opinion of what is going to happen. In the later part of Year 2, the case is settled when West pays Smith $280,000 in cash. What is the impact on income reported by these companies in Year 2?

	Smith	West
A.	$120,000 gain	$20,000 gain
B.	$280,000 gain	$120,000 gain
C.	$280,000 gain	$120,000 loss
D.	$120,000 gain	$50,000 loss

ANSWERS: CONTINGENCIES AND OTHER LOSSES AND LIABILITIES

1. **D** The $50,000 advance payment should be reclassified as a current asset, Advance to Suppliers. The checks recorded on 12/29/06 incorrectly reduced the accounts payable balance by $100,000. The $100,000 reduction should not have been recorded until the checks were mailed on 1/5/07. The 12/31/06 accounts payable must be increased by $100,000. Therefore, the corrected 12/31/06 accounts payable is $510,000 ($360,000 + $50,000 + $100,000).

2. **D** Accrued interest payable at 12/31/06 is interest expense which has been incurred by 12/31/06, but has not yet been paid by that date. The notes were issued on 3/1/05 and interest is payable in full at maturity at 2/28/05. Therefore, there is 1 year and 10 months of unpaid interest at 12/31/06.

   Interest for the first year is $1,200 ($10,000 × 12%). Because interest is compounded annually, the new principal amount for the second year includes the original principal ($10,000) plus the first year's interest ($1,200). Therefore, accrued interest for the ten months ended 12/31/06 is $1,120 ($11,200 × 12% × 10/12) and total accrued interest at 12/31/06 is $2,320 ($1,200 + $1,120).

3. **C** The $4,000,000 note is due March 15, Year 6, and would normally be classified as a current liability in the December 31, Year 5 financial statements. However, SFAS 6 states that a short-term obligation can be reclassified as long-term if the company intends to refinance the obligation on a long-term basis and the intent is supported by the ability to refinance.

   Maui demonstrated its ability to refinance by actually issuing bonds and refinancing the note prior to the issuance of the December 31, Year 5 financial statements. Since the proceeds from the bonds exceeded the amount needed to retire the note, the entire $4,000,000 notes payable would be classified as a noncurrent liability, with separate disclosure of the note refinancing required by SFAS 6.

4. **C** A key to solving this problem is understanding that the employee advances do not affect the accrued salaries payable. When advances are made to employees, they are a cash payment separate from the payroll function. The advances made, therefore, are not reflected in salaries expense ($420,000) or gross salaries paid ($390,000).

   Analyze the salaries payable account as follows: Beginning salaries payable balance ($40,000) is increased by salaries expense ($420,000) and decreased by salaries paid ($390,000), resulting in a 12/31/06 balance of $70,000.

5. **D** An accrued liability is an expense which has been incurred but has not yet been paid. Of the $500 advertising bill, $375 has been incurred as an expense as of 12/31/06 and should be reported as an accrued liability at that time.

   For the store lease, the fixed portion ($1,200 per month) is payable on the 16th of each month for the preceding month. Therefore, on 12/16/06, rent was paid for the period 11/16/06 to 12/15/06. An additional one-half month's rent expense (1/2 × $1,200 = $600) has been incurred but not paid as of 12/31/06.

   The variable portion of the rent [5% × ($550,000 − $300,000) = $12,500] was incurred during Year 6, but will not be paid until 1/31/07. It, too, is an accrued liability at 12/31/06. Total 12/31/06 accrued liabilities are $13,475.

Advertising	$375
Fixed rent	$600
Variable rent	$12,500
Total	$13,475

6. **B** When a company issues gift certificates for cash, the following journal entry is made: debit cash, credit deferred revenue. When the gift certificates are subsequently redeemed, the following journal entry is made: debit deferred revenue, credit revenue. However, if the gift certificates are not redeemed and lapse, the following journal entry is made: debit deferred revenue, credit gain on lapse of certificates.

Note that although different accounts are credited depending on whether the certificates are redeemed or lapsed, the deferred revenue account is decreased in both cases.

7.   **B**   At June 30, Year 6, Nathan should report the coupon transactions as unearned revenues because the sale of the coupons is not the culmination of the earnings process (i.e., Nathan must allow customers to exchange the coupons for merchandise or refund the cost of the coupons at some later date). The unearned revenues should be recorded at the amount of the cash received by debiting cash and crediting an unearned revenue account.

The retail price of the merchandise for which coupons may be redeemed does not impact the monetary amount of Nathan's liability to its customers, and each coupon redeemed will ultimately result in the recognition of sales of $10, the amount of cash previously received.

8.   **D**   All contract sales are made evenly during the year. Therefore, the Year 5 contracts range from one year expired (if sold on 12/31/05) to two years expired (if sold on 1/1/05), for an average of 1.5 years expired [(2 + 1)/2].

Similarly, the Year 6 contracts range from zero years expired to one year expired, for an average of 0.5 years expired [(0 + 1)/2].

The average unearned portion of the Year 5 contracts is 0.5 years, the last half of the second contract year. The amount of unearned revenue related to Year 5 contracts is computed as follows: $500,000 × 60% × 1/2 = $150,000.

The average unearned portion of the Year 6 contracts is 1.5 years, the last half of the first contract year and all of the second contract year. The amount of unearned revenue related to the Year 6 contracts is computed as follows: ($600,000 × 40% × 1/2) + ($600,000 × 60%) = $480,000.

9.   **C**   Revenue is earned by Toddler as time goes by and care is provided. Therefore, revenue should be recognized on a straight-line basis regardless of the timing of cash receipts. The monthly fees can simply be recognized on a monthly basis, but the initial payment must be deferred and recognized as revenue on a straight-line basis over the 12-month period. The 12/31/06 deferred revenues are $6,600 as computed below:

($500 × 8/12 × 15) + ($200 × 8/12 × 12) = $6,600.

Because the total initial payments received are given $9,900, a shortcut is to simply multiply that amount by 8/12.

10. **B**   Per SFAS 5, a loss contingency should be accrued if it is probable that a liability has been incurred at the balance sheet date and the amount of the loss is reasonably estimable. With respect to unfiled claims, the company must consider the probability of an unfavorable outcome. Although it is probable that claims will be asserted against Sarnia, it is only reasonably possible that the claims will be successful.

Therefore, this contingent liability should not be accrued, but it should be disclosed. The potential loss to be disclosed is $250,000 because the additional amount above the deductible would be covered by the insurance policy, and therefore it is not a loss or a liability for Sarnia. The explosion occurred after December 31, Year 5.

11. **C**   ARB 43 states that current liabilities are obligations whose liquidation is reasonably expected to require the use of current assets or the creation of other current liabilities. This means that, generally, current liabilities are the liabilities that are due within one year of the balance sheet date.

Clearly, accounts payable ($55,000) and accrued expenses ($35,000) are current liabilities. Notes payable ($400,000) and bonds payable ($1,000,000) are usually considered to be long-term, but the maturity dates given (7/1/Year 6 and 3/31/Year 6 respectively) indicate they are current liabilities at 12/31/Year 5.

The contingent liability ($450,000) and deferred tax liability ($25,000) will not be settled until Year 7 and Year 8 and, therefore, should be classified as long-term at 12/31/Year 5.

Thus, the 12/31/Year 5 current liabilities total is $1,490,000.

12. **A** The lawsuit damages must be accrued as a loss contingency in accordance with SFAS 5 because an unfavorable outcome is probable and the amount of the loss is reasonably estimable. Per FASB Interpretation 14, when a range of possible loss exists, the best estimate within the range is accrued. When no other amount within the range is a better estimate than any other amount, the dollar amount at the low end of the range is accrued (in this case, $500,000) and the dollar amount of the high end of the range is disclosed.

13. **C** Per SFAS 5, a loss contingency should be accrued if it is probable that a liability has been incurred at the balance sheet date and the amount of the loss is reasonably estimable. This loss must be accrued because it meets both criteria.

Notice that even though the lawsuit was not initiated until 1/12/07, the liability was incurred on 11/5/06 when the accident occurred.

FASB Interpretation 14 requires that when some amount within an estimated range is a better estimate than any other amount in the range, that amount is accrued. Therefore, a loss of $300,000 should be accrued. If no amount within the range is a better estimate than any other amount, the amount at the low end of the range is accrued and the amount at the high end is disclosed.

14. **A** SFAS 5 states that gain contingencies are not reflected in the accounts until realized. Since the case is unresolved at 12/31/06, none of this contingent gain should be recorded as income in Year 6. Adequate disclosure should be made of the gain contingency, but care should be taken to avoid misleading implications as to the likelihood of realization.

15. **A** SFAS 43 states that accrual of a liability for future vacation pay is required if all four conditions below are met:
    1. Obligation arises from employee services already performed.
    2. Obligation arises from rights that vest or accumulate.
    3. Payment is probable.
    4. Amount can be reasonably estimated.

    The criteria are met for the vacation pay ($150 \times \$100 = \$15,000$), so North is required to report a $15,000 liability. The same criteria apply to accrual of a liability for future sick pay, except that if sick pay benefits accumulate but do not vest, accrual is permitted but not required because its payment is contingent upon future employee sickness. Therefore, no liability is required for these sick pay benefits ($75 \times \$100 = \$7,500$).

    Note that the unadjusted balance of the liability account ($21,000) does not affect the computation of the required 12/31/06 liability.

16. **B** Per SFAS 43, an employer is required to accrue a liability for employees' rights to receive compensation for future absences, such as vacations, when certain conditions are met. The Statement does not, however, specify how such liabilities are to be measured. Because vacation time is paid by Gable at the salaries in effect when vacations are taken or when employment is terminated, Gable adjusts its vacation liability and expense to current salary levels.

    Gable's Year 6 vacation pay expense consists of vacations earned for work in Year 6 (adjusted to current rates) of $30,000 plus the amount necessary to adjust its pre-Year 6 vacation liability for the 10% salary increase. The amount of this adjustment is equal to 10% of the preexisting liability balance at December 31, Year 6 [($35,000 – $20,000) × 10% = $1,500]. Therefore, total vacation pay expense for the period is equal to $31,500.

17. **D** The warranty expense of $30 for each machine sold, although it will be incurred over the three-year warranty period, is directly related to the sales revenue as an integral and inseparable part of the sale and recognized at the time of the sale.

    The warranty costs make their contribution to revenue in the year of sale by making the product more attractive to the customer. Therefore, in accordance with the matching principle, the warranty costs should be expensed when the machines are sold with a corresponding credit to accrued liabilities.

18. **D**   Case expects 120,000 coupons to be redeemed at a total cost of $0.50 per coupon ($0.45 + $0.05). Therefore, total expected redemptions are $60,000 (120,000 × $0.50). By 12/31/06, $25,000 has been paid on coupon redemptions, so a liability of $35,000 must be established ($60,000 – $25,000). Note that this liability would include both payments due for the 50,000 coupons on hand, and payments due on coupons to be received within the first 30 days after the expiration date.

19. **A**   ARB 43 states that current liabilities are obligations whose liquidation is reasonably expected to require the use of current assets or the creation of other current liabilities. This means that generally, current liabilities are liabilities due within one year of the balance sheet date.

    Clearly, accounts payable ($15,000) and dividends payable ($8,000) are current liabilities. Generally, bonds payable are a long-term liability; however, because these bonds are due in Year 7, they must be reported as a current liability at 1/31/Year 7 ($25,000 fair value less $3,000 discount = $22,000). Therefore, total current liabilities are $45,000 ($15,000 + $8,000 + $22,000). The notes payable ($20,000) are classified as long-term because they are not due until Year 8.

20. **C**   For a contingency, a probable loss is recognized. When that number can only be estimated to within a range, the most likely figure within that range is used. However, if no number in the range is most likely, the lowest number should be recognized. Thus, in Year 1, a loss of $100,000 is recognized. In Year 2, when the actual loss turned out to be $118,000, an additional loss of $18,000 had to be recognized.

21. **B**   A number of requirements must be met before a liability must be recognized for termination costs. However, the specific identity of the people to be terminated is not necessary for the amount of the liability to be reported.

22. **C**   Because of the matching principle, the company estimates and recognizes an expense in Year 1 of $9,000 (600 toasters expected to break × $15 each in cost). Eventually, though, that cost amounts to $10,150 (250 toasters × $15 plus 400 toasters × $16). The extra $1,150 in expense is recognized in Year 2 when it became known that the originally estimation was wrong and had to be adjusted.

23. **D**   In Year 1, Coleman should recognize a contingent liability of $90,000. When a company can only estimate a contingent loss within a range and no number in that range is more likely, the lowest number is recognized. When the contingency is eventually settled for $136,000, the additional $46,000 loss must be recognized.

24. **C**   As the potential winner, Smith will recognize no gain until the process is substantially completed. That happens in Year 2. Therefore, the entire profit is recognized when the case is settled in Year 2.

    As the potential loser, West will recognize a loss as soon as the amount becomes probable. Here, that is in Year 1. When the amount can only be estimated to within a range, the most likely number in the range is used. If no number is most likely, the lowest number in the range is recognized. For that reason, West recognized a $160,000 loss in Year 1 which then had to be increased in Year 2 by $120,000 to arrive at the actual figure of $280,000.

CHAPTER 14 – ACCOUNTING FOR INCOME TAXES

STUDY TIP

The biggest enemy that any CPA exam candidate faces is procrastination. Adequate preparation requires a significant number of hours. It is easy to put off doing the studying that is necessary. There is always something that absolutely has to be done prior to studying: paying the bills, washing the dishes, taking out the garbage, mowing the grass, etc. Eventually, the dishes get washed but the candidate never manages to get around to studying. Study first so you can avoid procrastination.

CHAPTER 14 – ACCOUNTING FOR INCOME TAXES

FUNDAMENTALS OF DEFERRED TAX THEORY

A. There is pretax financial (book) income that follows GAAP, and there is taxable income that follows the Internal Revenue Code (IRC).

B. Pretax financial (book) income usually differs from taxable income so that income tax expense based on GAAP is not equal to income taxes payable based on the IRC.

C. Income tax expense equals the taxes actually owed (a current tax liability: income taxes payable) for the current period plus or minus the change during the current period in amounts payable in the future and in future tax benefits.

   1. By using this procedure, any possible income statement or balance sheet distortion that may result from differences in timing of revenue recognition or expense deductibility and asset or liability valuation between GAAP and the IRC is avoided.

TERMS USED IN ACCOUNTING FOR INCOME TAXES—TAX RETURN TERMINOLOGY

A. Taxable income.

   1. Income subject to tax based on the tax return.

B. Taxes payable (equal to current tax expense—see below).

   1. The tax liability on the balance sheet caused by taxable income.

   2. Taxable income times the tax rate.

C. Income tax paid.

   1. Actual cash flow for income taxes, including payments or refunds for other years.

D. Tax loss carryforward.

   1. The current net taxable loss that is used to reduce taxable income (and thus, taxes payable) in future years.

TERMS USED IN ACCOUNTING FOR INCOME TAXES—FINANCIAL REPORTING TERMINOLOGY

A. Pretax income.

   1. Financial statement income before the deduction of income tax expense.

B. Income tax expense.

   1. The expense recognized on the income statement that includes both taxes payable (or current expense) and deferred tax expense or deferred tax benefit.

   2. Essentially, it is cash taxes plus noncash items such as the change in deferred taxes.

C. Current tax expense (equal to taxes payable—see above).

   1. Cash taxes payable in the current period.

D. Deferred tax expense.

   1. The difference between income tax expense and current tax expense.

   2. Results from changes in deferred tax assets and liabilities.

DIFFERENCES (TEMPORARY AND PERMANENT DIFFERENCES)

A. Temporary differences.

   1. Some revenues and expenses are recognized for external financial reporting purposes in one period, but tax recognition occurs in a different period.

      a. These are referred to as *temporary differences* because they are expected to reverse themselves in future years.

      b. The most common way that temporary differences are created is when different depreciation methods are used on the tax return and the income statement.

   2. A temporary difference leads to a *deferred tax liability* if taxable income will be higher than book (accounting) income in the future, due to this particular temporary difference.

      a. A deferred tax liability indicates that a relatively higher tax payment (cash outflow) will be made in the future as compared to the GAAP-based calculation of expense now.

      b. Deferred tax liabilities are created when more expense is deducted on the tax return relative to the financial statements, leading to lower taxable income now and lower taxes payable on the tax return relative to the financial statements.

      c. Examples of lower taxable income now and higher taxable income later include:
         - Using different depreciation methods for external reporting and taxes (accelerated tax depreciation versus straight-line depreciation for GAAP-based financial statements in the early years of an asset's life—yielding a taxable income lower than the book income because the tax deduction is higher than the income statement expense). *Note: This is a temporary difference because over the life of the asset, the depreciation could very well be the same for tax and book purposes.* So, in the future, the "difference" will, as we say, "reverse itself."
         - Using accrual accounting for external reporting of sales (accelerated recognition), but the installment sales method for taxes (slower recognition). This results in higher book income now, but higher taxable income later.

- Using the equity method for the external reporting of an investment (accelerated recognition), but dividends collected for taxes (slower recognition)—this assumes a positive equity pick-up figure, of course. This results in higher book income now, but higher taxable income later.

3. A temporary difference leads to a *deferred tax asset* if taxable income will be lower than book income in the future, due to that temporary difference item.

   a. A deferred tax asset indicates a future benefit because income expected to be taxed will be relatively lower in the future as compared to book income.

   b. Deferred tax assets are created when less expense is deducted on the tax return, leading to higher taxable income now and greater taxes payable relative to the financial statements. Upon reversal in the future, the tax deduction will exceed the financial statement expense.

   c. Examples of higher taxable income now and lower taxable income later include:

      - Estimated warranty and contingency expense may be accrued on the financial statements, but it is not deductible currently. This creates a deferred tax asset because the asset represents the future tax savings that will result when the deduction is actually taken (when the warranty expense is actually paid).
      - Estimating bad debts for external reporting (accelerated deduction), but using actual losses for taxes (deduction later)—very similar treatment as above.
      - Recognizing revenues as earned for external reporting (slower recognition) but cash revenues collected in advance for tax (earlier recognition). Cash revenues are taxable on the tax return upon receipt.

   d. A tax loss carryforward is an example of a deferred tax asset that would lower taxable income later but did not arise from higher taxable income now.

   e. Following is a handy tip for remembering this:

      - Make a "pretend" journal entry to debit tax expense (a GAAP item) and credit tax payable (an IRS item).
      - If taxable income is expected to exceed GAAP income, that "pretend" journal entry will have a bigger credit (tax payable) than debit (tax expense). To balance the entry, you need a debit, or a deferred tax asset.
      - If taxable income is expected to be less than GAAP income, that "pretend" journal entry will have a bigger debit (expense) than credit (tax payable). To balance the entry, you need a credit, or a deferred tax liability.
      - Differences between the tax expense (GAAP) and the tax payable (IRS) can result from differences in expenses or differences in income for GAAP versus IRS.

B. Permanent differences.

1. Permanent differences between book income and taxable income will cause no future differences between book income and taxable income. Thus, they will not give rise to deferred tax assets or liabilities.

2. Examples of items that create permanent differences include:

   a. Municipal bond interest and life insurance are included in book income but never in taxable income.

   b. Federal taxes are expenses on the books but are not deductible for tax purposes. The same is true of life insurance premiums if the company is the beneficiary of the policy.

   c. A portion of dividends received from another domestic company is recognized but never taxed.

- This dividends-received deduction (DRD) is 70%, if less than 20% of the company is owned.
- The DRD is 80%, if 20% up to 80% of the company is owned.
- The DRD is 100% if 80% or more of the company is owned.

APPLICATION

A. A balance sheet approach is used for recognizing deferred taxes.

1. The amounts of all expected future temporary differences are scheduled each year, and deferred tax assets and liabilities are computed.

2. The changes in these accounts create the deferred income tax expense to be recognized.

B. Example to demonstrate the scheduling process is as follows:

An asset costs $200,000, has a depreciable life of four years, and has zero salvage value. It is expected to produce $150,000 in annual revenue. It is depreciated by the double declining balance (DDB) method for tax purposes and by the straight line method for financial reporting purposes.

Using the DDB method, depreciation will be $100,000, $50,000, $25,000, and $25,000 in each of the next four years. The relevant tax rate is 40%.

Tax return reporting

	Year 1	Year 2	Year 3	Year 4	Total
Revenue	$150K	$150K	$150K	$150K	$600K
Depreciation	$100K	$50K	$25K	$25K	$200K
Taxable income	$50K	$100K	$125K	$125K	$400K
Taxes payable	$20K	$40K	$50K	$50K	$160K
Net income	$30K	$60K	$75K	$75L	$240K

Financial statement reporting

	Year 1	Year 2	Year 3	Year 4	Total
Revenue	$150K	$150K	$150K	$150K	$600K
Depreciation	$50K	$50K	$50K	$50K	$200K
Pretax income	$100K	$100K	$100K	$100K	$400K
Income tax expense	$40K	$40K	$40K	$40K	$160K
Net income	$60K	$60K	$60K	$60K	$240K

The difference between pretax income on the financial statements, and taxable income on the tax return is attributable to different accounting treatments. For example, in Year 1, the difference between income tax expense and taxes payable is $40,000 – $20,000 = $20,000. Because the differences are expected to reverse, a balance sheet perspective recognizes a liability in the early years equal to the amount of tax that must eventually be paid back in later years.

The company will schedule out the following deferred tax liabilities on a worksheet and ultimately report them on the balance sheet:

	Year 1	Year 2	Year 3	Year 4
Income tax expense	$40K	$40K	$40K	$40K
Taxes payable	$20K	$40K	$50K	$50K
Deferred tax expense	$20K	$0	($10K)	($10K)
Deferred tax liability (per balance sheet)	$20K	$20K	$10K	$0

FINANCIAL REPORTING OF INCOME TAX AMOUNTS—SUMMARY

A. Items within book income for the current year are listed, and for each item, the list should have a current tax effect, a future tax effect, or no tax effect.

B. Temporary differences from past years are also included to show how they impact either current taxable income or future taxable income.

C. All items currently taxable are netted and multiplied by the enacted tax rate to get the current income tax payable and expense. These amounts are recognized on the financial statements.

D. For all future years, anticipated tax effects are determined and multiplied by the *enacted* future tax rates to get the various deferred tax asset and liability balances. For any deferred assets, the need for a valuation allowance is also determined.

E. At the end of each year, any (1) previous deferred tax liability, (2) deferred tax asset, and (3) valuation allowance already on the books are adjusted to the newly determined balances. The net amount of change is the deferred income tax expense figure recognized in the income statement.

TAX RATES—ALWAYS USE ENACTED TAX RATES

A. If the enacted tax rate increases, the following occurs:

   1. The increase in deferred tax liabilities increases the deferred tax expense, or the increase in deferred tax assets decreases the deferred tax expense.

   2. As long as deferred tax liabilities exceed deferred tax assets (generally the most common occurrence), the net impact of the increase in the tax rate will be to increase deferred tax expense, and that will increase income tax expense and decrease net income.

B. The opposite effects will occur if the tax rate decreases.

VALUATION ALLOWANCE FOR DEFERRED TAX ASSETS

A. Because of the conservative nature of accounting, recognition of a deferred tax asset requires a company to also consider recognition of a contra-account or allowance-account (called a *valuation allowance*) to reduce the reported value of an asset.

B. For deferred tax assets to be beneficial, the company must have future taxable income. An example of this would be a tax loss carryforward from prior years applied to taxable income in future years.

   1. If a company believes that it is more likely than not (over 50% likelihood) that it will generate sufficient taxable income for the temporary difference to reduce, no valuation allowance is needed.

   2. If it is more likely than not that the company will *not* generate sufficient taxable income for the temporary difference to reduce, and thus provide a benefit in the future, then a valuation allowance must be recorded to reduce the reported value of the deferred asset.

C. It is up to management to defend the recognition of all deferred tax assets.

   1. If a company has order backlogs or existing contracts that are expected to generate future taxable income, then a valuation allowance would not be necessary.

   2. However, if a company has cumulative losses over the past few years or a history of an inability to use tax loss carryforwards, then the company would need to use a valuation allowance to reflect the likelihood that the deferred tax asset would never be used.

D. From a big picture perspective, a valuation allowance reduces income from continuing operations. Because an increase (decrease) in the valuation allowance will serve to decrease (increase) operating income, changes in the valuation allowance are a common means of managing earnings, especially if the amounts are significant.

CLASSIFICATION OF DEFERRED TAX ACCOUNTS ON THE BALANCE SHEET

A. If a temporary difference relates to a noncurrent account, then the deferred tax liability or asset that results is also noncurrent.

B. The same applies if the temporary difference relates to a current account.

   1. If the "difference" relates to depreciation on a building, the related deferred tax account is considered noncurrent. If the "difference" relates to an accounts receivable balance, the deferred tax account is considered current.

C. All existing noncurrent deferred tax assets and liabilities are netted to arrive at a single figure to report on the balance sheet. In other words, they may be combined and allowed to offset one another.

D. The same applies for current deferred tax assets and liabilities.

   1. Remember that they are netted by "time."

DISCLOSURE REQUIREMENTS RELATING TO DEFERRED TAXES

A. All deferred tax assets and liabilities (specific items comprising the overall balance).

B. Any valuation allowance and the net change in the allowance over the period.

C. Tax loss carryforwards or tax credits.

D. Components of income tax expense.

E. Reconciliation of reported income tax expense with the hypothetical amount based upon the statutory tax rate.

SUMMARY

A. If taxable income (on the tax return) is less than pretax income (on the financial statements) and the cause of this difference will reverse in future years, then a deferred tax liability is created.

B. If taxable income is more than pretax income and the difference will reverse in future years, then a deferred tax asset is created.

QUESTIONS: ACCOUNTING FOR INCOME TAXES

1. Justification for the method of determining periodic deferred tax expense is based on the concept of:
    A. matching of periodic expense to periodic revenue.
    B. objectivity in the calculation of periodic expense.
    C. recognition of assets and liabilities.
    D. consistency of tax expense measurements with actual tax planning strategies.

2. Caleb Co. (Caleb) has three financial statement elements for which the December 31, Year 6 book value is different than the December 31, Year 6 tax basis:

	Book value	Tax basis
Equipment	$200,000	$120,000
Prepaid officers' insurance policy	$75,000	$0
Warranty liability	$50,000	$0

    As a result of these differences, future taxable amounts are:
    A. $50,000.
    B. $80,000.
    C. $155,000.
    D. $205,000.

3. For the year ended December 31, Year 6, Tyne Co. (Tyne) reported pretax financial statement income of $750,000. Its taxable income was $650,000. The difference is due to accelerated depreciation for income tax purposes. Tyne's effective income tax rate is 30% and Tyne made estimated tax payments during Year 6 of $90,000. What amount should Tyne report as current income tax expense for Year 6?
    A. $105,000.
    B. $135,000.
    C. $195,000.
    D. $225,000.

4. Tinseltown Corp. (Tinseltown) began operations on January 1, Year 5. For financial reporting, Tinseltown recognizes revenues from all sales under the accrual method. However, in its income tax returns, Tinseltown reports qualifying sales under the installment method. Tinseltown's gross profit on these installment sales under each method was as follows:

Year	Accrual method	Installment method
Year 5	$1,600,000	$600,000
Year 6	$2,600,000	$1,400,000

    The income tax rate is 30% for Year 5 and future years. There are no other temporary or permanent differences.

    In its December 31, Year 6 balance sheet, what amount should Tinseltown report as a liability for deferred income taxes?
    A. $360,000.
    B. $600,000.
    C. $660,000.
    D. $840,000.

Use the following information to answer Questions 5 and 6.

Zeffy, Inc. (Zeffy) prepared the following reconciliation of its pretax financial statement income to taxable income for the year ended December 31, Year 6, its first year of operations:

Pretax financial income	$160,000
Nontaxable interest received on municipal securities	(5,000)
Long-term loss accrual in excess of deductible amount	10,000
Depreciation in excess of financial statement amount	(25,000)
Taxable income	$140,000

Zeff's tax rate for Year 6 is 40%.

5. In its Year 6 income statement, what amount should Zeffy report as current income tax expense?
   A. $52,000.
   B. $56,000.
   C. $62,000.
   D. $64,000.

6. In its December 31, Year 6 balance sheet, what should Zeffy report as a deferred income tax liability?
   A. $2,000.
   B. $4,000.
   C. $6,000.
   D. $8,000.

7. Westwick Corp. (Westwick) leased a building and received the $36,000 annual rental payment on June 15, Year 6. The beginning of the lease was on July 1, Year 6. Rental income is taxable when received. Westwick's tax rates are 30% for Year 6 and 40% thereafter. There were no other permanent or temporary differences and no valuation allowance was required.

   What amount of deferred tax asset should Westwick report on its December 31, Year 6 balance sheet?
   A. $5,400.
   B. $7,200.
   C. $10,800.
   D. $14,400.

8. Orleans Co. (Orleans), a cash-basis taxpayer, prepares accrual basis financial statements. In its Year 6 balance sheet, Orleans' deferred tax liabilities increased compared to Year 5. Which of the following changes would cause this increase in deferred tax liabilities?

   I. An increase in prepaid insurance.
   II. An increase in rent receivable.
   III. An increase in warranty obligations.

   A. I only.
   B. I and II.
   C. II and III.
   D. III only.

9. At the end of Year 1, Cody Co. (Cody) reported a profit on a partially completed construction contract by applying the percentage-of-completion method. By the end of Year 2, the total estimated profit on the contract at completion in Year 3 had been drastically reduced from the amount estimated at the end of Year 1.

   Consequently, in Year 2, a loss equal to one-half of the year profit was recognized. Cody used the completed-contract method for income tax purposes and had no other contracts. Should the Year 2 balance sheet include a deferred tax?

	Asset	Liability
A.	Yes	Yes
B.	No	Yes
C.	Yes	No
D.	No	No

10. Quinn Co. (Quinn) reported a net deferred tax asset of $9,000 in its December 31, Year 5 balance sheet. For Year 6, Quinn reported pretax financial statement income of $300,000. Temporary differences of $100,000 resulted in taxable income of $200,000 in Year 6. At December 31, Year 6, Quinn had cumulative taxable differences of $70,000. Quinn's effective income tax rate is 30%.

    In its December 31, Year 6 income statement, what should Quinn report as deferred income tax expense?
    A. $12,000.
    B. $21,000.
    C. $30,000.
    D. $60,000.

11. On its December 31, Year 6 income statement, Rena Co. (Rena) had income taxes payable of $13,000 and a current deferred tax asset of $20,000 before determining the need for a valuation allowance. Rena had reported a current deferred tax asset of $15,000 at December 31, Year 5. At December 31, Year 6, Rena determined that it was more likely than not that 10% of the deferred tax asset would not be realized.

    In its Year 6 income statement, what amount should Rena report as total income tax expense?
    A. $8,000.
    B. $8,500.
    C. $10,000.
    D. $13,000.

12. Dix, Inc. (Dix), a calendar-year corporation, reported the following operating income (loss) before income tax for its first three years of operations:

    Year 4 $100,000
    Year 5   ($200,000)
    Year 6 $400,000

    There are no permanent or temporary differences between operating income/loss for financial and income tax reporting purposes. When filing its Year 5 income tax return, Dix did not elect to forgo the carryback of its loss for Year 5. Assume a 40% tax rate for all years.

    What amount should Dix report as its income tax liability at December 31, Year 6?
    A. $60,000.
    B. $80,000.
    C. $120,000.
    D. $160,000.

13. Bishop Co. (Bishop) began operations in Year 4 and had operating losses of $200,000 in Year 4 and $150,000 in Year 5. For the year ended December 31, Year 6, Bishop had pretax book income of $300,000. For the three-year period Year 4 to Year 6, assume an income tax rate of 40% and no permanent or temporary differences between book and taxable income. Because Bishop began operations in Year 4, the entire amount of deferred tax assets recognized in Year 4 and Year 5 was offset with amounts added to the valuation allowance account.

    In Bishop's Year 6 income statement, how much should be reported as current income tax expense?
    A. $0.
    B. $40,000.
    C. $60,000.
    D. $120,000.

14. At the most recent year-end, Eberman has a deferred income tax liability arising from accelerated depreciation that exceeded a deferred income tax asset relating to rent received in advance that is expected to reverse in the next year.

    Which of the following should be reported in Eberman's most recent year-end balance sheet?
    A. The excess of the deferred income tax liability over the deferred income tax asset as a noncurrent liability.
    B. The excess of the deferred income tax liability over the deferred income tax asset as a current liability.
    C. The deferred income tax liability as a noncurrent liability.
    D. The deferred income tax liability as a current liability.

15.   In Year 6, Rintoul, Inc. (Rintoul) reported for financial statement purposes the following items that were not included in taxable income:

Installment gain to be collected equally in Year 7 through Year 9	$1,500,000
Estimated future warranty costs to be paid equally in Year 7 through Year 9	$2,100,000

There were no temporary differences in prior years. Rintoul's enacted tax rates are 30% for Year 6 and 25% for Year 7 through 2009.

In Rintoul's December 31, Year 6 balance sheet, what amounts of the deferred tax asset should be classified as current and noncurrent?

	Current	Noncurrent
A.	$60,000	$100,000
B.	$60,000	$120,000
C.	$50,000	$100,000
D	$50,000	$120,000

16.   Because Jiri Co. (Jiri) uses different methods to depreciate equipment for financial statement and income tax purposes, Jiri has temporary differences that will reverse during the next year and add to taxable income. Deferred income taxes that are based on these temporary differences should be classified in Jiri's balance sheet as:
A. contra account to current assets.
B. contra account to noncurrent assets.
C. current liability.
D. noncurrent liability.

17.   In Year 1, a company has a profit of $700,000 before taxes. In addition, the company had one other sale for $500,000 with a gross profit of $100,000 that is being accounted for by accrual accounting for financial reporting purposes and by the installment sales method for tax purposes. The company collected $50,000 of the $500,000 this year and expects to collect that much each year for the next nine years. The enacted tax rate is 25% for Years 1 through 4 and 30% thereafter. What is the amount of deferred income tax liability that will be reported as noncurrent on the company's balance sheet?
A. $20,000.
B. $23,000.
C. $25,000.
D. $25,500.

18. In Year 1, a company has a warranty expense on its income statement of $120,000. However, the company expects these warranties to be satisfied as follows: $50,000 in Year 2, $40,000 in Year 3, and $30,000 in Year 4. The tax rates for each year are as follows: Year 2 – 22%, Year 3 – 24%, Year 4 – 25%. The company believes that there is 65% chance that it will have adequate taxable income in Year 2 to absorb the warranty expense but that the likelihood drops to 55% in Year 3, and 45% in Year 4. On its Year 1 income statement, what does this company report as its deferred income tax benefit?
    A. $11,000.
    B. $15,805.
    C. $20,600.
    D. $28,100.

19. A company ends Year 1 with a deferred income tax liability—noncurrent of $23,000, a deferred income tax asset—noncurrent of $7,000, and a deferred income tax liability—current of $11,000. The company ends Year 2 with a deferred income tax liability—noncurrent of $19,000, a deferred income tax asset—noncurrent of $10,000, a deferred income tax liability—current of $24,000, and a deferred income tax asset—current of $2,000. On its Year 2 income statement, what is reported as Income Tax Expense—Deferred?
    A. ($7,000).
    B. $4,000.
    C. $9,000.
    D. $31,000.

20. A company ends Year 1 with a noncurrent deferred income tax liability of $19,000, a noncurrent deferred income tax asset of $10,000, a current deferred income tax liability of $24,000, and a current deferred income tax asset of $2,000. Neither of the assets has a valuation allowance. On its Year 1 balance sheet, what is reported for deferred income taxes?
    A. A $43,000 deferred liability and a $12,000 deferred asset.
    B. A $31,000 deferred liability.
    C. A $9,000 noncurrent deferred liability and a $22,000 current deferred liability.
    D. All four figures should be shown separately.

21. A company is in its first year of business. Business operations are expected to be profitable in the foreseeable future. Sales are reported on the financial statements using accrual accounting. However, the installment sales method was used on the business's federal tax return because only 10% of the cash was received this year. What is the result of this situation?
    A. The company will recognize a deferred tax asset.
    B. The company will recognize no deferred taxes this year.
    C. The company will recognize a deferred tax liability.
    D. The company will recognize both a deferred tax asset and a deferred tax liability.

22. A company is in its first year of business. Business operations are expected to be profitable in the foreseeable future. The items being sold are covered by a warranty. No items were reported by customers as defective this year, but some are expected to fail in the near future. What is the result of this situation?
    A. The company will recognize a deferred tax asset.
    B. The company will note no deferred taxes this year.
    C. The company will recognize a deferred tax liability.
    D. The company will recognize both a deferred tax asset and a deferred tax liability.

23. A company reports net income before income taxes this year of $300,000. The enacted tax rate is 30%. The company has reported a $40,000 gain on an installment sale that will not be taxed for two years. The company has also reported $50,000 in interest revenue from State of Maine bonds. On the company's income statement, what is reported as "current income tax expense"?
   A. $63,000.
   B. $75,000.
   C. $78,000.
   D. $90,000.

24. A company reports net income on its Year 1 financial statements before its income tax expense of $500,000. The company has been profitable in the past and expects to continue to be profitable. The company had one $30,000 expense that will not be deductible for tax purposes until Year 4. The company also had a $70,000 revenue that will not be taxed until Year 3. The company also earned and reported municipal bond interest of $20,000. The enacted tax rate is 30%. On the company's income statement for Year 1, what should be reported as "deferred income tax expense"?
   A. $9,000.
   B. $12,000.
   C. $21,000.
   D. $30,000.

25. In Year 1, a company reports net income before taxes of $600,000. However, the company had $70,000 in income that will not be taxed until Year 3. In Year 2, the same company reports net income before taxes of $700,000. Of that amount, the company had $90,000 in income that will not be taxed until Year 4. The enacted tax rate in Year 1 was 30% but a new rate of 34% was enacted on January 1, Year 2. What amount of "deferred income tax expense" should this company recognize on its Year 2 income statement?
   A. $30,600.
   B. $31,500.
   C. $32,300.
   D. $33,400.

26. A company starts operations in Year 1 and reports net income of $200,000 before income taxes. The company had one expense deduction of $110,000 on its income statement that will not be deducted for tax purposes until Year 5. The company believes that there is only a 40% chance that it will have taxable income in the future to allow for the eventual deduction of this expense. If the enacted tax rate is 30%, what is the total amount of income tax expense that should be reported in the company's Year 1 income statement?
   A. $60,000.
   B. $73,200.
   C. $79,800.
   D. $93,000.

27. A company starts operations in Year 1 and reports net income of $300,000 before income taxes. The company had one expense deduction of $70,000 on its income statement that will not be deducted for tax purposes until Year 4. The company believes that there is only a 60% chance that it will have taxable income in the future to allow for the eventual deduction of this expense. If the enacted tax rate is 30%, what is the total amount of income tax expense that should be reported in the company's Year 1 income statement?

    A. $90,000.
    B. $98,400.
    C. $102,600.
    D. $111,000.

28. In Year 1, a company has an enacted tax rate of 30% and a $100,000 temporary tax difference created by depreciation. For tax purposes, the company will have less depreciation of $70,000 in Year 2 and $30,000 in Year 3. The company also has a $60,000 temporary tax difference created by a warranty. For tax purposes, the company will have an additional warranty expense of $40,000 in Year 2 and $20,000 in Year 3. What is reported on the company's balance sheet?

    A. A current deferred income tax liability of $9,000 and a noncurrent deferred income tax liability of $3,000.
    B. A current deferred income tax liability of $9,000, a noncurrent deferred income tax liability of $9,000, and a noncurrent deferred income tax asset of $6,000.
    C. A current deferred income tax liability of $21,000, a current deferred income tax asset of $12,000, a noncurrent deferred income tax liability of $9,000, and a noncurrent deferred income tax asset of $6,000.
    D. A current deferred income tax asset of $12,000 and a noncurrent deferred income tax liability of $24,000.

ANSWERS: ACCOUNTING FOR INCOME TAXES

1. **C** The objective of accounting for income taxes is to recognize the amount of current and deferred taxes payable or refundable at the date of the financial statements. Furthermore, this objective is implemented through recognition of deferred tax liabilities or assets. Deferred tax expense results from changes in deferred tax assets and liabilities.

2. **B** The officer insurance policy difference ($75,000) is a permanent difference that does not result in future taxable or deductible amounts. The warranty difference ($50,000) is a temporary difference, but it results in future deductible amounts in future years when tax warranty expense exceeds book warranty experience. However, the equipment difference ($80,000) is a temporary difference that results in future taxable amounts in future years when tax depreciation is less than book depreciation.

3. **C** Income tax expense must be reported in two components: the amount currently payable (current portion) and the tax effects of temporary differences (deferred portion). The current portion is computed by multiplying taxable income by the current enacted tax rate ($650,000 × 30% = $195,000). The deferred portion is $30,000 ($100,000 temporary difference × 30%). The estimated tax payments ($90,000) do not affect the amount of tax expense, although the payments would decrease taxes payable.

4. **C** Over the two years, accounting income on the accrual basis is $4,200,000 ($1,600,000 + $2,600,000) and taxable income using the installment method is $2,000,000 ($600,000 + $1,400,000). This results in future taxable amounts at December 31, Year 6 of $2,200,000 ($4,200,000 – $2,000,000). Therefore on December 31, Year 6, Tinseltown should report a deferred tax liability of $660,000 ($2,200,000 × 30%).

5. **B** The amount of tax currently payable, or current income tax expense, is computed by multiplying taxable income by the current enacted tax rate ($140,000 × 40% = $56,000).

6. **C** The deferred tax liability to be reported at December 31, Year 6 results from the net future taxable and deductible amounts that exist as a result of past transactions, multiplied by the appropriate tax rate. There is the requirement to net the current deferred tax assets and liabilities and the noncurrent deferred tax assets and liabilities.

   The nontaxable interest received on municipal securities ($5,000) is a permanent difference that does not result in future taxable or deductible amounts.

   The future deductible amount ($10,000) resulting from a loss accrual results in a long-term deferred tax asset of $4,000 ($10,000 × 40%) because it is related to a long-term loss accrual that likely will result in a future tax deduction.

   The future taxable amount ($25,000) caused by depreciation results in a long-term deferred tax liability of $10,000 ($25,000 × 40%) because it is related to a long-term asset (PP&E).

   Because these items are both long-term, they are netted, and a long-term deferred tax liability of $6,000 ($10,000 liability – $4,000 asset) is reported on the balance sheet.

7. **B** At December 31, Year 6, unearned rent for financial accounting purposes is $18,000 ($36,000 × 6/12). The amount of rent revenue recognized on the income statement is six of twelve months ($36,000 × 6/12) = $18,000. Rental income on the tax return is $36,000 because rental income is taxed when received. Therefore, the timing difference is $18,000, giving rise to a deferred tax asset on the balance sheet of $18,000 × 40% = $7,200. The deferred tax asset to be recorded is measured using the future enacted tax rate of 40%.

8. **B** The increase in prepaid insurance in Year 6 creates a deductible amount for income tax reporting purposes for the insurance paid; however, for financial reporting purposes the expense is not recognized until years subsequent to Year 6. As a result, net taxable income for future years is increased; thus, the deferred tax liability increases.

The increase in rent receivable in Year 6 also increases the deferred tax liability. For income tax purposes, rents are not included in income until received (i.e., years subsequent to Year 6). However, the amount of the receivable is earned and recognized in the income statement in Year 6.

The increase in warranty obligations results in warranty expense for Year 6 and will provide future deductible amounts because tax rules do not allow a deduction for warranty cost until such a cost is incurred. Future deductible amounts lead to deferred tax assets.

9. **B** A deferred tax liability is recognized for temporary differences that will result in net taxable amounts in future years. Although Cody has recognized a loss (per books) in Year 2 of the construction contract, the contract is still profitable over the three years. Therefore, in Year 3 when the contract is completed, Cody will recognize the total profit on its tax return and only a portion of the profit will be recorded in its income statement. Thus, the contract will result in a taxable income in Year 3 and a deferred tax liability exists. Note that this liability was recorded at the end of Year 1 and reduced by one-half at the end of Year 2 due to the change in estimated profit. Answers A and C are incorrect because no deferred tax asset is created. Answer D is incorrect because Cody will include a deferred tax liability on its balance sheet.

10. **C** The current portion of income tax expense is computed by multiplying taxable income by the current enacted tax rate ($200,000 × 30% = $60,000). The deferred portion is $30,000 ($100,000 temporary difference × 30%).

11. **C** From 12/31/Year 5 to 12/31/Year 6, the deferred tax asset increases by $5,000 (from $15,000 to $20,000). Income taxes payable at 12/31/Year 4 are $13,000. Based on this information, the following journal entries can be recreated:

Income tax expense—current	$13,000	
Income tax payable		$13,000
Deferred tax asset	$5,000	
Income tax expense—deferred		$5,000

An additional entry would be prepared by Rena to record an allowance to reduce the deferred tax asset to its realizable value (10% × $20,000 = $2,000).

Income tax expense—deferred	$2,000	
Allowance to reduce deferred tax asset		$2,000
to realizable value		

Based on these three entries, total Year 6 income tax expense is $10,000 ($13,000 – $5,000 + $2,000).

12. **C** Dix did *not* elect to forgo the loss carryback, so $100,000 of the $200,000 loss will be carried back to offset Year 4 income, resulting in a tax refund of $40,000 (40% × $100,000). The remaining $100,000 of the Year 5 loss will be carried forward to offset part of Year 6 income. Thus, the income tax liability at December 31, Year 6 will be $120,000 [40% × ($400,000 – $100,000)].

13. **A** For tax purposes, loss carryforwards should not be recognized until they are actually realized.

Income tax return analysis

	Year 4	Year 5	Year 6
Income or loss	($200,000)	($150,000)	$300,000
Carryforward	$200,000	$100,000	($300,000)
Unused carryforward	$0	$50,000	$0

The $200,000 loss carryforward in Year 4 is applied against the $300,000 of income in Year 6 first and then $100,000 of the loss carryforward in Year 5 is applied against the remaining $100,000 of income in Year 6. This leaves an unused carryforward amount of $50,000 relating to Year 5. Bishop would recognize (in the income statement) income tax expense of $0.

14. **C** Deferred tax assets and liabilities are classified as current or noncurrent based on the classification of the related asset or liability for financial statement reporting. Therefore, a deferred tax liability relating to depreciation of a fixed asset would be noncurrent in nature. The deferred tax asset relating to rent received in advance that is expected to reverse in the following year would be classified as current. No netting of net current amounts and net noncurrent amounts can occur.

15. **C** The warranty temporary difference results in future deductible amounts of $700,000 per year in Year 7 through Year 9 ($2,100,000/3). The installment temporary difference results in future taxable amounts of $500,000 per year in Year 7 through 2009 ($1,500,000/3). The portions of the resulting deferred tax asset and deferred tax liability that will be netted to find the amount of the current asset/current liability to be presented on the balance sheet are shown below:

Deferred tax asset:	$700,000 × 25%	$175,000
Deferred tax liability:	($500,000) × 25%	($125,000)
Current deferred tax asset shown on balance sheet:		$50,000

The noncurrent deferred tax asset is $100,000 [25% × ($2,100,000 – $1,500,000)] – $50,000 current portion.

16. **D** Deferred tax liabilities and assets are classified as current or noncurrent based on the related asset or liability. A deferred tax liability or asset is considered to be related to an asset or liability if reduction of the asset or liability will cause the temporary difference to reverse. If the deferred tax liability or asset is not related to any asset or liability, then it is classified based on the timing of its expected reversal or utilization date.

This deferred tax liability is related to the equipment, which is noncurrent, so the deferred tax liability should also be classified as a noncurrent liability.

Deferred taxes are always classified as assets or liabilities, rather than as contra accounts.

17. **B** Of the sales price, 90% will be collected in future years, so $90,000 of the gross profit is deferred for tax purposes. The $10,000 that relates to Year 2 will result in a current liability because it corresponds to a current receivable on the installment sale. Of the $80,000 that remains, $20,000 (Years 3 and 4) will be taxed at 25% ($5,000) and the remaining $60,000 (beyond Year 4) will be taxed at 30% ($18,000). That produces a noncurrent deferred tax liability of $23,000.

18. **C** Because the company believes that it is less likely than not (<50%) that it will have income in Year 4 to absorb the warranty expense in that period, the income statement effect is restricted to Year 2 and Year 3. That benefit is $50,000 × 22% ($11,000) and $40,000 × 24% ($9,600) for a total of $20,600. The benefit for Year 4 is too uncertain to justify recognition on the income statement.

19. **B** The amount to be reported as deferred income tax expense is the change that takes place during the year for each of the deferred asset accounts and the deferred liability accounts. At the beginning of the year, the two deferred liability accounts totaled $34,000 ($23,000 + $11,000). At the end of the year, they total $43,000 ($19,000 + $24,000) so they have increased by $9,000. The one deferred asset has a beginning balance of $7,000 but the two deferred assets total $12,000 ($10,000 + $2,000) at year's end, an increase of $5,000. The $9,000 jump in the deferred liabilities is offset partially by the $5,000 increase in the deferred assets so that the income tax expense-deferred balance for the year is $4,000.

20. **C** In reporting deferred tax liabilities and assets, all current balances are first combined and then all noncurrent balances are combined. The two resulting figures are reported.

21. **C** For financial reporting purposes, the income on the sale is recognized currently. However, the income is not taxable until later because use of the installment sales method defers recognition of the income until the cash is collected. Because of the matching principle, the tax expense is recognized now although payment has been delayed. That delayed payment leads to the recognition of a deferred tax liability.

22. **A**   The expense should be deducted in the current year for financial reporting purposes because of the matching principle. Since the sale is made this year, the related expense should also be recognized this year. However, for taxes purposes, a warranty can only be deducted when a payment is made and that will not happen until the future. Thus, taxable income currently will be higher (the expense is not yet allowed) but will be reduced in the future (when the expense is finally deducted). That impact is reported as deferred income tax asset.

23. **A**   Because state and municipal bond interest is non-taxable income, the company only has $250,000 of income that will ever be taxed. Of this amount, $40,000 will be taxed at a later date. Hence, only $210,000 is actually taxed in the current year. At the 30% enacted rate, an "income tax expense – current" figure of $63,000 is determined.

24. **B**   The $30,000 deduction in the future creates a deferred tax asset of $9,000 based on the 30% tax rate. The $70,000 revenue to be taxed in the future creates a deferred tax liability of $21,000 based on that same rate. Creating the $21,000 liability and the $9,000 asset leads to the recognition of a $12,000 net expense.

25. **D**   At the end of the first year, the company has a deferred income tax liability of $21,000 ($70,000 temporary difference × the 30% enacted rate). At the end of the second year, the company's deferred income tax liability has grown to $54,400 (the total of $160,000 in temporary differences that are still scheduled to be taxed in the future × the new enacted rate of 34%). The income tax expense-deferred balance on the income statement is created here by the change in the deferred income tax liability balance from $21,000 to $54,400.

26. **D**   Because the company cannot deduct the $110,000 expense this year, taxable income on the current tax return will be $310,000. Based on the 30% tax rate, that leads to the recognition of an income tax expense—current of $93,000. The $110,000 deduction will be allowed in the future and creates the recognition of a deferred income tax asset of $33,000 ($110,000 × 30%). However, because it fails to be more likely than not (51%) that the company will ever get to utilize the benefit from this deduction, an allowance account of $33,000 must also be recognized to reduce the asset (in this case to zero). Creating a $33,000 deferred tax asset along with an equal and offsetting $33,000 allowance means that no income tax expense – deferred balance is recognized on the income statement. The only income effect, therefore, is the $93,000 income tax expense—current.

27. **A**   Because the company cannot deduct the $70,000 expense this year, taxable income on the current tax return will be $370,000. Based on the 30% enacted tax rate, that leads to the recognition of an "income tax expense—current" of $111,000. The $70,000 deduction will be allowed in the future and creates the recognition of a deferred income tax asset of $21,000 ($70,000 × 30%). Because it is more likely than not (51%) that the company will be able to utilize the benefit from this deduction, an allowance account is not needed. Recording the deferred asset alone creates a $21,000 "income tax benefit—deferred" on the company's income statement so that the overall income tax expense is $90,000 ($111,000 less $21,000).

28. **D**   For balance sheet reporting, all deferred tax balances are classified as either current or noncurrent and the two resulting combined figures (current and noncurrent) are reported. If possible, the current-noncurrent status of every deferred income tax is based on the balance sheet cause. For example, depreciation results from fixed assets such as buildings and equipment. Because these assets accounts are noncurrent, any resulting deferred income taxes are also noncurrent. A warranty creates a warranty liability on the balance sheet. The portion of that liability that will be settled next year ($40,000) is current whereas any part of the liability that will be settled later ($20,000) is noncurrent. The deferred tax asset relating to the current liability (30% of $40,000 or $12,000) is current; the deferred tax asset relating to the noncurrent liability (30% of $20,000 or $6,000) is noncurrent.

    As a result, the company has a deferred tax liability—noncurrent from the depreciation of $30,000 ($100,000 temporary difference times 30%) as well as a deferred tax asset—current of $12,000 and a deferred tax asset—noncurrent of $6,000. The two noncurrent balances are netted together to arrive at a single deferred income tax liability—noncurrent of $24,000. The sole current balance does not have a deferred income liability—current for netting purposes and is, thus, reported as a deferred income tax asset—current of $12,000.

CHAPTER 15 – EQUITY METHOD OF ACCOUNTING FOR INVESTMENTS

STUDY TIP

When you are studying a complicated subject such as the equity method of accounting, it is good to remind yourself that you do not need to be perfect. There is no need to shoot for a grade of 100. You only have to make a grade of 75 in order to pass the CPA exam and that means that you can miss a lot of questions and still pass. That is quite different from school where teachers write most tests looking for students who can answer all of the questions. On the CPA exam, any score exceeding 75 indicates that the candidate studied too hard.

CHAPTER 15 – EQUITY METHOD OF ACCOUNTING FOR INVESTMENTS

OVERVIEW OF CONSOLIDATED AND COMBINED FINANCIAL STATEMENTS AND THE EQUITY METHOD COVERAGE ON THE CPA EXAM

The equity method is a subtopic covered in a section of the CPA exam called "Typical items: *recognition, measurement, valuation*, and *presentation* in financial statements in conformity with GAAP."

Consolidated and Combined Financial Statements is one subtopic covered in a section of the CPA exam called "Concepts and standards for financial statements."

Business Combinations is a subtopic that focuses on consolidated financial statements and is covered in a section of the CPA exam called "Specific types of transactions and events: *recognition, measurement, valuation*, and *presentation* in financial statements in conformity with GAAP."

ACCOUNTING FOR INVESTMENTS

A. Percentage of ownership is typically used as a practical guide to determine influence or control for financial reporting purposes. The conceptual distinction for determining reporting methods centers on the degree to which the investee is an integral part of the investor (parent company).

Ownership	Criterion (degree of influence)	Method
Less than 20%	No significant influence	Cost or market
20% to 50%	Significant influence	Equity
Greater than 50%	Control	Consolidation

B. Ownership of less than 20% is typically viewed as a noncontrolling interest, and the two companies are treated as separate entities. The accounting for intercorporate investments in previous discussions is an example of the cost or market method.

Note: A detailed discussion of the equity method and the consolidation method will follow below.

EQUITY METHOD

The equity method is used to account for an investment in shares where the owner has the ability to *significantly influence* (the critical test) the managing, operating, investing, and financing decisions of the investee.

A. Although the ability to apply significant influence is the only criterion, ownership of 20% to 50% of the investee's shares is generally accounted for by the equity method.

B. The investor may use the equity method in some cases even if less than 20% is held by the owner. This would occur if the investor has significant influence, for example, by having many seats on the board of directors.

C. Conversely, the investor should not use the equity method, even if over 20% is held, if the following conditions are present:

1. The investor does not have the ability to significantly influence because a majority shareholder controls the investee's operations.

2. There are other factors that indicate lack of significant influence on the part of the investor, such a lack of seats on the board of directors.

3. In applying the equity method, the investment is initially recorded at cost.

4. The owner recognizes income (or loss) as soon as the investee earns it based on the percentage of ownership. Income is recognized and the book value is raised (for income) or lowered (for loss).

5. Income is recognized regardless of whether the earnings are actually received (i.e., whether or not the investee pays out earnings as dividends).

6. Because income is recognized as earned, dividends received cannot also be recognized as revenue (this would be double counting).

7. Instead, dividends received from the investee are recorded as a reduction in the book value of the investment.

   • The journal entry would be to debit cash received and credit investment so that there is a direct offset on the assets side of the balance sheet.

8. Note that a payment of dividends exceeding the investor's share of the investee's income since acquisition would be treated as a return of capital. This would reduce the amount of the investment account.

Initial Recording of an Investment Under the Equity Method

A. The price of the investment may be in excess of the investee's underlying book value (or net assets). Recall that book value is determined by multiplying stockholders' equity by the percentage bought.

B. The excess of the amount of payment over the book value may be attributed to a specific asset such as land or building if the value of the item is greater than its book value on the records of the investee. Allocation to the change in value of the asset is based on the percentage of the investee company that is bought.

C. If any part of the price that exceeds the underlying book value cannot be assigned to a specific asset or liability, the remainder is assumed to be goodwill.

D. Any allocations of excess price (unless assigned to land) must be amortized.

1. If allocation is to a specific asset or liability such as buildings or equipment, the allocation is amortized over the useful life.

2. Goodwill is an exception to this rule, as it is not amortized. Additionally, it is not separately tested for impairment when it is within an equity method investment.

3. Amortization reduces the value of the investment account (allocations are not reported separately by the owner) and reduces the amount of income being reported from the investee.

4. Changes in fair value of investments recorded by the equity method are ignored. For fiscal years beginning after November 15, 2007, equity method investors can make an irrevocable election to report the investment on the balance sheet at fair value. In this case, changes in fair value are recognized in the investor's income statement.

Example of Implementing the Equity Method

A. Situation:

1. December 31, Year 4, the parent company (Parent) invests $1,000 in the subsidiary company (Sub) and receives 30% of the shares of Sub.

2. During Year 5, Sub earns $400 and pays dividends of $100.

3. During Year 6, Sub earns $600 and pays dividends of $150.

B. Analysis:

1. On December 31, Year 4, Parent will record the investment in Sub at its initial cost of $1,000.

2. For Year 5, Parent will recognize $120 ($400 × 30%) on its income statement as equity in the net income of Sub.

   a. Parent will increase the investment in the Sub account on the balance sheet by $120 to $1,120, reflecting the share of the net assets of Sub.

   b. Parent will receive $30 ($100 × 30%) in cash dividends from Sub and reduce its investment in Sub by that amount to reflect the decline in the net assets of Sub due to the dividend payment.

   c. At the end of Year 5, the carrying value of Sub on Parent's balance sheet will be $1,000 original investment + $120 proportional share of Sub's earnings – $30 dividend received = $1,090.

3. For Year 6, Parent will recognize income of $180 ($600 × 30%) and increase the investment by $180. Also, Parent will receive dividends of $45 ($150 × 30%) and will lower the investment account by $45. At the end of Year 6, the carrying value of Sub on Parent's balance sheet will be $1,225 ($1,090 for the carryover balance from Year 5 + $180 proportional share of Sub's earnings – $45 dividend received).

Accounting Issues with the Equity Method

A. Recall that if the investee company reported losses, the investor would have to write down the investment account (but not below zero) and recognize its share of the loss in net income.

B. This introduces the possibility of earnings management: a company that acquires stock in an unprofitable investee may try to keep proportional ownership just below 20% (so it doesn't have to recognize the loss).

C. Clearly, the use of the equity method makes sense when the investee's undistributed income is increasing.

D. Equity method goodwill is not separately tested for impairment. Rather, an impairment test is performed based on the book value and fair value of the investment account as a whole.

QUESTIONS: EQUITY METHOD OF ACCOUNTING FOR INVESTMENTS

1. If a company uses the equity method to account for an investment in another company, which of the following is true?
    A. Income is combined to the extent of ownership.
    B. Income to the investing company consists of actual dividends, interest, or capital gains.
    C. All of the investee's income is included in the investor's income except for income relating to intercompany transactions.
    D. Income of the investee is included in the investor's income but reduced by any dividends paid to the investor.

2. On January 2, Year 6, Rhea Co. (Rhea) purchased 10% of Lourdes Co.'s (Lourdes) outstanding common shares for $400,000. Rhea is the largest single shareholder in Lourdes and Rhea's officers are a majority on Lourdes' board of directors. Lourdes reported net income of $500,000 for Year 6 and paid dividends of $150,000.

    In its December 31, Year 6 balance sheet, what amount should Rhea report as investment in Lourdes?
    A. $385,000.
    B. $400,000.
    C. $435,000.
    D. $450,000.

3. Brad Co. (Brad) uses the equity method to account for its January 1, Year 6 purchase of Lamb Co.'s (Lamb) common stock. On that date, the fair values of Lamb's FIFO inventory and land exceeded their carrying amounts.

    How do these excesses of fair values over carrying amounts affect Brad's reported equity in Lamb's Year 6 earnings?

	Inventory Excess	Land Excess
A.	Decrease	Decrease
B.	Decrease	No effect
C.	Increase	Increase
D.	Increase	No effect

Use the following information to answer Questions 4 and 5.

Nikolai, Inc. (Nikolai) acquired 40% of the shares of Novikov, Inc. (Novikov) for $1.5 million on January 1, Year 6. During Year 6, Novikov earned $500,000 and paid dividends of $125,000.

4. Using the equity method, at the end of Year 6, Nikolai reported an investment in Novikov of:
    A. $1.5 million.
    B. $1.65 million.
    C. $1.7 million.
    D. $1.875 million.

5.   Using the equity method, Nikolai reported investment income in Year 6 of:
      A. $50,000.
      B. $150,000.
      C. $200,000.
      D. $500,000.

6.   In its financial statements, Longley Co. (Longley) uses the equity method of accounting for its 30% ownership of Autumn Co. (Autumn). At December 31, Year 6, Longley has a receivable from Autumn.

      How should the receivable be reported on Longley's Year 6 financial statements?
      A. None of the receivable should be reported, but the entire receivable should be offset against Autumn's payable to Longley.
      B. Report 70% of the receivable separately with the balance offset against 30% of Autumn's payable to Longley.
      C. The total receivable should be disclosed separately.
      D. The total receivable should be included as part of the investment in Autumn, without separate disclosure.

7.   On January 2, Year 6, Keats Co. (Keats) purchased a 30% interest in Ortiz Co. (Ortiz) for $250,000. On this date, Ortiz's stockholders' equity was $500,000. The carrying amount of Ortiz's identifiable net assets approximated their fair values except for land, whose fair value exceeded its carrying amount by $200,000.

      Ortiz reported net income of $100,000 for Year 6 and paid no dividends. Keats accounts for this investment using the equity method.

      In its December 31, Year 6 balance sheet, what amount should Keats report as investment in Ortiz?
      A. $210,000.
      B. $220,000.
      C. $270,000.
      D. $280,000.

8.   On January 2, Year 6, Saxton, Inc. (Saxton) purchased 20% of Cowley Co.'s (Cowley) common stock for $150,000. Saxton intends to hold the stock indefinitely. This investment did not give Saxton the ability to exercise significant influence over Cowley. During Year 6, Cowley reported net of income of $175,000 and paid cash dividends of $100,000 on its common stock. There was no change in market value of the common stock during the year.

      The balance in Saxton's investment in the Cowley account at December 31, Year 6 should be:
      A. $130,000.
      B. $150,000.
      C. $165,000.
      D. $185,000.

9.   Samia, Inc. (Samia) bought 40% of Marcello, Inc.'s (Marcello) outstanding common stock on January 2, Year 6 for $400,000. The carrying amount of Marcello's net assets at the purchase date totaled $900,000. Fair values and carrying amounts were the same for all items except for plant and inventory, for which fair values exceeded their carrying amounts by $90,000 and $10,000, respectively. The plant has an 18-year life. All inventory was sold during Year 6. During Year 6, Marcello reported net income of $120,000 and paid a $20,000 cash dividend.

What amount should Samia report in its income statement from its investment in Marcello for the year ended December 31, Year 6?
A. $32,000.
B. $36,000.
C. $42,000.
D. $48,000.

10.   The Greenpath Corporation's balance sheet shows assets of $800,000 and liabilities of $300,000. In addition, the company has an unrecorded intangible asset with a value of $100,000 and a 10-year useful life. On January 1, Year 1, the Montana Corporation acquires 30% of Greenpath's outstanding stock for $290,000. In Year 1, Greenpath reported net income of $90,000 and paid dividends of $20,000. In Year 2, Greenpath reported net income of $110,000 and paid dividends of $50,000. If the equity method is being applied to this investment, what is the reported balance for the asset at the end of Year 2?
A. $302,000.
B. $311,000.
C. $317,500.
D. $323,000.

11.   The Jamestown Corporation reported net income for the current year of $200,000 and paid cash dividends of $30,000. The Stadium Company holds 22% of the outstanding voting stock of Jamestown. However, another corporation holds the other 78% ownership and does not take Stadium's wants and wishes into consideration when making financing and operating decisions for Jamestown. What investment income should Stadium recognize for the current year?
A. $0.
B. $6,600.
C. $44,000.
D. $50,600.

12.   On January 1, Year 1, Big Company bought 30% of the outstanding stock of Little Company for $110,000 which provided Big with the ability to significantly influence the decisions of Little. Little reported assets of $400,000 and liabilities of $100,000 on that date. As part of its analysis before buying these shares, Big determined that Little owned a patent that had not been recorded despite having a remaining useful life of five years and a value of $20,000. During Year 1, Little reported net income of $70,000 and paid cash dividends of $30,000. What investment income should Big report for Year 1?
A. $9,000.
B. $17,000.
C. $19,800.
D. $21,000.

13.   In preparing its Year 1 income statement, a company has had the following transactions in connection with dividends received:
  • $4,000 cash from a company where the date of declaration was December 22, Year 1, the date of record was December 28, Year 1, and date of collection was January 6, Year 2.
  • $5,000 cash from a company that qualified as a liquidating dividend.
  • 10% stock dividend where the par value of the stock received was $2,000 but the market value was $8,000.
  • $7,000 cash from a company where the investment was being recorded by the equity method.

  What amount of investment income should the company report on its income statement for Year 1 as a result of these dividends?
  A. $0.
  B. $4,000.
  C. $9,000.
  D. $19,000.

14.   Grant, Inc. acquired 30% of South Co.'s voting stock for $200,000 on January 1, Year 1. Grant's 30% interest in South gave Grant the ability to exercise significant influence over South's operating and financial policies. On that date, South reported assets of $500,000 and liabilities of $100,000. South had equipment with a book value of $60,000 that was actually worth $160,000. The equipment had a remaining useful life of five years. During Year 1, South reported net income of $80,000 and paid dividends of $50,000. What amount of income should Grant recognize in Year 1 as a result of this investment?
  A. $4,000.
  B. $15,000.
  C. $16,750.
  D. $18,000.

ANSWERS: EQUITY METHOD OF ACCOUNTING FOR INVESTMENTS

1. **A**   With the equity method, only the proportional share of the investee's income (% ownership × investee earnings) is reported on the investor's income statement.

2. **C**   Ownership of less than 20% leads to the presumption of no substantial influence unless evidence to the contrary exists. Rhea's position as Lourdes' largest single shareholder and the presence of Rhea's officers as a majority of Lourdes' board of directors constitute evidence that Rhea does have significant influence despite less than 20% ownership.

    Therefore, the equity method is used. The investment account had a beginning balance of $400,000 (purchase price). This amount is increased by Rhea's equity in Lourdes' earnings (10% × $500,000 = $50,000) and decreased by Rhea's dividends received from Lourdes (10% × $150,000 = $15,000), resulting in a balance of $435,000.

3. **B**   When the equity method is used, the investor must amortize any portion of the excess of fair values over carrying amounts (differential) that relates to depreciable or amortizable assets held by the investee. Amortization of the differential results in a reduction of the investment account and a reduction in the equity of the investee's earnings.

    For inventory, an excess of FV over FIFO cost has the same effect on the investment account and equity in investee earnings in the period in which the goods are sold. Therefore, the portion of the differential that relates to inventory would decrease Brad's reported equity in Lamb's earnings, and answers C and D are incorrect. Land is not a depreciable asset, so there would be no amortization of the differential related to land.

4. **B** $1,500,000 + 0.40($500,000 – $125,000) = $1,650,000

5. **C** $500,000 × 40% = $200,000. Dividends are not included in income under the equity method. The dividends are included in cash flow, however.

6. **C**   Under the equity method, intercompany profits and losses are eliminated. However, receivables and payables are not eliminated as they are in the case of consolidated financial statements. On the December 31, Year 6 balance sheet, Longley should separately disclose the total amount of the receivable. Additionally, this receivable should be shown separately from other receivables.

7. **D**   The investment should have originally been recorded at the $250,000 purchase price. This amount would be increased by Keats' share of Ortiz's earnings (30% × $100,000 = $30,000), decreased by the amortization of cost over book value, and decreased by dividends received by Keats (none in this case).

    The book value Keats purchased is $150,000 (30% × $500,000), resulting in an excess of cost over book value of $100,000 ($250,000 – $150,000). This excess must be attributed to specific assets of Ortiz that have a fair value greater than their book value. Any amount not attributed to specific assets is attributed to goodwill. In this case, the excess would be attributed first to land (30% × $200,000 = $60,000) and the remainder of $40,000 to goodwill. The portion attributed to land and goodwill should not be amortized.

    The investment in Ortiz and December 31, Year 6 should be $250,000 + $30,000 = $280,000.

8. **B**   The equity method is to be used when the investor owns 20% of more of the investee's voting stock unless there is evidence that the investor does not have the ability to exercise significant influence over the investee. Because this is the case, Saxton must carry the stock in the available-for-sale category. Under this method, dividends received are to be recognized as income to the investor and the investment account is unaffected.

Also, under this method, the investor's share of the investee's net income is not recognized. Any changes in the market value of the stock would be reflected in the book value of the stock with a corresponding amount in a separate account in stockholders' equity.

As there has been no change in the market value, the investment account would still have a balance of $150,000 at December 31, Year 6.

Note that the dividends received by Saxton were distributed from Cowley's net accumulated earnings since the date of acquisition by Saxton. However, if dividends received had been in excess of earnings subsequent to the investment date, they are considered a return of capital and would be recorded as a reduction in the investment account.

9. **C**   Samia paid $400,000 for its 40% investment in Marcello when Marcello's net assets had a carrying amount of $900,000. Therefore, the book value Samia purchased is $360,000 (40% × $900,000), resulting in an excess of cost over book value of $40,000. This excess must be attributed to specific assets of Marcello; any amount not attributed to specific assets is attributed to goodwill.

In this case, the excess is attributed to plant assets (40% × $90,000 = $36,000) and inventory (40% × $10,000 = $4,000). The portion attributed to plant assets is amortized over 18 years, while the portion attributed to inventory is expensed immediately (because all inventory was sold during Year 6). Therefore, Samia's investment income is $42,000 as computed below:

Share of income (40% × $120,000)	$48,000
Excess amortization [($36,000/18) + $4,000]	(6,000)
	$42,000

10. **D**   Greenpath has a net book value of $500,000 ($800,000 assets – $300,000 in liabilities). A 30% ownership would equate to $150,000. Montana paid $290,000, or an extra $140,000. Part of that excess can be attributed to the unrecorded intangible asset. Because of its $100,000 value, $30,000 (30%) is assigned to this asset. The remaining $110,000 is unexplained and, hence, assigned to goodwill. The intangible asset allocation is amortized at the rate of $3,000 per year. The goodwill is not amortized. Under the equity method, Montana will increase its investment by 30% of Greenpath's income (30% of $90,000 and $110,000 or $60,000 in total). Montana will decrease its investment by 30% of Greenpath's dividends (30% of $20,000 and $50,000 or $21,000). After two years, the investment balance is the $290,000 cost + $60,000 – $21,000 – $6,000 in amortization (for two years) for a total of $323,000.

11. **B**   The equity method is normally applied to any investment where the owner holds between 20% and 50% of the outstanding voting stock. However, that is only a guideline. The actual rule states that the equity method is used where the owner has the ability to apply significant influence to the operating and financing decisions of the investee company. Here, despite holding 22% of the outstanding stock, it is clear that Stadium does not have that level of influence because of the actions of the other owner. Therefore, the only investment income would have been the 22% of the $30,000 dividends received by Stadium, or $6,600.

12. **C**   The equity method is used here because Big has obtained the ability to apply significant influence. In applying this method, a determination must be made as to whether any portion of the purchase price should be allocated to specific assets and liabilities as well as to goodwill. The net book value on the date of acquisition is $300,000 ($400,000 – $100,000). The underlying portion that equates to Big's acquisition is 30% of that figure or $90,000. Because Big paid an acquisition price of $110,000, there is an excess $20,000 that must be explained. A portion of that amount was paid in recognition of the value of the patent that was unrecorded. The patent was worth $20,000, but Big only bought 30% of the other company, so it is reasonable to believe that an extra $6,000 was paid to compensate the seller for the value of the patent. The remaining $14,000 of the excess amount is unexplained and, as such, is assigned to the intangible asset Goodwill. The patent has a life of five years so annual amortization will be $1,200 ($6,000/5 years). Goodwill is not subjected to amortization. The investment income, then, is 30% of the reported income $70,000, or $21,000 less the $1,200 amortization the patent for a net figure of $19,800.

13. **B**   No income is recorded in connection with the receipt of liquidating dividends, stock dividends, and dividends where the equity method is being applied. Normally, cash dividends are recorded as income by the owner on the date of record which, in the first dividend, was December 28, Year 1. That $4,000 is the only income to be recorded by the owner in Year 1.

14. **D**   Because Grant has the ability to exercise significant influence over South's operating and financial decisions, the equity method should be applied to this investment. The initial step in that process is an allocation of the $200,000 purchase price. On the date of acquisition, South has a net book value of $400,000 ($500,000 – $100,000). A 30% purchase equates to $120,000. However, Grant actually paid $200,000, and the $80,000 excess must be explained. South had equipment undervalued on its books by $100,000 ($160,000 less $60,000) and Grant would have paid more for the company's stock for that reason. Since 30% was bought, an allocation of $30,000 ($100,000 × 30%) is attributed to this equipment. With a 5-year useful life, that allocation is amortized at the rate of $6,000 per year.

That leaves $50,000 of the excess unexplained ($80,000 – $30,000). That residual is always assigned to goodwill, an intangible asset that is no longer amortized. In Year 1, Grant should recognize income of $24,000 (South's $80,000 reported income × 30%) and then the $6,000 annual amortization is removed to arrive at the reported income figure of $18,000.

CHAPTER 16 – CONSOLIDATED FINANCIAL INFORMATION

STUDY TIP

A key to passing the CPA exam is to break each topic into learnable segments. Normally, each topic is composed of several different specific steps. Break the topic into those steps and then learn each one individually. Passing the CPA exam becomes quite difficult when a candidate attempts to learn a major topic as a single whole. That is similar to trying to eat a watermelon without cutting it into pieces. People come to understand the topic better when they are faced with a segment of information that is small enough to be learnable.

CHAPTER 16 – CONSOLIDATED FINANCIAL INFORMATION

CONSOLIDATED FINANCIAL STATEMENTS

GENERAL FEATURES OF CONSOLIDATED FINANCIAL STATEMENTS

A. The concept of consolidated financial statements is that the resources of two or more companies are under the control of the parent company.

B. Consolidated statements are prepared as if the group of legal entities were one economic entity group.

C. Consolidated statements are presumed to be more meaningful for management, owners, and creditors of the parent company, and they are required for fair presentation of the financially related companies.

REQUIRED DISCLOSURE ITEMS FOR BUSINESS ACQUISITIONS

A. Business acquisitions require significant disclosure in the notes to the consolidated financial statements, especially if it is a material business combination.

1. Disclosure of the name and a brief description of the acquired entity and the percentage of voting equity interest acquired.

2. Disclosure of the primary reasons for a business combination and the allocation of the purchase price paid to the assets acquired and liabilities assumed by major balance sheet caption.

3. The period for which the results of the operations of the acquired entity are included in the income statement of the combined entity.

4. When the amounts of goodwill and intangible assets acquired are significant in relation to the purchase price paid, disclosure of other information about those assets is required, such as the amount of goodwill by reportable segment and the amount of the purchase price assigned to each major intangible asset class.

COMBINED FINANCIAL STATEMENTS

Combined financial statements is a term used to describe financial statements prepared for companies that are owned by the same parent company or individual.

A. These statements are often prepared when several subsidiaries of a common parent are not consolidated with the parent.

B. Combined financial statements are prepared by combining all of the separate companies' financial statement classifications but without the inclusion of the parent company.

C. Intercompany transactions, balances, and profit/loss should be eliminated in the same way as in consolidated statements. But without the parent, no arbitrary allocations or amortization are included, and that may make the information more useful.

CONSOLIDATION

A. As stated previously, the consolidation process brings together two or more sets of financial statements because the companies have common ownership. For external reporting purposes, the companies are viewed as a single entity even though the companies may be separate legal entities.

B. Total ownership is not necessary to form a business combination (consolidation accounting). Only control is required, and control is usually established through the direct or indirect ownership of over 50% of the voting shares. Consolidation is also required by the primary beneficiary of a variable interest entity (discussed later).

C. Note a few exceptions where control is temporary or if barriers to control exist, such as government intervention, bankruptcy.

   1. These exceptions exist to accommodate situations where the parent company cannot use the subsidiaries' assets or control its actions.

   2. In such cases, consolidation accounting would not be required.

D. Consolidated financial statements are prepared from worksheets that begin with the trial balances of the parent and subsidiary companies.

   1. Eliminating worksheet entries are made to reflect the two separate companies' results of operations and financial position as one combined economic entity.

   2. The entire consolidation process takes place only on a worksheet; no consolidation elimination entries are ever recorded on either the parent's or the subsidiary's books.

E. A purchase is viewed as an acquisition: one company clearly buys the other. It is often compared to a parent-child relationship.

F. All consolidations are now reported by use of the acquisition method (formerly known as the purchase method).

G. The pooling of interests method has been eliminated, although consolidations previously reported using this method are allowed to remain as poolings.

   1. It assumed a combining of stockholders' interests and the basis of valuation is the net book value of the net assets on the books of the acquired company.

   2. No goodwill is created at the date of combination.

   3. Financial statements of the acquired company are restated to show the operations and financial position of the pooled companies as if they had been pooled since inception.

PURCHASE PRICE

A. A purchase price is determined based on the fair value of the consideration (cash, stock, debt, etc.) given by the acquiring company. The assets and liabilities of the acquired company are revalued to their respective fair values at the combination date.

B. Direct costs incurred as a result of the acquisition (accounting, legal, and investment banking fees) are expensed as incurred. Costs incurred for the issuance of debt and equity securities are accounted for under other applicable GAAP.

C. An allocation of the purchase price is made at the date of acquisition. Any difference between price paid and the equivalent portion of the underlying book value of the subsidiary must be allocated.

D. Allocation is made to the acquired firm's identifiable assets and liabilities based on 100% of their fair values even if less than 100% is acquired. Unrecorded intangible assets such as an Internet URL, noncompetition agreements, or a database of customer information must be valued and included in the allocation process.

E. For example, suppose that a parent pays $100,000 over book value to acquire a subsidiary. The subsidiary had land that originally cost $50,000, but it is now worth $70,000.

   1. Of the excess purchase price, $20,000 is allocated to this land.

   2. If the parent had only bought 80% of the subsidiary, then the allocation to land is still $20,000 (or 100%) of the increase in value.

   3. Any excess purchase price that cannot be allocated to specific assets and liabilities is assigned to goodwill, an intangible asset.

   4. Goodwill is not subject to annual amortization but, rather, must be tested annually for impairment (more on that later).

ACCOUNTING ISSUES RELATED TO PURCHASE PRICE ALLOCATIONS

A. FASB wants the parent to consider whether any excess purchase price indicates the presence of identifiable intangible assets other than goodwill.

   1. It has been suggested to value assets such as customer lists, sales backlog, noncompetition agreements, database, and the like.

B. The acquired firm's in-process research and development is capitalized as an indefinite-lived asset until completion and tested annually for impairment. Upon completion, the asset is reclassified as a finite-lived intangible and amortized over its useful life. If abandoned, the asset is expensed immediately.

C. If, after all allocations are made to assets and liabilities, a negative amount remains, the remainder is recognized as a gain in the income statement as a component of continuing operations (not extraordinary).

GOODWILL

A. Goodwill should be tested for impairment on an annual basis and on an even more frequent basis if there is evidence to suggest that negative events have occurred.

B. The resulting consolidated company is divided into reporting units by much the same approach that is utilized for segment reporting.

   1. The goodwill is then assigned to these various units based on the expected benefits of the acquisition.

   2. Part of the goodwill can be attributed to a reporting unit within the parent if the unit is better off because of the takeover.

C. There are two steps in determining if goodwill of a reporting unit has been impaired. If the first step does not show impairment, then the second step is not even tested.

   1. First, unless the fair value of the reporting unit as a whole is below the carrying value of that unit, there is no impairment.

   2. Second, the fair value of the reporting unit as a whole is compared to the fair value of the individual assets of that same reporting unit.

     a. Any excess is the implied goodwill remaining on that day.

     b. If this impaired value is below the book value of goodwill assigned to that unit, then goodwill is written down to the implied valued, and a loss is recognized.

INTERCOMPANY TRANSACTIONS

A. The consolidation process eliminates reciprocal items that are shown on both the parent's and the subsidiary's books.

   1. These eliminations are necessary to avoid double counting the same items that would misstate the financial statements of the combined economic entity.

B. Intercompany debt (accounts receivable/accounts payable or investment in bonds/bonds payable) are offset against each other. All intercompany balances are removed, even if ownership is below 100%.

C. All balances recorded for inventory transfers between the parties must be removed. Both sales and COGS are reduced by the entire amount of the transfer price.

   1. If inventory is transferred between parties, any unrealized gain in connection with goods still held at year-end must also be eliminated.

   2. Profit must be deferred until it is actually realized.

   3. The amount of the unrealized gain remaining at the end of the year is found by multiplying the remaining goods times the profit. One of these figures has to be a percentage and the other a dollar amount.

   4. Deferral of the unrealized gain creates a reduction in the Inventory account and an increase in the COGS account.

D. If any other asset is transferred, all accounts must be returned to balances that would be applicable if the transfer had not occurred.

   1. Adjustments are made to the asset account, accumulated depreciation, depreciation expense, and any gain or loss, in order to align them with the balances that would have resulted.

E. Any "investment in subsidiary" account or "income of subsidiary" account must be removed on consolidation. Any intercompany dividends are also eliminated.

NONCONTROLLING INTEREST

A. Subsidiaries are consolidated in total regardless of whether 100% of the stock is owned.

1. If less than 100% is held within the business combination, the outside owners are referred to as a noncontrolling interest and their ownership is reflected as:

   a. Single figure in consolidated shareholders' equity.

   b. Reduction in the consolidated income statement.

B. Noncontrolling interest balances attributed to outside owners are computed by taking (1) the fair value of the subsidiary including goodwill and (2) the reported income of the subsidiary and multiplying both by the outside ownership percentage.

C. Goodwill is allocated to the controlling and noncontrolling interests.

Example:

Firm A acquires 75% of Firm B for $800 which includes a $50 control premium.

The fair value of firm B is $1,000.

The fair value of firm B's identifiable net assets is $700.

Required: allocate the acquisition goodwill to the controlling and noncontrolling interests.

Solution:

Fair value of Firm B	$1,000
Less: FV (100%) of B's net assets	700
Total goodwill	$300
Purchase price	$800
Less: FV (75%) of B's net assets	525
Goodwill – controlling interest	$275

Goodwill – noncontrolling interest $25 ($300 – $275)

Note the controlling interest's share is not 75% of total goodwill because of the control premium paid.

CONSOLIDATED AMOUNTS

A. At the date of a purchase, the following applies:

1. Each consolidated asset and liability is the sum of the two book values with the following adjustments:

   a. Plus or minus any allocation made of the purchase price based on the fair value of the subsidiary's accounts.

   b. Less any intercompany transactions.

2. Goodwill (if any) is included as an asset on the consolidated balance sheet.

3. The parent previously maintained an internal investment account to monitor its ownership of the subsidiary, but this account is always eliminated in the consolidation process.

B. Subsequent to the date of acquisition, the following applies:

    1. The current book values of the assets and liabilities are added together along with the original allocations.

    2. However, each of these allocations (except for goodwill and land) is reduced by amortization over the useful lives.

C. Consolidated revenues and expenses are the parent figures plus the subsidiary figures, but the subsidiary figures are used only for the period since the acquisition.

D. Amortization on any purchase price allocations must be included as expenses.

E. Any unrealized gains must be removed.

F. Any investment in subsidiary or income from subsidiary balances are removed.

G. To determine consolidated retained earnings or consolidated income, a determination of what has been included in the parent's figures is made.

    1. No second inclusion is needed if the parent has already done the following:

        a. Recognized its ownership percentage of the subsidiary's income.

        b. Removed any unrealized gain.

        c. Recorded amortization expense for the period.

H. Consolidated stockholders' equity is always the parent's balances plus any income effects relating to the subsidiary since the acquisition.

I. If the parent issued stock in taking over the subsidiary, then the value of those shares must be included in the consolidated equity figure.

PUSH-DOWN ACCOUNTING

A. *Push-down accounting* is a method used to prepare separate financial statements for significant, very large subsidiaries that are either wholly owned or substantially owned (90% or more).

    1. For publicly traded companies, the SEC requires a one-time adjustment under the purchase method to revalue the subsidiary's assets and liabilities to fair value based on the purchase price.

    2. This entry is made directly on the books of the subsidiary.

B. Push-down accounting requires the subsidiary to record an entry revaluing all assets and liabilities with a balancing entry to a revaluation capital account.

    1. The revaluation account will be eliminated in consolidation against the investment in subsidiary account.

C. Push-down accounting will have no effect on the presentation of the consolidated financial statements or the separate financial statements of the parent company.

   1. However, the subsidiary's financial statements would be reported at fair value rather than historical cost, so the consolidation process is simpler.

D. Advocates of push-down accounting believe that a change in ownership through a purchase combination justifies the use of a new basis for the acquired entity. Thus, the new basis should be pushed down or directly recorded on the acquired company's books.

VARIABLE INTEREST ENTITIES

A. Variable interest entities (VIEs) are often used as holding entities for passive activities (e.g., receivables or real estate) or as entities that provide services for other companies (e.g., R&D). The parent may control the VIE without owning 50% of its stock.

B. Consolidating VIEs involves a two-step test:

   1. Is the entity a VIE? If no, then consolidation is not required unless there is more than 50% ownership.

   2. If yes, then it must be determined who will consolidate it.

C. *Step 1*: An entity is a VIE subject to consolidation if either of the following conditions exist:

   1. The total equity investment at risk is not sufficient to permit the entity to finance its own activities without additional subordinated financial support from other parties (e.g., the equity investment at risk is less than the expected losses of the entity).

   2. As a group, the holders of the equity investment at risk lack one or more of the following three characteristics of a controlling financial interest:

      a. The direct or indirect ability to make decisions about an entity's activities through voting rights or similar rights.

      b. The obligation to absorb the expected losses of the entity if they occur.

      c. The right to receive the expected residual returns of the entity (if they occur).

   3. An equity investment of less than 10% of total assets should generally be considered insufficient to fund the entity's operations, unless there is clear evidence to the contrary, as demonstrated by satisfying each of the following criteria:

      a. The entity can get funds for its activities without additional subordinated financial support.

      b. The entity's funding is consistent with other entities with similar assets and whose track record indicates that less than 10% equity is reasonable and appropriate.

      c. The amount of equity invested exceeds any expected losses from the entity's activities.

   4. In practice, less than 10% generally means that the entity will be considered to be a VIE.

      a. Entities with 10% or more equity may or may not be considered VIEs, depending on the circumstances.

D. *Step 2*: Assuming the VIE test is met, the VIE should be consolidated by the company (the primary beneficiary) that will:

   1. Absorb the majority of the entity's expected losses (if they occur).

   2. Receive a majority of the entity's expected residual returns (if they occur).

E. In situations where one party receives a majority of the income/gains while another party is exposed to a majority of the losses, the party exposed to the losses must consolidate the VIE (a "tie breaker" rule).

   1. A VIE will not be consolidated by any party if the risk of the VIE is effectively disbursed among all parties involved.

   2. Nevertheless, each party is required to include its involvement in the VIE in its financial disclosures.

F. In addition to consolidation, the primary beneficiary should disclose the following:

   1. The nature, purpose, size, and activities of the VIE.

   2. The carrying amount and classification of consolidated assets that are collateral for the VIE's obligations.

   3. Lack of recourse if creditors of a consolidated VIE have no recourse to the general credit of the primary beneficiary.

G. Any party that holds a significant interest in a VIE that is not the primary beneficiary should disclose the following:

   1. The nature of its involvement with the VIE and when involvement began.

   2. The nature, purpose, size, and activities of the VIE.

   3. The party's maximum exposure to loss as a result of its involvement with the VIE.

QUESTIONS: CONSOLIDATED FINANCIAL INFORMATION

1. A business combination is accounted for appropriately as a purchase. Which of the following should be deducted in determining the combined company's net income for the current period?

	Direct costs of acquisition	General costs related to acquisition
A.	Yes	No
B.	Yes	Yes
C.	No	Yes
D.	No	No

2. On January 1, Year 6, Shaw Co. (Shaw) issued 100,000 shares of its $10 par value common stock in exchange for all of Crawford Co.'s (Crawford) outstanding stock. The fair value of Shaw's common stock on December 31, Year 5, was $19 per share. The carrying amounts and fair values of Crawford's assets and liabilities on December 31, Year 5, were as follows:

	Carrying Amount	Fair Value
Cash	$240,000	$240,000
Receivables	$270,000	$270,000
Inventory	$435,000	$405,000
PP&E	$1,305,000	$1,440,000
Liabilities	($525,000)	($525,000)

    What is the amount of goodwill resulting from the business combination?
    A. $0.
    B. $70,000.
    C. $105,000.
    D. $175,000.

3. Partita, Inc. (Partita) has a receivable from its parent, Concerto, Inc. (Concerto). Should this receivable be separately reported in Partita's balance sheet and in Concerto's consolidated balance sheet?

	Partita's balance sheet	Concerto's consolidated balance sheet
A.	Yes	No
B.	Yes	Yes
C.	No	No
D.	No	Yes

4. On June 30, Year 6, Panagakos Co. (Panagakos) exchanged 150,000 shares of its $20 par value common stock for all of Skylar Co.'s (Skylar) common stock. On that date, the fair value of Panagakos' common stock issued was equal to the book value of Skylar's net assets. Both corporations continued to operate as separate businesses, maintaining accounting records with years ending December 31. Information from separate company operations are as follows:

	Panagakos	Skylar
Retained earnings—December 31, Year 5	$3,200,000	$925,000
Net income—first six months of Year 6	$800,000	$275,000
Dividends paid—March 25, Year 6	$750,000	$0

    What amount of retained earnings would Panagakos report in its June 30, Year 6, consolidated balance sheet?
    A. $3,250,000.
    B. $3,525,000.
    C. $4,450,000.
    D. $5,200,000.

5. Intermezzo, Inc. (Intermezzo) owns 80% of Sonata, Inc.'s (Sonata) common stock. During Year 6, Intermezzo sold $250,000 of inventory to Sonata on the same terms as sales made to third parties. Sonata sold all the inventory purchased from Intermezzo in Year 6. The following information pertains to Intermezzo and Sonata's sales for Year 6:

	Intermezzo	Sonata
Sales	$1,000,000	$700,000
Cost of sales	$400,000	$350,000

    What amount should Intermezzo report as cost of sales in its Year 6 consolidated income statement?
    A. $430,000.
    B. $500,000.
    C. $680,000.
    D. $750,000.

6. Colette Co. (Colette) acquired a 70% interest in Ruby, Inc. (Ruby) in Year 4. For the years ended December 31, Year 5 and Year 6, Ruby reported net income of $80,000 and $90,000, respectively. During Year 5, Ruby sold merchandise to Colette for $10,000 at a profit of $2,000. The merchandise was later resold by Colette to outsiders for $15,000 during Year 6.

    For consolidation purposes, what is the minority interest's share of Ruby's net income for Year 5 and Year 6, respectively?
    A. $23,400 and $27,600.
    B. $24,000 and $27,000.
    C. $24,600 and $26,400.
    D. $26,000 and $25,000.

7. Prelude, Inc., Chorale ,Inc., and Fugue, Inc. established a variable interest entity (VIE) to perform leasing activities for the three companies. Which of the companies should consolidate the VIE?
   A. The company with the largest interest in the entity should consolidate.
   B. The company that will absorb a majority of the expected losses if they occur should consolidate.
   C. The company that has the most voting equity interest should consolidate.
   D. Each company should consolidate one-third of the VIE.

8. Andsnes, Inc. owns 90% of Barenboim Co.'s (Barenboim) common stock and 80% of Corigliano Co.'s (Corigliano) common stock. The remaining common shares of Barenboim and Corigliano are owned by their respective employees. Barenboim sells exclusively to Corigliano, Corigliano buys exclusively from Barenboim, and Corigliano sells exclusively to unrelated parties. Selected Year 6 information is as follows:

	Barenboim	Corigliano
Sales	$130,000	$91,000
Cost of sales	$100,000	$65,000
Beginning inventory	$0	$0
Ending inventory	$0	$65,000

   What amount should be reported as gross profit in Barenboim and Corigliano's combined income statement for the year ended December 31, Year 6?
   A. $26,000.
   B. $41,000.
   C. $47,800.
   D. $56,000.

9. During Year 6, Penny, Inc. (Penny) sold goods to its 80%-owned subsidiary, Sikora, Inc. (Sikora). At December 31, Year 6, one-half of these goods were included in Sikora's ending inventory. Reported Year 6 selling expenses were $1,100,000 and $400,000 for Penny and Sikora, respectively. Penny's selling expenses included $50,000 of freight-out costs for goods sold to Sikora.

   What amount of selling expenses should be reported in Penny's Year 6 consolidated income statement?
   A. $1,450,000.
   B. $1,475,000.
   C. $1,480,000.
   D. $1,500,000.

10. When is the determination made of whether an interest holder must consolidate a variable interest entity (VIE)?
   A. Each reporting period.
   B. When the interest holder initially gets involved with the VIE.
   C. Every time the cash flows of the VIE change significantly.
   D. Never.

Use the following information to answer Questions 11 through 15.

On January 1, Year 6, Polka Co. (Polka) and Strauss Co. (Strauss) had condensed balance sheets as follows:

	Polka	Strauss
Current assets	$70,000	$20,000
Noncurrent assets	$90,000	$40,000
Current liabilities	$30,000	$10,000
Long-term debt	$50,000	$0
Stockholder's equity	$80,000	$50,000

On January 2, Year 6, Polka borrowed $90,000 and used the proceeds to purchase 90% of the outstanding common shares of Strauss. This debt is payable in ten equal annual principal payments, plus interest, beginning December 30, Year 6. On the acquisition date, the fair value of Strauss was $100,000 and the excess cost of the investment over Strauss' book value of acquired net assets should be allocated 60% to inventory and 40% to goodwill.

11. Current assets on the January 2, Year 6 consolidated balance sheet should be:
    A. $79,000.
    B. $90,000.
    C. $96,000.
    D. $120,000.

12. Noncurrent assets on the January 2, Year 6 consolidated balance sheet should be:
    A. $130,000.
    B. $134,000.
    C. $136,000.
    D. $150,000.

13. Current liabilities on the January 2, Year 6 consolidated balance sheet should be:
    A. $30,000.
    B. $40,000.
    C. $49,000.
    D. $50,000.

14. Noncurrent liabilities on the January 2, Year 6 consolidated balance sheet should be:
    A. $55,000.
    B. $104,000.
    C. $109,000.
    D. $131,000.

15. Stockholders' equity on the January 2, Year 6 consolidated balance sheet should be:
    A. $80,000.
    B. $85,000.
    C. $90,000.
    D. $130,000.

16.   Giant Corporation buys 100% of the voting stock of Small, Inc. on January 1, Year 1. Small had a building with a 10-year life at a book value of $400,000 that was actually worth $540,000. Giant paid enough for Small so that $60,000 in goodwill was recognized. Subsequently, on December 31, Year 2, Giant reports have buildings with a book value of $900,000, and Small now reports buildings with a book value of $650,000. What is the book value for the consolidated Buildings account?

    A. $1,550,000.
    B. $1,587,000.
    C. $1,662,000.
    D. $1,690,000.

17.   On December 31, Year 1, Big Company transfers a building to its wholly-owned subsidiary (Little Company) at a gain of $50,000. The building should last for an additional ten years. The company is currently producing consolidated financial statements for Year 3. Which of the following statements is true?

    A. Consolidated net income in Year 3 will not be impacted by this transfer.
    B. Consolidated net income in Year 3 will be increased by $5,000 because of this transfer.
    C. Consolidated net income in Year 3 will be decreased by $5,000 because of this transfer.
    D. Consolidated net income in Year 3 will be decreased by $50,000 because of this transfer.

18.   Little Company has an excellent credit rating and also has an extensive database of potential customers. Neither of these is reported by the company as an asset. Big Company buys all of the outstanding stock of Little for significantly above book value. The parent pays an extra $30,000 because of the credit rating and an extra $50,000 because of the database. In consolidation, how are these balances reported?

    A. $30,000 is included in goodwill, and $50,000 is shown as a separate intangible asset.
    B. $30,000 is expensed immediately, and $50,000 is included in goodwill.
    C. Both of these amounts are included in goodwill.
    D. Both amounts are expensed immediately.

19.   A company has four asset balances and no liabilities: accounts receivable of $100,000, inventory of $100,000, equipment of $60,000, and intangible assets of $40,000. Each of these assets is worth an amount that is exactly equal to its book value. There are no unrecorded intangible assets. All of the outstanding stock of this company is acquired by the Kansas Corporation for $270,000 in cash. Consolidated statements are being produced immediately after the purchase. Which of the following statements is true?

    A. Accounts receivable will be consolidated at $90,000.
    B. Inventory will be consolidated at $85,000.
    C. Equipment will be consolidated at $51,000.
    D. Intangible assets will be consolidated at $40,000.

20.   A company has four asset balances and no liabilities: accounts receivable of $100,000, inventory of $100,000, equipment of $60,000, and intangible assets of $40,000. Each of these assets is worth exactly as much as its book value. There are no unrecorded intangible assets. All of the outstanding stock of this company is acquired by the Nebraska Corporation for $190,000 in cash. Consolidated statements are being produced immediately after the purchase. Which of the following statements is true?

    A. An extraordinary gain of $10,000 is reported.
    B. A regular gain of $110,000 is reported.
    C. Accounts receivable is reported as $95,000.
    D. Inventory is reported as $90,000.

21. Ajax and Thompson formed a business combination several years ago. One reporting unit of the combination has been assigned goodwill of $40,000. Currently, this reporting unit has a total book value of $550,000, but the fair value of the reporting unit is only $520,000. A total of fair values of all identifiable assets and liabilities of this reporting unit is $470,000. What amount of loss should be recognized because of the impairment of goodwill value?
    A. $0.
    B. $10,000.
    C. $30,000.
    D. $40,000.

22. On January 1, Year 1, Giant Company pays $900,000 for all of the outstanding shares of Small Corporation. On that date, Small has a net book value (assets – liabilities) of $700,000. In analyzing the company prior to the acquisition, Giant discovers that Small is working on several in-process research and development projects that are worth a total of $170,000 although none of the projects has yet reached the point of technological feasibility. Which of the following statements is true?
    A. Goodwill of $30,000 should be recorded as a result of this purchase.
    B. An expense of $170,000 should be recognized immediately at the date of acquisition.
    C. Any goodwill allocation will be amortized at the end of Year 1.
    D. The life attributed to any goodwill allocation will be 40 years or less.

23. Large Company bought all of the outstanding stock of Tiny Corporation several years ago. During the current year, Tiny sold inventory costing $80,000 to Large for $100,000. By the end of the year, 60% of this merchandise had been resold to unrelated parties. At the end of the year, Large reported cost of goods sold of $400,000, and Tiny reported cost of goods sold of $200,000. What is the consolidated cost of goods sold for that year?
    A. $500,000.
    B. $508,000.
    C. $520,000.
    D. $568,000.

24. On January 1, Year 1, the Kincaid Corporation buys all of the outstanding shares of Patterson, Inc., for a price of $800,000 in excess of Patterson, Inc.'s book value. At that time, Kincaid held buildings with a ten-year remaining life and no expected salvage value that had a book value of $4 million and a fair value of $4.3 million. On the same day, Patterson owned buildings with a 10-year remaining life and no expected salvage value that had a book value of $2 million and a fair value of $2.2 million. During the following year, both companies bought additional buildings so that, by December 31, Kincaid's buildings had a book value of $5 million and a fair value of $5.5 million, while Patterson's buildings had a book value of $3 million (excluding any value allocated to Patterson's buildings because of Kincaid's purchase of Patterson) and had a fair value of $3.2 million. What was the reported balance for the Buildings account on the consolidated financial statements at the year end?
    A. $8,180,000.
    B. $8,200,000.
    C. $8,500,000.
    D. $9,100,000.

25.   The Max Corporation buys a controlling interest in Min Corporation and now must produce consolidated financial statements. Max paid an amount in excess of Min's book value and must now allocate that balance to specific subsidiary assets and liabilities and to goodwill. The accountant has suggested that each of the following four has a value and should be recognized in consolidation as an intangible asset separate from goodwill. Which of these four cannot be shown as a separate asset?
    A.   Internet domain name.
    B.   Database.
    C.   Noncompetition agreement.
    D.   Education costs expended on members of management.

26.   Two years ago, Company A bought all of the outstanding stock of Company Z. As a result of this acquisition, $1 million has been reported in the consolidated statements as goodwill. Company Z is comprised of two reporting units: wood and plastics. At the date of acquisition, $700,000 of the goodwill was assigned to the Wood unit, and $300,000 was assigned to the Plastics unit. The Wood unit has done poorly and there is a question as to whether the Goodwill balance has been impaired. Today, this unit's book value is $5 million, but its fair value is only $5.1 million. The total fair value of all of its identifiable assets and liabilities is $4.8 million. What amount of loss should be recognized as a result of goodwill impairment in connection with the Wood reporting unit?
    A. $0.
    B. $400,000.
    C. $600,000.
    D. $700,000.

27.   Two years ago, Company X bought all of the outstanding stock of Company Y. As a result of this acquisition, $2 million has been reported in the consolidated statements as goodwill. Company Y is comprised of two reporting units: paper and food services. At the date of acquisition, $1.3 million of the goodwill was assigned to the paper unit and $700,000 assigned to food services. The paper unit has done poorly financially since the acquisition and now there is a question as to whether or not the goodwill balance has been impaired. Today, this unit's book value is $9 million, but its fair value is only $8.8 million. The total fair value of all of its identifiable assets and liabilities is $8.4 million. What amount of loss should be recognized as a result of goodwill impairment in connection with the Paper reporting unit?
    A. $0.
    B. $400,000.
    C. $700,000.
    D. $900,000.

28.   On January 1, Year 1, the Pop Corporation buys 100% of the outstanding stock of Son, Inc. for $4 million. On that date, Son reports assets of $5 million and liabilities of $2 million. Upon investigation, Pop uncovers a potential intangible asset held by Son. It has a value of $200,000. Son has contractual rights to this asset but it cannot be separated and sold. Pop also discovers a second potential intangible asset held by Son. It has a value of $300,000. This asset can be separated from Son and sold, but the company does not hold contractual rights to it. In consolidated financial statements prepared immediately after the purchase, what amount should be reported as goodwill?
    A. $500,000.
    B. $700,000.
    C. $800,000.
    D. $1,000,000.

29. Company A acquired 100% of Company Z several years ago. During the current year, Company Z bought inventory for $120,000 and sold it to Company A for $150,000. Of this merchandise, Company A resold $100,000 (at the transfer price) to outsiders prior to the end of that year. Consolidated statements are now being prepared. Which of the following is not correct?
    A. Inventory must be reduced by $10,000.
    B. Cost of goods sold must be reduced by $140,000.
    C. Sales must be reduced by $150,000.
    D. Gross profit must be reduced by $20,000.

30. One of the separate units of a company reports a net book value of $3 million, which contains goodwill of $200,000. Currently, this unit has a fair value of only $2.9 million. Which of the following is true?
    A. Goodwill is not impaired.
    B. Goodwill might be impaired.
    C. Goodwill is impaired.
    D. Goodwill impairment is tested for the company as a whole and not for individual units.

ANSWERS: CONSOLIDATED FINANCIAL INFORMATION

1. **B** Both the direct costs of acquisition and general costs related to the acquisition are expensed when incurred in determining the combined firm's net income for the current period.

2. **B** In a business combination accounted for as a purchase, the fair value of the net assets is used as the valuation basis for the combination. In this case, Crawford's assets have an implied fair value of $1,900,000, equal to the market value of the common stock issue (100,000 shares × $19). The value assigned to goodwill is $70,000, which is the value of the stock minus the fair value of Crawford's identifiable assets.

3. **A** When a subsidiary prepares separate financial statements, intercompany receivables (and payables) should be reported in the balance sheet as a separate line item. When consolidated financial statements are prepared by the parent company, all intercompany receivables and payables should be eliminated to avoid overstating assets and liabilities.

4. **A** In a business combination accounted for as a purchase, the FV of net assets is used as the valuation basis for the combination. The investment is recorded at the fair value of the net assets, common stock is recorded at par value (150,000 × $20 = $3,000,000), and any difference is recorded as APIC.

   The subsidiary's retained earnings are not recorded in a purchase. Therefore, the June 30, Year 6 consolidated retained earnings is equal to Panagakos' separate June 30, Year 6 retained earnings of $3,250,000 ($3,200,000 + $800,000 – $750,000).

5. **B** When preparing the consolidated income statement, the objective is to restate the accounts as if the intercompany transactions had not occurred. As a result of the intercompany sale, Intermezzo has recorded $250,000 of sales and Sonata has recorded $250,000 cost of sales that should be eliminated (note that Intermezzo's cost of sales on the original sale is the amount left in consolidated cost of sales, and Sonata's sales when the goods were sold to outside parties is the amount left in consolidated sales). Therefore, Intermezzo should report $500,000 as cost of sales in the Year 6 consolidated income statement ($400,000 + $350,000 – $250,000).

6. **A** Without the intercompany transaction, the minority interest income from Ruby in Year 5 would be $24,000 (30% × $80,000). In Year 6, the minority interest income would be $27,000 (30% × $90,000). On the consolidated statements in Year 5, the $2,000 intercompany profit will be eliminated because from a consolidated viewpoint, an arm's length transaction has not occurred with third parties. The elimination entry will be to credit inventory on the books of Colette for $2,000, and debits will be made of $1,400 to majority interest income and $600 to minority interest income.

   In Year 6, when Colette sells the inventory to outsiders, the $2,000 profit has effectively been earned. In Year 6, an entry will be made on the consolidated books to effectively recognize this profit and allocate it to the majority and minority interest. Thus, the 2005 minority interest income will be reduced by $600 to $23,400, and Year 6 minority interest income increased by $600 to $27,600.

7. **B** A VIE should be consolidated by the company that will absorb the majority of the VIE's expected losses if they occur, or receive the majority of the residual returns if they occur, or both.

8. **B** Combined financial statements are prepared for companies that are owned by the same parent company or individual but are not consolidated. These statements are prepared by combining the separate companies' financial statement classifications. Intercompany transactions, balances, and profit/loss should be eliminated.

   Therefore, to determine the gross profit of Barenboim and Corigliano's combined income statement, the intercompany profit resulting from Barenboim's sales to Corigliano should be eliminated. Corigliano sold to outsiders 50% ($65,000/$130,000) of the inventory purchased from Barenboim. The cost of sales to the combined entity is thus 50% of the $100,000 cost of sales reported by Barenboim. Gross profit of the combined entity amounts to $41,000, equal to $91,000 of sales to unrelated companies less $50,000 cost of sales.

9. **A**   Penny's selling expenses for Year 6 include $50,000 in freight-out COGS to Sikora, its subsidiary. This $50,000 becomes part of Sikora's inventory because it is a cost directly associated with bringing the goods to a saleable condition. One-half of the goods sold to Sikora by Penny remained in Sikora's inventory at the end of Year 6. Therefore, one-half of the $50,000 ($25,000) flowed out as part of COGS and one-half remains in ending inventory. Thus, none of the $50,000 represents a selling expense for the consolidated entity, and $1,450,000 ($1,100,000 + $400,000 – $50,000) should be reported as selling expenses in the consolidated income statement.

10. **B**   The determination of whether an entity is a VIE and which company should consolidate the VIE is made at the time the company initially gets involved with the VIE. The determination does not change unless there is a fundamental change in the nature of the VIE or in the relationship between the interest holders.

11. **D**   Under the purchase method, assets and liabilities of the acquired entity are reported at 100% of their fair values. Acquisition goodwill is equal to $20,000 as follows:

Fair value of Strauss	$100,000
Less: BV (100%) of Strauss	50,000
Excess of fair value over book value	50,000
Less: Excess allocated to inventory	30,000 ($50,000 excess × 60%)
Goodwill	$20,000

Consolidated current assets include 100% of the current assets of both firms, plus the excess of fair value allocated to the inventory. Thus, consolidated current assets are equal to $120,000 ($70,000 Polka + $20,000 Strauss + $30,000 excess allocated to inventory).

12. **D**   Under the purchase method, assets and liabilities of the acquired entity are reported at 100% of their fair values. Acquisition goodwill is equal to $20,000 as follows:

Fair value of Strauss	$100,000
Less: BV (100%) of Strauss	50,000
Excess of fair value over book value	50,000
Less: Excess allocated to inventory	30,000 ($50,000 excess × 60%)
Goodwill	$20,000

Consolidated noncurrent assets include 100% of the noncurrent assets of both firms plus the acquisition goodwill. Thus, consolidated noncurrent assets are equal to $150,000 ($90,000 Polka + $40,000 Strauss + $20,000 goodwill).

13. **C**   Consolidated current liabilities include 100% of the current liabilities of both firms plus the current portion of acquisition debt due within the next 12 months ($90,000 / 10 years = $9,000). Thus, consolidated current liabilities are equal to $49,000 ($30,000 Polka + $10,000 Strauss + $9,000 current portion of acquisition debt).

14. **D**   Consolidated noncurrent liabilities include 100% of the noncurrent liabilities of both firms plus the noncurrent portion of acquisition debt. Thus, consolidated noncurrent liabilities are equal to $131,000 [$50,000 Polka + ($90,000 acquisition debt – $9,000 current portion)].

15. **C**   In the consolidated balance sheet, neither the parent company's investment account nor the subsidiary's stockholders' equity is reported. These amounts are eliminated in the same journal entry that records the excess of cost over book value. Consolidated shareholders' equity is equal to Polka's equity *plus* the noncontrolling interest. The noncontrolling interest can be broken down into the proportional share of Strauss' net assets at fair value ($80,000 × 10%) and the noncontrolling goodwill ($20,000 total goodwill minus $18,000 controlling goodwill). Controlling goodwill is equal to $18,000 [$90,000 purchase price minus ($80,000 FV net assets × 90%)]. Thus, consolidated shareholder's equity is equal to $90,000 ($80,000 Polka + $10,000 noncontrolling interest).

16. **C**   Because the parent paid enough so that goodwill was recorded, a full allocation of $140,000 was made to the building account in recognition of the difference in its book value and actual value. With a 10-year life, that allocation will be depreciated at the rate of $14,000 per year. After two years, for consolidation purposes, the parent book value of $900,000 is added to the subsidiary's book value of $650,000 and then the allocation of $140,000 is included, but two years of amortization ($28,000) must be subtracted.

17. **B**   Because of the gain on the transfer, the building is overstated by $50,000 on the buyer's books, which means that depreciation expense each year is overstated by $5,000 (since the building has a 10-year life). Removing this excess depreciation expense each year causes consolidated net income to rise.

18. **A**   The company does not have a contractual right to the credit rating and it is not something that can be separated from the company and sold. Therefore, any extra amount included in the purchase price is part of the allocation attributed to goodwill. Conversely, the company does have a contractual right to the database and, therefore, it should be reported as a separate asset in consolidated statements. Furthermore, the database could be separated from Little and sold.

19. **D**   The parent has paid $30,000 less than the book value of the subsidiary ($270,000 – $300,000). This is a bargain purchase. There are no allocation amounts because book value is the same as fair value. Thus, the identifiable assets and liabilities will be reported on the consolidated balance sheet at their fair values. The remainder will be reported in the income statement as a part of continuing operations.

20. **B**   The parent has paid $110,000 less than the book value of the subsidiary ($190,000 – $300,000). There are no allocation amounts because book value is the same as fair value. That amount is reported immediately as a regular gain.

21. **A**   The fair value of this reporting unit is less than book value so a test of goodwill impairment does have to be made. However, if the reporting unit has a total value of $520,000 whereas the individual assets and liabilities are worth only $470,000, then current goodwill is $50,000 ($520,000 – $470,000). If the current goodwill is $50,000, it exceeds the $40,000 that is being reported. Thus, the goodwill is not impaired although some other assets of the reporting unit may be impaired.

22. **A**   In creating a business combination, any amount attributed to the value of in-process research and development must be recognized. Any portion of the purchase price in excess of the underlying book value of the subsidiary that cannot be assigned to an identifiable asset or liability is reported as the intangible asset Goodwill. Here, the purchase price was $900,000 and the book value was $700,000 so the excess was $200,000. Of that amount, $170,000 is assigned to in-process research and development. The remaining $30,000 is reported by the consolidated companies as goodwill. Goodwill is no longer amortized over a period of time but is rather checked periodically for impairment.

23. **B**   The two companies' cost of goods sold accounts total $600,000. However, this total includes the impact of the inter-company purchases of Large from Tiny. If we consider that Tiny's cost of goods sold for sales to outside customers for the period amounts to $168,000 ($200,000 COGS amount reported – $80,000 transfers to Large + $48,000 transfers actually sold to outside customers by Large (60% of $80,000)) and Large's COGS amount of $400,000 includes $60,000 of inter-company purchases recorded as sold that should be eliminated (because this duplicates and overstates what Tiny is reporting), consolidated COGS for the two companies would amount to $168,000 + $340,000, or $508,000.

24. **A**   When the acquisition took place, $800,000 was paid in excess of Paterson's book value. It appears reasonable to assume that $200,000 of this excess was allocated to the book value of Patterson's buildings. This was because of the comparison of FMV of the buildings ($2.2 million) with book value ($2 million). However, this allocation must be amortized to expense over the 10-year life of the building. The consolidated building account balance after one year will be the parent's book value balance on that date ($5 million) plus the subsidiary's book value ($3 million) plus the purchase price allocation ($200,000) less amortization of $20,000 ($200,000/10 years) for the one year that has now passed.

25. D   To be recognized separately as an intangible asset, the company must hold contractual or other legal rights in connection with the asset or the item must be something that can be separated from the subsidiary so that it can be sold, franchised, or the like. The education costs may actually make the employees more effective and efficient in the future, but that is not an asset where the company has contractual or legal rights or that can be separated and sold.

26. A   In checking for goodwill impairment, as long as the fair value of the reporting unit is larger than its book value, no impairment of goodwill is recognized. Here, the Wood reporting unit has a book value of $5 million but a fair value of $5.1 million. There is no goodwill impairment, and no loss is recognized.

27. D   Because the fair value of the reporting unit ($8.8 million) is below its book value ($9 million), a test must be made to see if the goodwill of that unit has been impaired. The unit has a total fair value of $8.8 million. Since the individual assets and liabilities at that date are only worth $8.4 million, the assumption is made that the current value of goodwill makes up the $400,000 difference. Goodwill on the books for this reporting unit is $1.3 million. Reduction to the current goodwill value of $400,000 necessitates recognition of a loss of $900,000.

28. A   Pop paid $1 million more than the underlying book value of Son ($4 million purchase price – $3 million net book value). For recording purposes, the parent must search for any assets and liabilities of the subsidiary that have a value that differs from book value. None are mentioned here. In addition, any unrecorded intangible assets held by the subsidiary must be uncovered and reported. To qualify, the company must have contractual rights to the asset or it must be something that can be separated from the company and sold. Both of the assets here meet one of these requirements and must be recognized. Reporting these values of $200,000 and $300,000 leaves only $500,000 of the $1 million excess payment unexplained. It is this unexplained residual that is reported as goodwill.

29. D   Gross profit of $30,000 occurred on the inter-company sales of Z to A (sales revenue of $150,000 minus $120,000 COGS). This sales price was a 25% markup on Z's cost: ($150,000 / $120,000) = 1.25. However, not all of this gross profit has been realized in sales to outside customers by year-end. A's ending inventory includes $50,000 in purchases from Z, or 1/3 of the original inter-company purchase amount. This $50,000 includes a mark-up 25%, or $10,000 ($50,000 / 1.25). Gross profit of $10,000 must be eliminated in consolidation.

This analysis, then, supports answer choice A (inventory must be reduced by $10,000) as being correct.

Cost of goods sold (for what is given in this question scenario) on a consolidated basis, amounts to only $80,000, 2/3 of Z's original inventory cost of $120,000. However, A would have reported $120,000 because of the sale of its inventory to A. A would have reported COGS of $100,000 because of its purchases from Z, minus its $50,000 ending inventory ($150,000 purchases – $100,000 sales). These two COGS figures amount to $220,000, $140,000 greater than consolidated COGS. This analysis supports Option "B" as being correct.

Answer choice C is also correct, as Z's inter-company sales would be eliminated in consolidation.

30. B   Goodwill impairment is tested for individual reporting units which are usually much the same as the segments of the business. Because the fair value of the unit is below its net book value, the reported goodwill figure might be impaired. However, further testing will be needed to determine if impairment has actually occurred. Had the fair value of the unit been greater than the net book value, no further testing for goodwill impairment would have been necessary.

CHAPTER 17 – GOVERNMENTAL ACCOUNTING

STUDY TIP

Forget the past. People often approach the CPA exam talking about previous failures, either on the exam itself or in school. "I was never a very good student" is a common refrain. The past is not important. If you use good, quality preparation materials and are willing to invest a sufficient amount of time studying, you can pass. Do not let something that occurred in the past hold you back from success today.

CHAPTER 17 – GOVERNMENTAL ACCOUNTING

Before reading this chapter, you may want to download a great set of financial statements for a government, the city of Scottsdale, AZ. Go to the following URL to see the most recent version. If you are taking the Online Review Course for CPA with Kaplan Schweser, you will also use these financial statements in your governmental class.

http://www.scottsdaleaz.gov/Assets/documents/finance/CAFR/cafrbasicfin.pdf

INTRODUCTION TO FUND ACCOUNTING

The accounting principles and financial statements used by profit-seeking businesses to measure their activities are not appropriate for all types of organizations. Most not-for-profit organizations need to adopt an approach that emphasizes accountability to outsiders rather than profit measurement. Governmental units accomplish this goal by using fund accounting.

Fund accounting is a system of record keeping and financial statement preparation that segregates the different resources of an entity into separate self-balancing sets of accounts, known as *funds*. Such an approach is particularly useful when resources have been restricted in some way. By keeping restricted resources in separate funds, better control can be maintained over them.

The seven major differences between governmental accounting and accounting for-profit business are as follows:

1. The absence of a profit motive, except for some governmental enterprises, such as utilities.

2. A legal emphasis that involves restrictions both in the raising and spending of revenues.

3. An inability to "match" revenues with expenditures, as revenues are often provided by persons other than those receiving the services.

4. An emphasis on accountability or stewardship of resources entrusted to public officials.

5. The use of fund accounting and reporting, as well as government-wide reporting.

6. The recording of the budget in some funds.

7. The use of modified accrual accounting rather than full accrual accounting in some funds.

Governmental units use fund accounting standards issued by the Governmental Accounting Standards Board (GASB). The GASB was created in 1984. Current pronouncements are reflected in the Codification of Governmental Accounting and Financial Reporting Standards issued by the GASB each year. The GASB has authority under the AICPA Ethics Rule 203, Accounting Principles.

The GASB has issued three statements that completely transform the accounting and financial reporting for state and local governments, including public colleges and universities.

1. **GASB 33,** *Accounting and Financial Reporting for Nonexchange Transactions*, was issued in December 1998 and is required to be followed for fiscal years ending after June 15, 2001.

2. **GASB 34,** *Basic Financial Statements and Management's Discussion and Analysis—for State and Local Governments*, was issued in June 1999. Implementation depends upon the size of the government (defined in terms of total annual revenues as of the first fiscal year ending after June 15, 2001). One of the requirements of GASB 34 is the recording and depreciating of infrastructure; that requirement was optional in the past. Prospective recording is required upon adoption of the statement. Retroactive recording of infrastructure acquired or significantly improved in fiscal years ending after June 30, 1980, is required four years after the date required for GASB 34 adoption, except that governments with total revenues less than $10 million are not required to report infrastructure retroactively.

3. **GASB 35,** *Basic Financial Statements—and Management's Discussion and Analysis—for Public Colleges and Universities*, incorporates public colleges and universities into GASB 34 reporting requirements for special-purpose entities.

THE REPORTING ENTITY

A reporting entity is made up of a primary government and its component units. A primary government is (1) a state government, (2) a general purpose local government, or (3) a special purpose local government that has a separately elected governing body, is legally separate, and is fiscally independent of other state or local governments. A component unit is a legally separate organization for which the elected officials of a primary government are financially accountable, or for which the nature and significance of its relationship with a primary government is such that omission would cause the primary government's financial statements to be misleading.

REPORTING COMPONENT UNITS

A. Discrete Presentation—Most component units are presented in the government-wide financial statements, in a separate column(s) to the right of the information related to the primary government.

B. Blended—Component units whose activities are so closely tied to the primary government as to be indistinguishable should be blended with the primary government figures.

THE GOVERNMENT REPORTING MODEL

A. GASB 34 provides requirements that constitute the minimum required to be in compliance with GAAP. These requirements for general-purpose governmental units (states, municipalities, counties) include:

1. Management's Discussion and Analysis (MD&A)—This is considered required supplementary information (RSI).

2. Government-wide Financial Statements.

   a. Statement of Net Assets.

   b. Statement of Activities.

3. Fund Financial Statements.

    a. Governmental Funds.

        - Balance Sheet.
        - Statement of Revenues, Expenditures and Changes in Fund Balance.

    b. Proprietary Funds.

        - Statement of Net Assets (or Balance Sheet).
        - Statement of Revenues, Expenses, and Changes in Fund Net Assets (or Fund Equity).
        - Statement of Cash Flows.

    c. Fiduciary Funds.

        - Statement of Fiduciary Net Assets.
        - Statement of Changes in Fiduciary Net Assets.

4. Notes to the Financial Statements.

5. Required Supplementary Information (other than MD&A).

    a. Schedule of Funding Progress (for entities reporting pension trust funds).

    b. Schedule of Employer Contributions (for entities reporting pension trust funds).

    c. Budgetary Comparison Schedules.

    d. Information about infrastructure assets (for entities using the modified approach).

    e. Claims development information (for entities who sponsor a public entity risk pool).

B. Other additional supplementary information, such as combined statements for nonmajor funds, may be included.

SPECIAL PURPOSE GOVERNMENTS

Special purpose governments include park districts, tollway authorities, school districts, and sanitation districts. GASB has categorized special purpose governments into the following four categories:

1. Governmental activities

2. Business-type activities

3. Fiduciary activities

4. Both governmental and business-type activities

Special purpose governments that are engaged in governmental activities and have more than one program and special purpose governments that are engaged in both governmental and business-type activities must prepare both the government-wide and fund financial statements. Special purpose governments that are engaged in a single governmental activity (such as a cemetery district or a school) may combine the government-wide and fund financial statements or use other methods allowed by GASB. Special purpose governments that are engaged in only business-type activities or fiduciary activities are not required to prepare the government-wide statements but only prepare the proprietary or fiduciary fund statements. All governments must include the MD&A, the Notes, and the RSI.

A Comprehensive Annual Financial Report (CAFR) is not required of special purpose governments. Following are the three major sections that should be included in a CAFR:

1. Introductory Section—Includes a letter of transmittal, an organizational chart, and a list of principal officials.

2. Financial Section—Includes an auditor's report, the required information, and supplementary information listed above.

3. Statistical Section—Includes a number of schedules, such as net assets by component, changes in net assets, revenue sources, debt capacity, and demographic and economic statistics.

MANAGEMENT'S DISCUSSION AND ANALYSIS (MD&A)

FORMAT AND CONTENT OF MANAGEMENT'S DISCUSSION AND ANALYSIS

A. The purpose of MD&A is to provide users of the financial statements with an introduction, an overview, and an analysis of the financial statements. The specific topics that a government should address in its MD&A include:

1. A discussion of the basic financial statements.

2. Condensed financial data from the government-wide financial statements and individual fund statements with comparisons to the prior year.

3. An analysis of the overall financial position and results of operations and information as to whether that position has improved or deteriorated.

4. An analysis of the significant balances and operations of individual major funds. Significant changes in fund balances or fund net assets should be discussed.

5. An analysis of significant variations between the original budget, final budget, and actual results for the year.

6. A description of significant capital asset and long-term debt activity for the year.

7. Governments that use the modified approach to infrastructure should discuss all of the following in their MD&A:

   a. Significant changes in the condition levels of infrastructure.

   b. How current condition levels compare with target condition levels.

   c. Significant differences between the amount estimated to be necessary for maintaining and preserving infrastructure assets at target conditions levels and the actual amounts of expense incurred for that purpose.

8. Other potentially significant matters such as the acceptance of a major grant awarded, a significant lawsuit, reassessment of taxable property, increases in tax rates, etc.

B. MD&A is required supplementary information (RSI) and for that reason, a government may not address additional topics not found on the above list. MD&A, like all RSI, is subject to a limited degree of auditor involvement. Accordingly, highly subjective information should be reported in the letter of transmittal rather than in the MD&A.

GOVERNMENT-WIDE FINANCIAL STATEMENTS

Government-wide financial statements include the Statement of Net Assets and the Statement of Activities. They are both prepared with the economic resources measurement focus and the accrual basis of accounting (discussed later). All activities of the primary government except fiduciary activities are reported on these statements. Fiduciary funds are not reported in the government-wide financial statements because these assets must be conveyed to a party outside of the government and therefore are not available to be used by the government.

Both fixed assets and long-term debt are reported in the government-wide financial statements. They are also reported in the proprietary fund financial statements. Fixed assets and long-term debt are not reported in governmental funds. GASB 34 requires that infrastructure (roads, bridges, storm sewers, etc.) be included in fixed assets. All new infrastructure items must be capitalized at cost on the government-wide financial statements and depreciated. A government may choose to use a modified approach for recording charges for infrastructure assets rather than charge depreciation. Under the modified approach, if a government meets certain criteria for maintaining its infrastructure, expenditures to extend service life would be reported as expenses in lieu of depreciation. A fixed asset management system must be in place that meets certain criteria, and extensive disclosures are required. Any infrastructure assets acquired prior to GASB 34 do not have to be capitalized immediately. Most governments have an additional four years to determine a book value for infrastructure assets acquired prior to GASB 34.

A. Statement of Net Assets—This statement is much like a balance sheet. It reports all assets and liabilities of the primary government except the fiduciary funds, as stated earlier. The difference between assets and liabilities is labeled "Net Assets," and it is reported with three classifications, Capital Assets Net of Related Debt, Restricted Net Assets, and Unrestricted Net Assets. This statement is separated into the following columns:

1. Governmental Activities—Those activities that are financed primarily through taxes and other nonexchange transactions and include all governmental funds and internal service funds.

2. Business-Type Activities—Those activities that are normally financed through user charges and include all enterprise funds.

3. Total Primary Government—This is simply the total of the Governmental Activities and the Business-Type Activities columns.

4. Component Units—Each discretely presented component unit is normally presented in a separate column. If a government has more component units than can be displayed effectively in the Statement of Net Assets, then the detail of each component unit should be disclosed in the notes to the financial statements.

B. Statement of Activities—This statement reports revenues and expenses on the full accrual basis. It is a consolidated statement, except that interfund transactions are not eliminated when those transactions are between governmental and business-type activities and between the primary government and discretely presented component units. This is called an "all-inclusive activity" statement. The separate elements of the statement are as follows:

1. Expenses—These are reported first and classified by function such as "general government" and "public safety." Depreciation expense is recognized and allocated to the specific functions. Primary government functions are listed first, followed by business-type functions and component units.

2. Program Revenues—These are reported next and are deducted from expenses to arrive at net expense or revenue. Program revenues include charges for services, operating grants and

contributions, and capital grants and contributions that are all reported in separate columns. Charges for services are deducted from the function that creates the revenues. Grants and contributions are reported in the function to which their use is restricted.

3. Net Expense (Revenue)—The net expense or revenue is broken out among governmental activities, business-type activities, and component units. Governmental activities and business-type activities are totaled and reported first followed by a reporting of each component unit.

4. General Revenues—These are deducted from Net Expense (Revenue) to arrive at the Change in Net Assets. General revenues include all taxes levied by the reporting government and other nonexchange revenues not restricted to a particular program such as investment earnings.

5. Special Items—These are events that are within the control of management that are either unusual in nature or infrequent in occurrence, such as a gain on the sale of park land. Separate additions or deductions are made for special items.

6. Extraordinary Items—These are events that are both unusual in nature and infrequent in occurrence. Separate additions or deductions are made for extraordinary items.

7. Transfers—A separate addition or deduction is made for transfers between categories.

8. Net Assets—Beginning and end of year net assets are reconciled.

FUND FINANCIAL STATEMENTS

A. In addition to government-wide statements, GASB 34 requires a number of fund financial statements. Most governments use fund accounting internally and prepare the fund financial statements first, making worksheet adjustments to arrive at the government-wide statements previously discussed. A **fund** is defined as:

A fiscal and accounting entity with a self-balancing set of accounts recording cash and other financial resources, together with all related liabilities, residual equities, balances, and changes therein, that are segregated for the purpose of carrying on specific activities or attaining certain objectives in accordance with special regulations, restrictions, or limitations.

B. There are now 11 fund types that are classified into the following 3 general categories:

1. Governmental Funds—These funds focus on the current financial resources raised and expended to carry out general government purposes. They include the following:

   a. General Fund—Each government has only one general fund. The general fund is always considered to be a major fund (discussed later). It accounts for all financial resources except those required to be accounted for in another fund.

   b. Special Revenue Funds—These funds account for specific revenue sources that are legally restricted to be expended for specified purposes.

   c. Debt Service Funds—These funds account for the accumulation of resources for and the payment of general long-term debt and interest.

   d. Capital Projects Funds—These funds account for financial resources to be used for the acquisition or construction of major capital facilities, other than those financed by proprietary funds or trust funds.

e. Permanent Funds—These funds are used to report resources that are legally restricted to the extent that only earnings, and not principal, may be used to support government programs.

2. Proprietary Funds—These funds focus on total economic resources, income determination, and cash flow presentation. They include the following:

    a. Internal Service Funds—These funds report any activity that provides goods or services to other funds of the primary government on a cost-reimbursement basis. Examples might include print shops, motor pools, and self-insurance activities.

    b. Enterprise Funds—These funds may be used to provide goods or services to external users for a fee. Enterprise funds must be used if (a) the activity is financed with debt that is secured solely by a pledge of the net revenues from fees and charges of that activity, (b) laws or regulations require that the activity's cost of providing service be recovered with fees and charges, rather than from taxes or similar revenues, or (c) the pricing policies of the activity establish fees and charges designed to cover its costs including capital costs (e.g., depreciation and debt service). Examples might include water utilities, airports, and swimming pools.

3. Fiduciary Funds.

    a. Agency Funds—These funds report only assets and liabilities.

    b. Pension and Other Employee Benefit Trust Funds—These funds account for funds held in trust for the payment of employee retirement and other benefits. These trust funds exist when the government is the trustee for the pension plan. Accounting for these plans is covered by GASB 25 and 43.

    c. Investment Trust Funds—These funds are used to report the external portions of investment pools when the reporting government is the trustee.

    d. Private Purpose Trust Funds—These are used to report all other trust arrangements where the principal and income benefit individuals, private organizations, and other governments. An example might be a public school that has a fund to report scholarship funds contributed by individuals and businesses.

The fund financial statements for the governmental and enterprise funds categories report major funds separately and combine all other non-major funds into one column. Consequently, one of the first steps in preparing the fund financial statements is to determine which funds are major funds. The general fund is always reported as a major fund. Other major funds will include governmental or enterprise funds meeting *both* of the following criteria:

1. Total assets, liabilities, revenues, *or* expenditures/expenses of that individual governmental or enterprise fund are at least 10% of that corresponding total for all funds of that category or type.

2. Total assets, liabilities, revenues, *or* expenditures/expenses of that individual governmental or enterprise fund are at least 5% of the corresponding total for all governmental and enterprise funds combined.

Additionally, a government may choose to call any fund "major" if it feels that reporting that fund would be useful to the financial statement user. As stated earlier, the nonmajor funds are aggregated and reported in a single column. Combining statements for nonmajor funds are shown as "Other Supplementary Information."

A. Two governmental fund financial statements are required. Both statements are prepared on the current financial resources measurement focus and the modified accrual basis (discussed later).

    1. Balance Sheet—This statement shows current financial resources and claims on current financial resources. The difference in these assets and liabilities is known as the "fund balance" and can be classified as reserved or unreserved based upon the government's ability to make use of the financial resources. Capital assets and long-term debt are not reported.

    2. Statement of Revenues, Expenditures, and Changes in Fund Balance—This report presents revenues, expenditures, other financing sources, other financing uses, and special items. Only expenditures are reflected in this statement—not expenses (including depreciation expense). Capital asset outlays and long-term debt payments are reported as expenditures because they use current financial resources.

B. Three proprietary fund financial statements are required. They are prepared using the economic resources measurement focus and the full accrual basis (discussed later).

    1. Statement of Net Assets (or Balance Sheet)—GASB permits the more traditional balance sheet format (Assets = Liabilities + Fund Equity) for the proprietary fund statements. Internal service funds are grouped together and shown separately from the enterprise funds.

    2. Statement of Revenues, Expenses, and Changes in Net Assets (or Fund Equity)—Major enterprise funds are shown separately, along with a total of all enterprise fund activity, and the total of internal service funds is shown separately. GASB requires an operating income figure, with operating revenues and expenses shown separately from nonoperating revenue and expenses. Capital contributions, transfers, extraordinary items, and special items are to be shown after the nonoperating revenues and expenses. GASB requires that depreciation be shown separately as an operating expense and that interest be shown as a nonoperating expense. Interest related to fixed assets is capitalized.

    3. Statement of Cash Flows—This statement contains six major differences from the familiar business cash flow statement required by FASB, as follows:

        a. Only the direct method is acceptable, and a reconciliation is required.

        b. The reconciliation is from operating income to net cash provided by operating activities—not from net income to net cash.

        c. There are four categories (rather than three) included in the statement. These are: operating, noncapital financing, capital and related financing, and investing.

        d. Cash receipts from interest are classified as investing activities—not operating activities.

        e. Cash payments for interest are classified as financing (either noncapital or capital and related)—not as operating activities.

        f. Purchases of capital assets (resources provided by financing activities) are considered financing activities—not investing activities.

C. Two fiduciary fund financial statements are required. They are prepared using the economic resources measurement focus and the full accrual basis. The fiduciary fund statements report totals for each of the four fund types (Agency, Pension and Other Employee Benefit Trust, Investment Trust, and Private Purpose Trust. However, each individual pension or employee benefit trust fund report must be reported in the notes if separate reports have not been issued. If separate reports have been issued, the notes to the financial statements must indicate how the user can obtain the reports.

1. Statement of Fiduciary Net Assets—This statement is prepared in this form: Assets - Liabilities = Net Assets.

2. Statement of Changes in Fiduciary Net Assets—This statement uses the terms "additions" and "deductions" instead of revenues and expenses. Like all other GASB operating statements, this statement includes a reconciliation of the beginning and ending net assets at the bottom of the statement. Because agency funds have only assets and liabilities, they do not appear on this statement.

NOTES TO THE FINANCIAL STATEMENTS

GAAP requires that the basic financial statements be accompanied by Notes to the Financial Statements. Some of the major disclosures include a summary of significant accounting policies (SSAP); a description of the reporting entity; budgetary information including material violations, expenditures in excess of appropriations, budgetary basis of accounting, and a reconciliation between the budgetary basis of accounting and GAAP; information on cash deposits and investments; contingent liabilities; outstanding encumbrances; subsequent events; employer participation in defined benefit, defined contribution, insured and special funding pension plans; material violations of finance-related legal and contractual provisions; debt service requirements to maturity; lease obligations; lease receivables; capital assets; long-term liabilities; deficits in individual funds; interfund receivables and payables; property taxes; related party transactions; and joint ventures.

Some of the disclosure brought about by GASB 34 includes a description of the government-wide statements; the policy for capitalizing fixed assets and estimating useful lives; segment information for enterprise funds; and the policy for recording infrastructure, including the use of the modified approach, if applicable.

REQUIRED SUPPLEMENTARY INFORMATION (RSI) OTHER THAN MD&A

A. GASB requires four types of information that should be included immediately after the notes to the financial statements. These four items, along with MD&A (discussed previously) are considered RSI. RSI is presented outside the basic financial statements and is not covered by the audit opinion. However, omission of RSI, incomplete RSI, or misleading RSI does require comment by the auditor. RSI includes:

1. Pension Schedules—These schedules are required when a government reports a defined benefit pension plan.

   a. Schedule of Funding Progress—This schedule provides actuarial information regarding the actuarial value of assets, the actuarial accrued liability, and the unfunded actuarial liability, if any.

   b. Schedule of Employer Contributions—This schedule reflects the amount contributed compared with the amount required to be contributed.

2. Schedule of Revenue and Claims Development—This schedule is required when the government is a sponsor of a public entity risk pool.

3. Budgetary Comparison Schedule—This schedule presents the original budget, the final budget, and the actual revenues and expenditures computed on the budgetary basis for the general fund

and all major special revenue funds for which an annual budget has been passed by the government unit. A variance column may or may not be used. The format may be that of the original budget document or in the format, terminology, and classification in the Statement of Revenues, Expenditures, and Changes in Fund Balances. Information must be given either in this schedule or in notes to the RSI that provides a reconciliation from the budgetary basis to GAAP if the government prepares its budget on a non-GAAP basis.

4. Infrastructure Schedules—This information is presented only when the government is using the modified approach for reporting infrastructure. A government has the option of not depreciating its infrastructure assets if it adopts this approach. The government must meet certain requirements. First, it must manage the eligible infrastructure assets using an asset management system that (1) keeps a current inventory of infrastructure assets, (2) performs condition assessments using a measurement scale, and (3) estimates the cost each year to preserve the infrastructure assets at the condition level established and disclosed by the government. Secondly, the government must document that the infrastructure has been preserved at the level established by the government. The following two schedules are required:

   a. A schedule reflecting the conditions of the infrastructure.

   b. A comparison of the needed and actual expenditures to maintain the infrastructure.

THE FINANCIAL REPORTING PROCESS

MEASUREMENT FOCUS AND BASIS OF ACCOUNTING

GASB Standards require two methods of accounting, each used in certain parts of the financial statements. The government-wide financial statements, the proprietary fund statements, and the fiduciary fund statements are reported using the *economic resources measurement focus and accrual basis of accounting*. This method measures all of the economic resources available to the government. Fixed assets are recorded and depreciated. Long-term debt is also recorded. Revenues are recognized when earned, and expenses are recognized when incurred.

The governmental fund financial statements are reported using the *current financial resources measurement focus and modified accrual basis of accounting*. This method measures only the current financial resources available to the government. With this measurement focus, only current assets and current liabilities are generally included on the balance sheet. Fixed assets and long-term debt are not accounted and reported on this balance sheet. Revenues are recognized when measurable and available to finance expenditures of the current period. Property taxes may be considered "available" when collected within 60 days of year-end. This approach differs from the manner in which the governmental activities of the government-wide financial statements are prepared. Therefore, governmental fund financial statements include a reconciliation with brief explanations to better identify the relationship between the government-wide statements and the statements for governmental funds.

ACCOUNTING FOR NONEXCHANGE TRANSACTIONS

Revenues include both exchange transactions (those for which goods or services of equal or approximate equal value are exchanged) and nonexchange transactions (those for which a government receives value without directly giving equal value in exchange). Revenues from exchange transactions are recognized in accordance with generally accepted accounting principles. They are recognized when earned under the full accrual accounting method, and they are recognized when measurable and available to finance expenditures of the current period.

GASB 33, *Accounting and Financial Reporting for Nonexchange Transactions*, classifies nonexchange transactions into four categories, and revenue recognition depends upon the category. Each category and the corresponding revenue recognition rule according to GASB 33 are summarized below. These rules are written under the presumption that an entity is following full accrual accounting; therefore, the rules apply to the government-wide financial statements only. In order to be recognized on the fund financial statements (reported on the modified accrual basis), the revenues must also be available. "Available" means that the financial resources will be collected soon enough to be used to pay for current period expenditures. Available is often defined as anything accrued in the current period that will be collected within 60 days of the beginning of the subsequent period. The number of days, though, can vary and should be disclosed in the notes to the financial statements.

1. Derived tax revenues—These result from taxes assessed by governments on an underlying exchange transaction or event. Examples include sales taxes, income taxes, and motor fuel taxes. Receivables and revenues are recognized when the underlying transaction (the sale or income) takes place.

2. Imposed nonexchange transactions—These are taxes and other assessments by governments that are not derived from underlying transactions. Examples include property taxes, special assessments, fines, and forfeitures. A receivable is recognized when an enforceable legal claim exists or when the resources are received, whichever occurs first. In the case of property taxes, this would normally be specified in the enabling legislation, such as the lien or assessment date. Revenues for property taxes should be recognized net of estimated refunds and estimated uncollectible taxes in the period for which the taxes are levied or assessed regardless of the enforcement or collection date. Under the modified accrual method, property taxes may not be recognized unless collected within 60 days after the end of the fiscal year.

3. Government-mandated nonexchange transactions—These revenues usually represent grants or similar receipts given to a government to help pay for the cost of a legally required action imposed by the providing government; for example, a state government that requires a city to clean up an environmental hazard and then provides funding for that purpose. The receivable and the revenue are both reported when all eligibility requirements have been met. In some cases, the government must spend the money first and then apply for reimbursement. Revenues are recognized in these cases when the money is properly expended.

4. Voluntary nonexchange transactions—These are grants, entitlements, and donations given to a government (often for a specified purpose) for which the provider does not impose specific requirements. For example, a state provides a grant for new technology for school districts but does not require those school districts to accept the grant or to utilize the technology. Even though the use of the grant would be restricted to the new technology, the use is not required; the school district can decide not to use the grant at all. Therefore, this grant would be a voluntary nonexchange transaction. Purpose restrictions may or may not be specified for voluntary nonexchange transactions. The recognition of receivables and revenue would be when all eligibility requirements have been met. Any restrictions on the funds should be disclosed by showing a restriction in the net assets (government-wide financial statements) or a fund balance reserve (fund financial statements).

BUDGETARY ACCOUNTING

GASB requires governments to adopt an annual budget. It also requires that the accounting system provide the basis for appropriate budgetary control and that common terminology and classification be used consistently throughout the budget, the accounts, and the financial reports of each fund. Recall that a budget to actual comparison is required in RSI or as a basic financial statement for the general fund and all major special revenue funds that have a legally adopted annual budget.

Budgetary accounts (e.g., Estimated Revenues, Appropriations, Estimated Other Financing Sources, Estimated Other Financing Uses, Budgetary Fund Balance) are incorporated into governmental accounting systems to provide legislative control over revenues and other resource inflows and expenditures and other resource outflows. The entries that follow illustrate the budgetary accounts used by the general and special revenue funds.

The first entry made on the books of the general fund each fiscal year will be to record the budgetary accounts. The legislative body will estimate the various sources of revenue, such as property taxes, sales taxes, income taxes, and licenses and permits. It will also identify other financing sources (proceeds from general obligation bond issues and/or operating transfers from other funds). The legislative body will also authorize various expenditures for the year, known as appropriations. In addition, there may be other financing (operating transfers to other funds). Unless revenues and other sources equal appropriations and other uses, an adjustment will be made to the unreserved and undesignated fund balance, an account similar to unappropriated retained earnings of a private business. The budgetary entry will be reversed at year-end. The entry to record the initial budget is as follows:

Estimated Revenues	$3,900,000		
Estimated Other Financing Sources	$250,000		
Appropriations		$4,000,000	
Estimated Other Financing Uses		$100,000	
Budgetary Fund Balance		$50,000	(anticipates surplus)

To record the annual budget.

All of the above accounts, with the exception of the fund balance, are control accounts. Actual records will usually reflect a more detailed breakdown of each account such as "Estimated Revenues—Property Taxes" and "Appropriations—Supplies." As actual resource inflows and outflows occur during the year, they are recorded in the revenue and expenditure accounts, and the detail is posted to the subsidiary ledgers to facilitate budget versus actual comparisons. To prevent the overspending of an item in the appropriations budget, an additional budgetary account is maintained during the year. This budgetary account is called *encumbrances.* When goods (or services) are ordered, appropriations (specific items in the subsidiary ledger) are encumbered (restricted) with the following entry:

Encumbrances	$5,000	(Cost estimate)
Budgetary Fund Balance—Reserved for Encumbrances	$5,000	(Cost estimate)

To record the encumbrance of goods ordered.

This reduces the amount that can still be obligated or expended for an individual budget line item. When the goods or services are received, the encumbrance entry is reversed and the actual expenditure is recorded.

Budgetary Fund Balance—Reserved for Encumbrances	$5,000	
Encumbrances		$5,000

To reverse the encumbrance of goods received.

Expenditures	$5,200	
Accounts Payable		$5,200

To record the receipt of goods ordered.

The encumbrance account does not represent expenditure; it is a budgetary account that represents the estimated cost of goods or services that have yet to be received. In effect, the recording of encumbrances represents the recording of contracts that is essential to prevent overspending of an appropriation (normally an illegal act). If encumbrances are outstanding at the end of a period, that account is closed to the Fund Balance—Reserved for Encumbrances that is reported in the fund balance section of the balance sheet.

Assume that at the end of the fiscal year, a government had actual revenues of $4,005,000, actual expenditures of $3,950,000, and encumbrances outstanding at year-end were $100,000. The following entries would be required:

Appropriations	$4,000,000	
Estimated Other Financing Uses	$100,000	
Budgetary Fund Balance	$50,000	
Estimated Revenues		$3,900,000
Estimated Other Financing Sources		$250,000

To reverse the budgetary entry and close the budgetary accounts.

Revenue	$4,005,000	
Expenditures		$3,950,000
Encumbrances		$100,000
Fund Balance—Unreserved		$450,000

To close revenue and expenditures to Fund Balance.

Budgetary Fund Balance—Reserved for Encumbrances	$100,000	
Fund Balance—Reserved for Encumbrances		$100,000

To record outstanding encumbrances at year-end.

REVENUE CYCLE IN THE GENERAL FUND

Revenues come from many sources such as income taxes, property taxes, sales and use taxes, licenses, permits, fines and forfeitures, and charges for services and grants. Generally, a government's accounts are recorded using the modified accrual method, and worksheet adjustments are made at year-end to prepare the government-wide financial statements on a full accrual method. Modified accrual accounting only allows revenues to be recognized when measurable and available; therefore, the majority of revenues will not be recognized until received. A major exception is made for property tax revenue that is billed by the government and assessed against property, thus becoming measurable and available before actual collection. Assume a government levies a property tax in the current year and the tax bills total $4,000,000, and $200,000 of that amount is estimated to be uncollectible. When property taxes are levied, the following entry would be made if collections will be made in time to finance expenditures of the current period.

Property Taxes Receivable—Current	$4,000,000	
Allowance for Uncollectible Taxes—Current		$200,000
Property Tax Revenue		$3,800,000

To record the current tax levy and the amount estimated to be uncollectible.

Note that the reference to receivables and uncollectibles as being current indicates that these amounts are due but not delinquent. If the available criteria are not met, then the property tax levy would be recorded with a credit to "Deferred Revenue," a liability account, rather than to "Revenues."

If cash is needed to pay for expenditures before the property taxes receivables are collected, it is not uncommon for governmental units to borrow on tax anticipation notes. The receivable serves as security for this loan, and as taxes are collected, the anticipation warrants are liquidated.

If the government collects $3,850,000 in property taxes, the following entry will be made:

Cash	$3,850,000	
Allowance for Uncollectible Taxes—Current	$50,000	
Property Taxes Receivable—Current		$3,850,000
Property Tax Revenue		$50,000

To record collections of property tax.

The entry to the allowance for uncollectible taxes is required because it was overstated by $50,000. Note that the estimate was $200,000 in the entry above. Because tax revenues actually exceeded the anticipated amount of $3,800,000 for the current year, an increase in revenues is required. Notice that all entries involving uncollectible taxes affect revenues and not expenditures. This approach is radically different from accrual accounting, in which uncollectible amounts are treated as an expense.

If taxpayers pay property taxes that have not been billed yet, the early receipts will be reported as deferred revenue (a liability).

Cash	$250,000	
Deferred Revenue		$250,000

To record property tax receipts for unbilled property taxes.

Property tax revenues that are recognized in the current period include amounts collected during the period and amounts expected to be collected during the first 60 days of the subsequent period. Amounts expected to be collected after the 60 days and amounts estimated to be uncollectible are excluded from the current period's revenues. After the due date has been reached for property tax bills, uncollected amounts are generally reclassified as delinquent. If the government believes that an estimated $25,000 of the previously classified uncollectible taxes will now be collected, the following entries would be made:

Allowance for Uncollectible Taxes—Current	$25,000	
Property Tax Revenue		$25,000

To adjust the allowance for uncollectible property taxes at year-end.

Property Taxes Receivable—Delinquent	$150,000	
Allowance for Uncollectible Taxes—Current	$125,000	
Property Taxes Receivable—Current		$150,000
Allowance for Uncollectible Taxes—Delinquent		$125,000

To reclassify property taxes receivable from current to delinquent at the end of the year.

Revenues from taxpayer assessed taxes, such as sales or income taxes, should be recognized in the period in which they become susceptible to accrual, net of estimated refunds. Other revenue collections, such as permits and licenses, are usually not measurable until the cash is collected. Revenues, therefore, are recorded when the cash is collected.

Cash	$100,000	
Revenues		$100,000

To record the receipt of revenue from permits.

Transfers should be recognized in the accounting period in which the interfund receivable and payable arise. The transfer accounts are closed at the end of the year. Assume the general fund received a $20,000 transfer from a special revenue fund.

Due from Special Revenue Fund	$20,000	
Other Financing Sources—Transfer In		$ 20,000

To record the interfund receivable for the transfer due from the Special Revenue Fund.

Cash	$20,000	
Due From Special Revenue Fund		$20,000

To record the receipt of the interfund transfer.

The special revenue fund would record a payable as follows:

Other Financing Uses—Transfers Out	$20,000	
Due to General Fund		$20,000

To record the interfund payable in the special revenue fund.

EXPENDITURES CYCLE IN THE GENERAL FUND

Besides the budget entries, the expenditures cycle includes ordering, receiving, vouching, and paying for goods and services. Assume a government ordered equipment costing $24,000. When an order is placed for goods or services, the purchase commitment is recorded as follows:

Encumbrances	$24,000	
Budgetary Fund Balance—Reserved for Encumbrances		$24,000

To record and order for goods or services.

The amount encumbered is the best cost estimate available at the time the order is placed. The encumbrances account is a control account. Normally, each encumbrance will be detailed by type, such as "Encumbrances—Supplies." Recording the encumbrances prevents overspending line-item appropriations. When the order is received, an entry will be made to cancel the encumbrance.

Budgetary Fund Balance—Reserved for Encumbrances	$24,000	
Encumbrances		$24,000

At the same time, a voucher will be issued to the provider for the amount owed, and an expenditure will be recorded. This amount often is different from the cost estimate used for the encumbrance entries because estimates often are incorrect. If the actual cost was $23,500, the entry would be as follows:

Expenditures	$23,500	
Vouchers Payable		$ 23,500

To record the voucher issued to the provider.

The expenditures account is a control account, and actual entries provide additional detail as to the category of expenditure. Expenditures are normally grouped by object classification (e.g., salaries and wages) with further detail by program, function, and activity if the government desires.

Finally, the voucher will be presented for payment, and the obvious entry will be made to record the cash outlay:

Vouchers Payable	$23,500	
Cash		$23,500

To record the payment for the equipment.

Some expenditures are not encumbered because there is no purchase order issued, or it is a recurring, known amount. An example is payment of salaries and wages.

Claims against a governmental unit may result in a judgment, establishing a liability. Prior to litigation, a liability may be estimated. Claims and judgments that will be liquidated with funds that are currently expendable are recorded as expenditures and liabilities of the governmental units. Any remaining amounts are reported in the government-wide financial statements only.

Note that the purchase of fixed assets and inventory will be treated in the same manner as other expenditures in the fund financial statements. Fixed asset acquisitions and disposals will be reflected in the government-wide financial statements.

CLOSING ENTRIES FOR THE GENERAL FUND

At the end of the fiscal year, closing entries are prepared, just as in accrual accounting. The closing entries, however, must include the budgetary accounts along with the nominal accounts. The closing entry for the budgetary accounts will literally reverse the entry that was used to record the budget. It might appear as follows:

Appropriations	$4,000,000	
Estimated Other Financing Uses	$100,000	
Budgetary Fund Balance	$50,000	
Estimated Revenues		$3,900,000
Estimated Other Financing Sources		$250,000

Appropriate closing entries might appear as follows:

Revenues	$4,015,000	
Other Financing Sources	$250,000	
Fund Balance—Unreserved		$235,000
Expenditures		$3,750,000
Encumbrances		$200,000
Other Financing Uses		$80,000

To close revenue, other financing sources, expenditures, and other financing uses to fund balance.

Budgetary Fund Balance—Reserved for Encumbrances	$200,000	
Fund Balance—Reserved for Encumbrances		$200,000

To record outstanding encumbrances at year-end.

The balances in all of the control accounts are eliminated by the first entry. Notice that the closing entry includes any encumbrances that are still open at the end of the year, but not the fund balance—reserved for encumbrances. This remains in the fund equity section of the balance sheet. Because appropriations include all authorizations to spend for the current year, it should be compared (through this closing entry) with all items that were received as well as any other items from the current budget that were ordered and not yet received. Therefore, the fund balance is increased or decreased by the net difference between budgeted spending and actual spending.

Inventories are generally recorded under the purchases method as expenditures when received. As an alternative, funds may keep track of existing inventories, if material, using the consumption approach. Under this approach, expenditures are allocated among periods as amounts are used. A similar approach is used for prepayments, such as prepaid insurance. It is common to keep track of existing year-end inventories through the use of two accounts that will always equal each other. These accounts are adjusted at the end of each fiscal year to reflect the net increase or decrease in inventory levels. In a period of inventory increase, under the purchases method, the entry would be as follows:

Inventories	$75,000	
Fund Balance—Reserved for Inventories		$75,000

In a period of decline, of course, the fund equity account is debited and the asset account credited. Notice that accounting for inventories in this manner does not negate the principle of recording inventory purchases as expenditures because the entry to adjust inventory does not affect any spending accounts.

Although the above entries appear to complete the annual cycle, two problems exist relative to the orders placed but not received by year-end. First, with the fund balance—reserved for encumbrances that remain on the books—there must be some means of eliminating them when the orders are filled. Second, if the receipt of the goods or services in a year subsequent to the appropriation is recorded as an expenditure, it could appear that actual spending exceeded the budget of that subsequent year.

When the goods or services are ultimately received on the $200,000 prior-year encumbrance, a voucher will be issued for the actual cost and the expenditure will be identified as pertaining to the prior year:

Expenditures—Prior Year	$190,000	
Vouchers Payable		$190,000

At the end of the year, a closing entry is prepared to eliminate the remaining balance of the fund balance reserved for encumbrances that had been set up in the previous year.

Fund Balance—Reserved for Encumbrances	$200,000	
Fund Balance—Unreserved		$10,000
Expenditures—Prior Year		$190,000

Using this approach, current period budgetary and actual accounts are kept separate from prior period accounts, enhancing the fund's capacity to analyze results and determine compliance.

ACCOUNTING FOR SPECIAL REVENUE FUNDS

Special revenue funds account for earmarked revenue as opposed to the many revenue sources that are accounted for in the general fund. The earmarked revenue is then used to finance various authorized expenditures. For example, a city might place its share of the state's gasoline tax revenues into a Street Maintenance Fund that would then be used to maintain streets. Many times grants are reported in special revenue funds, often in a separate fund in compliance with grant requirements.

The accounting for special revenue funds parallels that of the general fund. One type of transaction that often takes place in a special revenue fund is a "reimbursement" grant from a federal or state government. GASB 33 lists reimbursement grant requirements as one of the conditions that must be satisfied before a revenue can be recognized, either for accrual or modified accrual accounting. With a reimbursement grant, the granting government will not provide resources unless the receiving government provides evidence that an appropriate expenditure has taken place; GASB 33 requires that the expenditure must be recognized prior to a revenue being recognized.

For example, assume a municipality with a calendar fiscal year receives a state grant award on November 1, 2005 in the amount of $30,000. (No entry would be recorded either as receivable or revenue until the expenditure takes place.) Also, assume that the actual expenditure takes place March 1, 2006. The following entries would be made on March 1, 2006:

Expenditures	$30,000	
Cash		$30,000

To record the expenditure of funds.

Grants Receivable	$30,000	
Grant Revenues		$30,000

To record the receivable for the grant due from the state.

The cash is received from the state on April 1, 2006 and the following entry is made:

Cash	$30,000	
Grants Receivable		$30,000

To record the receipt of the grant from the state.

CAPITAL PROJECTS FUND

Capital projects funds account for the acquisition and use of resources for the construction or purchase of major, long-lived fixed assets, except for those that are financed by internal service, enterprise, and trust funds. Resources for construction or purchase normally come from the issuance of general long-term debt, from government grants and from interfund transfers.

Project budgets for estimated resources and expenditures must be approved before the project can begin. Although encumbrances and other elements of modified accrual accounting apply, the capital projects fund will usually not record the annual budget. Resources are reported as revenues or other financing sources when received.

Assume a government approved the construction of a new community center at an estimated cost of $8,000,000 and that general obligation long-term serial bonds were authorized for issuance in the face amount of $8,000,000. If the bonds are issued for $8,100,000, the premium would be transferred to a debt service fund for the eventual payment of the debt. When bonds are issued at a premium, the premium is transferred to the debt service fund to be used for servicing the bond. A discount, on the other hand, generally reduces the amount recorded as other financing sources. Neither a discount nor a premium is amortized in the debt service fund. Also, bond issue costs and debt insurance are not amortized; they are recorded as expenditures when incurred. The following entries are made in the capital projects fund:

Cash	$8,100,000	
Other Financing Sources—Proceeds of Bonds		$8,100,000

To record the proceeds of general obligation bonds.

Other Financing Uses—Transfers Out	$100,000	
Cash		$100,000

To record the transfer of the bond premium to the debt service fund.

Assume the bond-issued proceeds are temporarily invested in a certificate of deposit (CD), and that they earn $50,000. The earnings are authorized to be sent to the debt service fund for the payment of bonds. The following entries are made in the capital projects fund:

Investments	$8,000,000	
Cash		$8,000,000

To record the investment of the bond proceeds.

Cash	$50,000	
Revenues—Interest		$50,000

To record the receipt of interest revenue.

Other Financing Uses—Transfers Out	$50,000	
Cash		$50,000

To record the transfer of the interest revenue to the debt service fund.

The lowest bid of $7,800,000 is accepted from a general contractor, and the contract is awarded:

Encumbrances	$7,800,000	
Fund Balance—Reserved for Encumbrances		$7,800,000

To record the contract award.

Progress billings due to the general contractor for work performed amount to $2,000,000. The contract allows 10% of the billings to be retained until final inspection and approval of the building. The contractor was paid $1,800,000 and $2,000,000 of the temporary investments are liquidated:

Cash	$2,000,000	
Investments		$2,000,000

To liquidate a portion of investments.

Fund Balance—Reserved for Encumbrances	$2,000,000	
Encumbrance Control		$2,000,000

To reverse encumbrances for progress billings.

Expenditures—Construction	$2,000,000	
Contracts Payable		$2,000,000

To record the progress billings to date.

Contracts Payable	$2,000,000	
Cash		$1,800,000
Contracts Payable—Retained Percentage		$200,000

To record the payment to the contractor for 90% of the progress billing.

Interest accrued on the CD at the end of the year amounted to $50,000. This was authorized to be sent to the debt service fund for the payment of the debt.

| Interest Receivable | $50,000 | |
| Revenue—Interest | | $50,000 |

To record the interest revenue from the CD.

| Other Financing Uses—Transfers Out | $50,000 | |
| Due to Other Funds | | $50,000 |

To record the interest due to the debt service fund.

| Due to Other Funds | $50,000 | |
| Cash | | $50,000 |

To record the payment of interest due to the debt service funds.

Often, capital projects are financed by grants received from other governmental entities or outside agencies. If a grant is unrestricted, then revenues can be recorded when the grant is made. However, if the grant is restricted to a specific project or activity, then revenues should be deferred until the funds are expended. For example, assume a grant of $100,000 is received for the construction of the new community center. The receipt of funds is accounted for as follows:

| Cash | $100,000 | |
| Deferred Revenue | | $100,000 |

To record the grant award for the new community center.

As funds are expended, entries are made to record the expenditures and recognize the revenues in equal amounts. Assume the entire grant was used in the current year for authorized purposes.

| Expenditures—Construction | $100,000 | |
| Cash | | $100,000 |

To record the grant expenditures.

| Deferred Revenue | $100,000 | |
| Revenue—Grants | | $100,000 |

To recognize grant revenue.

Closing entries for the capital projects fund would appear as follows:

Revenue—Interest	$90,000	
Revenue—Grants	$100,000	
Other Financing Sources—Proceeds of Bonds	$8,100,000	
Fund Balance—Unreserved		$200,000
Encumbrances		$5,800,000
Expenditures—Construction		$2,100,000
Other Financing Uses—Transfers Out		$190,000

To close the accounts in the capital projects fund at year-end.

DEBT SERVICE FUND

Debt service funds usually handle the repayment of general obligation long-term debt and interest. This type of debt is secured by the good faith and taxing power of the governmental unit. Repayment of internal service and enterprise long-term debt is accounted for in those individual funds. Consequently, debt service funds are normally established as the result of issuing general obligation bonds for capital projects. The bond liability to be extinguished is not recorded in the debt service fund until it matures. General long-term debt is only reported in the government-wide financial statements.

Budgetary accounts are used at the option of the legislature. Where the legislative body of the government has not adopted a formal annual budget, such accounts are not used. Because the debt service fund is limited to collecting, investing, and disbursing liquid resources used in connection with general obligations, the encumbrance system is not used.

Continuing the earlier scenario, assume a government authorizes a debt service fund for the general obligation serial bonds issued to finance a community center. The debt service fund is also authorized to pay the 5% interest on $8,000,000 of debt on December 31 and June 30. This fiscal year-end is June 30. Assume the bonds were issued on July 1. Additionally, assume that $250,000 of the bonds mature each six months, starting June 30. The debt service fund makes the following entries in connection with the receipt of resources form the capital projects fund as stated above:

Cash	$100,000	
Other Financing Sources—Transfers In		$100,000

To record the transfer of the bond premium from the capital projects fund.

Cash	$50,000	
Other Financing Sources—Transfers In		$50,000

To record the transfer of interest revenue from the capital projects fund.

Cash	$50,000	
Other Financing Sources—Transfers In		$50,000

To record the transfer of accrued interest revenue from the capital projects fund.

If the property tax levy contains an $500,000 portion allocable to the debt service fund, and $20,000 of this is estimated to be uncollectible, the following entry would be made:

Property Taxes Receivable—Current	$520,000	
Allowance for Uncollectible Taxes—Current		$20,000
Revenues—Property Taxes		$500,000

To record property tax levy.

On December 31, the semi-annual interest is paid ($8,000,000 × 5% / 2):

Expenditures—Interest	$200,000	
Matured Interest Payable		$200,000

To record the semi-annual interest expense.

Matured Interest Payable	$200,000	
Cash		$200,000

To record the payment of the semi-annual interest expense.

Because the debt service fund uses modified accrual accounting, interest is not systematically allocated to the loan period. Instead, interest on debt is recorded in each period that it becomes due and payable. Next, assume the government collects $480,000 of property taxes during the year and then reclassifies the remaining property taxes:

Cash	$480,000	
Property Taxes Receivable—Current		$480,000

To record the receipt of property taxes.

Property Taxes Receivable—Delinquent	$40,000	
Allowance for Uncollectible Taxes—Current	$20,000	
Property Taxes Receivable—Current		$40,000
Allowance for Uncollectible Taxes—Delinquent		$20,000

To reclassify delinquent property taxes at year-end.

On June 30, the semi-annual interest is paid ($8,000,000 × 5% / 2) and the general fund transferred $50,000 to the debt service fund:

Expenditures—Interest	$200,000	
Matured Interest Payable		$200,000

To record the semi-annual interest expense.

Matured Interest Payable	$200,000	
Cash		$200,000

To record the payment of the semi-annual interest expense.

Due from the General Fund	$50,000	
Other Financing Sources—Transfers In		$50,000

To record the payable due from the General Fund.

Cash	$250,000	
Due from the General Fund		$250,000

To record the transfer of funds from the General Fund.

On June 30, the first $250,000 principal payment became due.

Expenditures—Principal	$250,000	
Matured Bonds Payable		$250,000

To record the principal payment due June 30.

Matured Bonds Payable	$250,000	
Cash		$250,000

To record the payment of principal due June 30.

The following closing entry would be made based upon the above information:

Revenues—Property Taxes	$500,000	
Other Financing Sources—Transfers In	$250,000	
Expenditures—Interest		$400,000
Expenditures—Principal		$250,000
Fund Balance—Reserved for Debt Service		$100,000

To record closing entries in the Debt Service Fund.

PERMANENT FUNDS

GASB 34 requires the use of another category of governmental funds called the permanent fund type. Permanent funds account for nonexpendable funds provided and held for some governmental purpose. The income for those investments will be recorded as revenues.

A common example of this type of fund would be a cemetery perpetual care fund set up by a citizen who was concerned about the deplorable condition of the city cemetery. If the citizen contributed a large sum of money to the city with the stipulation that the funds be invested and held and that the income only be used for the purpose of maintaining the city cemetery, then the contribution would be held in a permanent fund.

PROPRIETARY FUNDS

There are two types of proprietary funds: internal service funds and enterprise funds. Both the enterprise and internal service funds use full accrual accounting, as would a private business. Fixed assets and interest during construction are capitalized. Long-term liabilities are also recorded. Revenues and expenses (not expenditures) are recorded as any other accrual entity would, including depreciation on fixed assets and interest on debts. Premiums and discounts on debt issuances, as well as debt issue costs, are recorded with the debt and amortized over the life of the bonds. Neither budgetary nor encumbrance accounts are maintained. Revenues, expenses, capital contributions, and transfers are closed out to net assets at year-end. Three categories of net assets exist: invested in capital assets, net of related debt, and restricted and unrestricted (the same categories used in the government-wide statements).

Internal service funds are established to account for the provision of goods and services by one department of the government to other departments within the government, generally on a cost-reimbursement basis. Uses of internal service fund services are budgeted through the budgets of the user departments. Internal service funds are normally established for the following types of activities: central garages, motor pools, central printing and duplicating, stores departments, and self-insurance.

A special problem exists with self-insurance funds that are often classified as internal service funds. Governments transfer resources from other funds to self-insurance funds, from which claims are paid. To the extent that the transfers do not exceed the actuarially determined liability of the government, the transfers are recorded as expenses. Any transfers in addition to the actuarially determined liability are classified as transfers.

Enterprise funds account for activities, for which the government provides goods and services that are rendered primarily to the general public, are financed substantially or entirely through user charges and are intended to be self-supporting. Enterprise funds are usually established for public utilities, airports, toll roads and bridges, transit systems, golf courses, and solid waste landfills.

Another special problem exists with municipal waste landfills that are often classified as enterprise funds. Many of the solid waste landfills in the United States are operated by local governmental units. The problem that arises in accounting for municipal landfills is that most revenue is earned early in the useful life of the landfill as various persons and organizations pay to dispose of waste; conversely, a significant portion of the costs termed *closure* and *post closure* care costs as defined by U.S. Government regulations occur up to 20 to 30 years later. The GASB requires that these future costs be estimated and charged against periodic revenues on a "units of production" basis according to the amount of landfill capacity consumed during each period. If a municipal waste landfill is operated as an enterprise fund, expenses and liabilities are accounted for on a full accrual basis and recorded directly in the enterprise fund. If the municipal waste landfill is operated through a governmental fund, the expenditure and fund liability would be limited to the amount that will be paid with currently available resources, and the remaining liability would be reported in the government-wide statements.

FIDUCIARY FUNDS

Fiduciary funds (trust and agency funds) account for resources invested or to be expended for the benefit of other governments, private organizations, or individuals. Included in the fiduciary fund category are pension (and other employee benefit) trust funds, investment trust funds, private-purpose trust funds, and agency funds.

Pension (and Other Employee Benefit) Trust Funds—These funds are maintained when the government is trustee for the pension (or other employee benefit) plan. These funds use accrual accounting, and investments are reported at fair value. Pension trust funds are required to have two statements and two schedules included in RSI. The pension trust funds are included in the Statement of Fiduciary Net Assets and the Statement of Changes in Fiduciary Net Assets. The Statement of Fiduciary Net Assets should provide information on the fair value of the net assets and on their composition. The statement should be prepared on an accrual basis. The Statement of Changes in Fiduciary Net Assets should provide information on additions, deductions, and changes in the plan net assets for the year. Additions to plan net assets include employer, plan member, or other contributions, and net investment income (including net appreciation or depreciation in the fair value plan investments). Deductions include benefits and refunds paid to plan members and beneficiaries and total administrative expenses. It is prepared on the accrual basis of accounting.

The two RSI schedules are the Schedule of Funding Progress that gives historical trend information about the actuarially determined funded status of the plan and progress made toward accumulation of assets needed to pay benefits when due, and the Schedule of Employer Contributions that includes historical trend information about the annual required contributions of the employer and the contribution made by the employer relating to this requirement.

Defined benefit pension plans do not include the accrued actuarial liability in the statement of fiduciary net assets. Rather, the actuarial liability is reported in the schedule of funding progress and in the notes. Extensive note disclosures are required both for the Public Employees Retirement System (PERS) and for the government as employer, whether or not it is trustee of the pension plan. Under defined contribution plans, the government is liable only for the required contributions not made.

Internal Revenue Code (IRC) Section 457 authorizes state and local governments to establish deferred compensation plans, provided certain requirements are met. In many cases, these plans will not be recorded; however, when the plan meets the criteria for inclusion in a government financial statement, GASB 34 requires that a pension trust fund be used.

Investment Trust Funds—These funds are required when a government sponsors an external investment pool. They are reported in a manner similar to Pension Trust Funds. Statements of Net Fiduciary Assets and of Changes in Fiduciary Net Assets are required.

Private Purpose Trust Funds—These funds represent all other trust arrangements under which principal and income benefit other governments, private organizations, or individuals. Private-purpose trust funds may be nonexpendable or expendable. A nonexpendable trust fund is one in which the principal cannot be expended but that provides that income may be expended for some agreed-upon purpose. Sometimes this is called an *endowment*. Expendable private purpose trust funds are accounted for in the same manner, except that the principal as well as investment income may be expended.

Another use of a private purpose trust fund is for escheat property. This is property that reverts to a governmental entity in the absence of legal claimants or heirs. Generally, such property is reported in the governmental or proprietary fund to which the property will ultimately revert. If the escheat property is being held for another governmental entity, it should be reported as a private purpose trust fund. Escheat revenue should be reduced and a fund liability reported to the extent that it is probable that the escheat property will be reclaimed and paid to claimants.

Agency Funds—These funds are used to account for activities where the government is acting as an agent for others. Agency funds have only assets and liabilities; no fund equity, revenue, or expenditures accounts are used. Agency funds are sometimes used for special assessments. Special assessments are levied for projects to be paid primarily by the property owners who benefit from them (e.g., street lighting or sidewalk repair). GASB requires the use of agency funds for special assessments where the government is not liable in any way for the debt; however, if the government is either primarily or potentially liable for the debt, the accounting will take place as if it were any other capital improvement and financing transaction. Construction activities will be recorded in a capital projects fund and debt principal and interest activities will be recorded in a debt service fund. For the government-wide financial statements, the capital asset is recorded at cost along with any related debt; the capital asset is depreciated over its estimated life, and collections from property owners are recorded as revenues. For the fund-based financial statements, an expenditure is recorded within the capital projects funds, the proceeds from any debt issued to finance the project are reported as an other financing source; and cash received from the property owner is shown as revenue.

Another common use of an agency fund is to account for property taxes. Property taxes are usually remitted to a county treasurer who places the monies in a county agency fund. The taxes are held until such time as they are remitted to each of the other local governments within the county. Often a fee is charged that decreases the amount that is distributed to the other local government.

INTERFUND TRANSACTIONS

GASB 34 requires that interfund activity be shown between individual funds in fund financial statements and between business-type and governmental-type activities in the government-wide financial statements. An interfund transaction occurs when one fund disburses cash to another. These may result from interfund loans or advances, interfund services provided and used (known as *quasi-external transactions* in pre-GASB 34 terminology), interfund transfers, or interfund reimbursements.

1. An interfund loan or advance is a transaction in which one fund provides resources with a requirement for repayment. These simply result in the creation of interfund receivables and payables in the affected funds. Short-term transactions are recorded with "Due From" and "Due To" accounts. Long-term transactions use the terms "Advance To" and "Advance From." If a governmental fund makes a long-term loan to another fund, it is necessary to reserve fund balances as the resources are not available for expenditure.

2. Interfund services provided and used results from a fund providing goods or services to another fund and received payment as it would if services were rendered to unrelated entities. Common examples include payments to an internal service fund for goods and services received and contributions to a pension trust fund for employees covered under the plan. The paying fund would record an expenditure or expense and the recipient fund a revenue.

3. Interfund transfers are nonreciprocal transfers between funds. They represent movement of resources between funds where payment is not expected. The amounts transferred do not represent either revenues or spending by the government as a whole, and they are kept separate from such accounts, reported as "Other Financing Sources and Uses" in modified accrual funds, and as Operating Transfers in accrual funds.

4. An interfund reimbursement occurs when one fund has paid costs that are obligations of another fund and then receives repayment of the costs. The paying fund will record the expenditure or expense, and the recipient fund will reduce the expenditure or expense it had previously recorded when it paid the costs.

REVERSE REPURCHASE AGREEMENTS

A governmental unit may enter into a reverse repurchase agreement in which a financial institution or a broker transfers cash to the governmental entity. The entity transfers securities to the broker or institution and promises to repay the cash plus interest in exchange for the return of the same securities. Typically, such an arrangement transfers neither the risks nor the benefits of ownership to the purchaser. Instead, the arrangement functions essentially as a form of collateralized loan with the government in the role of the borrower.

The governmental entity should disclose the carrying value and market value of the underlying securities using a caption such as "Investment Held by Brokers under Reverse Repurchase Agreements." Credit risk related to the agreements will also be disclosed.

ACCOUNTING FOR INVESTMENTS

GASB provides that investments in debt securities and in equity securities with determinable fair values be reported at fair value. Changes in fair value should be reported as a part of operations, using modified accrual or accrual accounting as appropriate. No distinction is to be made on the face of the financial statements between realized and unrealized gains and losses, although disclosure may be made of realized gains in the notes. When investments are pooled, investment income should be reported in the fund for which investments are held.

ACCOUNTING FOR LEASES

A government can acquire assets through a lease. Many times these arrangements must be capitalized. The criteria for requiring capitalization of a lease are the same as that used in a for-profit business. In the government-wide financial statements, the reporting is also the same as that used in a for-profit business. The asset is reported at the present value of the minimum lease payments and depreciated over the period of use. The liability is also recorded at present value. Each payment is partially recognized as interest expense and partially recognized as principal payment. On the fund financial statements, if the lease is acquired by a governmental fund, both an expenditure and another financing source are recorded for the present value of all minimum lease payments. When payments are subsequently made, an expenditure is recorded, part for interest and part for the principal.

ACCOUNTING FOR COMPENSATED ABSENCES

Government employees can earn amounts for vacations, holidays, and the like. When financial statements are being produced, any amounts due to employees for such compensated absences should be recognized if based on past services. In the government-wide financial statements, the expense is recognized as the liability is incurred. For the fund-based financial statements, an expenditure is recognized along with a liability, but only for the amount of the debt that will be paid from current financial resources.

ACCOUNTING FOR SUPPLIES AND PREPAID EXPENSES

In the government-wide financial statements, supplies and prepaid expenses are reported as in a for-profit business. The asset is recorded at cost and reclassified to expense as it is used. However, for fund-based financial statements, supplies and prepaid expenses cause special reporting problems because they are neither financial resources nor capital assets. On the fund-based statements, the following are two ways that can be used to report such assets:

1. Consumption Method—This method records cost as an asset when acquired and then reclassifies this amount to an expenditures account as the asset is consumed either by use or over time. At the end of the year, if any asset is still being reported, an equal amount of the unreserved fund balance should be switched to a fund balance reserved for supplies (or the prepaid item) to show that a portion of the asset being reported is not a financial resource that can be spent.

2. Purchase Method—This method records entire cost as an expenditure when purchased. Any asset remaining at the end of the year is recorded directly on the balance sheet with an offsetting entry to a fund balance reserved for supplies (or the prepaid item) account.

DEBT REFUNDINGS REPORTED BY PROPRIETARY FUNDS (GASB STATEMENT NO. 23)

A refunding entails issuing new debt so that the proceeds from this new debt can be used to pay off the old debt. If the repayment is done immediately, it is a current refunding. If the new debt is placed in an escrow account and invested to pay the old debt at some point in the future, it is an advance refunding. Of course, with advance refunding, the old debt remains outstanding until the call date or maturity. In substance, there is little difference between a current refund and an advance refunding. Accordingly, GAAP requires that most advance refunding transactions be accounted for just as though the old debt had been redeemed upon issuance of the refunding bonds by removing both the old debt and the related escrow assets from the financial statements. A general description of the transaction is required in the notes to the financial statements.

ARTWORKS AND HISTORICAL TREASURES

To qualify as an artwork or historical treasure, an item must be for exhibit, education, or research, and it must be protected and preserved. Additionally, a policy must be in place that the proceeds of any sale will be used to replace the sold item with a similar item.

If artworks and historical treasures are acquired by purchase, then such items are recorded as assets in the government-wide financial statements and as expenditures in the fund financial statements. The assets must be depreciated unless the item is considered to be inexhaustible.

If artworks and historical treasures are acquired by donation, then such items are recorded as assets and revenue at fair value in the government-wide financial statements. The assets must be depreciated unless the item is considered to be inexhaustible. A government may choose to record the donated item as an expenditure and a revenue rather than an asset and a revenue in the government-wide financial statements. It is not necessary to record donated items in the fund financial statements because current financial resources were not affected.

CONVERSION FROM FUND FINANCIAL STATEMENTS TO GOVERNMENT-WIDE FINANCIAL STATEMENTS

As stated previously, most state and local governments will keep their books on a fund basis in order to facilitate the preparation of fund financial statements and to prepare the budget to actual schedule as part of RSI. This means that transactions are recorded using the modified accrual basis for governmental funds and the accrual basis for proprietary and fiduciary funds. At year-end, worksheets are prepared in order to convert the fund financial statements to the government-wide financial statements. The following are the major changes that will be necessary to convert the fund financial statements to the government-wide financial statements.

GENERAL FIXED ASSETS

When general fixed assets are acquired through governmental funds, they are recorded as expenditures. In order to prepare the government-wide financial statements, the fixed assets must be eliminated from the expenditure accounts and recorded as fixed assets. Additionally, depreciation expense must be calculated and charged. The entry to record the fixed assets will be a debit to "Fixed Assets" and a credit to the expenditure account where the original purchase was recorded.

LONG-TERM DEBT

When general long-term debt is issued, governmental funds credit "Other Financing Sources—Proceeds from Debt." Premiums and discounts are not amortized but added or deducted from the amount of resources available. In order to prepare the government-wide financial statements, the former entries must be eliminated and the debt must be recorded as a liability. Any premium or discount must also be associated with the liability and amortized over the life of the bonds. If the bonds were issued at par, the entry to record the debt will be a debit to "Other Financing Sources—Proceeds from Debt" and a credit to "Bonds Payable."

DEBT SERVICE PAYMENTS

When making principal payments on long-term debt, governmental funds debit expenditures. In order to prepare the government-wide financial statements, those expenditures will need to be eliminated and replaced with a debit to the debt principal. The entry to record the principal payment would be a debit to "Bonds Payable" and a credit to the expenditure account where the original payment was recorded. Additionally, governmental funds do not accrue interest payable, but record expenditures on the maturity date. An accrual of interest payable will be required for the government-wide statements (see "Accrual of Expenses" below).

REVENUE RECOGNITION

Governmental funds recognize revenues only when measurable and available to finance expenditures of the current period. In the case of property taxes, revenues cannot be recognized if those revenues will be collected more than 60 days after the end of the fiscal year. When preparing the government-wide financial statements, some adjustments will be required to recognize all revenues net of uncollectible receivables in accordance with revenue accounting for exchange and nonexchange transactions.

ACCRUAL OF EXPENSES

Governmental funds record expenditures using the modified accrual accounting method so that expenditures are only recorded for items that are to be paid from current recourses. Therefore, in order to prepare the government-wide statements on the full accrual method, adjustments must be made to record interest payable and the noncurrent portion of certain liabilities such as claims and judgments, compensated absences, and so on. The entry to record these expenditures would be a debt to expenditures and a credit to liabilities.

OTHER

Some governments use the purchases method to record governmental fund inventories, and these must be changed to the consumption method when using accrual accounting. Other governments do not record and amortize certain prepaid items such as prepaid insurance and prepaid rent. Adjustments must also be made for these items.

RECLASSIFICATIONS

Fund financial statements are represented separately for governmental, proprietary and fiduciary fund categories. Government-wide financial statements have columns for governmental activities, business-type activities, and component units. In order to make the transition from fund financial statements, the fiduciary funds will be eliminated. Internal service funds, which are proprietary funds, are to be classified as governmental activities in the government-wide statements. Discretely presented component units that are not presented at all in the fund financial statements will be added when preparing the government-wide financial statements.

QUESTIONS: GOVERNMENTAL ACCOUNTING

1. Government-wide statement of net assets reports capital assets:
    A. at estimated fair value.
    B. at historical costs including any capitalized interest.
    C. as part of the fixed asset group.
    D. in the statement of capital assets.

2. Which of the following accounts of a governmental unit is credited when the budget is recorded?
    A. Reserve for encumbrances.
    B. Encumbrances.
    C. Appropriations.
    D. Estimated revenues.

3. SGAS 34 requires that budgetary comparison schedules should:
    A. not be reported.
    B. be reported for all proprietary funds.
    C. be reported for the permanent funds.
    D. be reported for the general fund and each major special revenue fund with a legally adopted budget.

4. The budgetary fund balance reserved for encumbrances account of a governmental fund type is increased when:
    A. a purchase order is approved.
    B. supplies previously ordered are received.
    C. appropriations are recorded.
    D. the budget is recorded.

5. Interest paid on capital debt and leases must be reported on public colleges' cash flow statements as cash from:
    A. investing activities.
    B. operations.
    C. capital and related financing activities.
    D. noncapital financing activities.

6. When the budget of a governmental unit, for which the estimated revenues exceed the appropriations, is adopted and recorded in the general ledger at the beginning of the year, the budgetary fund balance account is:
    A. debited at the beginning of the year and credited at the end of the year.
    B. credited at the beginning of the year and no entry made at the end of the year.
    C. debited at the beginning of the year and no entry made at the end of the year.
    D. credited at the beginning of the year and debited at the end of the year.

7. Cash flows from a public university bookstore would appear on the statement of cash flows as cash flows from:
    A. operations.
    B. investing activities.
    C. financing activities.
    D. noncapital financing.

8. A budgetary fund balance reserved for encumbrances in excess of a balance of encumbrances indicates a(n):
    A. excess of vouchers payable over encumbrances.
    B. recording error.
    C. excess of purchase orders over invoices received.
    D. excess of appropriations over encumbrances.

9. Which event(s) below support interperiod equity as a financial reporting objective of a governmental unit?

    I.   A balanced budget is adopted.
    II. Residual equity transfers out, equal residual equity transfers in.

    A. I only.
    B. II only.
    C. Both I and II.
    D. Neither I nor II.

10. Harbor City's appropriations control account at December 31, 2004, had a balance of $7,000,000. When the budgetary accounts were closed at year-end, this $7,000,000 appropriations control balance should have:
    A. appeared as a contra account.
    B. been credited.
    C. remained open.
    D. been debited.

11. According to SGAS 34, notes to the financial statements:
    A. are a part of the required supplemental information (RSI).
    B. are an integral part of the financial statements because they present information essential to fair presentation that is not reported on the face of the financial statements.
    C. are a part of the management's discussion and analysis.
    D. give equal focus to the primary government and its component units.

12. A state government collected income taxes of $8,000,000 for the benefit of one of its cities that imposes an income tax on its residents. The state remitted these collections periodically to the city. The state should account for the $8,000,000 in the:
    A. internal service funds.
    B. general fund.
    C. agency funds.
    D. special assessment funds.

13. Which of the following accounts of a governmental unit is credited when taxpayers are billed for property taxes, assuming they will be available this year?
    A. Appropriations.
    B. Revenues.
    C. Taxes receivable—current.
    D. Estimated revenues.

14. ABC City opens a landfill in Year 1 that is expected to take ten years to fill. Currently, the city expects a total of $1,000,000 in closure costs and $500,000 in post-closure cost. During Year 1, the city makes an initial payment of $40,000 on the closure cost and the landfill is 8% full. Assuming that the landfill is part of the general fund, what account and amount would be debited for the landfill cost for year one using fund-based reporting?
    A. Expenditures-landfill closure cost—$40,000.
    B. Expense-landfill closure cost—$40,000.
    C. Expense-landfill closure cost—$120,000.
    D. Expenditures-landfill closure cost—$120,000.

15. Assuming that the landfill cost is being reported on government-wide financial statements, what account and amount would be debited for the cost of the landfill for year one?
    A. Expenditures-landfill closure cost—$40,000.
    B. Expenditures-landfill closure cost—$120,000.
    C. Expense-landfill closure cost—$40,000.
    D. Expense-landfill closure cost—$120,000.

16. Assume that the landfill cost is being reported on government-wide financial statements. What account and amount would be debited to record the initial payment on the closure cost?
    A. Asset-landfill—$120,000.
    B. Other financing uses-landfill—$40,000.
    C. Landfill closure liability—$40,000.
    D. Asset-landfill—$40,000.

17. The following information pertains to property taxes levied by Oak City for the calendar year 2005:

Collections during 2005	$500,000
Expected collections during the first 60 days of 2006	100,000
Expected collections during the balance of 2006	60,000
Expected collections during January 2007	30,000
Estimated to be uncollectible	10,000
Total levy	$700,000

    What amount should Oak City report for 2005 net property tax revenues?
    A. $600,000.
    B. $700,000.
    C. $690,000.
    D. $500,000.

18. Which of the following accounts of a governmental unit is debited when a purchase order is approved?
    A. Fund balance reserved for encumbrances.
    B. Appropriations control.
    C. Vouchers payable.
    D. Encumbrances control.

19. The Board of Commissioners of the City of Rockton adopted its budget for the year ending July 31, Year 2 that indicated revenues of $1,000,000 and appropriations of $900,000. If the budget is formally integrated into the accounting records, what is the required journal entry?

	Dr.	Cr.
A. Memorandum entry only		
B. Appropriations	$900,000	
General fund	$100,000	
Estimated revenues		$1,000,000
C. Estimated revenues	$1,000,000	
Appropriations		$900,000
Budgetary fund balance		$100,000
D. Revenues receivable	$1,000,000	
Expenditures payable	$900,000	
General fund balance		$100,000

    A. C.
    B. A.
    C. B.
    D. D.

20. Which of the following funds of a governmental unit integrates budgetary accounts into the accounting system?
    A. Special revenue.
    B. Enterprise.
    C. Internal service.
    D. Nonexpendable trust.

21. Ridge Township's governing body adopted its general fund budget for the year ended July 31, Year 5, comprised of estimated revenues of $100,000 and appropriations of $80,000. Ridge formally integrates its budget into the accounting records.

To record the appropriations of $80,000, Ridge should:
    A. credit estimated expenditures control.
    B. debit appropriations control.
    C. credit appropriations control.
    D. debit estimated expenditures control.

22. To record the $20,000 budgeted excess of estimated revenues over appropriations, Ridge should:
    A. credit budgetary fund balance.
    B. debit budgetary fund balance.
    C. debit estimated excess revenues control.
    D. credit estimated excess revenues control.

23. Gold County received goods that had been approved for purchase but for which payment had not yet been made. Should the accounts listed below be increased?

	Encumbrances	Expenditures
A.	Yes	No
B.	No	Yes
C.	Yes	Yes
D.	No	No

24. For the budgetary year ending December 31, Year 5, Maple City's general fund expects the following inflows of resources:

Property taxes, licenses, and fines	$9,000,000
Proceeds of debt issue	$5,000,000
Interfund transfers for debt service	$1,000,000

    In the budgetary entry, what amount should Maple record for estimated revenues?
    A. $15,000,000.
    B. $10,000,000.
    C. $14,000,000.
    D. $9,000,000.

25. Which capitalized assets must be depreciated in government-wide financial statements?
    A. All capitalized collections of art.
    B. All infrastructure assets.
    C. All capitalized collections that are exhaustible.
    D. All collections of historical treasures.

26. The following related entries were recorded in sequence in the general fund of a municipality:

1. Encumbrances Control	$12,000	
Fund balances reserved for encumbrances		$12,000
2. Fund balances reserved for encumbrances	$12,000	
Encumbrances Control		$12,000
3. Expenditures Control	$12,350	
Vouchers payable		$12,350

    The sequence of entries indicates that:
    A. the first entry was erroneous and was reversed; a liability of $12,350 was acknowledged.
    B. an adverse event was foreseen and a reserve of $12,000 was created; later the reserve was cancelled and a liability for the item was acknowledged.
    C. encumbrances were anticipated but later failed to materialize and were reversed. A liability of $12,350 was incurred.
    D. an order was placed for goods or services estimated to cost $12,000; the actual cost was $12,350 for which a liability was acknowledged upon receipt.

27. Governmental financial reporting should provide information to assist users in which situation(s)?

    I. Making social and political decisions
    II. Assessing whether current-year citizens received services but shifted part of the payment burden to future-year citizens

    A. Both I and II.
    B. I only.
    C. II only.
    D. Neither I nor II.

28. According to SGAS 34, Management's Discussion Analysis includes which of the following?
    A. Appears after the notes to the financial statements at the end of the financial report.
    B. A budgetary comparison of the actual versus budget financial statements for the general fund and the enterprise funds.
    C. A description of currently known facts, decisions, or conditions expected to have significant effects on financial activities.
    D. Is no longer required for governmental financial reports.

29. Infrastructure assets using the modified approach are:
    A. not depreciated.
    B. reported in the balance sheet for governmental funds.
    C. reported in government-wide statements at historical costs less accumulated depreciation.
    D. reported in the fixed asset group of accounts.

30. Which of the following funds of a governmental unit would include retained earnings in its balance sheet?
    A. Internal service.
    B. Expendable pension trust.
    C. Special revenue.
    D. Capital projects.

31. Taxes collected and held by Franklin County for a separate school district would be accounted for in which fund?
    A. Special revenue.
    B. Agency.
    C. Internal service.
    D. Trust.

32. A capital projects fund of a municipality is an example of what type of fund?
    A. Proprietary.
    B. Internal service.
    C. Governmental.
    D. Fiduciary.

33. Which of the following fund types should account for fixed assets in a manner similar to a "for profit" organization?
    A. General fixed assets account group.
    B. Special revenue fund.
    C. Capital projects fund.
    D. Enterprise fund.

34. The billings for transportation services provided to other governmental units are recorded by the internal service fund as:
    A. transportation appropriations.
    B. interfund exchanges.
    C. operating revenues.
    D. intergovernmental transfers.

35. Tott City's serial bonds are serviced through a debt service fund with cash provided by the general fund. In a debt service fund's statements, how are cash receipts and cash payments reported?

	Cash receipts	Cash payments
A.	Operating transfers	Expenditures
B.	Revenues	Expenditures
C.	Revenues	Operating transfers
D.	Operating transfers	Operating transfers

36. Lisa County issued $5,000,000 of general obligation bonds at 101 to finance a capital project. The $50,000 premium was to be used for payment of principal and interest. This transaction should be accounted for in the:
   A. capital projects funds and debt service funds only.
   B. capital projects funds, debt service funds, and the general long-term debt account group.
   C. debt service funds and the general long-term debt account group only.
   D. debt service funds only.

37. The special revenue fund of a governmental unit is an example of what type of fund?
   A. Proprietary.
   B. Governmental.
   C. Internal service.
   D. Fiduciary.

38. How would customers' security deposits that cannot be spent for normal operation purposes be classified in the balance sheet of the enterprise fund of a governmental unit?

	Restricted asset	Liability	Fund equity
A.	No	Yes	No
B.	Yes	No	Yes
C.	Yes	Yes	Yes
D.	Yes	Yes	No

39. According to SGAS 34, Agency Funds are:
   A. proprietary funds.
   B. governmental funds.
   C. fiduciary funds in which the assets should equal the liabilities in the statement of fiduciary net assets.
   D. permanent funds.

40. Which of the following accounts could be included in the balance sheet of an enterprise fund?

	Reserve for encumbrances	Revenue bonds payable	Retained earnings
A.	No	Yes	Yes
B.	No	No	Yes
C.	Yes	Yes	No
D.	No	No	No

41.   Through an internal service fund, Wood County operates a centralized data processing center to provide services to Wood's other governmental units. The internal service fund billed Wood's parks and recreation fund $75,000 for data processing services. What account should Wood's internal service fund credit to record this $75,000 billing to the parks and recreation fund?
   A. Interfund exchanges.
   B. Operating revenues control.
   C. Intergovernmental transfers.
   D. Data processing department expenses.

42.   The following balances are included in the subsidiary records of Burwood Village's Parks and Recreation Department at March 31:
   Appropriations—supplies $7,500
   Expenditures—supplies $4,500
   Encumbrances—supplies $750

   How much does the Recreation Department have available for additional purchases of supplies?
   A. $6,750.
   B. $0.
   C. $3,000.
   D. $2,250.

43.   The following information for the year ended June 30 pertains to a proprietary fund established by Burwood Village in connection with Burwood's public parking facilities:
   Receipts from users $400,000
       of parking facilities
   Expenditures
       Parking meters $210,000
       Salaries and other cash expenses $90,000
   Depreciation of parking meters $70,000

   For the year ended June 30, this proprietary fund should report net income (excluding depreciation) of:
   A. $30,000.
   B. $0.
   C. $240,000.
   D. $100,000.

44.   Oda County's expenditures control account at December 31st had a balance of $9,000,000. When Oda's books were closed, this $9,000,000 expenditures control balance should have:
   A. been debited.
   B. been credited.
   C. remained open.
   D. appeared as a contra-account.

45. An enterprise fund would be used when the governing body requires which of the following?

    I. Accounting for the financing of an agency's services to other government departments be on a cost-reimbursement basis.
    II. User charges cover the costs of general public services.
    III. Net income information be provided for an activity.

    A. II and III.
    B. I only.
    C. II only.
    D. I and III.

46. Repairs that have been made for a governmental unit, and for which a bill has been received, should be recorded in the general fund as a debit to an:
    A. appropriation.
    B. encumbrance.
    C. expense.
    D. expenditure.

47. Fiduciary trust funds include:
    A. expendable trust funds.
    B. private purpose trust funds.
    C. permanent funds.
    D. nonexpendable trust funds.

48. Under SGAS 34, capital assets and non-current debt are reported in the:
    A. governmental funds balance sheet.
    B. fixed asset and long-term debt group of accounts.
    C. governmental-wide statement of net assets.
    D. no longer reported under SGAS 34.

49. Under SGAS 34, a special revenue fund may be reported as a major fund if:
    A. total liabilities of the fund are 10% of the total liabilities of all government funds and 5% of the total liabilities of all governmental and enterprise funds combined.
    B. total revenues of the fund are 5% of the total revenues of all governmental funds and 10% of the total revenues of all governmental and enterprise funds combined.
    C. total assets of the fund are 10% of the total assets of all governmental funds and 5% of the assets for all governmental funds and the internal service fund combined.
    D. total expenditures of the fund are 10% of the total expenditures of all governmental funds and 5% of the expenditures for all the governmental funds and the permanent funds combined.

50. Customers' security deposits that cannot be spent for normal operating purposes were collected by a governmental unit and accounted for in the enterprise fund. A portion of the amount collected was invested in marketable securities. How would the portion in cash and the portion in marketable securities be classified in the balance sheet of the enterprise fund?

	Portion in cash	Portion in marketable securities
A.	Unrestricted asset	Restricted asset
B.	Unrestricted asset	Unrestricted asset
C.	Restricted asset	Unrestricted asset
D.	Restricted asset	Restricted asset

51. With regard to the statement of cash flows for a governmental unit's enterprise fund, items generally presented as cash equivalents are as follows:

	Two-month treasury bills	Three-month certificates of deposit
A.	No	Yes
B.	Yes	Yes
C.	Yes	No
D.	No	No

52. Revenues that are legally restricted to expenditures for specified purposes should be accounted for in special revenue funds, including:
    A. pension trust fund revenues.
    B. accumulation of resources for payment of general long-term debt principal and interest.
    C. gasoline taxes to finance road repairs.
    D. proprietary fund revenues.

53. Long-term liabilities of an enterprise fund should be accounted for in the following:

	Enterprise fund	Long-term debt account group
A.	Yes	No
B.	No	No
C.	No	Yes
D.	Yes	Yes

54. The revenues control account of a governmental unit is debited when:
    A. property taxes are collected.
    B. the budget is recorded at the beginning of the year.
    C. property taxes are recorded.
    D. the account is closed out at the end of the year.

55. The economic resources management focus is:
    A. used by the general fund for fund-based reporting.
    B. a focus on the overall entity perspective and records information about long-term stewardship of governmental resources.
    C. used by the permanent funds for fund-based reporting.
    D. a focus on the short-term results and the current inflows and outflows of governmental resources.

56. In accordance with SGAS 34, depreciation would be recorded on which of the following financial statements?

	Governmental funds statement of activities	Statement of revenues, expenses, and changes in fund assets for proprietary funds
A.	No	No
B.	Yes	Yes
C.	No	Yes
D.	Yes	No

57.   Fixed assets of an enterprise fund should be accounted for in the:
A.   enterprise fund and depreciation on the fixed assets should be recorded.
B.   general fixed asset account group but no depreciation on the fixed assets should be recorded.
C.   general fixed asset account group and depreciation on the fixed assets should be recorded.
D.   enterprise fund but no depreciation on the fixed assets should be recorded.

58.   The following equity balances are among those maintained by Cole City:
       Enterprise funds $1,000,000
       Internal service funds $400,000

       Cole's proprietary equity balances amount to:
A. $1,000,000.
B. $1,400,000.
C. $400,000.
D. $0.

59.   According to SGAS 34, the focus of governmental funds should be on which of the following?

	Economic resources measurement focus	Modified accrual basis	Current fin. resources measurement focus	Accrual basis
A.	No	Yes	Yes	No
B.	Yes	Yes	No	No
C.	Yes	No	No	Yes
D.	No	No	Yes	Yes

60.   The debt service fund of a governmental unit is used to account for the accumulation of resources to pay, and the payment of, general long-term debt, as follows:

	Principal	Interest
A.	No	No
B.	Yes	Yes
C.	No	Yes
D.	Yes	No

61.   Preparation of government-wide financial statements requires the elimination from fund-based statements of:
A.   other financing uses accounts—transfers out.
B.   due from general fund and due to special revenue fund accounts.
C.   other financing sources accounts—transfers in.
D.   all of these.

62.   For governmental fund types, which item is considered the primary measurement focus?
A.   Income determination.
B.   Flows and balances of financial resources.
C.   Capital maintenance.
D.   Cash flows and balances.

63. Which of the following funds of a governmental unit uses the same basis of accounting as an enterprise fund?
    A. Expendable trust.
    B. Special revenue.
    C. Internal service.
    D. Capital projects.

64. The following funds are among those maintained by Arlong City:
    Enterprise funds $2,000,000
    Internal service funds $800,000

    Arlong's proprietary funds amount to:
    A. $2,800,000.
    B. $0.
    C. $800,000.
    D. $2,000,000.

65. A state governmental unit should use which basis of accounting for each of the following types of funds?

	Governmental	Proprietary
A.	Modified accrual	Modified accrual
B.	Cash	Modified accrual
C.	Modified accrual	Accrual
D.	Accrual	Accrual

66. Which of the following funds of a governmental unit uses the modified accrual basis of accounting?
    A. Nonexpendable trust funds.
    B. Enterprise funds.
    C. Internal service funds.
    D. Special revenue funds.

67. Which of the following funds of a governmental unit would include contributed capital in its balance sheet?
    A. Internal service.
    B. Expendable pension trust.
    C. Special revenue.
    D. Capital projects.

68. Under which basis of accounting for a governmental unit should revenues be recognized in the accounting period in which they are earned and become measurable?

	Accrual basis	Modified accrual basis
A.	No	No
B.	No	Yes
C.	Yes	No
D.	Yes	Yes

69. Lake City incurred $300,000 of salaries and wages expense in its general fund for the month ended May 31st. For this $300,000 expense, Lake should debit:
    A. fund balance—unreserved, undesignated.
    B. expenditures control.
    C. encumbrances control.
    D. appropriations control.

70. The basis of accounting for a capital projects fund is the:
    A. modified accrual basis.
    B. cash basis.
    C. accrual basis.
    D. modified cash basis.

71. SGAS 34 requires that proprietary funds present which of the following statements?
    A. Statement of Cash Flows (direct method).
    B. Statement of Activities.
    C. Statement of Cash Flows (indirect method).
    D. Statement of Revenues, Expenditures, and Changes in Fund Balances.

72. SGAS 34 requires that the statement of net assets:
    A. report assets classified into current and noncurrent categories.
    B. display net assets in three categories.
    C. report liabilities classified in current and non-current categories.
    D. use a balance sheet format.

73. The following information pertains to Wood Township's long-term debt:
    General long-term obligations $350,000
    Proprietary fund obligations $100,000

    How much of these cash accumulations should be accounted for in Wood's debt service funds?
    A. $100,000.
    B. $0.
    C. $350,000.
    D. $450,000.

74. Gem City's internal service fund received a residual equity transfer of $50,000 cash from the general fund. This $50,000 transfer should be reported in Gem's internal service fund as a credit to:
    A. revenues.
    B. contributed capital.
    C. other financing sources.
    D. accounts payable.

75. Interperiod equity is an objective of financial reporting for governmental entities. According to the Governmental Accounting Standards Board, is interperiod equity fundamental to public administration and is it a component of accountability?

	Fundamental to public administration	Component of accountability
A.	Yes	Yes
B.	No	Yes
C.	No	No
D.	Yes	No

76. Eureka City should issue a statement of cash flows for which of the following funds?

	Eureka City Hall capital projects fund	Eureka Water enterprise fund
A.	Yes	No
B.	No	No
C.	Yes	Yes
D.	No	Yes

77. Kew City received a $15,000,000 federal grant to finance the construction of a center for rehabilitation of drug addicts. The proceeds of this grant should be accounted for in the:
A. capital projects funds.
B. special revenue funds.
C. general fund.
D. trust funds.

78. Which of the following types of revenue would generally be recorded directly in the general fund of a governmental unit?
A. Revenues from internal service funds.
B. Receipts from a city-owned parking structure.
C. Interest earned on investments held for retirement of employees.
D. Property taxes.

79. In connection with Albury Township's long-term debt, the following cash accumulations are available to cover payment of principal and interest on:

Bonds for financing of water treatment plant construction	$1,000,000
General long-term obligations	$400,000

The amount of these cash accumulations that should be accounted for in Albury's debt service funds is:
A. $1,000,000.
B. $0.
C. $400,000.
D. $1,400,000.

80. According to SGAS 34, a summary reconciliation of the government-wide and fund financial statements:
A. must be presented at the bottom of the fund statements or in an accompanying schedule.
B. is not required.
C. must accompany the notes to the financial statements.
D. must be presented as a part of the management's discussion analysis.

81. Fixed assets should be accounted for in which of the following?

	Capital projects fund	Internal service fund
A.	No	No
B.	No	Yes
C.	Yes	No
D.	Yes	Yes

82. The activities of a municipal employees' retirement and pension system should be recorded in a(n):
    A. internal service fund.
    B. general fund.
    C. capital projects fund.
    D. trust fund.

83. Which of the following bases of accounting should a government use for its proprietary funds in measuring financial position and operating results?

	Modified accrual basis	Accrual basis
A.	No	Yes
B.	Yes	No
C.	No	No
D.	Yes	Yes

84. On the statement of net assets for a public university, the restricted net assets are divided between nonexpendable and expendable net assets. The nonexpendable net assets allow for the expenditures of:
    A. earnings only.
    B. principal only.
    C. principal and earnings.
    D. neither principal nor earnings.

85. Which of the following accounts should Moon City close at the end of its fiscal year?
    A. Fund balance—reserved for encumbrances.
    B. Vouchers payable.
    C. Fund balance.
    D. Expenditures.

86. Government-wide financial statements use which of the following concepts?

	Accrual resources basis	Modified accrual	Economic resources measurement focus	Current financial measurement focus
A.	Yes	No	Yes	No
B.	Yes	No	No	Yes
C.	No	No	No	No
D.	No	Yes	Yes	No

87. Under SGAS 34, which financial statements must be presented for governmental funds?
    A. A statement of activities.
    B. A statement of cash flows.
    C. A financial statement in balance sheet format.
    D. A statement of revenues, expenses, and changes in fund balances.

88. The restricted net assets account reported in the net asset section of the Statement of Net Assets:
    A. may include expendable but not non-expendable endowments.
    B. includes capital assets restricted by external entities or by law (constitutional provisions or enabling legislation).
    C. are included in the combined net assets section of the Statement of Net Assets.
    D. may include nonexpendable but not expendable endowments.

89. Which category of funds is not reported in government-wide financial statements?
    A. Fiduciary funds.
    B. Governmental funds.
    C. Enterprise funds.
    D. Proprietary funds.

90. The modified accrual basis of accounting should be used for which of the following funds?
    A. Proprietary fund.
    B. Enterprise fund.
    C. Pension trust fund.
    D. Capital projects fund.

91. According to SGAS 34, a summary reconciliation of government-wide and fund-based financial statements:
    A. must be presented at the bottom of the fund-based statements or in an accompanying schedule.
    B. is not required by SGAS 34, but is recommended.
    C. must be presented in the notes to the financial statements.
    D. must be presented in the required supplemental information.

92. Customers' security deposits that cannot be spent for normal operating purposes were collected by a governmental unit and accounted for in the enterprise fund. A portion of the amount collected was invested in marketable debt securities and a portion in marketable equity securities. How would each portion be classified in the balance sheet?

	Portion in marketable debt securities	Portion in marketable equity securities
A.	Unrestricted asset	Unrestricted asset
B.	Restricted asset	Restricted asset
C.	Restricted asset	Unrestricted asset
D.	Unrestricted asset	Restricted asset

93. Maple City's public employee retirement system (PERS) reported the following account balances at June 30:

Reserve for employer's contributions	$5,000,000
Actuarial deficiency in reserve for employer's contributions	$300,000
Reserve for employee's contributions	$9,000,000

    Maple's PERS fund balance at June 30 should be:
    A. $14,300,000.
    B. $5,000,000.
    C. $5,300,000.
    D. $14,000,000.

94. Taxes collected and held by Eldorado County for a school district would be accounted for in which of the following funds?
    A. Special revenue.
    B. Trust.
    C. Agency.
    D. Internal service.

95. The operating statements of governmental units should embody the:
    A. Current performance approach.
    B. All-inclusive approach.
    C. Prospective approach.
    D. Retroactive approach.

96. SGAS 34 requires budgetary comparison schedules:
    A. be presented for the government-wide financial statements.
    B. be presented for each of the governmental funds.
    C. compare actual amounts with only the final budget.
    D. be presented for the general fund and each special revenue fund with a legally adopted budget.

97. In accordance with SGAS 34, governmental funds should report which of the following financial statements?

    I. Income statement.
    II. Statement of activities.
    III. Statement of revenues, expenses, and changes in net assets.
    IV. A statement of net assets.
    V. Balance sheet.

    A. V.
    B. I, IV.
    C. V, II, IV.
    D. III, IV.

98. For governmental units, depreciation expense on assets acquired with capital grants externally restricted for capital acquisitions should be reported in which type of fund?

	Governmental fund	Proprietary fund
A.	Yes	Yes
B.	No	No
C.	No	Yes
D.	Yes	No

99. The estimated revenues control account balance of a governmental fund type is eliminated when:
    A. the budgetary accounts are closed.
    B. the budget is recorded.
    C. property taxes are recorded.
    D. appropriations are closed.

100. SGAS 34 requires that a statement of revenues, expenditures, and changes in fund balances be reported for governmental funds. In that statement:
   A. revenues are classified by function.
   B. proceeds from the issue of long-term bonds should be reported in the other financing sources and uses section.
   C. expenditures are classified by source.
   D. other financing sources-transfers are classified as revenues.

101. The government-wide statement of activities should report which of the following categories of program revenues?

   I. Charges for services.
   II. Capital grants and contributions.
   III. General property taxes.
   IV. Property taxes levied for debt service.

   A. I, II.
   B. I only.
   C. I, II, III.
   D. I, II, III, IV.

102. The town of Hill operates municipal electric and water utilities. In which of the following funds should the operations of the utilities be accounted for?
   A. Special revenue fund.
   B. Internal service fund.
   C. Agency fund.
   D. Enterprise fund.

103. Which of the following is an appropriate basis of accounting for a proprietary fund of a governmental unit?

	Cash basis	Modified accrual basis
A.	No	Yes
B.	Yes	Yes
C.	No	No
D.	Yes	No

104. The modified accrual basis of accounting is appropriate for which of the following fund categories of a county government?

	Governmental	Proprietary
A.	Yes	No
B.	No	No
C.	Yes	Yes
D.	No	Yes

105. SGAS 34 requires that general capital assets and general long-term liabilities be reported on:
   A. statement of net assets in the governmental activities column.
   B. governmental funds balance sheet.
   C. special revenue funds balance sheet.
   D. fixed assets and long-term debt group of accounts.

106. In accordance with SGAS 34, governmental funds include which of the following?
    A. Private-purpose trust funds.
    B. Internal service funds.
    C. Investment trust funds.
    D. Permanent funds.

107. Which of the following funds of a governmental unit recognized revenues in the accounting period in which they become available and measurable?

	General fund	Enterprise fund
A.	No	Yes
B.	Yes	No
C.	No	No
D.	Yes	Yes

108. The government-wide statement of activities reports:
    A. by function the expenses minus program revenues and general revenues as they apply to governmental and business-type activities.
    B. only the activities of the proprietary funds using the economic resources measurement focus and accrual accounting.
    C. includes the fiduciary funds using the economic resources measurement focus and accrual accounting.
    D. includes by function the expenses minus the revenues for the fixed assets and the long-term debt groups.

109. Bay Creek's municipal motor pool maintains all city-owned vehicles and charges the various departments for the cost of rendering those services. In which of the following funds should Bay account for the cost of such maintenance?
    A. Internal service fund.
    B. General fund.
    C. Special revenue fund.
    D. Special assessment fund.

110. In analyzing a set of financial statements for a city government, a reader sees a building being reported at a cost of $1.3 million along with accumulated depreciation of $400,000. In which of the following is the reader not looking?
    A. Government-wide financial statements for governmental activities.
    B. Fund-based financial statements for proprietary funds.
    C. Fund-based financial statements for governmental funds.
    D. Government-wide financial statements for business-type activities.

111. In governmental accounting, what is meant by the term "interperiod equity"? The:
    A. surplus or deficit carried over by a government from one year to the next.
    B. fund balance of a fund that is assigned to the interim periods of a year.
    C. difference in reporting between the consumption method and the purchases method.
    D. reconciliation that is necessary between government-wide statements and fund-based statements.

112. In the financial statements of a state or municipal government, the Management's Discussion and Analysis (MD&A) is:
  A. optional in a comprehensive annual financial report.
  B. required supplemental information in a comprehensive annual financial report.
  C. included in the notes to the government-wide financial statements.
  D. included in the notes to the fund-based financial statements.

113. The City of Wayside appoints a majority of the board for a local city tourist bureau. The government is required to approve the annual budget and fee structure for the tourist bureau but has no other connections to this entity. What is the *most likely* relationship between the tourist bureau and the city?
  A. They are probably viewed as unrelated.
  B. The tourist bureau is most likely to be a related organization.
  C. The tourist bureau is most likely to be a discretely presented component unit.
  D. The tourist bureau is most likely to be a blended component unit.

114. The City of Wayside appoints a majority of the board of a city tourist bureau. There are no other connections between the city and the bureau. What is the *most likely* relationship between the tourist bureau and the city?
  A. They are probably viewed as unrelated.
  B. The tourist bureau is most likely to be a related organization.
  C. The tourist bureau is most likely to be a discretely presented component unit.
  D. The tourist bureau is most likely to be a blended component unit.

115. A city built a major street in 1969. A major renovation of the street took place in 1988. In 1969 and in 1988, the amount spent was recorded by the city as an expenditure with no other reporting. What should be shown for this street in the current statement of net assets on the government-wide financial statements? The road should:
  A. not be reported at all.
  B. be reported at cost but only if that cost can be determined.
  C. be reported at an estimated cost figure if historical cost is no longer known.
  D. be reported at an estimated book value if historical cost is no longer known.

116. A city has only one function: public safety. For the current year, direct expenses were $400,000, program revenues were $100,000, state grants received in connection with public safety were $130,000, property tax revenues were $90,000, and sales tax revenues were $70,000. On a statement of activities in the government-wide financial statements, what should be reported as the net expense for this function?
  A. $10,000.
  B. $80,000.
  C. $170,000.
  D. $300,000.

117. A city has a special item of $700,000. How is that reported within its comprehensive annual financial report? A special item:
  A. is another financing source reported on the statement of revenue, expenditures, or other changes in fund balance.
  B. appears on the statement of activities after the city's general revenues are listed.
  C. appears as an asset in statement of net assets after the infrastructure items.
  D. appears as an asset on the balance sheet despite not being a current financial resource.

118. A city has one relatively small special revenue fund and two separate capital projects funds that are both relatively large. Which of the following is *most likely* to be true as far as reporting on the fund-based financial statements? There will be:
    A. a separate column for each of the capital projects, but the special revenue fund will be included in an "other funds" column.
    B. one column reported for the special revenue fund and one column reported for the two capital projects.
    C. one column reported for the special revenue fund and two separate columns for the two capital projects.
    D. one column reported for the capital projects, and the special revenue will be included in an "other funds" column.

119. The General Fund transfers $43,000 cash to a capital projects fund. Which of the following statements is false? On the:
    A. government-wide financial statements, both a transfer-in and a transfer-out are shown and then offset.
    B. government-wide financial statements, transfers between governmental and business-type activities are reported.
    C. fund-based financial statements, an other financial source is reported by the capital projects fund.
    D. fund-based financial statements, an other financial use is reported by the General Fund.

120. A government is reporting a statement of cash flows. Which of the following is true?
    A. The statement of cash flows is part of the government-wide financial statements.
    B. The statement of cash flows must include the transactions of the government's General Fund.
    C. A proprietary fund has to report a statement of cash flows.
    D. The statement of cash flows has a single column for cash flows from financing activities.

121. A city collects a sales tax. At the end of Year 1, sales have been made so that $800,000 of sales tax should be received. That amount will be received 68 days into Year 2. Which of the following is true about recognition of this revenue? It:
    A. is reported on the government-wide financial statements in Year 1 but cannot be reported on the fund-based financial statements in Year 2.
    B. has to be reported on both the government-wide financial statements and the fund-based financial statements in Year 1.
    C. is reported on neither the government-wide financial statements nor the fund-based financial statements in Year 1 because it will not be received within 60 days of year end.
    D. is reported on the government-wide financial statements in Year 1 but the reporting for the fund-based financial statements depends on the government's definition of available current financial resources.

122. A city government operates a swimming pool for the public where each person is charged 25 cents per day to swim. Which of the following statements is false?
    A. If the fee was set at an amount that would recover the cost of operating the swimming pool, it must be reported within an enterprise fund.
    B. Because the fee is so small, the swimming pool will be accounted for within the General Fund.
    C. Even if the fee is viewed to be small, the swimming pool can still be accounted for within an enterprise fund.
    D. If the debts of the swimming pool are secured solely by the revenues generated, it must be reported within an enterprise fund.

123. The policy in the city of Abrams confiscates $120,000 in cash from an illegal drug operation. Where is this money initially reported?
      A. The general fund.
      B. An agency fund.
      C. A permanent fund.
      D. A private-purpose trust fund.

124. On the balance sheet for the General Fund of a city, an account balance titled "Fund Balance— Reserved for Encumbrance" is reported. Which of the following is true?
      A. The government owes that much money at the end of the year.
      B. The eventual expenditure balance will be equal to the amount reported here.
      C. The government has issued a purchase order or incurred some other commitment for this amount of money.
      D. Money of this amount has been restricted by an outside donor.

125. Which of the following is an imposed nonexchange revenue?
      A. A forfeiture of a deposit.
      B. Sales tax.
      C. Income tax.
      D. A grant given by a nongovernment organization.

126. A government has investments in shares of stock that are reported on a major US stock exchange. The shares had an original cost of $67,000 but have risen to $82,000 in value by year's end. What reporting is appropriate?
      A. Only if the investments are classified as "trading securities" will the gain be reported by the government.
      B. Only if the investments are classified as "available for sale" will the gain be reported by the government.
      C. The investments must continue to be reported at cost with no gain recognized.
      D. The investments must be reported at fair value with the gain being reported by the government.

127. The City of Williams operates a print shop as an internal service fund. In the current year, this print shop does $19,000 worth of work for the school system which is reported as a Special Revenue Fund. The $19,000 is paid in cash prior to the end of the year. What reporting is appropriate for fund-based financial statements for the internal service fund?
      A. A transfer-in of $19,000.
      B. Nothing is reported because it is within the government.
      C. An other financial source of $19,000.
      D. A revenue of $19,000.

128. A school building is constructed by a city on the first day of the current year. The school system is reported within a special revenue fund. Which of the following is incorrect?
      A. Depreciation should not be reported in the fund-based financial statements.
      B. If the modified approach is used by the city government, depreciation is not required.
      C. Depreciation should be reported in the government-wide financial statements.
      D. At the end of the year, the building should be reported in the government-wide financial statements at its cost less accumulated depreciation.

129. Fund-based financial statements are being produced for the governmental funds of the City of Atkins. On the balance sheet, which of the following assets will not appear?
     A. Taxes receivable to be collected 45 days into the subsequent year.
     B. Investments in marketable securities.
     C. Supplies.
     D. Computer.

130. A city government maintains a garage to keep its police vehicles in good running condition. This garage is recorded by the city as an internal service fund. In the government-wide financial statements, how will this internal service fund be reported? As:
     A. a governmental activity.
     B. a business-type activity.
     C. an enterprise fund.
     D. a proprietary fund.

131. In Year 1, a city government levies a property tax of $1 million. The government has an immediate enforceable claim and the money can be used in Year 1. The government anticipates collecting $940,000 during Year 1 and the remaining $60,000 exactly three months into Year 2. How will the reporting of the property taxes on Year 1 statements differ between government-wide financial statements and fund-based financial statements? On government-wide statements, revenues of:
     A. $940,000 will be recognized, and in fund-based financial statements the same $940,000 is recognized.
     B. $940,000 will be recognized, and in fund-based financial statements $1 million in revenues is recognized.
     C. $1 million will be recognized, and in fund-based financial statements $940,000 in revenues is recognized.
     D. $1 million will be recognized, and in fund-based financial statements the same $1 million is recognized.

132. The state government provides a grant of $1 million to the City of Bexley. The money has to be used to teach first graders in that city to read because reading levels have fallen below the national average, and the states wants to encourage improvement. What type of revenue is this?
     A. Derived tax revenue.
     B. Imposed nonexchange transaction.
     C. Government-mandated nonexchange transaction.
     D. Voluntary nonexchange transaction.

133. The school system in Meckleston County may be a special-purpose local government that must produce its own individual set of financial statements. Which of the following is not a requirement for the school system to qualify as a special-purpose local government? It must:
     A. have a separately-elected governing body.
     B. have specifically defined geographic boundaries.
     C. have corporate powers to prove that it is legally independent.
     D. be fiscally independent.

134. An art museum is operated within the City of Liston as a legally separate organization. However, the museum meets the definition of a discretely-presented component unit. Which of the following is true? The:
    A. museum's financial position and operations will not be reported by the city, but extensive disclosure will be required in its financial statements.
    B. museum will be reported by the city as if it were simply another one of its own funds.
    C. museum's financial position and operations will be reported on the government-wide financial statements on the right side of the figures for the primary government.
    D. museum will be reported as a major fund in the fund-based financial statements of the city's governmental funds.

135. A local government operates a solid waste landfill as an enterprise fund. If the landfill had been closed on December 31, Year 1, closure costs would have been $6 million. By December 31, Year 2, closure costs had grown to $7 million. The landfill was 19% filled at the end of Year 1. In Year 2, another 8% was filled so that it was 27% filled at the end of that year. The landfill will not actually be covered and closed until Year 8. What amount of expense should be recognized in Year 2 for the future closure costs?
    A. $0.
    B. $560,000.
    C. $690,000.
    D. $750,000.

136. A city has a police department that spends the following cash amounts this year: salaries—$80,000, police car—$90,000, transfer to debt service fund—$10,000, and payment on principal of long-term liability—$30,000. On fund-based financial statements, on the statement of revenues, expenditures, and changes in fund balance for the General Fund, what is the change created by these transactions in the fund balance?
    A. $80,000.
    B. $90,000.
    C. $110,000.
    D. $210,000.

137. A city has a police department that spends the following cash amounts this year: salaries—$80,000, police car—$90,000, transfer to debt service fund—$10,000, and payment on principal of long-term liability—$30,000. On government-wide financial statements, on the statement of activities, what is the change created by these transactions in the net assets of the governmental activities?
    A. $80,000.
    B. $90,000.
    C. $110,000.
    D. $210,000.

138. A government spends $13 million to build a road. The road should last for an extended period of time if properly maintained. Which of the following is false?
   A. The $13 million is reported as an expenditure on the fund-based financial statements and not as a capital asset.
   B. The $13 million is reported as a capital asset on the government-wide financial statements and not as an expenditure.
   C. Unless the modified approach is applied, depreciation expense is required on government-wide financial statements.
   D. Because the road qualifies as infrastructure, the modified approach is required on the government-wide financial statements.

139. The police department of a city government collects $32,000 in parking meter and speeding tickets. The government itself collects $900,000 from a local sales tax. Government-wide financial statements are currently being prepared. Which of the following is correct?
   A. The $32,000 is a program revenue, and the $900,000 is a general revenue.
   B. The $32,000 is a general revenue, and the $900,000 is a program revenue.
   C. Both of these amounts represent program revenues
   D. Both of these amounts represent general revenues.

140. Which of the following is correct about the preparation of a statement of cash flows for a for-profit business and for a proprietary fund of a state or local government?
   A. Both types of organizations may use either the indirect or the direct method for reporting cash flows from operating activities.
   B. Both types of organizations use a statement that has three separate sections.
   C. The issuance of a bond to generate cash to build a new office building by a government proprietary fund is reported as a cash flow from a capital and related financing activity.
   D. The issuance of a bond to generate cash to build a new office building by a for-profit business is reported as a cash flow from investing activities.

ANSWERS: GOVERNMENTAL ACCOUNTING

1. **B** At historical costs including any capitalized interest.

2. **C** Appropriations—the entry to record the budget:

Estimated revenue control	$XXX	
Appropriation control		$XXX
Budgetary fund balance		$XXX

    This entry assumes that estimated revenue exceeds appropriations, which is the normal condition.

3. **D** SGAS 34 requires that budgetary comparison schedules be reported for the general fund and each major special revenue fund with a legally adopted budget.

4. **A** A purchase order is approved. When a purchase order is approved, the following entry is made:

Encumbrances control	$XXX	
Budgetary fund balance reserved for encumbrances		$XXX

    A credit balance is the normal balance for this account; hence it is increased when a purchase order is approved. When supplies orders are received, the above entry is reversed, decreasing the balance. The account's function is to measure obligations outstanding not recorded as liabilities.

5. **C** Interest paid on capital debt and leases must be reported on public colleges' cash flow statements as cash from capital and related financing activities.

6. **D** Credited at the beginning of the year and debited at the end of the year.

    Beginning of the year opening entry:

Estimated revenue control	$1,000,000	
Appropriations		$950,000
Budgetary fund balance		$50,000

    End of year—reverse the above entry.

7. **A** Cash flows from a public university's bookstore would be cash from operations.

8. **B** Only an error would cause a difference in balance.

When a purchase order is approved—		
Encumbrances	$100	
Reserve for Encumbrances		$100
When the order arrives the entry is reversed—		
Reserve for Encumbrances	$100	
Encumbrances		$100

9. **A** Interperiod equity assumes that the revenues of a period will at least equal the expenditures of the period. This financial objective assumes that a balanced budget will be adopted. Residual equity is not related to interperiod equity.

10. **D** When the budget is initially recorded appropriations control is credited. At year-end the budget entry is reversed; thus the appropriations control account would be debited to close it out.

11. **B** The notes are a distinct part of financial reporting and are not a part of any other disclosure requirements. The main focus is on the primary unit, not the component units.

12. **C** Funds collected by one governmental unit for the benefit of another governmental unit are recorded in agency funds.

13. **B** Property taxes are recognized as revenue as soon as they are available. If these taxes were not available until the following year, they would be recorded in a liability account, *Deferred Revenue*.

Property taxes receivable	$100	
Allowance for uncollective account		$10
Revenues		$90

14. **A** The general fund has a current resources focus so the only journal entry would be a debit to expenditures-landfill closure cost and a credit to cash for $40,000.

15. **D** The government-wide statements record an expense of $120,000 (8% × $1,500,000). The journal entry would be a debit to expense-landfill closure cost and a credit to landfill closure liability.

16. **C**

Landfill closure liability	$40,000	
Cash		$40,000

17. **A** Property taxes are recognized as a receivable when they are levied; however, recognition must happen when they are both measurable and available.

Collections during the year 2004	$500,000
Expected collections during the first 60 days of 2005	100,000
Total net property tax revenue	$600,000

The other expected collections of $90,000 (60,000 + 30,000) would be recorded as a deferred revenue. The $10,000 estimated to be uncollectible would not be considered, because revenues are recorded net.

18. **D** Encumbrances control. When a purchase order is approved, the entry is

Encumbrances control	$XXX	
Fund balance reserved for encumbrances		$XXX

When the order is received, this entry is reversed.

19. **A**

Estimated revenues	$1,000,000	
Appropriations		$900,000
Budgetary fund balance		$100,000

20. **A** In special revenue governmental funds, budgetary accounts are used. This is not the case with proprietary and fiduciary funds.

21. **C** Appropriation would be credited for $80,000.

The entry to record the budget would be as follows:

Estimated revenue	$100,000	
Appropriations		$80,000
Budgetary fund balance		$20,000

22. **A** If estimated revenue exceeds appropriations, budgetary fund balance would be credited for $20,000.

---

23. **B** Encumbrances are established when the purchase order is written. When the goods arrive, the encumbrance is reduced, and the actual expenditure and liability is recorded for the amount of the invoice. Thus the encumbrances decrease and the expenditures increase.

24. **D** Only the property taxes, licenses, and fines of $9,000,000 would be classified as estimated revenue. Proceeds of debt issue of $500,000 and interfund transfers for debt service of $1,000,000 are both other financial sources and are not part of the estimated revenue.

25. **C** The correct answer is all capitalized collections that are exhaustible. Infrastructure assets using the modified approach are not depreciated. All works of art or historical treasures are not depreciated. If the collections are held for the use of public service and not for gain, preserved, cared for, and kept unencumbered, and, if sold, the proceeds are used to obtain items for the collection, they do not have to be capitalized or depreciated.

26. **D** The sequence of entries is explained by the answer choice. The incorrect answer choices are foreign to fund accounting. An encumbrance is the recording of an obligation to incur an expenditure. When this obligation becomes a liability, it is reversed and the expenditure/liability is recorded.

27. **A** Governmental financial reporting should provide information to assist users in making social and political decisions and in assisting users in assessing whether current-year citizens receive services whose payment is shifted to future years.

28. **C** A description of currently known facts, decisions, or conditions expected to have significant effects on financial activities.

29. **A** The balance sheet of governmental funds does not record fixed assets. SGAS 34 eliminated the use of the fixed asset group of accounts.

30. **A** Internal Service is a proprietary fund. The accounting and reporting for such funds is similar to that of for-profit entities (GAAP).

31. **B** Agency funds are primarily clearing accounts for cash and other resources that are held for a brief period and disbursed to authorized recipients.

32. **C** Governmental funds include general, special revenue, debt service, capital projects, and permanent funds.

33. **D** Enterprise funds are proprietary or "business-type" funds and, as such, use the full accrual basis of accounting. The accounting for enterprise funds is similar to "for profit" enterprises and thus fixed assets and depreciation are accounted for as if the entity uses a "for profit" organization.

34. **C** Billings for services provided by the internal service fund to other funds of the same governmental entity are reported as revenues.

35. **A** The cash received from the general fund is recorded as an operating transfer. The payments for interest are operating activities of the fund and are recorded as expenditures.

36. **A** The $50,000 premium is initially recorded in the capital projects fund. An entry is made, however, to transfer the premium to the debt service fund. Cash is received in the debt service fund.

37. **B** The special revenue fund is a governmental fund by definition.

38. **D** A restricted asset would be appropriately classified in the balance sheet with the credit side shown as a liability. Because the deposit must at some point be returned or applied to a customer's account, it could not properly be part of fund equity.

39. **C** Agency Funds are fiduciary funds.

40. **A** Enterprise funds carry their own bonds and have a retained earnings account, but do not use budgetary accounts.

41. **B** The internal service fund recognizes revenue in the same manner as "regular" business entities. Thus operating revenues is credited when sales are made.

42. **D** $2,250 (7,500 – 4,500 – 750). Appropriations represent the budgeted amount. Expenditures represent amounts already spent. Encumbrances represent orders, so $750 is already committed.

43. **C** A careful reading of the facts reveals that the $210,000 for parking meters is a capital expenditure. Because this is an enterprise fund, this amount is capitalized and depreciation is recorded. GAAP is followed. $400,000 – $90,000 – $70,000 = $240,000 net income.

44. **B** The normal balance of the expenditures control account is a debit. Therefore, to close the account at year-end it is credited.

45. **A** An enterprise fund is used for a self-supporting activity that charges the public for services, and measurement of income is important. Services provided to other departments on a cost reimbursement basis are accounted for by the internal service fund.

46. **D** Expenditures include current operating expenses that require the current or future use of net current assets, debt service, and capital outlays.

47. **B** Fiduciary trust funds include private purpose trust funds. Expendable-trust funds and nonexpendable trust funds were eliminated by SGAS 34. Permanent funds are a part of governmental funds.

48. **C** Under SGAS 34, capital assets and noncurrent debt are reported in the governmental-wide statement of net assets.

49. **A** The main operating fund (the general fund) is always reported as a major fund, and any governmental or enterprise fund believed to be particularly important to users may also be reported in this way. Moreover, any fund must be reported as major if revenues, expenditures/expenses, assets, or liabilities (excluding revenues and expenditures/expenses reported as extraordinary items) of the fund are (1) at least 10% of the corresponding total for all funds of the same category or type, that is, for all governmental or all enterprise funds, and (2) at least 5% of the corresponding total for all governmental and enterprise funds combined.

50. **D** If the funds cannot be spent for normal operating purposes, the funds are restricted whether cash, marketable securities, or something else.

51. **B** Cash equivalents are defined in GASB 9 as short-term, highly liquid investments that are readily convertible into known amounts of cash and are near maturity so that the changes in rates represent insignificant risks (three months or less).

52. **C** Gasoline taxes to finance road repairs. Special revenue funds are used to account for revenues derived from specific taxes or other earmarked revenue sources.

53. **A** Enterprise funds carry their own long-term debt. SGAS 34 eliminated the use of long-term debt account groups.

54. **D** The account is closed out at the end of the year. At year-end revenues control is debited in the amount of its credit balance. Likewise, expenditures are credited in the amount of its debit balance. Any difference becomes part of fund balance.

55. **B** The answer is a definition of economic resources management focus.

56. **C** Governmental funds do not have a Statement of Activities as a financial report. Because Proprietary funds are on accrual basis and report their property, plant, and equipment, they would record depreciation on their equivalent of an income statement.

57. **A** Enterprise fund and depreciation on the fixed assets should be recorded. Enterprise funds (proprietary) carry their own assets, record depreciation, follow GAAP and match costs and revenue as much as possible.

58. **B** The proprietary funds include both:

Enterprise funds	$1,000,000
Internal service funds	400,000
Total proprietary balance	$1,400,000

59. **A** According to SGAS 34, the focus of governmental funds should be Modified Accrual Basis and Current Financial Resources Measurement Focus. Donated fixed assets should be recorded at their estimated fair value at the time received.

60. **B** Funds may be accumulated, however, in debt service to pay both principal and interest of such debt.

61. **D** All intrafund transfers are eliminated.

62. **B** The primary measurement focus of governmental fund types is the inflows, outflows, and balances of financial resources.

63. **C** Proprietary funds use the accrual basis of accounting. Internal service and enterprise are proprietary funds.

64. **A** Proprietary funds, sometimes referred to as "income determination," "nonexpendable," or commercial-type funds, include both enterprise and internal service funds.

65. **C** GASB standards require that governmental funds must use the modified accrual method and proprietary funds use the accrual method.

66. **D** Nonexpendable trust, enterprise, and internal service funds use the accrual method. Special revenue is a governmental fund that uses the modified method.

67. **A** An internal service fund receives such capital to provide the services necessary to carry out its mission. The other funds have no such account.

68. **C** "Earned and measurable" are attributes of the accrual method.

69. **B** Salaries and wages and other similar type recurring items are not ordinarily subject to being recorded as encumbrances such as equipment or supplies. This is the only nonbudgetary account listed.

70. **A** A capital projects fund is a governmental fund for which the modified accrual basis is recommended.

71. **A** SGAS 34 requires that proprietary funds present a Statement of Cash Flows using the direct method.

72. **B** SGAS 34 requires that net assets be reported in three categories: investment in capital assets net of related debt, restricted net assets, and unrestricted net assets. SGAS 34 does not require classified statements and prefers a statement of net assets and does not require a balance sheet format.

73. **C** Proprietary funds maintain their own cash accumulations for payment of debt. General long-term obligations, however, would be paid from cash accumulated in a debt service fund.

74. **B**   Equity transfers to proprietary funds should be reported as additions to contributed capital.

75. **A**   GASB believes that interperiod equity is a significant part of accountability and is fundamental to public administration.

76. **D**   A statement of cash flows is required for all proprietary funds but not for governmental funds. Capital projects fund is a governmental fund while the enterprise fund is a proprietary fund.

77. **A**   Monies received for the construction of governmental-owned assets is recorded in the capital projects fund.

78. **D**   Property taxes, unless otherwise designated, would be general fund revenue.

79. **C**   Bonds for the water treatment plant construction are accounted for in an enterprise fund that handles its own debt. Funds accumulated to pay the general obligation bonds would be accumulated in the debt service fund.

80. **A**   According to SGAS 34, a summary reconciliation of the government-wide and fund financial statements must be presented at the bottom of the fund statements or in an accompanying schedule.

81. **B**   Fixed assets are not reported in the capital projects fund. Fixed assets are accounted for within the internal service fund and depreciation is computed on fixed assets so that costs can be properly allocated to users.

82. **D**   A trust fund is used to account for money or property received from non-enterprise fund sources to be held in the capacity of a trustee, custodian or agent. In a retirement system trust fund the focus is on the Economic Resources Measurement Concept.

83. **A**   The modified accrual basis of accounting is used by the governmental-type funds. The full accrual basis is used by the proprietary-type funds.

84. **A**   Nonexpendable net assets allow for the expenditure of earnings but not principal.

85. **D**   Expenditures is a temporary account that must be closed at year-end. The other choices are balance sheet accounts that are permanent and not closed at year-end.

86. **A**   Government-wide financial statements use Accrual Resources Basis and Economic Resources Measurement Focus.

87. **C**   SGAS 34 requires governmental funds to report a balance sheet and the statement of revenues, expenditures, and changes in fund balances.

88. **B**   Restricted net assets may include both expendable and nonexpendable endowments. Combined net assets is not a section of the Statement of Net Assets.

89. **A**   Because fiduciary funds are not available for governmental use, they are not included in government-wide reports but are included in fund-based reports.

90. **D**   All governmental fund types use the modified accrual basis of accounting. The capital projects fund is a governmental fund. The others use full accrual.

91. **A**   The summary reconciliation is required and must be presented at the bottom of the statements or in an accompanying schedule.

92. **B**   Because the customer deposits are not available to be spent for normal operating purposes, the investments cannot be accounted for as an unrestricted asset. The key factor here is the fact that the funds are restricted and are not available for current use.

93. **A** The fund balance of Maple City's is composed of the following:

Reserve for employer's contributions	$5,000,000
Actuarial deficiency for contributions	$300,000
Reserve for employee's contributions	$9,000,000

94. **C** Assets that are held for disbursement to a different entity are recorded in the agency fund. Eldorado County is an intermediary that has custody of these funds.

95. **B** GASB requires that operating statements embody the all-inclusive approach. It means that all governmental fund types, revenues, expenditures, and similar trust funds are combined to determine the changes in fund balance.

96. **D** SGAS 34 requires budgetary comparison schedules be presented for the fund-based general fund and each special revenue fund with a legally adopted budget. The schedule is a comparison of the actual results versus the original budget, the first appropriated budget, and the final appropriated budget. A variance column may or may not be used.

97. **A** Governmental funds should report a balance sheet and a statement of revenues, expenditures, and changes in fund balances.

98. **C** Depreciation expenses on assets are not recorded for governmental funds but are recorded for all depreciable assets in the proprietary funds.

99. **A** The budgetary accounts are closed. The budgetary accounts are set up as opening entries as follows:

Estimated revenues control	$XXX	
Appropriations control		$XXX
Budgetary fund balance		$XXX

At the end of the accounting period, the above entry is reversed.

100. **B** Proceeds from the issue of long-term bonds should be reported in the other financing sources and uses section.

101. **A** The categories for program revenues are charges for services, capital grants and contributions, and operating grants and contributions.

102. **D** Enterprise funds are used to account for those "business-type" activities in which income determination is desired. Utilities are usually self-supporting entities that should measure income.

103. **C** The accrual basis is required for proprietary funds.

104. **A** The modified accrual basis of accounting is recommended for all governmental fund entities. The "accrual" basis of accounting is recommended for proprietary funds.

105. **A** The correct answer is the statement of net assets in the governmental activities column. This governmental funds balance sheet uses a current resources focus that would exclude capital assets and long-term debt. SGAS 34 eliminated the fixed assets and long-term debt group of accounts.

106. **D** The governmental funds include permanent funds. The other choices are fiduciary funds.

107. **B** The general fund is a governmental fund, and recognizes revenue when they become available and measurable. The enterprise fund uses the accrual method of revenue recognition.

108. **C** The statement of activities includes governmental activities, business type activities, and component units if they are discretely presented. Expenditures and program revenues are presented by function and general revenue is allocated to the governmental and business-type activities.

109. **A** Internal service funds are used to account for financing of goods or services provided by one department or agency to the other departments or other agencies on a cost reimbursement basis.

110. **C** The government-wide financial statements report all of the economic resources of the government, including assets such as buildings. The fund-based statements for the proprietary funds are reported in the same manner. However, the fund-based statements for governmental funds only report current financial resources, and a building is not a current financial resource.

111. **A** Future generations are affected by the taxing and spending decisions made currently by a government. If surplus resources are carried over from one year to the next, there can be more money to utilize in the future or tax rates can be lowered. Conversely, if deficits are carried from one period to the next, the tax burden will have to be higher or services reduced. Interperiod equity refers to the surpluses or deficits that occur and the impact on citizens in the future.

112. **B** The MD&A is a narrative overview and analysis of the government's financial activities. It appears in front of the basic financial statements in the comprehensive annual financial report and is required supplemental information to enhance the data presented in the financial statements.

113. **C** Because the city approves the budget and the fee structure, the tourist bureau is viewed as fiscally dependent on the city. As such, the tourist bureau is considered a component unit. However, because the two entities are not really intertwined, the financial information for the bureau is discretely presented to the right side of the government-wide financial statements rather than being blended in with the funds of the government.

114. **B** The city is accountable for the tourist bureau because it appoints the board. However, fiscal dependency does not exist. No other connection has been established. Hence, the tourist bureau is merely a related organization. No financial information for the bureau is presented along with that of the city but disclosure must be made in the city's comprehensive annual financial report of the existence of the related organization.

115. **D** All major infrastructure assets that were bought, constructed, renovated, restored, or improved since June 30, 1980 should be reported in the government-wide financial statements. If cost figures are no longer available, cost should be estimated and then reduced by an appropriate amount of depreciation for the years since the cost was incurred.

116. **C** The net expense (or revenue) for any government function is its direct expenses offset by any program revenues and any grants or other gifts specifically designed for that function. Thus, the net expense for public safety would be the $400,000 direct expense less the program revenues of $100,000 and the state grant of $130,000.

117. **B** A special item is a gain or loss that is either unusual or infrequent but is still within management's control. It is often a gain or loss from the sale of an asset. To highlight the unusual nature (or infrequency) of the transaction, in the government-wide financial statements, it is shown separately on the statement of activities after the general revenues.

118. **A** There has to be a separate column reported for the General Fund and for each "major" activity fund. Each of the two capital projects would appear to be a major fund because they are relatively large. All funds that are not viewed as major are aggregated and reported within an "other funds" column.

119. **B** In the fund-based statement, every fund reports transactions as it sees them. So, the General Fund has an other financial use of its current financial resources, whereas the capital projects fund has an other financial source. On the government-wide financial statements, transfers are reported only if they are between a governmental activity and a business-type activity. This transfer occurs solely within the governmental

activities so that no "net" change takes place. The described accounting entries (transfer-in and transfer-out and then offset) would not take place on the government-wide financial statements. No reporting is thus needed in the government-wide financial statements.

120. **C** The only required statement of cash flows is for the proprietary funds in the fund-based financial statements. That statement is different, however, from the one reported by a for-profit organization. One variation is that, rather than having a single cash flows from financing activities presentation, both "cash flows from noncapital financing activities" are reported as well as "cash flows from capital and related financing activities."

121. **D** The government-wide financial statements are reported using accrual accounting so the length of time for receiving the revenues is not relevant. The fund-based financial statements for the governmental funds use modified accrual accounting which says revenues are recognized when measurable and available. For property taxes, "available" is defined as being within 60 days. However, for other revenues, the government selects a period of time that is often 60 or 90 days.

122. **B** Whenever an operation is open to the public for a user fee, the government is always allowed to report the activities as an enterprise fund. However, that reporting is mandated if the fee is set at an amount large enough to recover costs. Use of an enterprise fund is also required if the fee serves as the sole security for the debts of the operation.

123. **D** The money is not simply passing through the government to a designated individual or other government so that it is not recorded in an agency fund. Instead, it is to be held by the government until the proper legal use can be made of the money. In such cases, the money is reported in a private-purpose trust fund.

124. **C** This balance indicates that a commitment (often a purchase order) for this amount of money has been incurred in the current period that will require current financial resources in the following period. It is not yet a liability but will become so subsequently. The amount of the eventual liability is often slightly different than the amount recorded as the encumbrance because of taxes or transportation charges or other costs not anticipated precisely by the government.

125. **A** An imposed nonexchange revenue occurs when the government gains money without an underlying event or transaction such as a sale or the creation of income by a taxpayer. A property tax is the primary example of an imposed nonexchange transactions, although fines and forfeitures are also used by GASB as common examples. A grant or gift has to be either a government-mandated nonexchange transaction or a voluntary nonexchange transaction.

126. **D** The accounting for state and local governments requires that such investments be reported at fair value with any gains or losses in value being immediately reported on the financial statements.

127. **D** This is an internal exchange transaction because, although it occurred totally within the government, the transaction was the same as could have taken place with an outside party. On fund-based statements, internal exchange transactions are reported just as if they had taken place with a party outside of the government.

128. **B** For governmental funds, depreciation is not recorded in the fund-based financial statements but is reported in the government-wide financial statements so that the asset can be reported at its net book value. The modified approach does eliminate the necessity of reporting depreciation, but it is only used when conditions are met for infrastructure assets such as sidewalks and roads.

129. **D** The fund-based financial statements for the governmental funds report the current financial resources that can be expended by elected and other officials. These resources include cash, receivables (if collected soon enough to pay for current year expenditures – often set as 60 days), and marketable securities. Although not actually current financial resources, supplies and prepaid expenses are included as assets because they relate to daily operations and expenditures. Capital assets (such as a computer) are not reported in the fund-based financial statements for the governmental funds because they do not represent current financial resources.

130. **A** On fund-based financial statements, internal service funds are reported within the proprietary funds. However, on the government-wide financial statements, the placement of an internal service fund depends on the type of activity that is being benefited. Because this garage services the police department, which is a governmental activity, the internal service fund is also labeled as a governmental activity.

131. **C** In government-wide financial statements, revenues are recognized on accrual accounting. Property taxes, more specifically, are recognized when the resources are required to be used or in the first period when use is allowed (Year 1). In fund-based financial statements, for governmental funds, modified accrual accounting is utilized that also says that the resources must be "available," which means that the resources will be collected soon enough to be used for current year claims. For property taxes, a specific period of 60 days is allowed. Because $50,000 will not be collected quickly enough in Year 2 to pay for Year 1 expenditures, recognition of that revenue is deferred until Year 2.

132. **D** A grant is labeled as either a government-mandated nonexchange transaction or a voluntary nonexchange transaction. A grant is only classified as a government-mandated nonexchange transaction if the grant is given to help a government meet a legal requirement that has been passed. There is no indication here that the state has established any law mandating that reading levels in the school system be brought up to the national average.

133. **B** A special-purpose local government is one where there is an independent government function being carried out without specified boundaries that are usually associated with state or local governments. In many areas of the United States where school board members are publicly elected, the school system will qualify as a special-purpose local government.

134. **C** A discretely-presented component unit is reported along with the primary government in government-wide financial statements but to the far right side so that the reader is aware of the separation.

135. **D** At the end of Year 1, a liability of $1.14 million should be reported (19% of $6 million). At the end of Year 2, that liability needs to be $1.89 million (27% of $7 million). A $750,000 expense should be recognized for Year 2 to adjust the liability from the old balance to the new.

136. **D** In fund-based financial statements for governmental funds, the fund balance shows increases and decreases in current financial resources (usually cash, investments in marketable securities, and receivables to be collected soon enough so that the money can be used in connection with current expenditures). Here, all four of these transactions reduce the amount of current financial resources being held, and hence, decrease the fund balance.

137. **A** On the government-wide financial statements, all economic resources are being reported, including all assets and all liabilities. The acquisition of the police car has no net effect because one asset increases while the other decreases. The payment of the long-term liability has no net effect because an asset goes down but so does a liability. The transfer has no net effect since the money is moved entirely inside of the governmental activities. The only change in economic resources is caused by the payment of the salary expense.

138. **D** Infrastructure assets such as roads, bridges, sidewalks must be depreciated unless the modified approach is utilized. That approach ensures that the infrastructure is maintained at a predetermined standard and, if so, no depreciation need be recorded. However, the government must elect to use the modified approach.

139. **A** The $32,000 is classified as a program revenue because it is generated by a particular function, here the police department. The sales tax is a general revenue because it is applied to all citizens making purchases.

140. **C** A proprietary fund's cash flow statement has four sections rather than three, and the cash flows from operations must be determined by the direct method. A for-profit business reports the issuance for a bond as a financing activity. However, a government has a separate section solely relating to the issuance of debts and acquisition of capital assets.

CHAPTER 18 – STATEMENT OF CASH FLOWS

STUDY TIP

Believe in yourself. Thousands of people just like you pass the CPA exam each year. They are no smarter and no better educated than you are. They just use good quality materials, and they put in the time and the energy. You can do it also. The CPA exam is challenging, but it is certainly not impossible to pass. People will constantly tell you that you cannot pass. Tell them to go away. There is nothing more important that you can bring to the CPA exam than a belief that you can do the work and make it happen.

CHAPTER 18 – STATEMENT OF CASH FLOWS

STATEMENT OF CASH FLOWS

A. The primary purposes of the statement of cash flows (SCF) are as follows:

1. Provide information about where a company's cash was obtained and how it was used. Any investment bought within three months of maturity is included as a cash item.

2. Disclose information about the financing and investing activities of a company.

B. This statement should help the users of the statements assess the following:

1. A company's ability to generate positive future cash flows.

2. A company's ability to meet its obligations and pay dividends.

3. The reasons for differences between income and cash flow.

4. The cash and noncash aspects of a company's investing and financing transactions.

C. The reporting of a SCF is required for each year in which an income statement is presented. Essentially, the SCF can be derived by using elements from both the income statement and the balance sheet.

1. All cash inflows and outflows are reported within one of three classifications that are presented on the SCF in the following order:

    a. *Operating activities* are transactions involving the regular course of daily operations, such as delivering or producing goods for sale and providing services.

        • Examples would include cash received from customers, cash paid to suppliers, cash paid for operating expenses, and cash paid for income taxes.
        • Interest revenue, interest expense, and dividend revenue are all viewed as operating activity cash flows and not the result of investing or financing activities.

    b. *Investing activities* are transactions involving assets that do not change in the regular course of daily operations.

        • Examples would include the purchase or sale of equipment or land and the purchase or sale of marketable securities (longer-term holding period).

    c. *Financing activities* are transactions involving stockholders' equity or liabilities that do not change in the regular course of daily operations.

        • Examples would include paying dividends, issuing bonds or stocks, and repaying loans.

D. Noncash investing and financing activities should be excluded from the formal SCF as they involve no cash inflows or outflows. However, they have a significant effect on the prospective cash flows of a company. Such noncash items must be reported in a separate schedule or in the footnotes to the financial statements.

1. Examples include conversion of debt to equity, issuance of stock to purchase assets, and stock dividends and splits.

OPERATING ACTIVITIES

There are two methods permitted under GAAP. The direct method is preferred by the FASB, but the indirect method is the most commonly encountered in practice. Both the direct and indirect methods are frequently tested on the CPA exam.

Direct Method

A. Reports the cash flows from individual types of operating transactions.

    1. Must report cash collected from customers, cash paid to suppliers, cash paid for operating expenses, cash paid/received for interest expense/income, and cash paid for taxes.

    2. The various income statement amounts for operations items are converted from accrual to cash basis amounts.

    3. Income statement items related to investing and financing transactions are not reported here. Examples are gains/losses from sales of assets.

    4. Noncash expenses, such as depreciation and amortization, are also omitted.

B. Sales less any increase in receivables during the year or plus any decrease in receivables equals *cash collected from sales*. As a way of arriving at the cash flow figure, the accountant can make a journal entry to simulate the recording of sales for the period, as well as the change in the receivable account with the balancing figure being the cash inflow. For example: If sales were $100 and accounts receivable increased by $5, the simulated "journal entry" would be as follows, showing cash from customers of $95:

Accounts receivable $5
Cash $95 (balancing amount)
   Sales $100

Note the following formula for calculating cash received from customers:

Net sales – (ending Accounts Receivable + Accounts Receivable written off – beginning Accounts Receivable) = Cash received from customers during accounting period

C. A journal entry can be made with COGS and changes in inventory and accounts payable to derive *cash paid for purchases*. For example, assume the following: COGS of $40, increase in AP of $10, decrease in inventory of $5. The simulated "journal entry" would be as follows, showing cash paid to suppliers of $25:

COGS $40
   AP $10
   Inventory $5
   Cash $25   (balancing amount)

The formula for calculating cash paid to suppliers is as follows:

COGS – (beginning Inventory + ending Accounts Payable) + (ending Inventory + beginning Accounts Payable)

D. For any expense account, first remove any noncash item, such as depreciation. A journal entry can then be made to record the remaining figure, and that consists of changes in related accrued expenses and prepaid expenses to arrive at *cash paid for operating expenses*. For example, assume the following:

Prepaid expenses decreased by $15, accrued expenses decreased by $10, operating expenses were $50. The simulated "journal entry" would be as follows, showing cash paid for operating expenses of $45:

Operating Expenses	$50	
Accrued Expenses	$10	
Prepaid Expenses		$15
Cash (paid for operating expenses)		$45

Following is the formula for cash paid for operating expenses:

> Operating Expenses – Depreciation – beginning Prepaid Expenses + ending Prepaid Expenses – ending Accrued Expenses Payable + beginning Accrued Expenses Payable = Cash paid for operating expenses during accounting period.

E. For cash paid for income taxes, the simulated "journal entry" would consist of the amount recorded for tax expense, along with the changes to deferred taxes and taxes payable. For cash paid/received for interest expense/revenue, the simulated journal entry would consist of the amount recorded for interest, along with changes to prepaid and/or accrued interest.

Note: Remember, this simulated or hypothetical "journal entry" is a technique to determine the cash payment. It is not an actual journal entry. Any of these amounts (sales, expenses, operational assets, and liabilities) would be recorded in numerous journal entries throughout the reporting period. This is simply an easy way to remember the effect on cash when you are analyzing the various categories required for the direct method operations section of the SCF.

F. Gains and losses on the income statement are nonoperational and simply omitted from the reporting of cash flows from operating activities.

G. Summary:

Direct Method:

Cash Inflows	Cash Outflows
Operating	
Collections from sales	Payments to suppliers and employees
Interest income received	Payments for interest expense
Dividend income	Payments for taxes
Proceeds from sale of trading securities	Payments for purchases of trading securities
Miscellaneous income received	Payments for miscellaneous expenses

H. Example of a presentation of the direct method:

Cash flows from operating activities			
Cash received from dividends	$500		
Cash received from interest	1,000		
Cash received from the sale of goods	8,000		
Cash provided by operating activities		$9,500	
Cash paid to suppliers	5,000		
Cash paid for operating expenses	500		
Cash paid for interest	500		
Cash paid for taxes	500		
Cash disbursed from operating activities		6,500	
Net cash flows from operating activities		$3,000	

Indirect Method: Reconciliation of Net income to Cash Flows from Operations

A. Start with net income and then remove all items that are either (1) noncash amounts or (2) that do not occur in the regular course of business (i.e., are nonoperations items, so they do not belong in the Operating section of the SCF). In this approach, you are starting with net income and making the necessary adjustments to convert it to net cash received or paid from the usual operating activities of the business. Remember: Some items that belong in net income do not belong in the operating section of the SCF (e.g., gains/losses on the sale of long-term assets such as land). The cash associated with this transaction would appear in the investing section as the total cash received from the sale. The cash flow is the total amount received, not the gain/loss.

1. By starting with net income, you are making an "assumption" (just for the purposes of creating the SCF) that all revenues were received in cash and all expenses were paid in cash. However, you know this is not true, but it greatly simplifies the process of creating a SCF.

2. So, you must make any adjustments that are necessary because (a) not all revenues and expenses were cash transactions, as well as the fact that (b) some items included in net income are not properly included in operating cash flows, but actually belong in a different section of the SCF.

3. The best example is depreciation: It was an expense in calculating net income, so it reduced net income, but it was *not* a cash outlay. (No one ever wrote a check for depreciation expense.) So, you add it back to net income in the conversion of *net income* to *cash from operations*. And, no, you are not adding it back because it was a positive cash flow. You are adding it back because it was a subtraction in arriving at net income, so you are actually *removing* it.

B. Removal of noncash and nonoperations items requires the:

1. subtraction of items that are ordinarily included in net income as positives (i.e., an income item), and

2. addition of items that are ordinarily included in net income as negatives (i.e., an expense item).

C. The major noncash items include:

1. Depreciation and amortization expense.

2. Equity income reported in excess of cash dividends received from the equity method investee.

D. Noncash items also include the changes in operational assets and liabilities. *Changes in these accounts represent further plus or minus adjustments to net income in reconciling to cash flows from operations.* These are primarily current assets and current liabilities. Remember, you started with net income, pretending it was all cash. However, if *accounts receivable increased* for the year, some of the revenue was not collected in cash, so net income is more than net cash receipts, requiring a "minus" adjustment to net income. If *accounts receivable decreased* for the year, you collected more cash than the revenue, causing net income to be less than net cash receipts, requiring a "plus" adjustment to net income. This type of analysis can be applied to all the operational accounts.

Consider this example: Let's say revenue was $100, and beginning A/R was $20. The starting point of net income includes $100. However, if ending A/R was $30, you only collected $90 of that $100. So your adjustment to net income would be a minus $10. If ending A/R was $5, you collected all the revenue of $100 plus $15 of the beginning balance of $20, so your adjustment to net income would be *plus* $15.

On the liabilities side, let's say operating expenses were $200, beginning accrued expenses (a current liability) were $40, and ending accrued expenses were $25. This means you included $200 in the calculation of net income, but you actually paid $15 ($40 – $25) more than you expensed. So, your cash *outlay* for operating expenses was really $215. This results in an adjustment to net income of *minus $15* to arrive at cash flows from operations. *Be sure to fully comprehend this example of A/R and A/P before reading further.*

When analyzing the changes in operating accounts, be sure to consider accounts receivable, inventory, prepaid expenses, accounts payable, and accrued expenses.

An easy way to remember what to do with these operational assets is to think of a hypothetical journal entry, where one side represents the *change* in the current asset or liability, and the assumed offset is to cash for the same amount. If current assets increase (debit), the effect on cash flows would, therefore, be a decrease (credit cash) when preparing the SCF. If current liabilities increase (credit), the effect on cash flows would be an increase (debit cash) when preparing the SCF.

Account	Change in balance for the year	Therefore, the effect on cash would be a/an	"Assumed Journal Entry" when preparing the Statement of cash flows
Current asset	increase	decrease	Debit current asset, credit cash (cash decreases) = "minus" to net income to arrive at cash.
Current asset	decrease	increase	Debit cash (cash increases), credit current asset = "plus" to net income to arrive at cash.
Current liability	increase	increase	Debit cash (cash increases), credit current liability = "plus" to net income to arrive at cash.
Current liability	decrease	decrease	Debit current liability, credit cash (cash decreases) = "minus" to net income to arrive at cash.

E. Nonoperational items that must be removed from net income include most gains and losses, such as a gain or loss on the sale of a long-lived asset. The gain or loss would be included in net income, but should not be included in cash flows from operations. Therefore, you must remove it by adding back the losses and subtracting out the gains. (Remember, cash flows associated with selling long-lived assets are included in a different section of the SCF: the investing section.)

F. Summary:

RECONCILIATION OF NET INCOME TO NET CASH PROVIDED
BY OPERATING ACTIVITIES

Overview

Net Income

Add	*Deduct*
Depreciation expense	
Amortization (bond discount)	Amortization (bond premium)
Amortization of deferred charges and intangibles	Decrease in deferred tax liabilities
Increase in deferred tax liabilities	Increase in deferred tax asset
Decrease in deferred tax asset	Increases in investments accounted for under the equity method
Decreases in investments accounted for under the equity method	Gains on sale of property, plant, and equipment or investments other than trading securities
Losses on sale of property, plant, and equipment or investments other than trading securities	Increase in receivables
Decrease in receivables	Increase in inventories
Decrease in inventories	Increase in prepaid expenses
Decrease in prepaid expenses	Decrease in accounts payable and accrued liabilities
Increase in accounts payable and accrued liabilities	Payments for acquisitions of trading securities
Minority interest in net income of subsidiary	
Decreases in trading securities due to sales	

Equals: Net cash provided by operating activities

The following is a summary of the items to be included in the Investing and Financing sections of the SCF.

Investing	
Proceeds from sale of property, plant and equipment	Payments for purchases of property, plant and equipment
Proceeds from sale of debt or equity securities of other entities other than trading securities	Payments for purchases of debt or equity securities of other entities other than trading securities
Collections of loans (principal portion) made to other entities	Payments for loans (principal portion) made to other entities
Financing	
Proceeds from issuance of debt (notes and bonds)	Repayment of debt (principal portion)
Proceeds from issuance of equity securities	Payments for reacquisition of equity securities (treasury stock)
Investments by partners	Payments of dividends to stockholders
	Disinvestment by partners
	Partners' drawings

Remember: When including the cash flows from the sale of property, plant, and equipment, it is the total amount of cash received. In a journal entry, to remove the property from the books, the total debit to cash becomes an investing activity. When considering the collections or payments of loan amounts, it is only the principal that goes in the investing section. Interest paid or received is an operating item.

QUESTIONS: STATEMENT OF CASH FLOWS

1. Which of the following pieces of information should be included in Melay, Inc.'s (Melay) Year 6 summary of significant accounting policies?
    A. Property, plant, and equipment is recorded at cost with depreciation computed principally by the straight-line method.
    B. During Year 6, the Delay business component was sold.
    C. Business component revenues in Year 6 are Alay $1 million, Delay $2 million, and Celay $3 million.
    D. Future common share dividends are expected to approximate 60% of earnings.

2. Miri, Inc. (Miri) was incorporated on January 1, Year 6, with proceeds from the issuance of $750,000 in stock and borrowed funds of $110,000. During the first year of operations, revenues from sales and consulting amounted to $82,000, and operating costs and expenses totaled $64,000. On December 15, Miri declared a $3,000 cash dividend, payable to stockholders on January 15, Year 7. No additional activities affected owner's equity in Year 6. Miri's liabilities increased to $120,000 by December 31, Year 6.

    On Miri's December 31, Year 6 balance sheet, total assets should be reported at:
    A. $875,000.
    B. $878,000.
    C. $882,000.
    D. $885,000.

3. When preparing a draft of its Year 6 balance sheet, Montecristo, Inc. (Montecristo) reported net assets totaling $875,000. Included in the asset section of the balance sheet were the following:

Treasury stock of Montecristo at cost, which approximates market value on December 31	$24,000
Idle machinery	$11,200
Cash surrender value of life insurance on corporate executives	$13,700
Allowance for decline in market value of noncurrent equity investments	$8,400

    At what amount should Montecristo's net assets be reported on the December 31, Year 6 balance sheet?
    A. $834,500.
    B. $842,600.
    C. $850,100.
    D. $851,000.

4. Brocket Corp. (Brocket) reports operating expenses in two categories: (1) selling, and (2) general and administrative. The adjusted trial balance on December 31, Year 6 included the following expense and loss accounts:

Accounting and legal fees	$120,000
Advertising	$150,000
Freight-out	$80,000
Interest	$70,000
Loss on sale of long-term investment	$30,000
Officers' salary	$225,000
Rent for office space	$220,000
Sales salaries and commissions	$140,000

One-half of the rented premises is occupied by the sales department.

Brocket's total selling expenses for Year 6 are:
A. $360,000.
B. $370,000.
C. $400,000.
D. $480,000.

5. At December 31, Year 6, Kato Co. (Kato) had the following balances in the accounts it maintains at First State Bank:

Checking account #101	$175,000
Checking account #102	($10,000)
Money market account	$25,000
90-day certificate of deposit, due 2/28/Year 7	$50,000
180-day certificate of deposit, due 3/15/Year 7	$80,000

In its December 31, Year 6, balance sheet, what amount should Kato report as cash and cash equivalents?
A. $190,000.
B. $200,000.
C. $240,000.
D. $320,000.

6. The primary purpose of a statement of cash flows is to provide relevant information about which of the following?
A. Differences between net income and associated cash receipts and disbursements.
B. A company's ability to generate future positive net cash flows.
C. The cash receipts and cash disbursements of a company during a period.
D. A company's ability to meet cash operating needs.

7.   Alpine, Inc. (Alpine) had the following activities during Year 6:
   - Acquired 2,000 shares of stock in Geneva, Inc. (Geneva) for $26,000. Alpine intends to hold the stock as a long-term investment.
   - Sold an investment in Bern, Inc. (Bern) for $35,000 when the carrying value was $33,000.
   - Acquired a $50,000, 4-year certificate of deposit from a bank. During the year, interest of $3,750 was paid to Alpine.
   - Collected dividends of $1,200 on stock investments.

   In Alpine's Year 6 statement of cash flows, net cash used in investing activities should be:
   A. $37,250.
   B. $38,050.
   C. $39,800.
   D. $41,000.

8.   On July 1, Year 6, Davis, Inc. (Davis) signed a 20-year building lease that it reported as a capital lease. Davis paid the monthly lease payments when due. How should Davis report the effect of the lease payments in the financing activities section of its Year 6 statement of cash flows?
   A. An inflow equal to the present value of future lease payments at July 1, Year 6, less Year 6 principal and interest payments.
   B. An outflow equal to the Year 6 principal and interest payments on the lease.
   C. An outflow equal to the Year 6 principal payments only.
   D. The lease payments should not be reported in the financing activities section.

9.   On January 1, Year 6, Bretagne, Inc. (Bretagne) installed cabinets to display its merchandise in the customers' store. Bretagne expects to use these cabinets for five years. Bretagne's Year 6 multi-step income statement should include:
   A. 1/5 of the cabinet costs in COGS.
   B. 1/5 of the cabinet costs in selling, general, and administrative expenses.
   C. all of the cabinet costs in COGS.
   D. all of the cabinet costs in selling, general, and administrative expenses.

Use the following information to answer Questions 10 and 11.

In preparing its cash flow statement for the year ended December 31, Year 6, Reza Co. (Reza) collected the following data:

Gain on sale of equipment	($6,000)
Proceeds from sale of equipment	$10,000
Purchase of bonds (par value $200,000)	($180,000)
Amortization of bonds discount	$2,000
Dividends declared	($45,000)
Dividends paid	($38,000)
Proceeds from sale of treasury stock (carrying amount $65,000)	$75,000

10.   In its December 31, Year 6 statement of cash flows, what amount should Reza report as net cash used in investing activities?
   A. $170,000.
   B. $176,000.
   C. $188,000.
   D. $194,000.

11. In its December 31, Year 6 statement of cash flows, what amount should Reza report as net cash provided by financing activities?
    A. $20,000.
    B. $27,000.
    C. $30,000.
    D. $37,000.

12. On September 1, Year 6, El Polo, Inc. (El Polo) sold used equipment for a cash amount equaling its carrying amount for both book and tax purposes. On September 15, El Polo replaced the equipment by paying cash and signing a note payable for new equipment. The cash paid for the new equipment exceeded the cash received for the old equipment. How should these equipment transactions be reported in El Polo's Year 6 statement of cash flows?
    A. Cash outflow equal to the cash paid less the cash received.
    B. Cash outflow equal to the cash paid and note payable less the cash received.
    C. Cash inflow equal to the cash received and a cash outflow equal to the cash paid and note payable.
    D. Cash inflow equal to the cash received and a cash outflow equal to the cash paid.

13. Which of the following pieces of information should be disclosed in the summary of significant accounting policies?
    A. Refinancing of debt subsequent to the balance sheet date.
    B. Guarantees of indebtedness of others.
    C. Criteria for determining which investments are treated as cash equivalents.
    D. Adequacy of pension plan assets relative to vested benefits.

14. The following costs were incurred by Griffin, Inc. (Griffin), a manufacturer, during Year 6:

Accounting and legal fees	$25,000
Freight-in	$175,000
Freight-out	$160,000
Officers' salaries	$150,000
Insurance	$85,000
Sales representatives' salaries	$215,000

    What amount of these costs should Griffin report as general and administrative expenses for Year 6?
    A. $260,000.
    B. $550,000.
    C. $635,000.
    D. $810,000.

15. Smyrski Co's (Smyrski) wages payable increased from the beginning to the end of the year. In Smyrski's statement of cash flows in which the operating activities section is prepared under the direct method, this cash paid for wages would be:
    A. salary expense plus wages payable at the beginning of the year.
    B. salary expense plus the increase in wages payable from the beginning to the end of the year.
    C. salary expense less the increase in wages payable from the beginning to the end of the year.
    D. the same as salary expense.

16.   Linus Co.'s (Linus) worksheet for the preparation of its Year 6 statement of cash flows included the following:

	December 31	January 1
Accounts receivable	$29,000	$23,000
Allowance for uncollectible accounts	$1,000	$800
Prepaid rent expense	$8,200	$12,400
Accounts payable	$22,400	$19,400

Linus' Year 6 net income is $150,000.

What amount should Linus include as net cash provided by operating activities in the statement of cash flows?
A. $145,400.
B. $148,600.
C. $151,000.
D. $151,400.

17.   Craig Co.'s (Craig) income statement for the year ended December 31, Year 6 reported net income of $74,100. The auditor raised questions about the following amounts that had been included in net income:

Unrealized loss on decline in market value of noncurrent investments in stock classified as available-for-sale (net of tax)	($5,400)
Gain on early retirement of bonds payable (net of $11,000 tax effect)	$22,000
Adjustment to profits of prior years for errors in depreciation (net of $3,750 tax effect)	($7,500)
Loss from fire (net of $7,000 tax effect)	($14,000)

The loss from the fire was an infrequent, but not unusual occurrence in Craig's line of business.

Craig's December 31, Year 6 income statement should report net income of:
A. $65,000.
B. $66,100.
C. $81,600.
D. $87,000.

18.   In analyzing a company's financial statements, which financial statement would a potential investor primarily use to assess the company's liquidity and financial flexibility?
A. Balance sheet.
B. Income statement.
C. Statement of retained earnings.
D. Statement of cash flows.

Use the following information to answer Questions 19 and 20.

Vine Co.'s (Vine) trial balance of income statement accounts for the year ended December 31, Year 6 included the following:

	Debit	Credit
Sales		$575,000
Cost of sales	$240,000	
Administrative expenses	70,000	
Loss on sale of equipment	10,000	
Sales commissions	50,000	
Interest revenue		25,000
Freight-out	15,000	
Loss on early retirement of long-term debt	20,000	
Uncollectible accounts expense	15,000	
Totals	$420,000	$600,000

Other information:
Finished goods inventory:

January 1, Year 6	$400,000
December 31, Year 6	$360,000

Vine's income tax rate is 30%.

19. In Vine's Year 6 multiple-step income statement, what amount should Vine report as the cost of goods manufactured?
    A. $200,000.
    B. $215,000.
    C. $280,000.
    D. $295,000.

20. In Vine's Year 6 multiple-step income statement, what amount should Vine report as income after income taxes from continuing operations?
    A. $126,000.
    B. $129,500.
    C. $140,000.
    D. $147,000.

Use the following information to answer Questions 21 through 23.

The differences in Beatrix, Inc.'s (Beatrix) balance sheet accounts at December 31, Year 6 and Year 5 are presented below:

Assets	Increase/Decrease
Cash and cash equivalents	$120,000
Available-for-sale securities	300,000
Accounts receivable, net	0
Inventory	80,000
Long-term investments	(100,000)
Plant assets	700,000
Accumulated depreciation	0
	$1,100,000

Liabilities and Stockholders' Equity	
Accounts payable and accrued liabilities	($5,000)
Dividend payable	160,000
Short-term bank debt	325,000
Long-term debt	110,000
Common stock, $10 par	100,000
Additional paid-in capital	120,000
Retained earnings	290,000
	$1,100,000

The following additional information relates to Year 6:
- Net income was $790,000.
- Cash dividends of $500,000 were declared.
- A building costing $600,000 and having a carrying amount of $350,000 was sold for $350,000.
- Equipment costing $110,000 was acquired through issuance of long-term debt.
- A long-term investment was sold for $135,000. There were no other transactions affecting long-term investments.
- 10,000 shares of common stock were issued for $22 per share.

21. In Beatrix's Year 6 statement of cash flows, net cash provided by operating activities was:
    A. $705,000.
    B. $920,000.
    C. $1,040,000.
    D. $1,160,000.

22. In Beatrix's Year 6 statement of cash flows, net cash used in investing activities was:
    A. $1,005,000.
    B. $1,190,000.
    C. $1,275,000.
    D. $1,600,000.

23. In Beatrix's Year 6 statement of cash flows, net cash provided by financing activities was:
    A. $20,000.
    B. $45,000.
    C. $150,000.
    D. $205,000.

Use the following information to answer Questions 24 through 27.

Debbie's Dish Shops, Inc.
Balance Sheets

	Dec 31/Year 6	Dec 31/Year 5
Assets		
Current assets:		
Cash	$300,000	$200,000
Accounts receivable – net	840,000	580,000
Merchandise inventory	660,000	420,000
Prepaid expenses	100,000	50,000
Total current assets	$1,900,000	$1,250,000
Long-term investments	$80,000	
Land, building, and fixtures	1,130,000	600,000
Less: accumulated depreciation	(110,000)	(50,000)
	$1,100,000	$550,000
Total assets	$3,000,000	$1,800,000
Liabilities and stockholders' equity		
Current liabilities:		
Accounts payable	$530,000	$440,000
Accrued expenses	140,000	130,000
Dividends payable	70,000	
Total current liabilities	$740,000	$570,000
Note payable—due 2008	$500,000	
Stockholders' equity:		
Common stock	$1,200,000	$900,000
Retained earnings	560,000	330,000
Total stockholders' equity	$1,760,000	$1,230,000
Total liabilities and stockholders' equity	$3,000,000	$1,800,000

Debbie's Dish Shops, Inc.
Income Statements

	Year ended Year 6	December 31, Year 5
Net credit sales	$6,400,000	$4,000,000
Cost of goods sold	5,000,000	3,200,000
Gross profit	$1,400,000	$800,000
Expenses (including income taxes)	1,000,000	520,000
Net income	$400,000	$280,000

Additional information available includes the following:

- All accounts receivable and accounts payable related to trade merchandise. Accounts payable are recorded net and always are paid to take all of the discounts allowed. The allowance for doubtful accounts at the end of Year 6 was the same as at the end of Year 5; no receivables were charged against the allowance during Year 6.
- The proceeds from the note payable were used to finance a new store building. Capital stock was sold to provide additional working capital.

24. Cash collected during Year 6 from accounts receivable amounted to:
    A. $5,560,000.
    B. $5,840,000.
    C. $6,140,000.
    D. $6,400,000.

25. Cash payments during Year 6 on accounts payable to suppliers amounted to:
    A. $4,670,000.
    B. $4,910,000.
    C. $5,000,000.
    D. $5,150,000.

26. Net cash provided by financing activities for Year 6 totaled:
    A. $140,000.
    B. $300,000.
    C. $500,000.
    D. $700,000.

27. Net cash used in investing activities during Year 6 was:
    A. $80,000.
    B. $530,000.
    C. $610,000.
    D. $660,000.

28. Financial statements shall include disclosures of material transactions between related parties except:
    A. nonmonetary exchanges by affiliates.
    B. sales of inventory by a subsidiary to its parent.
    C. expense allowances for executives that exceed normal business practice.
    D. a company's agreement to act as surety for a loan to its chief executive officer.

29. Dino Co. (Dino) acquired 100% of Fred Co. (Fred) prior to Year 6. During Year 6, the individual companies included in their financial statements the following:

	Dino	Fred
Officers' salaries	$75,000	$50,000
Officers' expenses	$20,000	$10,000
Loans to officers	$125,000	$50,000
Intercompany sales	$150,000	$0

What amount should be reported as related-party disclosures in the notes to Dino's Year 6 consolidated financial statements?
   A. $150,000.
   B. $155,000.
   C. $175,000.
   D. $330,000.

30. Zero Corp. (Zero) suffered a loss that would have a material effect on its financial statements on an uncollectible trade account receivable due to a customer's bankruptcy. This occurred suddenly due to a natural disaster ten days after Zero's balance sheet date, but one month before the issuance of the financial statements.

Under these circumstances:

	Adjust statements	Disclose in statements but do not adjust accounts
A.	Yes	No
B.	Yes	Yes
C.	No	No
D.	No	Yes

31. Holmquist, Inc. (Holmquist) acquired 25% of its capital stock after year-end and prior to the issuance of the financial statements. Which of the following is required?
   A. An adjustment to the balance sheet to reflect the acquisition.
   B. Issuance of pro forma financial statements giving effect to the acquisition as if it had occurred at year-end.
   C. Disclosure of the acquisition in the notes to the financial statements.
   D. No disclosure nor adjustment is necessary.

32.   An accountant compiled the following information for Universe, Inc. for the year ended
       December 31, Year 4:
       • Net income was $850,000.
       • Depreciation expense was $200,000.
       • Interest paid was $100,000.
       • Income taxes paid were $50,000.
       • Common stock was sold for $100,000.
       • Preferred stock (8% annual dividend) was sold at par value of $125,000.
       • Common stock dividends of $25,000 were paid.
       • Preferred stock dividends of $10,000 were paid.

       Equipment with a book value of $50,000 was sold for $100,000.

       Using the indirect method, what was Universe, Inc.'s cash flow from operations (CFO) for the year
       ended December 31, Year 4?
       A. $1,015,000.
       B. $1,000,000.
       C. $1,050,000.
       D. $1,040,000.

33.   A company has the following changes in its balance sheet accounts:

Net sales	$500
An increase in accounts receivable	$20
A decrease in accounts payable	$40
An increase in inventory	$30
Sale of common stock	$100
Repayment of debt	$10
Depreciation	$2
Net Income	$100
Interest expense on debt	$5

       The company's cash flow from financing is:
       A. $110.
       B. ($10).
       C. $90.
       D. $100.

34. Financial information for Jefferson Corp. for the year ended December 31 was as follows:

Sales	$3,000,000
Purchases	$1,800,000
Inventory at beginning	$500,000
Inventory at ending	$800,000
Accounts receivable at beginning	$300,000
Accounts receivable at ending	$200,000
Other operating expenses paid	$400,000

Based upon this data and using the direct method, what was Jefferson Corp.'s cash flow from operations for the year ended December 31?
A. $1,200,000.
B. $1,100,000.
C. $900,000.
D. $800,000.

35. Which of the following items would not be used to compute the cash flow from *operations*?
A. Change in long-term debt.
B. Depreciation.
C. Net income.
D. Change in inventory levels.

36. All of the following should be classified as cash flows from financing (CFF) by Gordon, Inc. except:
A. the portion of long-term debt principal payable within the current year operating cycle of the business.
B. proceeds from the issuance of 8% preferred stock of Gordon, Inc.
C. preferred stock dividends paid by Gordon, Inc. to its preferred shareholders at 8% of par value.
D. preferred stock dividends paid to Gordon, Inc. on account of Gordon's ownership of 9% par value preferred stock in Venture, Inc.

37. Which of the following does not represent a cash flow relating to operating activity?
A. Interest paid to bondholders.
B. Cash received from customers.
C. Dividends paid to stockholders.
D. Cash paid for salaries.

38.   What is the difference between the direct and indirect method of calculating cash flow from operations?
   A.   The indirect method starts with gross income and adjusts to cash flow from operations, while the direct method starts with gross profit and flows through the income statement to calculate cash flows from operations.
   B.   The direct method starts with sales and follows cash as it flows through the income statement, while the indirect method starts with net income and adjusts for non-cash charges and other items.
   C.   Balance sheet items are not included in the cash flow from operations for the direct method, while they are included for the indirect method.
   D.   The direct method will result in a lower or higher cash flow figure for operating activities as it details all of the income statement items, while the indirect method only uses net income.

39.   Which of the following would not be a component of cash flow from investing?
   A.   Purchase of securities.
   B.   Purchase of equipment.
   C.   Sale of land.
   D.   Dividends paid.

40.   The following information is from the balance sheet of Silverstone Company:

Net Income for 5/1/05 to 5/31/05: $8,000

Balance 5/01 Year 5	Account	Balance 5/31 Year 5
$2,000	Inventory	$1,750
$1,200	Prepaid exp	$1,700
$800	Acc depreciation	$975
$425	Accounts payable	$625
$650	Bonds payable	$550

Using the indirect method, calculate the cash flow from operations for Silverstone Company as of 5/31 Year 5.
   A.   Increase in cash of $8,125.
   B.   Increase in cash of $8,025.
   C.   Increase in cash of $7,725.
   D.   The indirect method cannot be calculated from the information provided.

41. Use the following information to calculate cash flows from operations using the indirect method:

Net income	$12,000
Depreciation expense	$1,000
Loss on sale of machinery	$500
Increase in accounts receivable	$2,000
Decrease in accounts payable	$1,500
Increase in income taxes payable	$500
Repayment of bonds	$3,000

   A. Decrease in cash of $8,500.
   B. Increase in cash of $10,500.
   C. Increase in cash of $7,500.
   D. Increase in cash of $9,500.

42. Use the following financial data for Moose Printing Corporation to calculate the cash flow from operations using the indirect method:

Net income	$225
Increase in accounts receivable	$55
Decrease in inventory	$33
Depreciation	$65
Decrease in accounts payable	$25
Increase in wages payable	$15
Decrease in deferred taxes	$10
Purchase of new equipment	$65
Dividends paid	$75

   A. Increase in cash of $248.
   B. Increase in cash of $183.
   C. Increase in cash of $173.
   D. Decrease in cash of $108.

43.   Using the following information, calculate operating cash flows using the direct method for Carlisle Cosmetics Corporation:

Carlisle Cosmetics Corporation
Income Statement
May 31, 2005

Net sales	$50,000
Cost of goods sold	38,000
Gross margin	$12,000
Operating expenses	2,500
Operating income	$9,500
Other income	
Interest expense	500
Income before taxes	$9,000
Income taxes	1,800
Net income	$7,200

- Cash sales are $35,000.
- Inventory increased by $3,000.
- Accounts payable increased by $2,000.
- Depreciation expense for May was $750.
- Income taxes payable decreased by $200.
- Carlisle Cosmetics Corporation purchased equipment for $10,000.

Cash dividends were paid in the amount of $3,000.
A. Decrease in cash of $7,800.
B. Decrease in cash of $9,950.
C. Increase in cash of $4,950.
D. Decrease in cash of $8,250.

44. Laurel, Inc.'s net income after taxes for the year ended December 31, Year 4, was $10,000,000. Laurel's balance sheet showed the following as of the beginning and end of Year 4:

	January 1, Year 4	December 31, Year 4
Cash	$12,000,000	$19,000,000
Accounts receivable	6,000,000	8,000,000
Inventory	13,000,000	17,000,000
Property, plant & equip.	24,000,000	24,000,000
Accumulated depreciation	(10,000,000)	(13,000,000)
Total assets	$45,000,000	$55,000,000
Accounts payable	$9,000,000	$8,000,000
Long-term debt	12,000,000	15,000,000
Deferred taxes	1,500,000	4,000,000
Common stock	8,000,000	9,000,000
Retained earnings	14,500,000	19,000,000
Total liabilities and equity	$45,000,000	$55,000,000

Using the indirect method, net cash provided (used) by operating activities for the year ended December 31, Year 4 was:

A. $8,500,000.
B. $16,500,000.
C. $9,500,000.
D. $12,500,000.

45. Land costing $50,000 was sold by Jimmy Corporation for a gain of $10,000. Assuming Jimmy uses the indirect method for presenting operating cash flow, how will the sale of land be reflected on its statement of cash flows? Cash flow from investing activities will increase by:

A. $50,000; cash flow from operating activities will require a negative adjustment to net income of $10,000.
B. $60,000; cash flow from operating activities will require a positive adjustment to net income of $10,000.
C. $60,000; cash flow from operating activities will require a negative adjustment to net income of $10,000.
D. $50,000; cash flow from operating activities will require a positive adjustment to net income of $10,000.

46. Carver, Inc. has computed that its cash collections for Year 4 were $67,000,000, and other cash outflows and costs were $22,000,000. Information on Carver's inventory activities in Year 4 was as follows:

Inventory at January 1	$23,000,000
Inventory at December 31	$21,000,000
Inventory purchases	$39,000,000

One-third of the inventory purchases in Year 4 were obtained by increasing Carver's credit with its suppliers. There were no other net changes in Carver's accounts payable.

Using the direct method, cash provided or used by Carver, Inc.'s operating activities in Year 4 was:
A. $19,000,000.
B. $32,000,000.
C. $21,000,000.
D. $17,000,000.

47. When using the indirect method for computing cash flow from operating activities, a change in accounts payable will require which of the following?
A. A negative adjustment to net income regardless of whether accounts payable increases or decreases.
B. A positive adjustment to net income regardless of whether accounts payable increases or decreases.
C. A negative (positive) adjustment to net income when accounts payable increases (decreases).
D. A positive (negative) adjustment to net income when accounts payable increases (decreases).

48. When calculating cash flow from operations (CFO) using the indirect method, which of the following is true?
A. When recognizing a gain on the sale of fixed assets, part of the amount may be a deduction to operating cash flows.
B. The indirect method requires an additional schedule to reconcile net income to cash flow.
C. In using the indirect method, each item on the income statement is converted to its cash equivalent.
D. Accumulated depreciation would be a deduction to calculate the net cash flow, because this is a non-cash activity.

49. Using the direct method, calculate net cash flow from operations with the following information:
- Net income $87,000
- Increase in accounts receivable $65,000
- Depreciation expense $4,500
- Increase in prepaid expense $21,750
- Decrease in income taxes payable $650
- Sale of furniture $4,000
- Decrease in common stock $25,000

A. Decrease in cash of $4,750.
B. Net cash flow cannot be calculated using the direct method, because the income statement is required.
C. Increase in cash of $5,400.
D. Decrease in cash of $4,900.

50.   Convenience Travel Corp.'s financial information for the year ended December 31, Year 4, included the following:

Property, plant & equipment $15,000,000
Accumulated depreciation $9,000,000

The only asset owned by Convenience Travel in Year 5 was a corporate jet airplane. The airplane was being depreciated over a 15-year period on a straight-line basis at a rate of $1,000,000 per year.

On December 31, Year 5, Convenience Travel sold the airplane for $10,000,000 cash. Net income for the year ended December 31, Year 5, was $12,000,000.

Based on the above information, and ignoring taxes, what is cash flow from operations (CFO) for Convenience Travel for the year ended December 31, Year 5?
    A. $12,000,000.
    B. $13,000,000.
    C. $11,000,000.
    D. $8,000,000.

51.   Favor, Inc.'s capital and related transactions during Year 5 were as follows:
    •   On January 1, $1,000,000 of 5-year 10% annual interest bonds were issued to Cover Industries in exchange for old equipment owned by Cover.
    •   On June 30, $50,000 of interest was paid to Cover.
    •   On July 1, the bonds were returned to Favor in exchange for $1,500,000 par value 6% preferred stock.
    •   On December 31, preferred stock dividends of $45,000 were paid to Cover.

Favor, Inc.'s cash flow from financing (CFF) for Year 5 is:
    A. ($1,045,000).
    B. ($95,000).
    C. ($45,000).
    D. ($1,095,000).

52.   Which of the following items would not be included in cash flow from *financing*?
    A. Dividends paid to shareholders.
    B. Gain on sale of stock of a subsidiary.
    C. Purchase of treasury stock.
    D. Issuance of common stock.

53.   If Jackson Ski Company issues common stock and uses the proceeds to purchase fixed assets such as equipment:
    A. both cash flow from operations and cash flow from financing would increase.
    B. cash flow from financing would decrease and cash flow from investing would increase.
    C. both cash flow from operations and cash flow from financing would decrease.
    D. cash flow from financing would increase and cash flow from investing would decrease.

54. Which of the following statements about accounting procedures and their impact on the statement of cash flows is *least* valid? All else equal:
    A. a nonprofitable company that uses LIFO to account for inventory will have higher total cash flow than a nonprofitable company that uses FIFO during a period of rising prices.
    B. a company that finances through common stock issues may have the same cash flow from financing as a firm that issues debt.
    C. the cash flow from operations for a company that has a capital lease will be overstated compared to that of a firm that has an operating lease.
    D. the cash flow from operations for a company that issues a bond at a premium will be understated compared to a firm that issues a bond at par.

55. In Year 2, Copper, Inc. completed a $4,000,000 bond issue to finance the purchase of equipment used in its operations. The bonds were convertible into common stock at a conversion rate of 100 shares per $1,000 bond. In Year 5, the market price of Copper, Inc.'s common stock rose above $10 per share, and all of the outstanding bonds were converted into common stock when the common stock was selling for an average price of $15 per share.

    Copper, Inc. prepares its Statement of Cash Flows using the indirect method.

    Given the above information, Copper's Statement of Cash Flows for the year ended December 31, Year 5, should include:
    A. no reporting of the transaction in the Statement of Cash Flows, except for a footnote describing the conversion of the bonds into common stock.
    B. under Cash Flow from Financing, "Retirement of Bonds: $4,000,000" and "Issuance of Common Stock: $4,000,000."
    C. under Cash Flow from Financing, "Retirement of Bonds: $4,000,000" and "Issuance of Common Stock: $6,000,000" and under Cash Flow from Investing, "Loss on Retirement of Bonds: $2,000,000."
    D. no reporting of the transaction.

56. Which of the following should be disclosed as supplemental information in the statement of cash flows?

	Cash flow per share	Conversion of debt to equity
A.	Yes	Yes
B.	Yes	No
C.	No	Yes
D.	No	No

57. Bee Co. uses the direct write-off method to account for uncollectible accounts receivable. During an accounting period, Bee's cash collections from customers equal sales adjusted for the addition or deduction of the following amounts:

	Accounts written-off	Increase in accounts receivable balance
A.	Deduction	Deduction
B.	Addition	Deduction
C.	Deduction	Addition
D.	Addition	Addition

58. Which of the following cash flows per share should be reported in a statement of cash flows?
    A. Both primary and fully diluted cash flows per share.
    B. Primary cash flows per share only.
    C. Fully diluted cash flows per share only.
    D. Cash flows per share should not be reported.

59. A company reports net income of $300,000. The company reported depreciation expense of $60,000. It also reported a $23,000 increase in accounts receivable and a $9,000 increase in accounts payable. On a statement of cash flows, what is the cash flow from operating activities?
    A. $337,000.
    B. $346,000.
    C. $360,000.
    D. $369,000.

60. A company buys a building for $360,000 by signing a long-term liability. Later, cash of $23,000 was paid: $20,000 on the note and $3,000 as interest expense. The company also sold equipment with a cost of $200,000 and accumulated depreciation of $60,000 at a gain of $11,000. On a statement of cash flows, which of the following statements is correct?
    A. Under investing activities, a $360,000 cash outflow should be shown because of acquisition of this building.
    B. Under financing activities, a $23,000 cash outflow should be shown because of the payment in connection with the long-term liability.
    C. Under investing activities, a $151,000 cash inflow should be shown because of the payment in connection with the sale of the equipment.
    D. Under investing activities, a $139,000 cash inflow should be shown because of the payment in connection with the sale of the equipment.

61. A company is producing a statement of cash flows and is reporting operating activities by means of the direct method. The company reports insurance expense of $60,000 on its income statement. During the year, prepaid insurance on one policy went up by $11,000. At the same time, an insurance liability on a different policy went down by $3,000. How much cash did the company pay during the year on insurance?
    A. $46,000.
    B. $52,000.
    C. $68,000.
    D. $74,000.

62. A company started the current year with a building costing $300,000 and a book value of $180,000. During the year, depreciation expense of $12,000 was recognized on this building before it was sold at a loss of $20,000. On a statement of cash flows, what is reported under investing activities?
    A. Cash inflow of $148,000.
    B. Cash inflow of $160,000.
    C. Cash inflow of $168,000.
    D. Cash inflow of $180,000.

ANSWERS: STATEMENT OF CASH FLOWS

1. **A**   Per APB 22, disclosure of accounting policies should identify and describe the accounting principles followed by the reporting company and methods applying those principles.

    Answer A is correct because the method of recording and depreciating assets is an example of such a required disclosure. Answers B and C are incorrect because both represent detail presented elsewhere in the financial statements. Answer D is incorrect because it is an estimate of earnings rather than an accounting policy.

2. **D**   Miri began operations on 1/1/Year 6 with the following balance sheet elements:

    Assets ($860,000) = Liabilities ($110,000) + Owners' equity ($750,000)

    During Year 6, liabilities increased to $120,000, and owners' equity increased to $765,000 [$750,000 beginning balance + $18,000 net income ($82,000 revenues – $64,000 expenses) – $3,000 dividends declared].

    Therefore, 12/31/Year 6 assets must be $885,000.

    Liabilities ($120,000) + Owners' equity ($765,000) = Assets ($885,000)

3. **D**   Idle machinery ($11,200) and cash surrender value of life insurance ($13,700) are both assets. The allowance for decline in market value of noncurrent marketable equity securities ($8,400) is a contra-asset that is properly included in the asset section of the balance sheet (as a deduction).

    The only item listed that should not be included in the asset section of the balance sheet is the treasury stock ($24,000). Although the treasury stock account has a debit balance, it is not an asset; instead, it is reported as a contra equity account.

    Therefore, the $24,000 must be excluded from the asset section, reducing the net asset amount to $851,000 ($875,000 – $24,000).

4. **D**   Advertising ($150,000) and sales salaries and commissions ($140,000) are clearly selling expenses, as is the rent for the office space occupied by the sales department ($220,000 × 0.5 = $110,000). Additionally, freight-out ($80,000) is a selling expense because shipping the goods from the point of sale to the customer is the final effort in the selling process. The total selling expense is, therefore, $480,000 ($150,000 + $140,000 + $110,000 + $80,000).

    The remaining expenses given are general and administrative expenses, except for interest and the loss on sale of long-term investment that are nonoperating items (other expenses and losses).

5. **C**   The 12/31/Year 6 cash and cash equivalents balance is $240,000, as computed below:

Checking account #101	$175,000
Checking account #102	(10,000)
Money market account	25,000
90-day certificate of deposit	50,000
Total cash and cash equivalents	$240,000

    Bank overdrafts (such as account #102) are normally reported as a current liability. However, when available cash is present in another account in the same bank, as in this case, offsetting is required. The money market account of $25,000 and the 90-day certificate of deposit are considered cash equivalents because they had original maturities of three months or less. The 180-day certificate of deposit of $80,000 is excluded because its original maturity was more than three months.

6. **C** Per SFAS 95, the primary purpose of a statement of cash flows is to provide relevant information about the company's cash receipts and cash payments during a period. Answers A, B, and D are incorrect because, although they represent uses of the statement of cash flows, they are not the primary use.

7. **D** Investing activities include all cash flows involving assets, other than operating items. The investing activities are as follows:

Purchase of investment in stock	($26,000)
Sale of investment in stock	35,000
Acquisition of certificate of deposit	(50,000)
Net cash used	($41,000)

The gain on sale of investment in Geneva ($35,000 – $33,000 = $2,000), the interest earned ($3,750), and dividends earned ($1,200) are all operating items. Note that the sale of investment is reported in the investing section at the cash inflow amount ($35,000), not at the carrying value of the investment ($33,000). If the certificate had been for three months instead of four years, it would be part of "cash and cash equivalents" and would not be shown under investing activities.

8. **C** Financing activities include the repayment of debt principal or as in this case, the payment of the capital lease obligation. Thus, the cash outflow is equal to the 2004 principal payments only. The interest on the capital lease is classified as an operating cash outflow.

9. **B** In Year 6, Bretagne would report one-fifth of the cabinet costs as depreciation expense in selling, general, and administrative expenses, while four-fifths of the cabinet cost would remain capitalized as fixed assets at the end of Year 6. The cabinets are considered fixed assets and not part of COGS.

10. **A** Investing activities include all cash flows involving assets other than operating items. The investing activities are as follows:

Proceeds from sale of equipment	$10,000
Purchase of bonds	(180,000)
Net cash used in investing activities	($170,000)

The gain on sale of equipment ($6,000) and amortization of bond discount ($2,000) are net income adjustments in the operating section, while dividends paid ($38,000) and proceeds from the sale of treasury stock ($75,000) are financing items. The excess of dividends declared over dividends paid is a noncash financing activity.

11. **D** Financing activities include all cash flows involving liabilities and owners' equity other than operating items. The financing activities are as follows:

Dividends paid	($38,000)
Proceeds from the sale of treasury stock	75,000
Net cash provided by financing activities	$37,000

The excess of dividends declared over dividends paid is a noncash financing activity. The gain on sale of equipment ($6,000) and amortization of bond discount ($2,000) are net income adjustments in the operating section, while the proceeds from the sale of equipment ($10,000) and purchase of bonds ($180,000) are investing items.

12. **D** Per SFAS 95, companies are required to report the gross amounts of cash receipts and cash payments, rather than net amounts. Therefore, the gross cash inflow from the sale of equipment and the gross outflow for the payment of new equipment should be reported.

Answer A is incorrect because both gross inflow and outflow should be reported, rather than reporting the net cash flow from the transaction.

Answer B is incorrect because gross cash flows, not net, are reported and because a note payable is not reported because the transaction results in no actual inflow or outflow in the period in which the payable occurs. This noncash activity would be reported in a separate schedule or in the footnotes. Noncash transactions commonly recognized in a separate schedule in the financial statements include conversion of debt to equity and acquisition of assets by assuming liabilities, including lease obligations.

Answer C is incorrect because the note payable is not reported on the statement of cash flows; rather, it is shown in a separate schedule.

13. **C.** Per APB 22, disclosure of accounting policies should identify and describe the accounting principles followed by the reporting entity and methods of applying those principles. The criteria for determining which investments are treated as cash equivalents is an example of how the company applies accounting principles. APB 22 states that these disclosures should not duplicate details presented elsewhere as part of the financial statements.

Answers A, B, and D are not disclosures of accounting policies and also would be presented elsewhere in the financial statements.

14. **A** Operating expenses are usually divided into two categories: selling expenses and general and administrative (G&A) expenses. Selling expenses are related to the sale of a company's products, while G&A expenses are related to the company's general operations. Therefore, Griffin should include the following costs in G&A expense:

Accounting and legal fees	$35,000
Officers' salaries	150,000
Insurance	85,000
Total	$260,000

Freight-in ($175,000) is an inventoriable cost that should be reflected in COGS and ending inventory. Freight-out, the cost of delivering goods to customers ($160,000), is included in selling expenses. Sales representatives' salaries ($215,000) is also a selling expense.

15. **C** In a statement of cash flows in which the operating activities is prepared using the direct method, the cash paid for wages would be equal to the accrual-basis salaries expense plus/minus any decrease/increase in the wages payable account. The logic is essentially the same as an accrual-basis to cash-basis adjustment. In this case, the wages payable account increased, so the correct sign would be minus.

16. **D** Based only on the items given, net cash provided by operating activities is $151,400 as computed below:

Net income	$150,000
Increase in net accounts receivable	
[($29,000 – 1,000) – ($23,000 – 800)]	(5,800)
Decrease in prepaid rent ($12,400 – $8,200)	4,200
Increase in accounts payable ($22,400 – $19,400)	3,000
Cash provided by operations	$151,400

The increase in net accounts receivable is deducted from net income because it indicates that cash collected is less than sales revenue. The decrease in prepaid rent is added because it reflects rent expense that was not a cash payment, but an allocation of previously recorded prepaid rent. Finally, the increase in accounts payable is added because it also represents an expense (COGS) that was not yet paid.

17. **D**   Net income as reported ($74,100) properly included the gain on early retirement of bonds payable ($22,000) and the loss from fire ($14,000). The fact that the gain and loss were reported net of taxes in the income statement was incorrect, but does not cause the net income amount to be in error.

However, the other two items should not be reported in the income statement at all. An unrealized loss on noncurrent investments in stock ($5,400) is reported in other comprehensive income, not in net income. A correction of an error ($7,500) is treated as a prior period adjustment. It is reported in the financial statements as an adjustment to the beginning balance of retained earnings, rather than in the income statement. Because both of these items were subtracted in the computation of reported net income, they must be added back to compute the correct net income of $87,000 ($74,100 + $5,400 + $7,500).

18. **A**   Although the statement of cash flows provides information about liquidity, solvency, and financial flexibility, a potential investor would primarily use the balance sheet to assess liquidity and financial flexibility. The balance sheet helps users analyze the company's ability to use current assets to pay current liabilities (liquidity) and the company's ability to alter the amounts and timing of future cash flows to adapt to unexpected needs or to take advantage of opportunities (flexibility).

19. **A**   Cost of goods manufactured has to be computed indirectly in this case, using the cost of sales formula, as follows:

Beginning finished goods	$400,000
+ Cost of goods manufactured	?
– Ending finished goods	($360,000)
Cost of sales	$240,000

Solving for the missing amount, cost of goods manufactured is $200,000.

20. **A**   All of the revenues, gains, expenses, and losses given in this question are components of income from continuing operations. Income before taxes is $180,000 as computed below:

Revenues ($575,000 + $25,000)	$600,000
Expenses and losses ($240,000	
+ $70,000 + $10,000	
+ $50,000 + $15,000	
+ $15,000 + $20,000)	(420,000)
Income before income taxes	$180,000
Income taxes (30%)	(54,000)
Income from continuing operations	$126,000

To compute income from continuing operations (after taxes), income taxes ($180,000 × 30% = $54,000) must also be deducted ($180,000 – $54,000 = $126,000).

21. **B**   There is not enough information to use the direct method, so we use the indirect approach. Net income is adjusted for noncash items as shown below:

Net income	$790,000
Add: Depreciation expense	250,000
Gain on sale of long-term investment	(35,000)
Increase in inventory	(80,000)
Decrease in accounts payable and accrued liabilities	(5,000)
	$920,000

Accumulated depreciation did not show any net decrease or increase during Year 6. But we know it was decreased by $250,000 when the building was sold ($600,000 cost less $350,000 carrying amount). Therefore, depreciation expense of $250,000 must have increased the accumulated depreciation account to result in a net effect for the year of $0. Depreciation expense is added back because it is a noncash expense.

The long-term investment was sold for $135,000 and the listing of accounts shows a decrease in long-term investments of $100,000. The resulting gain on sale of $35,000 is deducted because the total cash effect of this transaction ($135,000) will be reported as an investing activity.

Two of the working capital accounts that changed are related to net income. The increase in inventory ($80,000) is deducted because cash was used to increase inventory. The decrease in accounts payable and accrued liabilities ($5,000) is deducted because cash was used to pay these liabilities.

The increase of $300,000 for available-for-sale securities is an investing activity.

22. **A**   The common stock issued is a financing activity. The changes in the inventory and accumulated depreciation accounts are operating items. The cash flows involving the other assets listed below are investing activities:

Purchase of available-for-sale securities	($300,000)
Sale of long-term investments	135,000
Sale of plant assets	350,000
Purchase of plant assets	(1,190,000)
	($1,005,000)

The amounts above were given except for the purchase of plant assets, the amount of which can be determined as follows:

Cost of equipment acquired	$110,000
Cost of building sold	(600,000)
Cost of plant assets purchased	?
Net increase	$700,000

Solving for the debit, we arrive at $1,190,000.

The equipment acquired through issuance of long-term debt is a noncash investing and financing activity so it does not affect net cash used in investing activities.

23. **D**   The change in the accounts payable and accrued liabilities account is an operating item. The part of the change in retained earnings caused by net income ($790,000) is also an operating item. The cash flows involving the other liability and equity accounts, listed below, are financing activities:

Payment of dividends ($500,000 – $160,000)	($340,000)
Issuance of short-term debt	325,000
Issuance of common stock (10,000 × $22)	220,000
	$205,000

The question states that $500,000 of dividends were declared and this is confirmed by the change in the retained earnings account ($790,000 net income – $500,000 dividends declared = $290,000 net increase). However, because dividends payable increase by $160,000, only $340,000 of dividends were paid.

The issuance of long-term debt for equipment ($110,000) is a noncash financing and investing activity, so it does not affect net cash provided by financing activities.

The issuance of common stock is confirmed by the increases in the common stock and additional paid-in capital accounts ($100,000 + $120,000 = $220,000).

24. **C** The allowance account has no effect on this analysis because the question states that the balance in this account has not changed and no accounts receivable were written off. Net credit sales are the only debit to accounts receivable because all accounts receivable relate to trade merchandise.

Dec 31/Year 5 net accounts receivable balance	$580,000
Year 6 collections	?
Year 6 net credit sales	6,400,000
Dec 31/Year 6 net accounts receivable balance	$840,000

Solving for the missing credit amount, we determine that $6,140,000 was collected on account during Year 6.

25. **D** The COGS statement can be used to compute purchases:

Beginning inventory	$420,000
+ Purchases	?
– Ending inventory	(660,000)
COGS	$5,000,000

   Purchases = $5,000,000 – ($420,000 – $660,000) = $5,240,000

Dec 31/Year 5 net accounts payable balance	$440,000
Purchases	5,240,000
Payments to suppliers	?
Dec 31/Year 6 net accounts payable balance	$530,000

Solving for the missing debit amount, we determine that the payments to suppliers were $5,150,000 during Year 6.

26. **D** The note payable was issued for cash, and the proceeds were used to purchase a building. Cash inflows from financing activities include proceeds from long-term borrowing and issuance of capital stock:

Proceeds from long-term note	$500,000
Proceeds from issuance of common stock	300,000
	$800,000

To determine the amount of dividends paid, it is necessary to analyze both the retained earnings and the dividends payable accounts.

Dec 31/Year 5 retained earnings balance	$330,000
Net income for Year 6	400,000
Less: Dividends declared	?
Dec 31/Year 6 retained earnings balance	$560,000

Solving for the missing debit amount, we determine that the dividends declared were $170,000 during Year 6.

Dec 31/Year 5 dividends payable balance	$0
Dividends declared in Year 6	170,000
Less: Dividends paid	?
Dec 31/Year 6 dividends payable balance	$70,000

Solving for the missing debit amount, we determine that the dividends paid were $100,000 during Year 6.

Therefore, net cash flows provided by financing activities is $700,000 ($800,000 – $100,000).

27. **C**   The two assets other than those related to operations shown on the balance sheet (long-term investments and land, building, and fixtures) have increased from 12/31/Year 5 to 12/31/Year 6, indicating cash purchases, because the additional information does not suggest any other means of acquisition.

   Therefore, cash outflows from investing activities include $80,000 for long-term investments and $530,000 ($1,130,000 – $600,000) for land, building, and fixtures. Notice that the building was purchased for $500,000, so fixtures or land must have been acquired for $30,000.

28. **B**   Because sales of inventory between subsidiary and parent are eliminated in preparing consolidated financial statements, such sales need not be disclosed as a related-party transaction.

   Nonmonetary exchanges by affiliates are not specifically exempted from disclosure by SFAS 57, and therefore, must be disclosed as related-party transactions.

   In this case, the expense allowances are in excess of normal business practice, and therefore, must be disclosed.

   Surety and guarantee agreements between related parties are not specifically exempted from disclosure by SFAS 57, and therefore must be disclosed as related-party transactions.

29. **C**   The officers' salaries and expenses fall into the first category of exemptions in SFAS 57 (compensation agreements and expense allowances). The intercompany sales fall into the second category (will be eliminated on consolidation). Therefore, only the loans to officers ($125,000 + $50,000 = $175,000) are reported as related-party disclosures.

30. **D**   Answer D is correct because a customer's major casualty loss after year-end will result in a financial statement note disclosure with no adjustment to the financial statements.

31. **C**   Answer C is correct because the transaction described is a Type 2 subsequent event (because the acquisition provided evidence of a condition that came into existence after year-end) and therefore the accounting approach would be note disclosure rather than adjustment.

   Answer A is incorrect because adjustments are only appropriate for Type 1 subsequent events (events that provide evidence the condition was in existence at year-end). Answer B is incorrect because the pro forma statements are optional and not mandatory. Based on the above, Answer D is clearly incorrect because at a minimum, disclosure in the footnotes is required.

32. **B**   Cash flow from operations (CFO) using the indirect method is computed by taking net income plus noncash expenses (i.e., depreciation) less gains from the equipment sale. Note that cash flow from operations must be adjusted downward for the amount of the gain on the sale of the equipment. Cash flow from operations is [$850,000 + $200,000 – ($100,000 – $50,000)] = $1,000,000. Note that interest and income taxes paid are expenses shown on the income statement and will already be factored into net income. The other information relates to financial and investing cash flows.

33. **C**

Sale of common stock	$100
Repayment of debt	(10)
Financing cash flows	$90

34. **C**   Cost of goods sold was (beginning inventory plus purchases less ending inventory) $500,000 + $1,800,000 – $800,000 = $1,500,000. Cash flow from operations under the direct method is calculated by:

   Cash collections from customers: $3,100,000 (net sales plus decrease in accounts receivable) of [$3,000,000 + ($300,000 – $200,000)].

Less cash paid to suppliers: $1,800,000 (cost of goods sold plus increase in inventory) of ($1,500,000 + $300,000).

Less other cash outflows of $400,000 for operating expenses.

Cash flow from operations = $3,100,000 – $1,800,000 – $400,000 = $900,000.

35. **A** Long-term debt would be a financing cash flow.

36. **D** Dividend income is considered cash from operations (CFO). Debt proceeds and payments, other than interest paid or received, are considered to be cash flows from financing (CFF).

37. **C** Dividends paid to stockholders are considered cash flow relating to financing activity. However, U.S. GAAP requires interest paid to bondholders to be considered an operating activity.

38. **B** The main difference between the direct and indirect methods of calculating cash flows is the way that cash flow from operations is calculated. The direct method starts with sales and follows cash as it flows through the income statement, while the indirect method starts with income after taxes and adjusts backwards for noncash and other items. Both methods will have the same result for operating cash flows. The direct and indirect method calculates the financing and investing cash flows the same way, and both methods will result in the same cash flow figure.

39. **D** Dividends paid is not a component of cash flow from investing; it is a component of cash flow from financing. The other items are all components of cash flow from investing

40. **A** Silverstone Company's cash flow from operations would be calculated as Net income $8,000 + Inventory $250 – Prepaid expense $500 + Depreciation $175 + A/P $200 = $8,125. Bonds payable is a financing activity and would not be included in the cash flow from operations. The indirect method takes the change in the noncash accounts and decreases or increases net income to get to the change in cash flow.

41. **B** Cash flow from operations would be calculated as Net income $12,000 + Depreciation $1,000 + Loss on sale of machinery $500 – A/R $2,000 – A/P $1,500 + Income taxes payable $500 = $10,500. Repayment of Bonds is a financing activity and would not be included with operating activities. Depreciation is not a cash flow activity and is therefore always added back to net income to calculate CFO. The loss on the sale of machinery is not a cash outflow, so it is also added back to calculate CFO. Accounts receivable is subtracted when there is an increase as this increases net income but does not affect cash.

42. **A** Cash flows from operations for Moose Printing Corporation is calculated as follows: Net income $225 – A/R $55 + Inventory $33 + Depreciation $65 – A/P $25 + Wages payable $15 – Deferred taxes $10 = $248. The purchase of new equipment would be an investing activity and, therefore, would not be included in the cash flows from operations. Dividends paid would be a financing activity and would not be included in the cash flows from operations.

43. **D** Operating cash flows would be calculated as follows:

Cash receipts from sales	$35,000
Cash payments for:	
Purchases ($38,000 + $3,000 – $2,000)	(39,000)
Operating expenses ($2,500 – $750)	(1,750)
Income taxes ($1,800 + $200)	(2,000)
Interest paid	(500)
Net cash flows from operations	($8,250)

The purchase of equipment is an investing activity and would not be included in the operating activities. A dividend paid is a financing activity and would also not be included with the operating activities. When calculating cash flow using the direct method, the balance sheet items need to be considered because they affect cash.

44. **A**   To compute net cash provided by operating activities for Year 4 using the indirect method, start with net income and add (subtract) the following amounts:

Net income	$10,000,000
Less: Accounts receivable increase	(2,000,000)
Less: Increase in inventory	(4,000,000)
Add: Depreciation expense	3,000,000
Less: Accounts payable decrease	(1,000,000)
Add: Increase in deferred taxes	2,500,000
Cash flows from operating activities	$8,500,000

Changes in long-term debt, common stock, and retained earnings do not affect cash flows from operations.

45. **C**   The sale of land has generated cash of $60,000 ($50,000 cost plus $10,000 gain), and all of this will need to be disclosed as a cash flow from investing activities. Since the $10,000 gain is included in net income, net income will need to be adjusted downward to reflect the correct cash flow from operating activities and to avoid double counting.

46. **A**   Under the direct method, cash provided by operating activities is cash collections less cash inputs less other cash outflows. Cash inputs are cost of goods sold plus increase (or less decrease) in inventory plus decrease (or less increase) in accounts payable. Cost of goods sold for Carver in 2004 was beginning inventory plus purchases less ending inventory ($23,000,000 + $39,000,000 – $21,000,000 = $41,000,000). The decrease in inventory was $23,000,000 – $21,000,000 = $2,000,000. The increase in accounts payable was $39,000,000 × 1/3 = $13,000,000. Cash inputs were $41,000,000 – $2,000,000 – $13,000,000 = $26,000,000. Cash provided by operating activities for Carver, Inc. in 2001 was $67,000,000 – $26,000,000 – $22,000,000 = $19,000,000.

47. **D**   A decrease in accounts payable represents an outflow. Hence, a negative adjustment will be required. Conversely, an increase represents an inflow and a positive adjustment.

48. **A**   When recognizing a gain on the sale of fixed assets, part of the amount may be a deduction to operating cash flows. This is because the gain may be greater than the book value and would be double counted in the investing section and in net income. Therefore, the gain amount greater than the book value must be removed from net income. The direct method of cash flow calculation converts the income statement items to their cash equivalents, not the indirect method. When calculating cash flow from operations, the current period depreciation (expense) amount should be used and not total accumulated depreciation. Also, depreciation is added to net income in order to calculate CFO using the indirect method.

49. **B**   When calculating net cash flow using the direct method, the income statement is required or the accounts on the income statement are required. The direct method takes each item on the income statement and determines its effect on cash flow to calculate net cash flow. When calculating net cash flow from operations (CFO), sale of furniture is not included in this section as it is an investing activity. Common stock is a financing activity and would not be reflected in operations on the statement of cash flows. Note that using the information given, CFO using the indirect method is equal to $4,100 (87,000 – 65,000 + 4,500 – 21,750 – 650).

50. **D**   Using the indirect method, CFO is net income increased by Year 5 depreciation ($1,000,000) and decreased by the gain recognized on the sale of the plane [$10,000,000 – ($15,000,000 – $10,000,000)].

51. **C**   Issuing bonds in exchange for equipment does not affect cash flow. Interest paid is an operating cash flow. Exchanging bonds for stock does not affect cash, but should still be disclosed in a footnote to the Statement of Cash Flows. Dividends paid are considered financing activities. In this case, only the preferred stock dividends paid would be considered CFF.

52. **B**   Gains or losses will be found in cash flow from investments.

53. **D**   Cash flow from financing increases when stock is issued, while cash flow from investing decreases when spending for purchases of fixed assets.

54. **A**   Because of the impact of income taxes, a *profitable* company that accounts for inventory using LIFO will have higher total cash flow than a *profitable* company that uses FIFO. The company that uses LIFO will have higher cost of goods sold, resulting in lower net income and, thus, lower taxes.

   The other statements are correct. A company that issues common stock is *not* required to pay dividends (which would reduce cash flow from financing). Thus, it may have the same CFF as a firm that issues debt since interest paid on debt is a component of cash flow from operations (CFO).

   The cash flow from operations for a company that has a capital lease will be overstated compared to that of a firm that has an operating lease. The interest portion of a capital lease payment reduces cash flow from operations, and the principal portion reduces cash flow from financing. The rental payments on an operating lease reduce cash flow from operations only.

   The cash flow from operations for a company that issues a bond at a premium will be understated compared to a firm that issues a bond at par. When a company issues bonds at a premium, the coupon payment is "too big" (reduces CFO) and, thus, interest expense is reduced by the amount of the amortization of the premium (increases CFF).

55. **A**   A conversion of bonds into common stock does not affect cash flow, but the conversion should be disclosed in a footnote to the Statement of Cash Flows.

56. **C**   Per FAS 95, cash flow per share shall not be reported in financial statements. Neither cash flow per share, nor any component thereof, is an acceptable alternative to net income or earnings per share as a measure of performance. Per FAS 95, noncash investing and financing activities that affect recognized assets or liabilities shall be reported in related disclosures (either narrative or summarized in a schedule).

57. **A**   The write-off of accounts receivable is a noncash decrease in accounts receivable. Therefore, the increase (decrease) in accounts receivable for the period does not represent the true uncollected sales (additional collections). The write-off, as a noncash decrease in accounts receivable, would be deducted from sales to determine cash collections from customers. The increase in accounts receivable represents (results from) uncollected sales, and would be deducted from sales to determine cash collections from customers.

58. **D**   Cash flow per share should not be reported in financial statements. Neither cash flow per share, nor any component thereof, is an acceptable alternative to net income or earnings per share as a measure of performance.

59. **B**   To determine cash flows from operations, the depreciation expense must be removed because it is not a cash flow. Because the expense is a negative in net income, its removal is done through addition. The receivables went up, which means that $23,000 less cash was collected so that figure needs to be subtracted. The payables went up, which means that $9,000 less cash was paid so that figure needs to be added. Cash flows from operations is $300,000 plus $60,000 less $23,000 plus $9,000 or $346,000.

60. **C**   The acquisition of the building was done through signing a liability so no cash flows were used. The payment was a $20,000 financing activity (in connection with the liability) and a $3,000 operating activity (in connection with the interest). The equipment had a book value of $140,000 and was sold at an $11,000 gain so that $151,000 must have been received. Because an asset was sold, it is an investing activity.

61. **D**   The prepaid insurance went up indicating that the company made $11,000 in excess payments on that particular policy. The insurance payable went down $3,000, so the company overpaid on the second policy. Consequently, although $60,000 was reported as the expense for the period, the company actually paid an additional $11,000 and $3,000 or $74,000 in total.

62. **A**   The book value of the equipment prior to being sold was reduced from $180,000 to $168,000. Because this equipment was sold at a loss, the company only received $148,000.

CHAPTER 19 – ACCOUNTING FOR NOT-FOR-PROFIT ORGANIZATIONS

STUDY TIP

Always focus on learning the essentials of each topic. The CPA exam rarely gets into much depth on any topic, but instead prefers to focus on testing a very broad range of questions. It is better to know the essentials about every topic than to know any topic in serious depth and detail.

CHAPTER 19 – ACCOUNTING FOR NOT-FOR-PROFIT ORGANIZATIONS

INTRODUCTION

Not-for-profit (NFP) organizations provide socially desirable services without the intention of realizing a profit. They are financed by user charges, contributions from donors and/or foundations, investment income, and government grants. The nature and extent of support depends upon the type of NFP. These organizations include a wide array of organizations, such as public and private colleges, hospitals, charities, churches, and the like. NFP organizations are either in the private sector (nongovernmental) or in the public sector (governmental).

- **Private NFP Organizations**—Accounting for private NFP organizations, such as colleges, private sector health care entities operated by religious or other NFP organizations, voluntary health and welfare organizations, charities, and churches, falls under the authority of the Financial Accounting Standards Board (FASB). Accounting for these organizations resembles that used by for-profit businesses.
- **Public NFP Organizations**—Accounting for public NFP organizations, such as public colleges and universities, government hospitals, and government museums falls under the authority of the Governmental Accounting Standards Board (GASB).

In 1993, the FASB issued SFAS No. 116, *Accounting for Contributions Received and Contributions Made*, and SFAS No. 117, *Financial Statements of NFP Organizations*. These standards drastically changed the reporting for private NFPs. Prior to issuance of these standards, all NFP organizations reported on a fund accounting basis.

- As a result of these standards, funds for nongovernmental NFP can now be used only for internal reporting or as supplementary information to the new reporting requirements.
- The AICPA has developed two Audit Guides that correspond and add to the new FASB principles, one for NFP organizations and one for health care organizations.
- The NFP guide applies only to private sector NFPs. The health care guide applies to all health care entities, including private for-profit, private NFPs, and governmental.

Private NFPs follow the rules of the FASB. Therefore, any testing pertaining to private NFPs should follow the rules as set forth by the FASB (unless the NFP is specifically exempt from the application of the FASB). In addition, the NFPs must apply the FASB statements that pertain solely to those entities.

The new standards do not apply to governmental organizations, including public hospitals and public colleges, because these organizations are governed by GASB. Therefore, unless otherwise specified, the CPA exam questions on public hospitals and public colleges and universities should be answered by applying the rules as set forth by GASB. These entities are accounted for as enterprise funds.

FASB AND AICPA STANDARDS FOR PRIVATE SECTOR NOT-FOR-PROFITS

FINANCIAL STATEMENTS

SFAS No. 117 establishes standards for general purpose external reporting of NFP organizations. The reporting focus is on the entity as a whole rather than the disaggregated fund-by-fund reporting that was prevalent prior to the issuance of this statement. In addition to certain footnote disclosures, the four required financial statements for NFP organizations are as follows:

1. Statement of financial position—similar to a Balance Sheet.

2. Statement of activities—similar to an Income Statement.

3. Statement of cash flows.

4. Statement of functional expenses (only for voluntary health and welfare organizations, such as the American Red Cross, a mental health association, or a Big Brothers/Big Sisters organization).

STATEMENT OF FINANCIAL POSITION

A. The focus of the statement of financial position is the entity as a whole. Minimum display requirements are organization-wide total assets, total liabilities, and total net assets. In addition, total net assets must be presented in categories of permanently restricted, temporarily restricted, or unrestricted.

   1. **Permanently Restricted Net Assets** have donor-imposed restrictions that stipulate that resources be permanently maintained but permit the organization to expend the income. These may be donor-restricted gifts, such as artwork that must be used for a certain purpose and may not be sold; or a donor-restricted gift to be invested, with the principal preserved and the income available for expenditure; or land, when the land must be held in perpetuity.

   2. **Temporarily Restricted Net Assets** have donor-imposed restrictions that limit the assets' use. The restriction is satisfied with either the passage of time or by the accomplishment of the donor-imposed purpose. An example of a temporarily restricted net asset is a term endowment, where the principal must be kept intact for a period of time, but may be expended when the time restriction has passed. Donor-restricted gifts to be expended for certain purposes, such as for a special program or project, is another example of a temporarily restricted asset. The donor-restricted gift might be restricted to a specific fund, such as the building and equipment fund.

   3. **Unrestricted Net Assets** are contributions and assets that either have no restrictions or the restrictions have expired. Examples include assets from operations; unrestricted gifts of cash or other assets; temporarily restricted assets released due to satisfaction of the donor's provisions; or board-designated funds (funds restricted by the governing board rather than a donor external to the organization). Resources are presumed to be unrestricted, unless evidence exists that donor-imposed restrictions exist.

B. Assets and liabilities may be classified or reported in order of liquidity and payment date. Assets restricted for long-term purposes must be reported separately from those that are not. A comparative format is optional, as NFP organizations may report balances for only one year.

C. An entity may or may not capitalize "collections." These are works of art, historical treasures, and similar assets if those assets meet three specific conditions. (See the discussion on donated works of art below.) If collections are not capitalized, revenues (contributions) would not be recognized for donated collections. Extensive note disclosures regarding accessions, disposals, etc., are required.

D. Investments in all debt securities and investments in equity securities that have readily determinable fair values (except equity securities accounted for under the equity method and investments in consolidated subsidiaries) are to be reported at fair value in the statement of net assets.

E. Example: A sample statement of financial position follows:

Not-For-Profit Organization

STATEMENT OF FINANCIAL POSITION

June 30, 20X1 and 20X2

(in thousands)

Assets	20X2	20X1
Cash and cash equivalents	$ 75	$ 460
Accounts and interest receivable	2,130	1,670
Inventories and prepaid expenses	610	1,060
Contributions receivable	3,025	2,700
Short-term investments	1,400	1,000
Assets restricted to investment in land, buildings, and equipment	5,210	4,500
Land, buildings, and equipment	61,700	63,590
Long-term investments	218,070	203,500
Total assets	$292,220	$278,480
Liabilities and Net Assets		
Liabilities		
Accounts payable	$2,570	$1,050
Refundable advance		650
Grants payable	875	1,300
Notes payable		1,140
Annuity obligations	1,685	1,700
Long-term debt	5,500	6,500
Total liabilities	10,630	12,340
Net Assets		
Unrestricted	115,228	103,670
Temporarily restricted	24,342	25,470
Permanently restricted	142,020	137,000
Total net assets	281,590	266,140
Total liabilities and net assets	$292,220	$278,480

STATEMENT OF ACTIVITIES

A. The focus of the statement of activities is the entity as a whole. It shows the changes in unrestricted, temporarily restricted, permanently restricted, and total net assets. The full accrual basis of accounting is used.

   1. Revenues and expenses that are major or related to the central operations of the entity should be reported at gross amounts. Revenues could be netted with direct costs only if the activities are peripheral or incidental transactions (e.g., sale of a building or expenses associated with investment income).

   2. Revenues are recognized for each category of net asset. Revenue is presumed to be unrestricted, unless donor-imposed restrictions apply, either permanent or temporary.

   3. Revenue from contributions is recognized in accordance with the rules of SFAS No. 116. Unconditional contributions are to be recorded as assets (contributions receivable) and as revenues (contribution revenue). However, a donor-imposed condition causes a NFP organization to not recognize either a receivable or a revenue. A donor-imposed condition specifies a future or uncertain event whose occurrence or failure to occur gives the promisor a right of return of the assets transferred or releases the promisor from its obligation to transfer the assets promised.

   4. Multiyear contributions receivable are recorded at the present value of the future collections. Moneys to be collected in future years are presumed to be temporarily restricted revenues (based on time restrictions) and then reclassified in the year of receipt. The difference between the previously recorded temporarily restricted revenue at present value amounts and the current value would be recorded as contribution revenue, not interest. All contributions should be recorded at fair value as of the contribution date.

   5. SFAS 136 requires that when a NFP organization is an intermediary or an agent for the transfer of assets to another NFP organization, that intermediary or agent would not recognize a contribution, unless it is granted variance power to redirect the resources or it is financially interrelated. The receipt of resources would be offset with the recognition of a liability to the recipient organization. If variance power exists, the recipient organization would recognize contribution revenue. SFAS 136 also requires that the recipient organization recognize a revenue when the intermediary or agent recognizes a liability. When the intermediary or agent and the beneficiary are financially interrelated, the intermediary or agent would recognize contribution revenue; the beneficiary would recognize its interest in the net assets of the intermediary or agent.

   6. Exchange revenues (tuition, membership dues, charges for services, etc.) are increases in unrestricted net assets and are recognized in accordance with GAAP, as applied to business enterprises.

   7. Contributed services, when recognized, are recognized as both revenue and expense. However, contributed services should be recognized only when the services:

      a. Create or enhance non-financial assets.

      b. Require specialized skills and are provided by individuals possessing those skills and would typically be purchased if not provided by donation.

      *Note: See further discussion on **Contributed Services** later in this chapter.*

   8. Expenses are reported as reductions to unrestricted net assets.

9. Expenses using resources that are temporarily restricted, including depreciation of plant, would be matched by a reclassification of resources from temporarily restricted to unrestricted net assets. The reclassification category of the statement of activities is unique. Sometimes "Reclassifications" are called "Net Assets Released from Restrictions." Reclassifications generally include satisfaction of program restrictions, satisfaction of equipment acquisition restrictions, satisfaction of time restrictions, and expiration of term endowment.

10. If the provisions of a temporary restriction are met in the period of the gift, the revenue and expenses may be reported in the unrestricted category.

11. Expenses are required to be reported by functional classification, either on the face of the statement or in the notes to the financial statements. Functional classifications include major classes of program services and supporting services. Program services are activities that result in goods and services being distributed that fulfill the mission of the organization. A university's major programs would include instruction and research. A health care provider's major programs would include patient care and research. Supporting services include management and general, fundraising, and membership development activities (activities that are not program activities). Other classifications, such as operating income, maybe be included but are not required, except for health care organizations. Combined costs that include elements of both program service and supporting services should be allocated between the two types in a rational manner.

12. Fund-raising expenses must be disclosed in the notes, if not in the statement of activities.

13. Unlike SFAS 115 for business enterprises, all unrealized gains and losses are to be reflected in the statement of activities, along with realized gains and losses in the appropriate net asset class.

14. Gains and losses can be recognized in all three categories of net assets.

B. Example: A statement of activities follows:

Note: Organizations have flexibility as to the format of the statement. It should be presented so it is useful and understandable to its users.

Not-for-Profit Organization

STATEMENT OF ACTIVITIES

Year Ended June 30, 20X1

(in thousands)

	Unrestricted	Temporarily Restricted	Permanently Restricted	Total
Revenues, gain, and other support:				
Contributions	$8,640	$8,110	$280	$17,030
Fees	5,400			5,400
Income on long-term investments	5,600	2,580	120	8,300
Other investment income	850			850
Net unrealized and realized gains on long-term investments	8,228	2,952	4,620	15,800
Other	150			150
Net assets released from restrictions:				
Satisfaction of program restrictions	11,990	(11,990)		
Satisfaction of equipment acquisition restrictions	1,500	(1,500)		
Expiration of time restrictions	1,250	(1,250)		
Total revenues, gains and other support	$43,608	($1,098)	$5,020	$47,530
Expenses and losses:				
Program A	13,100			13,100
Program B	8,540			8,540
Program C	5,760			5,760
Management and general	2,420			2,420
Fund raising	2,150			2,150
Total expenses	$31,970			$31,970
Fire loss	80			80
Actuarial loss on annuity obligations		30		30
Total expenses and losses	$32,050	$30	$-0-	$32,080
Change in net assets	11,558	(1,128)	5,020	15,450
Net assets at beginning of year	103,670	25,470	137,000	266,140
Net assets at end of year	$115,228	$24,342	$142,020	$281,590

STATEMENT OF CASH FLOWS

A. NFPs must present a statement of cash flows similar to the statement required of business enterprises. In general, the FASB rules for cash flow statement, required by SFAS 95 apply to NFP organizations. The statement must show cash flows from operating, cash flows from investing, and cash flows from financing activities in three separate sections. The total changes from the three sections should be the total change in cash from the beginning to the end of the year.

1. Unlike the statement of financial position and statement of activities, there is no distinction in the statement of cash flows for donor-imposed restrictions.

2. Operating activities include cash flows from the ongoing operations of the entity, including unrestricted gifts.

3. Investing activities include purchase or sale of plant, property, or equipment, and purchase or sale of investments.

4. Financing activities include issuance or repayment of debt and the receipt of both temporarily and permanently restricted resources stipulated by the donor to be used for long-term purposes. Related interest and dividends that are donor-restricted for long-term purposes are also shown as cash receipts from financing activities.

5. Cash flows from operating activities can be prepared using either the direct or indirect methods. If the direct method is used, there should be a reconciliation using the indirect method to show the change in total net assets from the activities statement to net cash used by operating activities.

6. Noncash gifts, such as investments or furniture, are disclosed as noncash investing and financing activities.

B. Example: A sample statement of cash flows follows:

Not-for-Profit Organization

STATEMENT OF CASH FLOWS

Year Ended June 30, 20X1

(in thousands)

Cash flows from operating activities:

Cash received from service recipients	$5,220
Cash received from contributors	8,030
Cash collected on contributions receivable	2,615
Interest and dividends received	8,570
Miscellaneous receipts	150
Interest paid	(382)
Cash paid to employees and suppliers	(23,808)
Grants paid	(425)
Net cash used by operating activities	($30)

Cash flows from investing activities:

Insurance proceeds from fire loss on building	250
Purchase of equipment	(1,500)
Proceeds from sale of investments	76,100
Purchase of investments	(74,900)
Net cash used by investing activities	($50)

Cash flows from financing activities:

Proceeds from contributions restricted for:	
Investment in endowment	200
Investment in term endowment	70
Investment in plant	1,210
Investment subject to annuity agreements	200
Cash Flows from Restricted Contributions	$1,680

Other financing activities:

Interest and dividends restricted for reinvestment	300
Payments of annuity obligations	(145)
Payments on notes payable	(1,140)
Payments on long-term debt	(1,000)
Cash Flows from Other Financing Activities	($1,985)
Net cash used by financing activities	($305)
Net decrease in cash and cash equivalents	($385)
Cash and cash equivalents at beginning of year	$460
Cash and cash equivalents at end of year	$ 75

Reconciliation of change in net assets to net cash used by operating activities:

Change in net assets	$15,450

Adjustments to reconcile change in net assets to net cash used by operating activities:

Depreciation	3,200
Fire loss	80
Actuarial loss on annuity obligations	30
Increase in accounts and interest receivable	(460)
Decrease in inventories and prepaid expenses	390
Increase in contributions receivable	(325)
Increase in accounts payable	1,520
Decrease in refundable advance	(650)
Decrease in grants payable	(425)
Contributions restricted for long-term investment	(2,740)
Interest and dividends restricted for long-term investment	(300)
Net unrealized and realized gains on long-term investments	(15,800)
Net cash used by operating activities	$ (30)

Supplemental data for noncash investing and financing activities:

Gifts of equipment	$140
Gift of paid-up life insurance, cash surrender values	$80

STATEMENT OF FUNCTIONAL EXPENSES

A. Voluntary health and welfare organizations must present a statement of functional expenses along with their other financial statements. This statement provides information by functional classification (program services and supporting services) and by natural classification (salaries, rent, electric, interest expense, depreciation expense, etc.) in a matrix format.

B. Example: A sample statement of functional expenses follows:

Voluntary Health and Welfare Organization

STATEMENT OF FUNCTIONAL EXPENSES

Year Ended June 30, 20X1

(in thousands)

		Program			Management	
	Total	A	B	C	& General	Fundraising
Salaries, wages, and benefits	$15,115	$7,400	$3,900	$1,725	$1,130	$960
Grants to other organizations	4,750	2,075	750	1,925		
Supplies and travel	3,155	865	1,000	490	240	560
Services and professional	2,840	160	1,490	600	200	390
Office and occupancy	2,528	1,160	600	450	218	100
Depreciation	3,200	1,440	800	570	250	140
Interest	382				382	
Total Expenses	$31,970	$13,100	$8,540	$5,760	$2,420	$2,150

NOTES TO FINANCIAL STATEMENTS

A. NFP organizations must have notes to accompany their financial statements. Disclosure and display requirements as set by GAAP are applicable to nonprofit organizations, unless there is a specific exemption from the requirement. For example, NFP organizations should apply the disclosure and display provisions for financial instruments; loss contingencies; extraordinary, unusual, and infrequently occurring events; and accounting changes.

1. Specific requirements of SFAS No.117 include:

a. Policy disclosures of choices related to restricted contributions received and expended in the same period.

b. Policy disclosures related to the recording of plant as temporarily restricted or unreserved.

c. More detailed information regarding the nature of temporarily and permanently restricted resources.

2. In addition, information about the nature and amounts of permanently, temporarily, and unrestricted net assets must either be reported on the face of the financial statement or in the notes to the statements.

3. The FASB specifically encourages note disclosures on the following:

a. Detail of reclassification.

b. Detail of investments.

   c.   Breakdown of expenses by function and natural classifications (except for voluntary health and welfare organizations that must include this information in the Statement of Functional Expenses).

4.   FASB requires that fund-raising expenses be reported either on the face of the financial statements or in the notes. AICPA Statement of Position 98-2 indicates that when an activity might involve fund-raising and either program or management and general activities, such as a mailing, it is presumed to be fund raising unless three criteria exist. Those criteria are as follows:

   a.   Purpose. The activity has more than one purpose as evidenced by whether compensation or fees for performing the activity are based strictly on the amount raised or on the performance of some program and/or management and general activity.

   b.   Audience. If the audience is selected on the basis of its likelihood to contribute to the NFP, this criterion is not met.

   c.   Content. In order for this criterion to be met, the mailing or event must include a call to action other than raising money. For example, a mailing from the American Cancer Society might call for recipients to have regular check-ups, exercise, eat the right kinds of food, etc.

CONTRIBUTIONS

A.   *Contributions* are unconditional transfers of cash or other assets to an entity, or the settlement or cancellation of an entity's liabilities. The transfer must be nonreciprocal, meaning the donor receives no direct benefit from this exchange. In general, contributions received, including unconditional promises of cash or other assets, are recognized as revenue in the period received at their fair value.

1.   Contributions without donor-imposed restrictions are reported as unrestricted revenue that increases unrestricted net assets.

2.   Restricted contributions are contributions that limit the use of the donated asset. These contributions are recognized as revenue when the pledge is made. The revenue would be classified as either increasing temporarily restricted or permanently restricted net assets, depending upon the nature of the restriction.

   a.   Temporarily restricted assets would include unconditional promises to contribute in the future. These pledges would be recorded at the present value of the estimated future cash flows. A provision for uncollectible pledges should be established.

   b.   Conditional promises are pledges that will occur only if a specified future event takes place. These contributions are recognized when the condition upon which the donation is based is substantially met (becomes unconditional). Assets received subject to conditions are accounted for as refundable advances until the conditions are met. A conditional contribution is considered unconditional if the possibility the condition will not be met is remote.

   Note: Conditions create barriers that must be overcome before assets are transferred, whereas restrictions put limitations on how the assets can be used after they are transferred. Both conditions and restrictions can exist in the same gift.

   When a donor receives an item in return for the contribution, the contribution revenue is calculated by deducting the fair value of the item the donor receives from the amount of the donation. For example, if a nonprofit organization receives a donation of $250, but the donor receives theater tickets with a fair value of $50, the contribution revenue is $200.

Contributed Services

A. Contributions of services are recognized at fair value as unrestricted revenue and an offsetting expense, if the services received meet either of the following two criteria:

1. The donated services create or enhance nonfinancial assets (e.g., materials and labor donated by a construction company to renovate a hospital wing or an architect's services to design the wing would enhance the value of the hospital).

2. The donated services require specialized skills, are provided by people possessing those skills, and would typically be purchased if they had not been donated (e.g., accountants, architects, doctors, lawyers, teachers, electricians, and plumbers).

B. If the above criteria are not met, donated services are not recorded. The following contributions of services would not be recognized as revenue because they do not meet either of the aforementioned two criteria:

1. Donated telemarketing services performed by a professional telemarketing company.

2. Advice on general business matters provided by an attorney who is an uncompensated trustee of the NFP, provided the attorney typically suggests the organization seek the opinion of legal counsel on substantive or complex legal questions.

3. Services of local high school students who provide services, such as reading and playing chess with elderly patients of a hospital's long-term care program.

Donated Fixed Assets Including Works of Art

Fixed assets donated to a NFP organization are generally recorded at fair value on the date of the gift as an asset with an offsetting credit to unrestricted revenue (or restricted, if applicable). As an option, a time-implied restriction can be presumed and the donation can be reported as temporarily restricted net assets. If that is done, an amount equal to depreciation expense should be reclassified each period to reduce the temporarily restricted column and increase the unrestricted column. The same alternative is available if a long-lived asset is acquired with the use of temporarily restricted net assets.

A. An entity has the option not to record contributions of works of art, historical treasures, and similar assets, if the collections meet all of the following criteria:

1. The collections are held for public exhibition, education, or research in furtherance of public service rather than financial gain.

2. The collections are protected, kept unencumbered, cared for, and preserved.

3. The collections are subject to an organizational policy that requires the proceeds from sales of collection items to be used to acquire other collections.

B. In addition, works of art and historical treasures with extraordinarily long lives need not be depreciated.

ACCOUNTING FOR CERTAIN INVESTMENTS HELD BY NFP ORGANIZATIONS

A. NFP organizations are required to report certain equity securities (equity securities with readily determinable fair values not accounted for under the equity method or as investments in consolidated subsidiaries) and all debt securities at fair value.

1. Realized or unrealized gains and losses on investments resulting from a change in the market value of the securities are reported in the statement of activities in the period in which the change in value occurs. These gains and losses are shown as a change in unrestricted net assets unless the use is temporarily or permanently restricted by explicit donor stipulations or by law.

2. Interest and dividends are recognized as an increase in unrestricted net assets, unless their use is temporarily or permanently restricted by explicit donor stipulations or by law. If a restriction exists that will be met in the same period as the revenue or the gain occurs, the revenue or gain can be reported as unrestricted.

3. Investment income includes the interest, dividend, and realized and unrealized gains and losses on investments resulting from the change in the market value of the securities.

4. The options available to account for donor-restricted endowment funds are limited as follows:

   a. If the donor stated, or if applicable laws require, that gains are to be added to endowment principal, the gain should be shown as an increase in permanently restricted net assets.

   b. If there are no requirements to add gains to endowment principal, the gain will be added to temporarily restricted net asset, if there is a restriction as to how or when the income can be spent.

   c. If there are no restrictions, the gains are added to unrestricted net assets.

   d. If a realized or unrealized loss is sustained that reduces the balance of the endowment below its historical cost (usually the original amount of the gift or the original amount of the gift adjusted by inflation), it cannot reduce the permanently restricted net assets below the historical cost of the endowment. The loss must be recognized as a reduction in either of the following:
      - Temporarily restricted net assets (if in prior years appreciation in the endowment had been recognized in this category of net asset and the appreciation has not yet been spent).
      - Unrestricted net assets (if the loss exceeds the net appreciation remaining in the temporarily restricted asset category).

   e. If the loss is recovered in subsequent years, the unrealized and realized gain must first be recognized as an increase in unrestricted net assets to the extent that they were previously written down. Additional gains follow the normal rules for gains.

ACCOUNTING FOR HEALTH CARE ORGANIZATIONS

As mentioned earlier, the AICPA has issued an AICPA Audit and Accounting Guide (AICPA Guide) for health care organizations. This guide applies to both private sector and governmental health care organizations. NFP health care providers are required to follow FASB guidance. They may use fund accounting for internal accounting records or as supplemental information to the minimum reporting requirements.

Governmental health care organizations are not allowed to use the principles established in SFAS No. 116 and No. 117 for NFP organizations. The AICPA Guide does, however, attempt to present accounting and reporting principles allowed by the GASB in as close a fashion as possible to private sector health care organizations. Whether the organization is NFP, investor-owned, or governmental, accounting and reporting for all types should be similar when possible.

Requirements of the AICPA Guide apply to clinics, medical group practices, individual practice associations, individual practitioners, emergency care facilities, laboratories, surgery centers, other ambulatory care organizations, continuing care retirement communities, health maintenance organizations, home health agencies, hospitals, nursing homes, and rehabilitation centers.

Sometimes, a fine line is drawn between those organizations considered health care entities and those considered voluntary health and welfare organizations that are not covered by the AICPA Guide. The distinction is made by the source of revenues, not by the services provided.

- A NFP organization providing health care service in return for payment (an exchange transaction) by the recipient of the service, by a third-party payer (such as an insurance company), or a government program would be considered a health care organization.
- A NFP organization providing health care service, funded primarily by voluntary contributions (from persons or organizations not receiving a service), would be considered a voluntary health and welfare organization.

BASIS OF ACCOUNTING

Health care providers should use the accrual basis of accounting and should match revenues with expenses.

FINANCIAL STATEMENTS

The basic financial statements of health care organizations consist of a balance sheet, statement of operations, statement of changes in net assets, cash flow statement, and notes to the financial statements.

NFP organizations present these statements following the minimum display requirements previously set forth. The governmental organizations may provide individual fund statements and then combine these statements to be part of the enterprise fund presented in accordance with GASB 34.

BALANCE SHEET

NFP organizations, except for continuing care retirement communities, must present a classified balance sheet and give information about the liquidity of assets and liabilities. The assets of the balance sheet may be divided into categories, such as current, assets limited as to use, and plant. The equity section must show unrestricted, temporarily restricted, permanently restricted, and total net assets.

STATEMENT OF OPERATIONS

NFP health care organizations have special reporting requirements including the following:
- A performance indicator should be reported in the statement of operations, as well as in the statement of net assets.
- The performance indicator should be clearly labeled with a descriptive term, such as revenue over expenses, revenues and gains over expenses and losses, earned income, or performance earnings. The notes to the financial statements should include a description of the nature and composition of the performance indicator.

- Dividends, interest, and other similar investment income, realized gains and losses on investments, unrealized gains and losses on trading securities, and other than temporary impairment losses are included in the performance indicator, if the assets are unrestricted.

The AICPA Guide specifically indicates that the following six items (at least) must be reported separately from (or underneath) the performance indicator (this is a partial list):

1. Equity transfers involving other entities that control the reporting entity, are controlled by the reporting entity, or are under the common control of the reporting entity.

2. Receipt of restricted contributions.

3. Contributions of (and assets released from donor restrictions related to) long-lived assets.

4. Unrealized gains and losses on investments not restricted by donors or by law (except for those investments classified as trading securities as noted above).

5. Investment returns restricted by donors or by law.

6. Other items required by GAAP to be reported separately, such as extraordinary items, the effect of discontinued operations, and accounting changes.

REVENUE

A. Revenue from Health Care Services—Revenue is classified based on the type of service rendered or contracted to be rendered. Gross patient service revenue is derived from fees charged for patient care. It is recorded on an accrual basis at the provider's established rates, regardless of whether the health care organization expects to collect that amount. Patient service revenue does not include charity care because these services are never expected to result in cash inflows. Net patient service revenue is calculated by deducting contractual and other adjustments, such as workers' compensation, no-fault insurance, and courtesy or employee discounts, from gross service revenue. The net patient service revenue is shown on the statement of operations. Significant revenue under capitation agreements (revenues from third-party payers based on number of employees to be covered, etc., instead of services performed) is to be reported separately. *Note: Disclosure should indicate the methods of revenue recognition and description of the types and amounts of contractual adjustments.*

  1. Premium revenue is earned as a result of an agreement to provide health care, rather than from the actual provision of services.

  2. Resident service revenue is related to maintenance fees, rental fees, or amortization of advance fees.

  3. Other revenue and gains include interest and dividends, certain realized changes in market values of marketable securities, rentals of health care facility space, fees charged for transcripts for lawyers and insurance companies, revenue from educational programs, auxiliary activities (e.g., gift shop, cafeteria, parking lot), and donated medicines and supplies. In governmental health care organizations, restricted funds are recognized as other operating revenue only when the funds are expended and only to the extent of the amount spent. Donated fixed assets, such as equipment, are directly recorded as a credit to fund balance in the general fund, not to revenue.

  4. Contribution revenue is recorded at fair value on the date of the contribution.

Note: Money held in a permanent trust by a bank, where the hospital does not control the funds but only gets the earnings, is not an asset of the hospital and, therefore, is not recorded. A memorandum entry would only be sufficient disclosure.

EXPENSES

Expenses are decreases in unrestricted net assets. Expenses may be reported on the face of the financial statements using either a natural classification or a functional presentation. NFP organizations are required to disclose expenses by functional classification in the notes, if the natural classification is used on the face of the operating statement. Functional classifications should be based on full-cost allocations. Unlike organizations subject to the NFP guide, health care organizations may report depreciation, interest, and bad debt expense, along with functional categories.

Typical hospital functional classifications include the following:

- Nursing Services.
- Other Professional Services.
- General Services.
- Administrative Services.
- Uncollectible Accounts.
- Depreciation.
- Interest.

THIRD PARTY CONSIDERATIONS

Some third party payers reimburse the health care organization on an interim basis and retrospectively determine final amounts reimbursable for services rendered based on allowable costs. The health care provider should estimate the receivable from or the payable to these payers in the same period the services are rendered.

GOVERNMENTAL HEALTH CARE ORGANIZATIONS

A. Governmental health care organizations are permitted by GASB 34 to report as special-purpose entities engaged in governmental or business-type activities, or both. Most will choose to report as special-purpose entities engaged in business-type activities.

B. Governmental health care organizations reporting as special-purpose entities engaged in business-type activities will prepare the statements required for proprietary funds. These are the balance sheet, the statement of revenues, expenses, and changes in net assets and the statement of cash flows.

C. GASB principles must be followed in the separate reports of governmental health care organizations. For example, net assets are to be categorized as invested in capital assets net of related debt, restricted and unrestricted. The GASB cash flow format should be used.

D. To the extent possible, the principles in the AICPA health care guide should also be followed.

ACCOUNTING FOR COLLEGES AND UNIVERSITIES

GASB Statement No. 35, *Basic Financial Statements—and Management's Discussion and Analysis—for Public Colleges and Universities* permits public colleges to report as special-purpose entities engaged in governmental or business-type activates, or both. Most 4-year institutions are expected to report as special-purpose entities engaged only in business-type activities. Some community colleges may choose to report as special-purpose entities engaged in governmental activities, due to the extent of state and local government tax support.

Colleges and universities, like hospitals, may be private NFP organizations, or they may be public institutions.

- Private institutions must follow the rules as set by the FASB and, therefore, must present the same three financial statements (statement of financial position, activities statement, and statement of cash flows) and meet the same minimum display requirements of all other nonprofit organizations.
- Public colleges and universities must follow the rules as set by the GASB. They have the option to use either the governmental or AICPA audit guide reporting models.

REVENUE

A. Typical revenues of a college or university include the following:

   1. Student tuition and fees. These amounts are reported net of refunds. Amounts not collected as a result of scholarships, tuition remissions to relatives of school employees, tuition waivers, and provisions for uncollectible accounts should not reduce revenues, but should instead be reported separately in a revenue deduction account as in the following example:

Cash	8,000	
Revenue Deduction—Student Scholarships	2,000	
Revenue—Student Tuition and Fees		10,000

   2. Further, student graduate assistantships and other amounts given as tuition remissions (e.g., for full-time employees) given in return for services provided to the institution are charged as expenses to the department and function where the services are provided.

Cash	8,000	
Expense—Instruction (Accounting Department)	2,000	
Revenue—Student Tuition and Fees		10,000

   3. When tuition payments that are applicable to future years are received, they should be reported as deferred revenues and treated as liabilities until the appropriate term.

      a. Government aid, grants, and contracts.

      b. Private gifts and grants.

      c. Endowment income.

      d. Sales and services of educational activities.

      e. Sales and services of auxiliary enterprises, such as residence halls, food services, intercollegiate athletics, and college stores.

DEPRECIATION EXPENSE

The AICPA Guide specifically states that operation and maintenance of physical plant is not to be reported as a functional expense. Those costs, including depreciation, are to be allocated to other functions.

NET ASSETS

The changes in net assets must be shown separately for unrestricted, temporarily restricted and permanently restricted net assets.

EXPENSES AND LOSSES

Expenses are reported as decreases in unrestricted net assets. Losses may be reported as decreases in any of the net asset classes.

ACCOUNTING FOR OTHER GOVERNMENTAL NFP ORGANIZATIONS

Other governmental NFP organizations (essentially governmental voluntary health and welfare and "other" NFP organizations) may also be considered special-purpose entities that may be engaged in either governmental or business-type activities, or both. However, GASB 34 specifically permits these organizations that were using the AICPA Not-for-Profit Model to report as special purpose entities engaged in business-type activities upon adoption of GASB 34. These entities will present proprietary fund statements. The AICPA guide for NFP organizations applies only to private sector organizations as previously described.

QUESTIONS: ACCOUNTING FOR NON-FOR-PROFIT ORGANIZATIONS

1. Public colleges use a(n):
    A. economic resources measurement focus.
    B. current resources focus.
    C. modified accrual accounting approach.
    D. cash basis accounting approach.

2. According to SGAS 35, a public university is required to report:
    A. fund-based financial statements.
    B. institution-wide (government-wide) financial statements.
    C. a balance sheet for the general fund.
    D. an actual versus budget report for the special revenue fund.

3. A management's discussion and analysis report for public colleges:
    A. is optional.
    B. should be reported as part of the footnotes.
    C. is required and should precede the financial statements.
    D. is required and should follow the presentation of each financial statement.

4. According to SGAS 35, cash flow statements for public universities are:
    A. optional.
    B. required and must use the indirect method.
    C. optional, but if disclosed, must use the indirect method.
    D. required and must use the direct method.

5. Under SGAS 35, public colleges must capitalize infrastructure assets. Which of the following items is not an infrastructure asset?
    A. Road.
    B. Bridge.
    C. Sidewalk.
    D. Computer equipment.

6. Capital assets of universities:
    A. must be depreciated.
    B. should not be depreciated.
    C. must be depreciated by private colleges but not by public colleges.
    D. may not be depreciated by private colleges but must be depreciated by public colleges.

7. SGAS 35 requires that public universities that have university hospitals should report these as:
    A. separate funds.
    B. component units.
    C. primary institutions.
    D. a major fund.

8. Expenses of public colleges should be reported by:
    A. object.
    B. function.
    C. either object or function.
    D. character.

9. The cost of construction of a university dormitory would be shown on a cash flow statement as cash flows from:
    A. operations.
    B. investing activities.
    C. financing activities.
    D. noncapital financing.

10. Cash flows from a public university bookstore would appear on the statement of cash flows as cash flows from:
    A. operations.
    B. investing activities.
    C. financing activities.
    D. noncapital financing.

11. Public universities must disclose separately in their cash flow statements capital and noncapital related:
    A. investing activities.
    B. financing activities.
    C. operational activities.
    D. changes in net assets.

12. Interest paid on capital debt and leases must be reported on public colleges' cash flow statements as cash from:
    A. operations.
    B. investing activities.
    C. capital and related financing activities.
    D. noncapital financing activities.

13. The cost of construction of a university dormitory would be shown on a cash flow statement as cash flows from:
    A. investing activities.
    B. operations.
    C. financing activities.
    D. noncapital financing.

14. On the statement of net assets for a public university, the restricted net assets are divided between nonexpendable and expendable net assets. The nonexpendable net assets allow for the expenditures of:
    A. principal only.
    B. principal and earnings.
    C. earnings only.
    D. neither principal nor earnings.

15. SFAS 117 requires which of the following financial statements for private not-for-profit organizations?
    A. Statement of financial position, statement of activities and changes in net assets, and a statement of cash flows.
    B. Balance sheet and income statement.
    C. Statement of cash flows, statement of revenues expenses and changes in net assets, and a statement of financial position.
    D. Balance sheet income statement for each fund.

16. Private not-for-profit organizations should report a statement of cash flows using the:
    A. direct method.
    B. working capital method.
    C. indirect method.
    D. indirect or direct method.

17. On the statement of activities for a private college, expenses should be deducted from:
    A. temporarily unrestricted revenues.
    B. unrestricted revenues.
    C. unrestricted revenues and temporarily unrestricted revenues.
    D. permanently restricted revenues.

18. On the statement of activities for a private university, expenses are reported by:
    A. character.
    B. department.
    C. object.
    D. function.

19. On the statement of activities and changes in net assets for private not-for-profit institutions, the changes in net assets should be presented for:
    A. unrestricted and permanently restricted net assets.
    B. unrestricted, temporarily restricted, and permanently restricted net assets.
    C. unrestricted net assets only.
    D. unrestricted and temporarily restricted net assets.

20. On the statement of activities for a private not-for-profit institution, net assets released from restrictions, would be shown under revenues, gains, and other support as a decrease in:
    A. permanently restricted and an increase in temporarily restricted net assets.
    B. restricted and an increase in temporarily restricted net assets.
    C. temporarily restricted and increase in permanently restricted net assets.
    D. temporarily restricted and increase in unrestricted net assets.

21. A statement of functional expenses is required for which of the following private not-for-profit institutions?
    A. Hospital.
    B. Voluntary health and welfare organization.
    C. Fraternal organization.
    D. College.

22. The statement of financial position for a private not-for-profit college should show separate dollar amounts for:
    A. all accounts in its equity section.
    B. unrestricted net assets only.
    C. unrestricted net assets and temporarily restricted net assets.
    D. unrestricted net assets, temporarily restricted net assets, and permanently restricted net assets.

23. According to SFAS 117, the financial statements for a not-for-profit entity should focus on the:
    A. economic resources measurement approach.
    B. current resources measurement approach.
    C. basic information for the organization as a whole.
    D. modified accrual approach.

24. The cash flows from operating activities section of the cash flow statement for a private not-for-profit college using the indirect method would begin with:
    A. net income from operations.
    B. net change in working capital.
    C. change in unrestricted net assets.
    D. total changes in net assets.

25. The statement of cash flows for a private not-for-profit performing arts center should report cash flows according to which of the following classifications?
    A. Operating activities, investing activities, and financing activities.
    B. Operating activities, noncapital activities, and capital activities.
    C. Investing activities, capital activities, and financing activities.
    D. Financing activities, noncapital activities, and capital activities.

26. Guil College, a private not-for-profit college, received the following cash inflows:
    • $400,000 from students for tuition.
    • $200,000 from a donor who stipulated that the money be invested indefinitely and the earnings used for student scholarships.
    • $100,000 from a donor who stipulated that the money be spent according to the wishes of the board of trustees.

    Which amounts of these cash flows should be shown on the cash flow statement as cash from operating activities?
    A. $700,000.
    B. $400,000.
    C. $600,000.
    D. $500,000.

27. Smith College, a private not-for-profit college, received the following cash inflows:
    - Cash contributions of $200,000 to be permanently invested.
    - Cash dividends and interest of $10,000 for purchase of video equipment for the accounting department.

    How would these cash inflows be disclosed on the Smith College cash flow statement?
    A. $10,000 from operations and $200,000 from financing activities.
    B. $210,000 from operating activities.
    C. $210,000 from financing activities.
    D. $210,000 from investing activities.

28. SFAS 117, *Financial Statements of Not-for-Profit Organizations,* focuses on:
    A. basic information for the organization as a whole.
    B. standardization of funds nomenclature.
    C. inherent differences of not-for-profit organizations that impact reporting presentations.
    D. distinctions between current fund and noncurrent fund presentations.

29. A large not-for-profit organization's statement of activities should report the net change for net assets that are:

	Unrestricted	Permanently restricted
A.	Yes	Yes
B.	Yes	No
C.	No	No
D.	No	Yes

30. Lea Meditators, a not-for-profit religious organization has adopted FASB Statement No. 116, *Accounting for Contributions Received and Contributions Made.* A storm broke glass windows in Lea's building. A member of Lea's congregation, a professional glazier, replaced the windows at no charge. In Lea's statement of activities, the breakage and replacement of the windows should:
    A. not be reported.
    B. be reported by note disclosure only.
    C. be reported as an increase in both expenses and contribution revenue.
    D. be reported as an increase in both net assets and contribution revenue.

31. On December 30, 20X4, Leigh Museum, a not-for-profit organization, received a $7,000,000 donation of Day Co. shares with donor stipulated requirements as follows:
    - Shares valued at $5,000,000 are to be sold with the proceeds used to erect a public viewing building.
    - Shares valued at $2,000,000 are to be retained with the dividends used to support current operations.

    Leigh has adopted SFAS 117, *Financial Statements of Not-for-Profit Organizations.* As a consequence of the receipt of the Day shares, how much should Leigh report as temporarily restricted net assets on its 20X4 statement of financial position?
    A. $0.
    B. $2,000,000.
    C. $5,000,000.
    D. $7,000,000.

32.　The Jones family lost its home in a fire. On December 25, 20X4, a philanthropist sent money to the Amer Benevolent Society to purchase furniture for the Jones family. During January 20X5, Amer purchased this furniture for the Jones family. Amer, a not-for-profit organization has adopted SFAS 116, *Accounting for Contributions Received and Contributions Made*. How should Amer report the receipt of the money in its 20X4 financial statements?
　　A.　As an unrestricted contribution.
　　B.　As a temporarily restricted contribution.
　　C.　As a permanently restricted contribution.
　　D.　As a liability.

33.　Glen Hope, a voluntary Health and Welfare organization, received a cash donation from George Swinney to purchase equipment for the organization's kitchen. The donation was received in 20X1, but the equipment was not purchased until 20X2. For 20X1 Glen Hope should report the donation on the statement of activities as:
　　A.　nonoperating revenue.
　　B.　unrestricted revenue.
　　C.　endowment fund revenue.
　　D.　temporarily restricted revenue.

34.　CIBA, a nonprofit performing arts organization, received a contribution of a term endowment and a regular endowment. These endowments should be reported on the statement of activities as follows:

	Term endowments	Regular endowments
A.	Permanently restricted	Permanently restricted
B.	Temporarily restricted	Permanently restricted
C.	Temporarily restricted	Temporarily restricted
D.	Unrestricted	Temporarily restricted

35.　Vista, a voluntary health and welfare organization, received a donation of $100,000 to be spent in accordance with the wishes of the institution's board of trustees. This donation should be reported on the statement of activities as:
　　A.　unrestricted revenue.
　　B.　other income—gifts.
　　C.　temporarily restricted revenue.
　　D.　permanently restricted revenues.

36.　Gray College, a private not-for-profit institution, received a contribution of $100,000 for faculty research. The donation was received in 20X1 and $80,000 was spent in 20X1. As a result of these transactions, Gray College should report on its 20X1 statement of activities a:
　　A.　$20,000 increase in temporarily restricted net assets.
　　B.　$100,000 increase in temporarily restricted net assets.
　　C.　$80,000 increase in temporarily restricted net assets.
　　D.　$100,000 increase in unrestricted net assets.

37. Clay University, a not-for-profit university, earned $300,000 from bookstore revenue and spent $100,000 for faculty research in 20X1. The $100,000 for faculty research came from a $150,000 research grant received in the previous year. What is the effect of these events on unrestricted net assets in 20X1?
    A. Increase $300,000.
    B. Increase $400,000.
    C. Increase $450,000.
    D. Increase $200,000.

38. Ellen College, a private not-for-profit institution, received a $100,000 grant for faculty research in 20X1. The grant money was not spent until 20X2. For 20X1, Ellen College should report the contribution as:
    A. unrestricted revenue.
    B. temporarily restricted revenue.
    C. other operating revenue.
    D. other nonoperating revenue.

39. Which of the following transactions of a private voluntary health and welfare organization would *increase* temporarily restricted net assets in the statement of activities for the current year?

    I. In the current year, received a contribution of $20,000 from a donor who stipulated that the money not be spent until the following year.
    II. Spent $25,000 for fund raising during the current year from a donation from the previous year.

    A. I only.
    B. I and II.
    C. II only.
    D. Neither I nor II.

40. In November 20X1, Gilmore Heating and Air Conditioning Service repaired the air conditioning system for GenCare, a voluntary health and welfare organization, and mailed an invoice for $3,000. On December 25, a note was received by GenCare indicating that Gilmore was canceling the invoice and that repairs were being donated. For the year ended, December 31, 20X1, GenCare should report these contributed services as:
    A. a footnote.
    B. nothing; no disclosure is required, but a thank-you note was mailed to Gilmore.
    C. an increase in unrestricted revenues and an increase in expenses on the statement of activities.
    D. an increase in temporarily restricted net assets in the statement of activities.

41.   The Granger Community Foundation, a private not-for-profit institution, received the following contributed services:

I.   Ernst and Dalton, a legal firm, contributed advice to the foundation in relation to the handling of the organization's endowment funds.

II.   Senior citizens participated in a telethon to raise money for the new computer equipment for the organization.

Which of these services would be recorded on the statement of activities?
A.   I and II.
B.   I only.
C.   Neither I nor II.
D.   II only.

42.   On December 31, 20X1, the board of trustees of a private, not-for-profit college designated $5,000,000 of unrestricted net assets for the construction of an addition to the music building. What effect does this designation have on the college's unrestricted and temporarily restricted net assets shown on the statement of financial position on December 31, 20X1?

	Unrestricted net assets	Temporarily restricted net assets
A.	Decrease	Increase
B.	Decrease	No effect
C.	No effect	Increase
D.	No effect	No effect

43.   The following contributions were received by a private voluntary health and welfare organization. Which of these would not be recorded as an increase in unrestricted revenue?
A.   A carpenter donated labor and materials for the construction of a deck.
B.   A painter donated paint and labor to paint all the meeting rooms.
C.   A retired college professor donated reading services to senior citizens. The organization would not have paid for these services if they had not been donated.
D.   A CPA firm donated its services to audit the financial statements for the past year.

44.   A local voluntary health and welfare organization had the following expenditures:

Administrative salaries	$20,000
Work to help elderly citizens	$60,000
Fund-raising costs	$5,000
Child care services provided for indigent families	$40,000

How should these items be reported by the organization?

	Program service expense	Supporting service expense
A.	$120,000	$5,000
B.	$100,000	$25,000
C.	$105,000	$20,000
D.	$ 80,000	$45,000

45. Which one of the following is not a required financial statement for a private voluntary health and welfare organization?
     A. Statement of Financial Position.
     B. Statement of Activities and Changes in Net Assets.
     C. Statement of Fund Balance.
     D. Statement of Cash Flows.

46. Gerlack College, a private, not-for-profit institution, received a donation of $2,000,000 as a challenge grant. If the college raises an additional $2,000,000 within the next two years, it may keep the donation. If it fails, the $2,000,000 must be returned to the donor. How would the college record the receipt of the grant?
     A. Unrestricted revenue.
     B. Temporarily restricted revenue.
     C. Note to the financial statement.
     D. Refundable advance.

47. Which one of the following is a voluntary health and welfare organization?
     A. Charity raising money for underprivileged children.
     B. Nursing home.
     C. Clinic.
     D. Hospital.

48. A private not-for-profit performing arts center receives the following three donations:
     • A gift of $90,000 that is unrestricted.
     • A gift of $125,000 restricted for payment of salaries.
     • A gift of $200,000 that is restricted forever but the income from the gift may be used for current expenditures.

     Which of the following is false?
     A. The temporarily restricted net assets increased by $125,000.
     B. The permanently restricted net assets increased by $325,000.
     C. When the money is spent for salaries, unrestricted net assets increase and decrease by the same amount.
     D. When the money is spent for salaries, temporarily restricted net assets decrease.

49. A voluntary health and welfare organization had the following asset inflows:

Cash gifts	$40,000
Membership dues	$8,000
Dividend income	$5,000
Interest income	$3,000
Donated supplies	$2,000

     How should these items be reported?

	Revenues	Public support
A.	$16,000	$42,000
B.	$8,000	$50,000
C.	$56,000	$2,000
D.	$10,000	$48,000

50. A private, not-for-profit college holds debt securities in current assets and in noncurrent assets. How would these items be reported on the statement of financial position?

	Debt securities in current assets	Debt securities in noncurrent assets
A.	Fair value	Carrying value
B.	Carrying value	Fair value
C.	Fair value	Fair value
D.	Carrying value	Carrying value

51. Vista, a private, not-for-profit health and welfare organization, purchased stock in XYZ Corp., using unrestricted net assets and paid $50,000. The investment represents less than 2% interest in XYZ. At the end of the year, Vista received a cash dividend of $3,000, and the value of the XYZ stock at year-end was $65,000. On its statement of activities from the current year, what amount would Vista report from XYZ?

A. $18,000 increase in unrestricted net assets.
B. $15,000 increase in temporarily restricted net assets.
C. $3,000 in unrestricted net assets.
D. $15,000 increase in unrestricted net assets.

52. Electra, a not-for-profit performing arts organization, held some donor restricted endowment funds that are invested in stocks listed on the New York Stock Exchange, so the fair values are readily determinable. Most of the investments represent amounts between 2% and 5% of the outstanding common stock of the invested corporations. However, Electra does own stock in one company, which gives it the ability to exercise significant influence over the operating and financing policies of the invested company. How should these two types of investments be reported on Electra's statement of financial position at year end?

	Equity securities 2%–5% ownership	Equity securities significant influence
A.	Fair value	Fair value
B.	Equity method	Equity method
C.	Fair value	Equity method
D.	Fair value	Carrying value

53. A hospital has the following account balances:

Amount charged to patients	$500,000
Revenue from newsstand	$15,000
Undesignated gifts	$40,000
Contractual adjustments	$70,000
Interest income	$12,000
Salaries expense–nurses	$120,000
Bad debts	$8,000

What is the hospital's net patient service revenue?
A. $422,000.
B. $430,000.
C. $500,000.
D. $540,000.

54. According to the AICPA audit and accounting guide, which one of the following is not a required financial statement for a health care organization?
    A. Statement of operations.
    B. Balance sheet.
    C. Statement of changes in equity.
    D. Statement of functional expense.

55. Which one of the following is not one of the financial statements required for a health care organization?
    A. Statement of operations.
    B. Statement of cash flows.
    C. Balance sheet.
    D. Income statement.

56. Which account would be credited in recording a gift of medicine to a nursing home from an outside party?
    A. Non-Operating Gain—Donations.
    B. Contractual Adjustments.
    C. Patient Service Revenues.
    D. Other Revenues—Donations.

57. A private, not-for-profit organization has received a valuable historical document worth $190,000. Officials of this organization do not want to record this donation as both an asset and a revenue. Which of the following would necessitate the other organization's recording of the gift?
    A. The item will be used solely for exhibition purposes.
    B. The item will be used solely for research purposes.
    C. The organization makes a commitment to preserve the document for the foreseeable future.
    D. The organization has no formal plan to use any money received if the document is ever sold.

58. In accounting for hospitals, what are third-party payers?
    A. Drug companies who supply free drugs for charity patients.
    B. Doctors who reduce fees for poor patients.
    C. Insurance companies, Medicare, and other groups that pay a significant portion of medical fees for patients.
    D. A computer company who repairs the hospital's computers without charge.

59. What is a contractual adjustment?
    A. An adjusting entry made at year-end to accrue unpaid patient service revenue.
    B. A reduction of patient service revenue for charity care.
    C. An allocation of the cost of patient care to the departments that supply the patient care.
    D. A reduction in patient service revenue because of agreements with third-party payers that allow them to pay a health care entity based on the agreed upon determination of reasonable cost.

60.   Fike Hospital, a private, not-for-profit institution, receives an unrestricted gift of common stock with a fair value of $100,000. The donor had paid $40,000 for the stock five years earlier. The gift should be recorded as an:
   A.   increase in temporarily restricted net assets of $100,000.
   B.   increase in unrestricted net assets of $100,000.
   C.   increase in temporarily restricted net assets of $40,000.
   D.   increase in unrestricted net assets of $40,000.

61.   Which of the following types of health care organizations follow FASB statements?

	Investor-owned health care enterprises	Private not-for-profit organizations	Governmental health organizations
A.	Yes	Yes	No
B.	Yes	Yes	Yes
C.	No	No	Yes
D.	Yes	No	Yes

62.   Which of the following types of health care organizations recognize depreciation expense?

	Investor-owned health care enterprises	Governmental not-for-profit organizations	Health care organizations
A.	Yes	Yes	No
B.	Yes	No	Yes
C.	No	No	Yes
D.	Yes	Yes	Yes

63.   In accruing patient charges for the current month, which one of the following accounts should a hospital credit?
   A.   Accounts Payable.
   B.   Patient Service Revenues.
   C.   Unearned Revenue.
   D.   Deferred Revenue.

64.   According to the AICPA Audit Guide, hospitals should prepare which of the following financial statements?

	Statement of Changes in Net Assets	Statement of Operations
A.	Yes	No
B.	Yes	Yes
C.	No	Yes
D.	No	No

65.   The Weyman Hospital, a private, not-for-profit institution, reported the following information:

Gross patient service revenue	$1,000,000
Allowance for discounts to hospital employees	$20,000
Bad debt expense	$40,000
Contractual adjustments	$100,000

What amount should the hospital report as net patient service revenue?
A. $840,000.
B. $900,000.
C. $880,000.
D. $980,000.

66.   A private not-for-profit hospital provided $150,000 in charity care for the current year. The hospital should report this charity care as:
A. net patient service revenue of $150,000 and patient care expense of $150,000.
B. net patient service revenue of $150,000 on the statement of operations.
C. only in the notes to the financial statements.
D. an unpaid accounts receivable on the balance sheet.

67.   The Johnson Hospital, a private not-for-profit hospital, received the following revenues in the current year:

Proceeds from sales of the hospital's flower shop	$60,000
Dividends and interest revenue not restricted	$20,000
Cash contributions for the renovation of the children's ward in the hospital	$200,000

Which of these amounts should be reported as other revenues and gains (other revenue) on the statement of operations?
A. $280,000.
B. $60,000.
C. $80,000.
D. $260,000.

68.   The Whitlow Hospital, a private, not-for-profit hospital, uses as its performance indicator revenues and gains over expenses and losses. Which of the following items would be included in the calculation of this indicator?
•   Unrealized gains on other than trading securities. The securities are included in the unrestricted net assets.
•   Contributions received from a donor in the current year that cannot be spent until the following year.

A. Neither.
B. Both.
C. Unrealized gains only.
D. Contribution only.

69.   The AICPA Audit Guide requires that private not-for-profit hospitals report a performance
        indicator on its statement of operations. Which of the following items would be included in the
        calculation of the performance indicator?
        •   Proceeds from cafeteria sales to non-patients.
        •   Net assets released from restrictions used for operating expenses.

        A. Both.
        B. Neither.
        C. Proceeds from cafeteria sales.
        D. Net assets released from restrictions used for operating expenses.

70.   On December 31, 20X1, Dahlia, a nongovernmental, not-for-profit organization, purchased a
        vehicle with $15,000 unrestricted cash and received a donated second vehicle having a fair value of
        $12,000. Dahlia expects each vehicle to provide it with equal service value over each of the next
        five years and then to have no residual value. Dahlia has an accounting policy implying a time
        restriction on gifts of long-lived assets. In Dahlia's 20X2 statement of activities, what depreciation
        expense should be included under changes in unrestricted net assets?
        A. $0.
        B. $2,400.
        C. $3,000.
        D. $5,400.

71.   Home Care, Inc., a nongovernmental voluntary health and welfare organization, received two
        contributions in 20X3. One contribution of $250,000 was restricted for use as general support in
        20X4. The other contribution of $200,000 carried no donor restrictions. What amount should
        Home Care report as temporarily restricted contributions in its 20X3 statement of activities?
        A. $450,000.
        B. $250,000.
        C. $200,000.
        D. $0.

72.   The University of Sea Land is a public, not-for-profit school that views its entire operation as
        being an enterprise fund. Which of the following is true?
        A. The amount spent for capital assets should be reported as an expenditure.
        B. The university is only required to produce government-wide financial statements.
        C. The university must report a statement of cash flows.
        D. The university will report both a government-wide set of financial statements and a fund-
            based set of statements.

73.   A private, not-for-profit organization receives donated services valued at $19,000. These services
        did not require a specialized skill. Under what condition should these services be reported by the
        organization on its financial statements?
        A. Only if they would have been acquired by the organization if not donated.
        B. Under no condition should they be reported.
        C. Only if they enhance a nonfinancial asset.
        D. All donated services should be recognized if they have a value that can be determined.

74. A private, not-for-profit university receives $100,000 that, according to the donor, must be spent for computers. On the last day of the year, $67,000 of this amount was properly spent. No time restriction was set for the use of these computers. In addition, students were charged tuition of $300,000 but were also awarded $110,000 in financial aid. For unrestricted net assets, what was the total amount of revenue, contributions, and reclassifications?
    A. $400,000.
    B. $367,000.
    C. $290,000.
    D. $257,000.

75. For a private, not-for-profit organization, how are expenses reported?
    A. As decreases in unrestricted net assets, temporarily restricted net assets, or permanently restricted net assets, depending on the donors stipulations.
    B. As decreases in unrestricted net assets or temporarily restricted net assets, depending on the donor's stipulations.
    C. As decreases in unrestricted net assets or permanently restricted net assets, depending on the donor's stipulations.
    D. As decreases in unrestricted net assets.

76. A private, not-for-profit organization receives a pledge from a past donor for another gift of $125,000 in cash. Under what condition should the pledge be recognized.
    A. Only if the pledge is viewed as an unconditional gift.
    B. Only if the money is received within the next 12 months.
    C. In all cases, pledges are recognized.
    D. Only if the pledge is viewed as a conditional gift where the condition will eventually be met.

77. Mr. Rich gives $100,000 to United Charity on Monday, with the stipulation the money will be given to the National Association for Dolphin Protection (NADP). However, prior to the actual conveyance, Mr. Rich has the right to divert the gift to a different beneficiary. If the financial statements are produced on Tuesday and United Charity is still holding the money, how much contribution revenue should United Charity recognize, and how much contribution revenue should NADP recognize at that time?

	United Charity	NADP
A.	$0	$0
B.	$100,000	$0
C.	$0	$100,000
D.	$100,000	$100,000

ANSWERS: ACCOUNTING FOR NOT-FOR-PROFIT ORGANIZATIONS

1. **A** SGAS 35 requires public colleges to use an economic resources measurement focus and accrual accounting.

2. **B** Answers A, C, and D are incorrect because they are fund-based reports, and fund-based reports are not required by SGAS 35.

3. **C** The management's discussion and analysis is required and should precede the financial statements.

4. **D** Cash flow statements must be presented, and the direct method is required.

5. **D** Roads, bridges, and sidewalks are all examples of infrastructure assets.

6. **A** Capital assets must be depreciated by both private and public colleges.

7. **B** Answers A and D are incorrect because public universities are not required to report fund-based statements. Answer C is incorrect because the university, not the hospital, is the primary institution.

8. **C** Expenses may be reported using either object or function according to SGAS 35.

9. **B** Construction cost would be an investing activity.

10. **A** Cash flows from a public university's bookstore would be cash from operations.

11. **B** Public universities must disclose capital-related and noncapital-related financing activities separately in their cash flows statements.

12. **C** It must be reported as cash from capital and related financing activities.

13. **A** Construction cost is an investing activity.

14. **C** Nonexpendable net assets allow for the expenditure of earnings but not principal.

15. **A** SFAS 117 requires statement of financial position, statement of activities and changes in net assets, and a statement of cash flows.

16. **D** SFAS 117 states that either the direct or indirect method may be used.

17. **B** Expenses are deducted from unrestricted revenues.

18. **D** Expenses must be reported by function.

19. **B** SFAS 117 requires a disclosure of unrestricted, temporarily restricted, and permanently restricted net assets.

20. **D** Net assets released from restrictions would cause a decrease in temporarily restricted and an increase in unrestricted net assets.

21. **B** SFAS 117 requires a statement of functional expenses for voluntary health and welfare organizations. The statement is optional for all other not-for-profit private institutions.

22. **D** SFAS 117 requires separate dollar amounts for unrestricted net assets, temporarily restricted net assets, and permanently restricted net assets.

23. **C** SFAS 117 requires that financial statements focus on basic information for the organization as a whole.

24. **D** The cash flow statement would begin with total changes in net assets.

25. **A** The statement of cash flows should be classified as operating activities, investing activities, and financing activities.

26. **D** The $200,000 donation would be an investing activity, and the other two amounts would be operating activities.

27. **C** The $200,000 cash contribution is a financing activity, and because the cash dividends and interest are restricted for purchase of video equipment and not available for operations, they are also considered financing activities.

28. **A** SFAS 117 focuses on the entity concept and views not-for-profits as a single unit rather than prior concepts that viewed the entity as being made up of component parts (fund accounting concepts).

29. **A** The statement of activities reports the changes in all classes of net assets (unrestricted, temporarily restricted, and restricted).

30. **C** SFAS 116 states that contributed services should be recognized if the services (1) require specialized skills and (2) they would typically need to be purchased if not provided by donation. When recognizing donated services, that entity would record the fair value of the service as a contribution and an expense.

31. **C** SFAS 117 states that there are three classifications of net assets—unrestricted, temporarily restricted, and permanently restricted. Temporarily restricted net assets are subject to a time or task requirement to use funds in a particular way. Leigh Museum received $5,000,000 of temporarily restricted assets (building construction) and $2,000,000 of permanently restricted funds (amount never to be spent).

32. **B** The contribution received was for a specific purpose. It could only be spent for furniture for the Jones family. Therefore, the contribution is restricted for that purpose and no other.

33. **D** Because it was not spent in the current year, the donation should be considered temporarily restricted revenue.

34. **B** Because the term endowment allows a portion of the principal to be spent each period, it is temporarily restricted. The regular endowment does not allow any of the principal to be spent; therefore, it is permanently restricted.

35. **A** Because the donation is not restricted, it should be shown as unrestricted revenue.

36. **A** The initial receipt of $100,000 would increase temporarily restricted net assets by $100,000, but the $80,000 that was spent is a classification reduction in temporarily restricted net assets for a net increase of $20,000.

37. **A** The $300,000 in bookstore revenue increased unrestricted net assets by $300,000. The reclassification of the $100,000 for research from temporarily restricted to unrestricted increased unrestricted net assets by $100,000, but this was offset by the $100,000 expenditure that decreased unrestricted net assets. The net effect is a $300,000 increase in unrestricted net assets.

38. **B** Because the contribution was not spent in the current year, it should be classified as temporarily restricted revenue.

39. **A** The $20,000 contribution is time restricted and cannot be spent in the current year; therefore, it should increase temporarily restricted net assets. The $25,000 for fund raising would decrease temporarily restricted net assets because it would be reclassified and transferred to unrestricted net assets for the current year.

40. **C** Because this donation replaces skilled services that would ordinarily have been paid for, it is recorded as expenses and unrestricted revenues.

41. **B** Contributions of skilled advice the organization would normally pay for are recorded as expenses and unrestricted revenues. The senior citizens' contribution does not require special skills and would not be recorded by the organization.

42. **D** Because the restriction is an internal, not an external, restriction, the classification of unrestricted net assets does not change.

43. **C** A, B, and D are all contributions of skilled labor the organization would ordinarily have paid for. The reading services do not require any special skills and would not be recorded.

44. **B** Child care and work with the elderly are program services that total $100,000. Administrative salaries and fund raising costs are supporting services that total $25,000.

45. **C** Because fund accounting is no longer required, a statement of fund balances is not reported.

46. **D** SFAS 116 states that a conditional grant should be recorded as a refundable advance.

47. **A** B, C, and D are health care organizations.

48. **B** Permanently restricted net assets would increase $200,000 for the gift that is restricted forever. When the salaries are going to be paid, the temporarily restricted net assets are reclassified (decreased) to unrestricted net assets (increased). When the salaries are actually paid out of unrestricted net assets, unrestricted net assets decrease.

49. **A** Revenues are membership dues, dividend income, and interest income for a total of $16,000. Public support consists of cash gifts and donated supplies for a total of $42,000.

50. **C** SFAS 124 requires the assets be reported at fair value.

51. **A** According to SFAS 124, the unrealized gain on XYZ of $15,000 and the dividend revenue ($3,000) from the unrestricted investments would be included in the statement of activities.

52. **C** The 2% to 5% ownership is covered by SFAS 124 and should be reported at fair value. SFAS 124 does not cover investments with significant influence, but APB #18 would require the use of equity method.

53. **B** Amount charged to patients minus contractual adjustments equals $430,000.

54. **D** Only voluntarily health and welfare organizations are required to issue a statement of functional expenses.

55. **D** Health care organizations are required to issue a statement of operations, not an income statement.

56. **D** A gift of medicine would be credited to other revenues—donations.

57. **D** A private, not-for-profit organization has the option to omit the reporting of an art work or museum piece, but only if three specific rules are met: (1) the item is used for research, education, or exhibit, (2) the item is protected and preserved, and (3) a policy is in place so if the item is ever sold, the money will be used to acquire a similar replacement item.

58. **C** A, B, and D are examples of donated services or supplies.

59. **D** Answer D is the only one that involves a contract with an outside party.

60. **B** Donations of unrestricted net assets should be recorded at fair value in the unrestricted net assets.

61. **A** Governmental health care organizations follow GASB statements.

62. **D** All health care organizations are required to recognize depreciation expense.

63. **B** Patient charges are accrued as patient service revenues.

64. **B** The AICPA Audit Guide requires a balance sheet, a statement of operations, a statement of changes in net assets, and a statement of cash flows.

65. **C**   Gross patient service revenue less the allowance for discounts to hospital employees and less contractual adjustments equals net patient service revenue of $880,000.

66. **C**   The AICPA Audit Guide requires the amount of charity care and the policy for providing charity care to be disclosed in the footnotes.

67. **C**   The revenue from the flower shop and the unrestricted dividends and interest should be reported as other revenues and gains for a total of $80,000.

68. **A**   Answers B and D are incorrect because the contributions should be included in temporarily restricted net assets. The unrealized gains are not a part of the performance indicator, according to the AICPA Audit Guide, but should be reported on the statement of operations after the performance indicator.

69. **A**   Both the sales from the cafeteria and the net assets released from the restrictions used for operating purposes would be included in the performance indicator.

70. **D**   A nongovernmental, not-for-profit organization would calculate the depreciation just like a corporation. Total cost of $27,000 divided by 5 years equals $5,400.

71. **B**   Because the $250,000 cannot be spent until 20X4, a time restriction applies and the contribution would be classified as temporarily restricted in the 20X3 financial statements. The $200,000 contribution is not restricted and would be reported as unrestricted revenue.

72. **C**   As an organization that is open to the public for a user fee, public, not-for-profit organizations can often view themselves as solely an enterprise fund. If that decision can be justified, the organization does not have to produce both government-wide and fund-based financial statements because they are quite similar for a proprietary fund. Only fund-based financial statements are required because enterprise funds are reported very much like a for-profit organization, rather than like governmental funds.

73. **C**   Donated services can only be recognized by a private, not-for-profit organization under one of two situations. First, the service requires a specialized skill that the donor has and that would have been acquired if not donated. These donated services did not require a specialized skill so this path is not appropriate. The only other situation where recording is required is when a nonfinancial asset, such as a building or computer, is enhanced.

74. **D**   Tuition revenue is always reported net of scholarships and financial aid. Thus, the net tuition revenue is shown as $190,000. Because the gift is designated by the donor, the $100,000 is initially reported as an increase in temporarily restricted net assets. When $67,000 is properly spent, that amount is reclassified for temporarily restricted to unrestricted net assets. Thus, the total increase is $190,000 plus $67,000, or $257,000.

75. **D**   All operating expenses are reported as decreases in unrestricted net assets. In that way, the organization is able to report its changes in unrestricted net assets as the equivalent of an operating statement. Expenses are not spread over several classifications but are all grouped within unrestricted net assets.

76. **A**   Pledges are only recognized as receivables if they are unconditional in nature. In other words, the organization is not required to do anything in order to qualify for the gift. The donor has made a commitment to make the gift, but it will not be conveyed until a future point in time.

77. **A**   Because of the rights retained by Mr. Rich, he is still in control of the ultimate utilization of the money. United Charity can make no use of the money and has no revenue; NADP is not sure it will actually get the money and has no revenue.

CHAPTER 20 – INTANGIBLE ASSETS

STUDY TIP

The AICPA provides a free 6-month subscription to their research database for candidates who have received their Notice to Schedule (NTS). Have you subscribed to this excellent free resource? If not, please go to *www.cpa-exam.org* and do so now. It's a tremendous benefit for practicing your research skills for the simulations.

CHAPTER 20 – INTANGIBLE ASSETS

INTANGIBLE ASSETS

A. Intangible assets are used to generate revenues but have no physical substance. As compared to a tangible operational asset, intangibles have a much less certain future economic benefit.

    1. Intangibles can be purchased from outside the company, or they can be developed internally. Purchased intangibles are amortized, unless they have an unlimited life. Internally developed intangibles are generally expensed (R&D).

    2. An exception to the immediate expensing of internally developed intangibles is any cost(s) incurred to maintain or protect that intangible after it is developed (e.g., legal and filing fees).

B. Common examples include the following:

    1. Patents.

    2. Goodwill.

    3. Leasehold improvements (the right to use improvements in leased property).

    4. Copyrights.

C. Examples arising out of purchase accounting (consolidation method), where the purchase price reflects items contained in the subsidiary, include the following:

- Internet domain names.
- Customer lists.
- Noncompetition agreements.
- Databases.

ACCOUNTING FOR INTANGIBLE ASSETS

A. Intangible assets are normally amortized using the straight-line method over the useful life of the asset. (Some intangibles have a longer *legal life*; but useful life is the key for amortization.)

B. The useful life is determined based on the use to be made of the asset, any legal life restrictions, the expected action of competitors, et cetera. Think of "useful life" as the "revenue-generating life" of the intangible asset. The legal life of a copyright on a book may be a lot longer than the period of time the book will actually sell and generate revenues for the company.

C. There is no maximum period restriction for amortization of intangibles.

D. Remember the following:

    1. Organization costs and start-up costs are expensed immediately.

    2. Leasehold improvements are amortized over the life of the improvement or the life of the lease, whichever is shorter.

3. Goodwill is not amortized. Rather, it is tested each year for possible impairment.

4. Development stage enterprises are those that have not started their principal operations or have not earned significant revenues from those principal operations. GAAP requires these companies to follow the same principles for expensing and capitalizing amounts as established enterprises. Therefore, normal operating expenses are still expensed.

E. Intangible assets are subject to the impairment rules discussed earlier under Tangible Operational Assets.

1. Intangible assets with finite lives follow the same rules as for tangible assets with finite lives discussed above.

2. Intangible assets with infinite lives follow a different procedure.

a. They are tested for impairment annually or more frequently if circumstances indicate that an asset may be impaired.

b. To determine impairment, compare the fair value of the asset with its book value. If book value is greater, the difference between fair and book values is recorded as an impairment loss.

c. There is no recoverability test for intangible assets with indefinite lives (as there was for assets with definite lives) because the "recoverability" is indefinite.

d. If there is an impairment loss recorded on an infinite life intangible, the new book value is the basis of future amortization, and the write-down can never be recovered.

e. Remember: Impairment rules need to be applied separately for (1) tangible assets and intangibles with limited lives, and (2) intangibles with unlimited lives.

ACCOUNTING FOR GOODWILL

A. Goodwill is unique among intangible assets: it is not separable from the company as a whole, and therefore, goodwill cannot be identified with any specific right or benefit.

B. Goodwill is only acquired in connection with the acquisition of another company.

C. In an acquisition, goodwill represents the difference between the purchase price of the acquisition and the fair value of the assets making up the acquisition. In effect, goodwill represents the value of the assets taken as a whole, as opposed to the value of a group of individual assets purchased separately.

D. Goodwill is not amortized, but it is examined at least annually for impairment. As with other intangibles that have unlimited lives, if circumstances indicate, goodwill may be examined for impairment more than once a year.

The steps are as follows:

1. If the fair value of a **reporting unit** is less than its book value, an impairment loss is recorded.

2. A reporting unit is an operating segment or part of an operating segment that provides discrete financial information, and for which the company regularly reviews the operating results.

3. If goodwill is being examined for impairment at the same time as other operational assets, the other assets must be examined and written down (if appropriate) first.

4. The fair value of the goodwill asset must be implied from the fair value of the reporting unit taken as a whole.

    a. The fair values of the identifiable assets in the reporting unit are determined.

    b. The fair value of the reporting unit is determined.

    c. The fair value of the goodwill is the fair value of the reporting unit in excess of the fair values of the identifiable assets added together.

5. The fair value of the goodwill thus determined is compared to the book value of the goodwill. If book value exceeds fair value, an impairment loss is recorded for the difference.

ACCOUNTING FOR RESEARCH AND DEVELOPMENT (R&D) COSTS CONTAINED IN SFAS 2

A. **Research** (R) is the search for and discovery of new knowledge for potential profit.

B. **Development** (D) is the translation of research into a plan for a profitable product.

C. Research and Development (R&D) costs are expensed immediately. In this way, all companies handle these costs in a comparable manner that is not subject to any manipulation or judgment. The principle behind this treatment is the great deal of uncertainty inherent in the entire process of developing new products and processes; a high percentage of new products fail each year.

    1. This expensing includes the costs of long-lived assets such as buildings and equipment if acquired for use in a specific project with no alternative future use.

    2. The cost of a long-lived asset acquired for R&D is not expensed immediately if it has alternative future uses. The cost is capitalized with subsequent amortization classified as R&D expense for any project in which it is used.

    3. In a purchase consolidation, any amount paid because the subsidiary has in-process R&D should be expensed immediately.

D. Note that the capitalized cost of a patent is the total of the legal costs of establishing and perhaps successfully defending the patent in any lawsuit. Such costs do not need to be expensed immediately. (Patents purchased from others are capitalized. Patents developed internally are expensed immediately, except for these additional legal expenses to defend it.)

E. R&D costs are usually those incurred prior to the start of commercial production of a new product, service, or process. Costs incurred after commercial production might be expensed or charged to inventory, depending upon their nature.

F. Examples of R&D: (1) laboratory research aimed at the discovery of new knowledge; (2) searching for applications of new research findings; (3) design, construction, and testing of preproduction prototypes and models; and (4) modification of the formulation or design of a product or process.

G. Examples that are not R&D: (1) anything on the CPA exam that says "commercial production"; (2) routine ongoing efforts to improve an existing product; and (3) items that include the term "continuing commercial activity."

H. R&D Performed for Others is expensed as a cost of goods sold.

ACCOUNTING FOR THE DEVELOPMENT OF SOFTWARE THAT IS TO BE SOLD, LEASED, OR OTHERWISE MARKETED PER SFAS 86

A. Until a product reaches the stage of technological feasibility (when a company has a *program design* or *working model*), all costs are recorded as R&D expenses.

B. After a product has achieved technological feasibility, further software development costs are capitalized. Technological feasibility occurs at the completion of all planning, designing, coding, and testing necessary to meet design specifications. Capitalized costs may include coding and testing, and the creation of product masters. Amortization begins when the product is available for general release to customers. Capitalized development costs are amortized to the income statement each year using the greater of:

   1. Straight-line figure.

   2. The percentage of current sales to total expected sales.

C. Actual production costs are reported as inventory.

D. *Note*: Software purchased for internal use is normally capitalized, although software developed internally is usually expensed.

QUESTIONS: INTANGIBLE ASSETS

1. On January 2, Year 3, Lava, Inc. (Lava) purchased a patent for a new consumer product for $90,000. At the time of purchase, the patent was valid for 15 years; however, the patent's useful life was estimated to be only ten years due to the competitive nature of the product. On December 31, Year 6, the product was permanently withdrawn from sale under government order because of a potential health hazard in the product. What amount should Lava charge against income during Year 6, assuming amortization is recorded at the end of each year?
    A. $9,000.
    B. $54,000.
    C. $63,000.
    D. $72,000.

2. Which of the following statements concerning patents is correct?
    A. Legal costs incurred to successfully defend an internally developed patent should be capitalized and amortized over the patent's remaining economic life.
    B. Legal fees and other direct costs incurred in registering a patent should be capitalized and amortized on a straight-line basis over a 5-year period.
    C. Research and development contract services purchased from others and used to develop a patented manufacturing process should be capitalized and amortized over the patent's economic life.
    D. Research and development costs incurred to develop a patented item should be capitalized and amortized on a straight-line basis over 17 years.

3. On December 31, Year 5, Byte Co. (Byte) has capitalized software costs of $600,000 with an economic life of four years. Sales for Year 6 were 10% of expected total sales of the software. At December 31, Year 6, the software had a net realizable value of $480,000. In its December 31, Year 6 balance sheet, what amount should Byte report as net capitalized cost of computer software?
    A. $432,000.
    B. $450,000.
    C. $480,000.
    D. $540,000.

4. Cody Corp. (Cody) incurred the following costs during Year 6:

Design of tools, jigs, molds, and dies involving new technology	$125,000
Modification of the formulation of a process	$160,000
Troubleshooting in connection with breakdowns during commercial production	$100,000
Adaptation of an existing capability to a particular customer's need as part of continuing commercial activity	$110,000

    In its Year 6 income statement, Cody should report research and development expense of:
    A. $125,000.
    B. $160,000.
    C. $235,000.
    D. $285,000.

5.　　On January 1, Year 6, Jamin Corp. (Jamin) purchased equipment for use in developing a new product. Jamin uses the straight-line depreciation method. The equipment could provide benefits over a 10-year period. However, the new product development is expected to take five years, and the equipment can be used only for this project. Based on the above, Jamin's Year 6 depreciation included in R&D expense equals:

A. $0.
B. 1/10 of the total cost of the equipment.
C. 1/5 of the total cost of the equipment.
D. The total cost of the equipment.

6.　　On December 31, Year 5, Billy Co. (Billy) has capitalized costs for a new computer software product with an economic life of five years. Sales for Year 6 were 30% of expected total sales of the software. At December 31, Year 6, the software had a net realizable value equal to 90% of the capitalized cost. What percentage of the original capitalized cost should be reported as the net amount on Billy's December 31, Year 6 balance sheet?

A. 70%.
B. 72%.
C. 80%.
D. 90%.

7.　　In January Year 6, Mosario Co. (Mosario) purchased a mineral mine for $2,640,000 with removable ore estimated at 1,200,000 tons. After it has extracted all the ore, Mosario will be required by law to restore the land to its original condition at an estimated cost of $220,000. The present value of the estimated restoration costs is $180,000. Mosario believes it will be able to sell the property afterwards for $300,000. During Year 6, Mosario incurred $360,000 of development costs preparing the mine for production and removed and sold 60,000 tons or ore. In its Year 6 income statement, what amount should Mosario report as depletion?

A. $135,000.
B. $144,000.
C. $150,000.
D. $159,000.

8.　　Wind Co. incurred organization costs of $6,000 at the beginning of its first year of operations. How should Wind treat the organization costs in its financial statements in accordance with GAAP?

A. Never amortized.
B. Amortized over 60 months.
C. Amortized over 40 years.
D. Expensed immediately.

9.　　Tech Co. bought a trademark on January 2, two years ago. The intangible was being amortized over 40 years. The carrying value at the beginning of the current year was $38,000. It was determined that the cash flow will be generated indefinitely at the current level for the trademark. What amount should Tech report as amortization expense for the current year?

A. $0.
B. $922.
C. $1,000.
D. $38,000.

10. On January 1, Year 1, a company leases a building to the Waterson Corporation for 20 years with the lessee having the option to extend the lease for an additional ten years. Both parties feel it is very reasonable to assume that this option will be taken because of the low rental rates being offered. Both parties report this lease as a capital lease. Immediately after signing the lease, Waterson constructs several walls inside of the building as well as attaching some book shelves. These additions had a cost of $100,000 and are expected to last for 25 years. At the end of Year 1, which of the following should be reported by Waterson?
    A. An intangible asset with a net book value of $95,000.
    B. An intangible asset with a net book value of $96,000.
    C. A tangible asset labeled building improvement with a net book value of $95,000.
    D. A tangible asset labeled building improvement with a net book value of $96,000.

11. The Gatewood Corporation is working to develop a computer software program that can be sold to the public. The company spends $800,000 to get the product to the point at which it is viewed as technologically feasible. The company spends another $110,000 to take the product from technological feasibility to the point at which it is ready to be sold. Which of the following statements is true?
    A. $910,000 is capitalized.
    B. $800,000 is expensed, and $110,000 is capitalized.
    C. $910,000 is expensed.
    D. $800,000 is capitalized, and $110,000 is expensed.

12. During Year 1, Jamison Corporation incurred research costs of $200,000 and development costs of another $120,000. On July 1, Year 1, a patent was granted in connection with this research and development work. The costs of registering this patent were $85,000. The patent has a legal life of 17 years, but an expected useful life of 10 years. On December 31, Year 1, what is the net book value of the intangible assets reported by Jamison?
    A. $80,750.
    B. $82,500.
    C. $194,750.
    D. $384,750.

13. Which of the following costs of goodwill should be capitalized?

	Maintaining goodwill	Developing goodwill
A.	Yes	No
B.	No	No
C.	Yes	Yes
D.	No	Yes

14. Hy Corp. bought Patent A for $40,000 and Patent B for $60,000. Hy also paid acquisition costs of $5,000 for Patent A and $7,000 for Patent B. Both patents were challenged in legal actions. Hy paid $20,000 in legal fees for a successful defense of Patent A and $30,000 in legal fees for an unsuccessful defense of Patent B. What amount should Hy capitalized for patents?
    A. $162,000.
    B. $112,000.
    C. $65,000.
    D. $45,000.

15.   During 20X5, Jase Co. incurred research and development costs of $136,000 in its laboratories relating to a patent that was granted on July 1, 20X5. Costs of registering the patent equaled $34,000. The patent's legal life is 17 years, and its estimated economic life is 10 years. In its December 31, 20X5, balance sheet, what amount should Jase report as patent, net of accumulated amortization?
A. $32,300.
B. $33,000.
C. $161,500.
D. $165,000.

16.   On January 2, 20X5, Judd Co. bought a trademark from Krug Co. for $500,000. Judd retained an independent consultant, who estimated the trademark's remaining life to be 50 years. Its unamortized cost on Krug's accounting records was $380,000. Judd decided to amortize the trademark over the maximum period allowed. In Judd's December 31, 20X5, balance sheet, what amount should be reported as accumulated amortization?
A. $7,600.
B. $9,500.
C. $10,000.
D. $12,500.

17.   On January 2, 20X5, Rafa Co. purchased a franchise with a useful life of ten years for $50,000. An additional franchise fee of 3% of franchise operation revenues must be paid each year to the franchisor. Revenues from franchise operations amounted to $400,000 during 20X5. In its December 31, 20X5, balance sheet, what amount should Rafa report as an intangible asset-franchise?
A. $33,000.
B. $43,800.
C. $45,000.
D. $50,000.

18.   On January 1, 20X5, Kew Corp. incurred organization costs of $24,000. For tax purposes, Kew is amortizing these costs over the maximum period allowed by the IRS. For financial reporting purposes, Kew is following GAAP. What portion of organization cost would Kew defer to years subsequent to 20X5?
A. $22,400.
B. $19,200.
C. $4,800.
D. $0.

19.   On January 1, 20X5, Nobb Corp. signed a 12-year lease for warehouse space. Nobb has an option to renew the lease for an additional 8-year period on or before January 1, 20X9. During January 20X7, Nobb made substantial improvements to the warehouse. The cost of these improvements was $540,000, with an estimated useful life of 15 years. At December 31, 20X7, Nobb intended to exercise the renewal option. Nobb has taken a full year's amortization on this leasehold. In Nobb's December 31, 20X7, balance sheet, the carrying amount of this leasehold improvement should be:
A. $486,000.
B. $504,000.
C. $510,000.
D. $513,000.

20.   Which of the following costs is included in research and development expense?
       A.   Ongoing efforts to improve existing products.
       B.   Troubleshooting in connection with breakdowns during commercial production.
       C.   Periodic design changes to existing products.
       D.   Design, construction, and testing of preproduction prototypes and models.

21.   West, Inc. made the following expenditures relating to Product Y:
       •   Legal costs to file a patent on Product Y are $10,000. Production of the finished product
            would not have been undertaken without the patent.
       •   Special equipment to be used solely for development of Product Y costs $60,000. The
            equipment has no other use and has an estimated useful life of four years.
       •   Labor and material costs incurred in producing a prototype model are $200,000.
       •   Cost of testing the prototype is $80,000.

       What is the total amount of costs that will be expensed when incurred?
       A. $280,000.
       B. $295,000.
       C. $340,000.
       D. $350,000.

22.   Miller Co. incurred the following computer software costs for the development and sale of
       software programs during the current year:
       Planning costs $50,000
       Design of the software $150,000
       Substantial testing of the project's
         initial stages $75,000
       Production and packaging costs for
         the first month's sales $500,000
       Costs of producing product masters
         after technology feasibility
         was established $200,000

       The project was not under any contractual arrangement when these expenditures were incurred.
       What amount should Miller report as research and development expense for the current year?
       A. $200,000.
       B. $275,000.
       C. $500,000.
       D. $975,000.

ANSWERS: INTANGIBLE ASSETS

1. **C** Before Year 6, Lava would record total amortization of $27,000 [($90,000 × 1/10) × 3 years], resulting in a 12/31/Year 5 carrying amount of $63,000 ($90,000 – $27,000). Because the patent became worthless at 12/31/Year 6 due to government prohibition on the product, the entire carrying amount ($63,000) should be charged against income in Year 6 as an impairment loss.

2. **A** Costs incurred in connection with securing a patent, as well as attorney's fees and other unrecovered costs of a successful legal suit to protect the patent, can be capitalized as part of patent costs. Therefore, answer A is correct because legal fees and other costs incurred to successfully defend a patent should be amortized along with the acquisition cost over the remaining economic life of the patent.

   Answer B is incorrect because legal fees and other direct costs incurred in registering a patent should be capitalized and amortized on a straight-line basis over its economic life, not five years.

   Answers C and D are incorrect because research and development costs related to the development of the product, process, or idea that is subsequently patented must be expensed as incurred, not capitalized and amortized.

3. **B** The software should be valued at the lower of its unamortized cost or its net realizable value. The software's unamortized cost is $450,000, which is equal to $600,000 – $150,000 ($600,000/4). Answer C is incorrect because the software's unamortized cost is less than its net realizable value.

4. **D** Research and development (R&D) costs are defined in SFAS 2. SFAS 2 provides detailed lists of examples of activities that would be included in R&D costs and expenses, and that would be excluded from R&D costs and possibly capitalized.

   Among those items listed as being part of R&D costs are design of tools, jigs, molds, and dies involving new technology ($125,000) and modification of the formulation of a process ($160,000), for a total R&D expense of $285,000.

   Included in the items listed in SFAS 2 as not being part of R&D costs are troubleshooting breakdowns during production ($100,000) and adaptation of existing capability for a specific customer ($110,000).

5. **A** SFAS 2 requires research and development costs to be expensed as incurred except for fixed assets, intangible assets, or materials purchased that have alternative future uses. Jamin purchased equipment to be used for research and development, but that equipment can only be used for that project. Therefore, the cost of the equipment must be expensed in Year 6 as R&D costs, as it has no alternative future uses. The equipment will not be depreciated, based on the applicable accounting guidelines.

6. **A** Per SFAS 86, the annual amortization of capitalized software costs shall be the greater of the: ratio of the software's current sales to its expected total sales or straight-line method over the economic life of the product.

   In this case, the ratio of current to expected total sales is 30% (given). The annual straight-line rate is 20% per year (1/economic life of five years). The 30% amortization should be recorded in Year 6, because it is the higher of the two. The unamortized cost on the 12/31/Year 6 balance sheet should, therefore, be 70% (100% – 30% amortization). Note that SFAS 86 requires that the unamortized cost of capitalized software products must be compared to the net realizable value of those assets at each balance sheet date. Any excess of the amortized cost over the net realizable value must be written off. In this case, the net realizable value (90%) was above the unamortized cost (70%), so no additional write-off was required.

7. **B** The depletion charge per unit is depletion base (net cost of the resource) divided by the estimated units of the resource. Mosario's depletion base is $2,880,000, as computed below:

Cost of mine	$2,640,000
Development cost	360,000
Restoration cost	180,000
Residual value	(300,000)
	$2,880,000

Note that the present value of the restoration costs is recorded as required by SFAS 143. The depletion charge is $2.40 per ton ($2,880,000/1,200,000 tons). Because 60,000 tons were removed and sold, depletion of $144,000 (60,000 × $2.40) is included in Mosario's Year 6 income statement.

Note that the amount of depletion included in the income statement depends on the tons sold. If more tons were removed than sold, part of the depletion would be included in the cost of ending inventory rather than in the income statement.

8. **D** Although such costs are amortized for tax purposes, for financial reporting purposes, they must be expensed when incurred.

9. **A** Intangible assets with an indefinite life are not amortized. The information now shows that situation so amortization is no longer appropriate.

10. **B** Because the walls and book shelves have been attached to the leased building, they are legally owned by the lessor and Waterson only has the right to use them. This intangible asset is known as a Leasehold Improvement and is amortized over its expected useful life. Because it is reasonable to expect Waterson to take the option to extend the lease contract, Waterson should get the full 25-year usage of these improvements. Annual amortization, therefore, would be $4,000 per year ($100,000/25 years).

11. **B** For the development of computer software that is to be sold, all costs associated with achieving technological feasibility are expensed as incurred as research and development costs. Any additional costs beyond that point (other than costs such as marketing and packaging) are reported as an intangible asset to be amortized over the sales life of the product.

12. **A** Research and development costs are expensed as incurred and, therefore, have no impact on the amount of intangible assets being reported. The patent registration cost is capitalized and then amortized over its expected useful life. Here, the $85,000 should be written off at the rate of $8,500 per year for ten years. Because only six months pass in Year 1, the amount is reduced to $4,250. The intangible asset balance is then $80,750 or $85,000 minus $4,250.

13. **B** Goodwill is capitalized when incurred in the purchase of another entity. The cost of maintaining or developing goodwill is not capitalized because there is not an objective basis for measuring its value.

14. **C** Since the legal action for Patent B was unsuccessful, the related costs would be written off. Only the costs for Patent A are carried as an asset including the legal fees.

15. **A** The research development costs should be expensed because of the uncertainty associated with any R & D effort. However, the cost of registering the patent should be capitalized because it benefits future periods and should be amortized over its useful life of ten years. In this case, the amortization for the last six months of 20X5 would be $1700 ($34,000 divided by 10 years × 6/12). The amount presented on the balance sheet would be the cost of $34,000 less the $1700 amortization or $32,300.

16. **C** $500,000 / 50 years = $10,000 per year.

Note: SFAS 142 eliminated the arbitrary limit of 40 years for amortization of intangibles.

17. **C**

Cost	$50,000
Less 2000 Amortization	
$50,000 / 10 years	(5,000)
December 31, 2000 Balance	$45,000

The 3% franchise fee is a current variable expense and should not be capitalized because it does not benefit future periods.

18. **D** SOP 98-5 requires that organization cost be expensed as incurred. Therefore, none of the organization cost may be deferred.

19. **B** Since the estimated life of the improvements (15 years) was less than the remaining lease term plus the option period (10 + 8 years), the 15-year amortization period is used:

Cost of improvements	$540,000
20X7 amortization ($540,000 × 15)	(36,000)
Carrying value 12/31/Year 7	$504,000

20. **D** Research and development expenses are incurred prior to the production process in researching and developing a new product or process. Answers A, B, and C are incurred after production was in process. Only D is a pre-production R&D expense.

21. **C** All costs incurred for producing and testing the prototype are R&D costs. The legal costs are capitalized as part of the cost of the patent. The special equipment, having no alternative use, is considered an R&D cost, and it is not depreciated.

22. **B** The key concept for cost incurred in the development of computer software is "technology feasibility."

All R&D cost incurred prior to the attainment of technology feasibility should be charged to R&D expense. Therefore, the planning cost, design of the software, and the testing cost should be R&D expense:

$50,000 + $150,000 + $75,000 = $275,000

All the other costs in the problem were incurred after the attainment of technology feasibility.

CHAPTER 21 – ACCOUNTING FOR PENSION COSTS AND POSTEMPLOYMENT BENEFITS

STUDY TIP

To pass the CPA exam, you need to invest an adequate amount of study time. The amount will vary significantly based on a number of factors, but most people need to plan on spending at least 60 to 120 hours in preparing for Financial Accounting & Reporting. Before getting started, make sure you know when you will have enough time available. It is very difficult to pass this exam without enough study hours.

Chapter 21 – Accounting for Pension Costs and Postemployment Benefits

Employee Benefits

Pensions

Although the topic, employee benefits, is considered a more challenging section because of all the terminology involved, a basic outline will help you keep all the material together. Remember the following four key points:

1. Differentiate between the two types of pension plans.

2. Understand pensions from a balance sheet perspective: the calculation of pension liability or asset and the items shown in other comprehensive income.

3. Understand pensions from an income statement perspective—calculation of pension expense.

4. Know and appreciate some of the basic financial disclosure requirements.

A. Defined contribution plans.

   1. Employee makes contributions, and the employer company may be obligated to make periodic contributions (through matching programs) to the retirement accounts of eligible employees.

   2. The company makes no promise to the employee regarding the amount of funds that will accumulate in the plan over time.

   3. Investment decisions for the funds are left to the employees, who bear all of the shortfall risk at retirement.

   4. Accounting for these plans is fairly simple:

      a. During the period, a liability will accrue to the employing company. This liability is for the company's own contribution to the plan on behalf of the employee, and, at least temporarily, the liability for contributions withheld from the employee's paycheck prior to the time they are transferred to the trustee of the plan.

      b. Following the company's payment of the contribution (say at the end of the period), the company no longer has any asset or liability relating to the pension.

B. Defined benefit plans.

   1. The company promises to pay a certain amount at retirement.

      a. This amount may or may not be related to an employee's salary level.

      b. The company, not the employee, assumes the risks and rewards associated with the plan assets and liabilities.

c. The actual calculation of the amount expected to be paid to the employee is an actuary's job, not an accountant's job. Therefore, you will not have to actually calculate this amount on the exam. (Auditors, of course, will review the assumptions underlying those numbers.)

2. The accounting is more complex than for a defined contribution plan.

    a. It requires management to calculate the value of plan assets and obligations based on estimates of the future for length of service, salary levels, and life expectancy.

    b. Based on those factors, the plan may be overfunded (plan assets > plan benefit obligations) or underfunded (plan assets < plan benefit obligations).

3. Changes in the relative values of plan assets and liabilities are reflected on the company's financial statements, typically as:

    a. Net pension expense on the income statement.

    b. Net pension liability or asset and other comprehensive income on the balance sheet.

4. Because pension-related estimates are subjective, pension accounting gives management an opportunity to manage the earnings stream by changing the assumptions used to estimate the value of plan assets and obligations.

Note that the remainder of the discussion on pensions will relate only to defined benefit plans.

PENSION BENEFIT OBLIGATION MEASURES

A. Projected benefit obligation (PBO).

1. The total liability (actually the present value of the estimated future pension payments) a company has incurred to date, based on future salary amounts.

2. The PBO increases because of the annual service cost (i.e., the present value of the future benefits actually earned in the period) and interest cost that accrues on the PBO.

3. PBO decreases when payments are made to retirees.

4. PBO can go up or down if:

    a. The plan is amended (called a prior service cost). PSC is the present value of the future benefits added when the pension plan is amended retroactively.

    b. One or more of the assumptions is changed (called an actuarial or unrecognized gain or loss). Here is an example of this: Pat, the actuary, has been using an interest rate assumption of 10% when making the necessary present value calculations. Actuary Pat determines that the interest rate is more likely to be 8%. Therefore, all of his previous 10% calculations must be revised based on 8%. [This would cause the PBO (present value of future benefits payments) to increase. Remember, in PV, smaller rates yield higher PV and vice versa.]

    c. Retroactive amendments to the pension plan will usually cause future benefits to improve; this will increase the PBO. At the point that this determination is made, the company will debit PSC and credit the pension liability. When the PBO changes due to changes in assumptions, the PBO could increase or decrease. The change will be recorded as unrecognized gains or losses.

6. FAS #158 changed some of the accounting requirements for pensions. Prior service cost (PSC) and gains and losses (net of G/L) are now recognized on the employer company's balance sheet as a component of other comprehensive income. When PSC is determined, a journal entry is required:

Debit prior service cost $XXX
    Credit pension liability $XXX

Note: prior service cost is recorded in stockholders' equity as a component of other comprehensive income. The pension liability is reported in the liability section of the company's balance sheet.

When actuarial gains or losses are determined, a journal entry is also required:

Debit losses $XXX
    Credit pension liability $XXX

Or

Debit pension liability $XXX
    Credit gains $XXX

Note: Any gains or losses are recorded in stockholder's equity as a component of other comprehensive income. The pension liability is reported in the liability section of the company's balance sheet.

7. The calculation (the components to be discussed separately below) and disclosure are as follows:

PBO at the beginning of the year

+ Service cost

+ Interest cost

+/– Actuarial gains and losses

+/– Prior service costs from plan amendments

+ Contributions by plan participants that increase plan benefits

– Benefits paid

= PBO at the end of the year

B. Accumulated benefit obligation (ABO).

1. The total estimated liability a company has incurred to date.

2. Similar to PBO, except that each person's *current* salary level is used (ignores future increases unlike PBO).

3. Would be appropriate if the company expects to liquidate and pay off its pension obligations.

FUNDING AND THE MEASURE OF PENSION ASSETS

A. Plan assets.

1. The total amount of assets already set aside to pay pension benefits.

2. Funding and any income earned on the investments in the fund will increase the plan assets.

3. Overall calculation and disclosure are as follows:

Plan assets opening balance
+ Employer contribution
+ Plan participant contributions
+ Actual return on assets
– Expenses (any amounts paid to the plan's investment professionals for managing the plan assets)
<u>– Benefits paid</u>
= Plan assets closing balance

B. Funding.

The amount of cash actually set aside by the employer company as a contribution to the plan assets.

C. Funded status.

Fair value of plan assets – PBO (The over- or under-funded status of the plan is now reported on the balance sheets, rather than only in footnote disclosures. And, the minimum liability is no longer a part of pension accounting. That calculation has gone away!)

COMPONENTS OF PENSION EXPENSE

(These components are added to calculate pension expense. Be sure to know these for the exam.)

A. Service cost.

1. *Service cost* is the increase in the amount of pension obligation because of work done by employees in the current year. When the employee works one more year, pension to be paid upon retirement will be higher. Present value of increase in benefits to be received at retirement is the service cost for each year.

2. This is a recurring plan expense that results in an increase in PBO.

3. Reported service cost is very sensitive to changes in assumptions that management uses to determine the pension obligations, such as the discount rate and the rate of compensation increase.

B. Interest cost.

1. The increase in the amount of pension obligation due to the passage of time; it is a recurring expense each year.

2. Even if no additional benefits are earned in a given year, the PBO will rise due to the time value of money.

3. Calculated by multiplying the PBO at the beginning of the period by the discount rate.

C. Expected return on plan assets.

The expected earnings of the plan assets decrease pension expense.

D. Prior service cost.

1. An increase in the PBO because of an amendment in the plan or because of the start-up of a plan, where the employees are granted credit for service before the current year. In either case, benefits (i.e., future payments to the retiree) are granted for employee service in earlier years.

2. Example: Plan beneficiaries have been promised 50% of the average of the last three years of their salary as a pension benefit when they retire. If the plan is amended so all employees are offered 60% instead of 50%, the change in the PBO that would result is referred to as prior service cost.

3. PBO immediately increases by the present value of all those new benefits, and PSC in other comprehensive income (stockholders' equity) is increased by the same amount. The related expense is only recognized gradually through amortization over future years.

4. Two methods approved for use in determining the assignment of prior service cost are as follows:

   a. Expected years of service method.

   b. Straight-line basis over the average remaining service period of active employees method.

   c. It's likely that on the exam, you will use the straight-line method, and the exam will provide the "average remaining service period."

E. Actuarial (unrecognized) gains and losses.

   1. These occur in two ways:

      a. Changes in the PBO because of a change in an actuarial assumption (examples: it is estimated that people will live longer, changes in compensation rate increase, change in discount rate).

      b. The difference in the expected return on plan assets and the actual return on plan assets (as measured by the change in market value after the payments and collections are removed).

   2. These two amounts are combined. The amounts are recorded in other comprehensive income in stockholders' equity as a debit (loss) or credit (gain) with the offset to pension liability on the balance sheet. Then, they are amortized into the income statement over the expected remaining service lives of the current employees.

F. Net pension expense (annual computation).

   The expense to be recognized and reported for a specific year after all of the above items are considered to be equal to the sum of the following:

   1. Service cost for the period.

   2. Plus interest cost (based on PBO and on a discount rate).

   3. Minus expected income on plan assets. Note this is expected return on plan assets, based on expectations as of the beginning of the year. We do not use actual return on plan assets. The difference between expected and actual is included in net gains and losses. If actual exceeds expected, the difference is a gain. If actual is below expected, the difference is a loss.

   4. Plus amortization of any prior service cost (amortized over the remaining service life of the employees benefited).

   5. Plus or minus amortization of actuarial or unrealized gains or losses. Amortization is ignored when the unamortized balance of net gains/losses (in stockholders' equity) is below a certain amount, which is called the "corridor." The corridor is equal to 10% of the PBO or the plan assets, whichever is greater. This corridor calculation is made at the *beginning* of the year. So, if plan assets are $100 and the PBO is $85, we would say the plan is overfunded by $15, and the corridor is $10. Only if the unamortized balance of net gains/losses (in stockholders' equity) is larger than $10 would we amortize it. In the next year, this whole calculation starts over again with the beginning

of *that* year's balances. On the CPA exam, you will be given the average remaining service lives of the employees, and you will use that number as the period for amortization.

RECORDING THE PENSION COSTS—EFFECTS ON INCOME STATEMENT AND BALANCE SHEET

FAS 158 requires certain journal entries for pensions:

A. Prior service cost and gains/losses: Initial recognition of total amount.

Remember that when either actuarial gains and losses *or* prior service cost is first determined, the original amounts are recorded on the employer company's books:

Prior service cost:

Debit Prior service cost—shown in other comprehensive income in stockholders' equity
    Credit Pension liability—shown in the liability section of the employer company's balance sheet

On the CPA exam, these amounts would be provided for you if you were asked to make this journal entry.

Actuarial losses:

Debit Net gains/losses—shown in other comprehensive income in stockholders' equity
    Credit Pension liability—shown in the liability section of the employer company's balance sheet

Actuarial gains:

Debit Pension liability—shown in the liability section of the employer company's balance sheet
    Credit Net gains/losses—shown in other comprehensive income in stockholders' equity

Remember: the journal entries above occur when the prior service cost or actuarial gains/losses are initially determined. The new pension rules from FAS 158 require that the initial amounts be recorded; the old pension rules did not. Under the old rules (which you may have learned in college, depending on when you took Intermediate accounting), the initial amounts were kept on an "off books" worksheet, and only the **amortization** of these amounts was actually recorded on the company's books as a part of pension expense. Be careful… new rules here!

B. Recording pension expense for each period.

Realize that under the new rules, the Prior Service Cost amortization and the Net Gains/Losses Amortization will be handled differently than under the old pension rules. FAS 158 requires the following entries:

Debit Pension expense
    Credit Prior service cost **

**The total amount is in Stockholders Equity, carried in Other Comprehensive Income; this is just the portion being amortized this period, based on the average remaining service lives of the employees.

Debit Pension expense
    Credit Unrecognized net gains/losses

This would be the journal entry for Pension Expense if the balance in Other Comprehensive Income was a net loss. If the total balance in OCI-Stockholders' Equity was a net gain, the entry would be a credit to pension expense and a debit to Unrecognized Net Gains/Losses in OCI-Stockholders' Equity.

So, the other journal entry required to properly record pension expense follows:

Debit Pension expense
    Credit Pension liability

- Both of these accounts are carried on the books of the employer company.
- The amount recorded in this entry is the sum of the following components:
  - Service cost (for this current period).
  - Interest cost (on the beginning of the year PBO).
  - Expected return on plan assets (remember: not the Actual but the expected, as determined at the beginning of the year).

C. Recording transactions in the plan assets.

Debit Pension liability
    Credit Cash (contributions by employer to plan assets)

This is another important change under FAS 158. The over- or under-funded status of the pension plan will now be shown on the books of the company. This is not the whole PBO balance, but the amounts that will eventually be paid by the employer company to the pension plan asset fund.

D. Let's summarize.

1. The PBO is equal to the service cost + interest cost +/- prior service cost – benefits paid to retirees. The actual PBO is carried on the books of the pension plan trustee, not on the books of the company.

2. The Plan Assets are equal to contributions by the company + any contributions that may be made by employees + actual returns due to investment income – benefits paid out to employees.

3. The Expense each period is equal to service cost + interest cost + amortization of prior service cost [+ amortization of losses (or) – amortization of gains] – expected return on plan assets.

4. The Pension Liability carried on the company's books will always now be the amount by which the plan is underfunded. If the plan is overfunded, there will be a Prepaid Pension rather than a Pension Liability. Assuming a liability, the balance is equal to amounts expensed but not funded + unamortized amounts of prior service + unrecognized amounts of losses – unamortized amounts of gains.

5. Self Quiz: True/False Questions

   1. If the company always funds an amount exactly equal to pension expense, will the pension liability be zero?

   2. Is the pension liability on the company's books equal to the PBO?

   3. Are the plan assets always equal to the pension liability on the books?

   4. Are the plan assets always equal to the PBO?

   5. Where are the PBO and Plan Assets recorded?

   6. Where is the minimum liability calculation?

6. Answers to True/False

    1. Not necessarily; there may be prior unamortized service cost and unamortized gains and losses. These would be offset in the pension liability account.

    2. No, the PBO is the liability for all future payments to the retirees. The pension liability on the books of the company is for the unfunded amounts, where the company has recorded the expense or the amounts in stockholders' equity, but has not contributed cash to the asset fund in the same amount.

    3. No, the liability is the unfunded portion; the plan assets have been funded.

    4. No, the plan can be over- or under-funded. The over- or under-funded amount is recorded in the pension liability account.

    5. On the books of the trustee of the pension plan and no longer on the books of the employer.

    6. Thank goodness… that no longer exists under FAS 158. Good news. You can forget that now. It was discontinued due to the fact that we now show the entire company liability on its books. (How? By recording PSC and unrecognized gains/losses in Other Comprehensive Income.)

EXAMPLE OF PENSION CALCULATIONS

The financial statements of Tanner Corp. (Tanner) for the year ended December 31, Year 6, include the following (in $ millions):

PBO at January 1, Year 6	$435
Service Cost	63
Interest cost	29
Benefits paid	(44)
PBO at December 31, Year 6	$483
Fair value of plan assets at January 1, Year 6	$522
Actual return on plan assets	$77
Employer contributions	$48
Benefits paid	($44)
Fair value of plan assets at December 31, Year 6	603
Average remaining years of service for employees	10
Expected return on plan assets: 12 months ended 12/31/Year 6	$32

There were no deferred or amortized amounts as of January 1, Year 6.

Calculate:

1. Pension expense for Year 6.

2. Overfunded or underfunded amount at 12/31/Year 6.

3. Amortization of gains in Year 7.

Solution:

1. Where there is no amortization, pension expense is calculated by subtracting expected return from the sum of interest cost and service cost ($63 + $29 – $32 = $60).

---

2. A plan is overfunded when the fair value of plan assets exceeds PBO. This plan is ($603 – $483) = $120 overfunded.

3. Amortization begins when gains exceed 10% of the greater of fair value of plan assets or PBO. Here, the difference between actual gains and expected gains is $45 million ($77 – $32). This is less than 10% of the greater of the two amounts (fair value is $603, and PBO is $483), so amortization will not begin in Year 7.

OTHER POSTEMPLOYMENT BENEFITS (OPEB)

A. The cost of postretirement health care for retired workers until their death is an example of an OPEB.

B. As employees work, this obligation is estimated and recorded as an expense in much the same way as a pension.

C. The obligation must be fully accrued by the employer company by the full eligibility date of the employee, even if the employee is to render additional services beyond that date.

D. In contrast with pensions, the accumulated postretirement benefit obligations (APBO) are not usually funded, and the obligations are less well-defined. Thus, they are more difficult to estimate.

DISCLOSURES

Given the complexities of pension accounting, notes to the financial statements are necessary in providing adequate information.

Required Pension Disclosures

A business entity that sponsors one or more benefit plans shall disclose the following information in the notes to its annual financial statements, separately for pension plans and other postretirement benefit plans:

A. For each statement of income presented, the amounts recognized in other comprehensive income, showing separately the net gain or loss and net prior service cost or credit. Those amounts should be separated into amounts arising during the period and reclassification adjustments of other comprehensive income as a result of being recognized as components of pension expense for the period.

B. For each annual statement of financial position presented, the amounts in accumulated other comprehensive income that have not yet been recognized as components of pension expense, showing separately the net gain or loss and the net prior service cost or credit.

C. The amounts in accumulated other comprehensive income expected to be recognized as components of net periodic benefit cost over the fiscal year that follows the most recent annual statement of financial position presented, showing separately the net gain or loss and the net prior service cost or credit.

D. The amount and timing of any plan assets expected to be returned to the business entity during the 12-month period, or operating cycle if longer, that follows the most recent annual statement of financial position presented.

QUESTIONS: ACCOUNTING FOR PENSION COSTS AND POSTEMPLOYMENT BENEFITS

1. Which of the following statements regarding pension accounting is false?
    A. The service cost is affected by all of the assumptions employed in the determination of the pension obligation.
    B. The ABO is the present value of pension benefits that are earned as of the balance sheet date based on current salaries.
    C. A plan is described as overfunded if the value of the pension assets exceeds the plan obligation.
    D. There is a positive relation between the discount rate and the calculated PBO; that is, a higher discount rate will result in a higher PBO.

2. Victor has been asked to do some accounting for the Alexeeff Corp. pension plan. At the beginning of the period, the ABO is $10 million, PBO is $12 million, and the fair value of plan assets is $8 million. The discount rate is 9%, expected return on assets is $960,000, and the anticipated compensation growth rate is 4%.

    At the end of the period, it was determined that the actual return on assets was 14%, plan assets were $9 million, and the service cost for the year was $900,000. Ignore amortization of unrecognized prior service costs and deferred gains and losses.

    Pension expense for the year is closest to:
    A. $720,000.
    B. $860,000.
    C. $900,000.
    D. $1,020,000.

3. Jamestown Corp. (Jamestown) obtains the following information from its actuary. All amounts are as of January 1, Year 6 (beginning of the year).
Projected benefit obligation	$1,530,000
Market-related asset value	$1,650,000
Unrecognized net loss	$235,000
Average remaining service period	5.5 years

    What amount of unrecognized net loss should be recognized as part of pension expense in Year 6?
    A. $12,727.
    B. $14,909.
    C. $42,727.
    D. $70,000.

4. The following information pertains to Saida Co. (Saida) pension plan:
Actuarial estimate of PBO at 1/1/Year 6	$72,000
Assumed discount rate	10%
Service costs for Year 6	$18,000
Pension benefits paid during Year 6	$15,000

    If no change in actuarial estimates occurred during Year 6, Saida's PBO at December 31, Year 6 is:
    A. $64,200.
    B. $75,000.
    C. $79,200.
    D. $82,200.

5. Jan Corp. (Jan) amended its defined benefit pension plan, granting a total credit of $100,000 to four employees for services rendered prior to the plan's adoption. The employees, A, B, C, and D, are expected to retire from the company as follows:
    A will retire after three years.
    B and C will retire after five years.
    D will retire after seven years.

    What is the amount of prior service cost amortization in the first year?
    A. $0.
    B. $5,000.
    C. $20,000.
    D. $25,000.

6. A company started a defined benefit plan on the first day of Year 1. The service cost was $200,000 per year, and the funding was $150,000 per year (funding is always made on January 1 of each year). The discount rate used for interest calculations is 10%. Earnings on plan assets are expected to be 8% per year but actually turn out to be 9%. No employee has yet retired. What is the projected obligation at the end of the second year?
    A. $378,150.
    B. $383,440.
    C. $407,610.
    D. $420,000.

7. A company started a defined benefit plan on the first day of Year 1. The service cost was $200,000 per year, and the funding was $150,000 per year (funding is always made on January 1 of each year). The discount rate used for interest calculations is 10%. Earnings on plan assets are expected to be 8% per year but actually turn out to be 9%. What is the net pension cost to be reported on the company's income statement for the second year?
    A. $194,920.
    B. $195,040.
    C. $208,000.
    D. $220,000.

8. At the end of the current year, a company has projected benefit obligation of $300,000, plan assets of $280,000, net pension cost of $90,000, and funding for the year of $83,000. What is the current period adjustment to the pension liability based on the information given?
    A. $0.
    B. $7,000.
    C. $20,000.
    D. $27,000.

9. A company has had a defined benefit pension plan for its employees for a number of years. On January 1, Year 2, a prior service cost is incurred because provisions of the pension plan have been amended, which caused a decrease in the projected benefit obligation. The prior service cost was $500,000. On that date, the average remaining service life of the employees affected is 20 years. What is the effect of the prior service cost on the computation of net pension cost (the pension expense) in Year 2?
    A. There is no impact on the Year 2 net pension cost.
    B. The entire $500,000 impacts net pension cost in Year 2.
    C. Net pension cost is increased in Year 2 by $25,000.
    D. Net pension cost is decreased in Year 2 by $25,000.

10. The Wilson Corporation covers its employees by paying them 3% of their highest salary level after they retire for each year they worked. For example, if an employee works 20 years and has a highest salary level of $150,000, that person will receive $90,000 per year after retirement (3% × 20 × $150,000). What kind of plan is this?
    A. Defined contribution pension plan.
    B. Defined benefit pension plan.
    C. Post-retirement benefit plan.
    D. Contributory stock appreciation plan.

11. A company has projected a benefit obligation in connection with its defined benefit pension plan on January 1, Year 1, of $1 million and plan assets of $800,000. The service cost for Year 1 was $300,000, and the company funded an additional $250,000 on December 31, Year 1. The discount or interest rate in connection with the projected benefit obligation is 8%, and the expected earnings rate on plan assets is 5%. What is the net pension cost (the pension expense figure) to be recognized for Year 1?
    A. $50,000.
    B. $90,000.
    C. $340,000.
    D. $351,500.

12. On January 1, Year 1, a company has a projected benefit obligation of $3 million and plan assets of $2 million. On that date, the company amends its pension contract to make the benefits larger and this change creates a prior service cost of $400,000. The discount or interest rate in connection with the projected benefit obligation is 6%, and the expected earnings rate on plan assets is 4%. The average remaining service life of those employees impacted by the amendment is estimated to be ten years. The service cost for the year is $290,000. No funding occurred during the year. What is the net pension cost (the pension expense figure) to be recognized for Year 1?
    A. $430,000.
    B. $454,000.
    C. $790,000.
    D. $814,000.

13. On December 31, Year 1, a company has an unrecognized net loss on its defined pension benefit plan of $600,000. The projected benefit obligation on that date is $4 million, whereas the plan assets total to $3.7 million. The average remaining service life of the company's employees on that date is estimated to be ten years. Which of the following is true, concerning the impact of this unrecognized loss on the net pension cost (the pension expense)?
    A. Net pension cost will go up by $60,000 on December 31, Year 1.
    B. Net pension cost will go up by $20,000 on December 31, Year 1.
    C. Net pension cost will go up by $20,000 on January 1, Year 2.
    D. Net pension cost will go up by $60,000 on January 1, Year 2.

14. A company has plan assets of $5 million in its defined pension benefit plan. The company expects to earn 6% each year on these assets but, in the current year, actually earned 7%. Which of the following statements is false?
    A. The $50,000 difference between the expected rate and the actual right impacts net pension cost recognized on the income statement in the current year.
    B. The net pension cost figure reported on the income statement is adjusted so the pension income included is equal to the expected rate of return.
    C. The amount of plan assets should be increased to reflect the actual rate of return.
    D. When the actual rate of return on plan assets differs from the expected rate of return, a deferred (or unrecognized) gain or loss balance must be maintained so the net pension cost is not immediately affected.

15. At the end of the first year of a defined pension benefit plan, a company has a net pension cost of $123,000, a projected benefit obligation of $546,000, and plan assets of $120,000. Funding of plan assets for that first year was $110,000. What amount should this company report on its balance sheet?
    A. $3,000.
    B. $13,000.
    C. $268,000.
    D. $426,000.

16. The Welsh Corporation has maintained a defined benefit pension plan for a number of years. At the end of the current year, the company has a net pension cost of $177,000, a projected benefit obligation of $829,000, and plan assets of $580,000. What is the total amount of liability this company should recognize on its balance sheet, in connection with this pension plan?
    A. $116,000.
    B. $122,000.
    C. $177,000.
    D. $249,000.

ANSWERS: ACCOUNTING FOR PENSION COSTS AND POSTEMPLOYMENT BENEFITS

1. **D** The discount rate is inversely related to the PBO. All the other statements are clearly true.

2. **D** Pension expense = service cost + interest cost – expected return on assets

   Service cost = $0.90 million (given)

   Interest cost = PBO at the beginning of the period × discount rate = $12 million × 0.09 = $1.08 million

   Expected return on plan assets = $0.96 million (given)

   Total pension expense = $0.90 million + $1.08 million – $0.96 million = $1.02 million

3. **A** The requirement is to determine the amount of unrecognized net loss to be recognized as a part of pension expense in Year 6. Per SFAS 87, the corridor approach is to be used to determine gain or loss amortization. Under this approach, only the unrecognized net gain or loss in excess of 10% of the greater of the PBO or the market-related asset value is amortized.

   In this case, the market value ($1,650,000) is larger than the PBO ($1,530,000). The corridor is $165,000 (10% × $1,650,000). The unrecognized net loss ($235,000) exceeds the corridor by $70,000 ($235,000 – $165,000). This excess is amortized over the average remaining service period of active employees expected to participate in the plan ($70,000/5.5 = $12,727).

4. **D** The PBO is the actuarial present value of the pension obligation at the end of the period. Because there were no changes in actuarial estimates during the year, the end of period PBO is computed as follows:

PBO, 1/1/Year 6	$72,000
Service cost	18,000
Interest on PBO (10% × $72,000)	7,200
Benefit payments	(15,000)
PBO, 12/31/Year 6	$82,200

   Note that service cost and interest on the PBO increase the PBO; benefit payments decrease the PBO.

5. **C** There are two methods approved for use in determining the assignment of prior service cost: the expected years of service method, and the straight-line basis over the average remaining service period of active employees method.

   Under the expected future years of service method, the total number of employee service years is calculated by grouping employees according to the time remaining to their retirement and multiplying the number in each group by the number of periods remaining to retirement [(1 person × 3) + (2 people × 5) + (1 person × 7) = 20]. To calculate the amortization of prior service costs for a given year, the number of employee service years applicable to that period is used as the numerator of the fraction, and the denominator is the total employee service years based on all the identified groups (4/20 × $100,000 = $20,000).

   For the straight-line basis over the average remaining service period method, the total number of service years (calculated above) is divided by the number of employees to find the weighted-average service life of each employee (20/4 = 5 years). The $100,000 of prior service cost will be amortized over the five years, or at $20,000 ($100,000/5 = $20,000) per year.

6. **D** The projected benefit obligation is the current value of the total liability for the pension. At the end of the first year, it is $200,000 because of the service cost recognized on the last day of that year. During the second year, interest of $20,000 (10%) is added to that amount opening balance. At the end of the second year, a second $200,000 is added as the service cost for that period to bring the total to $420,000.

7. **A** At the end of Year 2, the service cost is $200,000, and the interest on the beginning projected benefit obligation for the year is $20,000 ($200,000 × 10%). To compute the net pension cost, a reduction is made for the earnings on plan assets. For the income statement, that figure is adjusted from the actual return for the year to the expected return. At the end of Year 1, the plan assets would total $163,500 (the $150,000 funding

+ actual earnings of $13,500). Earnings of 9% were recognized in Year 1, because the funding was done at the first of the year. On the first day of the second year, funding of another $150,000 is made to bring the actual plan assets up to $313,500. The income figure used in determining the pension expense is based on the expected return of 8% or $25,080. This income reduces the expense from $220,000 to $194,920.

8. B   The expense for the period was $90,000, but the company only funded $83,000. The $7,000 difference is credited to pension liability.

9. D   Any prior service cost is amortized into the net pension cost normally over the average remaining service lives of the employees impacted by the change. The annual amount here is $25,000 or $500,000/20 years. The prior service cost in this problem is measuring an event that reduced the company's projected benefit obligation. That is the equivalent, to the company, of a gain. Thus, the amortization being computed reduces the expense figure: the net pension cost.

10. B   The benefits to be derived by the employee are set by formula so the amount to be received is simply determined through a computation and is not impacted (unless stated in the formula) by rises and falls in stock prices.

11. C   A defined benefit pension plan can have up to five components that must be used to determine net pension cost each year. Hence, there are only three of these components. First, the service cost for the year is $300,000. Second, the interest on the projected benefit obligation is $1 million times 8% or $80,000. Third, the income on the plan assets is $800,000 times 5% or $40,000. No income is computed on the funding since that took place on the last day of the year. The net pension cost is $300,000 plus $80,000 less $40,000 or $340,000.

12. B   A defined benefit pension plan can have up to five components that must be used to determine net pension cost each year. Here, there are four of these components. First, the service cost for the year is $290,000. Second, the projected benefit obligation is increased from $3 million to $3.4 million by the prior service cost, so the interest on the projected benefit obligation is $3.4 million times 6% or $204,000. Third, the income on the plan assets is $2 million times 4% or $80,000. Fourth, the prior service cost is amortized to the net pension cost over the average remaining service life of the employees. That amortization increases the cost by $40,000 ($400,000 divided by ten years). Hence, the net pension cost is $290,000 plus $204,000 less $80,000 plus $40,000 or $454,000.

13. C   To reduce the temptation to manipulate the amount of net pension cost being recognized at the end of each year, the amortization of a deferred gain or loss is always computed and recorded at the very beginning of each new year. The amortization is only computed on the portion of this gain or loss that exceeds a "corridor" amount, which is 10% of the larger of the projected benefit obligation and the plan assets on that date. Here, the projected benefit obligation is $4 million, which is larger than the amount of the plan assets. 10% of the projected benefit obligation is $400,000. The deferred loss of $600,000 is $200,000 larger than that boundary figure. It is the $200,000 excess that is amortized over the 10-year expected service life of the employees. That increases net pension cost (the pension expense) by $20,000 at the start of Year 2.

14. A   Initially, the actual rate of return on plan assets increases the amount of those plan assets and decreases the net pension cost balance, However, to avoid significant swings in income, the amount shown in the net pension cost is then adjusted to the expected rate of return. That adjustment is maintained in a deferred (or unrecognized) gain or loss account and only impacts net income if, at the beginning of any future year, it is larger than 10% of the larger of the projected benefit obligation of the plan assets.

15. D   SFAS 115 requires the reporting of the under- or over-funding status of the pension plan. Therefore, only the difference between the pension benefit obligation (PBO) and the plan assets of $426,000 will be reported on the balance sheet. It will be reported as a liability since the PBO exceeds the plan assets.

16. D   According to FASB 158, only the under- or over-funded amount of the pension plan is reported by the employer. This amount is the difference between the Projected Benefit Obligation and the Plan Assets, or $249,000 ($829,000 – $580,000) in this case.

CHAPTER 22 – INVENTORY

STUDY TIP

Never think about failing. When studying for the CPA exam, it is easy to become obsessed with failure. That attitude can sap your energy and prevent you from putting out your best effort. You should focus entirely on one goal: adding points to your score. That is the one and only obsession that will eventually get you to a passing score.

CHAPTER 22 – INVENTORY

INVENTORY AND COGS

COSTS CAPITALIZED IN CONNECTION WITH THE ACQUISITION OF INVENTORY

A. Base purchase price of the goods, plus

B. Costs incurred in preparing the inventory for its intended use:

1. Freight-in.

2. Repackaging costs (such as putting labels on merchandise).

    (Note that freight-out is a cost associated with the sale of inventory and, therefore, would be treated as a selling expense.)

C. Remember the following simple but very useful formula for calculating cost of goods sold (COGS):

    COGS = Beginning Inventory + Net Purchases – Ending Inventory

PERIODIC VS. PERPETUAL SYSTEMS

Both inventory and COGS can be monitored on an *ongoing* basis by a perpetual system or only at the *end of the year* by a periodic system.

A. Periodic system.

1. A charge is made to the *purchases* account when acquisitions are made.

2. At the close of the period, a physical count is required to determine the amount of inventory on hand.

3. The inventory is then valued, using FIFO, LIFO, average cost, or specific identification, in order to determine the COGS and the resulting gross margin.

B. Perpetual system.

1. A charge (debit) is made to the *inventory* account when acquisitions are made.

2. As sales are made, in order to record the cost of goods sold and remove the cost from inventory, there is an entry made in addition to the sales entry:

    Dr   COGS

        Cr   Inventory

C. Differentiate between the two systems.

1. *Perpetual* system is advantageous in that the inventory account reflects the amount that should be on hand at any given time. As a result, discrepancies are easily identified.

2. *Periodic* system does not provide amounts for inventory or COGS without the taking of a physical count. As a result, discrepancies are *not* easily identified.

3. *Perpetual* system is advantageous in that COGS can be easily and accurately measured and a company can evaluate the results of its operations at any given time, such as for interim reporting purposes. *Periodic* system is limited to using an inventory estimation approach for such purposes.

4. *Periodic* system is advantageous in that it is much less expensive to administer than a *perpetual* system.

INVENTORY COSTING METHODS

The following costing methods are used to determine the cost of the inventory and cost of goods sold from an accounting perspective. The actual physical flow of product may or may not follow the "cost flow assumption."

AVERAGE COST METHOD

A. Weighted-average method involves assigning the same unit price to items in inventory and items in COGS.

B. The cost assigned is the average cost for the period computed as follows: [(Cost of beginning inventory + Cost of units purchased during the period)/ total number of units].

C. This method has theoretical support as it does not tend to emphasize either the income statement or the balance sheet, and both are fairly stated.

D. In addition, it is often difficult to determine which specific units are being sold, so an averaging method may be assumed to match the actual flow of goods.

E. Inventory and COGS computed under this method will be different for companies using a periodic system than for those using a perpetual system.

F. This method is often referred to as the "moving average" method when applied to a perpetual system.

FIFO METHOD

A. FIFO (first-in, first-out) implies that the items that were acquired first will be sold first. FIFO computes COGS by using the oldest prices for the period and computes ending inventory using the most recent prices.

B. As a result, the method tends to emphasize fair statement of inventory on the balance sheet.

C. In addition, when inventory turns over regularly, the prices used for COGS are fairly recent, resulting in fair statement of COGS.

D. Inventory computed under the FIFO method will be the same regardless of whether a periodic or perpetual system is in use.

LIFO METHOD

A. LIFO (last-in, first-out) implies that the items that were acquired most recently will be the first sold.

   1. COGS is computed using the most recent prices.

   2. Ending inventory is computed using the oldest prices.

B. As a result, this method tends to emphasize the matching principle by matching current costs with current sales on the income statement.

C. Over time, however, the inventory prices used for balance sheet purposes may become outdated and unrealistic.

Issues to Consider in Using LIFO

A. LIFO is particularly popular during periods of rapid inflation.

B. There is concern with FIFO that as prices are rising, COGS is being recorded using older prices, resulting in an overstatement of profit.

C. By using LIFO, this can be avoided to some degree but at the sacrifice of fair presentation on the balance sheet. LIFO results in the inventory asset account being carried at the older costs.

D. When LIFO is used for tax purposes, it *must* be used to compute income for financial reporting purposes as well.

Criticisms of LIFO

A. One major criticism of the use of LIFO is that it gives management some manipulative power over reported profit by controlling purchases at year-end, assuming periods of rising prices.

B. When management buys excessive inventories at year-end under the LIFO method, the following occurs:

   1. Costs of the most recent purchases will be included in COGS.

   2. Costs of inventory purchased earlier in the period will now become part of ending inventory.

C. Management may increase income by refraining from purchasing inventory during the latter part of the period.

   1. If no merchandise is acquired toward the end of the period, merchandise that was included in beginning inventory may become part of COGS.

   2. This merchandise probably cost less than merchandise purchased *during* the period.

   3. As a result, COGS will include this low-cost inventory.

   4. Gross profit and net income will be higher.

Reporting Implications of Using LIFO

A. In periods of *rising* prices the following occurs:

   1. LIFO method will result in a *higher* amount reported as COGS than under the FIFO method.

2. LIFO method will result in a *lower* amount reported as inventory on the balance sheet than under the FIFO method.

3. The opposite is true in periods of *falling* prices.

B. When inventories carried under LIFO are allowed to drop below normal levels, the following happens:

1. Older (and generally lower) costs will be matched against current sales.

2. Gross profit and net income will be overstated.

3. Also, when those goods are replaced, the higher replacement prices will end up in inventory on the balance sheet.

Decision to Use FIFO vs. LIFO is Not a Physical Flow Decision

A. It is actually a cost flow decision.

B. When a company revises its **sales prices** (i.e., selling price to its customer) as the cost of replacing its inventory changes, it would be most appropriate for that company to use the LIFO method. This would best match the selling price and the cost, as each would be in current terms.

C. When a company maintains a pricing policy that is based on cost (setting current selling prices based on the actual cost of the goods), the FIFO method would be most appropriate.

"LIFO Layers"

A. Each purchase of inventory constitutes a new layer.

B. When inventory is disposed of, the goods are assumed to be taken from the most recently acquired layer.

C. Only when that layer has been eliminated in its entirety will a reduction occur in the next layer.

D. Once a layer has been eliminated, it cannot be re-established.

E. Instead, increases in inventory are recorded with the addition of new layers at that year's prices.

F. Because LIFO follows the assumption that the most recent costs are expensed first, as inventory quantities increase, layers can accumulate with costs from years earlier. If inventory quantities are then decreased, those older costs are being matched with current revenues. This is referred to as a LIFO liquidation. If inventory costs have risen over the years, a LIFO liquidation can create huge jumps in income. Thus, any LIFO liquidation must be disclosed and the effects explained.

LIFO Layers Under a Perpetual and a Periodic System

A. Inventory accounted for in a perpetual system may result in a partial or complete liquidation of an interim LIFO layer.

B. In a periodic system, LIFO liquidations come only from the layers that are added toward the end of the year.

C. As a result, perpetual and periodic systems may yield different inventory amounts when valued under LIFO.

LIFO Reserves

A. Some companies will maintain their "books and records" using an inventory valuation method *other than LIFO* to facilitate the preparation of internal reports.

B. However, they may use LIFO for external financial statement and tax purposes, in which case, a *LIFO reserve* is required as an adjustment to arrive at the appropriate LIFO amount. (Example: Inventory under FIFO – LIFO Reserve = Inventory under LIFO).

C. Each period, the company will measure the inventory under LIFO as of the balance sheet date, in addition to keeping track of inventory under the "books and records method."

   1. The LIFO reserve will be increased or decreased to adjust inventory to the proper amount.

   2. The offset will be to COGS.

VALUATION OF INVENTORY USING LOWER-OF-COST-OR-MARKET (LCM)

A. Because of obsolescence, inventory cost may have to be written down to a lower market value because GAAP requires the use of conservatism.

B. Cost is compared to market value, and the lower figure is reported.

C. Replacement cost is used as market value for comparison with cost of inventory unless replacement cost lies outside of two boundaries:

   1. The *ceiling* boundary is the estimated sales price less anticipated selling expenses. This is equal to the net realizable value (NRV) of the inventory. If the replacement cost is *above* the ceiling, the ceiling is used as market value.

   2. The *floor* boundary is the estimated sales price less anticipated selling expenses and normal profit. This is equal to the NRV (or ceiling) less normal profit. If replacement cost is *below* the floor, the floor figure is used as market value.

   3. If goods are damaged, cost should be reduced to NRV.

D. Example:

Example:

Consider the following data for Cornelia, Inc., a company that produces four distinct items.

Item	FIFO Cost	Replacement Cost	NRV	NRV Less Normal Profit
A	$10	$9	$13	$11
B	$15	$16	$14	$12
C	$20	$17	$18	$15
D	$35	$29	$37	$34

For each item, compute the values using LCM and the "ceiling and floor rules."

Solution:

Item A: Cost is $10. Market is $11 because replacement cost falls below the floor of $11 so the floor becomes market. Therefore, LCM is $10.

Item B: Cost is $15. Market is $14 because replacement cost falls above the ceiling of $14 so the ceiling becomes market. Therefore, LCM is $14.

Item C: Cost is $20. Market is $17 because replacement cost falls in between the ceiling and the floor so replacement cost becomes market. Therefore, LCM is $17.

Item D: Cost is $35. Market is $34 because replacement costs falls below the floor of $34 so the floor becomes market. Therefore, LCM is $34.

E. The LCM concept may be applied to inventories on an item-by-item basis, category-by-category basis, or it may be applied to the inventory as a whole.

F. The LCM rule is justified by the matching concept.

1. Under this approach, the maximum amount that can be presented as inventory is the NRV.

2. If inventory is stated above that amount, the sale (at NRV) will result in a loss.

3. By writing the goods down to the ceiling, a loss is recognized in the period in which the decline occurs and so there is no profit or loss recognized upon sale.

4. When the value of inventory falls below cost, the decline in value is generally recognized by reducing ending inventory with a resulting increase in COGS.

TIMING OF INVENTORY SALES AND PURCHASES

A. When items are sold or acquired near the year-end, the terms of shipment will determine whether or not the item will be included in the company's inventory and accounts receivable/payable at year-end. These terms also indicate when the seller records the sales revenue and removes the inventory from its records.

B. Although there are numerous types of shipping terms, the exam concentrates on goods that are shipped under two specific terms:

1. "FOB Destination" means they are included in the inventory of the purchaser when the goods are *received*. (*FOB Destination* means the goods are "free on board" at the destination, meaning the seller pays the freight to ship to the buyer, and the party paying the freight retains ownership until the buyer takes possession. Or, the seller owns the goods in transit.)

2. "FOB Shipping Point" means they are included in the inventory of the purchaser on the date the goods are *shipped* by the seller. (*FOB Shipping Point* means the goods are "free on board" at the point of shipment by the seller, so the buyer pays the freight from the time the goods are shipped until the buyer takes delivery. Because the buyer pays the freight, the buyer owns the goods in transit.)

INVENTORY ERRORS ARISING FROM INACCURATE RECORDING AND COUNTING

A. *Problem #1:* Errors can be made in recording the transfer of inventory, with either goods being bought or those being sold.

1. Transfer should be recorded based on "FOB Point" (either FOB Destination or FOB Shipping Point) as this is the point where legal title changes hands.

    2.   Because ending inventory is determined by count, an error in recording a purchase or sale does not necessarily affect the reporting of ending inventory.

B. *Problem #2:* Ending inventory can be counted incorrectly so that both ending inventory and COGS are incorrectly stated or there may be a simple clerical error.

    1.   If ending inventory is overstated, COGS is understated, and net income is overstated.

    2.   If ending inventory is understated, COGS is overstated, and net income is understated. (The ending inventory error automatically carries over to the next year's beginning inventory.)

    3.   If beginning inventory is overstated, COGS is overstated, and net income is understated.

    4.   If beginning inventory is understated, COGS is understated, and net income is overstated.

DISCOUNTS

PURCHASE TRADE DISCOUNTS

A. A *trade discount* is a percentage reduction in the invoice price given to retailers; it occurs when inventory is purchased for resale.

B. The price paid will often be determined on the basis of calculating trade discounts from the retail or list price.

C. A trade discount is not recorded; it is just used to establish the price to be charged.

D. If two percentages are given, the second one is applied on the net amount after the first discount is removed.

E. Example:

    1.   A company acquires merchandise with a list price of $10,000, subject to trade discounts of 10% and 5%.

    2.   The list price will be reduced by 10% ($1,000) to $9,000.

    3.   The $9,000 will be further reduced by 5% ($450) to $8,550.

    4. $8,550 will be recorded as the actual cost of the merchandise.

    In addition, inventory acquisitions may be subject to cash discounts if paid within a certain period of time.

CASH DISCOUNTS

A. A cash discount reduces the inventory cost if it is paid within a specified time.

B. A 2/15, n/30 discount, for example, gives a 2% discount if the net amount of the invoice is paid within 15 days. Otherwise, the gross amount is due within 30 days.

Recording Cash Discounts Under the Gross Method

A. Inventory, purchases, and accounts payable are recorded in the amount of the *total* purchase price (after any *trade* discounts).

B. Any cash discounts subsequently taken are recorded in a contra-purchase account.

Recording Cash Discounts Under the Net Method

A. Theoretically, inventory costs should be reduced even if the discount is not taken, because the additional inventory cost can be avoided by paying earlier.

B. Inventory, purchases, and accounts payable are recorded in an amount of the total purchase price (after any trade discounts) *minus* the cash discounts available.

C. Any cash discounts lost due to untimely payment are recorded as a period cost when the payable is settled. They are not capitalized (i.e., not recorded as a cost of the inventory).

PURCHASE COMMITMENTS AND THE RELATED DISCLOSURE REQUIREMENTS

A. Occasionally, a company will enter into an agreement to buy inventory (or supplies) in the future at a set price.

B. When the agreement is not cancelable on the part of the buyer, it is considered a firm purchase commitment.

C. In most cases, the commitment is entered into as a risk management strategy to ensure the availability of inventory in the future.

D. Such commitments have no special accounting implications but are generally disclosed if the amounts are material.

E. A *loss* will be reported in the amount of the difference between the agreed-upon purchase price and the reduced value of the item multiplied by the number of items the company is still obligated to purchase.

F. The same amount will be reported as an estimated liability (journal entry: debit loss, credit liability).

G. In subsequent periods, as the items are purchased at the agreed-upon price, inventory will be increased by the reduced value of the items. The excess will reduce the estimated liability set up above.

CONSIGNMENT INVENTORY

A. A consignment situation occurs when one company transfers inventory to another company without transferring title to that inventory.

B. In effect, merchandise is held for sale by one party (a consignee) although the goods are owned by another (a consignor).

C. The consignee deducts its reimbursable expenses incurred from the sale proceeds and usually also deducts an agreed-upon commission.

D. The remainder of the proceeds is forwarded to the consignor.

Accounting for Inventory Sold Through Consignment

A. The cost of consignment inventory is recorded on the financial statements of the consignor (at cost).

B. Therefore, the inventory is *not* reported on the financial statements of the consignee.

C. The consignor cannot record any receivable from the consignee (except for reimbursable expenses) until the goods are actually sold.

ESTIMATING INVENTORY

Reasons for Estimating Inventory

A. Preparing interim financial statements.

B. Providing a check figure for a physical inventory count.

C. Estimating fire and theft losses.

Retail Inventory Method

A. This method is used only if records are kept at both cost and retail amounts.

B. Ending inventory is first estimated at its retail value using the following formula:

Beginning Inventory + Purchases + Markups – Sales – Markdowns – Expenses (such as theft, breakage, and employee discounts)

C. Estimated ending inventory at retail is then converted to a cost figure by multiplying it by a cost-to-retail ratio.

D. Inventory at retail will not vary but there are several ways to determine the cost-to-retail ratio.

1. Average method for calculating cost-to-retail ratio.

   a. All cost figures (beginning inventory and purchases) are used.

   b. All retail figures (beginning inventory, purchases, markups, and markdowns) are used.

2. Conventional (or conventional lower-of-cost-or-market) is the same as averaging except that *markdowns* are left out of the retail part of the ratio.

3. FIFO is the same as averaging except that *beginning inventory* is left out of both cost and retail figures.

4. FIFO lower-of-cost-or-market is the same as averaging except that *beginning inventory* is left out of both cost and retail figures and *markdowns* are left out of the retail part of the ratio.

E. Example:

Example:

Papillons, Inc., a clothing retailer, has the following information regarding its inventory for the first quarter ended March 31, Year 6:

	Cost	Retail
Beginning inventory	$30,000	$40,000
Purchases	$160,000	$280,000
Freight-in	$20,000	
Net markups		$25,000
Net markdowns		$18,000
Sales		$275,000
Employee discounts		$2,000

Calculate the cost of inventory as of March 31, Year 6 using three ways:

1. Conventional retail method.

2. FIFO retail method, lower-of-cost-or-market.

3. FIFO retail method, cost.

Solution:

Begin by computing ending inventory at retail. This is the same for all three calculations.

Beginning inventory (at retail)	$40,000
Purchases	280,000
Net markups	25,000
Net markdowns	(18,000)
Sales	(275,000)
Employee discounts	(2,000)
Ending inventory (at retail)	$50,000

1. Conventional retail method

Compute the cost-to-retail percentage:

	Cost	Retail
Beginning inventory	$30,000	$40,000
Purchases	160,000	280,000
Freight-in	20,000	
Net markups		25,000
Total	$210,000	$345,000

Cost-to-retail percentage = $210,000 / $345,000 = 61%

Reduce ending inventory at retail down to cost:

$50,000 × 61% = $30,500

2. FIFO retail method (LCM)

Compute the cost-to-retail percentage:

	Cost	Retail
Purchases	$160,000	$280,000
Freight-in	20,000	
Net markups		25,000
Total	$180,000	$305,000

Cost-to-retail percentage = $180,000 / $305,000 = 59%

Reduce ending inventory at retail down to cost:

$50,000 × 59% = $29,500

3. FIFO retail method (Cost)

Compute the cost-to-retail percentage:

	Cost	Retail
Purchases	$160,000	$280,000
Freight-in	20,000	
Net markups		25,000
Net markdowns		(18,000)
Total	$180,000	$287,000

Cost-to-retail percentage = $180,000 / $287,000 = 63%

Reduce ending inventory at retail down to cost:

$50,000 × 63% = $31,500

Estimating Inventory Using the Gross Profit Method

A. This method is used when *only* cost figures are recorded.

B. COGS.

1. Normal gross profit percentage (gross profit/sales) computed from the past is multiplied by current sales to provide an estimate of current gross profit.

2. This figure is subtracted from sales to arrive at an estimate of the cost of inventory that has been sold in the current period (COGS).

C. Ending inventory.

1. Cost of beginning inventory is added to current purchases to get total goods available.

2. The estimated cost of the inventory that has been sold this period is subtracted to leave the estimated cost of the inventory still on hand.

D. Example:

Example:

Larravee, Inc. sells its merchandise at a gross profit of 30%. The following figures are among those pertaining to Larravee's operations for the six months ended June 30, Year 6:

Sales	$200,000
Beginning inventory	$50,000
Purchases	$130,000

On June 30, Year 6, all of Larravee's inventory was destroyed by fire. Calculate the estimated cost of the destroyed inventory.

Solution:

Beginning inventory	$50,000
Purchases	130,000
= Available for sale	$180,000
Estimated COGS (70% × $200,000)	(140,000)
Estimated cost of inventory destroyed	$40,000

DOLLAR VALUE LIFO

A. LIFO has some practical implementation problems that make it difficult to use.

B. Dollar value LIFO is one practical way to apply LIFO, as inventory is grouped into similar pools rather than handling items individually.

C. All LIFO systems start with a base inventory that is usually the quantity when LIFO is first applied times the price on that date.

    1. If inventory increases, a new layer is added as it is the additional quantity at the latest prices.

    2. If inventory decreases, cost is removed from the most recent layer(s).

D. When applying dollar value LIFO, the base inventory of a pool is also recorded.

    1. However, for each additional layer of inventory, the increase in quantity is measured in dollars and not units.

    2. For each additional layer, the latest price is measured as an index and not in dollars.

    3. The base inventory plus all of the additional layers gives ending inventory.

    4. A layer might be a $100,000 increase in quantity times an index of 1.15, for example, equaling $115,000.

E. An increase in quantity for the current period is the difference between the beginning inventory measured at base year prices and the ending inventory measured at base year prices. Because the prices are held constant, any difference is caused by quantity change.

F. The index for the current period is the ending inventory at end-of-year prices divided by the ending inventory at base year prices.

COMPUTING A PRICE INDEX IN DOLLAR VALUE LIFO

A. Simplified LIFO method.

    1. The company will use the price index for its industry as provided by government statistics.

    2. This method is generally tested on the CPA exam.

B. Link Chain method.

    1. The company will compute its own price level index.

    2. The company will compare the current year's inventory at current year prices to the current year's inventory at the previous year's prices.

    3. As a result, the index established each period is based on the increase (or decrease) in prices for the current year only.

    4. The index is not cumulative.

C. Double Extension method.

    1. The company will compute its own price level index.

    2. The company will compare the current year's inventory at current year prices to the current year's inventory at base year prices.

    3. The base year is the first year that the company uses the dollar value LIFO method.

    4. The index computed represents the cumulative increase in prices from the base year to the current year.

USING THE SIMPLIFIED LIFO APPROACH TO DOLLAR VALUE LIFO

A. The first year is considered to be the base year:

1. That period's inventory is considered the base layer and is stated at that period's prices both for financial reporting purposes in that year and for the purpose of subsequent dollar value LIFO calculations.

2. The inventory for that period may be valued under a variety of methods (moving average is commonly used).

B. In each subsequent period, inventory is measured using that year's prices. The amount is then converted to base year prices by dividing that period's price index (or the ratio of that price index to the index in the base year).

C. If the current period's inventory (valued at base year prices) is *higher* than the previous period's inventory (valued at base year prices), the quantity has increased, and a new layer is added:

1. The amount (at base year prices) will be used for future calculation.

2. The new layer, which is the increase stated at base year prices, is multiplied by the current year's price index (or the ratio of the current period's price index to the index in the base year) to convert the layer back to current year prices.

3. The new layer (at the current year's prices) is added to the amount that was reported as inventory of the previous period's financial statements.

4. The result will be the amount to be reported as inventory on the current period's financial statements.

D. If the current period's inventory (at base year prices) is *equal* to the previous period's inventory (at base year prices), the carrying value for financial reporting purposes is unchanged.

E. If the current period's inventory (at base year prices) is *lower* than the previous period's inventory (at base year prices), the most recent layer or layers are reduced or eliminated.

F. The remainder (at base year prices) will be used for future calculations.

G. Each of the remaining layers, at base year prices, is multiplied by the appropriate price index to determine the amount that will be used for financial reporting purposes.

H. Note that under the simplified LIFO method, industry price indexes will be given.

I. If the base year has a price index that is any amount other than 1.00, the conversion to or from base year prices will be done by using ratios:

1. To convert from current year prices to base year prices, use:

   Base Year Index/Current Year Index

2. To convert from base year prices to current year prices, use:

   Current Year Index/Base Year Index

J.   Example:

Example:

Ralph Co. manufactures a single product and adopted the dollar value LIFO inventory method on December 31, Year 3.

Inventory data:

Year ended Dec 31	Year-end prices	External price index (Year 3 base year)
Year 3	$5,000	1.00
Year 4	$8,400	1.20
Year 5	$9,750	1.50
Year 6	$11,200	1.40

Calculate the values for financial reporting of the inventory amounts at December 31, Year 3, Year 4, Year 5, and Year 6 using the (simplified) dollar value LIFO inventory method.

Solution:

Year 3—Because this is the base year, inventory will be valued at the current year's prices.

Base layer (Year 3): $5,000 × 1.00 = $5,000

Year 4—Inventory of $8,400 is valued at Year 4 prices when the index is 1.20. It is converted to base year prices by the formula $8,400/1.20 = $7,000.

Base layer (Year 3):	$5,000 × 1.00 = $5,000
Incremental layer (Year 4):	$2,000* × 1.20 = $2,400
Total	$7,400

*($7,000 – $5,000)

Year 5—Inventory of $9,750 is valued at Year 5 prices when the index is 1.50. It is converted to base year prices by the formula $9,750/1.50 = $6,500.

Base layer (Year 3)	$5,000 × 1.00 = $5,000
Incremental layer (Year 4)	1,500* × 1.20 = $1,800
Total	$6,800

*($6,500 – $5,000)

Year 6—Inventory of $11,200 is valued at Year 6 prices when the index is 1.40. It is converted to base year prices by the formula $11,200/1.40 = $8,000.

Base layer (Year 3)	$5,000 × 1.00 = $5,000
Incremental layer (Year 4)	1,500 × 1.20 = $1,800
Incremental layer (Year 6)	1,500* × 1.40 = $2,100
Total	$8,900

*($8,000 – $5,000 – $1,500)

USE OF THE DOUBLE EXTENSION METHOD OR THE LINK CHAIN METHOD

A. Double extension method.

1. The only difference between the double extension method and Simplified LIFO is that the company develops its own internal price index, rather than using the external price index provided.

2. In the first year, inventory is simply computed at the current year prices. This becomes the base year layer of inventory, and it is assumed that the price level index is 100.

3. In the second year, a price level index must be computed. This will be done by using the following procedures:

   a. The year-end quantities will be valued at *year-end* prices.

   b. The year-end quantities will also be valued at *base year* prices.

   c. The amount at year-end prices will be divided by the amount at base year prices. This will provide a price level index for the second year.

4. Example:

Example:

Assume the following information for Schubert, Inc.

	Product X	Product Y
Jan 1 Year 5 base year unit cost	$10.00	$15.00
Dec 31 Year 5 replacement unit cost	$12.00	$15.90
Dec 31 Year 5 quantity	20,000	10,000
Dec 31 Year 6 replacement unit cost	$11.00	$17.00
Dec 31, Year 6 quantity	22,000	8,000

Product X and Y are in the same inventory pool. Compute the internal conversion price indices for Year 5 and Year 6 using the double extension method.

Solution:

Ending quantities at year-end prices/ending quantities at base-year prices = internal conversion price index

Year 5:

Dec 31, Year 5 replacement cost

$(20,000 \times 12.00) + (10,000 \times 15.90) = \$399,000$

Jan 1, Year 5 base year cost

$(20,000 \times 10.00) + (10,000 \times 15.00) = \$350,000$

Index = 399,000 / 350,000 = 1.14

Year 6:

Dec 31, Year 6 replacement cost

$(22,000 \times 11.00) + (8,000 \times 17.00) = \$378,000$

Jan 1, Year 6 base year cost

$(22,000 \times 10.00) + (8,000 \times 15.00) = \$340,000$

Index = 378,000 / 340,000 = 1.11

B.   Link Chain method.

   1.   Under the link chain method, the procedures are similar.

   2.   The index is computed for the current period, however, by comparing the current period's prices to the previous period's prices rather than to the base year's prices.

   3.   On the CPA exam, knowing these *differences* between the Simplified LIFO method and the other methods might easily be tested in a conceptual multiple-choice question. So, even though the Simplified method is most often tested, do not forget about the others.

FINANCIAL RATIOS RELATING TO INVENTORY

A.   Inventory turnover.

   1.   COGS/Average Inventory.

   2.   Measures the number of times inventory was sold and reflects inventory order and investment policies.

B.   Number of days' supply in average inventory.

   1.   365/Inventory turnover.

   2.   Number of days that inventory is held before being sold and reflects the efficiency of inventory policies.

QUESTIONS: INVENTORY

1. Triana Distributors, Inc. (Triana) has determined its December 31, Year 5 inventory on a FIFO basis to be $200,000. Information pertaining to that inventory follows:

Estimated selling price	$204,000
Estimated cost of disposal	$10,000
Normal profit margin	$30,000
Current replacement cost	$180,000

    Triana records losses that result from applying the lower-of-cost-or-market rule. At December 31, Year 5, the loss that Triana should recognize is:
    A. $0.
    B. $6,000.
    C. $14,000.
    D. $20,000.

2. Chubb, Inc.'s (Chubb) accounts payable balance at December 31, Year 5 was $1,800,000 before considering the following transactions:

    Goods were in transit from a vendor to Chubb on December 31, Year 5. The invoice price was $100,000, and the goods were shipped FOB shipping point on December 29, Year 5. The goods were received on January 4, Year 6.

    Goods shipped to Chubb, F.O.B. shipping point on December 20, Year 5, from a vendor were lost in transit. The invoice price was $50,000. On January 5, Year 6, Chubb filed a $50,000 claim against the common carrier.

    In its December 31, Year 5 balance sheet, Chubb should report accounts payable of:
    A. $1,800,000.
    B. $1,850,000.
    C. $1,900,000.
    D. $1,950,000.

3. At December 31, Year 5, the following information was available from Schonfeld Co.'s (Schonfeld) accounting records:

	Cost	Retail
Inventory 1/1, Year 5	$147,000	$203,000
Purchases	833,000	1,155,000
Additional markups	0	42,000
Available for sale	$980,000	$1,400,000

    Sales for the year totaled $1,106,000. Markdowns amounted to $14,000. Under the approximate lower-of-cost-or-market retail method, Schonfeld's inventory at December 31, Year 5 was:
    A. $196,000.
    B. $215,600.
    C. $280,000.
    D. $308,000.

4.   Hardi Corp. (Hardi) had accounts payable of $100,000 recorded in the general ledger as of December 31, Year 5 before consideration of the following unrecorded transactions:

Invoice Date	Amount	Date Shipped	Date Received	FOB Terms
Jan 3, Year 6	$8,000	Dec 22, Year 5	Dec 24, Year 5	destination
Jan 2, Year 6	$13,000	Dec 28, Year 5	Jan 2, Year 6	shipping
Dec 26, Year 5	$12,000	Jan 2, Year 6	Jan 3, Year 6	shipping
Jan 10, Year 6	$9,000	Dec 31, Year 5	Jan 5, Year 6	destination

On Hardi's December 31, Year 5 balance sheet, the accounts payable should be reported in the amount of:
A. $100,000.
B. $108,000.
C. $121,000.
D. $142,000.

5.   The following information pertains to an inventory item:

Cost	$12.00
Estimated selling price	$13.60
Estimated disposal cost	$0.20
Normal gross margin	$2.20
Replacement cost	$10.90

Under the lower-of-cost-or-market rule, this inventory item should be valued at:
A. $10.70.
B. $10.90.
C. $11.20.
D. $12.00.

6.   In preparing its cash budget for the month of May, Year 6, Nora Co. (Nora) made the following projections:

Sales	$3,000,000
Gross margin (based on sales)	25%
Decrease in inventories	$140,000
Decrease in accounts payables for inventories	$240,000

For May, Year 6, Nora's estimated cash disbursements for inventories were:
A. $1,870,000.
B. $2,100,000.
C. $2,110,000.
D. $2,350,000.

7. On June 1, Year 6, Jordan Corp. (Jordan) sold merchandise with a list price of $5,000 to Andreas Corp. (Andreas) on account. Jordan allowed trade discounts of 30% and 20%. Credit terms were 2/15, n/40, and the sale was made FOB shipping point. Jordan prepaid $200 of delivery costs for Andreas as an accommodation.

    On June 12, Year 6, Jordan received from Andreas a remittance in full payment amounting to:
    A. $2,744.
    B. $2,940.
    C. $2,944.
    D. $3,140.

8. On October 20, Year 6, Greer Co. (Greer) consigned 40 freezers to Nelson Co. (Nelson) for sale at $1,000 each and paid $800 in transportation costs. On December 30, Year 6, Nelson reported the sale of ten freezers and remitted $8,500. The remittance was net of the agreed 15% commission.

    What amount should Greer recognize as consignment sales revenue for Year 6?
    A. $7,700.
    B. $8,500.
    C. $9,800
    D. $10,000.

9. Brandt, Inc.'s (Brandt) pricing structure has been formulated to yield a gross margin of 40%. The following data pertain to the year ended December 31, Year 5:

Sales	$600,000
Beginning inventory	$100,000
Purchases	$400,000
Physical inventory at year-end	$100,000

    Brandt is satisfied that all sales and purchases have been fully and properly recorded. How much might Brandt reasonably estimate as missing inventory at December 31, Year 5?
    A. $0.
    B. $40,000.
    C. $140,000.
    D. $160,000.

10. The following information applied to Facey, Inc. (Facey) for Year 6:

Merchandise purchased for resale	$400,000
Freight in	$10,000
Freight out	$5,000
Purchase returns	$2,000

    Facey's Year 6 inventoriable cost was:
    A. $400,000.
    B. $403,000.
    C. $408,000.
    D. $413,000.

11.   On December 28, Year 5, Kerr Manufacturing Co. (Kerr) purchased goods costing $50,000. The terms were FOB destination. Some of the costs incurred in connection with the sale and delivery of the goods were as follows:

Packaging for shipment $1,000
Shipping $1,500
Special handling charges $2,000

These goods were received on December 31, Year 5. On Kerr's December 31, Year 5 balance sheet, what amount of COGS should be included in inventory?
A. $50,000.
B. $52,000.
C. $53,500.
D. $54,500.

12.   In Year 5, Longley, Inc. (Longley) adopted the dollar value LIFO inventory method. At that time, Longley's ending inventory had a base-year cost and an end-of-year cost of $300,000. In Year 6, the ending inventory had a $400,000 base-year cost and a $440,000 end-of-year cost.

What dollar value LIFO inventory cost would be reported on Longley's December 31, Year 6 balance sheet?
A. $400,000.
B. $410,000.
C. $430,000.
D. $440,000.

13.   In general, which inventory costing method approximates *most* closely the current cost for COGS and ending inventory, respectively?

	COGS	Ending Inventory
A.	LIFO	FIFO
B.	LIFO	LIFO
C.	FIFO	FIFO
D.	FIFO	LIFO

14.   How should the following costs affect a retailer's inventory?

	Freight in	Interest on Inventory
A.	Increase	No effect
B.	Increase	Increase
C.	No effect	Increase
D.	No effect	No effect

15. The balance in Kern Co's accounts payable account at December 31, Year 5 was $900,000 before any necessary year-end adjustments relating to the following:

Goods were in transit to Kern from a vendor on December 31, Year 5. The invoice cost was $50,000. The goods were shipped FOB shipping point on December 31, Year 5 and were received January 4, Year 6.

Goods shipped FOB destination on December 21, Year 5 from a vendor to Kern were received on January 6, Year 6. The invoice cost was $25,000.

On December 27, Year 5, Kern wrote and recorded checks to creditors totaling $40,000 that were mailed on January 10, Year 6.

On Kern's December 31, Year 5 balance sheet, the accounts payable balance should be:
A. $940,000.
B. $950,000.
C. $975,000.
D. $990,000.

16. The following information was derived from the Year 5 accounting records of Samilski Co.:

	Goods in Central Warehouse	Goods Held by Consignees
Beginning inventory	$110,000	$12,000
Purchases	480,000	60,000
Freight in	10,000	
Transport to consignees		5,000
Freight out	30,000	8,000
Ending inventory	$145,000	$20,000

Samilski's COGS for Year 5 was:
A. $455,000.
B. $485,000.
C. $507,000.
D. $512,000.

17. Stone Co. had the following consignment transactions during December, Year 5:

Inventory shipped on consignment to Beta Co.	$18,000
Freight paid by Stone	$900
Inventory received on consignment from Alpha Co.	$12,000
Freight paid by Alpha	$500

No sales of consigned goods were made through December 31, Year 5. Stone's December 31, Year 5, balance sheet should include consigned inventory of:
A. $12,000.
B. $12,500.
C. $18,000.
D. $18,900.

18. Anders Co. (Anders) uses the moving-average method to determine the cost of inventory. During January, Year 6, Anders recorded the following information pertaining to its inventory:

	Units	Unit Cost	Total Cost
Balance on 1/1/Year 6	40,000	$5	$200,000
Sold on 1/17/ Year 6	35,000		
Purchased on 1/28/Year 6	20,000	$8	$160,000

What amount of inventory should Anders report on its January 31, Year 6, balance sheet?
A. $150,000.
B. $162,500.
C. $185,000.
D. $200,000.

19. Kewl Co.'s (Kewl) accounts payable balance at December 31, Year 5, was $2,200,000 before considering the following transactions:

Goods shipped to Kewl F.O.B. shipping point on December 22, Year 5, were lost in transit. The invoice cost of $40,000 was not recorded by Kewl. On January 7, Year 6, Kewl filed a $40,000 claim against the common carrier.

On December 27, Year 5, a vendor authorized Kewl to return, for full credit, goods shipped and billed at $70,000 on December 2, Year 5. The returned goods were shipped by Kewl on December 28, Year 5. A $70,000 credit memo was received and recorded by Kewl on January 5, Year 6.

Goods shipped to Kewl FOB destination on December 20, Year 5, were received on January 6, Year 6. The invoice cost was $50,000.

What amount should Kewl report as accounts payable on its December 31, Year 5 balance sheet?
A. $2,170,000.
B. $2,180,000.
C. $2,230,000.
D. $2,280,000.

20. Scarbo, Inc. (Scarbo) uses the conventional retail inventory method to account for inventory. The following relates to its Year 6 operations:

	Cost	Retail
Beginning inventory & purchases	$600,000	$920,000
Net markups		$40,000
Net markdowns		$60,000
Sales		$780,000

What amount should be reported as Scarbo's COGS for Year 6?
A. $480,000.
B. $487,500.
C. $520,000.
D. $525,000.

21. Ondine, Inc. (Ondine) paid the in-transit insurance premium for consignment goods shipped to Gibet ,Inc. (Gibet), the consignee. In addition, Ondine advanced part of the commissions that will be due when Gibet sells the goods. Should Ondine include the in-transit insurance premium and the advanced commissions in its inventory costs?

	Insurance premium	Advanced commissions
A.	Yes	Yes
B.	No	No
C.	Yes	No
D.	No	Yes

22. During periods of rising prices, when the FIFO inventory method is used, a perpetual inventory system results in an ending inventory cost that is:
   A. the same as in a periodic inventory system.
   B. higher than in a periodic inventory system.
   C. lower than in a periodic inventory system.
   D. higher or lower than in a periodic inventory system depending on whether physical quantities have increased or decreased.

23. Rabba Co. (Rabba) records its purchases at gross amounts but wishes to change to recording purchases net of purchase discounts. Discounts available on purchases recorded from October 1, Year 5 to September 30, Year 6 totaled $2,000. Of this amount, $200 is still available in the accounts payable balance. The balances in Rabba's accounts for the year ended September 30, Year 6, *before* the conversion are as follows:

Purchases	$100,000
Purchase discounts taken	$800
Accounts payable	$30,000

What is Rabba's accounts payable balance as at September 30, Year 6, *after* the conversion?
   A. $28,200.
   B. $28,800.
   C. $29,200.
   D. $29,800.

24. Jefferson, Inc. (Jefferson), a consignee, paid the freight costs for goods shipped from Chocolate, Inc. (Chocolate), a consignor. These freight costs are to be deducted from Jefferson's payment to Chocolate when the consignment goods are sold.

Until Jefferson sells the goods, the freight costs should be included in Jefferson's:
   A. COGS.
   B. freight-out costs.
   C. selling expenses.
   D. accounts receivable.

Use the following information to answer Questions 25 and 26.

During January, Year 6, Mazeppa Co. (Mazeppa), which maintains a perpetual inventory system, recorded the following information pertaining to its inventory:

	Units	Unit Cost	Total Cost	Units on Hand
Balance on 1/1 Year 6	1,000	$1	$1,000	1,000
Purchased on 1/7 Year 6	600	$3	$1,800	1,600
Sold on 1/20 Year 6	900			700
Purchased on 1/25 Year 6	400	$5	$2,000	1,100

25. Under the moving-average method, what amount should Mazeppa report as inventory at January 31, Year 6?
    A. $2,640.
    B. $3,225.
    C. $3,300.
    D. $3,900.

26. Under the LIFO method, what amount should Mazeppa report as inventory at January 31, Year 6?
    A. $1,300.
    B. $2,700.
    C. $3,900.
    D. $4,100.

27. The following items were included in Ota Co.'s (Ota) inventory account at December 31, Year 5:

Merchandise out on consignment, at sales price, including a 40% markup on selling price	$40,000
Goods purchased, in transit, shipped FOB shipping point	$36,000
Goods held on consignment by Ota (consignee)	$27,000

    By what amount should Ota's inventory account at December 31, Year 5 be reduced?
    A. $43,000.
    B. $51,000.
    C. $67,000.
    D. $103,000.

28.   Moses Co. (Moses) has determined its December 31, Year 5 inventory on a FIFO basis to be
        $400,000. Information pertaining to that inventory follows:

        Estimated selling price $408,000
        Estimated cost of disposal $20,000
        Normal profit margin $60,000
        Current replacement cost $360,000

        Moses records losses that result from applying the lower-of-cost-or-market rule. At December 31,
        Year 5, what should be the net carrying value of Moses' inventory?
        A. $328,000.
        B. $360,000.
        C. $388,000.
        D. $400,000.

29.   On December 1, Year 6, Novotny Department Store (Novotny) received 505 sweaters on
        consignment from Kinney Co. (Kinney). Kinney's cost for the sweaters was $80 each, and they
        were priced to sell at $100. Novotny's commission on consigned goods is 10%. At December 31,
        Year 6, five sweaters remained.

        In its December 31, Year 6, income statement what amount should Novotny report as payable for
        consigned goods?
        A. $40,400.
        B. $45,000.
        C. $45,400.
        D. $49,000.

30.   The following information pertains to Orosz Corp's (Orosz) COGS for Year 6:

        Inventory, 12/31 Year 5 $90,000
        Year 6 purchases   124,000
        Year 6 write-off of obsolete inventory   34,000
        Inventory, 12/31 Year 6 $30,000

        The inventory written off became obsolete due to an unexpected and unusual technological
        advance by a competitor.

        In its Year 6 income statement, what amount should Orosz report as COGS?
        A. $124,000.
        B. $150,000.
        C. $184,000.
        D. $218,000.

31.	On January 1, Year 6, Fialkowska Corp. (Fialkowska) signed a 3-year noncancelable purchase contract that allows Fialkowska to purchase up to 500,000 units (annually) of a computer part from Janina Supply Co. (Janina) at $0.10 per unit. A minimum annual purchase of 100,000 units is required.

   During Year 6, the part unexpectedly becomes obsolete, Fialkowska had 250,000 units of this inventory at December 31, Year 6, and believes that these parts can be sold as scrap for $0.02 per unit.

   What amount of probable loss from the purchase commitment should Fialkowska report in its Year 6 income statement?
   A. $8,000.
   B. $16,000.
   C. $20,000.
   D. $24,000.

32.	Drew Co. (Drew) uses the weighted-average cost inventory method for internal reporting purposes and LIFO for financial statement and income tax reporting. At December 31, Year 5, the inventory was $375,000 using average cost and $320,000 using LIFO. The unadjusted credit balance in the LIFO Reserve account on December 31, Year 5 was $35,000.

   What adjusting entry should Drew record to adjust from average cost to LIFO at December 31, Year 5?

	Debit	Credit
A.	COGS, $55,000	Inventory, $55,000
B.	COGS, $55,000	LIFO Reserve, $55,000
C.	COGS, $20,000	Inventory, $20,000
D.	COGS, $20,000	LIFO Reserve, $20,000

33.	Based on a physical inventory taken on December 31, Year 5, Foley Co. (Foley) determined its chocolate inventory (FIFO) to be $26,000, with a replacement cost of $20,000. Foley estimated that after further processing costs of $12,000, the chocolate could be sold as finished candy bars for $40,000. Foley's normal profit margin is 10% of sales.

   Under the lower-of-cost-or-market rule, what amount should Foley report as chocolate inventory on its December 31, Year 5 balance sheet?
   A. $20,000.
   B. $24,000.
   C. $26,000.
   D. $28,000.

34. On December 30, Year 5, Asper Corp. (Asper) sold merchandise for $75,000 to Brew Co. (Brew). The terms of the sale were net 30, FOB shipping point. The merchandise was shipped on December 31, Year 5 and arrived at Brew on January 5, Year 6.

   Due to a clerical error, the sale was not recorded until January, Year 6 and the merchandise, sold at a 25% markup, was included in Asper's inventory at December 31, Year 5.

   As a result, Asper's COGS for the year ended December 31, Year 5 was:
   A. correctly stated.
   B. understated by $15,000.
   C. understated by $60,000.
   D. understated by $75,000.

35. Brock Co. (Brock) adopted the dollar value LIFO inventory method as of January 1, Year 5. A single inventory pool and an internally computed price index are used to compute Brock's LIFO inventory layers.

   Information about Brock's dollar value inventory is as follows:

Date	Base Year	Current Cost	Dollar Value LIFO
1/1 Year 5	$40,000	$40,000	$40,000
Year 5 layer	$5,000	$14,000	$6,000
12/31 Year 5	$45,000	$54,000	$46,000
Year 6 layer	$15,000	$26,000	?
12/31 Year 6	$60,000	$80,000	?

   What was Brock's dollar value LIFO inventory value at December 31, Year 6?
   A. $60,000.
   B. $66,000.
   C. $74,000.
   D. $80,000.

36. A company has a unit of inventory that cost $65. Currently, though, this item can be acquired by the company for only $58. The company feels that, if it spends $9, the item being held can be sold for $78. The normal profit expected on the sale of this type of item is $6. The company uses the lower-of-cost-or-market value method for reporting its inventory. What figure should be reported for this inventory item?
   A. $58.
   B. $63.
   C. $64.
   D. $65.

37. A company buys 10 items of inventory for $9 each and then sells 8 of them. The company then buys another 10 items for $11 each and sells 8 of them. The company then buys a final 10 items for $12 each, and the year ends. The company holds 14 items at the end of the year. Which of the following statements is true?
   A. FIFO perpetual will give a higher ending inventory balance than FIFO periodic.
   B. LIFO perpetual will give an ending inventory balance of $160.
   C. LIFO periodic will give an ending inventory balance of $138.
   D. FIFO perpetual will give an ending inventory balance of $168.

38.   The Houston Corporation buys 10,000 units of inventory for $600,000. In process, 1,000 units
        are lost. The normal amount of lost units in this type of acquisition is 600; thus, the additional
        400 is viewed as an abnormal loss. What is the amount to be reported by the company for its
        Inventory account?
        A. $600,000.
        B. $576,000.
        C. $564,000.
        D. $540,000.

39.   A company holds one piece of inventory costing $5 and buys a second one for $7. It then sells one
        for $10 and buys a replacement piece for $8 per year. Finally, the company sells one item for $14
        and buys one final item for $9. If the company utilizes a perpetual inventory system with a LIFO
        cost flow assumption, what should be reported as its cost of goods sold?
        A. $17.
        B. $16.
        C. $15.
        D. $13.

40.   A company holds one piece of inventory costing $5 and buys a second one for $7. It then sells one
        for $10 and buys a replacement piece for $8 per year. Finally, the company sells one item for $14
        and buys one final item for $9. If the company utilizes a periodic inventory system with a LIFO
        cost flow assumption, what should be reported as its cost of goods sold?
        A. $17.
        B. $16.
        C. $15.
        D. $13.

41.   During the current year, the Midlothian Company shipped inventory costing $33 to a customer
        for a sales price of $45. Also, the Midlothian Company received inventory from a supplier at a cost
        of $42. Both of these shipments were shipped on December 29, Year 1 and arrived at the buyer on
        January 3, Year 2. Midlothian did not count either of these inventory items in arriving at its
        December 31, Year 1 physical inventory of $3,000. If both sales were made F.O.B. shipping point,
        what was the correct amount of Midlothian's inventory?
        A. $3,000.
        B. $3,033.
        C. $3,042.
        D. $3,075.

42.   A company begins Year 1 with inventory costing $80,000 and then buys $300,000 more in
        merchandise. The company does, though, get a discount on these purchases of $20,000. The
        transportation cost to get the merchandise to the company's stores was $14,000. The
        transportation cost to get the merchandise from the stores to the customers was another $18,000.
        At the end of the year, the company takes a physical inventory and finds inventory with a cost of
        $110,000 on hand. Sales for the period were $490,000. What was the company's gross profit?
        A. $208,000.
        B. $222,000.
        C. $226,000.
        D. $246,000.

ANSWERS: INVENTORY

1. **D** In applying the lower-of-cost-or-market rule to inventory, the replacement cost of $180,000 will be considered market, provided it falls between the floor and ceiling limitations.

    The ceiling is the net realizable value, which is the selling price of $204,000 minus the estimated cost of disposal of $10,000, or $194,000. The floor is the net realizable value of $194,000 minus a normal profit of $30,000, or $164,000.

    Because the replacement cost falls between the ceiling and the floor, it will be considered market value. In the lower-of-cost-or-market analysis, market value of $180,000 is lower than cost of $200,000. As a result, the inventory will be written down from $200,000 (cost) to $180,000 (market), indicating a loss of $20,000.

2. **D** Accounts payable of $1,800,000 will be increased by the goods in transit on December 31 because they were shipped FOB shipping point. The amount will also be increased by the goods lost in transit because the shipping terms were also FOB shipping point and the risk of loss is Chubb's. The adjusted accounts payable will be $1,800,000 + $100,000 + $50,000 = $1,950,000.

3. **A** Based on the figures provided, Schonfeld had a cost-to-retail ratio of $980,000 / $1,400,000 or 70%. Ending inventory at retail can be calculated by subtracting sales of $1,106,000 and markdowns of $14,000 from the amount available for sale, measured at retail, of $1,400,000 for a net amount of $1,400,000 – 1,106,000 – 14,000 = $280,000.

    The approximate lower-of-cost-or-market amount can be determined by multiplying the net retail amount by the cost-to-retail ratio at $280,000 × 70% = $196,000.

4. **C** The goods that were shipped on 12/22 Year 5 and received on 12/24 Year 5 should be included in accounts payable at 12/31/Year 5. Because the goods shipped on 12/28 Year 5 were shipped FOB shipping point, title would have transferred on 12/28 Year 5 and these goods should also be included in accounts payable. The goods shipped on 1/2/Year 6 and received on 1/3/Year 6 should be excluded, and the goods shipped on 12/31/Year 5 and received on 1/5/Year 6 were shipped FOB destination and would be excluded from accounts payable.

    Accounts payable at 12/31/Year 5 would include the recorded balance of $100,000 + $8,000 + 13,000 = $121,000.

5. **C** The replacement cost of $10.90 is first compared to the ceiling for market, which is net realizable value. In this case, the net realizable value equals the estimated selling price of $13.60 minus the estimated disposal cost of $0.20, or $13.40, so the replacement cost is below the ceiling. The floor for market is the net realizable value of $13.40 minus the normal gross margin of $2.20, or $11.20. Because replacement cost is below this floor, market is $11.20.

    Cost is $12, so the lower-of-cost-or-market is the market of $11.20 represented by the net realizable value less the normal gross margin.

6. **D** With sales of $3,000,000 and a gross margin of 25%, cost of sales represents 75%, or $2,250,000. In order for inventory to decrease by $140,000, purchases must have been less than cost of sales by that amount, or $2,110,000 total. A decrease in accounts payable for inventories of $240,000 indicates cash disbursements in excess of purchases by that amount, so that cash disbursements in total are $2,350,000.

7. **C** The terms of the purchase indicate that Andreas will be entitled to trade discounts of 30% and 20%. Based on a list price of $5,000, the initial discount will be 30% of the list price or $1,500, reducing the cost to $3,500.

    Andreas will then further reduce this by 20% or $700, resulting in a cost of $2,800. Because Andreas is paying for the merchandise within 15 days, the terms of 2/15, n/40 indicate that Andreas will be entitled to a 2% early payment discount or an additional $56. This will reduce Andreas' ultimate cost to $2,744.

Burr will remit this amount plus the $200 of delivery costs for a total of $2,944.

8. **D** Consignment sales revenues would be computed at ten freezers at $1,000 per unit or $10,000. The transportation costs of $800 would be included in cost of sales, and the $1,500 commission would be a sales-related expense.

9. **B** Actual cost of goods sold:

Beginning inventory	$100,000
Purchases	$400,000
Available	$500,000
Ending inventory	$100,000
Cost of goods sold	$400,000

Formulated cost of goods sold:

(60% × $600,000 sales) $360,000

Missing inventory $40,000 ($400,000 – $360,000)

10. **C** Merchandise purchased for resale of $400,000 is inventoriable. Freight in charges of $10,000 are included as well. Freight out charges are incurred in the sales process and are treated as selling expenses. Purchase returns of $2,000 reduce net purchases. The inventoriable cost is $400,000 + $10,000 – $2,000 = $408,000.

11. **A** Because the terms related to the purchase by Kerr were F.O.B. destination, the seller had the responsibility for packaging, shipping, and handling. Kerr's cost of the goods would have only included the invoice amount of $50,000. The shipping costs are not inventoriable.

12. **B** Longley's base inventory amount would be $300,000. The Year 6 ending inventory had a base year cost of $400,000 and a year-end cost of $440,000, indicating that prices had increased by 10%. The increase in inventory at base prices, $100,000, would be adjusted to Year 6 prices, increasing the amount to $110,000 ($100,000 × 110%). This layer would be added to the base layer of $300,000 to give ending inventory under dollar value LIFO of $410,000.

13. **A** In general, prices are rising. Under LIFO, cost of goods sold includes the cost of goods most recently purchased. Under FIFO, ending inventory includes the cost of goods most recently purchased.

14. **A** Freight in is included in the cost of inventory, while interest on inventory loans will be expensed as incurred.

15. **D** Goods costing $50,000 in transit to Kern that were shipped FOB shipping point will be the responsibility of Kern and will be added to accounts payable. The goods costing $25,000 shipped FOB destination do not become Kern's responsibility until received and would not be included in accounts payable. The checks amounting to $40,000 written to creditors on December 27, Year 5 but not mailed until January 10, Year 6 should not reduce accounts payable until mailed and would be added back.

As a result, accounts payable at 12/31/Year 5 would be $900,000 + 50,000 + 40,000 = $990,000.

16. **D** The COGS on the items in the central warehouse equals the beginning inventory of $110,000 plus purchases of $480,000 plus freight in of $10,000 minus ending inventory of $145,000, or $455,000.

The COGS on the items held by consignees equals the beginning inventory of $12,000 plus purchases of $60,000 plus transportation to consignees of $5,000 minus ending inventory of $20,000, or $57,000.

The COGS is $455,000 + $57,000 = $512,000.

Freight out costs are considered selling expenses and are not included in COGS.

17. **D**   Consignment inventories and related costs are reported on the financial statements of the consignor, not the consignee. As a result, Stone will include the inventory shipped to Beta on consignment in its balance sheet, but not the goods consigned to Stone from Alpha. The amount to be reported as consigned inventory will include the cost of $18,000 and the freight paid by Stone to ship the goods to Beta of $900 for a total of $18,900.

18. **C**   Moving-average is used in a perpetual inventory system. Under moving-average, the goods sold on 1/17 will reduce inventory at a cost of $5 per unit or $175,000, leaving 5,000 units at $5 or $25,000 in inventory. The purchase of 20,000 units on 1/28 at $8 would then increase inventory to $185,000. If additional units were sold prior to another purchase, the cost of the units sold would be calculated on the basis of $185,000/25,000 units or $7.40 per unit.

19. **A**   Accounts payable before adjustments is $2,200,000. Goods shipped FOB shipping point pass to the buyer when shipped, so that the $40,000 invoice cost is owed by Kewl. The fact that these goods were lost in transit simply means that Kewl will have an insurance claim. The vendor's $70,000 credit may be offset against accounts payable because authorization and return shipment has occurred in Year 5. Goods sent FOB destination do not pass to the buyer until arrival in Year 6.

Accounts payable balance is $2,200,000 + $40,000 – $70,000 = $2,170,000.

20. **D**   Under the conventional retail inventory method, beginning inventory and purchases of $600,000 will be divided by a retail amount including beginning inventory and purchases of $920,000 and net markups of $40,000 for a total of $960,000. The result is a cost-to-retail ratio of $600,000 / $960,000 or 62.5%.

Ending inventory at retail is computed by subtracting sales of $780,000 and net markdowns of $60,000 from the $960,000, giving an amount of $120,000. At a ratio of 62.5%, ending inventory at approximately lower-of-cost-or-market will be $75,000. Because beginning inventory and purchases were $600,000, cost of sales must be $525,000.

21. **C**   The insurance premium is part of the cost of transporting the consignment goods to the consignee and would be included as part of the cost of the consignment inventory. Commissions are selling expenses and not included in inventory. When paid in advance, they would be recorded as a prepaid expense.

22. **A**   Under the FIFO method of determining inventory cost, ending inventory would be the same amount regardless of whether a periodic system or a perpetual system was in use. The LIFO and average methods would derive different results under the different systems.

23. **D**   When purchases are recorded net of purchase discounts, the amount reported in accounts payable is equal to the purchase price of goods less discounts available. If discounts are forfeited, the amount of the lost discount is reported as an expense when the payable is settled. With an accounts payable balance of $30,000 and discounts available of $200, accounts payable will be reported at the net amount of $29,800.

24. **D**   A consignee is actually holding inventory for sale on behalf of the consignor. Any costs incurred by the consignee will be taken out of the proceeds from sale of the inventory, along with the consignee's fee or commission upon sale, before remitting the remainder to the consignor. As a result, costs incurred by the consignee are considered receivables.

25. **B**   Under the moving average approach, the 1,600 units on hand at 1/7/Year 6 would be divided into the total cost of $1,000 + $1,800 = $2,800, resulting in an average cost of $1.75 per unit. The 900 units sold on 1/20 would reduce inventory by 900 × $1.75 = $1,575, leaving inventory of 700 × $1.75 = $1,225. This would be increased by the purchase of 400 units at $5, or $2,000, resulting in inventory of $3,225.

26. **B**   Because a perpetual system is in use, LIFO inventory would be calculated as of each transaction. As a result, the 900 units sold on 1/20 would consist of the 600 units purchased on 1/7 and 300 of the units on hand at 1/1/Year 6. This leaves 700 units from beginning inventory at $1 or $700. This would be increased by the 400 units purchased on 1/25 at $5 giving inventory at 1/31/Year 6 of $2,700.

27. **A**   Ota's inventory would include the merchandise out on consignment, but at cost. The $40,000 would be reduced by the 40% markup based on selling price or $16,000. The goods in transit are properly included in inventory because the terms are FOB shipping point, indicating that they belong to Ota as of the date shipped. The goods held on consignment by Ota are improperly included in Ota's inventory and should be eliminated. As a result, inventory will be reduced by $16,000 + $27,000 = $43,000.

28. **B**   With a selling price of $408,000 and a cost of disposal of $20,000, the net realizable value, or ceiling, is $388,000. The floor is the ceiling of $388,000 less a normal profit of $60,000, or $328,000. Because the replacement cost of $360,000 is between the floor and ceiling, $360,000 will be considered market value. Because this is below the FIFO cost basis of $400,000, the carrying value of the inventory under the lower-of-cost-or-market approach will be $360,000.

29. **B**   As a consignee, Novotny is responsible to the consignor for the proceeds from the sale of consigned goods less any reimbursable expenses and less any commissions accruing to the consignee. Because Novotny received 505 sweaters and has 5 remaining as of the end of the year, it is assumed that 500 were sold at $100 each for total sales of $50,000. Novotny would deduct a 10% commission of $5,000 resulting in a liability of $45,000.

30. **B**   With a beginning balance of $90,000 and purchases of $124,000, cost of goods available for sale was $214,000. This would be reduced by the $34,000 of inventory written off as obsolete, which would be recognized as a loss because it was unexpected and unusual. As a result, cost of goods available for sale is reduced to $180,000. With ending inventory of $30,000, COGS would be the difference of $150,000.

31. **B**   As of 12/31/Year 6, Fialkowska is still obligated to purchase at least 100,000 units of the part for each of the next two years at $0.10 per unit. Because the parts are obsolete and are expected to be salable as scrap for $0.02 per unit, the difference of $0.08 per unit, or 200,000 × $0.08 = $16,000, will be recognized as a loss from the purchase commitment. In addition, the 250,000 units of inventory will be written down to the scrap value, but this will be considered a loss due to inventory decline, not part of the loss on the purchase commitment.

32. **D**   The LIFO reserve would be used to adjust the carrying value of inventory (under some method other than LIFO) to the LIFO balance for financial reporting purposes. With a value of $375,000 under average cost and $320,000 under LIFO, a reserve of $55,000 is needed. Because the reserve already has a credit balance of $35,000, a credit adjustment of $20,000 to the reserve is required. The offset to balance the entry will be a debit to COGS.

33. **B**   Because the inventory could be sold for $40,000, but would require further processing of $12,000, there is a net realizable value, or ceiling, of $28,000. With a normal profit margin of 10%, which is $4,000, the floor is $24,000. Because replacement cost of $20,000 is lower than the floor, market value will be $24,000. This is compared to the FIFO cost of $26,000 to result in inventory of $24,000 at the lower-of-cost-or-market.

34. **A**   We have no reason to assume that Asper's COGS balance for Year 5 is anything but correctly stated, using the information as it is presented in the question. Obviously, Asper would not want to include the merchandise in its Year 5 ending inventory.

35. **B**   Ending inventory at base year cost is $60,000, consisting of three layers. There is a 1/1/Year 5 layer with a base year cost of $40,000 and a dollar value LIFO amount of $40,000, a Year 5 layer with a base year cost of $5,000 and a dollar value LIFO cost of $6,000, and a Year 6 layer with a base year cost of $15,000.

    Because the total inventory has a base year cost of $60,000 and a current year cost of $80,000, the ratio of current year cost to base year cost is 8/6. This ratio can be applied to the Year 6 layer to give a dollar value cost of $15,000 × 8/6 = $20,000. This will be added to the previous balance of $46,000 to give ending inventory of $66,000 under dollar value LIFO.

36. **B**   The company must determine market value for this inventory item. That figure is normally replacement cost which, in this case, is $58. However, to qualify as market value, replacement cost cannot be outside of two boundaries which are often referred to as the ceiling and the floor. If replacement cost is above the ceiling,

that ceiling figure is used for market value. If replacement cost is below the floor, that floor figure is used for market value. The ceiling is the expected sales price ($78) less the cost to sell ($9) or $69. There is no problem here: replacement cost is not above that figure. The floor is the expected sales price ($78) less the cost to sell ($9) and the normal profit ($6) or $63. The replacement cost of $58 is below that figure. Consequently, $63 is used as the market value for this comparison. Because that determined market value figure is below the historical cost of $65, the $63 is reported.

37. **B**   FIFO perpetual and FIFO periodic systems always arrive at the same reported figures so that A cannot be correct. In either FIFO system, the ending inventory will be the last 14 items bought: 10 at $12 each ($120) and 4 at $11 each ($44) for a total balance of $164. Thus, D cannot be correct either.

   A LIFO periodic system simply assumes that the cost of the first 14 items would still be in ending inventory: 10 at $9 ($90) and 4 at $11 ($44) or $134. This means that C is not correct.

   A LIFO perpetual system moves the latest cost figures to cost of goods sold at the time of sale. When the first sale is made, 8 items go to cost of goods sold and 2 items remain in inventory with a cost of $9 each ($18). When the second sale is made, 8 more items go to cost of goods and 2 additional items remain with a cost of $11 each ($22). No sales occurred after the last purchase so all 10 of those items remain at $12 each ($120). Ending inventory is $18 plus $22 plus $120 (or $160).

38. **B**   In acquiring inventory, any abnormal costs are recording to net income immediately as a period cost. This inventory had a total cost of $600,000 or $60 per unit ($600,000/10,000 units). The abnormal loss was 400 units or $24,000 (at $60 each). Therefore, that amount is separated and recorded as a loss on the company's income statement. Only $576,000 remains in the asset account. The loss of the 600 units is simply viewed as a normal and necessary cost of making the acquisition.

39. **C**   In a perpetual inventory system, the company determines its cost of goods sold at the moment that each new sale is made. Under LIFO, that cost is always the cost of the most recent purchase. When the first sale is made, the most recent purchase before that sale was for an item at $7. When the second sale is made, the most recent purchase before that sale was for an item at $8.

40. **A**   In a periodic inventory system, the company determines its cost of goods sold at the very end of the period. Under LIFO, that cost is always the cost of the items bought at the latest part of the year. Here, two items were sold. As of the end of the year, the two items bought last were the $9 and $8 items.

41. **C**   When using F.O.B. shipping points, the inventory becomes the property of the buyer at the time of shipment. Since both shipments were made in Year 1, the inventory that Midlothian sold now belongs to the buyer (and it has been properly removed from Midlothian's Inventory balance). However, the inventory that Midlothian bought belongs to that company and should have been included in the year-end physical inventory.

42. **C**   Gross profit is the company's sales less its cost of goods sold. Because the Sales figure is given, only cost of goods sold must be computed. Beginning inventory is $80,000 and the Purchases balance for the year is $294,000. That is the $300,000 amount less the discounts received plus the transportation-in to the stores. The transportation cost to the customers is a delivery expense. Thus, had the company made no sales, it would be holding merchandise costing $374,000 ($80,000 plus $294,000). However, the company is actually in possession of $110,000 in merchandise. The missing inventory is assumed to be cost of goods sold: $374,000 minus $110,000 equals $264,000. Sales of $490,000 less cost of goods sold of $264,000 gives a gross profit of $226,000.

CHAPTER 23 – OTHER FINANCIAL ACCOUNTING TOPICS

STUDY TIP

Make sure that occasionally, probably once a week or so, you take a break and get completely away from preparing for the CPA exam. Everyone needs to recharge their batteries now and then. If you spend too much time studying, you will gradually wear down and become inefficient. On your calendar, program in time for rest and relaxation on a regular basis.

CHAPTER 23 – OTHER FINANCIAL ACCOUNTING TOPICS

SECTION 1: ACCOUNTING CHANGES

General Information—There has always been a problem when a company changes its accounting methods as to how the figures of past years would be reported. For the past several decades, those previously reported figures remained unchanged, while the impact on them caused by the new method was gathered and reported in the current year's income statement as the Cumulative Effect of an Accounting Change. This cumulative effect figure has always been reported at the very bottom of the company's income statement (along with discontinued operations and extraordinary gains and losses) net of any tax effect.

FASB 154 has now changed this process. All accounting changes are handled retrospectively. In other words, the previously reported figures are physically changed in order to conform to the newly adopted method. Thus, the need to report a Cumulative Effect of An Accounting Change has been eliminated.

There is one major exception to this change in reporting. If a company changes methods of depreciation (from straight-line, for example, to the double-declining balance method), this is viewed as a change in an estimation. Any change in estimation is viewed as having no impact on previously reported figures. Instead, the new depreciation method, or the new estimation, is simply applied in the current year and into the future.

A. Companies can decide to make changes in the accounting principles that are being applied. Normally, the company's independent auditor will only allow such changes if the move is to an acceptable alternative and if the company can show that the new method is preferable.

   1. Such changes are handled retroactively by restating all prior figures to those that would have been appropriate had the new method been used from the first day of the company's operations.

   2. For any period of time that is not being reported, the income impact on these earlier periods is shown as an adjustment (net of tax effect) to the earliest reported retained earnings balance. To illustrate, assume that a company began operations in Year 1 and is changing accounting principles in Year 5. If financial statements for only Years 4 and 5 are being presented, they are reported based on the new method. The income effect of the change on the first three years must be accumulated and reported as an adjustment to the opening retained earnings balance at the start of Year 4.

      a. If the previous effect of the change cannot be determined, the opening balance for the current year is based on the earlier method and then the new method begins to be applied.

      b. When a new official pronouncement is issued (such as by the FASB), the method of reporting figures from past years is normally explicitly detailed. If the handling of these earlier years is not established by the pronouncement, the change should be made retroactively.

   3. For a change in an estimation (such as the useful life of a building), there is no effect on any previously reported figure.

      a. To determine the amount to be reported for the current year, the beginning figures reported for the current year are used along with the new estimations.

4. If a change is both a change in an estimation and a change in a principle, it is reported as a change in an estimation. This is the approach by which a change in depreciation methods is reported. The old method is used until the first day of the current year and then the application of the new method is started. That is one change that is not applied retroactively.

SECTION 2: PARTNERSHIP ACCOUNTING

A. A **partnership** is an association of two or more persons to carry on a business as co-owners for profit. Many aspects of accounting for a partnership are the same as for a corporation, but there are unique features. For example, each partner has a separate capital account; the total of which replaces the stockholders' equity section of the balance sheet.

B. When a new partner is admitted into a partnership, any contributions are recorded by the partnership at market value, but the original book value is retained for tax purposes.

   1. A computation can be made so the new partner invests an amount that will be equal to the capital balance set up. This eliminates the need to record either goodwill or a bonus.

      a. The new partner's investment (NPI) can be set equal to the percentage of the business being acquired (%A) multiplied by the total capital of the business.

      b. Total capital would be the previous capital (PC) balance plus the new partner's investment. Thus, an equation would be set up and the new investment determined algebraically. NPI = %A × (PC + NPI) and solve for NPI.

   2. A new partner may have to contribute assets worth more than the percentage being acquired of the total capital, especially if it is a profitable partnership.

      a. This difference can be recorded by the **bonus method.** A partner is given a set capital balance or a percentage of total capital. Any difference from contribution (either positive or negative) is recorded to the original partners' capital accounts based on the previous method of allocating profits and losses.

      b. This difference can also be recorded using the **goodwill method.** The new partner receives a capital balance exactly equal to the contribution. The new partner's payment is then used to compute an implied value for the business as a whole. The investment is divided by the percentage acquired to get this valuation. The difference between this implied value and total capital (including the new investment) is viewed as goodwill and is recorded along with an offsetting entry to the capital accounts of the original partners based on the previous method of **allocating profits and losses**.

C. When revenues and expenses are closed out at the end of the year, the net profit or loss must be assigned to the partners' capital accounts. The actual amount paid to a partner is usually set by agreement and can differ from this allocation process.

   1. If there is no agreement, a split is always done on an even basis.

   2. If there is an agreement as to profit allocation but losses are not mentioned, the same method is used.

   3. Any agreements must be followed specifically. They can include several factors such as a salary allowance, interest, and a ratio. If more than one factor is included, the ratio is computed last.

D. At some point, a partnership may be liquidated, the assets sold off and the debts paid with any residual amounts going to the partners.

1. In liquidating noncash assets, any gains and losses are assigned to the partners based on normal profit and loss allocation.

2. Any residual cash goes to the partners based on the final balances in their capital accounts.

3. If enough money is set aside to pay all debts, available cash can be distributed to the partners before all noncash assets are sold. To determine distribution, maximum losses are assumed for all remaining noncash assets. If a partner has a negative capital balance after these simulated losses, that amount is also viewed as a loss to be absorbed by the remaining partners using their relative profit and loss percentages. When all remaining capital accounts have positive balances, those amounts are the safe capital amounts that can be distributed immediately.

SECTION 3: FINANCIAL INSTRUMENTS

A. Financial instruments are cash, investments in equities, or contracts to receive or pay cash or another financial instrument.

B. The term **financial instrument** includes traditional items such as accounts receivable and notes payable but also includes more complex arrangements such as forward currency exchange contracts.

DERIVATIVES

A. A particular type of financial instrument, a **derivative** is an exchange of promises where a "notional amount" is set by a contract, such as a number of shares of stock or barrels of oil that will be bought or sold or paid for in the future (often at a set amount).

B. An "underlying" such as the actual price of the shares of stock or oil on the market will give that contract a positive or negative fair value.

1. Formally, an **underlying** is any financial or physical variable that has either observable changes or objectively verifiable changes.

C. For example, a contract to buy one share of stock at $50 per share has a positive value if the stock is selling in the open market above $50 and a negative value if it is selling below $50.

1. The one share is the notional amount and the price of the stock is the underlying.

D. Derivatives require no initial net investment or an initial net investment that is smaller than would be required for other types of contracts that would be expected to have a similar response to changes in market factors.

1. Many derivative instruments require no net investment or simply a premium as compensation for the time value of money.

2. For example, futures contracts may require the establishment of a margin account with a balance equal to a small percentage (2% to 3%) of the value of the contract.

3. Another example would be the premium paid to purchase a call option on a stock being a fraction of the cost of the underlying stock.

E. Derivatives do one of the following with regards to settlement:

1. Require or permit net settlement, either within the contract or by a means outside of the contract. Net settlement means that a contract can be settled through the payment of cash rather than the exchange of specific assets referenced in the contract.

2. Provide for the delivery of an asset that puts the recipient in a position not substantially different from net settlement.

    a. For example, a futures contract may require one party to the contract to deliver an asset, but there is a "market mechanism" (such as an exchange) so that the asset can be readily converted to cash.

    b. Convertibility to cash requires an active market and is a determining factor in whether or not a financial instrument or any other contract will be treated as a derivative instrument.

EXAMPLES OF DERIVATIVE INSTRUMENTS

A. Options to purchase or sell either call or put exchange-traded securities.

B. Futures contracts.

C. Interest rate swaps.

D. Currency swaps.

E. Swaptions (an option on a swap).

F. Credit indexed contracts.

G. Interest rate caps/floors/collars.

BASIC ACCOUNTING FOR DERIVATIVES

A. All derivatives must be reported on the balance sheet. Depending on their nature, derivatives are shown as either assets or liabilities.

B. All derivatives are reported at their **fair values** (the current amount at which a financial instrument could be exchanged in a transaction between willing parties).

C. The change in fair value of a derivative is reported within current earnings or comprehensive income (depending on specific circumstances) for the period of the change.

EMBEDDED DERIVATIVE AND BIFURCATION

A. An **embedded derivative** is a feature of a financial instrument or other contract that, if the feature stood alone, would meet the definition of a derivative.

B. **Bifurcation** is the process of separating an embedded derivative from its host contract. The process is necessary so that hybrid instruments can be separated into their component parts, each being accounted for by using the appropriate valuation techniques.

HEDGES

A. Many derivatives are acquired to hedge other transactions or commitments where exposure to a change in value would create gains or losses.

B. A hedge is designed to cause an equal and offsetting gain or loss so that no net income effect will result. A derivative can be used for these purposes to balance out gains and losses from changes in value.

C. Most simply, which is how the exam tests this (thank goodness!), you are a party to a contract that may cause you a loss in the future when the contract is settled. So, you hedge (by buying a derivative that can cause you a gain in the future). When that future date arrives, you then have a loss on the original contract and a gain on the derivative, and they offset each other. An example would be a payable in a foreign currency; the original contract establishes a future payment in a foreign currency, which, when converted into U.S. dollars, could increase or decrease by the settlement date (due date) due to changes in foreign exchange rates. The derivative is purchased to settle at the same date, so whatever happens to the original contract happens in reverse to the derivative contract. Thus, there are gains and losses, which offset each other.

CRITERIA THAT MUST BE MET IN ORDER FOR A DERIVATIVE INSTRUMENT TO QUALIFY AS A HEDGE

A. Sufficient documentation such as the following must be provided at the beginning of the process to identify at a minimum:

1. The objective and strategy of the hedge.

2. The hedging instrument and the hedged item.

3. How the effectiveness of the hedge will be assessed on an ongoing basis.

B. The hedge must be "highly effective" throughout its life.

1. Effectiveness is measured by analyzing the hedging instrument's ability to generate changes in fair value that offset the changes in value of the hedged item.

2. At a minimum, its effectiveness will be measured every three months and whenever earnings or financial statements are reported.

3. A **highly effective hedge** has been interpreted to mean that "the cumulative change in the value of the hedging instrument should be between 80% and 125% of the inverse cumulative changes in the fair value or cash flows of the hedged item." So, if the original payable in foreign currency units increases in amount by $100, the derivative must change in value by between $80 and $125. The change in the payable, an increase in a liability, results in a loss. The change in the derivative must, therefore, result in a gain.

4. The method used to assess effectiveness must be used throughout the hedge period and must be consistent with the approach used for managing risk.

THREE KINDS OF HEDGES (SFAS 133)

Those derivative instruments that qualify under the definition of hedging instruments will be accounted for using hedge accounting, and hedge accounting generally provides for matching the recognition of gains and losses of the hedging instrument and the hedged asset or liability.

A. Fair value hedge.

    1. A hedge of the exposure to changes in the fair value of the following:

        a. A recognized asset or liability.

        b. An unrecognized firm commitment.

B. Cash flow hedge.

    1. A hedge of the exposure to variability in the cash flows of the following:

        a. A recognized asset or liability.

        b. A forecasted transaction.

C. Foreign currency hedge.

    1. A hedge of the foreign currency exposure of the following:

        a. An unrecognized firm commitment.

        b. An available-for-sale security.

        c. A forecasted transaction.

        d. A net investment in a foreign operation.

REQUIRED ACCOUNTING UNDER SFAS 133

The accounting for changes in the fair value of a derivative (that is, gains and losses) depends on the intended use of the derivative and the resulting designation. The following from FASB 133 describes that accounting.

A. For a derivative *designated as a hedge*, the following rules apply:

    1. For a derivative designated as hedging the exposure to changes in the fair value of a recognized asset or liability or a firm commitment (referred to as **a fair value hedge**), the gain or loss is *recognized in earnings in the period of change* together with the offsetting loss or gain on the hedged item attributable to the risk being hedged. The effect of that accounting is to reflect in earnings the extent to which the hedge is not effective in achieving offsetting changes in fair value.

    2. For a derivative designated as hedging the exposure to variable cash flows of a forecasted transaction (referred to as a **cash flow hedge**), the effective portion of the derivative's gain or loss is *initially reported as a component of other comprehensive income (outside earnings)* and subsequently reclassified into earnings when the forecasted transaction affects earnings. The ineffective portion of the gain or loss is reported in earnings immediately.

    3. For a derivative designated as hedging *the foreign currency exposure of a net investment in a foreign operation*, the *gain or loss is reported in other comprehensive income (outside earnings)* as part of the **cumulative translation** adjustment.

        a. The accounting for **a fair value hedge** described above applies to a derivative designated as a hedge of the *foreign currency exposure of an unrecognized firm commitment or an available-for-sale security.*

b. Similarly, the accounting for **a cash flow hedge** described above applies to a derivative designated as a hedge of the *foreign currency exposure of a foreign-currency-denominated forecasted transaction*.

B. For a derivative **not designated as a hedging instrument**, the gain or loss is recognized in earnings in the period of change.

C. Under this Statement, an entity that elects to apply hedge accounting is required to establish at the inception of the hedge the method it will use for assessing the effectiveness of the hedging derivative and the measurement approach for determining the ineffective aspect of the hedge. Those methods must be consistent with the entity's approach to managing risk.

DISCLOSURES RELATING TO FINANCIAL INSTRUMENTS, BOTH DERIVATIVE AND NONDERIVATIVE, THAT ARE USED AS HEDGING INSTRUMENTS

A. Objectives and the strategies for achieving them.

B. Context to understand the instrument.

C. Risk management policies.

D. A list of hedged instruments.

These disclosures have to be separated by type of hedge and reported every time a complete set of financial statements is issued.

REQUIREMENTS FOR DISCLOSURE OF RISKS ASSOCIATED WITH FINANCIAL INSTRUMENTS OTHER THAN DERIVATIVES

A. Fair value must be disclosed (in the body of the financial statements or in the notes) when practicable to do so.

1. Must include the method(s) and significant assumptions used in estimating fair value.

2. Must distinguish between financial instruments held/issued for trading purposes and for purposes other than trading.

B. Information pertinent to estimating fair value (carrying value, effective interest rate, maturity) must be disclosed if it is not practicable to estimate. It must also provide reasons why market value cannot easily be estimated.

C. No "netting" or aggregating of fair values between financial instruments that are derivatives, nonderivatives, or other derivatives.

D. If financial instruments are disclosed in more than one area of the financial statements, one note must contain a summary table cross-referencing the location of the other instruments.

REQUIREMENTS FOR DISCLOSURE OF CONCENTRATIONS OF CREDIT RISK FOR ALL FINANCIAL INSTRUMENTS OTHER THAN DERIVATIVES

A. Significant concentrations of credit risk must be disclosed.

1. **Credit risk** is the chance of loss resulting because another party fails to perform according to the terms of the contract.

   a. For example, a company guarantees the loan of another company and the debtor fails to pay.

2. A **significant concentration** is where a large amount of performance is required of a single party or by a group of similar parties (for example, in the same industry or the same geographical location).

   a. Must also indicate maximum potential accounting loss.

   b. Must also provide information about collateral and security requirements.

OFF-BALANCE SHEET RISK

A. Some financial instruments have off-balance sheet risk; in other words, a loss can be incurred that is larger than the amount being reported on the balance sheet.

B. For example: A company can have a commitment that is not being reported on the balance sheet that could still create a loss. An operating lease is a very basic example of this. There is no balance sheet liability for operating leases. There are other examples, but they are finance topics included in BEC.

GLOSSARY OF IMPORTANT TERMS

American option. An American option contract can be exercised at any time up to expiration. (See European option below.)

At-the-money. An option is said to be at-the-money when the price of the underlying asset is equal to the strike price of the option contract. An option contract that is at-the-money has no intrinsic value.

Buyer. The buyer of an option contract purchases from the writer the right to either purchase (call) or sell (put) the underlying asset from or to the writer, at a specified price, on or before a specified date. A buyer of the option is said to have a long position in the option.

Call. A call is an option contract that gives the holder the right to purchase the underlying asset at the strike price set in the contract.

European option. A European option contract can be exercised only at expiration.

Note that the terms *American* and *European* do not describe where options are traded but rather the type or style of option contracts. Although American and European options may have identical strike prices and expiration dates, they still differ in one important aspect. The owner of an American option may exercise the option at any time before or at expiration. The owner of a European option may exercise the option only at expiration.

Two options, one American and one European, that are otherwise alike in every respect, may have different values because of the American option's opportunity to exercise early. At expiration, the options will have the same value, but up until this time it is necessary to distinguish between the two styles in order to determine the option value.

If an American and a European option are identical in all ways (e.g., maturity, underlying stock, strike price), the value of the American option will always equal or exceed the value of the European option. The American contract has an option to exercise early, and the value of this ability to "exercise early" cannot be negative. If the option owner chooses not to exercise the American option early, it will have the same value as the European option on the expiration date. In most cases, the early exercise of an option on a nondividend-paying stock cannot be economically supported. However, early exercise in order to capture dividends or to gain power or influence (through voting rights) is often enticing to the holder of the option.

The vast majority of options traded throughout the world are American options, but most texts and training materials use examples of European options. European options are simpler to analyze than American options and can be used to effectively demonstrate the basic characteristics of options.

Exercise. Exercising an option forces the writer to fulfill their contractual obligation. The writer of a put must purchase the underlying asset at the strike price set in the contract. The writer of a call must sell the underlying asset at the strike price set in the contract.

Strike (exercise) price. The stated price at which the underlying asset may be purchased (call) or sold (put), usually designated by "X."

Expiration. The expiration of an option contract is the date at which the owner's option to exercise expires. After expiration, the contract is worthless because it cannot be exercised.

In-the-money. A call option is said to be in-the-money when the price of the underlying asset is greater than the strike price of the option contract. A put option is said to be in-the-money when the price of the underlying asset is less than the strike price of an option contract. Any option contract that is in-the-money has an intrinsic value greater than zero.

Intrinsic value. The intrinsic value is the amount the holder would receive if the option were exercised immediately.
- Call Option: $S - X$ (S = Asset Price, X = Strike Price)
- Put Option: $X - S$

Intrinsic value is the *greater* of: $S - X$ or zero for a call or $X - S$ or zero for a put. Intrinsic value cannot be negative.

Long. A long position in an option contract is the position held by the owner or buyer of the contract.

Offsetting order. An order that closes an existing order is called an offsetting order. An investor opens a position by buying an option and may later close the position before expiration by selling a similar option. Investors can also open a position by selling (writing) an option and later close the position by buying a similar option.

Out-of-the-money. A call option is said to be out-of-the-money when the price of the underlying asset is less than the strike price of the option contract. A put option is said to be out-of-the-money when the price of the underlying asset is greater than the strike price of an option contract. Any option that is out-of-the-money has an intrinsic value of zero.

Premium. The premium of an option contract is the price paid by the buyer to the writer of the contract for the right to exercise; usually designated as C for a call option and P for a put option.

Put. A put is an option contract that gives the holder the right to sell the underlying asset at the strike price set in the contract.

Short. A short position in an option contract is the position held by the writer or seller of the contract.

Time value. Prior to expiration, all American options and some European options will have value based upon the time remaining until expiration. The time value is equal to the difference between the option contract's market price and its intrinsic value.

Writer. The seller of an option contract. The writer assumes the obligation to buy or sell the underlying asset at the discretion of the option buyer. The writer of the option is said to hold a short position in the contract.

SECTION 4: EARNINGS PER SHARE

A. Earnings per share (EPS) is a common stock computation. It must be reported for each income period by all publicly held companies.

B. Keep in mind the financial statement assertion of disclosure.

   1. The individual items comprising net income have already occurred so we are not so concerned with the measurement and valuation issues.

   2. It is the presentation and disclosure of the EPS calculations that is paramount here.

C. Basically, the net income that is applicable to common stock is divided by the weighted average number of common stock shares outstanding.

D. Numerator:

   1. Any preferred stock dividends must be subtracted from net income to get the amount of income applicable to common stock.

   2. If preferred stock is cumulative, the annual dividend is subtracted each year whether declared or not. If noncumulative, it is only subtracted when declared.

E. Denominator:

   1. To get the weighted average number of common shares, the number of shares outstanding for a period is multiplied by that number of months.

   2. The resulting totals are added and divided by 12 to get the average for the year.

   3. For averaging purposes, shares issued as a stock dividend or split are assumed as having been issued at the earliest point in the computation.

F. Example:

Example:

Strauchan Co. (Strauchan) has one class of common stock outstanding and no other securities that are potentially convertible into common stock. During Year 5, 100,000 shares of common stock were outstanding. In Year 6, two distributions of additional common shares occurred:

- On April 1, 20,000 shares of treasury stock were sold.
- On July 1, a 2-for-1 stock split was issued.

Net income was $410,000 in Year 6 and $350,000 in Year 5.

What amounts should Strauchan report as EPS in its Year 6 and Year 5 comparative income statements?

Solution:

There were 100,000 shares of stock outstanding in Year 5. In Year 6, ignoring the stock split, the weighted average outstanding shares would include 100,000 for the entire year and 20,000 for 9/12 of the year for a total of 100,000 + 15,000 = 115,000. The stock split is given retroactive treatment as if there were 200,000 shares outstanding in Year 5 and the weighted average was 230,000 for Year 6.

The resulting EPS amounts would be $350,000/200,000 = $1.75 for Year 5 and $410,000/230,000 = $1.78 for Year 6.

DILUTED EPS

A. If a company has dilutive securities (that can be converted into common stock), it must also report a second figure called **diluted EPS**.

1. This computation gives weight to convertible items by assuming that conversion actually occurred.

2. This follows the basic accounting principle of *conservatism* in presenting financial results. Diluted EPS will always be lower or, at most, the same as Basic EPS.

3. In order to assure conformity, a set pattern must be used by every company to give weight to any convertible items. There is no flexibility; all companies must follow the same set of assumptions.

B. To include stock options or rights in the computation of diluted EPS, conversion is assumed, and the number of shares that would be issued is added to the denominator (*increases* the weighted average number of shares).

1. Converting options often requires payment of cash. If conversion is assumed, the cash coming into the company is also assumed.

2. It is further assumed that this cash is used to buy treasury stock at its average price for the period, and that *reduces* the weighted average number of outstanding shares.

C. To include convertible bonds in the computation of diluted EPS, conversion is assumed, and the number of shares that would be issued is added to the denominator (*increases* the weighted average number of shares).

1. Interest expense is a negative within net income.

2. Assumed conversion of the bonds would eliminate the interest, causing an increase in income used for this computation.

3. Don't forget to tax-effect the interest savings!

D. To include convertible preferred stock in the computation of diluted EPS, conversion is assumed, and the number of shares that would be issued is added to the denominator (*increases* the weighted average number of shares).

1. Preferred shares were previously subtracted in the numerator in arriving at the income applicable to common stock.

2. Assumed conversion of the preferred stock would eliminate the dividends, causing an increase in the income used for this computation.

E. Example:

Example:

Leslie, Inc. (Leslie) has 110,000 shares of common stock, 10,000 shares of preferred stock, and 8% bonds with a face value of $1,000,000, all outstanding on December 31, Year 6. During Year 6, Leslie paid dividends of $3.00 per share on its preferred stock. Net income for the year is $880,000. The income tax rate is 30%.

The preferred shares are convertible into 20,000 shares of common stock and the 8% bonds are convertible into 30,000 shares of common stock.

Calculate the fully diluted EPS for Year 6.

Solution:

To calculate fully diluted EPS, it will be assumed that all the convertible securities will be converted into common stock. If the convertible bonds had been converted into common stock, no interest on the bonds would have been paid. The numerator would be increased by the after-tax amount of bond interest.

Net income (less preferred stock dividends)		$850,000
Add: preferred dividends that would not be paid (10,000 × $3)		30,000
Add: bond interest ($1,000,000 × 8%)	$80,000	
Less: tax effect ($80,000 × 30%)	(24,000)	56,000
Adjusted net income		$936,000

The denominator would be increased for the 20,000 shares of common stock that the preferred stock can be converted into and increased for the 30,000 shares of common stock that the bonds can be converted into.

Number of shares	110,000
Preferred share conversion	20,000
Common share conversion	30,000
Adjusted number of shares	160,000

As a result, fully diluted EPS will be $936,000/160,000 = $5.85.

TREATMENT OF ANTIDILUTIVE ITEMS IN EPS CALCULATIONS

A. In computing EPS, any assumed conversion that causes the reported EPS figure to rise is referred to as **antidilutive**.

B. Antidilutive securities are simply ignored in the calculation.

C. Example:

Example:

Marko, Inc. had an EPS of $15.00 for Year 6 before considering the effects of any convertible securities. No conversion or exercise of convertible securities occurred during Year 6. However, possible conversion of convertible bonds would have reduced EPS by $0.75. The effect of possible exercise of common stock options would have increased EPS by $0.10.

What amount should Marko report as diluted EPS for Year 6?

Solution:

Diluted EPS takes into account the effect of all dilutive potential common shares that were outstanding during the period. Thus, the possible conversion of convertible bonds would be included because they are dilutive (i.e., EPS would be reduced), but the possible exercise of common stock options would not be included because they are antidilutive (i.e., EPS would be increased). Diluted EPS = $15.00 – $0.75 = $14.25.

EFFECT ON EPS OF CONTINGENTLY ISSUABLE SHARES

A. Per SFAS 128, the effect of contingently issuable shares is not included in basic EPS.

B. If shares are to be issued in the future with no restrictions on issuance other than the passage of time, they are to be considered issued and treated as outstanding in the computation of diluted EPS.

C. Example:

Example:

Cambridge Corp. has 1,200,000 shares of common stock outstanding on January 1 and December 1, Year 6. In connection with the acquisition of a subsidiary company in June Year 5, Cambridge is required to issue 50,000 additional shares of its common stock on July 1, Year 7, to the former owners of the subsidiary. Cambridge paid $200,000 in preferred stock dividends in Year 6, and reported net income of $3,400,000 for the year.

Calculate the diluted EPS for Year 6.

Solution:

The net income available to common shareholders is $3,200,000. This is the net income of $3,400,000 minus the preferred stock dividends of $200,000. The weighted average common shares outstanding is 1,250,000. This is computed as the actual common shares outstanding for the full year of 1,200,000 plus the contingent common shares of 50,000 that were outstanding for the full year because the contingency was incurred in Year 5. Thus, diluted EPS = $3,200,000/1,250,000 = $2.56.

RATIOS USING STOCKHOLDERS' EQUITY COMPONENTS IN THEIR CALCULATIONS

A. Dividend payout measures percentage of earnings distributed as dividends:

dividends per share / earnings per share

B. Rate of return on common stockholders' equity measures the return earned on the stockholders' investment in the company:

net income available to common stockholders / common stockholders' equity

C. Debt to equity shows creditors the company's ability to sustain losses:

total debt (all liabilities) / (stockholder's equity)

SECTION 5: FOREIGN CURRENCY BALANCES

Companies doing business on an international scale need to understand the relationship between amounts expressed in foreign currencies and amounts expressed in U.S. dollars. Principles have been established for circumstances involving the following:

- Companies with foreign subsidiaries that will be included in the preparation of consolidated financial statements.
- Companies with receivables or payables that will be settled by the receipt or payment of foreign currency.

EXCHANGE RATES

In applying the foreign currency principles, it is important to understand the use of exchange rates. The exchange rate at a specific date is referred to as the **spot rate**. If a receivable or payable is to be settled at a specific future date, the applicable rate would be referred to as the **future rate**.

For example, if a transaction on 11/1 were to result in a payable due after 90 days, it would be measured using the 90-day future rate. Upon preparing a balance sheet 60 days later on 12/31, the payable would be remeasured using the 30-day future rate.

When amounts are expressed in a foreign currency, the appropriate number of U.S. dollars (USD) is calculated by multiplying by a rate consisting of the ratio of USD1 to the amount of the foreign currency that USD1 is equivalent to.

If, for example, one Canadian dollar was equivalent to 90 cents of U.S. money, then the following would occur:

- The direct exchange rate would be $0.90/1 to convert Canadian amounts into U.S. amounts. This rate of 0.90 would be used to multiply by the number of Canadian dollars to convert them to their equivalent U.S. dollars. Example: 300 Canadian dollars × 0.9 = 270 U.S. dollars.
- The indirect exchange rate would be 1/$0.90. This rate, 1.11, represents the number of U.S. dollars that would equal 1 Canadian dollar. So, if you have 1 U.S. dollar, multiply it by 1.11 to determine the equivalent number of Canadian dollars.

FORWARD EXCHANGE CONTRACTS

When individuals or entities are involved in foreign currency transactions, they may enter into a particular type of transaction called a *forward exchange contract*. A forward exchange contract involves an agreement to either buy or sell a certain amount of foreign currency at a fixed exchange rate at some time in the future.

For example, if an individual was to believe that the rate at which dollars could be converted into euros was going to change such that in the future it will take more dollars to buy euros, he would enter into a contract to buy euros in the future at the current exchange rate. If his prediction is correct, he will buy the euros at the previous lower rate and sell them on the open market at the then current higher rate. If his prediction is incorrect, he will be buying at a higher rate and selling at a low rate.

Some forward exchange contracts are designed as protection against fluctuation in foreign currency exchange rates when an entity is involved in a foreign currency transaction to be settled in the future. If a company is to settle a note payable by paying a certain amount of euros at the end of one year, it can protect itself from a change in the exchange rate by entering into a forward exchange contract that will enable the company to buy the currency (euros) at the current rate when the note becomes due. This way, regardless of how much and which direction the exchange rate fluctuates, the entity will have to pay the same number of dollars to settle the liability. This is referred to as a **hedge**.

When a company has an effective hedge to protect a foreign currency commitment from fluctuations in the exchange rate, gains or losses are not recognized. This would apply to commitments for the purchase or sale of equipment or similar commitments. When a company enters into a forward exchange contract that is intended as a hedge against an existing receivable or payable that occurred in the ordinary course of business, gains and losses on the forward exchange contract are recognized. The amount of the gain or loss is measured by the change in the spot rate, similarly to the recognition of the gain or loss on the receivable or payable.

When a company enters into a forward exchange contract for speculative purposes, gains and losses resulting from changes in exchange rates are also recognized. The amount of the gain or loss is measured by the change in the forward rate.

FOREIGN CURRENCY TRANSACTIONS

Companies often have individual transactions denominated in a currency outside of their cash currency (formally known as the company's functional currency). For example, inventory or equipment can be bought or sold for balances to be conveyed in Japanese yen.

1. All transaction amounts denominated in a foreign currency are remeasured for reporting purposes into the reporting company's currency at the spot exchange rate as of the date of the transaction.

2. Assets or liabilities that require cash payments (as well as any assets or liabilities reported at fair value) are remeasured on an ongoing basis over time based on each new spot exchange rate.

3. Changes in the reported value of these specific assets and liabilities create gains and losses to be recognized in the company's income statement.

4. All other accounts remain reported based on the spot exchange rate as of the date of the transaction.

This is best described by an example.

A U.S. company, Usco, sells products to a customer, Canco, in Canada. The Canadian currency is the Canadian dollar (CAD) and the U.S. currency is the U.S. dollar (USD). The date of the transaction is December 1, Year 6, and the transaction amount is CAD10,000.

The CAD/USD spot exchange rate on December 1 is CAD1.20/USD. (1.20 Canadian dollars are required to purchase 1.00 U.S. dollars, or 1.20 CAD = 1 USD.)

Usco prepares its financial statements on December 31, Year 6. Assume that the exchange rate on December 31 is CAD1.16/USD.

The exchange of CAD10,000 to settle the transaction will occur on January 31, Year 7. Assume that the exchange rate on January 31, Year 7, is CAD1.18/USD.

A. Transaction date (December 1, Year 6).

    1. The amount at which Usco would record the transaction is as follows: CAD10,000/1.20 (CAD1.20 to USD1.00) = USD8,333

    2.
Accounts receivable	$8,333	
Revenue		$8,333

B. Financial statement preparation between transaction date and settlement date is as follows:

    1. It must restate foreign currency amounts to reflect the spot exchange rate as of the balance sheet date.

    2. Therefore, because the spot exchange rate changes between the transaction date and the balance sheet date, then there will be (unrealized) foreign exchange transaction gains or losses, depending on the direction of the change.

        CAD10,000/1.16 = USD8,621

    3. In this case, there is a gain of USD288 that is recorded as a credit to the foreign exchange gain account, not to the sales account, as follows:

Accounts receivable	$288	
Foreign currency transaction gain		$288

        a. The sale was a result of an operating decision, while the gain results from bearing the risk of fluctuating spot rates. The latter is the result of an investment decision.

        b. As we will see later, the risk of a foreign exchange transaction loss could have been avoided by either demanding immediate payment on the transaction date or by entering into a forward exchange contract to hedge the exposed asset (the accounts receivable).

C. Settlement date.

    1. Once again, it must restate the foreign currency amounts, this time to reflect the spot exchange rate as of the settlement date.

    2. CAD10,000/1.18 = USD8,475

    3. There is a loss of USD146 to be reported to the foreign exchange gain account and the receipt and conversion of foreign currency (CAD10,000) as follows:

Foreign currency	$8,475	
Foreign currency transaction loss	$146	
Accounts receivable		$8,621

Cash	$8,475	
Foreign currency		$8,475

D. Overall.

    1. Net effect of this foreign currency transaction is the receipt of $8,475 for a transaction originally measured at $8,333.

    2. Realized net gain is $142 over two periods—$288 gain in Year 6 and $146 loss in Year 7.

E. Financial statement disclosures required are as follows:

1. Aggregate transaction gain (loss) that is included in the company's net income.

2. Significant rate changes subsequent to the date of the financial statements, including the effects on unsettled foreign currency transactions.

ACCOUNTING FOR FORWARD EXCHANGE CONTRACTS

As above, the basics are best described by an example.

On December 12, Year 6, Dawson Corp. (Dawson) entered into a forward exchange contract to purchase €100,000 in 90 days to hedge a purchase of inventory on November 30, Year 6, for which the payable is due in March, Year 7.

The relevant exchange rates are as follows:

	Spot rate	Forward rate (for March 12, Year 7)
November 30, Year 6	$0.87**	$0.89
December 12, Year 6	$0.88	$0.90
December 31, Year 6	$0.92	$0.93

　　**$0.87 in U.S. currency = 1 Euro

A. On December 31, Year 6, Dawson needs to calculate the amount of foreign currency gain to include in income from this forward contract. This is because fair market valuation is required for foreign exchange contracts (see SFAS 133).

1. Each period, this is accomplished by marking the forward exchange contract to market by using the forward rate at the financial statement date. At December 31, Year 6, the forward rate is $0.93.

2. The difference between $0.93 and $0.90 (the latter being the forward rate on the date the contracts were entered into) times €100,000 is $3,000, the forward exchange gain that is included in income for Year 6. (This means that Dawson will be able to purchase the needed €100,000 for $90,000, but the value of the contract is $93,000. Dawson would get $93,000 of value for only $90,000, measured as of the year-end date of December 31.)

B. On December 31, Year 6, Dawson also needs to calculate the amount of foreign currency transaction loss to include in income from the revaluation of the accounts payable of 100,000 Euros incurred as a result of the purchase of inventory.

1. Exposed net assets denominated in foreign currency units need to be revalued at the current spot rate (see SFAS 52).

2. Therefore, at December 31, Year 6, there is a foreign exchange transaction loss of $5,000 [($0.92 − $0.87) × €100,000].

3. Keep in mind that the accounts payable was created on November 30, Year 6, hence the use of the $0.87 rate. The loss will be recorded in net income for Year 6.

FOREIGN CURRENCY TRANSLATION

A. Purpose:

1. To provide information relative to the expected economic effects of rate changes on a company's cash flows and equity.

2. To provide information in consolidated statements relative to the financial results and relationships of each individual foreign consolidated company as reflected by the functional currency of each reporting company.

FUNCTIONAL CURRENCY FOR THE PURPOSES OF TRANSLATION

A. All companies are said to have a functional currency, the currency in which the company primarily generates and expends cash (primary economic environment in which it operates).

B. As a simple example, for U.S. companies, the functional currency is the U.S. dollar.

C. If there is some doubt as to the identity of the functional currency, then the following seven factors must be examined:

1. Cash flows—Do the foreign entity's cash flows directly affect the parent's cash flows, and are they immediately available for remittance to the parent?

2. Sales prices—Are the foreign company's sales prices responsive to exchange rate changes and to international competition?

3. Sales markets—Is the foreign company's sales market in the parent's country or are sales denominated in the parent's currency?

4. Expenses—Are the foreign company's expenses (costs to acquire materials, pay labor, etc.) incurred in the parent's country?

5. Financing—Is the foreign company's major financing primarily from the parent or is it denominated in the parent's currency?

6. Intercompany transactions—Is there a high volume of intercompany transactions between the parent and the foreign company?

7. If the answers to the question above are predominantly yes, then the functional currency would be the reporting currency of the parent (i.e., the U.S. dollar). If the answers are predominantly no, the functional currency would be the foreign currency.

METHODS OF TRANSLATION: TRANSLATING FINANCIAL STATEMENTS OF A FOREIGN COMPANY WHEN THE FUNCTIONAL CURRENCY IS KNOWN

A. Prior to being reported in the consolidated financial statements, figures denominated in foreign currencies must be stated at their equivalent U.S. dollar values.

B. If the functional currency is the foreign currency, the **current rate** method is used.

C. If the functional currency is the reporting currency of the parent, the **temporal method** is used.

D. On a big picture level, the choice of functional currency is based on management judgment and may not be completely objective (once again, earnings management issues may come into play).

E. Summary:

1. In consolidation, if parent and sub have different functional currencies (quite frequently the case), turning the sub's numbers into the parent's functional currency is called a **translation**, and all assets and liabilities are translated at the current rate.

2. If parent and sub have the same functional currency, turning the sub's numbers into the parent's functional currency is called a **remeasurement**, and only monetary assets and liabilities are remeasured at the current rate.

RULES FOR APPLYING THE CURRENT RATE METHOD

A. All assets and liabilities are translated using the current rate at the balance sheet date (1.12 in the example below).

B. All revenues and expenses are translated at the rates in effect when these items are recognized during the period. Due to practical considerations, however, weighted-average rates can be used to translate revenues and expenses that were incurred throughout the year (1.10 in the example below).

C. Owners' equity accounts are translated using historical exchange rates (0.90 in the example below).

D. Dividends are translated at the historic rate on the date of declaration.

E. Because all assets and liabilities are constantly being translated at the new spot exchange rate, a net gain or loss will be created by the changes in reported value. For a translation (where the parent and the subsidiary have different functional currencies), these gains and losses are referred to as a "translation adjustment" and reported in other comprehensive income in the stockholders' equity section of the balance sheet. In translation, these gains and losses do not impact the computation of net income.

F.   Example of the current rate method:

Assets	Euros	Exchange rate	U.S. dollars
Cash	60	1.12	67.20
Accounts receivable	100	1.12	112.00
Land	200	1.12	224.00
Building	400	1.12	448.00
	760		851.20
Liabilities & Stockholders' Equity			
Accounts payable	100	1.12	112.00
Mortgage payable	200	1.12	224.00
Common stock	100	0.90	90.00
Retained earnings	360	income statement	352.00
Translation adjustment		plug	73.20
	760		851.20

Income Statement	Euros	Exchange rate	U.S. dollars
Revenues	260	1.10	286.00
Operating expenses	(140)	1.10	(154.00)
Depreciation expense	(20)	1.10	(22.00)
Net income	100		110.00
Retained Earnings			
Beginning amount	260	given	242.00
Net income	100		110.00
Closing amount	360		352.00

Note that the beginning retained earnings of 242 (U.S. dollars) is given and is taken from the prior period's translated financial statements; the amount cannot merely be translated using a single exchange rate.

RULES FOR APPLYING THE TEMPORAL METHOD

A.   Monetary assets and monetary liabilities are remeasured using the current rate at the balance sheet date (1.12 in the example below).

B.   Nonmonetary assets and liabilities (i.e., PP&E) that have historical cost balances are remeasured using historical rates at the date the item entered the subsidiary (0.90 in the example below).

C.   Owners' equity accounts, such as common stock and additional paid-in capital, are translated using historic rates (0.90 in the example below).

D.   Dividends are translated at the historic rate at the date of declaration.

E.   Retained earnings is brought forward from the translated statement of the previous year. Or it can simply be "plugged" to make the balance sheet balanced and then a subsequent "plug" is made for the remeasurement gain/loss.

F. Revenues and expenses that occur during a period are remeasured, for practical purposes, using the weighted-average exchange rate for the period (1.10 in the example below). However, revenues and expenses that represent allocations of historical balances (i.e., depreciation) are remeasured using the same historical exchange rates as used for those items on the balance sheet (0.90 in the example below).

G. Because all monetary assets and liabilities (and any recorded at fair value) are constantly being remeasured at the new spot exchange rate, a net gain or loss will be created by the changes in reported value. For a remeasurement (for individual transactions outside of a company's functional currency or for a consolidation where the parent and the subsidiary have the same functional currency), these gains and losses are computed and reported within the determination of net income.

H. The calculation of the remeasurement gain/loss is the result of the rules employed in the remeasurement process.

1. In mechanical terms, the remeasurement loss is the amount needed to "plug" so that the amounts balance.

2. In other words, since we already know ending retained earnings because it was "plugged" earlier, then we can solve for the remeasurement gain/loss on the income statement because we know or can calculate: opening retained earnings, translated income *before* remeasurement gain/loss, and dividends.

I. Example of the temporal method:

Assets	Euros	Exchange rate	U.S. dollars
Cash	60	1.12	67.20
Accounts receivable	100	1.12	112.00
Land	200	0.90	180.00
Building	400	0.90	360.00
	760		719.20
Liabilities & Stockholders' Equity			
Accounts payable	100	1.12	112.00
Mortgage payable	200	1.12	224.00
Common stock	100	0.90	90.00
Retained earnings	360	plugged (#1)	293.20
	760		719.20
Income Statement	Euros	Exchange rate	U.S. dollars
Revenues	260	1.10	286.00
Operating expenses	(140)	1.10	(154.00)
Depreciation expense	(20)	0.90	(18.00)
	100		114.00
Remeasurement loss		plugged (#2)	(40.80)
Net income	100		73.20
Retained Earnings			
Beginning amount	260	given	220.00
Net income	100	from above	73.20
Closing amount	360		293.20

Note that the beginning retained earnings of 220 (U.S. dollars) is given and is taken from the prior period's remeasured financial statements; the amount cannot merely be translated using a single exchange rate.

HYPERINFLATION

A. If the cumulative inflation rate is 100% or more over a 3-year period in a foreign country, the foreign currency statements of a company located in that hyperinflationary country are remeasured into the reporting currency (i.e., U.S. dollar).

B. In a hyperinflationary economy, the foreign currency will be rapidly depreciating against the reporting currency because the high inflation rate will quickly deteriorate the purchasing power of the foreign currency. In this case, using the current rate to translate all balance sheet amounts will result in very low values for all assets and liabilities after translation into the reporting currency.

C. In reality, the real value of nonmonetary assets and liabilities (i.e., PP&E) is typically not affected by hyperinflation because the local currency-denominated values increase to offset the impact of inflation (i.e., real estate values rise with inflation). As a result, the temporal method is more appropriate in this situation because it remeasures all nonmonetary accounts at the historical rate.

SUMMARY

A. Functional currency is the local currency of the foreign company,

1. Determinants of functional currency.

a. Subsidiary's operations are not integrated with parent's operations.

b. Buying and selling activities are primarily in local currency.

c. Cash flows are not immediately available for remittance to the parent.

2. Translation method is the current rate method.

a. All assets/liabilities translated using the current rate.

b. All revenues/expenses translated at the weighted-average rate.

c. Equity accounts translated at the historical rates.

3. Reporting.

a. Translation adjustments are reported as other comprehensive income under one of several acceptable reporting alternatives and as accumulated other comprehensive income in the equity section of the consolidated balance sheet.

b. Analysis of changes in accumulated translation adjustments are disclosed via footnote.

B. Functional currency is the U.S. dollar.

1. Functional currency determination.

a. Subsidiary's operations are integrated with the parent's operations.

b. Buying and selling activities are primarily in the United States and/or U.S. dollar.

    c.   Cash flows are immediately available for remittance to the parent.

    2.   Translation method is remeasurement (temporal method).

        a.   Monetary assets/liabilities use the current rate.

        b.   Historical cost balances (such as inventory, PP&E, prepaid expenses) use the historical rates.

        c.   Revenues/expenses use the weighted-average rates and historical rates, the latter for allocations such as depreciation expense.

    3.   Reporting.

        a.   Remeasurement gain/loss is reported on the consolidated income statement.

SECTION 6: DISCONTINUED OPERATIONS

A.   If an operation is discontinued by the reporting company, all of its operating results must be shown as a single figure net of income taxes at the bottom of the income statement just below income from continuing operations. The net figure is reported right before any extraordinary gains or losses.

B.   To qualify for this reporting, the assets being sold or abandoned must have operations and cash flows that are *clearly distinguished* by the company from the rest of the operations.

C.   While the company attempts to sell these assets, they should be reported as "held for sale" and shown at the lower of book value or fair value less cost to sell.

    1.   If assets qualify as held for resale, they should be separately identified on the balance sheet. Depreciation continues if the assets are still in operation. Depreciation ceases if the assets are no longer in operation.

    2.   If book value is below the fair value less the cost to sell, book value is maintained and no gain or loss is recognized. Because of conservatism, any gain is only recognized when it actually occurs.

    3.   If book value is greater than the fair value less the cost to sell, book value is reduced to the lower figure and a loss is recognized as soon as the asset qualifies as being held for sale.

    4.   Recognized gains and losses are reported as Other Income on the income statement unless the operations and cash flows of the asset have been clearly distinguished from the rest of the company. In that second situation, the gain or loss is reported at the bottom of the income statement (net of taxes) as part of discontinued operation. All revenues and expenses generated by the asset are also reported in this Discontinued Operation category. The recording of a discontinued operation begins when the assets are sold or (if earlier) when they qualify as held for sale.

    5.   When assets are reported as being a discontinued operation, all revenues and expenses for all prior years are accumulated and dropped to the bottom of the income statement. This classification does not change reported net income but separates continuing from discontinued operations for comparability purposes.

D.   Criteria for "held for sale."

    1.   Management commits to a plan of disposal.

    2.   The assets are available for sale.

3. An active program to locate a buyer has been initiated.

4. The sale is probable.

5. The asset is being actively marketed for sale at a fair price.

6. It is unlikely the disposal plan will significantly change.

E. Two other criteria to satisfy prior to reporting as discontinued operations are as follows:

1. The operations and cash flows of the component have been (or will be) eliminated from the ongoing operations of the company as a result of the disposal.

2. The company will not have any significant involvement in the operations of the component after the disposal.

SECTION 7: REPORTING SEGMENTS OF AN ENTERPRISE

A. The purpose of segment disclosure is to assist investors and lenders in assessing the future potential of a company by breaking down the information.

1. Trend, opportunities, and risk factors, for example, may get lost when data for a diversified company is merged into consolidated financial statements.

2. Most intersegment transactions that are eliminated from consolidated financial information can be found in segment information.

B. The company should first identify its operating segments based on the method management (the "management approach") uses to disaggregate the company for the making of internal operating decisions. The factors used to determine these segments must be disclosed.

1. Each operating segment must be engaged in business activities from which it earns revenues (even if only internally) and incurs expenses.

2. The operating results of each operating segment must be reviewed individually by the chief operating decision-maker within the company.

3. Some components of a company (i.e., central headquarters or the research and development department) may not be within any operating segment because they do not generate revenues.

4. Segments may be combined if they have the activities in the same geographic region even if the company disaggregates them for internal reporting purposes.

C. The company must disclose information about each operating segment of a significant size. Three tests are applied and every segment that meets at least one of these tests must be included in the disclosure.

1. Revenue test.

a. Any segment is viewed as significant if its revenue makes up 10% or more of the company's total.

b. Both sales to outsiders and intersegment revenues are included. Because intersegment revenues are included, they must use the same transfer prices for segment reporting purposes as are used internally (should reflect market prices).

2. Profit and loss test.

    a. Any segment is viewed as significant if its profit or loss is 10% of the greater of the profits of all profitable segments or the losses of all losing segments.

    b. Profit and loss should be determined in the manner that is used by the company internally to determine the profitability of its segments.

    c. Common costs should be allocated to segments if that is done so for internal decision-making purposes.

3. Asset test.

    a. Any segment is viewed as significant if its assets make up 10% or more of the company's total.

In addition to these three tests, there is an additional requirement as to the number of segments that are reported. This "75% rule" states that at least 75% of the unaffiliated revenue is reported by segments. If, after applying the three tests, this rule is not met, additional segments must be identified and reported separately.

D. Certain disclosures are required for the company as a whole even if the company only identifies itself as having one operating segment (more detailed information can be found in SFAS 131).

1. Revenue generated from external customers for each product and service.

2. For domestic operations, revenues from external customers and the amount of long-lived assets. The same disclosure is required for foreign operations.

3. Revenues and assets for any specific foreign country must also be disclosed if they are material.

4. If 10% or more of consolidated revenues come from a single customer, that fact must be disclosed. For this test, a group of customers under common control is viewed as a single customer.

E. A company may consider aggregating two or more operating segments if they have similar economic characteristics and if the segments are similar in each of the following areas:

1. The nature of the products and services.

2. The nature of the production processes.

3. The type of customer for their products and services.

4. The methods used to distribute their products or provide their services.

5. The nature of the regulatory environment.

F. Example:

Segment	Unaffiliated Revenue	Intersegment revenue	Operating profit (loss)	Segment assets
A	$90	$90	$20	$70
B	120	10	30	70
C	110	20	(40)	90
D	200	0	170	120
E	330	110	(100)	230
F	380	0	90	260
Total	$1,230	$230	170	$840

1. Revenues test: 10% × ($1,230 + $230) = $146.

Reportable segments are A, D, E, F.

Operating profit or loss test: 10% × $310 = $31 (must use the greater of operating loss or operating profit $310 = $20 + $30 + $170 + $90).

Reportable segments are C, D, E, F.

Segment assets test: 10% × $840 = $84.

Reportable segments are C, D, E, F.

Any segment that passes at least one of the 10% tests is ultimately reportable.

2. 75% test: 75% × $1,230 = $922.50.

Segments A, C, D, E, F have a combined total unaffiliated revenue of $1,110 and that is greater than the minimum required of $922.50. The 75% test is satisfied and no additional segments need to be reported.

QUESTIONS: OTHER FINANCIAL ACCOUNTING TOPICS

Section 1: Accounting Changes

1. On January 1, Year 3, Troy Co. (Troy) purchased a patent for $714,000. The patent is being amortized over its remaining legal life of 15 years and expiring on January 1, Year 18. During Year 6, Troy determined that the economic benefits of the patent would not last longer than ten years from the date of acquisition. What amount should be reported on the balance sheet for the patent, net of accumulated amortization, at December 31, Year 6?
   A. $428,000.
   B. $489,600.
   C. $504,000.
   D. $523,600.

2. Company X begins operations on January 1, Year 1. It uses the Green Method and determines an expense of $10,000 per year. During Year 5, the company decides to switch to the Blue Method (an allowable alternative) that would have reported an expense of $13,000 per year. The company is now going to report comparative financial statements for Years 4 and 5. Ignoring income tax effects, what is the amount that should be reported in Year 5 as the Cumulative Effect of Change in Accounting Method?
   A. $0.
   B. $6,000.
   C. $12,000.
   D. $15,000.

3. Company X begins operations on January 1, Year 1. It uses the Green Method and determines an expense of $10,000 per year. During Year 5, the company decides to switch to the Blue Method (an allowable alternative) that would have reported an expense of $13,000 per year. The company is now going to report comparative financial statements for Years 4 and 5. Originally, the company had reported net income of $200,000 for Year 4. Ignoring income tax effects, what will now be reported as the net income for Year 4?
   A. $200,000.
   B. $197,000.
   C. $188,000.
   D. $187,000.

4. On January 1, Year 1, Company X purchases equipment for $240,000 with an expected useful life of 12 years. During Year 4, company officials come to realize that the original useful life of the equipment had actually been 18 years. The company uses the straight-line depreciation method. The company is now reporting comparative financial statements for Years 3 and 4. What is reported as depreciation expense?
   A. $13,333 in Year 3 and $13,333 in Year 4.
   B. $13,333 in Year 3 and $20,000 in Year 4.
   C. $20,000 in Year 3 and $12,000 in Year 4.
   D. $20,000 in Year 3 and $13,333 in Year 4.

5.   On January 1, Year 1, Company X purchases equipment for $240,000 with an expected useful life of 12 years. The straight-line method is applied. During Year 4, company officials decide to switch to the double-declining balance method. No other change is made. What amount of depreciation expense is recognized by the company for Year 4?

      A. $23,148.
      B. $27,778.
      C. $30,000.
      D. $40,000.

6.   Both the blue method and the green method are viewed as generally accepted accounting principles. A company uses the blue method in Year 1 and it gives an expense of $20,000 and a net income of $100,000. The blue method is also used in Year 2 and Year 3. The expense is $30,000 (Year 2) and $40,000 (Year 3) so that net income is $120,000 (Year 2) and $130,000 (Year 3). On December 31, Year 3, the company decides to change to the green method which would give an expense of $16,000 (Year 1), $24,000 (Year 2), and $33,000 (Year 3). The independent auditor concurs with this change. What will be reported as the net income for Year 3? Ignore tax effects.

      A. $130,000.
      B. $137,000.
      C. $143,000.
      D. $147,000.

7.   A company buys a truck on January 1, Year 1 for $70,000 with a salvage value of $10,000 and an expected life of ten years. The straight-line method is being used based on the number of months the asset is held during the year. On January 1, Year 3, the company decides to switch to the double-declining balance method. At the end of Year 3, what is the amount of accumulated depreciation?

      A. $24,000.
      B. $26,500.
      C. $30,450.
      D. $34,160.

Section 2: Partnership Accounting

8.   The partnership agreement of Donn, Eddy, and Farr provides for annual distribution of profit or loss in the following sequence:

- Donn, the managing partner, receives a bonus of 10% of profit.
- Each partner receives 6% interest on average capital investment.
- Residual profit or loss is divided equally.

Average capital investments for 20X8 were:

Donn $80,000
Eddy $50,000
Farr $30,000

What portion of the $100,000 partnership profit for 20X8 should be allocated to Farr?

      A. $28,600.
      B. $29,800.
      C. $35,133.
      D. $41,600.

9. Fox, Greg, and Howe are partners with average capital balances during 20X6 of $120,000, $60,000, and $40,000, respectively. Partners receive 10% interest on their average capital balances. After deducting salaries of $30,000 to Fox and $20,000 to Howe, the residual profit or loss is divided equally. In 20X6, the partnership sustained a $33,000 loss before interest and salaries to partners. By what amount should Fox's capital account change?
   A. $7,000 increase.
   B. $11,000 decrease.
   C. $35,000 decrease.
   D. $42,000 increase.

10. On July 1, 20X8, a partnership was formed by Johnson and Smith. Johnson contributed cash. Smith, previously a sole proprietor, contributed property other than cash including realty subject to a mortgage, which was assumed by the partnership. Smith's capital account at July 1, 20X8, should be recorded at:
   A. Smith's book value of the property at July 1, 20X8.
   B. Smith's book value of the property less the mortgage payable at July 1, 20X8.
   C. the fair value of the property less the mortgage payable at July 1, 20X8.
   D. the fair value of the property at July 1, 20X8.

11. Roberts and Smith drafted a partnership agreement that lists the following assets contributed at the partnership's formation:

	Contributed by	
	Roberts	Smith
Cash	$20,000	$30,000
Inventory	$0	$15,000
Building	$0	$40,000
Furniture & Equipment	$15,000	$0

   The building is subject to a mortgage of $10,000, which the partnership has assumed. The partnership agreement also specifies that profits and losses are to be distributed evenly. What amounts should be recorded as capital for Roberts and Smith at the formation of the partnership?

	Roberts	Smith
A.	$35,000	$85,000
B.	$35,000	$75,000
C.	$55,000	$55,000
D.	$60,000	$60,000

12.   The following balance sheet is for the partnership of Able, Bayer, and Cain, which shares profits and losses in the ratio of 4:4:2, respectively.

Assets

Cash	$20,000
Other assets	180,000
	$200,000

Liabilities and Capital

Liabilities	$50,000
Able, Capital	37,000
Bayer, Capital	65,000
Cain, Capital	48,000
	$200,000

The original partnership was dissolved when its assets, liabilities, and capital were as shown on the above balance sheet and liquidated by selling assets in installments. The first sale of noncash assets having a book value of $90,000 realized $50,000, and all cash available after settlement with creditors was distributed. How much cash should the respective partners receive (to the nearest dollar)?

A.   Able $8,000; Bayer $8,000; Cain $4,000.
B.   Able $6,667; Bayer $6,667; Cain $6,666.
C.   Able $0; Bayer $13,333; Cain $6,667.
D.   Able $0; Bayer $3,000; Cain $17,000.

13.   The following condensed balance sheet is presented for the partnership of Cooke, Dorry, and Evans who share profits and losses in the ratio of 4:3:3, respectively:

Cash	$90,000
Other assets	820,000
Cooke, loan	30,000
	$940,000

Accounts payable	$210,000
Evans, loan	40,000
Cooke, capital	300,000
Dorry, capital	200,000
Evans, capital	190,000
	$940,000

Assume the partners decide to liquidate the partnership. If the other assets are sold for $600,000, how much of the available cash should be distributed to Cooke?

A. $170,000.
B. $182,000.
C. $212,000.
D. $300,000.

14. The following balance sheet is presented for the partnership of Davis, Wright, and Dover who share profits and losses in the ratio of 5:3:2 respectively:

Cash	$60,000
Other assets	540,000
	$600,000
Liabilities	$140,000
Davis, Capital	280,000
Wright, Capital	160,000
Dover, Capital	20,000
	$600,000

Assume that the assets and liabilities are fairly valued on the balance sheet and the partnership decided to admit Hank as a new partner with a one-fifth interest. No goodwill or bonus is to be recorded. How much should Hank contribute in cash or other assets?
   A. $120,000.
   B. $115,000.
   C. $92,000.
   D. $73,600.

15. Dunn and Grey are partners with capital account balances of $60,000 and $90,000, respectively. They agree to admit Zorn as a partner with a one-third interest in capital and profits, for an investment of $100,000, after revaluing the assets of Dunn and Grey. Goodwill to the original partners should be:
   A. $0.
   B. $33,333.
   C. $50,000.
   D. $66,667.

16. At December 31, 20X5, Reed and Quinn are partners with capital balances of $40,000 and $20,000, and they share profit and loss in the ratio of 2:1, respectively. On this date Poe invests $17,000 cash for a one-fifth interest in the capital and profit of the new partnership. Assuming that goodwill is not recorded, how much should be credited to Poe's capital account on December 31, 20X5?
   A. $12,000.
   B. $15,000.
   C. $15,400.
   D. $17,000.

17. Ames and Buell are partners who share profits and losses in the ratio of 3:2, respectively. On August 31, 20X6, their capital accounts were as follows:

Ames	$70,000
Buell	60,000
	$130,000

On date they agreed to admit Carter as a partner with a one-third interest in the capital and profits and losses, for an investment of $50,000. The new partnership will begin with a total capital of $180,000. Immediately after Carter's admission, what are the capital balances of the partners?

	Ames	_Buell_	_Carter_
A.	$60,000	$60,000	$60,000
B.	$63,333	$56,667	$60,000
C.	$64,000	$56,000	$60,000
D.	$70,000	$60,000	$50,000

Section 3: Financial Instruments

18. Which of the following is an "underlying"?
    A. A credit rating.
    B. A security price.
    C. An average daily temperature.
    D. All of the above.

19. Derivative instruments are financial instruments or other contracts that must contain:
    A. one or more underlyings or one or more notional amounts.
    B. no initial net investment or smaller net investment than required for similar response contracts.
    C. terms that do not require or permit net settlement or delivery of an asset.
    D. all of the above.

20. Which of the following statements is (are) true regarding derivative financial instruments?

    I. Derivative financial instruments should be measured at fair value and reported on the balance sheet as assets or liabilities.
    II. Gains or losses on derivative instruments not designated as hedging activities should be reported and recognized in earnings in the period of the change in fair value.

    A. I only.
    B. II only.
    C. Both I and II.
    D. Neither I nor II.

21. Examples of financial instruments with off-balance sheet risk include all of the following except:
    A. outstanding loan commitments written.
    B. recourse obligations on receivables.
    C. warranty obligations.
    D. futures contracts.

22. Whether recognized or unrecognized in a company's financial statements, disclosure of the fair values of the company's financial instruments is required when:
    A. it is practicable to estimate those values.
    B. the company maintains accurate cost records.
    C. aggregated fair values are material to the entity.
    D. individual fair values are material to the entity.

23. If the price of the underlying is greater than the strike or exercise price of the underlying, the call option is:
    A. at-the-money.
    B. in-the-money.
    C. on-the-money.
    D. out-of-the-money.

24. On October 15, Year 4, Gilmore, Inc. invested in a derivative designated as a hedge of the fair value of an asset. By December 31, Year 4, the fair value of the hedged asset had decreased by $200,000 but the fair value of the derivative had increased by $220,000. The net effect on Year 4 earnings would be:
    A. $200,000.
    B. $20,000.
    C. $0.
    D. $220,000.

25. On November 1, Year 4, Cox Corp. enters into a derivative contract to hedge the forecasted cash flows associated with a future sale of 100,000 bushels (notional amount) of corn. The future sale date is January 11, Year 5. The fair value of the derivative contract at December 31, Year 4 increased by $15,000, which was the same amount as the decrease in the value of corn. The fair value of the derivative contract increased by an additional $8,000 from January 1 to January 15, which again corresponded to the decrease in the value of the corn. On January 15, Year 5, the corn was sold and the derivative was settled. The gains from the derivative should be recognized in Year 4 and Year 5 as which of the following?

	Year 4 other comprehensive income	Year 5 net income
A.	$23,000	$23,000
B.	$15,000	$8,000
C.	$15,000	$23,000
D.	$0	$0

26. A gain on a forecasted cash flow hedge should be reported as:
    A. an extraordinary item.
    B. other comprehensive income.
    C. a change in accounting estimate.
    D. income from continuing operations.

27. Helgeson Corporation had the following transactions in the last quarter of the current year. Which of the transactions is most likely to result in a derivative subject to SFAS 133 Accounting for Derivative Instruments and Hedging Activities?
    A. Based on a forecasted purchase of cocoa beans, Helgeson bought a futures contract to protect itself from changes in market prices of cocoa beans.
    B. Invested in land with the anticipation of an increase in fair value.
    C. Purchased available-for-sale securities.
    D. Negotiated a 2-year loan with a Swiss bank to take advantage of lower European interest rates.

28. On December 12, Year 4, Imp Co. entered into three forward exchange contracts, each purchasing 100,000 euros in 90 days. The relevant exchange rates are as follows:

	Spot Rate	Forward Rate (for March 12, Year 5)
December 12, Year 4	$0.88	$0.90
December 31, Year 4	$0.98	$0.93

    Imp entered into the first forward contract to hedge a purchase of inventory in November Year 4, payable in March Year 5. At December 31, Year 4, what amount of gain should Imp include in income from this forward contract?
    A. $5,000.
    B. $0.
    C. $3,000.
    D. $10,000.

29. Imp entered into the second forward contract to hedge a commitment to purchase equipment being manufactured to Imp's specifications. At December 31, Year 4, what amount of gain should Imp include in income from this forward contract?
    A. $10,000.
    B. $0.
    C. $5,000.
    D. $3,000.

30. Imp entered into the third forward contract for speculation. At December 31, Year 4, what amount of gain should Imp include in income from this forward contract?
    A. $3,000.
    B. $0.
    C. $5,000.
    D. $10,000.

31. Disclosure of information about significant concentrations of credit risk is required for:
    A. all financial instruments.
    B. financial instruments with off-balance-sheet credit risk only.
    C. financial instruments with off-balance-sheet market risk only.
    D. financial instruments with off-balance-sheet risk of accounting loss only.

32. In its December 31 balance sheet, Butler Co. reported trade accounts receivable of $250,000 and related allowance for uncollectible accounts of $20,000. What is the total amount of risk of accounting loss related to Butler's trade accounts receivable, and what amount of that risk is off-balance sheet risk?

	Risk of accounting loss	Off-balance sheet risk
A.	$0	$0
B.	$230,000	$0
C.	$230,000	$20,000
D.	$250,000	$20,000

33. SFAS 133 defines a *derivative* as a financial instrument that has which of the following elements?
    A. One or more underlying and one or more notional amounts or payment provision or both; requiring either no initial investment or an immaterial net investment and requires or permits net settlement.
    B. One underlying; one notional amount; and a net settlement provision.
    C. An embedded contract; a conversion clause; and a net settlement amount.
    D. An underlying; a notional amount; and an effective hedge.

34. The loss from a decrease in the fair value of a derivative that is designated as a hedge would be included in current earnings if the derivative is a hedge of:
    A. cash flows.
    B. a foreign currency exposure of an available-for-sale security.
    C. a forecasted foreign currency transaction.
    D. a net investment in a foreign operation.

35. Which of the following risks are inherent in an interest rate swap agreement?

    I. The risk of exchanging a lower interest rate for a higher interest rate.
    II. The risk of nonperformance by the counterparty to the agreement.

    A. Neither I nor II.
    B. I only.
    C. II only.
    D. Both I and II.

36. A gain in the fair value of a derivative may be included in comprehensive income if the derivative is appropriately designated as a:
    A. hedge of a foreign currency exposure of a forecasted foreign currency denominated transaction.
    B. speculation in foreign currency.
    C. hedge of a foreign currency exposure of an available-for-sale security.
    D. hedge of a foreign currency firm commitment.

37. Which of the following is true about derivatives?
    A. A derivative is a particular type of financial instrument.
    B. Derivatives are different than financial instruments.
    C. Derivatives and financial instruments are the same.
    D. Most derivatives are financial instruments but not all.

Section 4: Earnings Per Share

38. The following is information on Jenghis Corp. (Jenghis) outstanding stock for Year 6:

Common stock, $5 par value
Shares outstanding, 1/1/Year 6   20,000
2-for-1 stock split, 4/1/Year 6   20,000
Shares issued, 7/1/Year 6   10,000

Preferred stock, $10 par value, 5% cumulative
Shares outstanding, 1/1/Year 6   4,000

What are the number of shares Jenghis should use to calculate Year 6 basic EPS?
A. 40,000.
B. 45,000.
C. 50,000.
D. 54,000.

39. Timpani, Inc. (Timpani) had the following common stock balances and transactions in Year 6:

1/1/ Year 6	Common stock outstanding	30,000
2/1/ Year 6	Issued a 10% common stock dividend	3,000
7/1/ Year 6	Issued common stock for cash	8,000
12/31/ Year 6	Common stock outstanding	41,000

What was Timpani's Year 6 weighted-average shares outstanding?
A. 30,000.
B. 34,000.
C. 36,750.
D. 37,000.

40. Henle Corp's (Henle) capital structure was as follows:

	Dec 31/Year 5	Dec 31/Year 6
Outstanding shares of stock		
Common	110,000	110,000
Convertible preferred	10,000	10,000

During Year 6, Henle paid dividends of $3.00 per share on its preferred stock. The preferred shares are convertible into 20,000 shares of common stock and considered common stock equivalents. Net income for Year 6 was $850,000. Assume that the income tax rate is 30%. The diluted EPS for Year 6 is:
A. $6.31.
B. $6.54.
C. $7.08.
D. $7.45.

41. In determining diluted EPS, dividends on nonconvertible cumulative preferred stock should be:
    A. disregarded.
    B. added back to net income whether declared or not.
    C. deducted from net income only if declared.
    D. deducted from net income whether declared or not.

42. A company reports net income in the current year of $500,000. During the year, the company paid $80,000 in cash dividends on its common stock and $30,000 in dividends on its nonconvertible preferred stock. The company has 15,000 shares of the preferred stock outstanding all year. The company starts the year with 100,000 shares of common stock outstanding. On July 1 of that year, 20,000 additional shares of common stock were issued as a stock dividend. What is the company's basic earnings per share figure (rounded)?
    A. $3.25.
    B. $3.55.
    C. $3.92.
    D. $4.27.

43. A company reports net income in the current year of $600,000. During the year, the company paid $50,000 in cash dividends on its common stock and $70,000 in dividends on its nonconvertible preferred stock. The company has 24,000 shares of the preferred stock outstanding all year. The company starts the year with 100,000 shares of common stock outstanding. On July 1 of that year, 20,000 additional shares of common stock were issued on the market for cash. What is the company's basic earnings per share figure (rounded)?
    A. $4.00.
    B. $4.36.
    C. $4.42.
    D. $4.82.

44. A company reports net income for the current year of $400,000 and has 80,000 shares of common stock outstanding. The company also has 5,000 shares of preferred stock outstanding that pays a dividend of $6 per share. Each share of this preferred stock can be converted into one share of common stock. The company's tax rate is 30%. What is the company's diluted earnings per share (rounded)?
    A. $4.71.
    B. $4.63.
    C. $4.60.
    D. $4.35.

45. The Raulston Corporation reports net income in the current year of $600,000. The company had a nonconvertible preferred stock paying $80,000 in cash dividends. Another $30,000 in dividends was paid to the common stockholders. There are 120,000 shares of this common stock outstanding throughout the year. In addition, the company has 20,000 stock options outstanding. For $5, each option can be converted into one share of common stock. The average price of the stock during the year was $20. The company has an effective tax rate of 40%. What is the company's diluted earnings per share (rounded)?
    A. $4.43.
    B. $4.33.
    C. $3.85.
    D. $3.71.

46.   The Nautical Corporation reports net income of $500,000. The company has 10,000 shares of nonconvertible preferred stock paying $4 per share each year in cumulative dividends. The company has 200,000 shares of common stock outstanding throughout the current year. In addition, the company has 5,000 convertible bonds outstanding. These bonds are each convertible into ten shares of common stock. Each bond pays interest each year of $30. The bonds were issued for face value. The effective tax rate is 30%. No preferred stock dividends were declared or paid this year. What is diluted earnings per share for the year (rounded)?
   A. $2.26.
   B. $2.30.
   C. $2.42.
   D. $2.44.

47.   A company reports net income for the year ending December 31, Year 1, of $400,000. The company paid $90,000 in cash dividends to its preferred stockholders and $40,000 in cash dividends to its common stockholders. The company had 30,000 shares of preferred stock outstanding all year. The company began the year with 100,000 shares of common stock outstanding but, on October 1, issued an additional 20,000 shares. What should the company report for the year as its basic earnings per share (rounded)?
   A. $2.25.
   B. $2.57.
   C. $2.58.
   D. $2.95.

48.   A company reports net income of $500,000 and pays its preferred stockholders cash dividends of $60,000. There are 100,000 shares of common stock outstanding so that the basic earnings per share to be reported is $4.40 ($500,000 minus $60,000 equals $440,000 divided by 100,000 shares). The company also has 10,000 bonds outstanding. Each bond was sold at face value and pays $7 in interest each year. Each bond can be converted into two shares of common stock. If the company has a tax rate of 30%, what should be reported as its diluted earnings per share for the period (rounded)?
   A. $3.08.
   B. $3.26.
   C. $4.08.
   D. $4.25.

49.   A company reports net income of $900,000 and pays its preferred stockholders cash dividends of $40,000. There are 200,000 shares of common stock outstanding so the basic earnings per share to be reported is $4.30 ($900,000 minus $40,000 equals $860,000 divided by 200,000 shares). The company also has 10,000 stock options outstanding. Each option can be converted into three shares of common stock. Each share can be obtained by the payment of $10.00 in cash. The average price of the stock for the year was $25.00 per share. If the company has a tax rate of 30%, what should be reported as its diluted earnings per share for the period (rounded)?
   A. $3.64.
   B. $3.74.
   C. $3.84.
   D. $3.94.

Section 5: Foreign Currency Balances

50. Linde, Inc. (Linde), a U.S. corporation, bought inventory items from a supplier in Argentina on November 5, Year 5, for 100,000 Argentine pesos, when the spot rate was $0.4295. At Linde's December 31, Year 5 year-end, the spot rate was $0.4245. On January 15, Year 6, Linde bought 100,000 pesos at the spot rate of $0.4345 and paid the invoice.

    How much should Linde report as part of net income for Year 5 and Year 6 as foreign exchange transaction gain or loss?

	Year 5	Year 6
A.	$500	($1,000)
B.	$0	($500)
C.	($500)	$0
D.	($1,000)	$500

51. In preparing consolidated financial statements of a U.S. parent company with a foreign subsidiary, the foreign subsidiary's functional currency is the currency:
    A. in which the subsidiary maintains its accounting records.
    B. of the country in which the subsidiary is located.
    C. of the country in which the parent is located.
    D. of the environment in which the subsidiary primarily generates and expends cash.

52. Sphinx Co. (Sphinx) records its transactions in U.S. dollars. A sale of goods resulted in a receivable denominated in Japanese yen, and a purchase of goods resulted in a payable denominated in Euros. Sphinx recorded a foreign exchange transaction gain on collection of the receivable and an exchange transaction loss on the settlement of the payable. The exchange rates are expressed as so many units of foreign currency to one dollar.

    Did the number of foreign currency units exchangeable for a dollar increase or decrease between the contract and settlement dates?

	Yen exchangeable for $1	Euros exchangeable for $1
A.	Increase	Increase
B.	Decrease	Decrease
C.	Decrease	Increase
D.	Increase	Decrease

53. A foreign subsidiary's functional currency is its local currency that has not experienced significant inflation. The weighted-average exchange rate for the current year would be the appropriate exchange rate for translating:

	Sales to customers	Wages expense
A.	No	No
B.	Yes	Yes
C.	No	Yes
D.	Yes	No

54.   On September 1, Year 5, Canope, Inc. (Canope), a U.S. corporation, sold merchandise to a foreign firm for 250,000 Botswana pula. Terms of the sale require payment in pula on February 1, Year 6. On September 1, Year 5, the spot exchange rate was $0.20 per pula. At December 31, Year 5 (Canope's year end), the spot rate was $0.19, but the rate increased to $0.22 by February 1, Year 6, when payment was received.

How much should Canope report as foreign exchange transaction gain or loss as part of Year 6 income?
A. $0.
B. $2,500 loss.
C. $5,000 gain.
D. $7,500 gain.

55.   A balance arising from the translation or remeasurement of a subsidiary's foreign currency financial statements is reported in the consolidated income statement when the subsidiary's functional currency is which of the following?

	Foreign currency	U.S. dollar
A.	No	No
B.	No	Yes
C.	Yes	No
D.	Yes	Yes

56.   Park Co.'s (Park) wholly owned subsidiary, Geneva, Inc. (Geneva), maintains its accounting records in Swiss francs. Because all of Geneva's branch offices are in the United Kingdom, its functional currency is the British pound. Remeasurement of Geneva's Year 6 financial statements resulted in a $7,600 gain and translation of its financial statements resulted in an $8,100 gain.

What amount should Park report as a foreign exchange gain as net income in its income statement for the year ended December 31, Year 6?
A. $0.
B. $7,600.
C. $8,100.
D. $15,700.

57.   Certain balance sheet accounts of a foreign subsidiary of Rowan, Inc. (Rowan) at December 31, Year 6, have been translated into U.S. dollars as follows:

	At current rates	At historical rates
Note receivable, long-term	$240,000	$200,000
Prepaid rent	$85,000	$80,000
Patent	$150,000	$170,000

The subsidiary's functional currency is the currency of the country in which it is located.

What total amount should be included in Rowan's December 31, Year 6 consolidated balance sheet for the above accounts?
A. $450,000.
B. $455,000.
C. $475,000.
D. $495,000.

58. Mazeppa, Inc. (Mazeppa) is a multicultural firm with its head office located in Toronto, Canada. Its main foreign subsidiary is in Paris, France but the primary economic environment in which the foreign subsidiary generates and expends cash is in the United States. Based on this information, which of the following statements is *most likely* true?
    A. The local currency is the U.S. dollar.
    B. The functional currency is the Euro.
    C. The reporting currency is the U.S. dollar.
    D. The reporting currency is the Canadian dollar.

59. The Tenstini Company assumes that the U.S. dollar is its functional currency. It buys inventory on credit on November 1, Year 1, for 60,000 Mexican pesos when one peso equals $0.083. On December 31, Year 1, the currency exchange rate is one peso equals $0.081. On January 19, Year 2, when the debt is paid, one peso equals $0.084. Which of the following is correct? Year 1 net income:
    A. increases $120.
    B. decreases $120.
    C. is not affected but comprehensive income increases $120.
    D. is not affected but comprehensive income decreases $120.

60. The Texas Company has a wholly-owned subsidiary, the Mexico Corporation. Texas uses the U.S. dollar as its functional currency whereas Mexico uses the Mexican peso as its functional currency. The subsidiary company buys inventory on credit on November 1, Year 1, for 60,000 Mexican pesos when one peso equals $0.083. On December 31, Year 1, the currency exchange rate is one peso equals $0.081. On January 19, Year 2, the inventory is sold and the debt is paid. On that date, one peso equals $0.084. Consolidated financial statements are now being prepared for Year 1. Which of the following is correct?
    A. Year 1 net income increases $120.
    B. Year 1 net income decreases $120.
    C. Year 1 net income is not affected but comprehensive income increases $120.
    D. Neither the Year 1 net income or the comprehensive income is affected.

61. A company is producing financial statements for Year 1. The company has a $400 currency exchange gain and a $300 positive translation adjustment for the period. Which of the following is true? Net income:
    A. increases by $700.
    B. increases by $400 and then comprehensive income increases by the other $300.
    C. increases by $300 and then comprehensive income increases by the other $400.
    D. is not affected but comprehensive income increases by $700.

Section 6: Discontinued Operation

62. On December 31, Year 6, Struan Co. (Struan) committed to a plan to dispose of its Howes (Howes) business component's assets. The disposal meets the requirements to be classified as discontinued operations. On that date, Struan estimated that the loss from the disposition of the assets would be $700,000 and Howes' Year 6 operating losses were $200,000. Disregarding income taxes, what net gain/loss should be reported for discontinued operations in Struan's Year 6 income statement?
    A. $0.
    B. ($200,000).
    C. ($700,000).
    D. ($900,000).

63. Which of the following criteria is not required for a component's results to be classified as discontinued operations?
    A. Management must have entered into a sales agreement.
    B. The component is available for immediate sale.
    C. The operations and cash flows of the component will be eliminated from the operations of the company as a result of the disposal.
    D. The company will not have any significant continuing involvement in the operations of the component after disposal.

64. On November 1, Year 6, management of Letourneau, Inc. (Letourneau) committed to a plan to dispose of Timmins Co. (Timmins), a major subsidiary. The disposal meets the requirements for classification as discontinued operations. The carrying value of Timmins was $8,000,000, and management estimated the fair value less costs to sell to be $6,500,000. For Year 6, Timmins had a loss of $2,000,000.

    How much should Letourneau present as a loss from discontinued operations before the effect of taxes in its Year 6 income statement?
    A. $0.
    B. $1,500,000.
    C. $2,000,000.
    D. $3,500,000.

Section 7: Reporting Segments of an Enterprise

65. Tecumseh Co. (Tecumseh), a publicly owned corporation, assesses performance and makes operating decisions using the following information for its reportable segments:

Total revenues	$768,000
Total profit and loss	$40,600

    Included in the total profit and loss are intersegment profits of $6,100. In addition, Tecumseh has $500 of common costs for its reportable segments that are not allocated in reports used internally.

    For purposes of segment reporting, Tecumseh should report segment profit of:
    A. $34,500.
    B. $35,000.
    C. $40,600.
    D. $41,100.

Use the following information to answer Questions 66 and 67.

Grimm Corp. (Grimm), a publicly owned corporation, is subject to the requirements of segment reporting. In its income statement for the year ended December 31, Year 6, Grimm reported revenues of $50 million, operating expenses of $47 million, and net income of $3 million. Operating expenses included payroll costs of $15 million.

Grimm's combined identifiable assets of all industry segments at December 31, Year 6, was $40 million. Reported revenues include $45 million of sales to external customers.

66.　In its Year 6 financial statements, Grimm should disclose major customer data if sales to any single customer amount to at least:
　　A.　$300,000.
　　B.　$1,500,000.
　　C.　$4,000,000.
　　D.　$5,000,000.

67.　External revenue reported by operating segments must be at least:
　　A.　$12,500,000.
　　B.　$15,000,000.
　　C.　$22,500,000.
　　D.　$37,500,000.

68.　The following information pertains to Aria Co. (Aria) and its operating segments for the year ended December 31, Year 6:

Sales to unaffiliated customers	$2,000,000
Intersegment sales of products	$600,000
Interest earned on loans to other industry segments	$40,000

Aria and all its divisions are engaged solely in manufacturing operations. Aria evaluates divisional performance based on controllable contribution by segments.

Aria has a reportable segment if that segment's revenue exceeds:
　　A.　$200,000.
　　B.　$204,000.
　　C.　$260,000.
　　D.　$264,000.

69.　A company is reporting revenues for the current year of $900,000, operating expenses of $500,000, and a gain of $120,000. This leaves income of $520,000. The tax rate is 30% so that income taxes are $156,000. Assume that the gain was from the sale of a portion of the company that is large enough to qualify as a discontinued operation. During the year, this operation had revenues of $200,000 and operating expenses of $100,000. On its current income statement, what should the company report as its net income before discontinued operations?
　　A.　$144,000.
　　B.　$210,000.
　　C.　$280,000.
　　D.　$300,000.

70.   The Moston Corporation has three operating segments. The company is currently looking into disclosures involved with its operating segments. For testing purposes, revenues are as follows: Blue segment – $500,000, Red segment – $120,000, Green segment – $680,000. Consolidated revenues (after intercompany eliminations) are $1,000,000. Which of the following statements is false?

A.   Revenues generated in a specific foreign country must be disclosed if the amount is viewed as material.

B.   If revenues of $100,000 or more are generated from a single customer, the existence of that customer must be disclosed in Moston's financial statements.

C.   Based on the revenue test only, disclosure of information is required of all three segments.

D.   These segments could be geographic segments or they could be industry segments.

ANSWERS: OTHER FINANCIAL ACCOUNTING TOPICS

Section 1: Accounting Changes

1. **B** This situation is a change in accounting estimate and should be accounted for currently and prospectively. From January 1, Year 3 to December 31, Year 5, patent amortization was recorded using a 15-year life. Yearly amortization was $47,600 ($714,000/15), accumulated amortization at December 31, Year 5 was $142,800 ($47,600 × 3), and the book value of the patent at December 31, Year 5 was $571,200 ($714,000 – $142,800). Beginning in Year 6, this book value must be amortized over its remaining useful life of seven years. Therefore, Year 6 amortization is $81,600 ($571,200/7) and the December 31, Year 6 book value is $489,600 ($571,200 – $81,600).

2. **A** Changes in an accounting principle are now reported retroactively. Thus, a "Cumulative Effect" balance is no longer used to report this type of accounting change.

3. **B** The only impact on Year 4 is that the reported expense will be changed from $10,000 to $13,000. Increasing the expense by $3,000 reduces the reported income by this same amount.

4. **C** In Years 1, 2, and 3, the depreciation expense will be reported as $20,000 ($240,000 divided by 12 years) and those figures are not changed. After these three years, the accumulated depreciation is $60,000 ($20,000 × 3 years) so the asset's book value is $180,000 ($240,000 – $60,000). The asset is now believed to have a useful life of eight years in total. However, three years of depreciation have already been recorded. That leaves 15 remaining years. The depreciation for Year 4 is the remaining depreciable value of $180,000 allocated over 15 remaining years, or $12,000.

5. **D** The change in depreciation methods is the one change in accounting principles that is handled as a change in estimation. For the first three years, depreciation expense is $20,000 per year ($240,000 / 12 years). This expense reduces the book value to $180,000. When the change is made, there are nine years left in the asset's life. Therefore, the fourth year expense is the $180,000 book value times 2/9 or $40,000.

6. **B** Accounting changes are now reported retroactively. Thus, here, the Year 1 figure, the Year 2 figure, and the Year 3 figure are all changed in the year reported. For Year 3, the $40,000 expense is reduced to $33,000 so that reported net income goes up by $7,000 to $137,000.

7. **B** Changes in depreciation method are now handled in the same manner as changes in an accounting estimation. The amounts that were recognized in previous years ($6,000 in Year 1 and in Year 2) are left as is. The current year figure is then computed based on the use of the new method. For Year 3, the book value is now $58,000 ($70,000 – $12,000 in accumulated depreciation), which is multiplied by 2/8 since there are eight years left in the asset's life when this new method is adopted. Current depreciation is $14,500 ($58,000 × 2/8) which increases accumulated depreciation from $12,000 to $26,500.

Section 2: Partnership Accounting

8. **A**

	Donn	Eddy	Farr	Total
Bonus (10% × $100,000)	$10,000	$ —	$ —	$ 10,000
Interest (6% Avg. Cap.)	4,800	3,000	1,800	9,600
	14,800	3,000	1,800	19,600
Excess in P/L ratio	26,800	26,800	26,800	80,400
Profit distribution	$41,600	$29,800	$28,600	$100,000

9. **A**

Partnership loss before interest and salaries to partners	$33,000
Partners' interest on average capital balances	
10% ($120,000 + $60,000 + $40,000)	22,000
Partners' salaries ($30,000 + 20,000)	50,000
"Residual" partnership loss	$105,000

Change in Fox's Capital Account:

Interest—10% × $120,000	$12,000
Salary	30,000
Share of "residual" partnership loss	
1/3 × $105,000	(35,000)
Increase in Fox's capital	$7,000

10. **C** For financial accounting purposes, non-cash contributions are recorded at the fair value of the net assets contributed as of the date of contribution.

11. **B** For financial accounting purposes, non-cash contributions are recorded at the fair value of the net assets contributed, as of the date of contribution. The mortgage balance attributable to the building reduces Smith's capital by the amount of the mortgage assumed by the partnership. Even though profits and losses will be split evenly, the capital balances do not need to be in that ratio.

12. **D**

	Cash	Assets	Other liabilities
Balances	$20,000	$180,000	$(50,000)
Sale of Assets			
($40,000 Loss in P/L Ratio)	50,000	(90,000)	0
Balances	$70,000	$90,000	$(50,000)
Allow for worst possible loss on			
remaining assets		(90,000)	
Payment to creditors	(50,000)		50,000
Balances	20,000	0	0
Distribution of Cash	(20,000)	0	0
Balances	$0		

		Capital Accounts	
	Able	Bayer	Cain
Balances	$(37,000)	$(65,000)	$(48,000)
Sale of Assets			
($40,000 Loss in P/L Ratio)	16,000	16,000	8,000
Balances	$(21,000)	$(49,000)	$(40,000)
Allow for worst possible loss on			
remaining assets	36,000	36,000	18,000
Payment to creditors	0	0	0
Balances	$15,000	$(13,000)	$(22,000)
Distribution of Able's deficit—			
4:2 ratio	(15,000)	10,000	5,000
Balances	0	(3,000)	(17,000)
Distribution of cash	0	3,000	17,000
Balances	$0	$0	$0

13. **B**

	Cooke	Dorry	Evans
Capital balances	$300,000	$200,000	$190,000
Offset Cooke Loan	(30,000)	0	0
Balances	$270,000	$200,000	$190,000
Distribution of loss on sale of assets in P/L ratio	(88,000)	(66,000)	(66,000)
Cash distribution	$182,000	$134,000	$124,000

Note: Evans' loan account would be offset to capital if his balance were negative; otherwise it would maintain its priority as a liability.

14. **B** $115,000. The investment by Hank must be an amount that, when added to the present capital, represents one-fifth of the new total capital. This can be expressed as follows (NC = new capital):

$$1/5 \text{ NC} + \$460,000 = \text{NC}$$
$$\$460,000 = 4/5 \text{ NC}$$
$$\text{NC} = \$575,000$$

New capital $575,000 – old capital $460,000 = $115,000.

15. **C** $50,000

Implied value of new partnership:

New partner's investment	$100,000
Multiple of interest acquired (1/3)	× 3
	$300,000

Less capital balance before recognition of goodwill:

Dunn	$60,000	
Grey	90,000	
Zorn (new partner)	100,000	250,000
Goodwill to original partners		$ 50,000

16. **C**

Reed capital	$40,000
Quinn capital	20,000
Poe's contribution	17,000
Total capital (New)	$77,000
Poe's interest in capital	× 1/5
Poe's capital balance	$15,400

Note: Bonus to old partners of $1,600 would result as Poe contributed $17,000; however only received a capital balance of $15,400.

17. **C**

Carter's capital ($180,000 × 1/3)	$60,000
Carter's investment	(50,000)
Bonus to Carter	$10,000

Bonus to Carter is shared by the old partners in their P/L ratio (Ames, 3/5; Buell, 2/5).

	Ames	Buell	Carter
Original capital balances	$70,000	$60,000	—
Carter's investment			$50,000
Bonus to Carter	(6,000)	(4,000)	10,000
New capital balances	$64,000	$56,000	$60,000

Note: Only Ames' new capital balance needs to be computed, as it is different for each of the possible answers.

Section 3: Financial Statements

18. **D**   All of the above meet the basic definition of an underlying, which is any financial or physical variable that has either observable changes or objectively verifiable changes.

19. **B**   Derivative instruments must contain one or more underlyings *and* one or more notional amounts. Derivative instruments do contain terms that require or permit net settlement or delivery of an asset.

20. **C**   Derivative instruments meet the definition of assets and liabilities. As such, they should be reported on the company's financial statements. The most relevant measure for reporting them is fair value. Thus, Statement I is true.

    If a derivative instrument does not qualify as a hedging instrument, then its gains or losses must be reported and recognized in current earnings. Thus, Statement II is also true.

21. **C**   The value of derivative financial instruments is typically derived from the value of an underlying asset or is tied to an index. As the price of the underlying asset changes, the price of the derivative changes. Outstanding loan commitments written, recourse obligations on receivables, and futures contracts are all tied to an asset account. Warranty obligations are the result of the sale of goods.

22. **A**   Companies must disclose the fair value of financial instruments, both assets and liabilities, whether recognized or not recognized in the balance sheet, for which it is practicable to estimate fair value. Pertinent descriptive information as to the fair value of the instrument is to be disclosed if an estimate of fair value cannot be made without incurring excessive costs.

23. **B**   A call option is in-the-money if the price of the underlying is greater than the strike or the exercise price of the underlying. An at-the-money option is one in which the price of the underlying is equal to the strike or exercise price. A call option is out-of-the-money if the strike or exercise price is greater than the price of the underlying.

24. **B.**   The net effect on Year 4 earnings of the gain from the derivative and the loss in the fair value of the asset is $20,000 ($220,000 – $200,000 = $20,000).

25. **C**   The $15,000 gain on the derivative in Year 4 is recognized in comprehensive income until the transaction is completed. When the transaction is completed in Year 5 (the corn is sold), the $15,000 gain is reclassified in Year 5 from other comprehensive income to current earnings. This reclassification plus the $8,000 gain in January would total at $23,000 gain in Year 5 ($15,000 + $8,000 = $23,000).

26. **B**   SFAS 133 requires that gains or losses from forecasted cash flow hedges be reported as other comprehensive income.

27. **A**   Helgeson's purchase of a futures contract to hedge against future market fluctuations would include the three elements in the SFAS 133 *Definition of a Derivative*.

28. **C**   SFAS 133 states that the change in the forward rate should be the basis for the calculation of the gain on the forward contract. The change in the forward rate is from $0.90 to $0.93 or $0.03 × €100,000 = $3,000.

29. **D**   SFAS 133 states that the change in the forward rate should be the basis for the calculation of the gain on the forward contract. The change in the forward rate is from $0.90 to $0.93 or $0.03 × €100,000 = $3,000.

30. **A**   SFAS 133 states that the change in the forward rate should be the basis for the calculation of the gain on the forward contract. The change in the forward rate is from $0.90 to $0.93 or $0.03 × €100,000 = $3,000.

31. **A**   SFAS 107 requires disclosure of information about significant concentrations of risk for all financial instruments. Concentrations of credit exist when a company has a business activity, economic characteristic, or location that is common to most of its financial instruments.

32. **B**   The risk of loss associated with the trade accounts receivable is the net realizable value of the receivables ($250,000 – $20,000 = $230,000). There is no off-balance sheet risk associated with trade accounts receivable.

33. **A**   The correct answer is the SFAS 133 *Definition of a Derivative.*

34. **B**   SFAS 133 requires that gains or losses on hedges of foreign currency exposure of an available-for-sale security must be recognized currently.

35. **D**   An interest rate swap agreement involves the exchange of cash flows determined by various interest rates. Fluctuations in interest rates after the agreement is entered into may result in the risk of exchanging a lower interest rate for a higher interest rate. Financial instruments, including swaps, also bear credit risk or the risk that a counterparty to the agreement will not perform as expected.

36. **A**   SFAS 133 requires that gains or losses on a derivative used as a hedge of a forecasted foreign-currency-denominated transaction should be included in comprehensive income because the transaction is not complete. When the transaction is complete, the gain will be reclassified from comprehensive income to current earnings.

37. **A**   Financial instruments are cash, investments in equities, or contracts to receive or pay cash or another financial instrument. A derivative is one particular type of financial instrument where promises are exchanged, such as a promise to pay cash for a certain amount of gold.

Section 4: Earnings Per Share

38. **B**   SFAS 128 states that for EPS purposes, shares of stock issued as a result of stock dividends or splits should be considered outstanding for the entire period in which they were issued. Therefore, both the original 20,000 shares and the additional 20,000 issued in the April 1 stock split are treated as outstanding for the entire year (20,000 × 2 = 40,000). The July 1 issuance of 10,000 shares results in a weighted average of 5,000 shares (10,000 × 6/12) because the shares were outstanding for only six months during the year. Therefore, Jenghis should use 45,000 shares (40,000 + 5,000) to calculate EPS.

39. **D**   The computation of weighted-average shares outstanding is:

Date	# of shares	Fraction	Weighted-average
Jan 1	30,000	12/12	30,000
Feb 1	3,000	12/12	3,000
Jul 1	8,000	6/12	4,000
			37,000

The 3,000 shares issued as a result of a stock dividend are weighted at 12/12 instead of 11/12 because for EPS purposes, stock dividends are treated as if they occurred at the beginning of the year.

40. **B**   Diluted EPS is based on common stock and all dilutive potential common shares. To determine if a security is dilutive, EPS, including the effect of the dilutive security, must be compared to the basic EPS. In this case, basic EPS is $7.45.

$$($850,000 – $30,000)/110,000 \text{ shares} = $7.45$$

The effect of the convertible preferred stock is to increase the numerator by $30,000 ($3.00 dividend per share × 10,000 shares) for the amount of the preferred dividends that would not be paid (assuming conversion) and increase the denominator by 20,000 shares. The security is dilutive because it decreases the EPS from $7.45 to $6.54.

$$($850,000 – $30,000 + $30,000)/(110,000 + 20,000) = $6.54$$

If the EPS increases due to the inclusion of a security, that security is antidilutive and should not be included.

41. **D**   Per SFAS 128, dividends on nonconvertible cumulative preferred shares should be deducted from net income, whether an actual liability exists or not. This is because cumulative preferred stock owners must receive any dividends in arrears before future dividend distributions can be made to common stockholders.

42. **C**   Earnings per share is a common stock computation. Thus, the "earnings" figure is the amount that can be assigned to the common stock. That is the total net income less any preferred dividends or $500,000 – $30,000 = $470,000. The "shares" figure is the weighted average number of common stock. A stock dividend (or split), though, is theoretically not viewed as the issuance of new shares but rather as a division of all earlier shares. A stock dividend, therefore, is viewed as occurring at the beginning of the period. For this computation, the company is viewed as having all 120,000 shares outstanding for the full year. Basic earnings per share is the $470,000 / 120,000 shares, or $3.92 per share (rounded).

43. **D**   Earnings per share is a common stock computation. Thus, the "earnings" figure is the amount can be assigned to the common stock. That is the total net income less any preferred dividends or $600,000 – $70,000 = $530,000. The "shares" figure is the weighted average number of common stock. For the first six months, the company had 100,000 shares outstanding and, for the next six months, the company had 120,000 shares outstanding. The weighted average would be 110,000 [= (100,000 × 6 + 120,000 × 6) / 12 months]. The basic earnings per share is $530,000 / 110,000 shares or $4.82 (rounded).

44. **B**   To compute diluted earnings per share, it is easier to begin by determining basic earnings per share. The net income should be reduced by the preferred stock dividends to arrive at earnings of $370,000 ($400,000 – $30,000) applicable to the common stock. That figure is divided by the 80,000 shares of common stock to arrive at $4.63. Then, assume that the convertible preferred shares were actually converted at the beginning of the year. The shares of common stock would increase by 5,000 to 85,000. In addition, the preferred stock dividends would not be paid if the shares had been converted. The $30,000 dividends are added back so earnings returns to $400,000. Diluted earnings per share is $4.71 ($400,000 / 85,000 shares). However, that figure is higher than basic earnings per share. The convertible preferred stock is antidilutive: it causes earnings per share to increase. The point of reporting diluted earnings per share is to show a worst-case scenario. Therefore, any antidilutive items should be removed from the computation which returns the diluted earnings per share back to $4.63 (rounded).

45. **C**   To compute diluted earnings per share, it is easier to begin by determining primary earnings per share. The net income should be reduced by the preferred stock dividends to arrive at earnings of $520,000 ($600,000 – $80,000) applicable to the common stock. That figure is divided by the 120,000 shares of common stock to arrive at $4.33. Then, assume that the stock options were all converted at the start of the year. That would increase the number of common shares by 20,000 to 140,000. The question, though, is what would happen to the $100,000 in cash (20,000 options at a conversion price of $5 each) received by the company. To enable conformity and comparability, all companies assume that money is used to buy treasury stock. That amount of money ($100,000) would allow the purchase of 5,000 shares ($100,000/$20 average price). Treasury stock acquisition reduces the outstanding shares from 140,000 to 135,000. Diluted earnings per share is $3.85 (= $520,000 / 135,000 shares) (rounded).

46. **A**   To compute diluted earnings per share, it is easier to begin by determining primary earnings per share. The net income should be reduced by the preferred stock dividends to arrive at earnings of $460,000 ($500,000 – $40,000) applicable to the common stock. A reduction is made for the preferred stock dividend even

though it was not declared because it was cumulative. The $460,000 figure is divided by the 200,000 shares of common stock to arrive at $2.30. Then, assume that the bonds were actually converted at the start of the year. That would add 50,000 shares to the common stock (5,000 bonds at 10 shares each). If the bonds were converted, though, no interest expense would have been paid. Thus, $150,000 in expense was saved (5,000 bonds × $30 interest). If the income goes up that much, the tax to be paid would have also gone up by $45,000 (30% of $150,000). So the "earnings" figure is $460,000 + $150,000 – $45,000 = $565,000. That is divided by 250,000 shares for a diluted earnings per share of $2.26 (rounded).

47. **D**   Earnings per share is a common stock computation. The net income for the year was $400,000, but cash dividends of $90,000 were paid to preferred stockholders, leaving $310,000 as the profit attributed to common stockholders. There were 100,000 shares outstanding for the first nine months (900,000) and 120,000 shares for the final three months (360,000). That provides a total of 1,260,000. To find the monthly average, divide by 12 to get 105,000 shares. Thus, basic earnings per share is computed as $310,000 / 105,000 shares = $2.95 (rounded).

48. **C**   In determining diluted earnings per share, the company begins with its basic earnings per share ($440,000 / 100,000 shares) and then gives some amount of weight to any items that can be converted into common stock. Here the bonds are convertibles. First, the company makes the assumption that they were actually converted into common stock. Because of the conversion ratio, 20,000 new shares would have to be issued (10,000 bonds at a two-for-one conversion ratio). That brings the number of shares up to 120,000. The conversion did not actually take place; the process is set up to show the potential effect of a conversion. If the bonds had actually been converted, the interest expense (10,000 bonds × $7, or $70,000) would not have been paid. Avoiding that expense would cause reported net income to rise. However, if net income goes up, the company would also have to pay an additional $21,000 in taxes (30% of $70,000). So, the potential impact on net income of the bond conversion is an increase of $70,000 (interest saved) and a decrease of $21,000 (additional taxes paid). For diluted earnings per share, the income is $440,000 + $70,000 – $21,000 = $489,000. When divided by the 120,000 shares, the company reports diluted earnings per share of $4.08 (rounded).

49. **D**   In determining diluted earnings per share, the company begins with its basic earnings per share ($860,000 / 200,000 shares) and then gives weight to any items that can be converted into common stock. Here, that is the stock options. First, the company makes the assumption that they were actually converted into common stock. Because of the conversion ratio, 30,000 new shares would have to be issued (10,000 options at a three-for-one conversion ratio). That brings the number of shares up to 130,000. The conversion did not actually take place; the process is set up to show the potential effect of a conversion. However, if conversion had taken place, the company would have received cash of $300,000 (30,000 shares at a conversion price of $10.00 each). The company could have used that money for an almost infinite number of purposes. However, to provide comparability across companies, every company must assume that such cash is used to buy treasury stock at the average market price per year. With that assumption, the company would have bought back 12,000 shares of treasury stock ($300,000 / $25 per share price). For diluted earnings per share, the income stays at $860,000. The shares start with 200,000, then goes up by 30,000 shares from the assumed conversion, and then down by 12,000 because of the assumed purchase of treasury stock for a total of 218,000 shares of common stock. When $860,000 is divided by the 218,000 shares, the company reports diluted earnings per share of $3.94 (rounded).

Section 5: Foreign Currency Balances

50. **A**   A transaction has occurred in which settlement will be made in Argentine pesos. Because Linde's functional currency is the U.S. dollar, a foreign exchange transaction gain (loss) will result if the spot rate on the settlement date is different than the rate on the transaction date (see SFAS 52). A provision must be made at any intervening year-end date if there has been a rate change.

Thus, in Year 5, a $500 foreign exchange transaction gain [100,000 × ($0.4295 – $0.4245)] would be recognized. In Year 6, a $1,000 foreign exchange transaction loss [100,000 × ($0.4245 – $0.4345)] would be recognized.

51. **D** Refer to the SFAS 52 Definition of Functional Currency.

52. **B** In the case of the receivable denominated in Japanese yen, a foreign exchange gain was recorded on the collection of the receivable. This means that more yen was received than was recorded in the receivables account. For that to happen, the rate of yen exchangeable for a dollar would have had to decrease, requiring more yen to be paid at the settlement date for the same amount of dollars at the contract date.

    On the other hand, there was a foreign exchange transaction loss on the payable denominated in euros. This means that at the settlement date, Sphinx had to pay more euros than were recorded in payable account. For this to occur, the rate of euros exchangeable for a dollar would have had to decrease, requiring more euros to be paid at the settlement date for the same amount of dollars at the contract date.

53. **B** The current rate method must be used for the translation of foreign currency financial statements when a foreign subsidiary's functional currency is its local currency. Using the current rate method, revenues and expenses should be translated into U.S. dollars at the weighted-average rate for the current year. Thus, both sales to customers and wages expense should be translated at the weighted-average rate.

54. **D** On September 1, Year 5, Canope obtained a receivable that will be collected in a foreign currency. A gain/loss will result if the exchange rate on the settlement date is different from the rate existing on the transaction date. A gain/loss must be recognized at any intervening balance sheet date, if necessary.

    Therefore, Canope would recognize a $2,500 foreign exchange transaction loss in its Year 5 income statement because a change in the exchange rate reduced the receivable (in U.S. dollars) from $50,000 on September 1, Year 5 (250,000 × $0.20) to $47,500 on December 31, Year 5 (250,000 × $0.19). In Year 6, a foreign exchange transaction gain of $7,500 is recognized because the receivable (in U.S. dollars) increased from $47,500 to $55,000 when received (250,000 × $0.22).

55. **B** Translation adjustments result from translating an entity's financial statements into the reporting currency. Such adjustments, which result when the company's functional currency is the foreign currency, should not be included in net income. Instead, such adjustments should be reported as other comprehensive income and accumulated other comprehensive income in the stockholders' equity section of the balance sheet.

    If the functional currency is the reporting currency (U.S. dollar), a remeasurement process takes place, with the resulting gain or loss included in net income.

56. **B** Geneva's accounting records are kept in Swiss francs, and its functional currency is the British pound. Before Geneva's financial statements can be consolidated with Park's financial statements, they must be remeasured from Swiss francs to British pounds. As a result of these restatements, there is a remeasurement gain of $7,600 and a credit translation adjustment of $8,100.

    A remeasurement gain or loss is included in net income, but a translation adjustment is not. Therefore, Park would report a foreign exchange gain of $7,600 in its Year 6 income statement.

57. **C** When the functional currency of a foreign subsidiary is the foreign currency, asset and liability accounts are translated using the current exchange rate (the rate of translation in effect at the balance sheet date). Therefore, these accounts should be included in the balance sheet at $475,000.

    Note that if the functional currency was the U.S. dollar, balance sheet accounts would be remeasured using a combination of historical and current rates.

58. **D** As a multinational firm, the location of Mazeppa's head office would most likely determine the currency to be used to prepare its final consolidated financial statements. That is the reporting currency, and, in this case, it is the Canadian dollar. Based on the facts, the local currency is the euro, and the functional currency is the U.S. dollar.

59. **A** Transactions that occur outside of a company's functional currency must be remeasured for reporting purposes. Under remeasurement, monetary accounts (cash, receivables, payables, and accounts stated at current fair value) are reported at the current exchange rate. All other accounts are reported using their historic exchange rates. Thus, only the value reported for the 60,000 peso account payable will be affected by changes in the exchange rate. It was initially $0.083 or $4,980 but, by the end of the year, was $0.081 or $4,860. A drop in the value of a liability creates a gain to be reported within net income.

60. **D** In consolidation, a translation takes place when the parent and the subsidiary have different functional currencies as they do here in this problem. The translation process uses current exchange rates for all assets and all liabilities. Therefore, both the 60,000 peso Inventory balance and the 60,000 peso Accounts Payable balance have to be retranslated from $0.083 to $0.081 on December 31, Year 1. The loss (a translation adjustment) on the reported value of the inventory is exactly offset by the gain (also a translation adjustment) on the account payable. No net effect remains to be reported.

61. **B** Currency exchange gains and losses result from remeasurements and are reported within net income. A translation adjustment results from a translation and is reported within accumulated other comprehensive income in the stockholders' equity section of the balance sheet. The changes each year in these other comprehensive income items are also used to convert net income to comprehensive income.

Section 6: Discontinued Operation

62. **D** The loss from discontinued operations would equal the loss from operations plus the estimated loss from disposal of the component.

63. **A** Refer to SFAS 44 for the list of requirements for the disposal of a component to be presented as discontinued operations. However, management is not required to have entered into a sales agreement. It is sufficient if management is committed to a disposal plan that is reasonable. The other items are all required for presentation as discontinued operations.

64. **D** In discontinued operations, it is required to present the income or loss from operations of the subsidiary *and* the gain or loss from disposal. Because the company met the requirements for "held for sale" status in Year 6, the subsidiary should be written down to its fair value less the cost to sell.

This would result in a loss of $1,500,000 ($8,000,000 carrying amount less $6,500,000 fair value). Therefore, the loss from discontinued operations would be $3,500,000 ($2,000,000 loss from operations + $1,500,000 loss on planned disposal).

Section 7: Reporting Segments of an Enterprise

65. **C** A company must report a measure of profit and loss based on the measure reported to the chief operating decision maker for purposes of making decisions. The information used by management includes intersegment profits and should be included, but common costs are not allocated to the segments when assessing performance and should not be included.

66. **D** If 10% or more of the revenue of a company is derived from sales to any single customer, that fact and the amount of revenue from each customer shall be disclosed. In this question, Grimm reported revenues of $50 million and thus should disclose major customer data if sales to any single customer amount to $5 million ($50 million × 10%).

67. **D** There must be enough segments reported so that the total of external revenues by operating segments equals at least 75% of total consolidated revenues (75% test). Consolidated revenues total $50 million, so external revenues reported by operating segments must be at least $37.5 million ($50 million × 75%).

68. **C**   Selected data for a segment must be reported separately if one of three criteria is met. One of these criteria is met when a segment's revenue is greater than or equal to 10% of the combined revenues of all industry segments. Combined revenue includes sales to unaffiliated customers and intersegment sales or transfers.

Thus, Aria has a reportable segment if that segment's revenues exceed $260,000 [($2,000,000 + $600,000) × 10%]. The $40,000 interest would not be included in combined revenue because it appears to be unrelated to the revenues of these segments and is not controllable at the segment level.

69. **B**   As a discontinued operation, all revenues, expenses, gains/losses, and taxes that relate to this operation are dropped to the bottom of the company's income statement. In this way, ongoing operations can be shown separately from discontinued operations. After removal of the discontinued operation, the company will report revenues of $700,000, operating expenses of $400,000, and no gain so that the income before taxes is $300,000. At a 30% tax rate, the tax figure is $90,000, leaving income before discontinued operations to be $210,000.

70. **C**   For disclosure purposes, a company must divide its operations into segments in the same manner as it does for internal decision-making purposes. In this testing of segment significance, the revenues of the segments include both external sales and internal transfers. For the revenue test, disclosure is required for any segment that makes up 10% or more of the total of all segments. The Red segment does not meet that standard ($120,000/$1,300,000 for the three segments as a whole is only 9.2%). Large sources of revenues must also be disclosed. Therefore, revenues from a specific country must be disclosed if material and revenues from a single customer must be disclosed if they make up 10% or more of consolidated revenues.

CRAM ESSENTIALS: CONTENTS

ACCOUNTS RECEIVABLE AND BAD DEBT EXPENSE

A. **Accounts Receivable**—amounts owed to the reporting entity, frequently owed to it by customers for sales made on credit.

1. Shown as a current asset unless payment is to be delayed.

2. Made up of four separate figures:

   a. Beginning balance for the period.

   b. Increased by credit sales for the period.

   c. Decreased by collections made.

   d. Decreased by balances written off because of returns or discounts or because they are uncollectible.

B. **Allowance for doubtful accounts**—an estimation of the amount of receivables being reported that will not be collected.

1. Balance is shown as a contra (negative) account to accounts receivable to report these receivables at net realizable value.

   a. **Net realizable value** is the amount (of any asset) that is expected to be collected in cash.

2. Final balance in the allowance account is a credit and is the result of four figures:

   a. Beginning balance for the period (starts with credit).

   b. Decreased by the write-off of an account receivable as bad.

   c. Increased by the subsequent collection of an account previously written off as bad. Cash is debited (increase) and allowance for doubtful accounts is credited (increase).

   d. Increased by the recognition of bad debt expense for the current period.

3. **Bad debt expense** is frequently recorded just prior to producing financial statements. Expense for current period is estimated and recorded so that it will be recognized in the same period as the sale—an example of the matching principle.

   a. Estimation can be made by the **percentage of sales method,** which calculates and then records bad debt expense based on an estimated percentage of sales. The percentage is derived from past experience. (sales × specified percentage = bad debt expense)

      • This calculated figure is the expense recognized for period with an accompanying increase in the allowance for doubtful accounts.
      • The sales figure for this computation can be "gross" or "net" (with discounts, allowances, etc., subtracted).

    b.   An alternative method is the **percentage of receivables method** (and the **aging method,** which is a variation). It calculates the ending credit balance for the Allowance account based on an estimated percentage of ending receivables (receivables × specified percentage = ending allowance balance).

- Allowance will already have a balance—in this method, that figure is increased to the credit balance previously computed.
- Bad debt expense is the increase in the allowance.

    c.   Company may use percentage of sales during the year for interim reporting and switch to receivables method at end.

- Expense is recognized during the year as a percentage of sales.
- Allowance is adjusted at end of year to appropriate balance based on percentage of receivables (or aging).

  4. Actual **write-off of a bad account** can occur at any time and is a debit to allowance (decrease) and a credit to accounts receivable (decrease). Has no effect on bad debt expense, net income, or the net balance reported for the receivables.

C. Direct write-off method—sometimes used by smaller businesses to report bad debts although it is not considered as generally accepted. No allowance account is established; bad debt expense is not recognized until account is written off.

  1. Accounts receivable is decreased and bad debt expense is increased.

  2. Receivable is reported at an amount above what will be collected. Expenses are not being matched in the same period as revenues.

D. Receivables can be used to generate immediate cash flows. Assignment and Pledging are ways to borrow cash using Receivables as collateral. In Assignment, certain specific Receivables are designated as collateral. The company makes a journal entry to debit Assigned A/R and credit A/R (regular A/R). In Pledging, no journal entry is required; the creditor has the right to claim any Receivables if the debtor does not pay. Both of these require footnote disclosures. Discounting refers to the sale of a note receivable whereas **factoring** and **securitization** reflect the sale of accounts receivable.

  1. Factoring usually indicates that a single party has bought some of a company's accounts receivable. The buyer will typically be responsible for collecting the receivables. Securitization means that many parties have bought the right to a portion of a company's receivables. The seller will continue to collect the receivables and convey all cash received to the buyer.

  2. In some situations, it may be difficult to determine if a sale has been made or if the receivables are simply being used as security for a debt. Both buyer and seller must recognize the assets and liabilities that they control. The financial component approach is used for this determination; it specifies that any element of the receivable is considered to be sold if three criteria have been met indicating a change in control.

    a.   The asset is isolated from the seller.

    b.   The buyer now has the right to sell or pledge the asset.

    c.   The seller has not retained control through agreements to repurchase or redeem the asset.

3. Receivables can be sold "**with recourse.**" If a receivable is not paid by customer when due, buyer can then demand payment from seller.

    a. To record the sale, the seller removes receivable and records cash received. However, because of potential liability, seller must also record the fair value of any "recourse obligation" that is expected to arise because of the failure of some customers to pay.

    b. The difference between the cash received and the summation of the asset lost and the recourse obligation incurred is recognized as a loss.

    c. If the receivable is sold without recourse so that the seller has no further obligation, the receivable is removed and the cash recognized and the difference is a loss. There is no recourse obligation.

PRESENT VALUE COMPUTATIONS

A. The concept of **present value:**

1. Generally accepted accounting principles state that all contractually set future cash flows must have an interest factor attached to them. Interest must be recognized virtually any time that money is paid or received over time. If cash is to be paid over time (a liability exists), interest expense is recognized; if cash is to be received (a receivable exists), interest revenue is recognized.

2. The interest factor can be explicitly stated in the contract and paid, thus causing no valuation problems. For example, if a $1,000 note payable pays 9% annual cash interest, $1,000 is the principal and $90 per year is the interest. Present value is not needed; a reasonable interest rate is stated and paid.

3. If a reasonable rate of interest is not stated and paid, the future cash is assumed to be part interest and part principal. For example, if land is acquired for a single payment of $2,000 to be made in two years, part of the $2,000 is viewed as principal (cost of the land) and the remainder is recorded as interest to be recognized over the 2-year period.

4. Present value computations are designed to compute the portion of any future cash flows that represents the principal.

    a. If a purchase is made that requires future cash payments, but a reasonable interest rate is not stated and paid, the present value is the cost assigned to the purchase.

    b. For a sale with future payments that do not include a reasonable interest, the present value is the amount of the sales revenue to be recorded immediately.

5. One major exception exists in connection with the use of present value. If all cash flows arise from normal business operations and are to be made within one year, present value computations are not used, even if no reasonable interest rate is stated and paid.

B. The **calculation of present value** is based on a formula: present value (or principal) is equal to the future cash flows multiplied by a conversion rate.

1. Future cash flows are usually specified in an agreement or contract.

2. Conversion rate comes from a table; specific rate is based on three variables.

    a. Number of time periods.

b.   A reasonable interest rate (sometimes called the yield rate or effective rate or market rate).

c.   Whether the cash flow is a single amount or an **annuity** (which is equal payments made at equal time intervals).

3.   If future cash flow is a single amount, conversion rate comes from "Present Value of 1" table. If future cash flow is an annuity, "Present Value of Annuity" table is used.

4.   If future cash flow is several unequal payments, "Present Value of 1" table is used. A separate conversion rate is used for each payment to get individual present values. These values are added to get total present value (principal).

5.   If future cash flow is both a single payment and an annuity (as it would be in many notes), the conversion rate for the annuity comes from the annuity table and the conversion rate for the single amount comes from the single amount table. Again, the individual present values are added to arrive at total.

C.   Annuities.

1.   An annuity where the payments are made at the end of each period is referred to as an **ordinary annuity**. Interest on a payable or receivable is usually paid at the end of the period.

2.   An annuity where the payments are made at the beginning of each period is referred to as an **annuity due**. Most rents and leases require payments at the beginning of the period.

3.   If necessary, an ordinary annuity table can be used to solve an annuity due problem. Remove the first cash payment and find the conversion rate for the remaining payments using the ordinary annuity table. Compute the present value of these remaining payments and then add the first payment. Since it is paid immediately, it is already stated at its present value.

D.   Future Values.

1.   Another set of conversion rates can be used to compute the amount that a set of cash flows will be worth at a specified point in the future. For example, if $1,000 is deposited in a savings account that adds 5% interest per year, a future value computation can be used to determine the amount in the account at any future point in time.

2.   Formula is: future value = cash flows × conversion rate. Once again, the conversion rate is based on the number of time periods, a reasonable interest rate, and whether a single amount or an annuity is involved. Conversion rate comes from a future value table.

LAND, BUILDINGS, AND EQUIPMENT (FIXED ASSETS)

A.   This balance sheet classification encompasses tangible, long-lived assets that are being used to generate revenues.

B.   For reporting purposes, the cost of **fixed assets** must be determined.

1.   For new acquisitions, all normal and necessary costs to acquire the asset and get it into a condition to be used follow the rules of **capitalization** (that is, they are added to an asset account rather than to an expense account). These amounts include:

a.   Invoice price (less any discounts).

b.   Sales taxes.

    c.   Cost of delivery.

    d.   Cost of installation.

2. In certain cases, **interest costs** are also capitalized.

    a.   Interest costs incurred during construction of fixed assets, and inventory if it is being specifically built for a customer, should be capitalized. The interest is added to the asset account rather than being recorded as interest expense.

    b.   The amount of interest to be capitalized is calculated each year by multiplying the average accumulated expenditures to date by the interest rate.

        • If a specific debt is incurred to finance the construction, the interest rate on that debt is used in this computation. Otherwise, the weighted average interest rate for all of the company's outstanding debt is used.

        • If the calculation of capitalized interest gives a figure that is more than the actual interest incurred during the period, only the actual interest is capitalized.

3. **Assets received as gifts** are initially recorded at fair value with a corresponding increase in a donated revenue account.

4. The ownership of some assets creates a liability that must be paid at the eventual point of retirement. For example, the acquisition of an off-shore oil or gas drilling facility may necessitate its eventual removal because of legal requirements.

    a.   As soon as this retirement obligation becomes probable, its current fair value must be determined and recognized as a liability. If a current fair value cannot be ascertained, the present value of the future obligation is recognized as the debt.

        • A credit-adjusted risk-free interest rate is used to determine the present value as well as the computation of the interest expense that should be recognized each period.

        • The credit-adjusted risk-free interest rate is the current interest rate for a United States government obligation for that period of time, adjusted upwards based on the credit rating of the company.

    b.   The liability that is recognized also serves to increase the capitalized cost of the asset. That impacts the annual recognition of depreciation expense.

5. For an asset already in use, any new expenditure is capitalized only if it is a betterment in some way: the life of the asset is extended beyond the original estimation, the asset becomes more efficient or productive, or operating costs are decreased. If an expenditure simply maintains the asset at its anticipated level of productivity and length of life, the cost is recorded as a maintenance expense.

C. Assets may be acquired (or sold) for future cash payments (a payable is created by a purchase, a receivable by a sale). If a reasonable interest rate is not stated and paid, the cost of the asset (or the revenue if it is a sale) will be the present value of the cash flows based on a reasonable interest rate.

1. In such cases, the asset (or sales revenue) is recorded at **present value.** The payable (or receivable) is reported at the total cash flow. A discount account is set up for the difference. This is a contra account to the payable (or receivable).

    a.   The discount represents the portion of the total cash flows that is viewed as interest rather than principal.

    b.   As an alternative, the payable (or receivable) could be reported as a single number net of the discount.

2. Over the life of the payable/receivable, the discount will gradually be reclassified (amortized) as interest.

    a. Reducing the discount causes an increase in the net balance of the payable/receivable.

    b. If payable/receivable is shown as a single net figure, recognition of interest within the cash flows increases the payable/receivable balance being reported.

3. Interest to be recognized each period is computed by multiplying the payable/receivable net of the discount by reasonable interest rate. This is referred to as the **effective rate method.**

4. As an alternative, if the results are not materially different, the straight-line method can be used to compute interest expense. The discount is divided evenly over the periods of time that payment will be made.

D. **Depreciation** is the process of assigning or allocating the cost of a fixed asset as an expense to the years in which it is used to generate revenues.

1. The amount is computed and recorded at the end of each year in which the asset is in use. It is also recorded at the date an asset is sold, traded, or otherwise disposed of.

    a. Recording entry is a debit (increase) to depreciation expense and a credit (increase) to accumulated depreciation. Depreciation expense is shown on the income statement and is closed out each year. **Accumulated depreciation** is a contra-account to the asset and, hence, is reported on the balance sheet so that it is not closed at the end of every period.

    b. Asset's book value (or carrying value) is its cost less total accumulated depreciation recognized to date.

    c. For convenience, a **half-year convention** (or some variation) can be used. Only one-half year of depreciation is recorded in the year of acquisition and again in the year of disposal, regardless of the exact dates of purchase or disposal.

    d. If an asset is not being used to generate revenues, it is reported as an "other asset" and depreciation is not reported.

2. **Straight-line method**—records the same expense for each full year. Annual figure is computed as follows: (cost – salvage value)/life.

3. **Accelerated depreciation** methods record high depreciation levels in the initial years of use (when the asset is most productive and subject to quick losses of value) but lower expense levels later. Several methods are available that create this pattern of cost allocation.

    a. **Double declining balance method** computes the current expense as follows: (cost – accumulated depreciation) × 2/life. Because accumulated depreciation gets larger each year, the resulting book value figure (and, hence, depreciation expense) will get smaller each year. An alternative method is 150% declining balance, which uses 1.5/life rather than 2/life.

    b. **Sum of the years' digits method** computes the annual expense as follows: (cost – salvage value) × fraction. The fraction is determined as follows:
- Denominator: the sum of the years of the asset's life. An asset with a five-year life would have a denominator of 15 (5 + 4 + 3 + 2 + 1).
- Numerator: the number in the asset's life that corresponds to the current year (in descending order). For an asset with a 5-year life, 5 would be used for the first year, 4 for the second, and so on.

4. **Group depreciation** (and the similar "composite" method) applies one straight-line rate to an entire group of assets that are all acquired in the same year but with different lives. For example, 20 different small machines might be depreciated as a group.

   a. In the year of acquisition, annual depreciation is computed for each asset. The total annual depreciation is divided by the total cost of these assets to get depreciation rate. Each year, this same rate is multiplied by the remaining cost of the group. Depreciation stops with the disposal of the last item in the group or when any remaining cost has been fully depreciated.

   b. For the disposal of an item within the group, cash received is recorded, the original cost of that particular asset is removed, and the difference is a reduction in accumulated depreciation. No gain or loss is recognized. The assumption is that all gains and losses within the group will eventually offset. Any residual gain or loss is recorded at the retirement of the last asset.

5. **Depletion of wasting assets,** such as oil wells and gold mines, is computed on the straight-line method, but based on units, not years.

   a. Rate is found by dividing the cost (less any anticipated residual value) by the number of expected units.

   b. When units are removed, the cost (the units times the rate) is first recorded in an Inventory account. At the eventual time of sale, the cost is reclassified from inventory to cost of goods sold.

   c. Because the number of units is an estimation, a new depletion rate may have to be computed each year. Estimated residual value is subtracted from remaining book value. The resulting figure is divided by the estimated number of units remaining.

   d. Depreciation can also be computed using an approach (known as the **units of production method**) that is similar to depletion computation. Depreciation of a taxicab, for example, could be based on the miles driven this year as a percentage of the total mileage of expected use.

E. Disposals—when an asset is sold, destroyed, or otherwise disposed of, depreciation is recorded to the date of disposal.

   1. Both the cost of the asset and the accumulated depreciation are then removed from the records.

   2. If the amount received is different from the book value being removed, a gain is recorded (if more is collected) or a loss (if less).

F. **Asset with an impaired value.**

   1. Impairment occurs when the total of expected net future cash inflows is less than current book value.

   2. If impaired, book value of asset is written down to fair value and a corresponding loss is recorded.

   3. If an asset's book value is written down because of an impairment, but the value subsequently increases, no write-up is allowed.

   4. A check for impairment should be made when there is a significant decline in the market price of an asset, there is a significant change in the use or condition of the asset, the cost was greater than expected, or the company plans to sell the asset before the end of its expected life.

5. In testing impairment, assets should be grouped at the lowest possible level for which cash flows can be identified.

   a. For that reason, a building and equipment might be tested separately or together.

   b. Cash flows should be determined for the life of the asset. If various assets are grouped, that life is the one for the **primary asset** in the group. The primary asset is the one that is most significant for generating cash flows. Any asset in the group with a longer life is assumed to be sold at the end of the primary asset's life.

   c. If a loss is determined for a group of assets, the loss is allocated to the various assets proportionally based on individual book values. No asset, though, should be reported below its current market value.

6. Assets to be sold must be reclassified on the balance sheet under certain conditions.

   a. The asset should be reclassified into a "held for sale" category when several requirements have been met including (1) the company is actively looking for a buyer, (2) sale is probable within one year, and (3) the asset is available for immediate sale.

   b. Any asset that qualifies as "held for sale" should be reported at the lower of its book value or net realizable value (expected sales price less anticipated costs necessary to sale).

7. If an asset is simply to be abandoned, the asset remains on the books and depreciation is continued as long as the asset is still in use. At the time of abandonment, the book value is removed and a loss recognized.

G. **Nonmonetary exchanges**—the trade of two items with little or no cash (sometimes referred to as "boot") involved. For example, trading one truck for another is a nonmonetary exchange as is trading a truck for a computer.

   1. The asset being surrendered may first have to be tested for impairment if its book value clearly exceeds its fair value. Impairment rules should be followed if this preliminary testing is needed.

   2. The book value of the asset or assets being surrendered are first removed, both the cost figure and the related accumulated depreciation.

   3. The asset being received is then recorded at the fair value of the item surrendered. However, if the fair value of the asset surrendered cannot be determined, then the new asset is recorded at its own fair value.

   4. Any difference between the book value of the asset being surrendered and the amount recorded for the new item is either a gain or loss to be recognized on the trade.

   5. If an exchange has no economic substance, then the new asset is recorded at the book value of the previously held asset so that no gain or loss is recognized.

      a. A trade is viewed as having no economic substance if the anticipated cash flows are virtually identical both before and after the exchange.

      b. Cash flows are viewed as virtually identical if they are expected to have the same amounts, the same timing, and the same amount of risk.

BONDS PAYABLE, NOTES PAYABLE, AND INVESTMENTS IN BONDS OR NOTES HELD TO MATURITY

A. **Bonds and notes** are formal promises to pay a certain amount of money along with a specified amount of cash interest at a certain time in the future. Can be negotiated with a single party or can be a negotiable instrument to be bought and sold at whatever price can be achieved.

   1. **Bonds** have several unique terms.

      a. **Serial bond**—interest and principal payments are made periodically.

      b. **Term bond**—interest is paid each period but principal is paid as a lump sum on maturity date.

      c. **Debenture bond**—debt is not secured by collateral or any other type of security.

      d. **Bond indenture**—this document gives the legal terms of a bond.

   2. **Bond issuance costs** paid by debtor (such as printing and legal fees) are reported as an asset and amortized to expense by straight-line method over life of bond. If bond is paid off early, any remaining cost must be removed.

B. Computation of the selling price of a bond on the market. Price is usually stated as a percentage of face value (a price of 98 would mean 98% of face value).

   1. If investors want an interest rate that is same as the cash rate stated on the indenture, they will pay an amount equal to the face value of the bond. **Stated interest rate** is multiplied by face value to determine annual amount of interest to be paid.

   2. If the investor and debtor negotiate an effective yield rate that is different than the stated cash interest rate, the price of the bond must be calculated. The present value of the cash flows set by the indenture is determined using the effective yield rate negotiated by the parties. The resulting price will be below face value if the negotiated yield rate is higher than the stated rate but will be above face value if the yield rate is below the stated interest rate.

   3. A present value computation is also necessary if stated interest rate is unreasonable (such as a zero rate). Interest is assumed to be hidden inside of the note or bond.

C. If a premium or discount is recorded on a bond, that amount must be amortized to interest over the life of bond.

   1. Amortization entries are made at the date of each interest payment, as well as at end of fiscal year.

   2. **Effective rate method** calculates true interest by multiplying current book value of the debt (face value plus premium or minus discount) times **effective interest rate.** The difference in this interest figure and the cash interest payment reduces the discount or premium. Because of change in discount or premium, book value of the bond or note changes each time amortization is recorded.

      a. Effective interest rate is the market rate at the time of the transaction or the rate the company could otherwise get.

   3. **Straight-line method** is sometimes used to amortize discount or premium, although effective rate method is preferred. It divides premium or discount evenly over life of bond; that amount is

amortized each period. Straight-line method can be used when recognized amounts are not materially different than figures that would have been reported by the effective rate method.

   a.   Under either method, interest to be recognized is the cash interest plus the amortization of any discount or less the amortization of any premium.

   4.   For a long-term bond, portion that should be reported as current is equal to any principal payment in the upcoming year less amortization of any discount or plus amortization of any premium.

D.   If a bond is called (paid off early) before its maturity date, a final amortization entry must be recorded to bring book value up to date. Bond issuance costs must be amortized as well as any discount or premium. Face value along with any remaining bond issuance costs and any unamortized discount or premium gives book value of bond.

   1.   The difference in this book value and cash payment is recognized as a gain or loss.

   2.   For the debtor, the gain or loss is classified as an ordinary part of net income. It is no longer viewed as an extraordinary item.

E.   A bond is sometimes sold along with **detachable stock warrants** for one price. For recording, price must be allocated between debt and equity.

   1.   If market value of only one item is known, that amount is assigned to that item. Remainder of price is allocated to other item.

   2.   If both items have a known fair value, price is allocated between debt and equity based on the relative market values.

F.   Some financial instruments have characteristics of both liabilities and equities, so classification on the balance sheet can be a problem. The following are considered to be liabilities rather than equities.

   1.   Any financial instrument (even a share of the company's own stock) is reported as a liability if assets will have to be used to satisfy a mandatory redemption. So, for example, preferred stock that must eventually be redeemed with cash is listed as a liability.

   2.   A financial instrument that must or may be settled by a variable number of the company's own equity shares is reported as a liability if the monetary amount is fixed (so that the number of shares required will vary based on market price) or the number of shares to be issued is based on some other value (such as the current price of gold).

G.   If a company has a debt coming due within 12 months of the balance sheet date, the debt is classified as long term if either one of two conditions is met before the financial statements are issued.

   1.   Debt is classified as long-term if (1) it is refinanced on a long-term basis or (2) a noncancellable agreement to refinance on a long-term basis is signed with a financially sound lending institution.

H.   A **troubled debt restructuring** occurs when a debtor faces default and the creditor gives more lenient terms in hopes of improving future collection.

   1.   If payment is made immediately with a noncash asset (such as land), the asset is first adjusted to market value so that debtor has an ordinary gain or loss. Difference between market value of asset and book value of debt is an ordinary gain or loss for debtor and an ordinary gain or loss for creditor.

2. If debt is restructured so that debtor has better terms, debtor and creditor record the restructuring differently. Debtor records a gain if new agreement calls for less to be paid (over the entire life of revised note) than is currently due (principal plus unpaid interest to date). If less is to be paid, debt is reduced to that amount and a gain is recognized.

    a. If gain or loss is recognized by debtor, no future interest is recorded even if a payment is called "interest."

    b. If more will be paid than is currently owed, no gain is recorded by debtor. That excess is recognized as interest over remaining life of the payments.

3. For a debt restructuring, creditor computes the present value of future cash flows (specified by the restructuring) based on the original rate of interest.

    a. If present value is less than current debt (principal plus accrued interest), creditor has a loss for difference.

    b. Future interest revenue to be recognized by creditor is original interest rate times book value, which is the present value of future cash flows.

MISCELLANEOUS FINANCIAL STATEMENTS

A. Interim Financial Statements.

    1. **Interim financial statements** are produced for any period less than one year, most frequently every three months (quarterly statements).

    2. Revenue recognition is same as in regular accounting. Revenues are recognized when earned and the transaction is substantially complete.

        a. Such income items as extraordinary items are recorded when incurred and not allocated over the entire year.

    3. Expenses are recorded in order to match them against the revenues they have helped to generate.

        a. Expenses (such as property taxes or rents) that are for longer than a single quarter must be allocated to the periods benefited.

    4. Income taxes must be anticipated and recognized each quarter.

        a. Each quarter, the effective tax rate for the entire year is estimated. This rate is multiplied times the total income to date to derive total income tax expense to date. Any tax expense previously recognized is subtracted to leave expense for current quarter.

    5. If **inventory declines in value** during a quarter, loss is not recognized if drop in value is considered temporary.

        a. If value decline is viewed as permanent, loss is recognized.

        b. If loss is recognized and value goes back up, a market recovery (or gain) is recorded. Market recovery cannot exceed loss that was reported.

B. Personal Financial Statements and Development Stage Enterprises.

1. **Personal financial statements** are prepared for individuals.

a. **Statement of financial condition** presents assets and liabilities at current values rather than historical cost. Difference is referred to as net worth.

- Because assets and liabilities are reported at fair value, the potential tax effects of realizing gains and losses in value must also be reported.
- Estimated tax effect on potential gains/losses is reported between liabilities and net worth section of balance sheet.

b. A **statement of changes in net worth** is also reported.

2. A **development stage enterprise** is a company that is working to establish its business and has not yet generated significant revenues.

a. Reporting process is normal except that income statement and cash flow figures are reported twice: for the current period and as cumulative amounts since the inception of the business.

STOCKHOLDERS' EQUITY

A. Corporations issue capital stock. Acquiring these shares of stock gives the buyer the right of ownership.

1. Depending on specific state law, ownership of **common stock** usually provides three rights:

a. Right to vote for members of the Board of Directors.

b. Right to share in any dividends that are declared.

c. Right to share in any assets remaining after liquidation.

2. Terminology in connection with capital stock.

a. **Shares authorized**—total number of shares that can legally be issued by a corporation.

b. **Shares issued**—number of shares that have been sold.

c. **Shares outstanding**—number of shares that are presently being held by the public.

d. **Par value**—a relatively arbitrary value attached to a share by the company. Anyone buying a share for less than par value risks having to make up the difference if the company ever goes bankrupt.

- When stock is sold, its par value is recorded in the stock account with any excess received recorded as additional paid-in capital (APIC).
- Stock issued in exchange for noncash assets or services is recorded at fair value.

e. **Subscribed stock**—shares that have been ordered by a potential investor but not yet fully paid. Usually, shares cannot be issued until fully paid.

3. Common stockholders can give up one or more of their basic rights to the owners of a second type of stock called **preferred stock.**

   a. The right given up is often connected with dividend payments. Preferred stock might be given a set dividend or one that is cumulative (all past dividends must be paid before common stock can receive any dividend).

      - If a **cumulative dividend** is not paid, it is referred to as **dividends in arrears** and must be disclosed. No dividend is viewed as a liability until declared by the company's board of directors.

4. Companies can never record a gain or loss on buying or selling their own stock. Differences increase or decrease APIC. If APIC is reduced to zero, any further reduction is recorded to the Retained Earnings account.

B. **Treasury stock** is the stock of a company that has been repurchased. It can be accounted for by using one of three methods.

   1. Under the cost method, the treasury stock is recorded at cost.

      a. If shares are later resold above cost, APIC is increased.

      b. If shares are later resold below cost, APIC is reduced. If APIC is not sufficient to cover difference, remainder is a reduction in retained earnings.

   2. Under the **par value method**, treasury stock is recorded at its par value with any APIC that was originally recorded being removed. Any difference in issuance price and the reacquisition price increases or decreases APIC. Retained earnings can be reduced.

      a. Under either cost or par value method, treasury stock is shown as a reduction figure within the Stockholders' Equity section of the balance sheet.

      b. Resale of shares is handled just like an original issuance.

   3. Stock can be bought back and then retired so that it is removed entirely from the records. Entry is same as repurchase entry under the par value method, except that common stock is reduced rather than treasury stock.

C. **Retained Earnings** account is a measure of net assets held by company that were generated originally by the operations.

   1. It is increased by net income but decreased by dividends on the date of declaration.

   2. If company has decided to limit dividends, retained earnings is shown as two figures: unappropriated (maximum amount of dividends that would be paid) and appropriated (remainder).

D. Incorporation of a sole proprietorship or partnership.

   1. All assets and liabilities are adjusted to fair value.

   2. Stock is issued to owners based on this total fair value.

   3. Retained earnings is set at zero since this is the beginning of a new corporation.

E. **Quasi-reorganization** is a technique used by company with approval of creditors in hopes of avoiding bankruptcy.

  1. Assets and liabilities are adjusted to fair value. Liabilities are also usually reduced by creditors. All gains and losses directly impact retained earnings.

  2. Par value of Common Stock account is reduced with an offsetting increase in additional paid-in capital.

  3. Negative balance in retained earnings is offset against APIC. Retained earnings is now reported as a zero balance.

F. Dividends are distributions made to stockholders as a reward of ownership.

  1. Three dates are important: (1) **date of declaration** (board of directors declares dividend so that it becomes a legal liability and retained earnings is reduced); (2) **date of record** (ownership of stock is established. Company makes no entry but owner records a receivable); (3) **date of payment.**

  2. **Property dividend** is a noncash distribution.

    a. Property is adjusted by company to fair value on date of declaration with a gain or loss being recognized. Dividend is then recorded.

G. **Stock dividend** is a distribution made in the stock of the company.

  1. Stockholders do not make a journal entry and do not record income but must reallocate book value over a greater number of shares.

  2. Company records dividend as a decrease in retained earnings and an increase in the Common Stock and possible increase in APIC accounts.

    a. If stock dividend is less than 20% (owner gets less than two shares for every ten being held), dividend is recorded at fair value of newly issued shares.

    b. If stock dividend is between 20% and 25%, company may choose to record dividend at fair value or par value of shares.

    c. If stock dividend is over 25%, dividend is recorded at par value of newly issued shares.

  3. In a **stock split,** the old shares are canceled and all new shares (with a new par value) are issued. No entry is necessary. Stock split does not affect stock accounts or retained earnings.

    a. Assume that 1,000 shares outstanding with a $100 par value are split 2 for 1. The company will now have 2,000 shares outstanding with a $50 par value. Total par value does not change; it was $100,000 both before and after the split.

H. A stock warrant is the right to acquire shares of stock at a set price known as an option price. Consequently, these are also referred to as stock options.

  1. If a stock warrant is sold by a company to raise capital, the inflow of assets is reflected through an increase in paid-in capital. If subsequently converted, the company records any additional cash received and removes the amount of the stock warrant. The new stock is then recorded at the total of these two amounts.

2. If such warrants are given away to owners as a type of dividend or to employees in a **noncompensatory plan**, no value is assigned by the company. If later these warrants are converted into shares of stock, the company makes the normal entry for the issuance for stock.

3. Stock warrants that are given to employees are deemed noncompensatory if substantially all employees share in the distribution on an equitable basis and the discount in price below market value is relatively small (under 5%). If there is a set purchase price, the employee must convert within 31 days to eliminate the chance for significant gains. If a percentage of market value is used to set the option price, the 31-day limitation is not necessary.

I. If stock warrants are given to employees and they do not qualify as noncompensatory, they are compensatory and an expense must be determined and recognized over the period that the employee is required to provide services.

1. The fair value of the warrants on the grant date is used to determine the amount of the expense.

2. An option pricing model, such as Black-Scholes-Merton, or a binomial model must be used to determine fair value of the options. No single model is required, but the one that is used must take a number of factors into account: exercise price, expected term of the option, current price of the stock, expected volatility of the stock price, expected amount of dividends, and a risk-free interest rate.

J. Stock appreciation rights can be awarded by a company to give a potential cash bonus to employees based on changes in the price of stock over a specified period of time. The company recognizes expense and creates a liability over the period that the services must be rendered.

1. At the end of each period, the value of these rights is determined using an option pricing model.

2. At the end of each period, the total benefit estimated at that time is multiplied by the percentage of the total time that has passed to get the benefits.

3. Any previous expense that has been recognized is subtracted from the benefits earned to date to arrive at the expense to be recognized for the current period.

4. In some cases, liability may have to be reduced so that a decrease in the expense is necessary.

ACCOUNTING FOR LEASES

A. One party (the lessor) owns property while a different party (the lessee) rents and uses the property.

B. A lease may be recorded as a **capitalized lease** if the rights and responsibilities of ownership are conveyed to the lessee. A capitalized lease is viewed as a transfer of ownership rights. A lease is viewed as a capitalized lease if it meets any one of the following four criteria:

1. Title of the property transfers to lessee at the end of the lease.

2. Lessee has the option to buy property at end of the lease for a price that is significantly below expected market value so that there is a reasonable expectation that the price will be paid. This arrangement is referred to as a **bargain purchase option.**

3. Life of the lease is 75% or more of the economic life of the item.

4. Present value of the minimum lease payments is 90% or more of the fair value of the leased item.

   a. Interest rate has to be used for this and other computations.

      • Lessor uses imputed interest rate built into the cash flows of the contract.

      • Lessee uses its incremental borrowing rate unless the lessor's imputed interest rate is known and it is less.

C. If none of the criteria are met, it is a rent and must be recorded as an **operating lease.**

   1. When the lease is signed, the lessee does not record an asset or liability. As incurred, rent expense is recognized.

   2. Lessor retains asset on its books and records rent revenue as it is earned.

   3. Unless periods of time differ, revenue (lessor) and expense (lessee) should be recorded as the same amount each period.

D. Lessee accounts for a capitalized lease as if property were being purchased over a period of time.

   1. Both asset and liability are recorded at present value of **minimum lease payments.** Liability can be shown as single figure or as a payable for total payments less a discount on lease account to reduce net balance to present value.

      a. Difference between total payments and present value is interest to be recognized over life of lease. Interest is recognized each period, based on effective rate method.

   2. Although not legally owned, lessee depreciates asset. Straight-line method is normally applied over useful life.

      a. If title transfers or if there is a bargain purchase option, depreciation is for life of asset. Otherwise, depreciation is for life of lease.

   3. Maintenance, property taxes, and the like are **executory costs.** Payments are not part of the minimum lease payments. Such payments are not included as part of the lease liability or the leased asset. Executory costs are expensed as incurred.

E. To account for a capitalized lease, lessor removes asset and recognizes revenue from lease. Two different methods can be used to determine pattern of revenue recognition.

   1. It is a **direct financing lease** if lessor is not a dealer or manufacturer of the product. Lessor leases item and does not sell it.

      a. Receivable and any cash immediately received are recorded.

      b. Asset is removed from books but no immediate gain is recorded. Difference is interest to be recorded over period of payments. It is initially recorded as unearned interest and then amortized to interest revenue using effective rate method.

   2. It is a **sales type lease** if lessor is a dealer or manufacturer who may also sell the item.

      a. Receivable and any cash immediately received are recorded. Asset is removed from books. Difference is total profit.

      b. Normal gain on sale is immediately recorded based on sales price of item. If sales price is not known, the present value of the minimum lease payments is used.

c. Any amount of the total profit in excess of the gain recorded on the sale is unearned interest to be recognized as interest over life of lease using the effective rate method.

F. Both parties to a capitalized lease base the computation on the **"minimum lease payments."** That figure includes the annual payment plus:

1. For the lessor, any amount to be received as a bargain purchase option is included in the minimum lease payments because collection is expected. However, if lessor anticipates getting the asset back because the title does not transfer and there is not a bargain purchase option, the expected value of the asset when returned is also viewed as a future collection.

2. For the lessee, any amount to be paid as a bargain purchase option is included as part of the minimum lease payments. If, instead, the asset is to be returned to the lessor, only a value that has been guaranteed is included by the lessee.

G. In a capitalized lease, lessor has a receivable to report whereas lessee has a liability. On the balance sheet, a part of each balance is shown as current with the rest being long-term. The current portion is the payment to be made in the next 12 months less the amount of interest to be recognized during that period.

H. Lessor may have to pay direct costs, such as legal fees and commissions associated with creating the lease agreement.

1. If it is an operating lease, these costs are recorded as an asset and amortized as an expense over the life of the lease.

2. If it is a sales type lease, cost is expensed immediately.

3. If it is a direct financing lease, cost is a reduction in the Unearned Interest account so that less interest revenue is recognized over the life of the lease.

I. There can be a **sale-leaseback arrangement.** Asset is sold and then leased back to original owner. If there is a loss, seller/lessee recognizes it immediately. If there is gain, seller/lessee may have to defer recognition of the gain.

1. If only a minor portion of the property is leased back, any gain is recognized by seller/lessee immediately. A minor portion is when present value of payments is 10% or less of market value.

2. If substantially all of the property is leased back, the entire gain is initially deferred. Deferred gain is written off to reduce depreciation expense over the life of the lease.

3. If leaseback is more than a minor portion but less than substantially all, seller/lessee recognizes part of gain and defers the rest of the gain. Deferred gain is written off to reduce depreciation expense over the life of the lease. Gain to be deferred is amount up to the present value of the payments. Any additional amount is recognized immediately as a gain.

MISCELLANEOUS ACCOUNTING CONCEPTS

A. The FASB issued several **Statements of Financial Accounting Concepts** to create a **Conceptual Framework.** It sets goals for accounting but not absolute rules. Concepts Statement Number 2 created a structure to describe useful information.

1. According to Concepts Statement Number 2, the one constraint for all accounting information is that the benefits derived from using the information must outweigh the cost of getting it.

2. To be useful for decision making, information should have several qualities.

   a. It should be relevant; the information can affect the decision making process. **Relevance** has three ingredients.

      - Timeliness—it is received quickly enough to impact a decision.
      - Predictive value—it helps to estimate future cash flows.
      - Feedback value—it confirms or corrects previous predictions of cash flows.

   b. It should be reliable; it can be trusted. **Reliability** has three ingredients.

      - Verifiability—it is objective and can be proven.
      - Neutral—it is free from bias.
      - Representational faithfulness—the reporting does mirror the actual event or transaction.

B. Statement of Financial Accounting Concepts 6 establishes definitions for reporting the elements of financial statements. Several of these definitions include the following:

   1. Asset—probable future economic benefit controlled by entity.

   2. Liability—probable future sacrifice of an economic benefit that arises from a present obligation which resulted from a past transaction or event.

   3. Comprehensive income—change in equity during a period from all nonowner sources.

   4. Revenues—increases in net assets during a period from delivering goods or services as part of the enterprise's central operations.

   5. Expenses—decreases in net assets during a period in connection with generating revenues from the enterprise's central operations.

   6. Gains—increases in equity from peripheral transactions.

   7. Losses—decreases in equity from peripheral transactions.

C. Recognition of revenues.

   1. Revenue is normally recognized when two factors are evident.

      a. Earning process must be substantially complete.

      b. Assets have been received that are readily convertible into cash.

      c. There are exceptions; revenues are recognized at other times.

         - Revenues on long-term construction projects are frequently recognized as the work is done using the percentage-of-completion method.
         - If uncertainty exists about collection, revenues are recognized as the cash is collected using either the installment sales method or cost recovery method.
         - If a sales price is assured, revenue is recognized when the product is received.

   2. If customer has the right to **return a purchase**, the point of sale is in question. Revenue is recognized when several events have occurred, including the following: (1) price is set, (2) the sale is not based on some future action (such as the resale of the item), and (3) amount of returns is subject to reasonable estimation. Revenue is recognized but also a contra account (Sales Returns) is estimated and recognized.

D. For adequate disclosure, **Summary of Significant Accounting Policies** (usually first footnote or presented just in front of the footnotes) indicates the accounting method being used when alternative methods are available (FIFO or LIFO as an example).

E. The amount of future cash payments must be disclosed. The amount to be paid as a result of present **long-term liabilities** in each of the next five years must be shown, as well as the cash payments required in total.

F. **Related party transactions** must also be disclosed.

1. A related party includes the following: one who owns 10% or more of the reporting entity, another company over which the entity can exert significant influence, members of the management and their immediate families.

2. For material related party transactions, nature of relationship is disclosed along with a description and terms of the transaction and the amounts as well as the balances still due.

G. To resolve conflicts that can arise between accounting rules, a **Generally Accepted Accounting Principles** (GAAP) Hierarchy was created to indicate which rules and pronouncements take precedent.

1. There are really three hierarchies: one for businesses and private not-for-profit organizations, one for state and local governments, and one for the federal government. Each hierarchy has several distinct levels. The higher levels have more authority than the lower levels.

2. Top level for businesses has three types of pronouncements: FASB statements, APB opinions, and AICPA research studies.

MARKETABLE SECURITIES

A. If a company has significant influence over another company (usually by ownership of 20% to 50% of its voting stock), the equity method is applied to account for the investment (covered in a later outline).

B. If a company has control over another company (by ownership of over 50% of its voting stock), consolidated financial statements are prepared (a topic covered in a later outline).

C. If a company owns bonds of another company and plans to hold these investments until maturity, the bonds are recorded at cost with any discount or premium amortized using the effective rate method as described previously in the Bonds and Notes outline. Straight-line method of amortization can be used if figures are not materially different.

D. All other stock and bond investments are placed in one of two categories.

1. Trading securities—stocks and bonds held for current resale.

   a. Portfolio is recorded at market value with change in value recorded on income statement.

   b. If sold, gain or loss is recognized as the difference between fair value at the beginning of current year and the amount received.

2. Available for sale—stocks and bonds are not actively traded but are not held with the intention of reaching maturity. Could be sold at any time if cash is needed.

   a. Portfolio is recorded at market value with change in value recorded within stockholders' equity.

   b. If sold, gain or loss on sale is the difference in original cost and sales price.

E. Determination of income effect or stockholders' equity effect created each year by the change in market value.

  1. Two "valuation allowance" accounts are established at the end of each year to adjust cost of each portfolio up to or down to market value. That balance remains until end of subsequent year.

  2. Annual change in Valuation Allowance account creates effect on net income (if created for the Trading Securities) or stockholders' equity (if created for the available-for-sale portfolio).

F. Securities can be transferred from one portfolio to another if the intentions of the owner changes.

  1. Only an investment in a debt instrument can be changed to the "held to maturity" classification. Market value (book value) of the old classification is removed and its face value is recorded in new classification along with a related discount or premium. Thus, the old and the new book values will agree. If transferred from "trading securities," the reclassification is complete. If transferred from "available for sale," any unrealized gain or loss in stockholders' equity remains. This balance is amortized to income over remaining life of the security.

  2. If a security is changed to either "trading securities" or "available for sale," the previous book value (along with any unrealized gain or loss in stockholders' equity) is removed and its current market value is recorded in new classification. If a difference exists, a gain or loss is recorded in the income statement (if changed to a trading security) or in stockholders' equity (if changed to an available for sale security).

G. Other accounting issues relating to marketable securities.

  1. Cash dividends are recorded as revenue on date of record.

  2. Stock dividends and splits are not recorded by the owner. Book value of investment is allocated over more shares.

  3. Liquidating dividend is a payment by a company that does not have income. Owner reduces investment account; no income recorded.

  4. Life insurance policy can have a cash surrender value, which is reported as an asset. Annual payment on policy less increase in cash surrender value is expense for the period.

  5. A bond sinking fund is money set aside to pay off a bond. If debt will be paid this year, sinking fund is a current asset; otherwise, the amount is a noncurrent investment.

LONG-TERM CONSTRUCTION CONTRACTS

A. For a construction job that will take over a year to complete, percentage of completion method is normally the method used for financial reporting purposes. It recognizes a percentage of total profit each year as the job progresses.

  1. A construction-in-progress account is maintained at cost plus the gain recognized to date.

  2. Percentage of work done is usually determined as the cost to date divided by the total of the estimated cost of the project.

  3. This percentage is multiplied by the total estimated profit to get the profit earned to date.

  4. Any previously recognized income is subtracted from profit earned to date to get profit to be recognized in current year.

5. If a loss is anticipated, 100% must be immediatcly recognized.

B. An alternative method to account for long-term construction projects is the completed contract method. It is not considered appropriate unless reasonable estimations cannot be made about a job. Usually some significant uncertainty exists.

   1. Cost is recorded in construction account with no income effect recognized until completed.

   2. Any anticipated losses must be recognized immediately.

C. Under either method, bills are sent out to the buyer periodically. The bills do not affect recognition of revenue. Accounts receivable and a billings account are both recorded.

   1. For balance sheet reporting, construction-in-progress and billings accounts are netted. If billings is higher, net amount is a liability; if the Construction account is higher, amount is reported as an asset.

INSTALLMENT SALES METHODS

A. Installment sales method is appropriately used to recognize profits for any sale when collection will take over a year and a significant uncertainty exists.

   1. No profit is recognized at time of sale, but rather when cash is collected. Until cash is collected, all profit is recognized in a deferred gain account.

   2. Profit to be recognized is the gross profit percentage times cash collected.

   3. Gross profit percentage is the profit divided by the sales price. This same percentage multiplied times the remaining receivable balance represents the gain still deferred.

B. Cost recovery method is appropriately used for any sale where collection is highly doubtful. For example, a sale is made to a company on the verge of bankruptcy.

   1. No profit is recorded until cash equal to cost of asset is collected. For all further collections of cash, a proportionate amount of profit is recognized.

STRUCTURE OF AN INCOME STATEMENT

A. An income statement can be reported by the single step format.

   1. All revenues and gains are listed first, followed by all expenses and losses.

B. Income statement can also be constructed using a multiple-step format.

   1. Revenues from major operations are listed first, followed by cost of goods sold to arrive at gross profit.

   2. Operating expenses are subtracted next. These expenses are usually presented as two categories: (1) selling expenses, such as commissions, advertising, and bad debt expense and (2) general and administrative expenses, such as insurance, repairs, and accounting.

   3. Other revenues and expenses are reported next. This category typically reports most gains and losses as well as interest revenues and interest expense.

   4. Gains or losses that are unusual in nature or infrequent in occurrence are reported next.

5. For most income statements, the final reduction is for income tax expense. As will be discussed in a later outline, this figure is frequently reported as two components: current expense and deferred expense.

6. If a company is publicly held, earnings per share information must also be reported along with each income statement.

C. Regardless of the format, two figures are always reported at the bottom of the income statement net of the applicable tax effect. They are:

1. The income effect of a discontinued operation, a topic that will be covered in a later outline.

2. Extraordinary gains and losses.

D. Extraordinary items are reported at the bottom of the income statement, net of any tax effect, just below discontinued operations, just below the reporting of discontinued operations.

1. To be classified as extraordinary, gains and losses must have three characteristics:

    a. Material in size. That means being of a size and/or nature that will affect the decision making of an outside party.

    b. Unusual in nature.

    c. Infrequent in occurrence.

2. Certain gains and losses cannot be considered extraordinary:

    a. Write-offs of assets not caused by a specific external event, such as the write-off of obsolete inventory or equipment.

    b. Gains and losses created by changes in the value of a foreign currency.

    c. Gains or losses resulting from a strike.

E. A company must now produce a statement of comprehensive income in order to report all changes in the net assets of a company other than investments by owners and distributions to owners.

1. Several changes that can be measured in a company's net assets are reflected in "accumulated other comprehensive income" shown in stockholders' equity instead of within net income. There are three primary examples:

    a. The translation of the financial statements of a foreign subsidiary creates a translation adjustment.

    b. Changes in the value of marketable securities classified as available for sale creates an unrealized gain or an unrealized loss.

    c. Recognition of the unamortized portions of prior service cost and net actuarial gains/losses in connection with pension plans.

2. The statement of comprehensive income starts with net income and adjusts that figure for changes during the period in each of these equity figures. For example, if marketable securities that are available for sale go up in value, the change is not reported in net income but would be reported in comprehensive income.

3. The net income figure may contain items that have been recognized previously in computing comprehensive income. For example, if available for sale securities go up in one year but are sold for a gain at the start of the following year, comprehensive income increases in the first year but net income increases in the second.

4. Comprehensive income can actually be shown as an entirely separate statement, as a combined statement of net income and comprehensive income, or as a part of the statement of stockholders' equity.

F. A prior period adjustment (PPA) is a change in an income statement item reported in a previous time period. It is not recorded on the income statement of the current period.

1. Prior period adjustments are made in only a few specific cases.

   a. A PPA is used if an error has occurred in applying an accounting principle or if a mathematical error has been made.

   b. The discovery of an incorrect estimation is not handled through a PPA (topic will be covered in a later outline).

2. If earlier income statement is being shown, change is made directly to it. If earlier statement is not shown, change is made as an adjustment to the earliest beginning retained earnings balance being reported.

   a. Regardless of reporting, actual journal entry adjusts the beginning retained earnings for the current year.

CONTINGENCIES AND OTHER LOSSES AND LIABILITIES

A. Contingent losses are caused by a past event but will only result in an actual loss if a future event also occurs. For example, a lawsuit has been filed but no actual loss exists unless jury finds the party guilty.

1. If chance of a loss is probable and amount is reasonably subject to estimation, loss must be immediately recognized with an accompanying liability being recorded or an asset reduced.

   a. If estimation is a range, the most likely figure within range must be recognized. If no figure is most likely, the lowest figure in the range is recognized with remainder of range disclosed.

2. If chance of loss is reasonably possible or if a reasonable estimation cannot be made, loss is disclosed but not recognized.

3. If chance of loss is only remote, no disclosure or recognition is required.

4. For a gain contingency, recognition is delayed until the earning process is substantially complete. Until then, only disclosure is required.

B. Contingencies such as guarantees and coupons are usually recorded because chance of loss is probable and the amount is subject to a reasonable estimation based on past history.

1. Amount to be paid is estimated and recognized immediately as an expense.

2. Amount that has not yet been paid is liability to be reported.

C. Gift certificates are also contingencies; company must give merchandise if redeemed.

   1. Initially recorded as a liability when customer acquires.

   2. Reclassified as a revenue when redeemed or when time expires.

D. Employer may have to report liability to employees for compensated absences such as vacations, as well as holiday and sick pay.

   1. Expense and liability are recognized when the following have occurred:

      a. Employee has performed services.

      b. Payment is probable.

      c. Amounts to be paid either vest (person is entitled to money without further work) or accumulate (carry over from year to year).

E. If a company plans to restructure its business by selling a line of business, closing particular locations, relocating operations or the like, a company may incur a liability because of the termination of employees and contracts.

   1. Such changes in a company are often referred to as exit activities or disposal activities.

   2. Liabilities for such costs should be recognized when they achieve the definition of a liability (they are probable and can be reasonably estimated) and should not be anticipated. The liability should be recognized at its fair value (often its present value).

   3. The cost of one-time termination of employees should be recognized when all of the following have been met and no further work is required. This information has to have been communicated to the employees.

      a. Termination plan has been approved.

      b. Number of employees to be fired is known along with their classifications and locations. The identity of the employees to be terminated does not have to be known.

      c. Benefit plans for employees have been set.

      d. It is unlikely the plan will be changed or withdrawn.

      e. If the employee must still do some work, the liability is recognized over that period of work instead of immediately.

DEFERRED INCOME TAXES

A. Some revenues and expenses are recognized for external reporting in one period but tax recognition occurs in a different period. These are referred to as temporary differences.

   1. A temporary difference leads to a deferred tax liability if taxable income will be higher than book (accounting) income in the future. A temporary difference leads to a deferred tax asset if taxable income will be lower than book income in the future.

      a. A deferred liability indicates that an additional tax payment will be made in the future; a deferred asset indicates a future benefit since income to be taxed will be reduced.

2. Examples of temporary differences that usually create less taxable income now and more taxable income later (creating a deferred tax liability) include (1) using different depreciation methods for external reporting and taxes, (2) using accrual accounting for the external reporting of sales but the installment sales method for taxes, and (3) using the equity method for the external reporting of an investment but dividends collected for taxes.

3. Examples of temporary differences that usually create more taxable income now and less taxable income later (creating a deferred tax asset) include (1) estimating warranty and contingency expenses for external reporting but using actual losses for taxes, (2) estimating bad debts for external reporting but using actual losses for taxes, and (3) recognizing revenues as earned for external reporting but revenues collected in advance for taxes.

4. Because of the conservative nature of accounting, recognition of a deferred tax asset requires a company to also consider recognition of a contra-allowance account to reduce reported value of asset.

    a. A deferred tax asset indicates that future book income will be reduced to arrive at a lower taxable income. The company only gets benefit if it has book income to reduce.

    b. If company believes that it is more likely than not (over 50% likelihood) that it will have future book income for the temporary difference to reduce, no allowance is needed.

    c. If it is more likely than not that company will not have book income for temporary difference to reduce, allowance must be recorded to reduce reported value of deferred asset.

    d. Likelihood of having future book income is anticipated by looking at many factors: history of profits, law suits in progress, backlog of orders, loss of patents or other rights, gaining or losing customers, etc.

B. A balance sheet approach is used for recognizing deferred taxes. The amount of all future temporary differences are scheduled each year, and deferred tax assets and liabilities are computed. The changes in these accounts create the income tax expense to be recognized.

C. Some differences between book income and taxable income will cause no future differences between book income and taxable income. Such items are known as permanent differences, and they do not create deferred tax assets or liabilities. Examples of items that create permanent differences include the following:

1. Municipal bond interest and life insurance proceeds are included in book income but never in taxable income.

2. Federal taxes are expenses on the books but are not deductible for tax purposes. The same is true of life insurance premiums if the company is the beneficiary of the policy.

3. A portion of dividends received from another domestic company is recognized but never taxed. This dividends received deduction (DRD) is 70% if less than 20% of the company is owned; the DRD is 80% if less than 80% but 20% or more of the company is owned; the DRD is 100% if 80% of more of the company is owned.

D. Computation of deferred income taxes is based on a scheduling process.

1. Items within book income for current year are listed.

    a. For each item, it should have a tax effect currently, a tax effect in the future, or no tax effect.

2. Temporary differences from past years are also included to show how they impact either current taxable income or future taxable income.

3. All items currently taxable are netted and multiplied by the enacted tax rate to get current income tax payable and expense. These amount are recognized.

4. For all future years, anticipated tax effects are determined and multiplied by enacted tax rates to get various deferred tax asset and liability balances. For any deferred assets, the need for an allowance is also determined.

5. If a temporary difference relates to a noncurrent account, the deferred tax liability or asset that results is noncurrent. If it relates to a current account, the deferred tax liability or asset is current. All current deferred tax assets and liabilities are netted to arrive at a single figure to report on the balance sheet. All noncurrent deferred assets and liabilities are also netted to arrive at a single figure to report on balance sheet.

6. At the end of each year, any previous (1) deferred tax liability, (2) deferred tax asset, and (3) allowance on any deferred tax asset balances already on the books are adjusted to the newly determined balances. The net amount of change is the deferred income tax expense figure recognized on the income statement.

EQUITY METHOD OF ACCOUNTING FOR INVESTMENTS

A. The equity method is used to account for an investment in stocks where the owner has the ability to significantly influence operating and financing decisions of the investee.

1. Although the ability to apply significant influence is the only criterion, ownership of 20% to 50% of the investee's shares is usually accounted for by the equity method.

   a. Owner can use equity method even if less than 20% is held if owner has ability to significantly influence, for example, by having membership on the Board of Directors.

   b. Should not use equity method even if over 20% is held if owner does not have ability to significantly influence.

B. In applying equity method, the investment is initially recorded at cost.

1. Owner recognizes income (or loss) as soon as the investee earns it, based on percentage of ownership. Income is recognized and book value of investment is raised (for income) or lowered (for loss).

2. Because income is recognized as earned, dividends received cannot be recognized as revenue. Dividends received from investee are recorded as a reduction in the book value of the investment.

C. The price of investment may be in excess of investee's underlying book value. Book value is determined by taking liabilities from assets or by stockholders' equity. Figure is multiplied by percentage bought.

1. Excess amount of payment may be attributed to a specific asset such as land or a building if the value of the item is greater than its book value on records of the investee. Allocation to the change in value of asset is based on percentage of the investee company that is bought.

2. If any part of the price that exceeds the underlying book value cannot be assigned to a specific asset or liability, that remainder is assumed to be goodwill.

3. Any allocations of excess price (unless assigned to land and/or goodwill) must be amortized.

    a. If allocation is to a specific asset or liability such as buildings or equipment, the allocation is amortized over useful life.

    b. Land and goodwill are exceptions. They are not amortized. In addition, goodwill is not separately checked for impairment when it is within an equity method investment.

    c. Amortization reduces the investment account (allocations are not reported separately by the owner) and reduces income being reported from investee.

CONSOLIDATED FINANCIAL INFORMATION

A. The consolidation process brings together two or more sets of financial statements because the companies have common ownership. For external reporting purposes, the companies are viewed as a single entity.

    1. Total ownership is not necessary to form a business combination. Only control is required, which is established through the ownership of over 50% of the voting stock.

        a. Subsidiaries are consolidated in total regardless of whether 100% of stock is owned. If less than 100% is held within the business combination, the outside owners are referred to as a minority interest and their ownership is reflected as a single figure in consolidated equity and also as a reduction in the consolidated income statement.

    2. All consolidations are now reported by use of the purchases method. The pooling of interests method has been eliminated, although consolidations previously reported using this method are allowed to remain as poolings.

B. A purchase is viewed as an acquisition: one company clearly buys the other. It is often compared to a parent-child relationship.

    1. A purchase price is determined based on the market value of the items given up and includes any direct consolidation costs except for stock issuance costs that are recorded as a reduction in additional paid-in capital.

    2. An allocation of this purchase price is made at the date of acquisition. Any difference between price paid and the equivalent portion of the underlying book value of subsidiary must be allocated. Allocation is made to specific assets and liabilities based on difference between their fair values and book values. Book value of subsidiary is its assets minus liabilities or its total stockholders' equity.

        a. For example, a parent pays $100,000 over book value to acquire a subsidiary. The subsidiary has land that originally cost $50,000 but which is now worth $70,000. Of the excess purchase price, $20,000 is allocated to this land. If the parent had only bought 80% of sub, the allocation to land is just $16,000 or 80% of the increase in value.

        b. Any excess purchase price that cannot be allocated to specific assets and liabilities is assigned to goodwill, an intangible asset. Goodwill is not subject to amortization but rather must be tested annually for impairment.

        c. The FASB encourages the parent to consider whether any excess purchase price indicates the presence of identifiable intangible assets other than goodwill. The Board has suggested valuing assets, such as customer lists, sales backlog, noncompetition agreements, databases, and the like. To be recognized in this way, the company must have legal contractual rights to the intangible asset or it must be something that can be separated from the subsidiary and sold.

    d. Any amount assigned to a particular research and development project with no alternative future uses will be expensed immediately.

    e. If, after all allocations are made to assets and liabilities, a negative amount remains, this reduction is assigned to noncurrent assets (except for investments) based on their relative market values. If negative amount is so large that it eliminates all of these noncurrent asset accounts, an extraordinary gain is established for any remainder.

3. At the date of a purchase, each consolidated asset and liability is the sum of the two book values plus or minus any allocation made of the purchase price based on the fair value of the sub's accounts. Any goodwill is also included.

    a. Parent maintains an Investment account to monitor its ownership of the sub, but this account is always eliminated in the consolidation process.

4. Subsequent to the date of acquisition, the current book values of the assets and liabilities are added together along with the original allocations. However, each of these allocations (except for goodwill and land) is reduced by amortization over its useful life.

5. In a purchase, consolidated stockholders' equity is always the parent's balances plus any income effects relating to the subsidiary since the merger. If parent-issued stock in taking over sub, those shares must be included in parent figures.

6. Consolidated revenues and expenses are the parent figures plus the subsidiary figures, but only for the period since the merger. Amortization on any purchase price allocations must be included as expenses, and any unrealized gains must be removed.

    a. To determine consolidated retained earnings or consolidated income, a determination of what has been included in parent's reported figures is made. No second inclusion is needed if parent has already (1) recognized its ownership percentage of the subsidiary's income, (2) removed any unrealized gains, and (3) recorded amortization expense for the period.

C. Goodwill should be tested for impairment on an annual basis and more often if there is evidence to suggest that negative events may have occurred.

1. The resulting consolidated company is divided into reporting units by much the same approach that is utilized for segment reporting. The goodwill is then assigned to these various units based on the expected benefits of the acquisition. Part of the goodwill can be attributed to a reporting unit within the parent if the unit is better off because of the takeover.

2. There are two steps in determining if goodwill has been impaired. If the first step does not show impairment, the second step is not even tested.

    a. First, unless the fair value of the reporting unit as a whole is below the carrying value of that unit, there is no impairment.

    b. Second, the fair value of the reporting unit as a whole is compared to the fair value of the individual assets of that same reporting unit. Any excess is the implied goodwill remaining on that day. If this implied value is below the book value of goodwill assigned to that unit, goodwill is written down to the implied value and a loss is recognized.

D. Some elements of a consolidation are the same for both purchases and poolings of interests.

   1. Intercompany debt (accounts receivable/accounts payable or investment in bonds/bonds payable) are offset against each other. All intercompany balances are removed even if ownership is below 100%.

   2. All balances recorded for inventory transfers between the parties must be removed. Both sales and cost of goods sold are reduced by the entire amount of the transfer price.

   3. If inventory is transferred between parties, any unrealized gain in connection with goods still held at year's end must also be eliminated. Profit is actually being deferred until realized.

      a. The amount of unrealized gain remaining at end of the year is found by multiplying remaining goods by the profit. One of these figures has to be a percentage; the other has to be a dollar amount.

      b. Deferral of unrealized gain creates a reduction in Inventory account and an increase in cost of goods sold account.

   4. If any other asset is transferred, all accounts must be returned to balances that would be applicable if transfer had not occurred.

      a. Adjustments are made to the asset account, accumulated depreciation, depreciation expense, and any gain or loss to align them with the balances that would have resulted.

   5. Any investment or income in the subsidiary account must be removed. Any intercompany dividend payments are also eliminated.

   6. Minority interest balances attributed to outside owners are computed by taking (1) the book value of the sub and (2) the reported income of the sub and multiplying both by the outside ownership percentage.

E. Other consolidation issues:

   1. "Combined" financial statements are consolidated statements of two or more subsidiaries without inclusion of the parent. Without the parent, no allocations or amortization are included, although all intercompany figures are removed as in any consolidation.

   2. Push-down accounting is an approach to consolidation where purchase price allocations and amortization are recorded directly on the sub's books rather than being added in each period through the consolidation process. It is supposed to make the process easier. It also enables the income reported by the subsidiary to mirror its impact on the consolidated statements.

GOVERNMENTAL ACCOUNTING—FUND ACCOUNTING AND FINANCIAL STATEMENTS

A. Because of the many and diverse activities of a state or local government (police and fire departments, airports, zoos, highway construction, etc.), the accounting and reporting functions are divided into a number of different funds. Each fund accounts for a specific activity and has its own unique accounting principles.

   1. Fund accounting promotes financial accountability, which is an underlying objective of government reporting. Readers of the financial statements should be able to determine the allocation of resources made to each activity and the use that the activity makes of those resources.

2. All funds are classified as either (1) governmental funds for public services, (2) proprietary funds where a user charge is assessed, or (3) fiduciary funds to report assets that will eventually be conveyed to a party outside of the government.

B. Traditionally, much of government accounting (in the governmental funds) has emphasized the measurement of the financial resources held by each activity and the inflow and outflow of those financial resources. The accounting process was designed to monitor the source of these resources, how those resources were used by the fund, and what resources are currently held. Modified accrual accounting was used to determine the proper timing for recognition by recording financial resources when they became both measurable and available.

1. Financial resources are basically monetary assets (cash, receivables, and investments). Under this approach, liabilities are only recognized if they represent claims that require the use of current financial resources.

2. Focusing on financial resources allows readers to see the utilization made by government officials of the public's money. In addition, it provided a measure of interperiod equity, the surplus or deficit carried over to future years. For example, if financial resources generated during a period will not cover expenditures, money has to be borrowed and then repaid by taxpayers in future years.

C. State and local governments must now report two separate sets of financial statements.

1. Government-wide financial statements move away from the financial resource approach to reporting. Instead, these statements measure all economic resources (all assets and all liabilities) and utilize accrual accounting to establish the timing of revenue and expense recognition. Thus these statements are produced in much the same way as the statements of a for-profit business.

    a. At least three basic columns are shown in each of the government-wide statements: a column for government activities, a column for business-type activities, and a total column. Inter-activity transactions between the activities in the first two columns are shown as internal balances and eliminated in arriving at the total column.

    Governmental activities are made up of the governmental funds. Thus, in contrast to the traditional approach to reporting, these statements measure economic resources and apply accrual accounting to the governmental funds. Most internal service funds (one of the proprietary funds) are also included as governmental activities but only if they were created primarily for the service of a governmental fund. Any transactions between the internal service funds and the governmental funds must be eliminated, though, to avoid any double counting.

    Business-type activities are made up of the enterprise funds, which is another category within the proprietary funds.

    Fiduciary funds are not reported in the government-wide financial statements because these assets must be conveyed to a party outside of the government and, therefore, are not available to be used by the government.

    b. Statement of net assets reports all assets and all liabilities of the governmental activities and the business-type activities (along with a total column). The difference in these assets and liabilities is known as "total net assets" and is reported within three classifications: (1) capital assets net of related debt, (2) restricted net assets that have to be used in a particular fashion, and (3) unrestricted net assets that can be used in any way.

c. Statement of activities reports all revenues and expenses of the governmental activities and the business-type activities.

Direct expenses are shown first and classified by function such as "general government" and "public safety." Depreciation expense is recognized and allocated to the specific functions.

For each function, program revenues are netted against these expenses to arrive at individual net revenue or net expense figures. Program revenues include charges for services and grants received. For example, "health and sanitation" should net any charge received for trash collection against the direct expenses of this function to determine a net revenue or expense figure, a measure of the burden or benefit of providing this service. Fines and forfeitures are also viewed as program revenues.

A total of the net figures for all of the functions is determined and then general revenues are added. General revenues include property taxes and other revenues such as investment income that are not associated with a specific function.

Special items are also included to arrive at a "change in net assets" for the governmental activities, the business-type activities and the total government. Special items are transactions within the control of management that are either unusual in nature or infrequent in occurrence.

2. Fund-based financial statements are also created to present information about each fund type. The method of reporting varies according to the type of fund being reported.

a. For the governmental funds, a balance sheet and a statement of revenues, expenditures, and changes in fund balance are produced. These statements reflect traditional government accounting: they measure financial resources and the flow of financial resources, while the timing of recognition is based on modified accrual accounting.

The balance sheet shows current financial resources and claims on current financial resources. Capital assets and long-term debt are not reported. The difference in the reported assets and liabilities is known as the "fund balance" which reflects the size of the fund. Some or all of this fund balance figure can be shown as "reserved" if an amount must be used for a certain purpose such as to fulfill a commitment or it can be "restricted" if an external party can compel the government to use assets in a certain manner. Amounts that can be spent totally at the discretion of officials are labeled as "unrestricted, unreserved."

The statement of revenues, expenditures, and changes in fund balance reports revenues, expenditures, other financing sources, other financing uses, and special items. Because expenditures are reflected here, expenses (including depreciation expense) are not reported. Capital asset outlays and long-term debt payments are reported as expenditures because they use up current financial resources.

For these fund-based financial statements, a separate column is shown for the General Fund and any other governmental fund that is considered major. All non-major governmental funds are accumulated into a single column. A major fund is one that makes up 10% or more of the governmental funds and 5% or more of the governmental funds plus the enterprise funds.

Because of the wide differences in the reporting between the government-wide financial statements and the fund-based financial statements, reconciliations must be reported. There is a reconciliation between the total fund balance for the governmental funds (fund-based statements) and the total net assets for the governmental activities (government-wide statements). There is also a reconciliation between the change in total fund balance and the change in total net assets. There are three major reasons for the differences: use of accrual accounting (government-wide statements) and modified accrual accounting (fund-based statements), measurement of economic resources (government-wide statements) and current financial resources (fund-based statements), and inclusion of internal service funds (government-wide statements) but not in the fund-based statements.

b. For the proprietary funds, a statement of net assets is reported along with a statement of revenues, expenses, and changes in fund net assets and a statement of cash flows.

These statements measure economic resources according to accrual accounting in the same way as in the government-wide statements.

A separate column is shown for each enterprise fund and for the internal service funds as a whole.

The cash flow statement has four classifications: operating activities (only the direct method can be used), noncapital financing activities (such as operating grants), capital and related financing activities (major construction and the debt incurred to finance it), and investing activities (buying and selling of investments).

c. For the fiduciary funds, statement of net assets is reported along with a statement of changes in net assets.

D. Governmental funds account for public services (police department, fire department, and the like). There are five separate fund types within the governmental funds. These funds traditionally measure financial resources, although a conversion to economic resources is necessary for government-wide financial statements. When measuring financial resources, no capital assets or long-term debts are reported. In addition, expenditures are reported when financial resources are reduced because of expenses, capital asset acquisitions, and long-term debt payments.

1. The General Fund is used when no other fund is appropriate. It is commonly utilized to record the receipts and expenditures of financial resources by on-going public service activities such as the fire department, police department, ambulance service, etc.

a. Most of the unique characteristics normally associated with governmental accounting can be found in the General Fund. Budgets and encumbrances are recorded. Expenditures are recognized for fixed asset and expense costs as well as payments on long-term liabilities.

b. Because capital assets are omitted from the governmental funds, no depreciation is recognized.

2. Special revenue funds account for all of the individual funds that monitor the receipt and expenditure of financial resources earmarked for specific operating purposes. For example, cash collected from a special tax, toll, or grant where the money must be used for a designated operating purpose would be recorded in this fund. In addition, this fund is used for gifts made to the government where both principal and any income must be utilized for a specified purpose.

3. Capital projects funds account for the receipt and expenditure of financial resources relating to construction or acquisition of long-lived assets. Because constructed assets are not financial resources, the actual asset is not recorded within this or any other governmental fund. Instead, the Capital Projects Fund measures the inflow and outflow of financial resources for a particular project.

4. Debt Service funds account for the receipt and expenditure of financial resources for the payment of long-term debts and related interest. Long-term debts are not recorded in this fund until they require the use of current financial resources.

5. Permanent funds account for resources (frequently gifts) where the principal cannot be spent, but any subsequent income can be used, often for a designated purpose.

E. Proprietary funds account for services that are financed (at least in part) by user charges. Accounting and reporting procedures are virtually identical to those found in profit-oriented businesses. As with any business, they use accrual accounting and report revenues, expenses, fixed assets, depreciation, long-term liabilities, retained earnings, etc. They are designed to measure the flow of economic resources.

1. Enterprise funds offer services to the public for a fee, such as a golf course, bus service, swimming pool, etc.

   a. Government officials are allowed to use an enterprise fund for accounting purposes whenever an activity has a user charge.

   b. Government officials must use an enterprise fund for accounting purposes when any one of the following occurs: the pricing policy for fees is set to recover costs; regulations specify that fees are supposed to recover costs; or debts are secured solely by the revenues generated by the activity.

2. Internal Service funds offer services to other areas of the government for a fee such as a print shop, data processing center, motor pool, etc. As indicated, for government-wide financial statements, the internal service funds are normally included within the governmental activities after elimination of any internal exchange transactions.

F. Fiduciary funds account for money being held by a government for a specific purpose. Use of these assets is not at the discretion of the government. Fiduciary Funds normally use accrual accounting to time recognition.

1. Agency funds hold money to be turned over to a person or to some other government (such as money withheld from employees for social security).

   a. Normally, they only have two account balances: cash and the related liability. No revenues, expenses, or expenditures are reported.

2. Pension Trust Funds hold money for employee retirement plans.

3. Investment Trust Funds record external investment pools. Governments will sometimes pool their investments in hopes of earning a higher rate of return. Thus a government could be holding investments actually owned by another government. If so, those investments are reported in an investment trust fund.

4. Private-purpose trust funds record property being held for the benefit of individuals, organizations, or other governments. For example, if a person dies without heirs and a will, any property may be held in this fund until disposition occurs. Confiscated property would also be monitored in this fund.

GOVERNMENTAL ACCOUNTING—FINANCIAL REPORTING PROCESS

A. Governmental funds will normally measure current financial resources for internal reporting purposes and for the fund-based financial statements. These figures will be converted to the measurement of economic resources in order to produce the government-wide financial statements. The proprietary funds measure economic resources internally so that no similar conversion is necessary.

B. To stress the stewardship function of a government, a budgetary journal entry is physically recorded at the start of the fiscal year by the General Fund and several other governmental funds. For the particular activity, it shows where resources will come from (debits) and what will be done with these resources (credits).

1. An estimated revenues account is debited and an appropriations (approved expenditures) account is credited.

2. To balance this entry, a budgetary fund balance account (or just a fund balance account) is established. A debit to this account indicates an anticipated deficit for the year, whereas a credit indicates that a surplus is expected.

3. Within the comprehensive annual financial report, this budgetary information is formally reported as required supplemental information (RSI). For the general fund and any other major special revenue fund that legally adopts a budget, the original budget is presented along with a final amended budget and the actual figures for the year. Rather than present this as RSI, a separate financial statement can also be presented to provide the same data.

C. Some governmental funds record commitments as encumbrances. To prevent overspending, commitments such as contracts and purchase orders are recorded when made. This is unique to governments; in a business, no formal entry is made for a commitment.

1. Entry is a debit to an encumbrances account and a credit to a reserved for encumbrances account (sometimes called Budgetary Fund Balance-Reserved for Encumbrances).

2. When commitment becomes a liability, the encumbrance entry is reversed off the books and liability is recognized. If liability is a different amount than was expected, the original Encumbrance balance is still removed.

3. Encumbrances are not reported on the government-wide financial statements. However, for the fund-based statements, recognition may be necessary for any encumbrances remaining at the end of the year. If the government plans to honor these outstanding commitments, a portion of the Fund Balance on the balance sheet is reported as reserved for encumbrance. This indicates that no liability yet exists, but a portion of the financial resources must be held to satisfy the commitment.

D. On the government-wide financial statements, expenses are recognized along with asset acquisitions and debt payments. However, on the fund-based financial statements, governmental funds measure financial resources. Thus, outflows of financial resources for expenses, capital asset acquisition, and the payment of long-term debt are all monitored in an expenditures account. Expenses, capital assets, and long-term debts are not separately recorded. The recognition of an expenditure is normally made when the cost becomes a legal liability and is a claim to current financial resources—usually to be paid within 60 days. At that point, financial resources are reduced.

1. For reporting purposes, expenditures can be classified in several different ways: by function (education and safety), by unit (fire department and police department), by activity (police administration and police training), by character (capital outlay and debt service), or by object (supplies and rent).

2. Although depreciation expense is recognized in the government-wide financial statements, it is not reported by the governmental funds in the fund-based statements because it does not affect current financial resources.

3. On government-wide statements, when a capital asset is sold, its cost and accumulated depreciation are both moved from the records and a gain or loss is recognized for the difference

between the amount received and the net book value. On fund-based financial statements, a revenue is recognized for the total amount received; the capital asset was not recorded and cannot be removed.

E. Capital assets are recorded on government-wide financial statements at cost and then depreciated over their useful lives. If received by donation, they are reported at fair value when received. For governmental funds on the fund-based financial statements, expenditures are reported so that capital assets do not appear and depreciation is not appropriate.

   1. Artworks and historical treasures can be received as donations. In such cases, a revenue must be recorded in the government-wide financial statements based on fair value when all eligibility requirements have been met.

   2. Recording of the asset in the government-wide statements is optional if three criteria are met: (1) the property is used for public exhibition, education, or research and not for financial gain; (2) the property is protected and preserved; and (3) there is a policy that the proceeds of any sale will be used to buy other items for the collection.

   3. If these criteria are met and the government chooses not to record the asset, an expense must be recognized to offset the reported revenue.

F. A capital asset is impaired if there is a decline in its service utility that is large in magnitude and the event or change in circumstance is outside the normal life cycle of the asset.

   1. If asset is no longer to be used, it is immediately recorded at the lower of its book value or fair value.

   2. If asset is to continue in use, a loss should be computed based on either the amount that would be needed to restore its value or the reduction in service utility that has occurred.

G. Infrastructure assets are stationary and have a relatively long life if properly maintained. Infrastructure includes bridges, roads, sidewalks and the like.

   1. All new infrastructure items must be capitalized at cost on the government-wide financial statements and depreciated. For the governmental funds, on the fund-based financial statements, expenditures are recorded rather than the infrastructure assets.

   2. For the government-wide financial statements, a modified approach can be used to avoid recognizing depreciation. Under this approach, the government can set a desired condition level for each network of infrastructure. All costs to keep the infrastructure at that level are then recognized as expenses instead of reporting depreciation.

   3. Any major infrastructure assets previously acquired, constructed, or renovated since 1980 must now be reported as assets in the government-wide financial statements. Under earlier rules, capitalization of these assets was not required, so the government may need to go back and estimate the book value of these previously obtained infrastructure items.

H. All of the revenues of a state or local government can be divided into four general classifications. Recognition varies by classification. Rules below are for government-wide financial statements. If reporting is for a governmental fund on the fund-based financial statement, the financial resource must also be available. Available means that the financial resources will be collected soon enough to be used to pay for current period expenditures. Available is often defined as anything accrued in the current period that will be collected within 60 days of the subsequent period. The number of days, though, can vary and that length of time being used should be disclosed. For property taxes, 60 days must be used.

1. Derived tax revenues—this is an assessment on an underlying transaction or event. Examples include sales taxes and income taxes. Asset (receivable or cash) and revenue are recognized in the same time period as the underlying transaction.

2. Imposed nonexchange revenues—this is an assessment on taxpayers that is not based on an underlying transaction or event. The best example is a property tax assessment. Asset is recognized when there is an enforceable legal claim (receivable) or cash is received if that is earlier. Revenue is recognized when the proceeds are required to be used or the first period in which use is permitted. For property taxes, revenue is recognized in the period for which the tax is levied. If the cash is received before it can be used, a deferred revenue is recognized.

3. Government-mandated nonexchange transactions—this is usually a grant or similar receipt given to a government to help pay for the cost of a legally required action. For example, this category is appropriate if the state requires a city to clean up its river and also provides funding for that purpose. The asset and revenue are both reported when all eligibility requirements have been met. In some cases, the government must spend the money first and then apply for reimbursement. Revenues are recognized in these cases when the money is properly spent.

4. Voluntary nonexchange transactions—this is a grant or a donation given to a government, often for a specified purpose. Once again, the asset and revenue are recognized when all eligibility requirements have been met. Any restriction on the funds should be disclosed by showing a restriction in the net assets (government-wide financial statements) and a fund balance reserved balance in the fund-based financial statement.

I. In the fund-based statements for the governmental funds, some changes in financial resources are neither revenues nor expenditures. For inflows, these transactions are recorded as Other Financing Sources (OFS); for outflows, the title Other Financing Uses (OFU) is applied. This does not apply to government-wide financial statements because they do not focus on financial resources.

1. A common OFS is the inflow of cash from the issuance of a bond. The governmental fund receiving the proceeds will debit cash and credit OFS. If the debt is not long-term, the liability rather than the OFS is reported. For the government-wide financial statements, cash is debited and the liability is always credited.

2. Governments often transfer money from one fund to another. Recording of these transfers depends on purpose.

   a. Operating transfers are made to move unrestricted funds in response to decisions made by government officials. For fund-based financial statements, the fund receiving the resources records inflow as an OFS; the fund giving up the resources records outflow as an OFU. There is no elimination of the two; both are shown. On government-wide financial statements, intra-activity transfers are within the governmental activities entirely or within the business-type activities entirely and are not shown because they offset. Inter-activity transfers are between the governmental activities and the business-type activities and are shown as positive and negative transfers. These figures are then offset in deriving totals for the government as a whole.

   b. Quasi-external transactions (or internal exchange transactions) are transfers (usually to an Internal Service Fund) to pay for work done or services performed. The fund getting money records inflow as a revenue; the fund losing the money records outflow as an expenditure. These balances remain on the fund-based statements but are removed on the government-wide financial statements if the internal service funds are reported within the governmental activities.

J. A government can acquire assets though lease, arrangements that must frequently be capitalized.

   1. The criteria for requiring capitalization of a lease are same as used in a for-profit business.

   2. For government-wide financial statements, the reporting is the same as a business: the asset is reported at the present value of the minimum lease payments and subsequently depreciated over the period of use. The liability is also recorded at present value. Each payment is partially recognized as interest expense (if time has passed) with the remainder serving to reduce the liability principal.

   3. On fund-based financial statements, if the lease is acquired by a governmental fund, both an expenditure and another financing source are recorded for the present value of all minimum lease payments. When payments are subsequently made, an expenditure is recorded, part for interest and part for the principal.

K. Government employees can earn amounts for vacations, holidays, and the like. When financial statements are being produced, any amounts due to employees for such compensated absences should be recognized if based on past services.

   1. For government-wide financial statements, the expense is recognized as the liability is incurred.

   2. In reporting governmental funds on the fund-based financial statements, an expenditure is recognized along with a liability, but only for the amount of the debt that will be paid from current financial resources.

L. Construction (such as sidewalks or other improvements) may be made and charged in whole or in part to the owners of the property being benefited. These are called special assessment projects.

   1. If the government has no obligation at all for the work, the money just flows through the government from the property owners to pay for the services. All recording is restricted to an Agency Fund so that no expenditures, revenues, expenses, or capital assets are reported by the government.

   2. If the government has any obligation, even if it is only secondarily liable, the cost of the project is recorded as a regular construction project.

      a. For the government-wide financial statements, the capital asset is recorded at cost along with any related debt. This capital asset is depreciated over its estimated life. Collections from property owners are recorded as revenues.

      b. For the fund-based financial statements, an expenditure is recorded within the Capital Projects Funds. The proceeds from any debt issued to finance the project are reported as another financing source whereas money paid on any long-term debt is an expenditure. Cash received from the property owners is shown as a revenue.

M. In government-wide financial statements, supplies and prepaid expenses are reported as in a for-profit business: the asset is recorded at cost and reclassified to expense as it is used. However, for fund-based financial statements, supplies and prepaid expenses cause special reporting problems because they are neither financial resources nor capital assets. On the fund-based statements, there are two ways that can be used to report such assets.

   1. Consumption method records cost as an asset when acquired and then reclassifies this amount to an expenditures account as the asset is consumed either by use or over time. At the end of the year, if any asset is still being reported, an equal amount of the unreserved fund balance should be

switched to a fund balance—reserved for supplies (or prepaid items) to show that a portion of the assets being reported is not a financial resource which can be spent.

2. Purchases method records entire cost as an expenditure when purchased. Any asset remaining at the end of the year is put directly onto the balance sheet, with an offsetting entry to a fund balance—reserved for supplies (or prepaid items) account.

N. Governments often operate solid waste landfills and are responsible for eventual clean-up costs. When a landfill reaches its total capacity, the government will have to expend funds to close and clean the site. Thus a liability is incurred as every landfill is being used.

1. A landfill can be recorded in an enterprise fund if there is a user charge or in the General Fund if the landfill is open to the public.

2. In the government-wide financial statements (and in the separate proprietary funds statements if accounted for in an enterprise fund), a liability should be accrued over the years based on the percentage of space that is filled. The liability to be reported is the percentage of the landfill capacity that is full times the estimated closure and postclosure costs. The annual adjustment to the liability is reported as an expense.

3. If the landfill is reported in the General Fund, the accounting on the fund-based financial statements will be different. Nothing is reported unless current financial resources are used or will be used. No long-term liability appears in the fund-based financial statements for the governmental funds.

O. Investments in stocks and bonds must be recorded at fair value. Unrealized gains and losses are reported along with realized gains and losses as a single number. Since investments are current financial resources, the accounting in the government-wide financial statements and the fund-based financial statements is basically the same.

P. A comprehensive annual financial report (CAFR) must be produced by every reporting entity.

1. A reporting entity is made up of a primary government and its component units.

    a. A component unit is a legally separate entity from the primary government, but elected officials of the primary government are still financially accountable for the component unit. A museum operating within a city might be an example if city officials must approve the museum's budget.

    b. Usually, the financial figures for a component unit are shown in the government-wide financial statements but to the far right side so as to separate them from the funds of the primary government. These are called discretely presented component units.

    c. A blended component unit is one that is so closely intertwined with the primary government that it is shown within the primary government's funds rather than being separately shown to the far right of the statement.

2. An activity (such as a school system) can qualify as a special-purpose government, which makes it a reporting entity that must produce a CAFR. To be a reporting entity, the special-purpose government must meet three criteria: it has a separately elected governing body, it is a legally separate entity, and it is fiscally independent (its officials can pass a budget, set tax rates, and issue bonded debt without approval from some other body.)

Q. The first part of the CAFR is the general purpose external financial statements that can also be issued by themselves. The general purpose statements are required to have each of the following items.

    1. Management's Discussion and Analysis (MD&A)—The MD&A provides a verbal explanation from city officials of the government's operations and financial position to help readers understand the measurements and results appearing in the statements. The MD&A should include the following:

        a. Information to determine whether financial position has improved or deteriorated.

        b. An analysis of the reasons for significant changes in fund balances or fund net assets within individual funds.

        c. An analysis of significant variations between original and final budget figures.

    2. Both sets of financial statements: government-wide financial statements and the fund-based financial statements. The two government-wide financial statements and the seven fund-based statements are identified above.

    3. Notes to the financial statements.

    4. Required supplemental information (RSI)—for example, the budgetary information described above would usually be included in this section, as well as a description of the modified approach if it is being used.

    5. In the CAFR, other information is presented beyond just these general purpose external financial statements, such as combining statements for the various funds and statistical information. A statistical section is included that must cover financial trends, revenue capacity, debt capacity, demographic and economic information, and operating information.

R. Public colleges and universities are not-for-profit organizations but must follow the accounting and reporting standards described above for state and local government units.

    1. These schools can choose to report as if they are only engaged in business-type activities, only engaged in governmental activities, or engaged in both business-type and governmental activities.

    2. Many schools will probably choose to report all activities as business-type. In that case, the school only has to prepare fund-based financial statements as would be done by a proprietary fund and does not have to produce government-wide financial statements because the two would be very similar.

STATEMENT OF CASH FLOWS

A. The reporting of a statement of cash flows (SCF) is required for each year in which an income statement is presented to show where cash was obtained and what was done with it. Any investment bought within three months of maturity is included as a cash item.

    1. All cash inflows and outflows are reported within one of three classifications.

        a. Investing activities are transactions involving assets that do not change in the regular course of daily operations. Examples would include the sale of equipment or the purchase of land.

        b. Financing activities are transactions involving stockholders' equity or liabilities that do not change in the regular course of daily operations. Examples would include paying a dividend and issuing a bond or common stock.

    c. Operating activities are transactions involving the regular course of daily operations. Examples would include paying an account payable or buying inventory.

    Interest revenue, interest expense, and dividend revenue are all viewed as operating activity cash flows and not the result of investing or financing activities.

B. To determine the cash flow effects to be reported, the changes during the year in each noncash account on the balance sheet are investigated.

    1. Accounts such as accounts receivable, inventory, prepaid expenses, accounts payable, and accrued liabilities change in the regular course of business and, therefore, only impact the reporting of cash flows from operating activities.

    2. The reason for the change in every other balance sheet account must be identified. The cash effect for each of these transactions is determined and classified as either an investing activity or a financing activity.

        a. In many cases, reproducing the journal entry will help to show the impact of the transaction and the change in cash.

        b. Examples: buying a patent is a cash outflow from an investing activity; paying a note is an outflow from a financing activity; selling treasury stock is an inflow from a financing activity.

        c. Only the cash flow is reported. For example, if a car is acquired by paying cash and signing a note, only the cash outflow is reported in the SCF.

        d. Exchanges are not included on the SCF but are separately disclosed as significant noncash transactions. Examples include land exchanged for a note and common stock issued to replace preferred stock.

        e. Stock dividends and splits are also events that do not appear on a statement of cash flows.

C. The goal of reporting operating activities is to show the net cash inflow or outflow. There are two methods to report operating activities. The indirect approach starts with net income and then removes all items that are either (1) noncash balances or (2) do not occur in the regular course of business (are nonoperational).

    1. Removal requires the subtraction of items that are included in net income as positives and the addition of items that are in net income as negatives.

    2. Noncash items include depreciation expense, amortization expense, and equity income reported in excess of the amount of dividends received.

    3. Noncash items also include the changes in operational assets and liabilities.

        a. Examples are accounts receivable, inventory, prepaid expenses, accounts payable, and accrued expenses.

        b. Changes in operational assets are removed by doing the opposite: an increase is subtracted, and a decrease is added.

        c. Changes in operational liabilities are removed by doing the same: an increase is added, and a decrease is subtracted.

    4. Nonoperational items include most gains and losses.

D. The direct approach to reporting operating activities reports the cash flows from individual types of operating transactions: cash collected from sales, cash paid for inventory purchases, cash paid for operating expenses, cash paid for taxes, etc. The various income statement accounts are converted to cash flow figures and reported.

1. Sales less any increase in receivables during the year or plus decrease in receivables equals cash collected from sales. As a way of arriving at the cash flow figure, the accountant can make a journal entry to simulate the recording of sales for the period as well as the change in the receivable account with the balancing figure being the cash inflow.

2. Journal entry can be made with cost of goods sold and changes in inventory and accounts payable to derive cash paid for purchases.

3. For any expense account, first remove any noncash item such as depreciation. Journal entry can then be made to record remaining figure and changes in related accrued expenses and prepaid expenses to arrive at cash paid for that expense.

4. Gains and losses on the income statement are nonoperational and omitted from the reporting of cash flows from operating activities.

E. A somewhat related topic is the conversion of cash financial records to accrual accounting.

1. Although accrual accounting is the appropriate generally accepted accounting principle, smaller operations often use cash basis accounting, which is another comprehensive basis of accounting.

2. Cash basis accounting is similar to the direct approach for reporting operating activities. Revenue is reported when cash is collected; expenses are reported when cash is paid.

3. Cash basis accounting does not record several balance sheet accounts: accounts receivables, accounts payables, accrued expenses, prepayments, and inventory that has not been paid for.

4. To change records from a cash basis to accrual accounting, two journal entries are made.

   a. Any balance sheet accounts that were left off the records as of the first day of the current year are recorded with a balancing entry made to beginning retained earnings.

   b. Any balance sheet accounts left off at the end of the year are recorded by adjusting the beginning balance to the year-end balance. The offsetting entry is made to the related income statement account (accounts receivable relates to sales; rent payable relates to rent expense; etc.).

ACCOUNTING FOR NOT-FOR-PROFIT ORGANIZATIONS

A. Not-for-profit (NFP) organizations have several sources of authoritative accounting principles.

1. Public colleges and universities such as the University of Virginia and the University of Kentucky follow the guidelines of the Governmental Accounting Standards Board (GASB). Financial reporting for these organizations follows the rules established above for governments and will not be discussed in this section.

2. Private not-for-profit organizations such as the University of Richmond and the Heart Fund follow the guidelines of the Financial Accounting Standards Board (FASB). The rules described below are for private organizations.

3. Private NFPs use accrual accounting. They record all capital assets and long-term debts. Neither budgetary entries nor encumbrances are formally recorded.

B. Financial statements are produced for NFPs to provide information for the various groups providing resources.

   1. The financial statements of a private NFP are designed to show the organization as a whole and are not intended to reflect fund accounting.

      a. Statement of financial position (balance sheet) reports all assets, all liabilities, and the balance of net assets (which is the "equity" section of the statement).

In the Net Assets section, three totals are shown: unrestricted, temporarily restricted, and permanently restricted.

The unrestricted net asset total discloses the amount of the organization's net assets (assets minus liabilities) that can be spent or used in any way that officials choose.

The temporarily restricted net asset total indicates the amount of the net assets that has been restricted by the donor for a specific purpose or for a specific period of time.

The permanently restricted net asset total is the amount of the net assets that has been restricted by the donor so that it must be held indefinitely. Income from these assets usually has to be used in a specified fashion.

      b. Statement of activities reports (usually in three columns) the changes during the current period in the amount of unrestricted net assets, temporarily restricted net assets, and permanently restricted net assets.

All three columns list increases first: revenues, gifts, gains and losses from sales, gains and losses in the value of investments, etc. Income generated on permanently restricted net assets is reported either in the temporarily restricted or the unrestricted net assets column depending on spending stipulations made by the donor.

All expenses are listed solely in the column for unrestricted net assets. Expenses are reported by function: according to the specific program benefited or as support to operate the organization (fund raising and administrative costs). Depreciation expense is recorded by not-for-profit organizations.

Just below the listing of increases, a line appears with a title such as "net assets released from restrictions" that shows an increase in unrestricted net assets and an equal decrease in temporarily restricted net assets. This figure reflects the amount of net assets that are no longer restricted because the funds were properly spent during the period or the time limitation was reached.

      c. Statement of cash flows looks like a statement produced by a for-profit business. It has three sections: operations, investing activities (asset transactions), and financing activities (liability and equity transactions). Unrestricted cash contributions are viewed as cash flows from operating activities, whereas cash contributions restricted for long-term projects appear under financing activities.

C. The recording of gifts depends on whether the assets are unrestricted, temporarily restricted, or permanently restricted.

   1. A gift that has to be spent for a particular purpose (or that cannot be spent for a period of time) is recorded in the statement of activities as an increase in temporarily restricted net assets.

2. When temporarily restricted amount is properly spent (or when required time passes), reclassification occurs: unrestricted net assets increase and temporarily restricted net assets decrease.

3. Long-lived assets or other property received as gifts should be reported at fair value on the date of the gift. Receipt of the asset can be recorded as an increase in unrestricted net assets. As an option, for long-lived assets, a time-implied restriction can be presumed and the gifts can be reported as temporarily restricted net assets. If that is done, an amount equal to depreciation expense should be reclassified each period to reduce the temporarily restricted column and increase the unrestricted column. This same alternative is available if a long-lived asset is acquired with the use of temporarily restricted net assets.

D. NFPs often receive pledges of future gifts. If an unconditional promise of a future gift is made (the organization has no obligation to do anything), a receivable is recorded at present value. An allowance for uncollectible accounts is also set up as a contra account for any expected defaults. The difference is the increase in net assets shown on the statement of activities. This amount is viewed as unrestricted if it is to be collected this year and use has not been designated. However, it is temporarily restricted if it is to be received later. It is temporarily or permanently restricted if use has been designated.

E. Contributions can also be made of art works, museum pieces, etc., such as valuable paintings. No recording at all is required if (1) the items are used for research, education, or exhibition, (2) they are protected and preserved, and (3) if sold, the money will be used to acquire similar items.

F. A donor can make a transfer to an NFP of assets that must be conveyed to a separate specific beneficiary. Normally, at that point, the donor removes the asset from its records and recognizes an expense. The NFP recognizes the asset along with a related liability (rather than a contribution revenue) at the asset's fair value, while the eventual recipient recognizes an asset (usually a receivable) and a contribution revenue.

1. However, if the donor retains the right to redirect the use of the assets or can revoke the gift, the donor continues to record the asset because it still has control. Once again, the NFP shows the asset along with a liability. The beneficiary makes no entry (until received) since the gift may never be obtained.

2. If the NFP is given variance powers so that the beneficiary could be changed, the donor records an expense and removes the asset. Because of its control, the NFP recognizes the asset along with a contribution revenue (rather than a liability). The beneficiary will not recognize the asset until received because of the uncertainty. Variance powers means the NFP can ignore the donor's instructions about the gift without seeking further approval.

G. Contributions can also be made of donated services; a person can do work for an NFP organization for free or for a reduced payment.

1. The value of the work donated is recorded as both a revenue and an expense, but only if the work enhances a nonfinancial asset or it (1) requires a specialized skill, (2) is provided by people with that skill, and (3) would be bought if not otherwise provided.

2. If these rules are not met, donated services are not recorded.

H. Private not-for-profit organizations often charge membership dues.

1. If members receive substantive benefits for these dues, they should be recorded as membership revenues by the NFP.

2. If members receive only negligible benefits for these dues, they should be reported as contribution revenues.

I. Investments in stocks and bonds are adjusted to fair value at the end of each year. Increases and decreases appear on the statement of activities. The net asset column that is affected is based on the restrictions (if any) attached to the investments and their changes in value.

J. If students in colleges and universities are given scholarships, the entire tuition charge is recorded as a revenue. The scholarship is then recorded as a direct reduction to the revenue (rather than being reported separately as an expense). The two are netted together for reporting purposes.

K. Voluntary health and welfare organization (VHWOs) and other types of charities report a separate statement of functional expenses in order to provide additional information about the use made of money. This statement is allowed for all NFPs but is required of VHWOs. Expenses are split between "program service expenses" (doing the stated work of the charity) and "supporting service expenses" (operating the charity and fund raising).

L. If a charity issues a fund-raising mailing along with other information, all mailing costs are considered to be fund-raising expenses unless certain criteria are met. If there is a specific call for action and the mailing is not directed solely at potential donors, some of the mailing costs may be considered a program service cost.

M. One common type of private not-for-profit organization is a health care entity such as a hospital or retirement home. For a health care entity, the net patient service revenue is a key figure reported to reflect the amount earned based on the people being served. The amount charged is reported but is then reduced by any contractual adjustments. A contractual adjustment is an accepted decrease in the amount of payment coming from a third-party payor (such as an insurance company) based on established rates. In addition, charges where the health care entity does not expect to collect (such as charity care) are not recorded rather than being recognized as both a revenue with an accompanying reduction.

INTANGIBLE ASSETS

A. Intangible assets are used to generate revenues but have no physical substance.

1. Most common intangibles are patents, goodwill, leasehold improvements (the right to use improvements in leased property), and organization costs. In a purchase consolidation, the purchase price can often indicate the necessity for recognizing intangible assets associated with the subsidiary such as Internet domain names, customer lists, noncompetition agreements, and databases. Intangible assets are only recognized in this situation if the company has a contractual right to them or if they can be separated from the subsidiary and sold.

2. Intangible assets are amortized (usually based on the straight-line method) over the useful life of the asset. The useful life is determined based on the use to be made of the asset, any legal life restrictions, the expected action of competitors, and the like. There is no maximum period of life; therefore, intangible assets with an unlimited life are not subject to amortization.

   a. Organization costs and start-up costs are expensed immediately.

   b. Leasehold improvements are amortized over the life of the improvement or the life of the lease, whichever is less.

   c. Goodwill is not amortized. Rather, it is checked each year for possible impairment.

B. Accounting for research and development costs. Research is the search and discovery of new knowledge for potential profit. Development is the translation of research into a plan for a profitable product.

   1. Research and development costs are expensed immediately. In this way, all companies handle these costs in a comparable manner that is not subject to manipulation or judgment.

      a. This expensing includes cost of long-lived assets, such as buildings and equipment if acquired for use in a specific project. Cost of long-lived assets acquired for research and development is not expensed immediately if it has alternative future uses. Cost is capitalized with subsequent amortization classified as a research and development expense.

      b. In a purchase consolidation, any amount paid because the subsidiary has in-process research and development should be expensed immediately.

   2. Since research and development is expensed, the capitalized cost of a patent is the legal costs of establishing and successfully defending the patent.

C. Accounting for the development of software that is to be sold.

   1. Until a product reaches the stage of technological feasibility when a company has a program design or working model, all costs are recorded as research and development expenses.

   2. After a product has achieved technological feasibility, further software development costs are capitalized.

      a. Capitalized development cost is amortized to expense each year using the greater of (1) the straight-line figure and (2) the percentage of current sales to total expected sales.

   3. Actual production costs are reported as inventory.

PENSION ACCOUNTING

A. If a company's pension is a defined benefit plan, the amount employees are entitled to receive when they retire is unknown because it is based on future factors, such as length of service, salary rates, how long they live, etc. Thus the expense incurred each year must be estimated based on assumptions about these variables.

In a defined contribution plan, the employer contributes a set amount of money each year; that amount is the expense.

B. Terminology of pension accounting is somewhat unique.

   1. Net pension cost is the expense to be recognized and reported for a specific year.

   2. Funding is amount of cash actually set aside by the employer.

   3. Service cost is the increase in the amount of pension obligation because of work done by employees in the current year.

   4. Projected benefit obligation (PBO) is the total liability (actually the present value of the estimated future pension payments) that a company has incurred to date based on the assumptions made of the variables, such as how long a person will live. One of the assumptions is what each person's highest salary will be.

      a. The PBO increases because of the annual service cost and interest that accrues on the PBO. PBO decreases when payments are made to retirees. PBO can go up or down if the plan is amended (called a prior service cost) or if one of the assumptions is changed (called an actuarial or an unrecognized gain or loss).

5. Accumulated benefit obligation is the total estimated liability that a company has incurred to date. It is just like PBO, except that each person's current salary level is used.

6. Plan assets is the total amount of assets already set aside to pay pension benefits. Funding and any income will increase the plan assets, whereas payments of benefits will reduce it.

7. Prior service cost is an increase in the projected benefit obligation because of an amendment in the plan or because of the start of the plan. PBO goes up immediately, but expense is recognized through amortization over future years.

8. Actuarial/unrecognized gains and losses are created in two ways.

   a. Changes in the PBO because of a change in an actuarial assumption (for example, it is estimated that people will live longer).

   b. The difference in the expected return on plan assets and the actual return on plan assets (as measured by the change in market value after the payments and collections are removed).

   The assumption is that actuarial/unrecognized gains and losses will even out over time; thus they are not allowed to affect income unless they become particularly large.

C. Annual computation of net pension cost starts with service cost for the period, adds interest expense on PBO (based on a settlement or discount rate), and subtracts expected income on plan assets.

   1. In addition, net pension cost includes amortization (almost always an increase in the expense) of any prior service cost which is usually written off over the remaining service life of the employees benefited.

   2. Net pension cost may also include amortization (can be an increase or a decrease) of any actuarial/ unrecognized gain or loss. Amortization is ignored unless balance is greater than 10% of larger of PBO and plan assets at the beginning of the year.

D. Recording of net pension cost is a debit to pension expense and a credit to pension liability. Funding of pension is a credit to cash and a debit to pension liability. If accrued pension liability has a credit balance, it is reported on balance sheet as a liability. If accrued pension liability has a debit balance, it is shown as a prepaid pension cost in the asset section of the balance sheet.

E. A recent new FASB Standard on pensions now requires the following:

   1. Prior Service Cost must be initially recorded by increasing PSC/Other Comprehensive Income in Stockholders' Equity and by increasing Pension Liability. As it is amortized to expense, these amounts on the balance sheet will decrease.

   2. Unrecognized Gains/Losses are initially recorded in the Stockholders' Equity and Pension Liability accounts as well. As these G/L are amortized, the balance sheet amounts will decrease.

   3. The result of this is that the "funded status" of the pension plan is reflected on the balance sheet of the company, rather than in the footnotes as required in the old FASB on pensions.

   4. No minimum liability is required; recording the normal period journal entries for Pension Expense, PSC and G/L will ensure that the proper Pension Liability (underfunded) or Pension Asset (overfunded) shows up on the balance sheet.

F. A company can also have an obligation for postretirement benefits other than pensions. For example, the company might agree to pay medical insurance premiums for retired workers until their death. As employees work, this obligation is estimated and recorded as an expense in much the same way as a pension.

   1. A few differences with pensions do occur: the amounts are not usually funded, and the obligations are less well defined and, thus, harder to estimate.

INVENTORY

A. Inventory is merchandise bought or constructed for resale purposes. It is recorded at cost. However, abnormal amounts paid for idle factory costs, freight, handling, wasted material, and the like should be expensed immediately rather than being capitalized.

B. Cost of goods sold (CGS) is computed by adding beginning inventory to purchases (including transportation in and any other normal and necessary costs) and then subtracting ending inventory. In contrast, transportation out is not an inventory cost but a delivery expense.

   1. Both inventory and cost of goods sold can be monitored on an ongoing basis by a perpetual system or only at the end of the year by a periodic system.

      a. Under a periodic system, the costs to be expensed are not determined until the end of the year.

      b. Under a perpetual system, the next costs to be expensed are determined every time that a new transaction occurs.

   2. Applying costs to units sold and units retained can be done by a FIFO (first-in, first-out) system, LIFO (last-in, first-out), or averaging.

      a. Periodic and perpetual systems give different results except when applying FIFO.

      b. For averaging in a periodic system (called weighted averaging), one average is determined at the end of the year; for averaging in a perpetual system (called moving averaging), a new average is computed each time a new purchase is made.

C. A cash discount reduces inventory cost if paid within a specified time. A 2/10, n/30 discount, for example, gives a 2% discount if bill is paid in ten days. Remaining (net) balance must be paid in 30 days.

   1. Theoretically, inventory cost should be reduced even if discount is not taken, since it is not a necessary cost of acquiring the inventory. This is called the net method, and any discount not taken is recorded as a loss rather than being capitalized. Can also record inventory at gross figure and record separate reduction at the time a discount is actually taken.

D. Because of obsolescence, inventory cost may have to be written down to a lower market value since accounting is conservative.

   1. Cost is compared to market value, and the lower figure is reported.

   2. Replacement cost is used as market value for comparison with cost of inventory unless replacement cost lies outside of two boundaries.

      a. The ceiling boundary is the estimated sales price less anticipated selling expenses. If the replacement cost is above the ceiling, the ceiling is used as market value.

  b. The floor boundary is the estimated sales price less anticipated selling expenses and normal profit. If replacement cost is below the floor, the floor figure is used as market value.

 3. If goods are damaged, cost should be reduced to net realizable value.

E. Errors in recording and counting inventory affect reported figures.

 1. Errors can be made in recording the transfer of inventory, with either goods being bought or those being sold.

  a. Transfer should be recorded at FOB point. This is point where legal title changes hands.

  b. Since ending inventory is determined by count, an error in recording a purchase or sale does not necessarily affect the reporting of ending inventory.

 2. As a second problem, ending inventory can be counted incorrectly so that both ending inventory and CGS are wrong.

  a. If ending inventory is overstated, CGS is too low, and net income is too high. If ending inventory is too low, CGS is too high, and net income is too low.

  b. Ending inventory error automatically carries over to the next year's beginning inventory. If beginning inventory is overstated, CGS is too high, and net income is too low. If beginning inventory is too low, CGS is too low, and net income is too high.

F. Inventory may need to be estimated for many reasons: preparation of interim financial statements, providing a check figure for a physical inventory count, estimating fire and theft losses, etc.

 1. Retail inventory method can be used to estimate inventory, but only if records are kept at both cost and retail.

  a. Ending inventory is first estimated at its retail value by taking the beginning inventory and adding purchases and mark ups and subtracting mark downs, losses (theft and breakage, for example), and sales.

  b. Estimated ending inventory at retail is then converted to a cost figure by multiplying it by a cost/retail ratio. Inventory at retail will not vary, but there are several ways to determine the cost/retail ratio. The Average Method is one common method for calculating the cost/retail ratio—all cost figures (beginning inventory and purchases) are used, and all retail figures (beginning inventory, purchases, mark ups, and mark downs) are used.

 2. Gross profit method of estimating inventory is used when only cost figures are recorded.

  a. Normal gross profit percentage (gross profit/sales) computed from the past is multiplied by current sales to provide an estimate of current gross profit. This figure is subtracted from sales to arrive at an estimate of the cost of inventory that has been sold in the current period.

  b. Cost of beginning inventory is added to current purchases to get total goods available. The estimated cost of the inventory that has been sold this period is subtracted to leave the estimated cost of the inventory still on hand.

G. Consignment inventory is merchandise held for sale by one party (a consignee) although the goods are owned by another (a consignor).

 1. Cost of consignment inventory is recorded by the owner (at cost) and not by the consignee. The party physically holding the items does not have them recorded.

2. Consignor cannot record receivable until goods are sold.

H. LIFO has some technical problems that make it difficult to use. Dollar value LIFO is one practical way to apply LIFO. For one thing, inventory is grouped into similar pools rather than handling items individually.

1. All LIFO systems start with a base inventory which is usually the quantity when LIFO is first applied times the price on that date. If inventory increases, a new layer is added: it is the additional quantity at the latest prices. If inventory decreases, cost is removed from the most recent layers.

2. When applying dollar value LIFO, the base inventory of a pool is also recorded. However, for each additional layer of inventory, the increase in quantity is measured in dollars and not units. For each additional layer, the latest price is measured as an index and not in dollars. The base inventory plus all of the added layers gives ending inventory. A layer might be a $10,000 increase in quantity times an index of 1.12 or $11,200.

3. An increase in quantity for the current period is the difference between the beginning inventory measured at base year prices and the ending inventory measured at base year prices. Since the prices are held constant, any difference is caused by quantity change.

4. The index for the current period is the ending inventory at ending prices divided by the ending inventory at base year prices.

ACCOUNTING CHANGES

A. Companies can decide to make changes in the accounting principles that are being applied. Normally, the company's independent auditor will only allow such changes if the move is to an acceptable alternative and if the company can show that the new method is preferable.

1. Such changes are handled retroactively by restating all prior figures to those that would have been appropriate had the new method been used from the first day of the company's operations.

2. For any period of time that is not being reported, the income impact on these earlier periods is shown as an adjustment (net of tax effect) to the earliest reported retained earnings. To illustrate, assume that a company began operations in Year 1 and is changing accounting principles in Year 5. If financial statements for only Years Four and Five are being reported, they are changed. In addition, the income effect on the first three years must be accumulated and reported as an adjustment to the opening retained earnings balance at the start of Year 4.

3. If the previous effect of the change cannot be determined, the opening balance for the current year is based on the earlier method and then the new method begins to be applied.

4. As discussed below, one major exception is a change in depreciation methods which is handled like a change in an estimation.

5. When a new official pronouncement is issued, the method of reporting past years is normally detailed. If not, the change must be applied retroactively also.

B. Changes in the reporting entity are also accounted for by restatement. A change in reporting entity is a change in the composition of consolidated statements without any change in ownership. For example, a subsidiary that used to be omitted from consolidation is now consolidated without any increase in ownership.

C. A company can change one of its estimations such as the bad debt percentage of the expected life of assets.

1. For changes in estimations, there is no effect reported on any previously reported figures.

2. To determine the reported amount for the current year, the beginning figures for the year are used and then the new estimations are applied.

3. If a change is both a change in an estimation and a change in a principle, it is reported as a change in an estimation. This is the method by which a change in depreciation methods is reported. The old method is used until the first day of the current year and then the application of the new method is started. That is one change that is not applied retroactively.

PARTNERSHIP ACCOUNTING

A. A partnership is an association of two or more persons to carry on a business as co-owners for profit. Many aspects of accounting for a partnership are same as for a corporation, but there are unique features. For example, each partner has a separate capital account, the total of which replaces the stockholders' equity section of the balance sheet.

B. When a new partner is admitted into a partnership, any contributions are recorded by partnership at market value, but original book value is retained for tax purposes.

1. A computation can be made so that a new partner invests an amount that will be equal to the capital balance set up. This eliminates the need to record either goodwill or a bonus.

a. The new partner's investment (NPI) can be set equal to the percentage of the business being acquired (%A) multiplied by the total capital of the business.

b. Total capital would be the previous capital (PC) balance plus the new partner's investment. Thus the equation would be set up and the new investment determined algebraically. NPI = %A × (PC + NPI), and solve for NPI.

2. A new partner may have to contribute assets worth more than the percentage being acquired of the total capital, especially if it is a profitable partnership.

a. This difference can be recorded by bonus method. The partner is given a set capital balance or a percentage of total capital. Any difference from a contribution (either positive or negative) is recorded to the original partners' Capital accounts based on previous method of allocating profits and losses.

b. This difference can also be recorded using the goodwill method. The new partner receives a capital balance exactly equal to the contribution. The new partner's payment is then used to compute an implied value for the business as a whole. The investment is divided by the percentage acquired to get this valuation. The difference between this implied value and total capital (including the new investment) is viewed as goodwill and recorded along with an offsetting entry to the capital accounts of the original partners based on the previous method of allocating profits and losses.

C. When revenues and expenses are closed out at the end of the year, the net profit or loss must be assigned to the partners' capital accounts. The actual amount paid to a partner is usually set by agreement and can differ from this allocation process.

1. If there is no agreement, split is always done on an even basis.

2. If there is an agreement as to profit allocation but losses are not mentioned, the same method is used.

3. Any agreements must be followed specifically. These can include several factors, such as a salary allowance, interest, and a ratio. If more than one factor is included, the ratio is computed last.

D. At some point, a partnership may be liquidated, the assets sold off, and the debts paid with any residual amounts going to the partners.

1. In liquidating noncash assets, any gains and losses are assigned to the partners based on normal profit and loss allocation.

2. Any residual cash goes to the partners based on the final balances in their capital accounts.

3. If enough money is set aside to pay all debts, available cash can be distributed to the partners before all noncash assets are sold. To determine distribution, maximum losses are assumed for all remaining noncash assets. If a partner has a negative capital balance after these simulated losses, that amount is also viewed as a loss to be absorbed by the remaining partners using their relative profit and loss percentages. When all remaining capital accounts have positive balances, those amounts are the safe capital amounts that can be distributed immediately.

FINANCIAL INSTRUMENTS

A. Financial instruments are cash, investments in equities, or contracts to receive or pay cash or another financial instrument.

1. The term "financial instrument" includes traditional items, such as accounts receivable and notes payable, but also more complex arrangements, such as forward currency exchange contracts.

2. A derivative is a particular type of financial instrument. A derivative is an exchange of promises where a "notional amount" is set by a contract, such as the number of shares of stock or barrels of oil that will be bought or sold or paid for in the future (often at a set amount). An "underlying," such as the actual price of the shares of stock or the oil on the market, will give that contract a positive or negative fair value. For example, a contract to buy one share of stock at $50 per share has a positive value if the stock is selling above $50 and a negative value if it is selling below $50. The one share is the notional amount, and the price of the stock is the underlying.

   a. All derivatives must be reported on the balance sheet. Depending on their nature, derivatives are shown as either assets or liabilities.

   b. All derivatives are reported at their fair values.

   c. The change in fair value of a derivative is reported within net income for the period of the change.

   d. Many derivatives are acquired to hedge other transactions or commitments where exposure to a change in value would create gains or losses. A hedge is designed to cause an equal and off-setting gain or loss so that no net income effect will result. A derivative can be used for this purpose to balance out gains and losses from changes in value.

   e. If a derivative is documented properly when acquired, it can be recorded as a hedge for a particular financial instrument. In that case, the financial instrument must also be reported at fair value each period, even if that is not the normal method of reporting.

3. Some financial instruments have off-balance sheet risk; in other words, a loss can be incurred that is larger than the amount being reported. For example, (1) a company can have a commitment that is not being reported on the balance sheet that could still create a loss, or (2) the company might have a payable reported as $100,000 that might actually require payment of $160,000.

4. Disclosure of risks associated with financial instruments.

   a. For all financial instruments, significant concentrations of credit risk must be disclosed. Credit risk is the chance of loss resulting because another party fails to perform. For example, a company guarantees the loan of another company and the debtor fails to pay. A significant concentration is where a large amount of performance is required of a single party or by a group of similar parties (for example, in the same industry or same geographical location).

   b. For all financial instruments, market value must be disclosed or an indication of why value cannot be determined.

EARNINGS PER SHARE

A. Earnings per share (EPS) is a common stock computation. It must be reported for each income period reported by all publicly held companies. Basically, the net income that is applicable to common stock is divided by the weighted average number of common stock shares outstanding.

   1. Any preferred stock dividends must be subtracted from net income to get amount of income applicable to common stock.

      a. If preferred stock is cumulative, the annual dividend is subtracted each year, whether declared or not; if noncumulative, it is only subtracted when declared.

   2. To get the weighted average of the common shares, the number of shares outstanding for a period is multiplied by that number of months. The resulting totals are added and divided by 12 to get the average for the year.

      a. For averaging purposes, shares issued as a stock dividend or split (or from a pooling of interests) are assumed as having been issued at the earliest point in the computation.

B. The above income divided by shares is termed basic earnings per share and is reported by all publicly held companies. If a company has dilutive securities (that can be converted into common stock), it must also report a second figure referred to as diluted earnings per share. This computation gives weight to convertible items by assuming that conversion actually occurred.

   1. To include stock options or rights in the computation of diluted earnings per share, conversion is assumed, and the number of shares that would be issued is added to the weighted average number of shares.

      a. Converting options often requires payment of cash. If conversion is assumed, the cash coming into the company is also assumed.

      b. It is assumed that this cash is used to buy treasury stock at its average price for the period which reduces the weighted average number of outstanding shares.

   2. To include convertible bonds in the computation of diluted EPS, conversion is assumed, and the number of shares that would be issued is added to the weighted average number of shares.

      a. Interest expense is a negative within net income. Assumed conversion of the bonds would eliminate the interest causing an increase (net of taxes) in income used for this computation.

3. To include convertible preferred stock in the computation of diluted EPS, conversion is assumed, and the number of shares that would be issued is added to the weighted average number of shares.

    a. Preferred stock dividends have been subtracted in arriving at the income applicable to common stock. Assumed conversion of the preferred stock would eliminate the dividends causing an increase in the income used for this computation.

C. In computing EPS, any assumed conversion that causes the reported figure to rise is referred to as antidilutive and is not included in the computation. For earnings per share, it is just ignored.

FOREIGN CURRENCY BALANCES

A. All companies have a functional currency. That is the currency in which most transactions are denominated. If in doubt as to the identity of functional currency, several factors should be examined: the currency of the primary sales markets, the currency used for major financing, the currency used to acquire materials and pay labor, etc. The dollar will be viewed here as the functional currency because it almost always is for U.S. companies.

B. Prior to being reported in financial statements, figures denominated in foreign currencies must be stated at their equivalent U.S. dollar values. Two different techniques have been established for this purpose.

    1. Financial statements of foreign subsidiaries of U.S. companies are translated into U.S. dollars for consolidation purposes if the functional currency of the sub is other than the dollar (which it normally is).

    2. Individual transactions of a U.S. company made in a foreign currency are remeasured into U.S. dollars. Although not as frequent, remeasurement is also used for the statements of a foreign sub if its functional currency is the U.S. dollar.

C. Both translation and remeasurement are based on multiplying the reported foreign currency balance by a fraction which is the value of desired currency/equivalent value of the foreign currency. In either case, there are two accounting problems to address.

    1. Should the restatement be based on historical exchange rates or current exchange rates (called spot rates)?

    2. If a balance is updated using the current rate, a change occurs in the reported figure. How is this effect measured and reported?

D. Translation of the financial statements of a foreign subsidiary.

    1. All accounts in the asset and liability sections (no exceptions) are translated into U.S. dollars at the current exchange rate in effect on the date of the balance sheet.

    2. All other accounts (revenues, expenses, paid-in capital, dividends, etc.) are translated into U.S. dollars at the historical exchange rate in effect at the time of the original recording of the account.

        a. Common stock, for example, is translated at rate in effect when stock was issued; dividends use the rate at the date of declaration.

            Since many income statement items (such as sales and rent expense) occur throughout the year, an average rate for the year can often be used.

            Because the date of recording is used, cost of goods sold and depreciation expense are translated at the average rate for the current year and not when the asset was bought.

3. Assets and liabilities use current exchange rates; thus, their balances will continually change. The effect of these changes is accumulated and reported in a Translation Adjustment account that appears with accumulated other comprehensive income within stockholders' equity.

    a. There is no net income effect created by a translation, but the change in the translation adjustment balance is used in converting net income to comprehensive income.

    b. The translation adjustment is computed as follows.

    The January 1 balance of net assets (or the equivalent stockholders' equity) is translated at the rate on that day.

    Any change in net assets during the year is translated at the rate on the date of the change. Dividends, income, and stock transactions are about the only possible changes in the net asset total.

    The above two translated figures are added.

    The December 31 balance of net assets is translated at the rate on that date.

    The value of the assets as they entered the company during the year (bullet 3 above) is compared to the ending value of the net assets (bullet 4). Difference is the change in value, which is the translation adjustment for the year.

E. Remeasurement of individual transactions (such as purchases and sales) denominated in a foreign currency. Remeasurement is also appropriate for a subsidiary that has the same functional currency as its parent.

1. At the time of the original transaction, all balances are remeasured at the exchange rate on that date.

2. Subsequently, any foreign currency monetary balances (cash, receivables, payables, and assets and liabilities reported at market value) must be remeasured at new current exchange rates.

    a. Monetary accounts could be remeasured every day, but for convenience they are remeasured at the time of subsequent transactions (a payable is collected, for example) and at the end of the fiscal period.

    b. Any time that a monetary account is remeasured and the value changes, a gain or loss is computed, that is reported on the income statement (and not within the stockholders' equity).

3. All other accounts (such as inventory, buildings, common stock, revenues, etc.) remain at historical rates and never change. For a remeasurement, that rate is the date of the initial transaction. Thus, depreciation uses the historical rate when the asset was bought; cost of goods sold is based on the rate when the inventory was acquired.

F. Forward exchange contracts are created so that one currency will be swapped for another currency in a specified period of time at a specified rate (called the forward rate).

1. As a derivative, the contract must be reported each period as either an asset or a liability based on its fair value (the fair market of the contract and not the fair value of the currency).

    a. Changes in the fair value of the contract are reported in net income each period.

    b. In one case, if the contract is bought to hedge a probable forecasted transaction, the gain or loss goes under "other comprehensive income" in stockholders' equity rather than in net income.

c. If a forward exchange contract is acquired in order to hedge an individual transaction or a commitment in a foreign currency (a fair value hedge), the change in the contract's fair value will tend to offset the change in the value of the balance that is denominated in the foreign currency. A forward exchange contract can also hedge a probable forecasted transaction but is known as a cash flow hedge.

DISCONTINUED OPERATIONS (FORMERLY DISPOSAL OF A SEGMENT)

A. If an operation is discontinued by the reporting company, all of the operation's results must be shown as a single figure net of income taxes at the bottom of the income statement just below income from continuing operations. The net figure is reported right before any extraordinary gains and losses.

B. To qualify for this reporting, the assets being sold or abandoned must have operations and cash flows that are clearly distinguished by the company from the rest of the operations.

C. While the company attempts to sell these assets, they should be reported as "held for sale" and shown at the lower of book value or fair value less cost to sell.

1. Thus, if the company anticipates a gain, the assets remain at book value and the gain is only recognized when it occurs.

2. Conversely, if the company anticipates a loss, the assets are written down to fair value less the cost to sell as soon as the loss can be anticipated.

D. All figures on past income statements related to this discontinued operation must also be separated and dropped to the bottom of the income statement for comparison purposes. This reporting does not change the previously reported net income totals, just the classifications.

REPORTING SEGMENTS OF AN ENTERPRISE

A. The company should first identify its operating segments based on the method the management uses to disaggregate the enterprise for the making of internal operating decisions. The factors used to determine these segments must be disclosed.

1. Each operating segment must be engaged in business activities from which it earns revenues (even if only internally) and incurs expenses.

2. The operating results of each operating segment must be reviewed individually by the chief operating decision maker within the company and not as part of some larger segment.

3. Some components of a company (central headquarters, for example, or the research and development department) may not be within any operating segment because they do not generate revenues.

4. Segments may be combined if they have the same activities in the same geographic region even if the company disaggregates them for internal reporting purposes.

B. The company must disclose information about each operating segment of a significant size. Three tests are applied and every segment that meets at least one of these tests must be included in the disclosure.

1. Revenue test—any segment is viewed as significant if its revenue makes up 10% or more of the company's total. Both sales to outsiders and intersegment revenues are included.

2. Profit and loss test—any segment is viewed as significant if its profit or loss is 10% of the greater of the profits of all profitable segments or the losses of all losing segments. Profit and loss should be determined in the manner that is used by the company internally to determine the profitability of its segments. Common costs should be allocated to segments if that is done so for internal decision making purposes.

3. Asset test—any segment is viewed as significant if its assets make up 10% or more of the company's total.

C. Certain disclosures are required for the company as a whole even if the company only identifies itself as having one operating segment.

1. Revenue generated from external customers for each product and service.

2. For domestic operations, revenues from external customers and the amount of long-lived assets. The same disclosure is required for foreign operations.

3. Revenues and assets for any specific foreign country must also be disclosed if they are material.

4. If 10% or more of consolidated revenues come from a single customer, that fact must be disclosed. For this test, a group of customers under common control is viewed as a single customer.

APPENDIX

Figure 1: Present Value of a Single Sum ($1)

Years	3.0%	3.5%	4.0%	4.5%	5.0%	5.5%	6.0%	6.5%	7.0%	7.5%	8.0%	8.5%
1	0.97087	0.96618	0.96154	0.95694	0.95238	0.94787	0.94340	0.93897	0.93458	0.93023	0.92593	0.92166
2	0.94260	0.93351	0.92456	0.91573	0.90703	0.89845	0.89000	0.88166	0.87344	0.86533	0.85734	0.84946
3	0.91514	0.90194	0.88900	0.87630	0.86384	0.85161	0.83962	0.82785	0.81630	0.80496	0.79383	0.78291
4	0.88849	0.87144	0.85480	0.83856	0.82270	0.80722	0.79209	0.77732	0.76290	0.74880	0.73503	0.72157
5	0.86261	0.84197	0.82193	0.80245	0.78353	0.76513	0.74726	0.72988	0.71299	0.69656	0.68058	0.66505
6	0.83748	0.81350	0.79032	0.76790	0.74622	0.72525	0.70496	0.68533	0.66634	0.64796	0.63017	0.61295
7	0.81309	0.78599	0.75992	0.73483	0.71068	0.68744	0.66506	0.64351	0.62275	0.60276	0.58349	0.56493
8	0.78941	0.75941	0.73069	0.70319	0.67684	0.65160	0.62741	0.60423	0.58201	0.56070	0.54027	0.52067
9	0.76642	0.73373	0.70259	0.67290	0.64461	0.61763	0.59190	0.56735	0.54393	0.52158	0.50025	0.47988
10	0.74409	0.70892	0.67556	0.64393	0.61391	0.58543	0.55840	0.53273	0.50835	0.48519	0.46319	0.44229
11	0.72242	0.68495	0.64958	0.61620	0.58468	0.55491	0.52679	0.50021	0.47509	0.45134	0.42888	0.40764
12	0.70138	0.66178	0.62460	0.58966	0.55684	0.52598	0.49697	0.46968	0.44401	0.41985	0.39711	0.37570
13	0.68095	0.63940	0.60057	0.56427	0.53032	0.49856	0.46884	0.44102	0.41496	0.39056	0.36770	0.34627
14	0.66112	0.61778	0.57748	0.53997	0.50507	0.47257	0.44230	0.41410	0.38782	0.36331	0.34046	0.31914
15	0.64186	0.59689	0.55527	0.51672	0.48102	0.44793	0.41727	0.38883	0.36245	0.33797	0.31524	0.29414
16	0.62317	0.57671	0.53391	0.49447	0.45811	0.42458	0.39365	0.36510	0.33874	0.31439	0.29189	0.27110
17	0.60502	0.55720	0.51337	0.47318	0.43630	0.40245	0.37136	0.34281	0.31657	0.29245	0.27027	0.24986
18	0.58740	0.53836	0.49363	0.45280	0.41552	0.38147	0.35034	0.32189	0.29586	0.27205	0.25025	0.23029
19	0.57029	0.52016	0.47464	0.43330	0.39573	0.36158	0.33051	0.30224	0.27651	0.25307	0.23171	0.21224
20	0.55368	0.50257	0.45639	0.41464	0.37689	0.34273	0.31181	0.28380	0.25842	0.23541	0.21455	0.19562
21	0.53755	0.48557	0.43883	0.39679	0.35894	0.32486	0.29416	0.26648	0.24151	0.21899	0.19866	0.18029
22	0.52189	0.46915	0.42196	0.37970	0.34185	0.30793	0.27751	0.25021	0.22571	0.20371	0.18394	0.16617
23	0.50669	0.45329	0.40573	0.36335	0.32557	0.29187	0.26180	0.23494	0.21095	0.18950	0.17032	0.15315
24	0.49193	0.43796	0.39012	0.34770	0.31007	0.27666	0.24698	0.22060	0.19715	0.17628	0.15770	0.14115
25	0.47761	0.42315	0.37512	0.33273	0.29530	0.26223	0.23300	0.20714	0.18425	0.16398	0.14602	0.13009

Figure 1: Present Value of a Single Sum ($1) (cont.)

Years	9.0%	9.5%	10.0%	10.5%	11.0%	11.5%	12.0%	12.5%	13.0%	13.5%	14.0%	14.5%	15.0%
1	0.91743	0.91324	0.90909	0.90498	0.90090	0.89686	0.89286	0.88889	0.88496	0.88106	0.87719	0.87336	0.86957
2	0.84168	0.83401	0.82645	0.81898	0.81162	0.80436	0.79719	0.79012	0.78315	0.77626	0.76947	0.76276	0.75614
3	0.77218	0.76165	0.75132	0.74116	0.73119	0.72140	0.71178	0.70233	0.69305	0.68393	0.67497	0.66617	0.65752
4	0.70843	0.69557	0.68301	0.67074	0.65873	0.64699	0.63552	0.62430	0.61332	0.60258	0.59208	0.58181	0.57175
5	0.64993	0.63523	0.62092	0.60700	0.59345	0.58026	0.56743	0.55493	0.54276	0.53091	0.51937	0.50813	0.49718
6	0.59627	0.58012	0.56447	0.54932	0.53464	0.52042	0.50663	0.49327	0.48032	0.46776	0.45559	0.44378	0.43233
7	0.54703	0.52979	0.51316	0.49712	0.48166	0.46674	0.45235	0.43846	0.42506	0.41213	0.39964	0.38758	0.37594
8	0.50187	0.48382	0.46651	0.44989	0.43393	0.41860	0.40388	0.38974	0.37616	0.36311	0.35056	0.33850	0.32690
9	0.46043	0.44185	0.42410	0.40714	0.39093	0.37543	0.36061	0.34644	0.33289	0.31992	0.30751	0.29563	0.28426
10	0.42241	0.40351	0.38554	0.36845	0.35218	0.33671	0.32197	0.30795	0.29459	0.28187	0.26974	0.25819	0.24719
11	0.38753	0.36851	0.35049	0.33344	0.31728	0.30198	0.28748	0.27373	0.26070	0.24834	0.23662	0.22550	0.21494
12	0.35554	0.33654	0.31863	0.30175	0.28584	0.27083	0.25668	0.24332	0.23071	0.21880	0.20756	0.19694	0.18691
13	0.32618	0.30734	0.28966	0.27308	0.25751	0.24290	0.22917	0.21628	0.20417	0.19278	0.18207	0.17200	0.16253
14	0.29925	0.28067	0.26333	0.24713	0.23200	0.21785	0.20462	0.19225	0.18068	0.16985	0.15971	0.15022	0.14133
15	0.27454	0.25632	0.23939	0.22365	0.20900	0.19538	0.18270	0.17089	0.15989	0.14965	0.14010	0.13120	0.12289
16	0.25187	0.23409	0.21763	0.20240	0.18829	0.17523	0.16312	0.15190	0.14150	0.13185	0.12289	0.11458	0.10687
17	0.23107	0.21378	0.19785	0.18316	0.16963	0.15716	0.14564	0.13502	0.12522	0.11616	0.10780	0.10007	0.09293
18	0.21199	0.19523	0.17986	0.16576	0.15282	0.14095	0.13004	0.12002	0.11081	0.10235	0.09456	0.08740	0.08081
19	0.19449	0.17829	0.16351	0.15001	0.13768	0.12641	0.11611	0.10669	0.09806	0.09017	0.08295	0.07633	0.07027
20	0.17843	0.16282	0.14864	0.13576	0.12403	0.11337	0.10367	0.09483	0.08678	0.07945	0.07276	0.06666	0.06110
21	0.16370	0.14870	0.13513	0.12286	0.11174	0.10168	0.09256	0.08429	0.07680	0.07000	0.06383	0.05822	0.05313
22	0.15018	0.13580	0.12285	0.11118	0.10067	0.09119	0.08264	0.07493	0.06796	0.06167	0.05599	0.05085	0.04620
23	0.13778	0.12402	0.11168	0.10062	0.09069	0.08179	0.07379	0.06660	0.06014	0.05434	0.04911	0.04441	0.04017
24	0.12641	0.11326	0.10153	0.09106	0.08171	0.07335	0.06588	0.05920	0.05323	0.04787	0.04308	0.03879	0.03493
25	0.11597	0.10343	0.09230	0.08240	0.07361	0.06579	0.05882	0.05262	0.04710	0.04218	0.03779	0.03387	0.03038

Figure 2: Present Value of an Ordinary Annuity ($1)

Years	3.0%	3.5%	4.0%	4.5%	5.0%	5.5%	6.0%	6.5%	7.0%	7.5%	8.0%	8.5%
1	0.97087	0.96618	0.96154	0.95694	0.95238	0.94787	0.94340	0.93897	0.93458	0.93023	0.92593	0.92166
2	1.91347	1.89969	1.88610	1.87267	1.85941	1.84632	1.83339	1.82063	1.80802	1.79557	1.78327	1.77111
3	2.82861	2.80164	2.77509	2.74896	2.72325	2.69793	2.67301	2.64848	2.62432	2.60053	2.57710	2.55402
4	3.71710	3.67308	3.62990	3.58753	3.54595	3.50515	3.46511	3.42580	3.38721	3.34933	3.31213	3.27560
5	4.57971	4.51505	4.45182	4.38998	4.32948	4.27028	4.21236	4.15568	4.10020	4.04589	3.99271	3.94064
6	5.41719	5.32855	5.24214	5.15787	5.07569	4.99553	4.91732	4.84101	4.76654	4.69385	4.62288	4.55359
7	6.23028	6.11454	6.00206	5.89270	5.78637	5.68297	5.58238	5.48452	5.38929	5.29660	5.20637	5.11851
8	7.01969	6.87396	6.73275	6.59589	6.46321	6.33457	6.20979	6.08875	5.97130	5.85730	5.74664	5.63918
9	7.78611	7.60769	7.43533	7.26879	7.10782	6.95220	6.80169	6.65610	6.51523	6.37889	6.24689	6.11906
10	8.53020	8.31661	8.11090	7.91272	7.72174	7.53763	7.36009	7.18883	7.02358	6.86408	6.71008	6.56135
11	9.25262	9.00155	8.76048	8.52892	8.30641	8.09254	7.88688	7.68904	7.49867	7.31542	7.13896	6.96898
12	9.95400	9.66333	9.38507	9.11858	8.86325	8.61852	8.38384	8.15873	7.94269	7.73528	7.53608	7.34469
13	10.63496	10.30274	9.98565	9.68285	9.39357	9.11708	8.85268	8.59974	8.35765	8.12584	7.90378	7.69096
14	11.29607	10.92052	10.56312	10.22283	9.89864	9.58965	9.29498	9.01384	8.74547	8.48915	8.24424	8.01010
15	11.93794	11.51741	11.11839	10.73955	10.37966	10.03758	9.71225	9.40267	9.10791	8.82712	8.55948	8.30424
16	12.56110	12.09412	11.65230	11.23402	10.83777	10.46216	10.10590	9.76776	9.44665	9.14151	8.85137	8.57533
17	13.16612	12.65132	12.16567	11.70719	11.27407	10.86461	10.47726	10.11058	9.76322	9.43396	9.12164	8.82519
18	13.75351	13.18968	12.65930	12.15999	11.68959	11.24607	10.82760	10.43247	10.05909	9.70601	9.37189	9.05548
19	14.32380	13.70984	13.13394	12.59329	12.08532	11.60765	11.15812	10.73471	10.33560	9.95908	9.60360	9.26772
20	14.87748	14.21240	13.59033	13.00794	12.46221	11.95038	11.46992	11.01851	10.59401	10.19449	9.81815	9.46334
21	15.41502	14.69797	14.02916	13.40472	12.82115	12.27524	11.76408	11.28498	10.83553	10.41348	10.01680	9.64363
22	15.93692	15.16713	14.45112	13.78443	13.16300	12.58317	12.04158	11.53520	11.06124	10.61719	10.20074	9.80980
23	16.44361	15.62041	14.85684	14.14778	13.48857	12.87504	12.30338	11.77014	11.27219	10.80669	10.37106	9.96295
24	16.93554	16.05837	15.24696	14.49548	13.79864	13.15170	12.55036	11.99074	11.46933	10.98297	10.52876	10.10410
25	17.41315	16.48152	15.62208	14.82821	14.09395	13.41393	12.78336	12.19788	11.65358	11.14695	10.67478	10.23419

Figure 2: Present Value of an Ordinary Annuity ($1) (cont.)

Years	9.0%	9.5%	10.0%	10.5%	11.0%	11.5%	12.0%	12.5%	13.0%	13.5%	14.0%	14.5%	15.0%
1	0.91743	0.91324	0.90909	0.90498	0.90090	0.89686	0.89286	0.88889	0.88496	0.88106	0.87719	0.87336	0.86957
2	1.75911	1.74725	1.73554	1.72396	1.71252	1.70122	1.69005	1.67901	1.66810	1.65732	1.64666	1.63612	1.62571
3	2.53130	2.50891	2.48685	2.46512	2.44372	2.42262	2.40183	2.38134	2.36115	2.34125	2.32163	2.30229	2.28323
4	3.23972	3.20448	3.16987	3.13586	3.10245	3.06961	3.03735	3.00564	2.97447	2.94383	2.91371	2.88410	2.85498
5	3.88965	3.83971	3.79079	3.74286	3.69590	3.64988	3.60478	3.56057	3.51723	3.47474	3.43308	3.39223	3.35216
6	4.48592	4.41983	4.35526	4.29218	4.23054	4.17029	4.11141	4.05384	3.99755	3.94251	3.88867	3.83601	3.78448
7	5.03295	4.94961	4.86842	4.78930	4.71220	4.63704	4.56376	4.49230	4.42261	4.35463	4.28831	4.22359	4.16042
8	5.53482	5.43344	5.33493	5.23919	5.14612	5.05564	4.96764	4.88205	4.79877	4.71774	4.63886	4.56208	4.48732
9	5.99525	5.87528	5.75902	5.64632	5.53705	5.43106	5.32825	5.22849	5.13166	5.03765	4.94637	4.85771	4.77158
10	6.41766	6.27880	6.14457	6.01477	5.88923	5.76777	5.65022	5.53643	5.42624	5.31952	5.21612	5.11591	5.01877
11	6.80519	6.64730	6.49506	6.34821	6.20652	6.06975	5.93770	5.81016	5.68694	5.56786	5.45273	5.34140	5.23371
12	7.16073	6.98384	6.81369	6.64996	6.49236	6.34058	6.19437	6.05348	5.91765	5.78666	5.66029	5.53834	5.42062
13	7.48690	7.29118	7.10336	6.92305	6.74987	6.58348	6.42355	6.26976	6.12181	5.97943	5.84236	5.71034	5.58315
14	7.78615	7.57185	7.36669	7.17018	6.98187	6.80133	6.62817	6.46201	6.30249	6.14928	6.00207	5.86056	5.72448
15	8.06069	7.82818	7.60608	7.39383	7.19087	6.99671	6.81086	6.63289	6.46238	6.29893	6.14217	5.99176	5.84737
16	8.31256	8.06226	7.82371	7.59622	7.37916	7.17194	6.97399	6.78480	6.60388	6.43077	6.26506	6.10634	5.95424
17	8.54363	8.27604	8.02155	7.77939	7.54879	7.32909	7.11963	6.91982	6.72909	6.54694	6.37286	6.20641	6.04716
18	8.75563	8.47127	8.20141	7.94515	7.70162	7.47004	7.24967	7.03984	6.83991	6.64928	6.46742	6.29381	6.12797
19	8.95012	8.64956	8.36492	8.09515	7.83929	7.59645	7.36578	7.14652	6.93797	6.73946	6.55037	6.37014	6.19823
20	9.12855	8.81238	8.51356	8.23091	7.96333	7.70982	7.46944	7.24135	7.02475	6.81890	6.62313	6.43680	6.25933
21	9.29224	8.96108	8.64869	8.35376	8.07507	7.81149	7.56200	7.32565	7.10155	6.88890	6.68696	6.49502	6.31246
22	9.44243	9.09688	8.77154	8.46495	8.17574	7.90269	7.64465	7.40058	7.16951	6.95058	6.74294	6.54587	6.35866
23	9.58021	9.22089	8.88322	8.56556	8.26643	7.98447	7.71843	7.46718	7.22966	7.00491	6.79206	6.59028	6.39884
24	9.70661	9.33415	8.98474	8.65662	8.34814	8.05782	7.78432	7.52638	7.28288	7.05279	6.83514	6.62907	6.43377
25	9.82258	9.43758	9.07704	8.73902	8.42175	8.12361	7.84314	7.57901	7.32999	7.09497	6.87293	6.66294	6.46415

Figure 3: Future Value of an Amount ($1)

Years	3.0%	3.5%	4.0%	4.5%	5.0%	5.5%	6.0%	6.5%	7.0%	7.5%	8.0%	8.5%	9.0%
1	1.03000	1.03500	1.04000	1.04500	1.05000	1.05500	1.06000	1.06500	1.07000	1.07500	1.08000	1.08500	1.09000
2	1.06090	1.07123	1.08160	1.09203	1.10250	1.11303	1.12360	1.13423	1.14490	1.15563	1.16640	1.17723	1.18810
3	1.09273	1.10872	1.12486	1.14117	1.15763	1.17424	1.19102	1.20795	1.22504	1.24230	1.25971	1.27729	1.29503
4	1.12551	1.14752	1.16986	1.19252	1.21551	1.23882	1.26248	1.28647	1.31080	1.33547	1.36049	1.38586	1.41158
5	1.15927	1.18769	1.21665	1.24618	1.27628	1.30696	1.33823	1.37009	1.40255	1.43563	1.46933	1.50366	1.53862
6	1.19405	1.22926	1.26532	1.30226	1.34010	1.37884	1.41852	1.45914	1.50073	1.54330	1.58687	1.63147	1.67710
7	1.22987	1.27228	1.31593	1.36086	1.40710	1.45468	1.50363	1.55399	1.60578	1.65905	1.71382	1.77014	1.82804
8	1.26677	1.31681	1.36857	1.42210	1.47746	1.53469	1.59385	1.65500	1.71819	1.78348	1.85093	1.92060	1.99256
9	1.30477	1.36290	1.42331	1.48610	1.55133	1.61909	1.68948	1.76257	1.83846	1.91724	1.99900	2.08386	2.17189
10	1.34392	1.41060	1.48024	1.55297	1.62889	1.70814	1.79085	1.87714	1.96715	2.06103	2.15892	2.26098	2.36736
11	1.38423	1.45997	1.53945	1.62285	1.71034	1.80209	1.89830	1.99915	2.10485	2.21561	2.33164	2.45317	2.58043
12	1.42576	1.51107	1.60103	1.69588	1.79586	1.90121	2.01220	2.12910	2.25219	2.38178	2.51817	2.66169	2.81266
13	1.46853	1.56396	1.66507	1.77220	1.88565	2.00577	2.13293	2.26749	2.40985	2.56041	2.71962	2.88793	3.06580
14	1.51259	1.61869	1.73168	1.85194	1.97993	2.11609	2.26090	2.41487	2.57853	2.75244	2.93719	3.13340	3.34173
15	1.55797	1.67535	1.80094	1.93528	2.07893	2.23248	2.39656	2.57184	2.75903	2.95888	3.17217	3.39974	3.64248
16	1.60471	1.73399	1.87298	2.02237	2.18287	2.35526	2.54035	2.73901	2.95216	3.18079	3.42594	3.68872	3.97031
17	1.65285	1.79468	1.94790	2.11338	2.29202	2.48480	2.69277	2.91705	3.15882	3.41935	3.70002	4.00226	4.32763
18	1.70243	1.85749	2.02582	2.20848	2.40662	2.62147	2.85434	3.10665	3.37993	3.67580	3.99602	4.34245	4.71712
19	1.75351	1.92250	2.10685	2.30786	2.52695	2.76565	3.02560	3.30859	3.61653	3.95149	4.31570	4.71156	5.14166
20	1.80611	1.98979	2.19112	2.41171	2.65330	2.91776	3.20714	3.52365	3.86968	4.24785	4.66096	5.11205	5.60441
21	1.86029	2.05943	2.27877	2.52024	2.78596	3.07823	3.39956	3.75268	4.14056	4.56644	5.03383	5.54657	6.10881
22	1.91610	2.13151	2.36992	2.63365	2.92526	3.24754	3.60354	3.99661	4.43040	4.90892	5.43654	6.01803	6.65860
23	1.97359	2.20611	2.46472	2.75217	3.07152	3.42615	3.81975	4.25639	4.74053	5.27709	5.87146	6.52956	7.25787
24	2.03279	2.28333	2.56330	2.87601	3.22510	3.61459	4.04893	4.53305	5.07237	5.67287	6.34118	7.08457	7.91108
25	2.09378	2.36324	2.66584	3.00543	3.38635	3.81339	4.29187	4.82770	5.42743	6.09834	6.84848	7.68676	8.62308

Figure 3: Future Value of an Amount ($1) (cont.)

Years	9.5%	10.0%	10.5%	11.0%	11.5%	12.0%	12.5%	13.0%	13.5%	14.0%	14.5%	15.0%
1	1.09500	1.10000	1.10500	1.11000	1.11500	1.12000	1.12500	1.13000	1.13500	1.14000	1.14500	1.15000
2	1.19903	1.21000	1.22103	1.23210	1.24323	1.25440	1.26563	1.27690	1.28823	1.29960	1.31103	1.32250
3	1.31293	1.33100	1.34923	1.36763	1.38620	1.40493	1.42383	1.44290	1.46214	1.48154	1.50112	1.52088
4	1.43766	1.46410	1.49090	1.51807	1.54561	1.57352	1.60181	1.63047	1.65952	1.68896	1.71879	1.74901
5	1.57424	1.61051	1.64745	1.68506	1.72335	1.76234	1.80203	1.84244	1.88356	1.92541	1.96801	2.01136
6	1.72379	1.77156	1.82043	1.87041	1.92154	1.97382	2.02729	2.08195	2.13784	2.19497	2.25337	2.31306
7	1.88755	1.94872	2.01157	2.07616	2.14252	2.21068	2.28070	2.35261	2.42645	2.50227	2.58011	2.66002
8	2.06687	2.14359	2.22279	2.30454	2.38891	2.47596	2.56578	2.65844	2.75402	2.85259	2.95423	3.05902
9	2.26322	2.35795	2.45618	2.55804	2.66363	2.77308	2.88651	3.00404	3.12581	3.25195	3.38259	3.51788
10	2.47823	2.59374	2.71408	2.83942	2.96995	3.10585	3.24732	3.39457	3.54780	3.70722	3.87307	4.04556
11	2.71366	2.85312	2.99906	3.15176	3.31149	3.47855	3.65324	3.83586	4.02675	4.22623	4.43466	4.65239
12	2.97146	3.13843	3.31396	3.49845	3.69231	3.89598	4.10989	4.33452	4.57036	4.81790	5.07769	5.35025
13	3.25375	3.45227	3.66193	3.88328	4.11693	4.36349	4.62363	4.89801	5.18736	5.49241	5.81395	6.15279
14	3.56285	3.79750	4.04643	4.31044	4.59037	4.88711	5.20158	5.53475	5.88765	6.26135	6.65697	7.07571
15	3.90132	4.17725	4.47130	4.78459	5.11827	5.47357	5.85178	6.25427	6.68248	7.13794	7.62223	8.13706
16	4.27195	4.59497	4.94079	5.31089	5.70687	6.13039	6.58325	7.06733	7.58462	8.13725	8.72746	9.35762
17	4.67778	5.05447	5.45957	5.89509	6.36316	6.86604	7.40616	7.98608	8.60854	9.27646	9.99294	10.76126
18	5.12217	5.55992	6.03283	6.54355	7.09492	7.68997	8.33193	9.02427	9.77070	10.57517	11.44192	12.37545
19	5.60878	6.11591	6.66628	7.26334	7.91084	8.61276	9.37342	10.19742	11.08974	12.05569	13.10099	14.23177
20	6.14161	6.72750	7.36623	8.06231	8.82058	9.64629	10.54509	11.52309	12.58686	13.74349	15.00064	16.36654
21	6.72507	7.40025	8.13969	8.94917	9.83495	10.80385	11.86323	13.02109	14.28608	15.66758	17.17573	18.82152
22	7.36395	8.14027	8.99436	9.93357	10.96597	12.10031	13.34613	14.71383	16.21470	17.86104	19.66621	21.64475
23	8.06352	8.95430	9.93876	11.02627	12.22706	13.55235	15.01440	16.62663	18.40369	20.36158	22.51781	24.89146
24	8.82956	9.84973	10.98233	12.23916	13.63317	15.17863	16.89120	18.78809	20.88818	23.21221	25.78290	28.62518
25	9.66836	10.83471	12.13548	13.58546	15.20098	17.00006	19.00260	21.23054	23.70809	26.46192	29.52141	32.91895

Figure 4: Future Value of an Ordinary Annuity ($1)

Years	3.0%	3.5%	4.0%	4.5%	5.0%	5.5%	6.0%	6.5%	7.0%	7.5%
1	1.00000	1.00000	1.00000	1.00000	1.00000	1.00000	1.00000	1.00000	1.00000	1.00000
2	2.03000	2.03500	2.04000	2.04500	2.05000	2.05500	2.06000	2.06500	2.07000	2.07500
3	3.09090	3.10622	3.12160	3.13703	3.15250	3.16803	3.18360	3.19923	3.21490	3.23063
4	4.18363	4.21494	4.24646	4.27819	4.31013	4.34227	4.37462	4.40717	4.43994	4.47292
5	5.30914	5.36247	5.41632	5.47071	5.52563	5.58109	5.63709	5.69364	5.75074	5.80839
6	6.46841	6.55015	6.63298	6.71689	6.80191	6.88805	6.97532	7.06373	7.15329	7.24402
7	7.66246	7.77941	7.89829	8.01915	8.14201	8.26689	8.39384	8.52287	8.65402	8.78732
8	8.89234	9.05169	9.21423	9.38001	9.54911	9.72157	9.89747	10.07686	10.25980	10.44637
9	10.15911	10.36850	10.58280	10.80211	11.02656	11.25626	11.49132	11.73185	11.97799	12.22985
10	11.46388	11.73139	12.00611	12.28821	12.57789	12.87535	13.18079	13.49442	13.81645	14.14709
11	12.80780	13.14199	13.48635	13.84118	14.20679	14.58350	14.97164	15.37156	15.78360	16.20812
12	14.19203	14.60196	15.02581	15.46403	15.91713	16.38559	16.86994	17.37071	17.88845	18.42373
13	15.61779	16.11303	16.62684	17.15991	17.71298	18.28680	18.88214	19.49981	20.14064	20.80551
14	17.08632	17.67699	18.29191	18.93211	19.59863	20.29257	21.01507	21.76730	22.55049	23.36592
15	18.59891	19.29568	20.02359	20.78405	21.57856	22.40866	23.27597	24.18217	25.12902	26.11836
16	20.15688	20.97103	21.82453	22.71934	23.65749	24.64114	25.67253	26.75401	27.88805	29.07724
17	21.76159	22.70502	23.69751	24.74171	25.84037	26.99640	28.21288	29.49302	30.84022	32.25804
18	23.41444	24.49969	25.64541	26.85508	28.13238	29.48120	30.90565	32.41007	33.99903	35.67739
19	25.11687	26.35718	27.67123	29.06356	30.53900	32.10267	33.75999	35.51672	37.37896	39.35319
20	26.87037	28.27968	29.77808	31.37142	33.06595	34.86832	36.78559	38.82531	40.99549	43.30468
21	28.67649	30.26947	31.96920	33.78314	35.71925	37.78608	39.99273	42.34895	44.86518	47.55253
22	30.53678	32.32890	34.24797	36.30338	38.50521	40.86431	43.39229	46.10164	49.00574	52.11897
23	32.45288	34.46041	36.61789	38.93703	41.43048	44.11185	46.99583	50.09824	53.43614	57.02790
24	34.42647	36.66653	39.08260	41.68920	44.50200	47.53800	50.81558	54.35463	58.17667	62.30499
25	36.45926	38.94986	41.64591	44.56521	47.72710	51.15259	54.86451	58.88768	63.24904	67.97786

Figure 4: Future Value of an Ordinary Annuity ($1) (cont.)

Years	8.0%	8.5%	9.0%	9.5%	10.0%	10.5%	11.0%	11.5%	12.0%	12.5%	13.0%	13.5%
1	1.00000	1.00000	1.00000	1.00000	1.00000	1.00000	1.00000	1.00000	1.00000	1.00000	1.00000	1.00000
2	2.08000	2.08500	2.09000	2.09500	2.10000	2.10500	2.11000	2.11500	2.12000	2.12500	2.13000	2.13500
3	3.24640	3.26223	3.27810	3.29403	3.31000	3.32603	3.34210	3.35823	3.37440	3.39063	3.40690	3.42323
4	4.50611	4.53951	4.57313	4.60696	4.64100	4.67526	4.70973	4.74442	4.77933	4.81445	4.84980	4.88536
5	5.86660	5.92537	5.98471	6.04462	6.10510	6.16616	6.22780	6.29003	6.35285	6.41626	6.48027	6.54488
6	7.33593	7.42903	7.52333	7.61886	7.71561	7.81361	7.91286	8.01338	8.11519	8.21829	8.32271	8.42844
7	8.92280	9.06050	9.20043	9.34265	9.48717	9.63404	9.78327	9.93492	10.08901	10.24558	10.40466	10.56628
8	10.63663	10.83064	11.02847	11.23020	11.43589	11.64561	11.85943	12.07744	12.29969	12.52628	12.75726	12.99273
9	12.48756	12.75124	13.02104	13.29707	13.57948	13.86840	14.16397	14.46634	14.77566	15.09206	15.41571	15.74675
10	14.48656	14.83510	15.19293	15.56029	15.93742	16.32458	16.72201	17.12997	17.54874	17.97857	18.41975	18.87256
11	16.64549	17.09608	17.56029	18.03852	18.53117	19.03866	19.56143	20.09992	20.65458	21.22589	21.81432	22.42036
12	18.97713	19.54925	20.14072	20.75218	21.38428	22.03772	22.71319	23.41141	24.13313	24.87913	25.65018	26.44711
13	21.49530	22.21094	22.95338	23.72363	24.52271	25.35168	26.21164	27.10372	28.02911	28.98902	29.98470	31.01746
14	24.21492	25.09887	26.01919	26.97738	27.97498	29.01361	30.09492	31.22065	32.39260	33.61264	34.88271	36.20482
15	27.15211	28.23227	29.36092	30.54023	31.77248	33.06004	34.40536	35.81102	37.27971	38.81422	40.41746	42.09247
16	30.32428	31.63201	33.00340	34.44155	35.94973	37.53134	39.18995	40.92929	42.75328	44.66600	46.67173	48.77496
17	33.75023	35.32073	36.97370	38.71350	40.54470	42.47213	44.50084	46.63616	48.88367	51.24925	53.73906	56.35958
18	37.45024	39.32300	41.30134	43.39128	45.59917	47.93170	50.39594	52.99932	55.74971	58.65541	61.72514	64.96812
19	41.44626	43.66545	46.01846	48.51345	51.15909	53.96453	56.93949	60.09424	63.43968	66.98733	70.74941	74.73882
20	45.76196	48.37701	51.16012	54.12223	57.27500	60.63081	64.20283	68.00508	72.05244	76.36075	80.94683	85.82856
21	50.42292	53.48906	56.76453	60.26384	64.00250	67.99704	72.26514	76.82566	81.69874	86.90584	92.46992	98.41541
22	55.45676	59.03563	62.87334	66.98891	71.40275	76.13673	81.21431	86.66062	92.50258	98.76908	105.49101	112.70149
23	60.89330	65.05366	69.53194	74.35286	79.54302	85.13109	91.14788	97.62659	104.60289	112.11521	120.20484	128.91619
24	66.76476	71.58322	76.78981	82.41638	88.49733	95.06985	102.17415	109.85364	118.15524	127.12961	136.83147	147.31988
25	73.10594	78.66779	84.70090	91.24593	98.34706	106.05219	114.41331	123.48681	133.33387	144.02081	155.61956	168.20806

Figure 4: Future Value of an Ordinary Annuity ($1) (cont.)

Years	14.0%	14.5%	15.0%
1	1.00000	1.00000	1.00000
2	2.14000	2.14500	2.15000
3	3.43960	3.45603	3.47250
4	4.92114	4.95715	4.99338
5	6.61010	6.67594	6.74238
6	8.53552	8.64395	8.75374
7	10.73049	10.89732	11.06680
8	13.23276	13.47743	13.72682
9	16.08535	16.43166	16.78584
10	19.33730	19.81425	20.30372
11	23.04452	23.68731	24.34928
12	27.27075	28.12197	29.00167
13	32.08865	33.19966	34.35192
14	37.58107	39.01361	40.50471
15	43.84241	45.67058	47.58041
16	50.98035	53.29282	55.71747
17	59.11760	62.02027	65.07509
18	68.39407	72.01321	75.83636
19	78.96923	83.45513	88.21181
20	91.02493	96.55612	102.44358
21	104.76842	111.55676	118.81012
22	120.43600	128.73249	137.63164
23	138.29704	148.39871	159.27638
24	158.65862	170.91652	184.16784
25	181.87083	196.69941	212.79302

Index

Notes

Notes